Seneca Philosophus

Seneca Philosophus

Edited by
Jula Wildberger
Marcia L. Colish

De Gruyter

ISBN 978-3-11-055493-9
e-ISBN 978-3-11-034986-3
ISSN 1868-4785

Library of Congress Cataloging-in-Publication Data
A CIP catalog record for this book has been applied for at the Library of Congress.

Bibliographic information published by the Deutsche Nationalbibliothek The
Deutsche Nationalbibliothek lists this publication in the Deutsche Nationalbibliografie; detailed bibliographic data are available in the Internet at http://dnb.dnb.de.

© 2017 Walter de Gruyter GmbH, Berlin/Boston
This volume is text- and page-identical with the hardback published in 2014.

Logo: Christopher Schneider, Laufen
Printing: CPI buch bücher.de GmbH, Birkach
∞ Printed on acid-free paper
Printed in Germany
www.degruyter.com

Trends in Classics — Supplementary Volumes

Edited by
Franco Montanari and Antonios Rengakos

Scientific Committee
Alberto Bernabé · Margarethe Billerbeck · Claude Calame
Philip R. Hardie · Stephen J. Harrison · Stephen Hinds
Richard Hunter · Christina Kraus · Giuseppe Mastromarco
Gregory Nagy · Theodore D. Papanghelis · Giusto Picone
Kurt Raaflaub · Bernhard Zimmermann

Volume 27

De Gruyter

Table of Contents

Introduction 1

Ilsetraut Hadot
Getting to Goodness: Reflections on Chapter 10 of Brad
Inwood, *Reading Seneca* 9

Antonello Orlando
Seneca on *Prolēpsis*: Greek Sources and Cicero's Influence 43

Jörn Müller
Did Seneca Understand Medea? A Contribution to the Stoic
Account of *Akrasia* 65

Marcia L. Colish
Seneca on Acting against Conscience 95

David H. Kaufman
Seneca on the Analysis and Therapy of Occurrent Emotions ... 111

Gareth D. Williams
Double Vision and Cross-Reading in Seneca's *Epistulae
Morales* and *Naturales Quaestiones* 135

Rita Degl'Innocenti Pierini
Freedom in Seneca: Some Reflections on the Relationship
between Philosophy and Politics, Public and Private Life 167

Jean-Christophe Courtil
Torture in Seneca's Philosophical Works: Between
Justification and Condemnation 189

Tommaso Gazzarri
Gender-Based Differential Morbidity and Moral Teaching
in Seneca's *Epistulae morales* 209

Elizabeth Gloyn
My Family Tree Goes Back to the Romans: Seneca's
Approach to the Family in the *Epistulae Morales* 229

Margaret R. Graver
Honeybee Reading and Self-Scripting: *Epistulae Morales* 84 .. 269

Linda Cermatori
The Philosopher as Craftsman: A Topos between Moral
Teaching and Literary Production 295

Martin T. Dinter
Sententiae in Seneca 319

Matheus De Pietro
Having the Right to Philosophize: A New Reading of
Seneca, *De Vita Beata* 1.1–6.2 343

Francesca Romana Berno
In Praise of Tubero's Pottery: A Note on Seneca,
Ep. 95.72–73 and 98.133 369

Madeleine Jones
Seneca's *Letters to Lucilius*: Hypocrisy as a Way of Life 393

Jula Wildberger
The Epicurus Trope and the Construction of a "Letter Writer"
in Seneca's *Epistulae Morales* 431

Abbreviations 467

Index of Passages Cited 469

Index of Modern Authors 495

General Index 505

Introduction

The purpose of this volume, most of whose contents were given as papers at an international conference "Seneca Philosophus" at the American University of Paris in May 2011, is to provide Anglophone readers with a range of current approaches to this important first-century Latin author. The contributors span scholarly generations and reflect diverse research cultures and agendas. In some cases this book makes the work of prominent scholars writing in other languages available in English for the first time. While these papers treat a variety of themes, often from contrasting disciplinary and methodological perspectives, they share many points of agreement about Seneca. Whether they focus on his epistemology, his ethics, his natural philosophy, his psychology, his political thought, or his conception of the body and of gender roles, the contributors see him as an author who draws with discrimination on other ancient traditions while developing an authentic, cogent, and original articulation of Roman Stoicism. Some papers in this collection emphasize Seneca's philosophy as such. Others focus on the ways in which his literary artistry serves to convey his ideas, accenting his strategies as a writer, his use of rhetorical devices and standard tropes, and the sophisticated techniques with which he constructs a literary as well as a philosophical persona, both in his prose and his dramatic works.

The first group of papers in this volume deals with Seneca the philosopher in the most immediate sense. Ilsetraut Hadot and Antonello Orlando engage the debate on how the earlier Stoics, and Seneca, think that we acquire the moral norms which we use in making moral decisions. Whereas Jörn Müller and Marcia L. Colish treat the problem of how we make such decisions when they contravene our accepted moral values, David H. Kaufman and Gareth D. Williams broaden this ethical topic in contrasting directions, focusing, respectively, on the allaying of irrational passions and the rejection of erroneous intellectual judgments in considering how Seneca presents himself as a moral therapist.

Against a popular empiricist understanding of the Stoic notion of the highest good and the concomitant view that Seneca might have been influenced by Platonic innatism, Ilsetraut Hadot argues that already the earliest Stoics assumed the existence of a basic innate pre-notion or "anticipated grasp" (*prolēpsis*) of the good, which she distinguishes both from the rudimentary notions acquired by experience or analogy during the development of reason and the fully formed correct notion of the good that can only be assimilated through philosophical education. Antonello Orlando's paper complements Hadot's approach with a detailed philological study of the wide range of Latin expressions used for rendering the Greek term *prolēpsis*. Orlando makes a case for considering lexical choices not only as a manner of aligning oneself with a particular school but also, at least for Seneca, as a necessary engagement with the terminology proposed by earlier Latin authors such as Cicero and the needs or expectations of a Roman readership.

Jörn Müller applies insights from his research on ancient and medieval concepts of *akrasia* ("weakness of will" or "lack of self-control") to the case study of Seneca's *Medea*, whose main character highlights the difficulties that arise when one tries to explain weak-willed behavior within the framework of a monist psychology. Müller distinguishes two basic types of Stoic explanations, for which he adduces evidence from Stoic sources in general and from the philosophical writings of Seneca himself. According to the "persistence model," an agent continues to maintain a passionate, uncontrollable state by the assent of his reason, so that it persists even when rational insight begins to suggest a different behavior. According to the "oscillation model," the mind of the akratic person switches rapidly between different judgments and thus simultaneously maintains conflicting passions, such as love or anger toward the same individual. According to Müller, Seneca shaped his Medea on the oscillation model rather. Right from the beginning, she appears torn between conflicting passions and solves her akratic conflict by complete abandonment to the full madness of one passion alone.

Marcia L. Colish examines "conscience" (*conscientia*) in Seneca philosophus and the other Imperial Stoics. She sees the originality of Seneca's approach in his reserving premeditation of future evils for sages, but also in the facts that self-examination appears as an activity conducted in various settings, also as a form of social exchange, and that Seneca presented his fictitious self as deeply unsettled by his public role. The importance of a good conscience as both the facilitator and the essence of a good life is showcased by Seneca's idiosyncratic use of well-known theatrical imagery for describing acts against conscience. In Seneca, responsibility is framed not as acting some stereotypic role but as performing one's own life on this world stage, which the agent plays well or badly according to his own volition.

David H. Kaufman studies Seneca's treatment of occurrent emotions, i.e. fresh passions that are intractable by reasoned argument according to Stoic orthodoxy. On the basis of an analysis of *De ira* 2.1–4, Kaufman argues that Seneca saw one cause of this problem in the fact that the beliefs correlated with the passion in its course are not the same as the beliefs which originally were the impassioned person's reasons for conceiving the passion in the first place. Kaufman further suggests that, as a result of this new understanding of the emotional pathology, Seneca added an Epicurean method to the Stoic therapist's first-aid kit: the treatment by stimulation of countervailing passions.

Gareth D. Williams argues that Seneca's *Naturales quaestiones* and *Epistulae morales* "in a sense *complete* each other as interdependent conceptual experiments" (137). He discusses the simultaneous composition and shared thematic concerns of the two works, for example the need to "do" something right now, which is highlighted in the first of the *Epistulae morales* and in the preface to the *Naturales quaestions*. According to Williams, the two works offer different but complementary forms of therapy with parallels in modern cognitive-behavioral therapy. It thus appears that the works addressed to the same dedicatee Lucilius, perhaps together with the *Libri moralis philosophiae*, were supposed to form a corpus that promotes a comprehensive philosophical as well as therapeutic agenda and, at the same time, the persona of an author sincerely devoted to a life in philosophical retreat.

The second group of papers in this collection analyzes a diverse range of topics, themes, and images related to political and social issues. Rita Degl' Innocenti Pierini and Jean-Christophe Courtil treat Seneca's critique of despotism, as it impinges on the freedom and physical integrity of others. Tommaso Gazzarri discusses how self-inflicted harm to the human body can acquire different moral significance depending on the gender of the agent, while Elizabeth Gloyn reviews the role of both male and female family members for the philosopher-in-progress in the *Epistulae morales* as a recurrent theme in a structured whole and as a marker of different stages in the progressor's development.

Rita Degl'Innocenti Pierini explores the refractions of Seneca's conception of freedom when applied to the political sphere in contrast to the ehtical perspective of the individual striving for consistency in his own life. She juxtaposes the mirror images of Cicero, the half-free ex-consul of *De brevitate vitae* 5 who bewails his imposed retreat from public life, and of Cato at the helm of the sinking state as he establishes freedom through his personal choice of suicide. On the basis of a careful comparison, she argues that for Seneca freedom is first of foremost a value of the private sphere and individual philosophical practice. All the same, exemplary sublimation of individual freedom can assume political importance and confirm freedom as a collective value, especially in the absence of political freedom. This picture is further refined by another comparison: In the political sphere as it is represented in *De clementia*, freedom dissolves into a paradox. Collective freedom depends on the absolute coercive power of the emperor, while that power presupposes the emperor's voluntary renunciation of his own individual freedom.

In a thorough study of references to torture in Seneca's prose works, Jean-Christophe Courtil argues that Seneca's frequent depiction of this practice stems not from a taste for the gruesome but from the horror and outrage at sadistic abuse of power which he seeks to inspire in his readers. Nevertheless, Courtil also provides evidence that Seneca did not reject all forms of torture and rather favors political pragmatism. He does not call into question the laws of the state permitting, or even prescribing, torture under certain circumstances. The apparent contradiction between these two attitudes is resolved by asserting the superiority of moral law. Reason must control all uses of torture, and torture must always serve a rationally justifiable remedial or legal purpose.

Tommaso Gazzarri contrasts gender-specific accounts of self-destruction and self-healing. As his starting point he takes a passage in the *Epistulae morales* in which Seneca explains the spread of male-specific diseases among the female population with the deviant behavior of the afflicted women. They suffer because they renounce their female nature by adopting dietary and sexual practices associated with masculinity. Also gender-related, and also drawing on medical imagery, is the presentation of the countervailing virtue which exemplary male heroes display when they assert their moral freedom by inflicting on themselves the "therapy" of suicide.

Elizabeth Gloyn takes Seneca's treatment of the family in the *Epistulae morales* as a showcase example of the manner in which this work functions as a systematically organized whole and integrates more general philosophical issues into a discourse focused on the practices, concerns, and moral development of its two protagonists, Seneca and Lucilius. Gloyn observes changes in the treatment of the theme as the reader advances through the work. After an initial phase in which the family is blanked out, references both to the theme in general and more specifically to Seneca's own family reappear. Warnings, but also acknowledgements of the obligations toward family members, gradually enable the progressor to take a rational stance and assign to his family the appropriate place within the framework of his ethical thought. His relatives sometimes give him support and good advice, but even their well-meaning interventions can hinder his progress. Seneca's treatment of the family thus serves as an extended case study of the tension between the sage's acceptance of his social responsibilities and his detachment from externals.

The final group of papers in this collection by Margaret R. Graver, Linda Cermatori, Martin Dinter, Matheus De Pietro, Francesca Romana

Berno, Madeleine Jones, and Jula Wildberger all accent ways in which Seneca uses imagery and literary strategies to fashion, express, and defend his own self or authorial persona.

In a discussion of *Epistula moralis* 84 and Michel Foucault's reading of that letter, Margaret R. Graver traces a "novel ontology of the self" (270). Seneca blends identifications of writers with their written work as we know them from Latin literature with a holistic application of the Roman concept of *ingenium* (one's "mind," "mindset," "talent," and what one produces with it). Thus he not only represents himself in his writings, the writings *are* his externalized "locus of identity" (270) and a means by which he can transcend himself whenever artistic achievement, understood as a unified whole created by both literary art and art of life, "surpasses and ultimately replaces one's unstable and fleeting sentience within the body with an externalized self that is more consistent and more admirable as well as more stable" (270).

The contributions of Linda Cermatori and Martin Dinter establish connections between Seneca's dramatic and philosophical works. In the tradition of studies that explore the interdependence of literary form and philosophical meaning, Linda Cermatori discusses the imagery of the artist and craftsman in various interrelated functions, most importantly the meta-literary construction of an authorial identity both as a philosopher and an educator. By confronting her findings in Seneca's philosophical prose with the use of similar imagery in the tragedies, Cermatori reveals striking inversions of the philosopher-educator evoked in the prose works: Characters in the plays are portrayed as ingenious fabricators of destructive machinations, while their victims become the objects of perverse craftsmanship, just as the soul of Lucilius in the *Epistulae morales* is the unformed matter out of which the philosopher-educator fashions Lucilius the Sage as his masterpiece.

Martin Dinter discusses another of Seneca's frequently noted devices, his taste for pithy maxims, not in his prose, however, but in his tragedies. Dinter suggests that Seneca might have written with a view to the contemporary practice of excerpting, to which the works of his father, Seneca the Elder, bear ample testimony, and that he composed his sententious plays in such a way that his authorial identity would be gleaned from the scattered sayings of his characters. Imitating the reading strategies of an orator on the hunt for striking formulations, Dinter identifies recurrent ideas which Seneca the Younger hammers home repeatedly in the tragedies. Themes thus articulated by the characters of his dramas turn out to yield positions consistent with those taken in his prose works.

Another feature of Seneca's style, repetitive accumulation of synonymous phrases expressing the same content, is given a new interpretation in

Matheus De Pietro's contribution. Analyzing a passage with descriptions of happiness and the supreme good in *De vita beata*, he shows that the allegedly aimless and rambling exuberance lambasted by ancient as well as modern critics is a literary device deliberately employed as a means of self-presentation. De Pietro indicates how this apparent chaos is carefully structured according to theoretical principles and points out features which serve an authorial purpose related to the apologetic function of the whole treatise: to parade Seneca's credentials as an expert Stoic philosopher.

Using the method of detailed inter- and intratextual comparison, Francesca Romana Berno throws into relief the nuances of Seneca's use of the example of proverbially frugal Q. Aelius Tubero. She is thus able to show the potential of this otherwise rather marginal figure to illustrate Seneca's views concerning his own role as a public figure. In contrast to the parallel accounts as they are attested in Cicero or Valerius Maximus, Seneca does not criticize Tubero's renunciation of public values and even presents such behavior as worthy of praise. Berno concludes that Seneca may have intended this assertion of consistency at the cost of a political career as a model for his own retreat from the political stage.

Madeleine Jones traces the complex antinomies implicit in the charge of hypocrisy raised, or expressly not raised, both within Seneca's work and in his reception. In a close reading of the eighty-seventh *Epistula moralis* and the metaphor of shipwreck placed prominently at the beginning of this letter, she argues that Seneca constructs his persona as a hypocrite both to forestall criticism and to express the confusion inherent in the Stoic condition. According to Jones, Stoicism appears as a system of thought which commits its adherents to hypocrisy: The man in progress espouses Stoic doctrine but, as someone who is not a sage, cannot live by it. For a Stoic like Seneca, the genre of the *Epistulae morales* as a moral discourse and, at the same time, familiar epistolary exchange between close friends requires a voice which highlights the distance between the sender's principles, his words (*verba*), and the facts (*res*) of his actual life (*vita*). However, since frank acknowledgement of one's own faults is also the necessary first step on the road to sagehood and since any philosopher casting himself in the Socratic mold must deny that he is wise, failure to meet the high standards one professes as a member of the Stoic sect, paradoxically, becomes a form of moral achievement. Hypocrisy, in the sense of preaching one thing and practicing another, thus is surreptitiously elevated to the closest approximation to virtue of which a non-wise philosopher-in-progress is capable.

Proposing a literary reading intended to elucidate the philosophical content of the *Epistulae morales*, Jula Wildberger argues that the engagement with Epicurus in the *Epistulae morales* is a multifaceted literary device essential to the fabric of what she calls an epistolary *Bildungsroman*.

According to her, the "Epicurus trope" supports the characterization of a Letter Writer "Seneca" and helps to endow the work with a dramatic structure. By presenting a pair of friends, *both* "Seneca" and "Lucilius," as appealing models of an exemplary philosophical lifestyle, the *Epistulae morales* serve as an introduction not just to Stoicism, but to philosophy itself. The Letter Writer progresses in the practices and methodologies any serious philosopher must master, including a progress from often naïve endorsement to a more carefully reflected, sophisticated account of Stoic thought. As part of this development, the Letter Writer draws increasingly sharper distinctions between his own views and Epicurean tenets, especially those on pleasure. Wildberger underscores the necessity to distinguish two layers of Epicurus' reception in the *Epistulae morales*: While the Letter Writer might be blissfully unaware of a theoretical problem and just read Epicurus in his own way, L. Annaeus, the author of this work, understood the other philosopher well enough to know exactly what he was doing when he cunningly and deliberately manipulated, misrepresented, or reinterpreted Epicurean tenets and expressions as it suited the Stoic mindset of his creation, the Letter Writer, at each specific point in the intellectual drama played out by this character in the letters.

Addressing classicists, philosophers, students, and general readers alike, this collection features a vitalizing diversity of contributions that emphasizes the unity of Seneca's work and his originality as a translator of Stoic ideas in the literary forms of imperial Rome. Individually and collectively, the contributions in this volume shed new light on his writings, each from their own historical, philosophical, literary, and theoretical perspectives. They will stimulate the study and understanding of Seneca with fresh analyses and solutions to issues that have been debated for some time and offer entirely new avenues of investigation.

We wish to thank Dr. Benedict Beckeld for his help with proofreading and both the Andrew W. Mellon Foundation and The American University of Paris for their support to the conference from which this volume arose.

Yale and Paris, March 2014   Marcia L. Colish & Jula Wildberger

Getting to Goodness: Reflections on Chapter 10 of Brad Inwood, *Reading Seneca**

Ilsetraut Hadot

While reading the set of interpretations of Seneca offered by Brad Inwood, *Reading Seneca: Stoic Philosophy at Rome*,[1] I was intrigued by, among other things, the chapter entitled "Getting to Goodness," which contains his interpretation of Seneca's *Letter to Lucilius* 120. The subject of this letter is the question: how have we acquired the knowledge of good and evil, and of what is morally good ("quomodo ad nos boni honestique notitia pervenerit")? We recall that for the Stoics, the only good was what is morally good, that a happy life was identical to a virtuous life as well as to a life according to nature, and that this conception of the good was obviously very far from the opinions of ordinary people. To state matters very briefly at the outset, Inwood is of the opinion that [a] to explain how man can be able to conceive the notion of the sovereign good, the Stoic method, since it is purely "empirical," is insufficient, and even incoherent,[2]

---

* The French version of this article was completed at the end of 2009 and then translated into English by Michael Chase to make it accessible to an Anglophone public. Only after this English version was submitted for publication in 2011, did the author become aware of Henry Dyson's *Prolepsis and Ennoia in the Early Stoa*, which had appeared in 2009. This book and the present publication often follow the same approach, but they disagree on a fundamental point: In contrast to Dyson the author of this paper argues that *prolēpseis*, as understood by Chrysippus, were *not* formed through perceptual experience. On the other hand, she is delighted to see that Antonello Orlando's contribution to this volume arrives at the same conclusion.

1 Inwood 2005.
2 I cite Inwood 2005, 281: "There was, then, a problem for Stoics in accounting for the possibility of our acquisition of the concept of good. It is clearly meant to be a concept open to us through natural, empirical means. Yet at the same time it seems to transcend the realm of ordinary experience and to embody an ideal of human perfection which we neither experience in our ordinary lives nor attain with any significant frequency. The starting points for coming to understand the good, the experience of what is mundanely useful or advantageous, are accessible enough; but the required development of such 'utility' towards the ideal of perfect moral utility is virtually impossible to account for within the framework of Stoic epistemology. It is one thing to set out a theory which builds on the assumption that we can learn about the good. But it is quite another to have a defensible account of

and [b] that Seneca tried, by means of arguments that are not completely orthodox, to find the beginnings of a solution to this difficulty, which would not be solved until Epictetus, who accepts the "reality of innate ideas."[3]

As these few citations show, and contrary to what the rather vast title of the chapter in question, "Getting to Goodness," seems to promise, Inwood's developments do not deal with all the means by which the Stoics thought they could become morally good. Instead, they focus on a single detail: the question of how, according to the Stoics, the notion of the sovereign good in particular, and ethical notions in general, are formed. And it is precisely because he thus reduces a complex theme to a question that belongs to the theory of knowledge alone, and because, in addition, he isolates *Letter* 120 from its context, which is initially the totality of the *Letters to Lucilius* and then the whole of Stoic philosophy – in short, it is because he limits his perspectives too much that, in my opinion, Inwood is led to reproach Seneca for incoherencies that are not to be found in him.

With regard to his interpretation of the Stoic theory of the formation of ethical notions, Inwood has obviously been deeply influenced by the thesis of F. H. Sandbach,[4] who, in opposition to Bonhöffer,[5] was of the opinion that the Stoics did not accept, above and beyond the empirical path (repeated sense perceptions → memory → experience) backed up by the analogical method, any complementary path which would be based on natural starting points toward virtue and innate pre-notions. Sandbach's viewpoint was accepted by most historians of ancient philosophy for about seventy years, but finally the recent article by M. Jackson-McCabe, entitled "The Stoic Theory of Implanted Preconceptions,"[6] seeks to rehabilitate Bonhöffer's thesis, which I have just mentioned.[7] Inwood could not have

---

how we are supposed to be able to do so within the context of Stoic epistemology. In our consideration of Seneca's contribution to this problem, we will need to focus on how this gap is to be bridged."

3 Inwood 2005, 301: "Seneca, I think, really did make a genuine advance over his Stoic predecessors in how he thought this gap might be bridged. But in so doing he brought Stoic moral epistemology to the threshold of Platonic recollection. Little wonder that, in the next generation, Epictetus seems to have taken the next step and accepted the reality of innate ideas."
4 Sandbach 1930, 44–51.
5 Bonhöffer 1890, 187–222.
6 Jackson-McCabe 2004, 323–347.
7 In fact, Jackson-McCabe has let some of Sandbach's criticisms of Bonhöffer persist, for instance 326 n. 18, where he joins Sandbach in condemning Bonhöffer, who supposedly identified "προλήψεις in general with the ἔμφυτοι προλήψεις in particular." Yet the following quotation shows, among other things, that Bonhöffer never committed such an identification. For he says (Bonhöffer 1890, 196): "Man kann nur soviel sagen, dass bei Epiktet die προλήψεις *vorzugsweise* [= *preferably*]

known this excellent article, which appeared one year before the publication of his own book, and I myself did not become aware of it until I had finished the first draft of the present article, which proposes, among other things, to rehabilitate the views of Bonhöffer, albeit on a broader basis. Since Jackson-McCabe's work refers in detail not only to Sandbach's article, which opposes Bonhöffer, but also, for important questions, to the partisans of both sides, I can refrain from referring to this older literature myself. However, since I am also attempting, unlike Jackson-McCabe, to prove that the use of certain technical terms was not constant throughout the history of Stoicism and that different terms in different authors might sometimes mean the same thing, and, conversely, that the same terms might designate different realities, I will take up in more detail, in the second part of this article, two texts which have already been well interpreted, in their broad outlines, by Jackson-McCabe: one by Diogenes Laertius (7.49–54) and the other by Aëtius (*Placita* 4.11).

I. Preliminary Research on the Meaning of Such Expressions as "Starting Points (*Aphormai*) toward Virtue," *Fundamenta* or *Semina Innata Virtutis*, *Prolēpsis Emphutos*, *Praesumptio* or *Praenotio*, etc.

Let us begin by asking ourselves whether the doctrine of the Stoics of the Hellenistic period concerning the formation of the concept of the sovereign good is incoherent, as Inwood thinks,[8] or not. To elucidate this question, I believe it is useful to first recall a few important general features of Stoic philosophy, which will facilitate the understanding of the texts that specifically concern the formation of notions, features that Inwood passes over in silence and of which Jackson-McCabe tackles only the doctrine of *oikeiōsis*, to which I will return in the second part of this article.

We recall that the Stoics' first principle can be called, indifferently, artisanal fire, nature, divine reason or divine breath (*pneuma*), God or Zeus.[9] Of this first principle under the aspect of primordial fire, Zeno, the founder of the Stoic school, says that it is "like a kind of seed (*sperma*) that contains within itself the reasons (*logous*) and the causes (*aitias*) of all

---

einen natürlichen, eingepflanzten Begriff bedeuten [...]." I lack the space here to provide an exhaustive list of the other critiques of Bonhöffer's theses, all of which are, I believe, based on misunderstandings.
8 Cf. above, p. 9 with note 2.
9 Cf. D.L. 7.147 = *SVF* 2.1021 and Sen. *Ben.* 4.7 = *SVF* 2.1024.

things,"[10] so that Zeno can speak of this principle as the "seminal reason (*logos spermatikos*) of the world."[11] The same thing can be affirmed of the first principle under the aspect of nature as breath: "Nature is a warm breath that moves itself, generates the seminal powers, and realizes and preserves man."[12] The soul is consequently defined as "a body composed of subtle particles that moves by itself in accordance with the seminal reasons."[13] Pohlenz rightly said that in the Stoic system, the seminal reasons replace Plato's ideas, in a sense.[14] This first principle, which permeates the totality of the world, is not, however, present everywhere with the same strength.

The Stoic system consequently distinguishes four echelons in the hierarchy of beings: The lowest echelon is that of inorganic beings, such as stones, in which nature or the *pneuma* is manifested in its most primitive form, as *hexis*, a term which, in this context, designates the "*pneuma* returning upon itself,"[15] and which ensures the internal cohesion of beings. At the second level, that of plants (*phuta*), the *pneuma* is also manifested in the form of nature (*phusis*), with the word *phusis* being taken here in the very narrow sense of "growth." At the third level, that of living mortal beings that lack reason, the *pneuma*, part of which is increasingly hot and dry, is also present under the aspect of the soul (*psuchē*), as the principle of autonomous motion and the guarantor, in different degrees, of sensory perceptions (*aisthēseis*) and their representations (*phantasiai*). Finally, at the fourth level, the *pneuma* manifests itself primarily as reason (*logos*)[16]

---

10 Eus. *P.E.* 15.14.1–2 = *SVF* 1.98. Unless indicated otherwise, translations are the author's own (translated from the original French into English by Michael Chase). See also [Gal.] *Definitiones medicae* 95, vol. 19, p. 371,4–9 and 12–14 Kühn = *SVF* 2.1133; Plu. *Comm. not.* 1077b = *SVF* 2.618; Philo, *De aeternitate mundi* 8 = *SVF* 2.619; Stob. 1.17.3, vol. 1, p. 153,7 Wachsmuth = *SVF* 1.497; Orig. *Cels.* 4.48, 15–24 = *SVF* 2.1074.
11 D.L. 7.135–136 (vol. 3, p. 355,5–6 Long) = *SVF* 1.102 (p. 28,26).
12 Ps.-Gal. *Definitiones medicae* 95, vol. 19, p. 371,4–9 and 12–14 Kühn = *SVF* 2.1133; Aëtius 1.7.33 = *SVF* 2.1027: "The Stoics declare that the god endowed with intelligence (θεός νοερός), the artisanal fire, which advances methodically toward the generation of the world, contains within itself all the seminal reasons (σπερματικοὶ λόγοι) according to which everything happens according to fate (καθ' εἱμαρμένην); and [that it is] a breath (πνεῦμα) that permeates the totality of the world, taking its denominations according to the changes of matter it passes through." Cf. D.L. 7.156 = *SVF* 2.774.
13 [Gal.] *Definitiones medicae* 29, vol. 19, p. 355,11–13 Kühn = *SVF* 2.780.
14 Pohlenz 1948, vol. 2, p. 45.
15 Alex. Aphr. *Mixt.* p. 224,23–25 Bruns = *SVF* 2.442 (near the end).
16 For instance, Gal. *In Hippocratis librum VI epidemiarum, commentarius V*, vol. 17b, p. 251,1–9 Kühn (Wenkebach) = *SVF* 2.715; [Gal.] *Introductio seu medicus*, p. 20,21–22 Petit = *SVF* 2.716.

and belongs to beings endowed with reason, some of whom are immortal, *viz.* the gods, and some of whom are mortal, *viz.* mankind.[17] This doctrine thus founds the Stoic belief in the existence of a certain similarity and kinship between the first principle, the gods, and mankind, a kinship that results from their common participation in reason,[18] albeit at very different degrees: the reason of the gods is perfect, whereas the reason of mankind is imperfect but perfectible.[19] It is so imperfect, in fact, that it does not manifest itself in early childhood, during which we remain more or less at the level of the higher animals, obeying our initial impulses toward self-preservation. Since, then, reason is the characteristic feature by which mankind not only is distinguished from animals and plants, but is also assimilated to a certain extent to the gods and to the first principle, the supreme good for mankind, the guarantor of a happy life, consists according to the Stoics in the perfect state of this reason, a state which is identical with virtue. Yet this perfect state of our reason – this is once again the common opinion of all the Stoics – is not a gift of nature in the sense of a natural biological development (*phusei*)[20] that realizes itself without our cooperation, but it is in conformity with our nature (*kata phusin*)[21] to be able to achieve it by dint of relentless intellectual labor.

---

17 Cf. Philo, *Legum allegoriae* 2.22 = *SVF* 2.458; *Quod deus sit immutabilis* 35 and 41 = *SVF* 2.458; *De aeternitate mundi* 75 = *SVF* 2.459; [Plu.] *Virt. mor.* 451b = *SVF* 2.460; Dexipp. *in Cat.* p. 50,31 Busse = *SVF* 2.461.

18 Although this doctrine, if one neglects its materialist basis, bears some resemblance to Platonic doctrines, it does not appear only at a late period of Stoicism, the Imperial period, but already at its beginnings.

19 Cf. Cic. *Leg.* 1.22 = *SVF* 3.339: "This subtle, far-sighted, complex, penetrating being, endowed with memory, full of reason and reflection whom we call 'man,' was created under a brilliant condition. Indeed, he is the only one, among so many kinds and natures of beings endowed with a soul, to participate in reason and in thought, whereas all the others are bereft of it [...]. Therefore, since there is nothing better than reason and since it is found both in man and in the god, there exists a primary community based on reason between man and the god." Cf. Sen. *Ep.* 66.12: "[Human] reason is nothing other than a part of the divine breath (*pars divini spiritus*) that has come down into the human body" and 92.27: "Reason is common to gods and men: It is complete in the former, but in us is apt to become so (*in illis consummata est, in nobis consummabilis*)."

20 Cf. Clem. Al. *Strom.* 7.3.19.3–4 = *SVF* 3.224; Clem. Al. *Strom.* 1.6.34.1–35.2 = *SVF* 3.225; Sen. *Ep.* 90.44, etc.

21 Cf. Stob. 2.7.5b8, vol. 2, p. 65, 7–10 Wachsmuth = *SVF* 1.566 (Cleanthes); D.L. 7.89 (vol. 2, p. 335, 2–5 Long) = *SVF* 3.228; Musonius in Stob. 2.9.8, vol. 2, p. 183f. and 31.126, vol. 2, p. 244f. Wachsmuth; Sen. *Ep.* 108.8; *Ep.* 31.9; *Ep.* 90.1. The idea that the virtues are given to us κατὰ φύσιν, and not φύσει, already appears in Aristotle, *E.N.* 2, 1103a–b: "Virtue thus has two forms: it is intellectual on the one hand, and on the other, moral. If it is intellectual, it is to a large extent to teaching that it owes its birth and growth [...] but if it is moral, it is the fruit of

This means that we are not born virtuous nor do we become virtuous automatically, but, because of the divine roots of our own reason, we nevertheless all have, unlike the animals, a predisposition to be able to achieve virtue, and this predisposition can only be innate. Centuries later, in Seneca, Cleanthes's famous dictum "All men possess by nature (*ek phuseōs*) starting points (*aphormai*)[22] toward virtue"[23] takes on the following

---

habit [...]. Whence it also appears that none of the moral virtues arises in us naturally (φύσει). Indeed, nothing natural is modified by habit. Thus, the stone which naturally tends downwards, cannot acquire the habit of tending upwards, even if we try to make it contract that habit by throwing it up in the air a thousand times [...] no natural behavior can be modified by habit. Consequently, it is neither naturally (φύσει) nor against nature (παρὰ φύσιν) that the virtues come to be within us. However, nature has made us able to receive them (πεφυκόσι [...] ἡμῖν δέξασθαι αὐτάς), but it is as we approach our perfection by means of habit that we acquire them. What is more, everything nature places at our disposition we first acquire in the form of abilities (δυνάμει), and then we respond to it by our acts, as we can see precisely in the case of the senses. Indeed, it is not from the frequent act of seeing or the frequent act of hearing that we derive our sense faculties, but the converse: it is because we possess them that we have made use of them, and it is not their use that has given us possession of them. But we derive the virtues from previous acts, as is the case with the other techniques" (English translation after the translation by Bodéüs 2004, 99–100). Unlike Aristotle, however, for the Stoics, who do not distinguish between intellectual and ethical virtues, the virtues develop equally by philosophical instruction and by habit acquired through spiritual exercises.

22 In general, *aphormai* is understood in the sense of *hormai* ("impulses"), and even more particularly of "initial impulses," despite the fact that the latter, as we shall see, lead only to the conservation of the individual and not to the notions of the good and of virtue, and that in this context the term *aphormē* designates "repulsion" among the Stoics, i.e. the contrary of an impulse (*hormē*). My translation, which follows the French version of R. Goulet in the first text of n. 23, is based on the ancient interpretations that I set forth below.

23 Stob. 2.7.5b8, vol. 2, p. 65,7–10 Wachsmuth = *SVF* 1.566. Cf. D.L. 7.89 = *SVF* 3.228, based on the translation of R. Goulet in M.-O. Goulet-Cazé 1999, 848: "But the rational animal is perverted, sometimes by the probabilities of the realities of the external world [R. Goulet is right to read πραγμάτων instead of πραγματειῶν], sometimes by the influence of those who share our lives, since nature supplies starting points (*aphormai*) that are exempt from all perversion." Cf. Stob. 2.7.5b3, vol. 2, p. 62 Wachsmuth = *SVF* 3.264: "Man possesses from nature starting points (*aphormai*) both for the discovery of what is appropriate (*to kathēkon*) and for the stability of impulses (*hormai*), for endurance, and for distributive justice." Cf. Orig. *Princ.* 2.1.3 (2), lines 38–43 Crouzel-Simonetti (SC) = *SVF* 2.988 (p. 288, 10–12), at the end of an evocation of the four echelons of being): "This is why, since in the nature of reason [sc. human reason] there are starting points for assessing (*aphormai tou theōrēsai*) good and evil, following which, once we have become able to assess good and evil, we choose good and refuse evil, we are praised if we practice good, and blamed in the contrary case." Cf. Cramer 1839, vol. 1, p. 171 (*Quomodo homines boni et mali fiant?*) = *SVF* 3.214; Sen. *Ep.* 49.11 = *SVF* 3.219.

turn: "Nature has given to all the foundations (*fundamenta*) and seeds (*semina*) of the virtues."[24] Indeed, when the Stoics think of their first principle as the seminal reason (*spermatikos logos*), these starting points are "seeds" or "germs" (*semina*), and when they conceive it as an artisanal fire, the starting points are "sparks." A text by Cicero combines these two images:

> If nature had created us such that we should be capable of viewing it and examining it attentively in itself[25] and if we could accomplish the course of our life with it as the best possible guide, in this case it would hardly be necessary to seek for philosophical instruction (*rationem ac doctrinam*). In reality, however, it has given us only tiny sparks (*parvulos nobis dedit igniculos*), which we, perverted by bad morals and bad opinions, smother so thoroughly and quickly that the light of nature appears nowhere. Indeed, germs of the virtues are innate in our intelligences (*ingeniis nostris semina innata virtutum*); if they were allowed to grow, nature itself would lead us toward the happy life. (Cic. *Tusc.* 3.2)[26]

Of what Greek term might the participle *innata* be the translation? The answer is provided by another text by Cicero, which is to be found in the first book of his *De Natura Deorum*, in an Epicurean context.[27] This text discusses the "implanted knowledge (*cognitiones insitas* [where *insitas* is the passive past participle of *insero*, 'to sow, to implant']) or rather innate (*innatas*) knowledge," of the gods. *Insita* is the literal translation of

---

24 Sen. *Ep.* 108.8. This sentence continues as follows: "We are all born for all those things [*sc.* for the virtues]: When someone comes to provide a stimulus, at that moment all these good things, which had as it were dozed off, reawaken." Cf. Sen. *Ep.* 94.29: "Souls bear within them the seeds of all things that are morally good, and these seeds are made to grow by admonitions (*admonitiones*), not unlike the way in which a spark, aided by a light breeze, unfolds its fire. Virtue stands up when it is touched and set under way."
25 This is a transposition into the Stoic system of an image utilized by Plato in the context of the same problem in the framework of his doctrine of reminiscence (*Phdr.* 250d): "Vision is the most acute of the senses that come to us by the intermediary of the body. By its means wisdom (*phronēsis*) cannot be seen. Indeed, it [wisdom] would provoke violent desires if it gave an image of itself that was as clear as that of beauty and touched the sense of sight [...]." Right from the outset, both Stoics and Platonists were of the opinion that the notions of the good, of virtue, and of justice were not accessible to sense presentations and to experience that is based on them. Cf. Sen. *Ep.* 115.3–4.
26 The text is not included in the *SVF*, but its Stoic origin is indubitable, owing, among other considerations, to the use of the terms "seeds" and "*igniculi*," which would have no meaning in a Platonic-Aristotelian context, in which one would speak instead of *dunameis* (abilities) or *epitēdeiotētes* (aptitudes). Cf. also Cic. *Leg.* 1.33.
27 Cic. *N.D.* 1.44. Seneca utilizes the same two translations of *emphutos* in such passages as *Ep.* 94.30 (*persuasiones innatae*) and 117.6 (*omnibus insita* [= *emphutos*] *de diis opinio*). Seneca translates *prolēpsis* by *praesumptio* in this context.

emphutos, while *innata* is its translation *ad sensum*. These few texts cited here and in the notes suffice to show that the belief that all mankind possesses an innate disposition toward virtue or the supreme good, a disposition that can be smothered under the influence of the surrounding world, does not appear in Stoicism only with Epictetus, as Inwood thinks, but was present from the beginning.

Yet this last text from Cicero is also important from another viewpoint, because in it the participle "implanted" (*emphutos*) or "innate" is combined with the translation of the Greek term *prolēpsis*. Indeed, in the exposition by the Epicurean Gaius Velleius[28] of the Epicurean doctrine concerning the gods, it is said that Epicurus had been the only one to prove the existence of the gods by the fact that nature itself had impressed (*impressisset*) the notion of the gods in the souls (*animis*) of all mankind.

> For which is the nation, or which is the kind of men that does not possess, without having been instructed (*sine doctrina*), a certain anticipated grasp (*anticipationem quandam*) of the gods, which Epicurus called *prolēpsis*, that is, a kind of idea of something anticipated by the soul (*anteceptam animo rei quandam informationem*), without which nothing can be understood, nor sought, nor discussed. We learn the strength and the usefulness of this modality (*rationis*) in the volume by the divine Epicurus that deals with the rule and judgment [that is, the treatise *Peri kritēriou* or *Kanōn*]. (Cic. *N.D.* 1.43)[29]

A bit farther on, in the text cited in note 29, Cicero translates this same Greek term *prolēpsis* less literally with "pre-notion" (*praenotio*). Later, Seneca was to translate this term by *praesumptio*.[30] Cicero must therefore

---

28 On this person see Castner 1988, 75–76.
29 The text continues (1.44) as follows: "That which is the base (*fundamentum*) of our enquiry, you thus see that it has been set down in an excellent way. Indeed, since the opinion has not been established by any institution, or by custom, or by law, and since unanimous and firm agreement endures, we must necessarily understand that the gods exist because we have an implanted, or better, innate knowledge of them (*insitas eorum vel potius innatas cognitiones habemus*); that about which the nature of everyone agrees is necessarily true; consequently, we must agree that the gods exist. And since this is a fact established for everyone, not only for philosophers but also for uneducated people, we must also admit as generally established the fact that we possess an anticipated grasp (*anticipationem*) – as I have called it before – or a pre-notion (*praenotionem*) of the gods (indeed, we must give new names to new things, as Epicurus himself called *prolēpsis* a thing that no one before him had called by that name) – we thus have a pre-notion according to which we believe that the gods are happy and immortal." I leave it up to specialists on Epicurus to determine the meaning of the term "nature" in this text (43–44) and to specify whether the term *emphutos prolēpsis* is compatible with what little we know from other sources about the *Kanōn* of Epicurus or whether we have to do instead with an expression due to Epicureans contemporary with Cicero. Gourinat 2005 gives only the reference to this text from Cicero, but does not interpret it.
30 Cf. *supra*, n. 27, and *infra*, p. 29.

have found in the Greek Epicurean texts he had available (but the explicit reference is to Epicurus' *Kanōn*) the term *emphutoi prolēpseis* in the sense of "innate anticipated grasps" with regard to the common opinion that the gods exist.

In the next book, the Stoic Balbus will accept this same common opinion, which he too declares to be innate,[31] as a proof of the gods' existence, a fact which did not prevent the Stoics from proving the existence of the gods by additional demonstrations. I mention this detail because some scholars follow Sandbach and his partisans in ignoring the protests of Bonhöffer[32] and the meaning of *emphutoi*, which is both evident and confirmed by ancient Latin translations.[33] Instead they persist in rendering this turn of phrase not by "innate" or "implanted anticipated grasps" (or, at a pinch, "pre-notions") but by "natural pre-notions" (that is: naturally *acquired* pre-notions), e.g. in the following quotation of Chrysippus by Plutarch. For example, Babut reads in accordance with an already lengthy tradition: "With regard to the doctrine of goods and evils of which he himself [sc. Chrysippus] was the promoter and the champion, he says that it is the one that is the most coherent with life and has the closest relation to the natural pre-notions (Τὸν περὶ ἀγαθῶν καὶ κακῶν λόγον [...] συμφωνότατον εἶναί φησι τῷ βίῳ καὶ μάλιστα τῶν ἐμφύτων ἅπτεσθαι προλήψεων)."[34]

Because in a text by Aëtius, which we shall interpret later on, *prolēpseis* are said to develop "naturally" (*phusikōs*) during the first seven years of our life, i.e. before the intervention of reason, by the accumulation of experiences based on sense perceptions, one assumes that this term can only have this one meaning everywhere. In opposition to this belief, I am of the opinion that in the Stoic system there is both an "innate anticipated grasp" and an "acquired anticipated grasp based on perception and experience,"[35] as there are common opinions of both these same kinds and "phantasms" with different meanings.

Furthermore, I understand Chrysippus's "innate anticipated grasps," which, according to the text of the quotation, have a connection with goods

---

31 Cic. *N.D.* 2.12. Cf. Sen. *Ep.* 117.6, quoted *infra*, p. 29.
32 Bonhöffer 1890, 187–208.
33 Cicero had available Hellenistic Greek sources that were incomparably richer than ours, and he also played host to a Greek Stoic philosopher until the latter's death.
34 Plu. *Stoic. rep.* 1041e = *SVF* 3,69, in Babut 2004, 49 (translated from the French). At page 181, note 218, Babut gives a very brief justification of this translation. Cf. also Babut 2002, 216–219, notes 332 and 333. Long and Sedley 1987 give this text as number 60B of their collection and translate (vol. 1, p. 369): "He [Chrysippus] says that the theory of good and bad things introduced and approved by himself is most in harmony with life and connects best with the *innate preconceptions*."
35 This is also the view of Jackson-McCabe (referred to above, pp. 10f.).

and evils, in a sense that is parallel, if not identical, to that of the innate "starting points" (*aphormai*), "foundations," "seeds" and "sparks" of which we have spoken. This will be confirmed by a text from Epictetus (p. 19).

To answer an objection that has been made to me, that the Latin translations of *emphutos* by *insitus* and *innatus* might be the result of a poor understanding of the Greek on part of Latin-speaking authors, I shall add the testimonies of two Stoic authors who taught and wrote in Greek and about whom there can be no doubt that they used Greek sources correctly: Musonius and Epictetus. I first quote a Greek text by Musonius, the diatribe to which Cora Lutz has given the title "That man is born with an inclination toward virtue."[36] Musonius wants to prove that *virtue is not entirely introduced in us from the outside* (as would be the case of the objects of sense perception and the experience that results from it), *but that there is something of it that is in us by nature*.[37] With this goal in mind, he gives as examples, among other things, such arts as medicine or the practice of the lyre, which no one claims to know without having studied them. In contrast, no one believes that only the philosopher is expected to be exempt from error in the conduct of life, despite the fact that the philosopher is the only one who concerns himself with the study of virtue. Rather, everyone is of the opinion that this is the case for each and every person. And Musonius concludes:[38]

> Clearly, then, there is no explanation for this other than that the human being is born with an inclination toward virtue. And this indeed is strong evidence of the presence of goodness in our nature (καὶ μὴν κἀκεῖνο μέγα τεκμήριον τοῦ μετεῖναι ἀρετῆς φύσει ἡμῖν), that all speak of themselves as having virtue and being good. For take the common man: when asked whether he is stupid or intelligent, not one will confess to being stupid; or again, when asked whether he is just or unjust, not one will say he is unjust. In the same way, if one asks him whether he is temperate or intemperate, he replies at once that he is temperate; and finally, if one asks whether he is good or bad, he would say that he is good, even though he can name no teacher of virtue or mention any study or practice of virtue he has ever made. Of what, then, is this evidence if not of the existence of an *innate inclination* of the human soul toward goodness and nobleness, and of the presence of the seeds of virtue in each one of us (τοῦτ' οὖν τίνος ἄλλου τεκμήριόν ἐστιν ἢ τοῦ φυσικὴν εἶναι ὑποβολὴν τῇ τοῦ ἀνθρώπου ψυχῇ πρὸς καλοκἀγαθίαν καὶ σπέρμα ἀρετῆς ἑκάστῳ ἡμῶν ἐνεῖναι)?

---

36 Lutz 1947, 37–39.
37 I quote the translation of Lutz (Muson. *Diatr.* 2, p. 37, 21–22, trans. p. 38): "And yet if the whole notion of virtue were something that came to us from without (εἰ ὅλον ἐπείσακτον τὸ τῆς ἀρετῆς ἦν), and we shared no part of it by birth (καὶ μηδὲν αὐτοῦ φύσει ἡμῖν μετῆν), just as in activities pertaining to the other arts no one who has not learned the art is expected to be free from error [...]."
38 Muson. *Diatr.* 2, p. 38, 1–14 Lutz, cited in the translation by Lutz, p. 37–39.

In this text, it is clearly said that the "totality of what concerns virtue" (Lutz translates: "the whole notion of virtue") does not come to us from outside, that is, not by the intermediary of the senses, but that a part of that is in us by nature (Lutz translates "by birth", cf. n. 37). The correctness of the Latin translations of *emphutos* by *insitus* and *innatus* is thus confirmed, and so these translations are valid proof for the occurrence of this Stoic doctrine in Cicero's Hellenistic Greek sources.

The *Diatribe*, or rather *Discourse* 2.11 of Epictetus reads like an echo of the diatribe of his teacher Musonius, which I have just quoted, but also contributes further important details. Epictetus begins by stating that we have all come into the world without being endowed by nature with the notion (*ennoia*), for instance, of a right-angled triangle, a diesis, or a semitone, but that it is thanks to technical instruction that we acquire these notions and that, for this reason, those who have not learned these arts do not claim to know them.[39] However, he continues:[40]

> Of the good and bad, of the (morally) beautiful and the ugly, of what is and is not appropriate, of happiness, of what is our duty and what is incumbent upon us, and of what we must do and not do, who *has come into the world without having an innate notion* (emphutos ennoia) *of this*? This is the reason why we use all these expressions, and try to adapt the anticipated grasps [*prolēpseis*, that is, what he has previously called "innate notions"] to particular substances (*epi merous ousiai*). Who among us uses these expressions with reserve? Who among us delays their use until the moment he is instructed about them, as is done by those who are ignorant of writing and sounds? The reason is *the fact of coming into the world as if, in this area, we had already learned some things (tina) by nature, from which we have set ourselves in motion and have added our opinion.*

In other words: we come into the world with anticipated grasps (*prolēpseis*) concerning the domain of ethics, which we use as starting points.[41] These we do not acquire after birth by means of sense perception. The *prolēpseis*, or anticipated grasps, which are here without any doubt innate, are thus identical to the *aphormai*, or starting points. The last sentence quoted thus brings a confirmation to what I said on pages 17f. with regard to the "anticipated grasps" of Chrysippus.

---

39 Arr. *Epict.* 2.11.2: "Ὀρθογωνίου μὲν γὰρ τριγώνου ἢ διέσεως ἡμιτονίου οὐδεμίαν φύσει ἔννοιαν ἥκομεν ἔχοντες, ἀλλ' ἔκ τινος τεχνικῆς παραλήψεως διδασκόμεθα ἕκαστον αὐτῶν [...]."

40 Arr. *Epict.* 2.11.3–6: "Ἀγαθοῦ δὲ καὶ κακοῦ καὶ καλοῦ καὶ αἰσχροῦ καὶ πρέποντος καὶ ἀπρεποῦς καὶ εὐδαιμονίας καὶ προσήκοντος καὶ ἐπιβάλλοντος καὶ ὅ τι δεῖ ποιῆσαι καὶ ὅ τι οὐ δεῖ ποιῆσαι τίς οὐκ ἔχων ἔμφυτον ἔννοιαν ἐλήλυθεν; 4 Διὰ τοῦτο πάντες χρώμεθα τοῖς ὀνόμασιν καὶ ἐφαρμόζειν πειρώμεθα τὰς προλήψεις ταῖς ἐπὶ μέρους οὐσίαις. [...] 6 Τούτου δ' αἴτιον τὸ ἥκειν ἤδη τινὰ ὑπὸ τῆς φύσεως κατὰ τὸν τόπον ὥσπερ δεδιδαγμένους, ἀφ' ὧν ὁρμώμενοι καὶ τὴν οἴησιν προσειλήφαμεν."

41 Arr. *Epict.* 2.11.6: "ἀφ' ὧν ὁρμώμενοι."

We need not be surprised that an innate disposition to virtue and seeds or germs of virtue (as in the text by Musonius) can be identical with anticipated grasps or innate ethical pre-notions: we recall that according to the general opinion of the Stoics, virtue is identical to "fully developed reason, accommodated to the intention of its nature."[42] The germs of virtue are thus the germs of reason that correspond to anticipated grasps, according to the Stoics, since human reason, as a fragment of divine reason, begins to manifest itself clearly only after the seventh year, remaining more or less latent until then. In the continuation of his development, except for a very brief allusion,[43] Epictetus gives no details concerning the process of deterioration undergone, right from birth, by these anticipated grasps of ethical notions under the influence of our surroundings (e.g. nursemaids or poorly educated parents) – a theme we have encountered above (pp. 14f.) in such authors as Chrysippus, Cicero, and Seneca – deterioration that is the cause of the variety in the moral judgments of adolescents and adults. Epictetus starts out immediately from the established fact of the deterioration of the anticipated grasps, which must now be remedied by the critical examination of each of these anticipated grasps deteriorated by the addition of our opinions from the angle of Stoic philosophy. This is the *diarthrōsis prolēpseōn*, or analysis of innate anticipated grasps.

II. Interpretation of the Texts Used, among Others, by Inwood as Testimonies to the Stoic Doctrine Concerning the Formation of Notions

Against this background, we finally come to the interpretation of the four main texts that deal with the acquisition of notions, of which Inwood has given a translation with commentary. Except for a few details, which I shall indicate, I agree with the interpretation of these same texts by Jackson-McCabe.[44] However, these short excerpts must be considered in their wider context. The first text is taken from Diogenes Laertius (7.52–53)[45] and has its source in the *Cursory Repertoire of Philosophers* by Diocles of

---

42 Cf., among other texts, Sen. *Ep.* 76.15–16: "ratio [...] recta et ad naturae suae voluntatem accommodata. Haec vocatur virtus, [...];" Cic. *Ac.* 1.38 = *SVF* 1.199 (Zeno); [Plu.] *Virt. mor.* 441c = *SVF* 1.202 (Zeno, Chrysippus, Aristo).
43 In the last sentence cited on p. 19 (Arr. *Epict.* 2.11.3), where Epictetus says that we add our own opinions to the innate anticipated grasps.
44 Jackson-McCabe 2004.
45 Cf. D.L. 7.50–54 (vol. 2, p. 318,16–320,10 Long) = *SVF* 2.55, 60, 61, 71, 84, 87 and 105.

Magnesia (first century CE). At paragraph 49 it is said that to end up with the definition of their criterion of truth, the Stoics believe one must begin by speaking of representation (*phantasia*) and sense perception (*aisthēsis*),

> insofar as the criterion, by which the truth of things is known, is generically a representation, and insofar as the theory of assent (*sunkatathesis*) – and that of the grasp or comprehension (*katalēpsis*) and conception (*noēsis*) – which comes before the others, cannot exist without representation. Indeed, representation comes first, followed by thought (*dianoia*), which is apt to speak (*eklalētikē*) and which expresses in speech what it experiences from representation.[46]

Paragraph 50 contains the distinction between representation (*phantasia*) and phantasm (*phantasma*), where the phantasm is a fancy (*dokēsis*) of thought (*dianoia*), as occurs in dreams, whereas the representation was, according to Chrysippus in the second book of his treatise *On the Soul*, not exactly an imprint, like the imprint left by a seal,[47] but an alteration of the soul produced by an existing object:

> Indeed, this imprint must not be understood as the mark left by a seal, since it is impossible for multiple marks to coexist simultaneously in the same place.[48] One conceives (*noeitai*) the representation as that which is engraved, struck, and imprinted from an existing object, in conformity with that object (*apo huparchontos kata to huparchon*), in such a way that it would not occur if the object did not exist.[49]

This last description, we might add, can only concern sense perception, for as we learn later on (61),[50] the phantasm of thought (*ennoēma*), since it does not represent a real object, "is neither something existent nor something qualified but something quasi-existent and quasi-qualified," and therefore cannot be a true imprint but only a certain modification of the guiding part of the soul (*hēgemonikon*) by itself.[51]

Paragraph 51 presents two divisions: [1] The first of these divides into representations based on sense perception (*phantasiai aisthētikai*), realized by one or more sense organs, and representations based on thought (*phantasiai dia tēs dianoias*), which, to judge by paragraphs 50 and 61, are also called "phantasms." We are thus already confronted by a certain inconsistency as far as terminology is concerned. The objects of the *phantasiai dia tēs dianoias* = *phantasmata* are the incorporeals, and all the objects grasped by reasoning, whereas the representations based on sense percep-

---

46 Translation based on the version by R. Goulet in M.-O. Goulet-Cazé 1999, 823, slightly modified.
47 Such was, it seems, the view of Cleanthes.
48 Compare Sext. Emp. *Math.* 7.228–229.
49 Translation based on the version by R. Goulet in M.-O Goulet-Cazé 1999, 823. Cf. below, note 53, the citation of Sextus Empiricus.
50 This time, the source of Diogenes Laertius is Diogenes of Babylon.
51 Cf. the quotation from Sextus Empiricus in note 53.

tion come from existent objects and are accompanied by a consent (*eixis*) and an assent (*sunkatathesis*).

[2] There follows a division into rational representations (*phantasiai logikai*), called conceptions (*noēseis*), and into irrational representations (*phantasiai alogoi*), which have not received a name. The former belong to living beings endowed with reason, the latter to living beings bereft of reason; some occur through learning (*phantasiai technikai*), and the others without learning (*phantasiai atechnoi*).

Paragraph 52, with which Inwood's quotation begins, starts off with an enumeration of the multiple meanings of the term "sense perception:"

> One calls sense perception (*aisthēsis*), according to the Stoics, the breath (*pneuma*) that extends from the guiding part [of the soul] to the senses (*aisthēseis*) as well as the grasp or comprehension (*katalēpsis*) that these senses ensure, and the equipment in sense organs, with regard to which some are crippled. But the action [of the senses] is also called sense perception.

The grasp or comprehension (*katalēpsis*) is then divided into comprehension realized by sense perception (the latter, as has been said, may be called "sense perception" *simpliciter*) and a comprehension realized by reason:

> As far as comprehension is concerned, that of things that are white, black, rough, or soft derives from sense perception, but that of the conclusions provided by demonstration, for instance that the gods exist and that they exercise providence, derives from reason (*logos*).[52]

The paragraph concludes with a division of the products of these comprehensions, the concepts:

> For among the concepts (*nooumena*), some are conceived by contact (*kata periptosin*),[53] others by similarity (*kat' homoiotēta*), others by analogy (*kat' analogian*),

---

52 That the gods exercise providence is no longer a common notion like that of their pure existence, so that it must be supported by demonstrations.

53 Κατὰ περίπτωσιν: "by the fact of falling upon," hence, probably, R. Goulet's translation "par contact," which I adopt. For according to the Stoics, sense perception always takes place by a corporeal contact with the object, even for vision and sight, and the following sentence of our text affirms that it is precisely sense objects (τὰ αἰσθητά) that are conceived by περίπτωσις. Cf. Sext. Emp. *Math.* 8.409: "[...] in this way some of the objects represented, such as white and black and the body in general, produce an imprint in the guiding part of the soul as if by touching and contact (οἱονεὶ ψαύοντα καὶ θιγγάνοντα τοῦ ἡγεμονικοῦ), while others are not of this nature since the guiding part gives rise to a representation resulting from them and not through their agency (τοῦ ἡγεμονικοῦ ἐπ' αὐτοῖς φαντασιουμένου καὶ οὐχ ὑπ' αὐτῶν), as in the case of incorporeal expressions." However, Inwood translates κατὰ περίπτωσιν by "on the basis of direct experience;" Bury, in his translation of Sext. Emp. *Math.* 8.56–57 for the Loeb Classical Library (1935), by "owing to experience;" and Jackson-McCabe by "by direct experience" (Jackson-McCabe 2004, 329). Κατὰ περίπτωσιν could also be

<others by transfer> (*kata metathesin*), others by synthesis (*kata sunthesin*), others by opposition (*kat' enantiōsin*).[54]

Paragraph 53 is entirely devoted to the explanation of the division of concepts:

> Sensible things are thus conceived by contact. By similarity, the things conceived on the basis of a neighboring object, as Socrates from his image. By analogy, in the sense of an increase in size, <for instance> Tityos or a Cyclops, or a diminution, for instance a pygmy. Likewise, the center of the earth is conceived by analogy with smaller spheres. [Other things are conceived] by transfer, like eyes on the chest. The Centaur is conceived by composition. Death, by opposition. Something is also conceived by deduction, like the expressibles (*lekta*) and place. *Something just (dikaion ti) and good is conceived (noeitai) in a natural way (phusikōs).*[55] And (other concepts are obtained) by privation, like a one-armed man. This is a sample of their doctrines concerning representation, sense perception, and conception (*noēsis*).[56]

Thus, after having discussed (in 51) representations based on sense perception (*phantasiai aisthētikai*) and representations based on thought (*phantasiai dia tēs dianoias*) – also called "phantasms" (*phantasmata*) in 50 as well as *phantasmata dianoias* and "intellections" (*ennoēmata*) in 61 – and then introduced (in 52) grasps or comprehensions (*katalēpseis*) resulting either from sense perception (*aisthēsis*) or reason (*logos*), Diocles deals at

---

> translated by "through encounter," but "experience" would rather be the translation of the Greek word ἐμπειρία, used in the text of Aëtius, which we will discuss below (pp. 26f., section [b]). There is a tendency to see a parallel to the sentence I have just cited in the text from Cic. *Fin.* 3.33 translated *infra*, p. 32: "Cumque rerum notiones in animis fiant, si aut usu aliquid cognitum sit aut coniunctione aut similitudine aut conlatione rationis [...]." According to this view, "usu" would be the translation of κατὰ περίπτωσιν, and "coniunctione," "similitudine," and "conlatione rationis" the translation of σύνθεσις, ὁμοιότης, and ἀναλογία (Pohlenz 1948, vol. 2, p. 34), which is correct for the last three notions. Yet there is no guarantee that "usu," which would be a very curious way to translate κατὰ περίπτωσιν, does not translate ἐμπειρία instead. In any case, modern translations should mark the etymological difference that exists between ἐμπειρία and περίπτωσις, but this is not the case either in Inwood's translation, or in that of Jackson-McCabe, which render both ἐμπειρία and περίπτωσις by "experience."

54 After the translation (modified) by R. Goulet in M.-O. Goulet-Cazé 1999, 824.
55 Inwood 2005, 272 translates the phrase "φυσικῶς δὲ νοεῖται δίκαιόν τι καὶ ἀγαθόν" thus: "And there is a natural origin too for the conception of something just and good," but there is no equivalent for "too" in the Greek text. The addition of this "too" places, without justification, the mode of conception of the just and the good on the same level as all the other conceptions named previously in [a] and [b], on p. 24, all of which would thus take place in a natural way instead of being distinct from one another. As I shall explain below (p. 29), this is a viewpoint I do not share.
56 After the translation of R. Goulet (824–825), slightly modified.

the end of 52 as well as in 53 with the different modes of generation of concepts (*ta nooumena*). These take place

[a] either by contact, that is, by sense perception of sensible things,

[b] or by operations of thought (but, as emerges from the context, on the basis of sensible things), such as assimilation, analogy, transfer, composition, opposition, privation (added at the end after c) and deduction,[57]

[c] or in a natural way (*phusikōs*).

Since, according to Cicero (*Fin.* 3.33, cited on p. 32), who depends on Hellenistic Greek sources, and later according to Seneca (*Ep.* 120), the concept of good is formed by analogy and is therefore classified in the category of concepts listed under [b], the "natural way" of conceiving, not the just and the good themselves, but "something just and good," must be different from the preceding modes of conception.[58] We note that Inwood speaks with regard to this sentence of the "mystery of this inference" (278). For my part, I would, with Jackson-McCabe,[59] tend to compare this mode of conceiving to the "innate anticipated grasps or comprehensions" (*prolēpseis emphutoi*) of Chrysippus.[60] I interpret it against the background of such texts as the diatribes of Musonius and Epictetus cited above (pp. 18–20), texts which show the indispensable role of anticipated grasps or pre-notions, implanted or innate, in the subsequent acquisition of true notions in the field of ethics. In Diocles, too, we therefore have an allusion to *prolēpseis emphutoi*, or pre-notions furnished by nature, in other words, innate.

Finally, paragraph 54, which, according to David E. Hahm, comes from another of Diogenes Laertius's sources, in particular from a Stoic "Introductory Handbook,"[61] returns to the criterion of truth:

> They say that it is the comprehensive representation (*kataleptikē phantasia*), that is, the one that comes from an existing object,[62] as is stated by Chrysippus in the

---

57 Among the operations of thought mentioned, deduction, like the demonstration mentioned in 52, is logically the one at the greatest remove from sensible objects.

58 Cf. the τι ("something") in the text by Diocles with the τινα ("some things") of the text by Arr. *Epict.* 2.11.6, cited p. 19.

59 Jackson-McCabe 2004, 329.

60 Cf. pp. 17f. above and pp. 24–26 below.

61 On this, cf. R. Goulet in M.-O. Goulet-Cazé 1999, 822 n. 1. This "Handbook" would be the source of D.L. 7.54–82. But the question of the extent of the quotation from Diocles cannot be solved with certainty (R. Goulet 1994, 757–777).

62 Cf. D.L. 7.46 (after the translation, slightly modified, by R. Goulet in M.-O. Goulet-Cazé 1999, 821): "The representation can be comprehensive or not comprehensive. The comprehensive representation, of which they [the Stoics] say that it is the criterion of realities (τῶν πραγμάτων), is the one that comes from an

second book of his *Physics*, Antipater and Apollodorus [...]. But Chrysippus [...] in the first book of his treatise *On Reason* says that the criteria are sense perception and anticipated grasp (*prolēpsis*). The anticipated grasp is a *natural* notion of what is general (*ennoia phusikē tōn katholou*).

It is highly likely that the quotation from Chrysippus ends after "anticipated grasp" (*prolēpsis*), for the following phrase has very much the character of a gloss, and was therefore not reproduced by H. von Arnim in *SVF* 2.94. Indeed, the possibility is by no means to be excluded that it is due to the author of the "Introductory Handbook" I have just mentioned, which, as D. E. Hahm suggests, is the source of this and the following paragraphs. The possible inauthenticity of this phrase, although mentioned briefly at his note 24, was not taken into account by Jackson-McCabe, for he subsequently treats this definition like an authentic statement by Chrysippus.[63] The explanation which the gloss tries to provide is not transparent. What precise meaning must we give here to the term *katholou*? Above all, a *prolēpsis* is *stricto sensu* not a notion (*ennoia*), but an anticipated grasp, or pre-notion. It is possible that here, as sometimes in Epictetus,[64] the term *ennoia* may be used in an imprecise way, but it is by no means certain that this imprecision is due to Chrysippus.

If we limit ourselves to the authentic text of Chrysippus, the criteria of truth mentioned are the following: in the second book of his *Physics* "the comprehensive representation (*kataleptikē phantasia*), that is, the one that comes from an existing object," and in the treatise *On Reason* sense perception (*aisthēsis*) and anticipated grasp (*prolēpsis*). That the latter corresponds to Chrysippus's "innate" or "implanted" anticipated grasp that I mentioned above (pp. 17f.), seems to me be proved by a text from Seneca (*Ep.* 117.6, cited below at p. 29), where the existence of the gods as an innate belief (*opinio insita*) or anticipated grasp (*praesumptio*) is men-

---

existing object and is imprinted and engraved in conformity with that existent object. Non-comprehensive are those which either do not come from an existent object or those which come from an existent object, but are not in conformity with the object (ἀπὸ ὑπάρχοντος μέν, μὴ κατ' αὐτὸ δὲ τὸ ὑπάρχον [as for instance the representations taken from memory]): those which are not clear or distinct." Comprehensive representations therefore belong to the category of representations based on immediate sense perception.

63 Jackson-McCabe 2004, 328.
64 Cf. Bonhöffer 1890, 197: "Wo es Epiktet darauf ankommt, das Apriorische des Begriffes hervorzuheben, bezeichnet er nicht bloss die ἔννοια, sondern auch die πρόληψις bestimmter als φυσική oder ἔμφυτος (II,11,2 etc.; II,17,7; I,22,9; vergl. 22,39 [...]). [...] Nichtsdestoweniger bedeutet in vielen Fällen die blosse ἔννοια (ohne den Zusatz φυσική) thatsächlich eine eingepflanzte Vorstellung, also eine πρόληψις im eigentlichen Sinne, während andererseits mit πρόληψις zuweilen auch ein empirisch (sei es durch Sinneswahrnehmung oder durch das Denken) gewonnener Begriff bezeichnet wird."

tioned as a criterion of truth.⁶⁵ Under no circumstances, it seems to me, can the *prolēpsis* of Chrysippus, in this specific text, have the same meaning as the *prolēpsis* (also called *ennoia*) of Aëtius, which we will discuss next. The latter is not innate, but occurs in a natural way (*phusikōs*), that is, by means of sense perception coming from outside and without a learning process. Otherwise, Chrysippus would have mentioned, in the authentic part of the quotation, the same thing – sense perception – twice as the criteria of truth.

The second text translated by Inwood is Aëtius 4.11= *SVF* 2.83, written about the end of the first century BCE and the beginning of the first century CE (the disposition into paragraphs is my own):

> How sense perception (*aisthēsis*), notion (*ennoia*), and inner language (*ho kata endiathesin logos*) take place.
>
> [a] The Stoics say: when a human being is born, the guiding part (*hēgemonikon*) of his soul resembles a papyrus leaf that has been well prepared in order to be written on. It inscribes each of the notions on it.⁶⁶

---

65 Unlike Jackson-McCabe 2004, 341–346, I see no difficulty in conceiving that the *communis opinio* according to which the gods exist could have been considered as innate as early as Old Stoicism, at least since Chrysippus. As we have seen (above, n. 19), Cicero bears witness to the fact that this viewpoint had already been adopted by Stoics belonging to the first half of the last century of the Hellenistic period, and not merely in the Imperial period. In any case, the indisputably ancient Stoic tenet mentioned above (p. 13), according to which a certain kinship exists between gods and men, a kinship based on their common participation (albeit to very different degrees) in divine reason, could have provided a sufficient explanation, both with a view to the presence of the "starting points," "seeds", and "germs" of virtue, innate within human souls, and of the innate traces of the memory of their origin. There is no need to seek any Platonic influence, other than that which is inherent in Stoic philosophy from the beginning.

66 It is astonishing that Aëtius did not take into account the correction made to Cleanthes' views by Chrysippus, even though it is useful. Chrysippus thought one should speak of an alteration of the *hēgemonikon* instead of an imprint (cf. above, p. 21 paragraph 50 and *SVF* 2.56). Indeed, to writing on a papyrus leaf, one could make the same objection as to the imprint of a seal in wax, for it is impossible for an unlimited quantity of writing signs to fit on the same leaf without the first ones having been gradually destroyed by erasure or superposition. In both cases, the possibility of storing representations and memorizing them would be excluded for the same reason. Although, from this viewpoint, the comparison of the guiding part of the soul, the *hēgemonikon*, with a papyrus leaf is unsatisfactory, the other element of the comparison – the fact of being well-prepared (*euergon*), one to be inscribed, the other to receive representations – is apt and deserves to be emphasized. If we move from metaphor to the psychic reality envisaged by the Stoics, this means that the human soul, like that of the animals, is by nature made capable of receiving modifications from sense perceptions, and is therefore not an empty leaf in the sense that it does not possess any qualification. This aptitude for having sensations (sense perceptions) is innate, that is, not acquired after birth. As we

[b] The first mode of inscription is that which takes place by the senses (*dia tōn aisthēseōn*). For when they perceive something, for instance white, they retain a memory (*mnēmē*) of it after it disappears. When there are many memories of the same kind, we call that "experience" (*empeiria*), for experience consists in a large number of representations (*phantasiai*) of the same kind.

[c] Of notions (*ennoiai*) some are produced *naturally* (*phusikōs*) in the way that has been mentioned and without technical elaboration (*anepitechnētōs*), while others are already produced by means of our teaching and solicitude. The latter are merely called "notions" (*ennoiai*), whereas the former are also called "anticipated grasps" (*prolēpseis*).

[d] Yet reason (*logos*), with regard to which we are called "rational," is said to be filled with anticipated grasps around the first hebdomad [= toward the age of seven].

[e] The "intellection" (*ennoēma*) is a *phantasma*[67] (representation) of the thought of the rational living being: when the *phantasma* comes into being in a rational soul, in this case it is called "intellection" (*ennoēma*), taking this name from the intellect (*nous*).

[f] This is why what comes into existence in living beings bereft of reason is a mere *phantasma*, but what comes into existence in us and in the gods, are generically (*kata genos*) *phantasmata* and specifically (*kat' eidos*) intellections, as denarii and staters, taken in themselves, are denarii and staters, but when they are given to hire a ship, at that moment, besides being denarii, they are also called "passage fare."

Already in Diocles, as transmitted by Diogenes Laertius (50 and 51) and another source of Diogenes Laertius (61), we noted a certain inconsistency in the use of terminology: the representation (*phantasia*) resulting from thought (*dianoia*) in dreams was designated by the term *phantasma*, but in the texts I have discussed subsequently the representations produced as well by sense perception as by thought are always called *phantasiai*. Similarly, Aëtius once (at the end of [b]) uses the word *phantasiai* for sensory representations and in the paragraphs [e] and [f] always the term *phantasmata*. When one compares Diocles's text with that of Aëtius, one notes that Aëtius generally employs the term *phantasma* where Diocles uses the term *phantasia*. For instance, compare the passage from Aëtius 4.11.4–5 =

---

have seen, however, the human soul is, in addition, naturally capable of acquiring virtue. It possesses starting points, germs, or sparks of virtue, which it may or may not develop, for, since human reason has a certain kinship with divine reason, it naturally possesses a basis of goodness, as well as certain innate anticipated grasps. Thus, the human soul possesses multiple predispositions at birth.

67 I maintain the transliteration of the Greek term *phantasma*, instead of translating it by "representation," which was the translation of *phantasia* in the text from Diocles, since I would like to emphasize the differences in terminology in Diocles and in Aëtius.

SVF 2.83, lines 24–28 and D.L. 7.51, p. 319, 5–7 Long.[68] Despite the difference in vocabulary, the two passages describe the same psychic realities, but Aëtius speaks of *phantasmata* and *ennoēma* where Diocles uses the terms *phantasiai* and *noēseis*. In the text from Aëtius, the notion of *phantasma* can therefore be both a generic term and a specific term, with the same functions being occupied by the term *phantasma* in Diocles. These different uses of the terms *phantasia* and *phantasma* also appear in other Stoic texts.

Another difference in meaning can be observed in the significations of the adverb *phusikōs* ("in a natural way") in Diocles's account at D.L. 7.53 and my paragraph [c] in the text of Aëtius. In Aëtius the "natural way" in which these kinds of notions, which can also be called "anticipated grasps" (*prolepseis*), occur is the one "that has just been mentioned" and thus the one that involves sense perception coming from outside. These *prolēpseis* that occur *phusikōs* are therefore not innate, and *phusikōs* means here "by means of sense perception." On the contrary, in paragraph 53 of Diogenes Laertius, a paragraph devoted entirely to the various modes of the genesis of concepts, the adverb *phusikōs* in the phrase "In a natural way (*phusikōs*) is conceived something just and good", can in no way be referred to genesis through sense perception, which was mentioned first. As I said above (p. 24), this mode of conception must rather be compared with the "innate anticipated grasps" of Chrysippus.

I believe these observations are important, for they warn us against the preconception that the same terms must always have exactly the same meaning within a single philosophy, in this case Stoicism.

From the two quoted texts placed side by side I draw the following information concerning the development of human reason: The first stage, shared by mankind with the animals, is that of sense perception, which, according to the opinion of Chrysippus and in opposition to Cleanthes, is not an imprint, but an alteration in the still-empty guiding part of the human soul. Sense perception takes place by physical contact (*periptōsis*) between a truly existent object and the guiding part, through the intermediary of the sense organs. The repetition of these sense perceptions (Diocles: *phantasiai aisthētikai*; Aëtius [b]: *phantasiai*) constitutes a memory, while

---

68 Aëtius: [...] τὸ γὰρ φάντασμα ἐπειδὰν λογικῇ προσπίπτῃ ψυχῇ, τότε ἐννόημα καλεῖται εἰληφὸς τοὔνομα παρὰ τοῦ νοῦ. Διόπερ τοῖς ἀλόγοις ζῴοις ὅσα προσπίπτει, φαντάσματα μόνον ἐστίν· ὅσα δὲ ἡμῖν καὶ τοῖς θεοῖς, ταῦτα καὶ φαντάσματα κατὰ γένος καὶ ἐννοήματα κατ' εἶδος.
Diocles: Ἔτι τῶν φαντασιῶν αἱ μέν εἰσι λογικαί, αἱ δὲ ἄλογοι· λογικαὶ μὲν αἱ τῶν λογικῶν ζῴων, ἄλογοι δὲ αἱ τῶν ἀλόγων. αἱ μὲν οὖν λογικαὶ νοήσεις εἰσίν, αἱ δ' ἄλογοι οὐ τετυχήκασιν ὀνόματος. Compare also D.L. 7.61: Ἐννόημα δέ ἐστι φάντασμα διανοίας, [...].

several memories of the same kind produce experience (*empeiria*). According to Aëtius, from the accumulation of these experiences, initially based on sense perception, there results in a natural way (*phusikōs*), without the intervention of thought, a first category of notions or concepts, that of "anticipated grasps" (*prolēpseis*), which are therefore not strictly speaking concepts, but a kind of pre-concepts or pre-notions.

On the basis of this text from Aëtius, and before the appearance of the article by Jackson-McCabe, the virtually universal opinion had been formed that the term "*phusikōs*" as well in D.L. 7.53 as in the turn of phrase *ennoia phusikē* of the gloss to paragraph 54 designates the process of the formation of pre-notions issuing from memorized sense perceptions, the accumulation of which constitutes experience. Yet as I have already said (p. 24), it is obvious that the *phusikōs* mode of conceiving "something just and good" in Diocles's account (D.L. 7.53) is not based on sense perception, for – and this is just one of many reasons – the concepts that take place by sense perception (by contact) were listed first in this text. As far as paragraph 54 is concerned, I refer to what has been said above at p. 25.

I therefore think that the meaning of the term *prolēpsis* is not the same in Chrysippus and in Aëtius. To judge by the following text, the *prolēpsis* or anticipated grasp of Chrysippus, which works like a criterion of truth, must be an innate common notion like the one mentioned above (pp. 17f.). It is Seneca who at *Ep.* 117.6 translates the Greek term *prolēpsis* literally by *praesumptio*:

> We [sc. the Stoics] are accustomed to accord a great deal of importance to the anticipated grasp (*praesumptio* = Greek *prolēpsis*) which is shared by all men, and for us something which seems true to all is a proof of truth (*argumentum veritatis*): Thus, we deduce the existence of the gods, among other things, from the fact that the conviction (*opinio*) [of the existence] of the gods is implanted (*insita* = Greek *emphutos* = "implanted, innate") in all men, and that nowhere does any race exist that has launched itself to such an extent outside the laws and morals that it no longer believes in some gods.

The innate character of this common opinion was already affirmed by the Stoic Balbus in Cicero, *N.D.* 2.12 (cf. above, p. 17).

I can leave aside the third text translated by Inwood (Sext. Emp. *Math.* 8.56 = *SVF* 2.88), for it contributes nothing new with regard to the first two texts.

Outside of the furtive mention of a natural possibility of knowing something just and good,[69] the texts by Diocles and Aëtius speak neither of the way the notions of good and the supreme good are formed, nor of the preparatory role played in this regard by Stoic *oikeiōsis*, a term which we translate by "appropriation." This is why Inwood has translated several

---

69 See above, p. 24.

texts by Cicero that pertain to this problem, some of which I will also take up. Cicero's demonstrations on the subject of *oikeiōsis* begin at *Fin*. 3.16–17, which I replace by the more concise parallel text of Diogenes Laertius, 7.85f. = *SVF* 3.178.[70] This text shows, moreover, that the parallel version in Cicero has the same source as Diogenes: Chrysippus's treatise *On Goals*, book 1.

> The primary impulse (*prōtē hormē*) possessed by the animate being (*zōon*) has as its goal, they say, self-preservation, owing to the fact that nature, right from the outset, appropriates it [to itself], as Chrysippus says in the first book of his treatise *On Goals*, when he says that for every animate being the first object proper to it is its own constitution and the consciousness it has of this constitution. Indeed, it would not be likely that [nature] had rendered the animate being alien [to itself], nor that, once it had made the animal, it did not render it either alien or appropriate [to itself]. It remains to say, therefore, that in constituting it, it has appropriated it to itself; indeed, in this way it rejects what is damaging to it and pursues what is proper to it. What some say: that the primary impulse in animate beings tends toward pleasure, they [sc. the Stoics] show that this is false. Indeed, they say that pleasure, if it really exists, is an accessory result, when nature itself and in itself, having sought what is in harmony with its constitution, seizes it: In this way animate beings give off a joy in living and plants prosper. And nature, they say, makes no distinction between plants and animate beings, since it governs the former as well, without impulse or sensation, and the vegetative character also occurs within us. Yet since impulse is added in animate beings, which they use to move toward what is proper to them, for these animate beings the [behavior] in conformity with nature consists in being governed in conformity with impulse. Yet when reason is granted to rational beings with a view to more perfect regulation, it is just that living in conformity to nature becomes for them living in conformity to reason.[71] Indeed, the latter comes as fulfillment as an artisan working on impulse.

In this text, which basically takes up the Stoic doctrine of the ranks in the hierarchy of beings mentioned above (pp. 12f.), it is the last two sentences that are the most interesting: For mankind, "living according to nature" means "living according to reason," and still more precisely according to right reason, which is his greatest good. It is reason that, as we recall, is not yet manifest in early childhood, which must so to speak work on or mold the primary impulses in order to arrive at this ultimate goal. What we must also retain from this text is the fact that these primary post-natal impulses, the *prōtai hormai*, which characterize the first stage of *oikeiōsis* and function only with a view to self-preservation and the proper use of the body, are common to human beings and to animals, and cannot be identified with Cleanthes's *aphormai pros aretēn* which we have discovered above (p. 14).

---

70 Translation after R. Goulet in M.-O. Goulet-Cazé 1999, 845–846, slightly modified.
71 Cf. Sen. *Ep.* 124.9–12.

We find some information on the second as well as the last stage of *oikeiōsis* in Cicero, *Fin.* 3.21 = *SVF* 3.188. Cicero begins by repeating that in the first stage, the small child is concerned with the preservation of his natural state, instinctively choosing the things that contribute to it and rejecting those that are contrary to it. Then, in the second stage, he must maintain himself in this state by continuing to make the right choice between what is and is not in conformity with nature. And, he says, once the child has discovered how to choose what is in conformity with nature and to reject what is not (*inventa selectione et item reiectione*), there follows choice according to what is appropriate (*cum officio selectio*: these are the imperfect duties). In the third stage, this choice becomes stable, and finally extremely constant, while remaining in accord with nature. It is in this choice, says Cicero, that "what can genuinely be called 'good' begins to be present and perceived."

Here, then, it is not in relation to a cognitive act, a conceptual grasp, that the good is mentioned, but with regard to an action and a *habitus*: It is in appropriate choice that has become a firm disposition, and which is the expression of virtue itself, and thus in the final stage of human perfection that is almost never achieved, that the genuine good is said to reveal itself for the first time. Yet this firm disposition is itself the result of a long apprenticeship, to which Cicero makes only a brief allusion in the words *inventa selectione et reiectione* and which is nothing other than the result of philosophical teaching, which he himself has mentioned in the text quoted above (p. 15) as necessary[72] for achieving virtue.

The formation of the notion of the good is dealt with in the continuation of this text, still at Cic. *Fin.* 3.21:

> First comes man's appropriation with the things that are in conformity with nature. Yet as soon as he has grasped a comprehension, or better a concept, which the Stoics call *ennoia*, and he sees the order of actions and, so to speak, their harmony (*concordia*), he appreciates this harmony much more than the things he loved previously, and this is how he arrives, with the help of analogy, at the conclusion (*observatione et ratione collegit*)[73] that this is the dwelling place of that famous supreme good of mankind, which is to be esteemed and sought for itself.

Taken in isolation, this text could lead us to believe that the concept of the sovereign good is formed, beginning with the age of reason, in a way that is exclusively empirical, with the help of observations and comparisons, for nothing is said about what, in the Stoics' view, makes us capable of

---

72 Cf. Sen. *Ep.* 90.46: "Virtue is accessible only to a soul trained and entirely instructed and brought to its culminating point by incessant exercises."
73 Cf. the following quote and Sen. *Ep.* 120.4: "[…] nobis videtur observatio collegisse [*sc.* the notion of virtue] et rerum saepe factarum inter se conlatio," a complex circumlocution which he translates in the following sentence by *analogia*.

distinguishing what is morally good, for instance, from what is useful but morally bad in our observations and comparisons. This problem is alluded to in another text by Cicero, which is also cited by Inwood:

> The good, which has so often come up in these discussions, may also be clarified by a definition. But their [sc. the Stoics'] definitions, although they differ very little among themselves, all end up at the same point. For my part, I approve of Diogenes, who defined the good as that which is complete according to nature. As a consequence, he has also declared that what is useful (as we would like to call the Greek *ōphelēma*) is the movement or state that results from this completed nature. Since the notions of things (*rerum notiones*) are formed in intellects (*in animis*) when something is conceived either by usage (*usu*),[74] synthesis (*coniunctione*), similarity (*similitudine*), or analogy (*collatione rationis*),[75] the notion of good was formed by this fourth operation, which I have listed last. Indeed, when our intellect (*animus*) rises with the help of analogy from the things that are in conformity with nature, at that moment it reaches the notion of the good. However, we do not feel (*sentimus*) this good itself and call it "good" either by adjunction or by increase[76] or by comparison with other things, but by its own force. Indeed, although honey is extremely sweet, it is not sensed as sweet in comparison with other things but by its own kind of taste, just so this good we are discussing is the one that is to be most esteemed, but this esteem is not based on its dimensions but on its [particular] kind. (Cic. *Fin*. 3.33–34 = *SVF* 3.72)

Inwood has cited but not commented on this passage, which, toward its end, opposes the notion of the good, which is formed by analogy, to the good itself, which is known not by analogy but makes itself known by its own force. And yet, this passage could have put him on the right track, for here, it is said, albeit in a somewhat roundabout way, that if we can elaborate the notion of the good with the help of the method of analogy, that is, by a cognitive procedure, it is because we already have previously a natural capacity, not to know it, but to "feel" it: that is, to have an existential experience of its value when we encounter it. In other words, the starting points, or seeds, or sparks of virtue that are innate within us, which we have discussed above in section I, enable us to have an instantaneous apprehension of the good when we encounter it in one form or another, as long as we do not allow our vices to annihilate or smother these seeds or sparks.

It is enough to read Seneca's *Letter* 94 to clarify the background of Cicero's text. This letter evokes the heresy of Aristo of Chios, a student of Zeno, the founder of the Stoic school, who objected to the Stoic division of

---

74 Cf. above, note 53 (toward the end, p. 23).
75 Cf. Sen. *Ep.* 120.4.
76 These are the modes of analogy: cf. above, p. 23 (D.L. 7.53) the enumeration of the various modes of analogy by enlargement or by diminution.

philosophy into two parts: a dogmatic part and a paraenetic part,[77] wishing to retain only the dogmatic part. Seneca, following Cleanthes, defends the general viewpoint of the Stoics by pleading in favor of the paraenetic part. I will limit myself here to citing only a few extracts from his plea:

> Souls bear within them the seeds of all things morally good (*omnium honestarum rerum semina*), which are made to emerge by admonition, not otherwise than a spark, aided by a light breeze, unfolds its fire. Virtue stands up straight when it is touched and set in motion. (Sen. *Ep.* 94.29)

To Aristo's objection that admonitions are not useful for anyone who does not possess correct tenets and is a slave of his vices, Seneca replies that they are useful precisely in helping him get rid of his vices:

> Indeed, in him the natural disposition (*indoles naturalis*) is not extinguished, but obscured and oppressed. Even in this state, it tries to get back up and strive against what is bad, and if it obtains assistance and is aided by precepts, it regains strength, unless, of course, a lengthy disease has not finally infected it and killed it, for when this happens, teaching in philosophy will no longer put it back in shape, even if this teaching has striven with all its might. (Sen. *Ep.* 94.31)

A bit farther on (*Ep.* 94.42), Seneca observes that examples have the same effects as precepts, that is, they awaken and reinforce our innate dispositions toward virtue, a remark that is very important for understanding the value of examples alongside paraenesis in Stoic philosophy. We shall return to this point with regard to *Letter* 120. Let us cite one more remark:

> But who will deny, indeed, that some precepts strike even the most ignorant? For instance these words, although they are so brief, nevertheless possess a great deal of weight: "Nothing in excess," "No gain satisfies a greedy mind," "Do not expect from others anything else than that what you would have done to another." *We do not hear such things without receiving a certain shock* (*cum ictu quodam*), and no one has the right to start to doubt and to say "Why is that?" *For the truth itself drags us along even without giving reasons.* (Sen. *Ep.* 94.43)[78]

From the beginning to the end of their history, the Stoics believed that the path toward virtue or the highest good is accomplished in the following way. At the beginning is the *conditio sine qua non*, that is, the innate starting points (*aphormai*) and anticipated grasps (*emphutoi prolēpseis*), seeds (*semina, logoi spermatikoi*), or sparks (*igniculi*) of virtue, which are, moreover, nothing other than the germs of right reason. They remain more

---

77 I have discussed this bipartition and the conclusions to be drawn from it at length in Hadot 1969, which will appear in an updated French version in 2014.
78 Cf. such passages as, once again, Sen. *Ep.* 108.8: "Nature has given the foundations and the seeds of virtue to all. We were all born for all those things [*sc.* for the virtues]: When a stimulus arrives, then all those good things which had dozed off, so to speak, are reawakened. Don't you see how the theaters resound with applause whenever something is said that we openly appreciate and whose truth we attest by our unanimity?"

or less latent during the first seven years of life, during which the young child is busy following his first impressions and appropriating what the Stoics call "the first gifts of nature (*prima naturae*)."[79] Even at this stage, however, during which the other, empirically acquired anticipated grasps are formed naturally (*phusikōs*) and without the intervention of thought, the negative influence of the environment can already have bad effects,[80] and this is why Chrysippus accorded the greatest importance even to the choice of nursemaids.[81] Beginning with the age of reason, the notions develop with the help of thought and instruction, and the predispositions to virtue can either be smothered by a hostile milieu or developed by means of a rational environment, and by the teaching of Stoic philosophy, the various forms of paraenesis, and good examples.[82] According to the Stoics, the life of a person lacking instruction can certainly give rise to phenomena that bear some resemblance to true virtue. These are, so to speak, the "matters" of true virtue (*materia virtutis*), but true virtue "is only accessible to a soul that has been trained, thoroughly instructed, and brought to its culminating point by incessant exercises" (Sen. *Ep.* 90.46). These exercises are spiritual exercises.

In view of the complexity of the conditions and formation of what, in the Stoics' view, is indispensable for achieving their highest good, and also in view of the fact that the Stoics' notion of the good is not constructed by the mere mechanism of purely cognitive acts, the rare texts collected in the *SVF* under the heading "On Notions,"[83] almost all of which we have interpreted, cannot inform us about the means foreseen by the Stoics for achieving the supreme good represented by virtue. Inwood is well aware of this, but he should have sought the answer to his question in the whole of Stoic literature instead of suspecting a gap in the Stoic doctrinal system.

III. Succinct Interpretation of Seneca's *Letter* 120

We now come to the interpretation of Seneca's *Letter* 120. After observing (120.3) that nothing is good that is not morally good (*honestum*), he pre-

---

79 Cf. Aulus Gellius 12.7, where the Platonist Taurus discusses the Stoic doctrine of good and evil.
80 Cf. *SVF* 3.228–236.
81 Cf. Quint. *Inst.* 1.4–5.
82 Cf. Sen. *Ep.* 94.45: "Virtue is divided into two parts: the contemplation of the true and action. Doctrinal teaching transmits contemplation, while admonition transmits action."
83 These are the texts of Aëtius and Diocles of Magnesia, interpreted above, and Sext. Emp. *Math.* 8.56 and 8.409.

pares to respond to Lucilius, who asks him how the first notion (*prima notitia*) of the good has reached us: "That, he says, Nature has not been able to teach us: she has given us the seeds (*semina*) of the knowledge [of the good], but not knowledge [itself]." Inwood comments: "Natural acquisition is ruled out (since nature only gives us the *semina scientiae*)." That is all.[84] He does not see that this sentence already contains the key to his problem: As we have seen, the seeds given by nature are nothing other than the innate starting points for a possible knowledge of the good. Seneca has no need to be explicit, for he has abundantly developed this subject in his previous letters.[85] Then (120.4), Seneca indicates (like Cicero)[86] the method of analogy as a formative element of the primary notion of the good, that is, that which is not yet the result of philosophical instruction, and he explains its mechanism as follows:

> We came to know the health of the body: On this basis, we thought there was also some health of the soul. We came to know the forces of the body: From this, we concluded to the existence of a vigor of the soul. Benevolent actions, full of humanity and courageous, had struck us with stupor (*obstupefecerant*): we began to admire them as if they had been perfect acts. Beneath were multiple vices hidden by external appearance (*species*) and the splendor of some remarkable act, and we concealed them. Nature orders us to magnify what is praiseworthy, and no one has evoked glory without going beyond the truth: From all this, then, we derived the appearance (*speciem*) of an immense good (*ingens bonum*). (Sen. *Ep.* 120.5)

According to Seneca, everything thus began with two notions obtained by the method of analogy: the health and vigor of the soul. But what follows is no longer a purely cognitive act: It is the instantaneous recognition of what is good in others by what is good in us, that is, by the "seeds," and the key words are "admiration" and "stupefaction." Like the *ictus* in the quotation from Seneca given above, p. 33, the verb *obstupefecerant* designates the salutary shock that awakens or reinforces our innate predispositions and which could only have been a shock because there was something within the soul that was apt to receive it and respond to it.

---

84   In a later publication, Inwood comments on *Letter* 120 as follows (2007, 324): "120.4 'nature could not have taught us'. Compare 90.44–6, 108.8. D.L. 7.89 notes that nature gives humans uncorrupted inclinations (*aphormai*) to virtue; these inclinations and the preconceptions which we develop naturally are among the 'seeds' referred to here. [...]" All the same, he still seems to believe that *fundamenta semenque virtutum* are the same as the innate anticipated grasps (*emphutoi prolēpseis*) since otherwise one would have expected him to clarify to his readers that his more recent understanding in the commentary of 2007 is contradictory to the opinions he had expressed in his paper "Getting to Goodness" quoted above in notes 2 and 3. For there, he regarded "innate ideas" as a later discovery by Epictetus.
85   Cf. the selection of examples contained in my quotations.
86   Cf. *supra*, pp. 31f.

Although Inwood nowhere refers to the existence in the Stoic system of those innate starting points, he nevertheless observes in his commentary (286) that Seneca claims "that this universal tendency to accentuate the praiseworthy is rooted in human nature by Nature and that this cognitive bias toward goodness is vital for our ability to derive, from the defective examples of good behavior which we actually observe in our experience, a sound notion of virtue, the *ingens bonum*. It is not at all clear that anyone who does not share a Stoic confidence in the providential care of Nature for our species should be reassured about the reliability of this process." As is shown by the continuation of his chapter, Inwood's last sentence is rather a critique of an argument he thinks is incomplete – indeed, taken in itself, the "command of nature" is bereft of doctrinal foundation – than a refusal to take the Stoic principles into consideration.

Paragraphs 6 and 7 of Seneca's *Letter* 120 mention two famous examples from Roman history, those of Fabricius and Horatius Cocles, which, as he says in paragraph 8, show us the image of virtue. The continuation (8–11) develops the warning against hidden vices, reminding Lucilius that one must know how to distinguish between evil under the appearance of virtue and true virtue. For instance, one must know how to tell the difference between the vice of prodigality and the virtue of generosity, between the vice of temerity and the virtue of courage. Here, in my opinion, and although Seneca does not point it out, we leave the stage of the formation of the first notion of the good, accessible to everyone, and move on to the higher stage of the differentiation between appearance and essence on the basis of Stoic teaching.

> This similarity [sc. between temerity and courage, etc.] obliges us, when we observe those whom a remarkable work has made famous, to be wary and to distinguish the things that are contiguous in their appearance, but are in reality diametrically opposed to one another. We began to observe that so-and-so had carried out an act in a generous spirit and with great zeal, but only once. We saw another being courageous at war, but timid in political life (*in foro*); a man who bore poverty undaunted, but dishonor in a base way: We praised the act, but we despised the man. 10 We saw another pleasant toward his friends, moderate toward his enemies, loyally and religiously administering both public and private affairs, lacking neither endurance in the things that must be undergone nor practical wisdom in what had to be done. We saw him give generously when it was time to distribute and when it was time to labor, be perseverant and obstinate, soothing bodily fatigue by strength of mind (*animo*). Apart from that, he was always the same and equal to himself in all his acts, being henceforth morally good not only by design but being led by habit to the point where not only could he act rightly, but he could not act in any other way than rightly (*iam non consilio bonus, sed more eo perductus ut non tantum recte facere posset, sed nisi recte facere non posset*). We realized that in him, virtue was perfect. 11 [...] By what, then, had we

discerned virtue? It was the orderly sequence (*ordo*) [87] that showed it to us, beauty and constancy (*constantia*), the harmony among all his acts, and his greatness, raising him above all things. (Sen. *Ep.* 120.9–11)

This text leads us, from two historical examples of acts that are heroic but not virtuous in the Stoic sense – one or even several correct or even outstanding acts are not yet virtues; they become so only if they are accompanied by an ethical conscience which is itself based on knowledge[88] – this text, then, leads us to a portrait of the Stoic sage, in whom occasional images of virtue have become a stable, constant way of being, and hence a *habitus*.[89] With regard to this portrait of the Stoic sage, Inwood says "[...] this sort of person is dispositionally good," but it is not clear if he understands by this a natural disposition or the *habitus* acquired by a long apprenticeship of Stoic doctrines combined with continuous exercises,[90] the *habitus* which is intended here by our text.

---

87 On the Stoic term "*ordo*," cf. Cic. *Off.* 1.142: "They [sc. the Stoics] define order as follows: an arrangement of things in their proper and appropriate places."

88 Cf. Sen. *Ep.* 95.57 = *SVF* 3.517: "An act will not be morally right (*actio recta non erit* ['*actio recta*' is the Latin translation of the Greek Stoic term κατόρθωμα]) unless intention (*voluntas* [a translation of προαίρεσις or βούλησις]) is so also: For action proceeds from intention. Conversely, the intention will not be morally right unless the *habitus* [a translation of the Greek Stoic terms διάθεσις or ἕξις] of the soul is morally right. Next, the soul's *habitus* will not [even] exist in the best [of men] (*in optimo* [cf. *Ep.* 90.46, quoted at n. 90, where in the same context *in optimis* has the meaning "in the best [by nature] of men"]), unless he has perceived the laws of all of life, measured which judgment must be brought to bear on each thing, and brought things back to truth (*nisi res ad verum redegerit*)." The Stoics knew the terminological distinction between ἕξις ("habit") and διάθεσις (*habitus*). Are called διαθέσεις the virtues and vices which, like the notion of the straight line, do not admit the more and the less (cf. Simp. *in Cat.* p. 237f. Kalbfleisch; Sen. *Ep.* 71.19); the ἕξεις, in contrast, are subject to intensification and relaxation (*SVF* 3.525). Yet this distinction is not always rigorously maintained, and the individual virtues are sometimes qualified as ἕξεις (*SVF* 3.265–270).

89 Cf. the previous note and Stob. 4.39.22, vol. 5, p. 906 Wachsmuth and Hense = *SVF* 3.510 (in this text, the term "happy life" can be replaced by "virtue," since the two terms were almost interchangeable among the Stoics): "From Chrysippus: He who is in the process of progressing toward the summit accomplishes what is appropriate (τὰ καθήκοντα = *media officia*) and omits nothing. However, his life is not yet happy, but the happy life will devolve upon him when these same middle acts (μέσαι πράξεις) acquire constancy (τὸ βέβαιον), habit (τὸ ἑκτικόν), and a kind of particular solidity (ἰδίαν πῆξίν τινα)."

90 Cf. Sen. *Ep.* 90.46: "They [sc. the men of ancient times] were innocent only by ignorance; there is a great difference between not wanting to sin and not knowing how. They lacked justice, they lacked prudence, they lacked temperance and courage. Their uncultivated life possessed some aspects similar to all these virtues, but virtue is accessible only to a soul that has been trained and thoroughly instructed and brought to its culminating point by incessant exercises. We are born for this,

From the notion of virtue as a *habitus*, illustrated by the portrait of the Stoic sage, Seneca can pass immediately to that of the happy life (*Ep.* 120.11–14), which is none other than the supreme good. Seneca emphasizes the content of this happy life by continuing the description of the Stoic sage, which culminates in the following observation:

> He had a perfect soul that had been brought to its summit, above which all that exists is the divine intellect, part of which has flowed into this mortal heart: This heart is never more divine than when it reflects on its mortality and when it knows that man was born to accomplish his life and that this body is not a home but a sojourn, and even a brief sojourn, with a host who must be left when you see you are a burden to him. (Sen. *Ep.* 120.14)

The last words provide a transition to a long paraenetic part in the form of the spiritual exercise of the preparation for death, the *praemeditatio mortis*.[91]

We should add, moreover, that Seneca's *Letter* 124 is a continuation of *Letter* 120. It deals with the question "whether it is by the senses or by the intellect (*intellectu*) that the good is grasped" (124.1) and contains an implicit critique of the Epicurean doctrine.[92] This text shows that the Stoic notion of the supreme good has little to do with sense perception. The doctrine that human reason is an emanation of the divine *pneuma* and that its perfect state makes man the equal of the gods goes back, as I have mentioned above (p. 13), to the beginning of Stoicism, and it is not useful to seek a Platonic influence on Seneca behind this text. Likewise, an exercise of preparation for death, in use both among the Stoics and the Platonists, cannot, in the mouth of a Stoic, have any other goal than perfect indifference with regard to one's body and the other *indifferentia* of this world.

---

but without it, and even in the best men (*in optimis*), before you instruct them, there is the matter of virtue (*virtutis materia*) but not virtue."

91 Yet the portrait of the Stoic sage himself is already, in a sense, a part of the paraenesis. As I mention in Hadot 1969 and 2014, a long tradition in antiquity had promoted the conviction that it was enough to set something praiseworthy before one's eyes in order to inspire imitation (cf. Sen. *Ep.* 115.6: "Let us propose something praiseworthy: an imitator will be found") and that the greatness of a splendid example combined with the very high artistic level of its description have an irresistible effect. At many places in his writings, Seneca evokes the figure of the Stoic sage with the force of a visionary apparition, with the goal of replacing by the plasticity of language the stronger and more persuasive impression that can only be provided by vision. Cf. above, p. 15 with n. 25.

92 Cf., for instance, 124.2: "All those who place pleasure at the summit judge that the good is accessible to the senses (*sensibile*); we, in contrast, who give the good to the soul, we judge that the good is accessible to our intelligence (*intellegibile*). If the senses were judges of what is good, we would not reject any pleasure [...] and in the contrary case we would not voluntarily undergo any pain, for every pain wounds the senses;" Cic. *Off.* 3.17.

Let us recall that for the Stoics, the things concerning the human body are *indifferentia* and that they identify man with his reason, which for them is also corporeal. Unlike Inwood,[93] I see no traces of Platonism other than those present in the early Stoa in all of *Letter* 120, nor, moreover, in the whole of Seneca's work.

IV. Conclusion

To return to Inwood's title, "Getting to Goodness," and to summarize briefly the various stages we have gone through in this article, I would insist on the distinction the Stoics made between the formation of the notion of the highest good, or of virtue, and the practice of this good or this virtue. The knowledge of the notion of the highest good does not imply its realization, and there is an abyss separating the two. According to them, the process of formation of the notion of the highest good is conditioned

[a] on the one hand, by the existence of innate starting points (*aphormai*), anticipated grasps (*prolēpseis, praesumptiones*), seeds (*semina*), or sparks (*igniculi*) of this good, which enable us, unless they have been hidden away or smothered, to recognize it as it were instinctively when we encounter it, and

[b] on the other hand, at the age of reason, by the application of the cognitive procedure of analogy to the representations (Diocles: *phantasiai*) based on sense perception, or to the anticipated grasps (Aëtius: *prolēpseis*) based on sense perception, and to the empirical notions that result from them; these "acquired" anticipated grasps are obviously different from the innate anticipated grasps I have just mentioned.

[c] However, to reach the notion of the Stoic highest good, so different from the highest good of most people, experience and analogy no longer suffice, and doctrinal teaching becomes necessary.

Point [b] is approximately documented by the few texts collected in the *SVF* under the heading "Περὶ ἐννοημάτων" (2.82–89), yet without expressly discussing the formation of the notion of the highest Stoic good, whereas point [a] is mentioned there only allusively, but is, like point [c],

---

93 Inwood writes on page 294: "But the most original contribution to this Stoic reflection on the epistemology of goodness comes from the 'platonic' excursus on the nature of the sage, which suggests that a ruthlessly clear recognition of the distinction between body and mind is the price one must pay for sustaining the consistency that is the mark of virtue. The platonism of the letter, if that is what it is, appears in the guise of what one must embrace in order really to understand the good."

amply dealt with in other texts belonging to all periods of the history of Stoicism. The road leading to the realization of the supreme good – the happy life or virtue – is long and complex. The teaching of Stoic philosophy will be necessary, which according to Seneca (*Ep.* 94 and 95) is divided since the beginning of Stoicism (cf. the controversy between Cleanthes and Aristo, mentioned p. 32f.) into two parts: the doctrinal part and the paraenetic part with, among other things, its spiritual exercises. For it is not enough to know the doctrines: One must digest them, assimilate them, let oneself be transformed by them with the help of incessant spiritual exercises. In short, as Seneca says (*Ep.* 124.12) about this supreme good constituted by perfect reason: "The youngest age (*infantia*) does not receive it in any way, so that childhood (*pueritia*) cannot expect it either, and adolescence (*adulescentia*) is imprudent to expect it: It goes well with old age (*senectus*), if it should reach it, by means of a long, tireless application."

Bibliography

Aristotle. 2004. *Éthique à Nicomaque*. See Bodéüs 2004.
Babut, Daniel, ed. and trans. 2002. *Plutarque, Œuvres morales: Tome XV, 1re partie: Traité 72: Sur les notions communes contre les stoïciens*. Paris: Les Belles Lettres.
Babut, Daniel, ed. and trans. 2004. *Plutarque, Œuvres morales: Tome XV, 2e partie: Traité 70: Sur les contradictions stoïciennes*. Paris: Les Belles Lettres.
Bodéüs, Richard, trans. 2004. *Aristote, Éthique à Nicomaque*. Paris: Flammarion.
Bonhöffer, Adolf Friedrich. 1890. *Epictet und die Stoa: Untersuchungen zur stoischen Philosophie*. Rpt. Stuttgart-Bad Cannstatt: F. Frommann, 1968.
Bury, Robert G., ed. and trans. 1939. *Sextus Empiricus in Four Volumes*. Vol. 3: *Against the Physicists; Against the Ethicists*. London; Cambridge: Heinemann; Harvard University Press. Reprint, 1967.
Castner, Catherine J. 1988. *Prosopography of Roman Epicureans from the Second Century B.C. to the Second Century A.D.* Frankfurt; New York: Peter Lang.
Cramer, John A., ed. 1839. *Anecdota Graeca e codd. manuscriptis Bibliothecae Regiae Parisiensis*. Vol. 1. Oxford: Typographeum Academicum.
Diogenes Laertius. 1999. See Goulet-Cazé 1999.
Dyson, Henry. 2009. *Prolepsis and Ennoia in the Early Stoa*. Berlin; New York: De Gruyter.
Goulet, Richard. 1994. "Dioclès de Magnésie." In *Dictionnaire des philosophes antiques*, edited by Richard Goulet. Vol. 2, 757–777. Paris: CNRS.
Goulet-Cazé, Marie-Odile, ed. and trans. 1999. *Diogène Laërce, Vies et doctrines des philosophes illustres*. Paris: Le Livre de Poche.
Gourinat, Jean-Baptiste. 2005. "L'origine des pensées: Un bien commun des épicuriens et des stoïciens." In *Cosmos et psychè: Mélanges offerts Jean Frère*, edited by Eugénie Vegleris, 271–291. Hildesheim; New York: Olms.
Hadot, Ilsetraut. 1969. *Seneca und die griechisch-römische Tradition der Seelenleitung*. Berlin: De Gruyter.
Hadot, Ilsetraut. 2014. *Sénèque: Direction spirituelle et pratique de la philosophie*. Paris: Vrin.

Hahm, David E. 1992. "Diogenes Laertius VII: On the Stoics." *ANRW* II 36.6: 4076–4182.
Inwood, Brad. 2005. *Reading Seneca: Stoic Philosophy at Rome*. Oxford; New York: Oxford University Press.
Inwood, Brad, trans. 2007. *Seneca, Selected Philosophical Letters: Translation with an Introduction and Commentary*. Oxford; New York: Oxford University Press.
Jackson-McCabe, Matt. 2004. "The Stoic Theory of Implanted Preconceptions." *Phronesis* 49: 323–347.
Long, Anthony, and David N. Sedley, eds. and trans. 1987. *The Hellenistic Philosophers*. 2 vols. Cambridge: Cambridge University Press.
Lutz, Cora Elizabeth, ed. and trans. 1947. *Musonius Rufus: "The Roman Socrates."* New Haven: Yale University Press.
Musonius Rufus. 1947. See Lutz 1947.
Plutarch. 2002. *Traité 72: Sur les notions communes contre les stoïciens*. See Babut 2002.
Plutarch. 2004. *Traité 70: Sur les contradictions stoïciennes*. See Babut 2004.
Pohlenz, Max. 1948. *Die Stoa: Geschichte einer geistigen Bewegung*. 2 vols. Göttingen: Vandenhoeck & Ruprecht.
Sandbach, Francis Henry. 1930. "Ἔννοια and Πρόληψις in the Stoic Theory of Knowledge." *CQ* 24: 44–51.
Seneca. 2007. *Selected Philosophical Letters*. See Inwood 2007.
Sextus Empiricus. See Bury 1939.

Seneca on *Prolēpsis*: Greek Sources and Cicero's Influence

Antonello Orlando
Università di Torino

> **EAMES:** We tried it, we got the idea in place, but it didn't take.
> **DOM COBB:** You didn't plant it deep enough?
> **EAMES:** Well, it's not about depth. You need the simplest version of the idea in order for it to grow naturally in the subject's mind. It's a very subtle art.
> (C. Nolan, *Inception*)

The meaning and use of the term *prolēpsis* seems not only confused but also stratified in the history of ancient philosophy. It is shared by Epicureans and Stoics, although with different features, and it plays a role even in Platonic epistemology. Far from claiming to resolve this difficult controversy, this short study will examine the only two references to *prolēpsis* by Seneca and compare them with those in Cicero. A discussion of Senecan *prolēpsis* would be incomplete if the comparison were limited to Stoic and Middle-Platonist antecedents or parallels; it must also consider the assimilation process carried out already by Cicero, especially with regard to the lexical field. In this way, it will be possible to uncover the peculiarities of the appropriation of the term in Seneca's Roman philosophy.

To begin with, it is necessary to outline the various meanings attributed to *prolēpsis* and its connections with the term *ennoia*. A suitable starting point for this is *De natura deorum* 1.44, where Cicero gives us the name of the "father" of *prolēpsis*: "For we are bound to employ novel terms to denote novel ideas, just as Epicurus himself employed the word *prolēpsis* in a sense in which no one had ever used it before."[1] According to Cicero, Epicurus introduced this word to the philosophical vocabulary of Hellenism. For the Epicurean *prolēpsis* we have Diogenes Laërtius' account, who describes *prolēpsis* as a concept made up of repeated experi-

---

1   Cic. *N.D.* 1.44: "Sunt enim rebus novis nova ponenda nomina, ut Epicurus ipse πρόληψιν appellavit, quam antea nemo eo verbo nominarat" (trans. Rackham).

ences and therefore as purely empirical.[2] For Stoicism the situation is more complicated. The term was not part of Zeno's vocabulary, and it joined the Stoic lexicon only with Chrysippus. While collecting evidence about Stoic *prolēpsis*, Sandbach[3] noticed a certain degree of confusion about *prolēpsis* in the narrow sense and the *koinai ennoiai* mentioned by Plutarch,[4] but a clear enough definition of *prolēpsis* is attested in the account of Diocles of Magnesia preserved by Diogenes Laërtius. There, *prolēpsis* is a natural concept of the general characteristic of an object.[5] Chrysippus had adopted the term for his theology and to describe the difference between good and evil. A testimony of Aëtius (4.11.1–4) adds a difference between *prolēpsis* and *ennoia*, which are otherwise often confused with one another. According to him, the former consists in direct and natural knowledge, while the latter derives from a rational elaboration. In fact, Long and Sedley (40E–F; vol. 1, p. 241) describe *prolēpseis* as "naturally acquired generic impressions" and *ennoiai* as "conceptions culturally determined or deliberately acquired."

Because of the fact that Epictetus' testimonies also focus on the *prolēpsis* of God and good and evil, Bonhöffer supposes that Chrysippus used to adopt the term *prolēpsis* only when speaking of these things.[6] Several scholars[7] have noticed a certain degree of fluidity in the Stoics' use of this term, especially when they were looking for the differences between *prolēpsis* and *ennoia*: according to Jackson-McCabe's distinction (2004, 328f.), *prolēpsis* would be the genre of which it is also a species, and at the same time also a particular species *ennoia* of the genre *ennoia*. *Prolēpsis* (as species) would differ from the species *ennoia* by its lack of rational origin, being essentially *phusikē* ("natural"),[8] something dormant that is activated by reality, then elaborated by reason, and finally changed into an *ennoia*, as Schofield (1980, 294) suggests.

According to Plutarch, a further characteristic in addition to naturalness is attributed to *prolēpsis* in Chrysippus' account: *prolēpsis* is also

---

2 D.L. 10.33: "Τὴν δὲ πρόληψιν λέγουσιν οἱονεὶ κατάληψιν ἢ δόξαν ὀρθὴν ἢ ἔννοιαν ἢ καθολικὴν νόησιν ἐναποκειμένην, τουτέστι μνήμην τοῦ πολλάκις ἔξωθεν φανέντος, οἷον τὸ Τοιοῦτόν ἐστιν ἄνθρωπος." About the Epicurean *prolēpsis* see the selected bibliography in Schofield 1980, 308, which may be complemented with Glidden 1985, 175–217; Hammerstaedt 1996; Asmis 1999, 276–283; Morel 2007, 25–48; Asmis 2009, 84–104.
3 Sandbach 1930.
4 Plu. *Comm. not.* 1059c, 1084f–1085c.
5 D.L. 7.54: "ἔστι δ' ἡ πρόληψις ἔννοια φυσικὴ τῶν καθόλου."
6 Bonhöffer 1890, 109–115, pointing to Arr. *Epict.* 2.11.6–7 and 8–14.
7 Sandbach 1930, 50; Lévy 1992, 304. See also Dyson 2009, 1–5.
8 See D.L. 7.54 (quoted in n. 5) and Aët. 2.11.1.

emphutos ("implanted").⁹ This is puzzling, since the Stoics are attested to have compared a child's soul after birth to a *tabula rasa*.¹⁰ An innate concept would be incompatible with the Stoic theory unless we believe with Sandbach that "Stoicism affects Platonism" in that system's later developments.¹¹ This feature of the innate corresponds to the description of Ideas by Plato (*Phdr.* 237d). On the other hand, Stoic gnoseology shared with Epicureanism an essentially empiricist approach, even though they differed from each other in their views about the formation and epistemic value of mental representations.

Jackson-McCabe¹² has tried to clarify this feature of Stoic *prolēpsis* in a different manner, without recourse to Plato; he focuses his attention on the fact that only the *prolēpsis* of good and evil is described as "implanted" in human beings. In his view, probably influenced by Pohlenz's intuition,¹³ the "moral" *prolēpsis* shares the feature of being implanted with *oikeiōsis*, the first appropriation of the animal to its own constitution, with the result that *prolēpsis* is genuinely Stoic and not contaminated with Platonism. This solution is a remarkable achievement. It prevents a philosophical hybridization, even though it runs the risk of minimizing the differences between *oikeiōsis* and *prolēpsis*. As I will try to show in the final part of this study, the nuance of innatism in Seneca's description of *prolēpsis* could be seen as only a part of a more general pedagogical strategy of providing a gnoseological foundation of ethics.

After this brief overview, I will examine the evidence for this concept in Seneca, analyzing in detail first the context of his references to *prolēpsis*, then the features of the *prolēpsis* of God (I). In the central part, I will broaden the perspective and conduct an investigation of the Roman lexicon for *prolēpsis* based on Cicero's and Seneca's philosophical works, with particular attention to moral *prolēpsis* and some Platonic nuances (II to V). In the last section (VI), I will suggest a new pedagogical reading of the Roman understanding of *prolēpsis* and of Seneca's contribution to its evolution.

---

9 Plu. *Stoic. rep.* 1041e: "Τὸν περὶ ἀγαθῶν καὶ κακῶν λόγον, ὃν αὐτὸς εἰσάγει καὶ δοκιμάζει, συμφωνότατον εἶναί φησι τῷ βίῳ καὶ μάλιστα τῶν ἐμφύτων ἅπτεσθαι προλήψεων." Cf. Dyson 2009, xxxi–xxxii.
10 Aët. 4.11.1; Long 1974, 91; Sharples 1996, 20; Lévy 2002, 127; Hankinson 2003, 63. Cf. Dyson 2009, xxiiif. on the impact of Locke's concept of the mind as a *tabula rasa* on modern readings of Stoic epistemology.
11 Sandbach 1930, 49.
12 Jackson-McCabe 2004, 327; 346–347. See also the contribution of Ilsetraut Hadot in this volume.
13 Pohlenz 1940, 89–93.

I. The *Prolēpsis* of God in Seneca and Cicero

Seneca's only explicit references to the concept of *prolēpsis* are in *Ep.* 117 and 120. Each of these letters is written in order to answer a precise question from Lucilius: in the first letter regarding the difference between *sapientia* ("wisdom") and *sapere* ("to be wise"), whether both are to be valued as goods;[14] in the second regarding the nature of the good and what is honorable (*honestum*) and the methods to obtain them. It may also be noted that the only two explicit occurrences of *prolēpsis* in Seneca are in these two letters. In the following two sections, I will examine separately the characteristics of the *prolēpseis* mentioned in each letter and compare it with the uses we can observe in Cicero.

In its first occurrence in Seneca's work, *prolēpsis* is described as follows:

> Multum dare solemus praesumptioni omnium hominum et apud nos veritatis argumentum est aliquid omnibus videri; tamquam deos esse inter alia hoc colligimus, quod omnibus insita de dis opinio est nec ulla gens usquam est adeo extra leges moresque proiecta ut non aliquos deos credat.

> We are accustomed to give considerable weight to the preconception of all people and our view is that it is an argument that something is true if all people believe it; for example, we conclude that there are gods for this reason among others, that there is implanted in everyone an opinion about gods and there is no culture anywhere so far beyond laws and customs that it does not believe in some gods. (Sen. *Ep.* 117.6, trans. Inwood 2007)

Seneca adduces common usage against the rigid distinction made by Stoic orthodoxy and asserts that there is no one who would not regard both wisdom and being wise as something good (*Ep.* 117.6). The *prolēpsis* about gods serves as evidence that Stoics do pay attention to such shared beliefs of all human beings, which they consider as "an argument that something is true." The same type of argument had already been used by Cicero – but not in order to present a specifically Stoic tenet – in *Tusc.* 1.30:

> Ut porro firmissimum hoc adferri videtur cur deos esse credamus, quod nulla gens tam fera, nemo omnium tam sit inmanis, cuius mentem non imbuerit deorum opinio (multi de diis prava sentiunt – id enim vitioso more effici solet. Omnes tamen esse vim et naturam divinam arbitrantur. Nec vero id conlocutio hominum aut consensus efficit, non institutis opinio est confirmata, non legibus; omni autem in re consensio omnium gentium lex naturae putanda est) [...] atque haec ita sentimus natura duce, nulla ratione nullaque doctrina.

> And this may further be brought as an irrefragable argument for us to believe that there are gods (that there never was any nation so barbarous, nor any people in the

---

14   For an analysis of Stoic logic and its Senecan treatment in *Ep.* 117, see Wildberger 2006, 163–178.

world so savage, as to be without some notion of gods. Many have wrong notions of the gods, for that is the nature and ordinary consequence of bad customs, yet all allow that there is a certain divine nature and energy. Nor does this proceed from the conversation of men, or the agreement of philosophers; it is not an opinion established by institutions or by laws; but, no doubt, in every case the consent of all nations is to be looked on as a law of nature.) [...] and we are led to this opinion by nature, without any arguments or any instructions. (Cic. *Tusc.* 1.30, trans. King, orthography and punctuation changed)

In this passage of the *Tusculanae disputationes*, Cicero is trying to demonstrate the immortality of the soul, starting first from some popular beliefs that are universally accepted and acquired without any reasoning or instruction ("nulla ratione nullaque doctrina"). The function of *prolēpsis* here is, as in Seneca, to establish an elementary and unquestionable foundation for further reasoning, namely the universal belief in gods. What Seneca seems to share with Cicero is the moral significance of the possession of this *prolēpsis*; in fact, Seneca, like Cicero, cannot imagine a nation so beyond legal and moral norms (*Ep.* 117.6: "adeo extra leges moresque") that it does not have this concept. In this sense, having certain kinds of *prolēpsis* seems in both Roman philosophers a sign of humanity as it is naturally given by Nature.

Both Cicero and Seneca introduce *prolēpsis* at the beginning of their treatment (*quaestiones*) and then characterize the universal consensus (*consensus omnium*) produced by a shared *prolēpsis* not only as evidence of truth but also as a prerequisite for civilization. However, this argument does not exhaust the rational process of demonstration. In *Ep.* 117.7[15] Seneca states that he will not stop at a simple *provocatio ad populum* ("an appeal to the people by a citizen") and intends to argue his point in Stoic terms as well. In the same way, Cicero does not limit himself to the mention of the belief (*opinio*) in gods but adds a discussion of Platonic and Aristotelian arguments for the immortality of the soul.

Apart from the passage in the *Tusculanae disputationes*, Cicero had spoken of the origin of the Stoic concept of a god in *De natura deorum*, where Balbus, the representative of this school, tells us:

> Itaque inter omnis omnium gentium summa constat; omnibus enim innatum est et in animo quasi insculptum esse deos. Quales sint varium est, esse nemo negat.
>
> Hence the main issue is agreed among all men of all nations, inasmuch as all have engraved in their minds an innate belief that the gods exist. As to their nature there are various opinions, but their existence nobody denies. (Cic. *N.D.* 2.12, trans. Rackham)

---

15 *Ep.* 117.7: "utor hac publica persuasione [...] Non faciam quod victi solent, ut provocem ad populum: nostris incipiamus armis confligere." Seneca seems to play with the metaphorical lexicon of gladiators and popular political consensus in order to prove that his arguments have their roots in common belief.

This passage is extremely similar to Seneca's words in *Ep.* 117.6: Both authors use the adjective *omnis* ("all"), repeated in form of a *polyptoton*, and also enhance the idea of universality by indicating that there is no nation (*gens*) that does not share the idea. However, Cicero adds an adjective that we do not find in Seneca: *innatus* ("innate"). The use of *innatus* could be compared with another passage of *De natura deorum*, in which Balbus returns to the *prolēpsis* of the divine:

> Sed cum talem esse deum certa notione animi praesentiamus, primum ut sit animans, deinde ut in omni natura nihil eo sit praestantius, ad hanc praesensionem notionemque nostram nihil video quod potius accommodem quam ut primum hunc ipsum mundum, quo nihil excellentius fieri potest, animantem esse et deum iudicem.

> But assuming that we have a definite and preconceived idea of a deity as, first, a living being, and secondly, a being unsurpassed in excellence by anything else in the whole of nature, I can see nothing that satisfies this preconception or idea of ours more fully than, first, the judgement that this world, which must necessarily be the most excellent of all things, is itself a living being and a god. (Cic. *N.D.* 2.45, trans. Rackham)

Here Cicero adopts the same term for *prolēpsis* which he had already used for translating divination (*praesensio*);[16] he also offers the more general and neutral translation *notio*, whose location is in the soul (*animus*), as in *N.D.* 2.12 ("in animo").[17]

Finally there is a passage in *De natura deorum* in which the Epicurean Velleius speaks about the *prolēpsis* of a god:

> Solus enim vidit primum esse deos, quod in omnium animis eorum notionem inpressisset ipsa natura. Quae est enim gens aut quod genus hominum quod non habeat sine doctrina anticipationem quandam deorum, quam appellat πρόλημψιν Epicurus, id est anteceptam animo rei quandam informationem, sine qua nec intellegi quicquam nec quaeri nec disputari potest. Quoius rationis vim atque utilitatem ex illo caelesti Epicuri de regula et iudicio volumine accepimus. Quod igitur fundamentum huius quaestionis est, id praeclare iactum videtis. Cum enim non instituto aliquo aut more aut lege sit opinio constituta maneatque ad unum omnium firma consensio, intellegi necesse est esse deos, quoniam insitas eorum vel potius innatas cognitiones habemus; de quo autem omnium natura consentit, id verum esse necesse est; esse igitur deos confitendum est. Quod quoniam fere constat inter omnis non philosophos solum sed etiam indoctos, fatemur constare illud etiam, hanc nos habere sive anticipationem, ut ante dixi, sive praenotionem deorum (sunt enim rebus novis nova ponenda nomina, ut Epicurus ipse πρόλημψιν appellavit, quam antea nemo eo verbo nominarat) – hanc igitur habemus, ut deos beatos et inmortales putemus. Quae enim nobis natura informationem ipsorum deorum dedit, eadem insculpsit in mentibus ut eos aeternos et beatos haberemus.

---

16 *Praesensio* appears in Cic. *Div.* 1.1, where it is used, with *scientia rerum futurarum*, as a translation for the Greek *mantikē*.
17 See n. 35.

For he alone perceived, first, that the gods exist, because nature herself has imprinted a conception of them on the minds of all mankind. For what nation or what tribe of men is there but possesses untaught some "preconception" of the gods? Such notions Epicurus designates by the word *prolēpsis*, that is, a sort of preconceived mental picture of a thing, without which nothing can be understood or investigated or discussed. The force and the value of this argument we learn in that work of genius, Epicurus' *Rule or Standard of Judgement*. You see therefore that the foundation (for such it is) of our inquiry has been well and truly laid. For the belief in the gods has not been established by authority, custom or law, but rests on the unanimous and abiding consensus of mankind; their existence is therefore a necessary inference, since we possess an instinctive or rather an innate concept of them; but a belief which all men by nature share must necessarily be true; therefore it must be admitted that the gods exist. And since this truth is almost universally accepted not only among philosophers but also among the unlearned, we must admit it as also being an accepted truth that we possess a "preconception," as I called it above, or "prior notion," of the gods. (For we are bound to employ novel terms to denote novel ideas, just as Epicurus himself employed the word *prolēpsis* in a sense in which no one had ever used it before.) We have then a preconception of such a nature that we believe the gods to be blessed and immortal. For nature, which bestowed upon us an idea of the gods themselves, also engraved on our minds the belief that they are eternal and blessed. (Cic. *N.D.* 1.43, trans. Rackham)

II. *Notitia*, *Notio* and *Opinio*

Lévy (1992, 102) counts six different names for *prolēpsis*, in Cicero's philosophical works alone. Cicero's use of these nouns seems to have evolved. We find *intellegentia* (only attested in *Leg.* 1.26 and *Fin.* 3.21), *anticipatio* and *praenotio* in an Epicurean context (*N.D.* 1.43), *praesensio* in a Stoic and Peripatetic one, *notitia*[18] in *Orat.* 116, and the more frequent and general *notio*. *Notio* and *notitia* are both deverbative abstract nouns, derived from the verb *nosco* "to get to know." When they first occur in Latin literature, in Plautus[19] and Terence,[20] they both mean "acquaintance among people." *Notio* is more frequently considered as active, *notitia* more often passive, derived from the past participle *notus*.[21] *Notitia* can also be translated with "practical knowledge," i.e. of a land or of a language.[22]

---

18 *Notitia* is considered "perfettamente analogo a *notio*" by Moreschini 1979, 122.
19 Plaut. *Truc.* 623: "quid tibi hanc notio est, inquam, amicam meam?"
20 Ter. *Haut.* 53: "quamquam haec inter nos nuper notitia admodumst."
21 Ernout and Meillet 1951, 790.
22 Caes. *Gal.* 6.24.5: "Gallis [...] transmarinarum rerum notitia multa ad copiam largitur ;" Caes. *Civ.* 1.31.2: "hominum et locorum notitia et usu eius provinciae nactus ;" Vell. 2.110.5: "non disciplinae tantummodo, sed lingua quoque notitia Romanae."

In Cicero's philosophical vocabulary, *notio* is used to translate both *prolēpsis* and *ennoia*, as pointed out by Cicero himself in *Top.* 31, regarding a terminology that was ambiguous also in its original language: "I call notion what the Greeks sometimes call *ennoia* and sometimes *prolēpsis*."[23] Both Moreschini and Lévy[24] point out the difficulties that the translation of *prolēpsis* could present to a Latin speaker, especially considering that *ennoia* and *prolēpsis* were terms shared by Platonism, Stoicism, and Epicureanism.

In Seneca we find thirty-two occurrences of *notitia* with a broad range of meanings. Apart from the general sense of "fame,"[25] *notitia* means "knowledge" of both divine and human subjects, which can be a physical-sensorial[26] form of knowledge or also ethnographical knowledge.[27] Often *notitia* expresses the general idea of "concept."

Just as Cicero employs the word *notio*, Seneca too uses *notitia* in order to express not only the technical Stoic concept of *ennoia-prolēpsis* but also a common knowledge gained by memory. Nevertheless, it seems possible to consider the *notitia boni* as the final step in the process of formation of human knowledge of the good.

In *Ep.* 117.6 Seneca uses the term *opinio*; this noun, derived from the verb *opinor* "to believe or opine," is frequently used in his work (110 occurrences), as it is by Cicero (more than 400 occurrences). *Opinio* is more general than *notitia* and has a broader range of meanings:[28] it is generally intended as "belief," often about a future event,[29] and also in the sense of "fame;"[30] in legal language it can mean "judgment"[31] or "military salary."[32]

Probably the most pertinent meaning of *opinio* is described thus in the *OLD* (s.v. 3): "the faculty of forming mental ideas, fancy, imagination;" "a mental picture, concept." Clearly, *opinio* means at the same time a process and a product of cognition. We have to note that Cicero chooses *opinio* in order to translate the Greek *doxa*, with a negative nuance that is easy to recognize. It is not by chance that in both Cicero and Seneca *opinio* is in-

---

23 "[...] notionem appello quod Graeci tum ἔννοιαν tum πρόληψιν" (trans. Reinhardt).
24 Moreschini 1979, 122; Lévy 1992, 302.
25 Sen. *Ep.* 19.3; 31.10; 79.14; *Ben.* 2.9.2 and 2.23.1.
26 *Nat.* 1.17.4; 2.51.1.
27 *Ep.* 104.15.
28 Ernout and Meillet 1951, 820–821; *OLD* 1968, s.v. *opinio*.
29 For example, Cic. *Catil.* 3.11.
30 E.g. Cic. *Phil.* 5.26; Sen. *Ep.* 123.11. Cf. Molenaar 1969, 174 for a "hierarchy" among *conscientia*, *fama*, and *opinio* in Seneca's lexicon.
31 *ThLL* IX.2, 716, 8–40; cf. also Berger 1953, s.v. *opinio*.
32 Davies 1967, 115–118.

cluded in expressions used for relativizing the thought of the author, such as *ut fert mea opinio* ("as I believe").[33] The relativity of *opinio* explains why Cicero adopts this term also in order to translate the Stoic term *hypolēpsis* for a false supposition in *Ac.* 1. 41 (= *SVF* 1.60). *Opinio* is like an empty container to be filled with every kind of concept, from rhetoric to ethics. If it is filled with a false judgment, as in the case of emotions like fear or anger, it still stands for a strong appearance of truth, as is indicated by Seneca in *Marc.* 19.1: "What tortures us, therefore, is an opinion."[34] In spite of the absence of real damage, the *opinio damni* can reproduce in human beings the same emotions as those caused by the actual damage itself. In this sense, *opinio* can be opposed to truth, nature and reality.

This quick survey has shown that neither *opinio* in Sen. *Ep.* 117.6 nor *notitia* in Sen. *Ep.* 120.4 are used as technical terms that would suffice to translate the full complexity of concepts like *prolēpsis* for a Roman reader. Like Cicero, Seneca sometimes prefers general and common terms, whose meaning is then narrowed down by modifying adverbs, adjectives, and locatives. Seneca follows Cicero's strategy of composing a larger lexical web in order to clarify a concept that could be difficult to understand if it were expressed with only one technical term in the target language.

III. The *Prolēpsis* of Moral Good

In this section I examine the second kind of *prolēpsis* which occurs in Seneca's philosophical works, that of moral good. Again I will pay attention to his lexicon and the possible parallels with usages in Cicero's philosophical treatises.

In *Epistle* 120 Seneca answers Lucilius' *quaestiuncula*, "how we have acquired our initial concept of the good and the honorable."

> Nunc ergo ad id revertor de quo desideras dici, quomodo ad nos prima boni honestique notitia pervenerit. Hoc nos natura docere non potuit: semina nobis scientiae dedit, scientiam non dedit. Quidam aiunt nos in notitiam incidisse, quod est incredibile, virtutis alicui speciem casu occucurrisse. Nobis videtur observatio collegisse et rerum saepe factarum inter se conlatio; per analogian nostri intellectum et honestum et bonum iudicant.

> So now I return to what you want me to discuss, how we have acquired our initial concept of the good and the honourable. Nature could not have taught us this; she has given us the seeds of knowledge. Certain people say that we just happened on the concept; but it is implausible that anyone should have come upon the form of

---

33 At Cic. *Ver.* 2.4.23; *Font.* 39; *Planc.* 48. In Seneca, "ut mea fert opinio" at *Ep.* 90.20; *Ben.* 2.31.1; *Cl.* 2.7.4.
34 "Opinio est ergo quae nos cruciat" (trans. Basore).

virtue by chance. We believe that it has been inferred by the observation and comparison of actions done repeatedly. Our school holds that the honourable and the good are understood by analogy. (Sen. Ep. 120.3–4, trans. Inwood 2007)

Seneca regards the *prolēpsis* of good not as a simple accident[35] but as a natural principle. This natural principle seems here incomplete, inchoate, and in need of the rational activity of human beings (carried out thanks to the mechanism of analogy[36] or *conlatio*) in order to become perfect. In fact, analogy is applied in paragraphs 6–7 to the virtuous examples of Fabricius[37] and Horatius Cocles,[38] which are often used by Cicero himself. Seneca also seems to share with Cicero a great interest in history as a pedagogical tool for Romanizing Greek philosophy. From this perspective Fox remarks:

> Because Cicero is determined to keep his philosophy relevant, to prevent it from becoming too abstract, or too foreign to the Roman context, any notion of a philosophical solution to Rome's problems will not be a dogmatic one with a single, foundational, historical narrative behind it. (2007, 317f.).

The historical examples are linked to moral *prolēpsis* not only by means of analogy but above all by their common matrix, namely nature, which produces the first notion of good and bad in the human soul and, at the same time, gives us a deeper and more structured phenomenological demonstration of these concepts. In Cic. *Fin.* 3.21 and 33, Cato the Younger gives an account of the *prolēpsis* of good and analyzes the production of the *ennoia* of good (*notio boni*). According to him, there are four modes of concept formation (likewise in D.L. 7.52), and only the *conlatio rationis* (analogy) is classified as a mechanism able to produce the notion of good. Seneca's description is less specific and articulate than Cicero's, even though both authors use *conlatio* as the Latin translation of analogy.[39] Both authors assign a leading role to nature, which gives us a fundamental but incomplete concept of good (*semina scientiae*). But the perfect knowledge of the good can be obtained only thanks to our reason.[40] Moreover, these two steps in the process seem to be defined in a way that is similar to the distinction between the formation of a *prolēpsis* and that of a *ennoia*.

---

35 A similar periphrasis ("cadere in notitiam") is also found in Sen. *Nat.* 2.3.1: "Omnia quae in notitiam nostram cadunt aut cadere possunt mundus complectitur."
36 See also Cic. *Tim.* 13: "Id optime adsequitur, quae Graece ἀναλογία, Latine (audendum est enim, quoniam haec primum a nobis novantur) conparatio proportiove dici potest."
37 Cic. *Parad.* 48; *Off.* 1.40.
38 Cic. *Parad.* 12; *Leg.* 2.10, where Horatius is mentioned as a human example of divine virtue. Cf. Inwood 2007, 323–324.
39 Varro *L.* 8.78; Cic. *Tusc.* 4.84; 5.85.
40 Sen. *Ep.* 120.4: "per analogian nostri intellectum et honestum et bonum iudicant."

There is another remarkable passage about the *prolēpsis* of the good in Cicero's *De finibus* that deserves consideration even though it does not pertain to the Stoic concept. The spokesman for Epicurean ethics, Lucius Manlius Torquatus, discusses the criterion for recognizing the supreme good and in this context explains the views of a peculiar faction in his school who rejects the strong empiricism traditionally defended by philosophers of the Garden:

> Sunt autem quidam e nostris qui haec subtilius velint tradere et negent satis esse, quid bonum sit aut quid malum, sensu iudicari, sed animo etiam ac ratione intellegi posse et voluptatem ipsam per se esse expetendam et dolorem ipsum per se esse fugiendum. Itaque aiunt hanc quasi naturalem atque insitam in animis nostris inesse notionem, ut alterum esse appetendum, alterum aspernandum sentiamus.
>
> Some Epicureans wish to refine this doctrine: they say that it is not enough to judge what is good and bad by the senses. Rather they claim that intellect and reason can also grasp that pleasure is to be sought for its own sake, and likewise pain to be avoided. Hence they say that there is as it were a natural and innate conception in our minds by which we are aware that the one is to be sought, the other shunned. (Cic. *Fin.* 1.31, trans. Annas and Woolf)

Obviously, there exists a strong lexical similarity between this account and Seneca's exposition in *Ep.* 120.4. Madvig (1876, 69) notes a "stoicizing-platonic colour," while DeWitt (1954, 133) assumes a simple contamination with Platonism. For our purposes it suffices to observe that the main difference between Epicurus' traditional gnoseology and this alternative view is essentially that according to the latter, pleasure can be perceived as the highest good not only through the senses but also through reason and the mind.

Cicero's Stoicism, Cicero's alternative Epicureanism (which is not attested elsewhere), and Seneca's Stoicism agree with each other in the localization of *prolēpsis* in the human mind, in the fundamental role of nature and, above all, in the use of the adjective *insitus*. In the next section I will focus my lexical analysis on this and one other feature of Cicero's, Seneca's, and also Lucretius' account of *prolēpsis*, the use and meaning of the words *insitus* and *semen*.

IV. *Insitus* and *Semen*

In the philosophical works of both Cicero and Seneca, the adjective *insitus* can be considered as a specification of the general idea of "concept," as it is described by Latin nouns like *notitia* and *opinio*. In *Tusc.* 1.57 Cicero uses *insitus* in order to qualify the Platonic Ideas (*notiones*). From an etymological point of view, Ernout and Meillet[41] explain the common meaning of *insitus* as "inserted" with a confusion between the two homographic verbs *insĕro* (respectively "to plait" and "to sow"). In Cicero's works, *insitus* is often construed with locative ablatives of *animus*[42] or *mentes* (*Orat.* 133). The agent of this external implantation can often be recognized as nature, as for example in the Epicurean context described in *N.D.* 1.43–45 and *Fin.* 1.31.[43] In both dialogues, nature seems to be the real creator of *prolēpsis*. In particular, the faction of Epicureans in *Fin.* 1.31 believes in a strange, probably innate, *prolēpsis* of pleasure. The difficulties raised by this text have caused much debate.[44] According to Reid,[45] the idea of innatism could have originated in a syncretistic mix of Epicurean *prolēpsis* and Stoic *ennoia*. However, there is no evidence for innatism in the genuine Stoic doctrine of *ennoia*.[46] The double use of *insitus* and *innatus* in *N.D.* 1.44 is for Asmis[47] only a redundant inelegance in Cicero's translation, an opinion also shared by Manuwald (1972, 12). At the same time, the adverb *quasi* in *Fin.* 1.31 is a clear pointer to the difficulty of interpreting intricate concepts such as *prolēpsis*. Seneca, on the other hand, relates *insita* to *opinio* without any periphrastic forms. While Cicero faces problems of translation with *prolēpsis*, Seneca appears to have been more at ease when treating the same subject.

At this point, a short comparison with another Roman philosopher could be useful. Already Lucretius had introduced a Latin translation of *prolēpsis* in his work. In two passages of *De rerum natura*,[48] he discusses *prolēpsis*, which he translates with *notities*. In the first passage *prolēpsis* is related to the origin of the world, in the second it is connected with the origin of language. Both times Lucretius opposes the idea that *prolēpsis* can occur within human beings independent of their experience. The adjective used to express the wrong understanding, that of an innate origin,

---

41   Ernout and Meillet 1951, 1091. Cf. also de Vaan 2008, 557.
42   Cic. *Ver.* 2.5.139; *Tusc.* 1.57, 3.63; *N.D.* 1.100. *Insitus* occurs with a genitive in *Fin.* 4.18.
43   Cic. *N.D.* 1.43: "Solus enim vidit primum esse deos, quod in omnium animis eorum notionem inpressisset ipsa natura;" 1.45: "quoniam insitas eorum [sc. deorum] vel potius innatas cognitions habemus; de quo autem omnium natura consentit, id verum esse necesse est." The full text is quoted on p. 48f. For *Fin.* 1.31, see p. 53.
44   See, e.g., Madvig 1876, 69; Bailey 1928, 245–248; DeWitt 1954, 133; Liebich 1954, 116–131; Reid 1968, 49; Manuwald 1972, 11–24; Gigon 1988, 424; Tsouna 2007, 68–73.
45   Reid 1968, *ad Fin.* 1.31.
46   See, however, the contribution of Ilsetraut Hadot in this volume.
47   Asmis 1984, 68–69. Cf. Asmis 2009, 92.
48   Lucr. 5.182 and 1046–1049.

is once again *insita*, as opposed to the only true *prolēpsis*, for instance of truth, that is, truth based on sense data, in 4.478.

In Seneca's work, *insitus* is attested seven times. In *Ben.* 4.6.6 we read: "All the ages of man, all his skills, have their germ within us. It is God, our teacher, who draws forth our genius from hidden depths."[49] Griffin and Inwood (2011, 89) translate *insita semina* with "inborn seeds." Apart from the metaphor of seeds, which also occurs in *Ep.* 120, there is also a specification of the identity of the sower in this passage: He is portrayed as a patient teacher and identified with God. Some lines later,[50] Seneca further identifies God with Nature. In this sense, *opinio* is *naturalis*, just like *notio* in *Fin.* 1.31.

The other four[51] occurrences of *insitus* in Seneca's works are related to Stoic *oikeiōsis*. *Oikeiōsis* could be defined as a natural instinct which drives a man to love himself (and consequently the entire world).[52] According to Seneca, it is inherent in human beings from their birth. The difference between *oikeiōsis* and a concept (the *ennoia* of Aëtius) is not insignificant: The former is a mere instinct, shared also by children before the complete development of their reason; the latter, especially according to the description in *Ep.* 120.4, is the result of rational activity performed through the mechanism of analogy. A connection between the *notitia boni* and *oikeiōsis* could perhaps be assumed, following Jackson-McCabe, who writes that "the formation of the preconception of 'good' and 'bad', in other words, is guaranteed by *oikeiôsis*" (2004, 339). Jackson-McCabe's solution suggests the possibility of a further improvement. Rather than a distinction of two levels, a threefold division could be more precise: The first step is *oikeiōsis*, which covers all living creatures. The second step, corresponding to the *prolēpsis* of God or of good, is *insitus* in the human soul at a point when the development of reason is still incomplete. Finally, in a third step, the acquisition of a *notitia boni*, an elaborate concept (*ennoia*) of the good, which is shaped and strengthened by reasoning in form of analogies drawn from perceived reality.

The intricacy of these three steps could explain the difficulties Cicero faced as a translator, and it no doubt contributed to the web of imagery in Cicero's descriptions (adjectives, such as *impressus*, *innatus*, *insculptus*,

---

49 "Insita sunt nobis omnium aetatum, omnium artium semina, magisterque ex occulto deus producit ingenia" (trans. Cooper and Procopé).
50 Sen. *Ben.* 4.7.1: "'Natura' inquit 'haec mihi praestat.' Non intellegis te, cum hoc dicis, mutare nomen deo?"
51 Sen. *Nat.* 1.17.6: "insitus amor sui;" *Ep.* 14.1: "insita caritas corporis nostri;" *Ep.* 82.15: "insita voluntas conservandi."
52 Cf. Cic. *Fin.* 3.62–68.

inchoatus, *involutus*) and motivated complex translations[53] introduced by qualifying particles, such as *quasi* or *vel potius*. Above all, it is the reason for the large number of abstract nouns and neologisms (*praeceptio*, *anticipatio*) which Cicero uses to designate *prolēpsis*. In Seneca, this elaborate figurative lexicon is reduced and simplified considerably, perhaps also owing to the refinement of his pedagogical technique. In order to represent *prolēpsis*, Seneca does not use any of Cicero's qualifiers, such as *quasi* or *vel potius*. *Impressus* is present, but only in his tragedies and in its primary physical meaning, while *inscupltus* does not occur at all.

The use of the metaphor of seed in *Ep.* 120.4, which had already been adopted by Cicero in a similar context,[54] may help us to understand better the process that leads to *notitia boni*. *Semen*, derived from *sero*,[55] has the primary meanings of "seed,"[56] "sperm" and, in poetic language, "parentage." However, in Cicero's work – in which the word is used thirty-nine times but never related to *scientia* ("knowledge") – the figurative meaning of "cause" can also be observed, at Cic. *Phil.* 2.55, where Cicero addresses Antonius as the cause of the civil war: "Thus, just as the cause of trees and shrubs is in their seeds, so you were the seed of this most lamentable war."[57] Seneca too, in *Ben.* 3.29.4,[58] describes seeds as causes, and in *Ep.* 94.29 he conjoins the metaphor of seeds to that of sparks, just as Cicero had done in *Fin.* 5.43. The continuity is more evident here thanks to the two authors' shared imaginative lexicon.[59]

The *prolēpsis* of the good is defined in *Ep.* 120.4 as a *semen scientiae* ("seed of knowledge") given by nature: The real knowledge, i.e. the complete formation of the concept or *ennoia* of the good, can be realized only through reason. It seems that the sower, whom we can easily identify with Nature or God, has implanted in human souls the *prolēpsis* of the good in order to provide them with a gradual process of moral cognition. This relation probably recalls the patience of the teacher with his pupils: in *Ep.* 38.2.[60] Seneca, who is trying to answer Lucilius' questions, appreciates his desire to learn and reflects on good pedagogy. He announces that his

---

53 Malaspina 1991, 62–64.
54 Cic. *Fin.* 5.43. Dyson 2009, xv–xvi.
55 On *insitus* see section IV.
56 Ernout and Meillet 1951, 1090; de Vaan 2008, 557.
57 "Ut in seminibus est causa arborum et stirpium, sic huius luctuosissimi belli semen tu fuisti" (trans. Ramsey and Shackleton Bailey).
58 Sen. *Ben.* 3.29.4: "nulla non res principia sua magno gradu transit. Semina omnium rerum causae sunt et tamen minimae partes sunt eorum, quae gignunt."
59 Cf. Cic. *Off.* 2.29 and Sen. *Ben.* 3.29.4.
60 Sen. *Ep.* 38.2: "facilius intrant et haerent; nec enim multis opus est sed efficacibus. *Seminis* modo spargenda sunt, quod quamvis sit exiguum, cum occupavit idoneum locum, vires suas explicat et ex minimo in maximos auctus diffunditur."

lessons will be few, but sensibly structured, like precious seeds. In this framework, the *prolēpsis* of good, imagined as a seed, is passively inserted in human minds, like an important lesson "implanted" by a skillful teacher.

Our investigation of the use and the occurrences of *insitus* and *semen* has shown a common foundation for both Cicero's and Seneca's understanding of *prolēpsis*. The last section of this paper will examine a possible Platonic nuance in Seneca's definition of this complex concept and in his use of the neologism.

V. Seneca's *Praesumptio* and a Possible Platonic Influence

The real innovation made by Seneca in the Latin lexicon for *prolēpsis* is his use of the deverbative substantive *praesumptio*. The word it not attested before him and therefore marks a further step beyond Cicero's efforts of translation. We have to note that Seneca introduces this term without any form of lexical elucidation, even though in other cases, such as *Ep.* 58.6, when speaking about *essentia*, and then in *Ep.* 120.4, a passage about *analogia*, he had taken care to refer to Cicero's authority.

Praesumptio is composed of the preverb *prae-* and the verbal root *sumo*. The preverb *prae-*[61] refers indifferently both to a spatial and a temporal anteriority and sometimes also to the causal acceptation of an impediment. The verb *sumo*, considered by Ernout and Meillet to be synonymous to *suscipio*, implies not only the action of gaining possession of something but is also meant to indicate that something acquires an object or property, showing in this way a passive or rather reflexive aspect, which is absent in the less receptive meaning of *capio*. This nuance of reception (or "adoption," according to the *OLD*)[62] is relevant for our concept. Cicero had used *prae-* in order to translate *prolēpsis* in *Part.*123, as the prefix to a noun *praeceptio*, thus preferring the root of the verb *capio*. On the other hand, in *Div.* 2.108,[63] speaking of the premises of syllogisms, Cicero translates "major premises" (*lemmata*) with *sumptiones* (or *sumpta* in *Ac.* 2.44)[64] and "minor premise" (*proslēpsis*) with *adsumptio*. The compound *praesumptio*, however, is not attested in Cicero's vocabulary.

Seneca's use of the neologism *praesumptio* thus indicates this author's willingness to provide a new translation of *prolēpsis*, which is perhaps more faithful than *notio* or *notitia* since these two words do not express the

---

61 Ernout and Meillet 1951, 937; de Vaan 2008, 485.
62 *OLD* 1968, s.v. *sumo*.
63 Pease 1958, *ad* 2.108.
64 Reid 1874, *ad* 2.44.

temporal dimension of the Greek prefix *pro-* and thus seem more suitable for translating the Stoic concept of *ennoia* (as shown in *Ep.* 120.4, where we find *notitia boni*).

Similar results derive from an analysis of *praesumo*. The verb is absent in Cicero's works but occurs eleven times in Seneca. In the majority of these cases,[65] *praesumo* is used in reference to future events. The *Thesaurus linguae Latinae*[66] notices a weakening of the temporal intensity of the preverb; on the other hand, it later acquires – as in Apul. *Met.* 8.28[67] – the negative acceptation of "excessive valuation" and from there becomes a denotation of a heretical thought against orthodoxy in the Christian age.[68]

Two other occurrences of this verb in the *Naturales quaestiones*[69] can perhaps help us to understand better the function of *prolēpsis* in Seneca's thought. In *Nat.* 7.11.1 He is about to review a short doxography of views about whirlwinds and comets, but before describing the ideas of the different philosophers, he states: "Before I begin to expound them, it must first be acknowledged that [...]."[70] Here he offers some core principles that are not open to discussion and serve as a foundation for what follows. This use does not seem very far removed from the use of the term *praesumptio* for the *prolēpsis* of a god, whose existence no one doubts even though there are several controversies about a god's precise characteristics.

As already noted, *praesumptio*, is introduced by Seneca as an alternative to Cicero's translations, whereas the use of *insitus* conforms to the older author's philosophical vocabulary. Yet another nuance can be observed in Seneca's use of *prolēpsis* in *Ep.* 58, where Seneca explains to Lucilius the subtle difference made in Platonist gnoseology between the Idea (*idea*) and the form (*eidos*).[71]

> Quid intersit quaeris? Alterum exemplar est, alterum forma ab exemplari sumpta et operi inposita; alteram artifex imitatur, alteram facit. Habet aliquam faciem statua: haec est idos. Habet aliquam faciem exemplar ipsum quod intuens opifex statuam figuravit: haec idea est.
>
> You ask, what is the difference between idea and form? The one is a model, while the other is a shape taken from the model and imposed on the work. The artisan imitates the one and produces the other. A statue has a certain appearance – this is

---

65 *Ep.* 24.1; 74.33; 91.8; 107.4; *De ira* 2.37.3; *Marc.* 7.4; *Ben.* 4.34.4.
66 *ThLL* X.2, 957, 8–15.
67 Apul. *Met.* 8.28: "mire contra plagarum dolores praesumptione munitus." Cf. also *Met.* 10.10: "offirmatus mira praesumptione."
68 A connotation of heresy in the word *praesumptio* is also attested at Apul. *Met.* 9.14: "in uicem certae religionis mentita sacrilega praesumptione dei."
69 Sen. *Nat.* 2.2.1; 7.11.1.
70 "[...] quas antequam exponere incipiam, illud praesumendum [...]" (trans. Hine).
71 Cf. Donini 1979, 180–189.

its form. The model itself has a certain appearance which the workman looked at when he shaped the statue. This is the idea. (Sen. Ep. 58.21, trans. Inwood 2007)

Aware of the difficulty of this subject, Seneca has recourse to the metaphorical repertoire of sculpture.[72] *Idea* is the model, while *eidos* is the shape that is defined as "taken (*sumpta*) from the model and imposed on the work." In this Platonic context, the verb *sumo* is used by Seneca not for a complete idea but in order to signify an intermediate concept, which is received by the artist and imposed by him onto his material. This parallel, which perhaps allows us to recognize a Platonic nuance in Seneca's thought, can in any case help us draw a conclusion about Seneca's method of translating the Stoic concept of *prolēpsis*.

VI. Conclusion

Seneca's attitude Stoic logic is characterized by Jonathan Barnes as follows: "Seneca, I think, was a logical utilitarian" (1997, 21). With its subtle distinctions, logic seems to have been only a propaedeutic discipline for him and subordinate to ethics. For a genuine utilitarian, having recourse to *prolēpsis* could represent only a stage on the way to other subjects. At both occurrences of the concept of *prolēpsis*, Seneca uses it as a starting point for addressing ethical conundrums, "little problems" (*quaestiunculae*) proposed to him by Lucilius. Especially in *Ep.* 117.6, *prolēpsis* is used in a moral sense and with a slight connotation of innatism. Even though it is not made explicit and no detailed explanation is provided, this characteristic of innateness can serve as an extraordinary foundation of ethics strong enough to penetrate even the barriers of Epicurean empiricism, as the example of the Epicurean faction in Cicero's *De finibus* shows.[73]

Regarding the controversy about the origin and the philosophical affiliations of *prolēpsis*, the present study has suggested a change of perspective, paying attention more to the lexical choices made by Seneca than to his philosophical affiliations. He seems to have considered not only the philosophical peculiarities of Greek concepts but also Cicero's several efforts at translation and the moral needs of Roman readers. Taking into account this pedagogical dimension, *praesumptio* might be an example of not only a philosophical but also a lexical hybrid of Stoicism and Platonism, as in the case of the definition of the moral and theological *prolēpsis*. The temporal dimension of the prefix *prae-*, the root of *sumo*, the adjective *insitus*, and the metaphor of the seed, which have examined in the previous

---

72 On metaphors of artistry, see also the paper by Linda Cermatori in this volume.
73 Cic. *Fin.* 1.31, quoted on p. 53.

sections, might be considered as linguistic tools of the same kind. All these elements are combined in order to trace an inborn concept common to all rational human beings. From this point of view, the instinct of *oikeiōsis* is *insitus* in the human soul as well as in animals and more general than and different from *prolēpsis*. A *prolēpsis* is a real concept, while *oikeiōsis* is a simpler instinct. The *ennoia* or *notitia boni* represents a further step: a complete product of human reason that, thanks to analogy, creates a strong impulse toward virtue in the human world. Yet, even though Seneca is referring to a certain kind of innatism, this does not reflect a direct adherence to Platonism, especially since his knowledge of Plato seems to have been filtered through Antiochus.[74] The matter is further complicated by the fact that, as Dyson suggests,[75] Chrysippus might have intended *prolēpsis* "as an alternative to the Platonic theory of recollection." Such issues could have induced Seneca to simplify his exposition, in tune with the pedagogical aims of the *Epistulae morales* and of all Roman philosophy.

Perhaps what is really inborn in human beings for Stoics is the tendency to form concepts on which discussions and structures of more complex reasoning can be built. According to this view, innatism could be considered as a tool which supplies the human mind with a strong basis[76] for the formation of concepts of both the good and God, a process with does not exclude the additional formation of more complex concepts, the *ennoiai* derived from other realities and legitimated by human reason. Middle Platonism seems to have provided a repertoire for Seneca's own lexicon, from which new philosophical, rhetorical, and pedagogical devices could be drawn, regardless of the differences among philosophical schools. Therefore, the Platonic nuances in Seneca's *prolēpsis* should not be taken as evidence for a philosophical commitment to this school of thought but as a lexical attempt to contribute to a more solid foundation of ethics. The resulting conceptual compromise in Seneca's renditions of the Greek term *prolēpsis* is in this way surprisingly similar to the one reached by the Epicurean innovators mentioned by Cicero in *Fin.* 1.31.

Bibliography

Annas, Julia, ed., and Raphael Woolf, trans. 2001. *Cicero, On Moral Ends*. Cambridge: Cambridge University Press.
Asmis, Elizabeth. 1984. *Epicurus' Scientific Method*. Ithaca: Cornell University Press.

---

74 Cf. Donini 1979, 275–295; Donini 1982, 191–197.
75 Dyson 2009, xxix.
76 In *De rerum natura* 4.465, Lucretius had used the existence of *prolēpsis* as an fundamental argument against Academic skepticism.

Asmis, Elizabeth. 2009. *Epicurean Empiricism*. In *The Cambridge Companion to Epicureanism*, edited by James Warren, 84–104. Cambridge: Cambridge University Press.
Bailey, Cyril. 1928. *The Greek Atomists and Epicurus*. Oxford: Clarendon Press.
Barnes, Jonathan. 1997. *Logic and the Imperial Stoa*. Leiden: Brill.
Basore, John W., ed. and trans. 1928–1935. *Seneca, Moral Essays*. 3 vols. London; New York: Heinemann; Putnam.
Berger, Adolf. 1953. *Encyclopedic Dictionary of Roman Law*. Philadelphia: The American Philosophical Society.
Bonhöffer, Adolf Friedrich. 1890. *Epictetus und die Stoa: Untersuchungen zur stoischen Philosophie*, Stuttgart: F. Enke.
Brittain, Charles. 2005. "Common Sense: Concepts, Definition and Meaning in and out of the Stoa." In *Language and Learning*, edited by Dorothea Frede and Brad Inwood, 164–209. Cambridge: Cambridge University Press.
Bugter, Stef E. W. 1987. "Sensus Communis in the Works of M. Tullius Cicero." In *Common Sense: The Foundations for Social Science*, edited by Frits L. van Holthoon and David R. Olson, 83–98. Lanham; New York; London: University Press of America.
Cicero. 1874. *Academica*. See Reid 1874.
Cicero. 1876. *De finibus bonorum et malorum libri quinque*. See Madvig 1876.
Cicero. 1924. *De Finibus Bonorum et Malorum libri 1, 2*. See Reid 1924.
Cicero. 1933. *De Natura Deorum; Academica*. See Rackham 1933.
Cicero. 1950. *Tusculan Disputations*. See King 1950.
Cicero. 1958. *De natura deorum: Liber secundus et tertius*. See Pease 1958.
Cicero. 1976. *Opere politiche e filosofiche 2: I termini estremi del bene e del male; Discussioni Tuscolane*. See Marinone 1976.
Cicero. 1988. *Über die Ziele des menschlichen Handelns*. See Gigon 1988.
Cicero. 2001. *On Moral Ends*. See Annas and Woolf 2001.
Cicero. 2003. *Topica*. See Reinhardt 2003.
Cicero. 2009. *Philippics 1–6*. See Ramsey and Shackleton Bailey 2009.
Cooper, John M., and J. F. Procopé, trans. 1995. *Seneca, Moral and Political Essays*. Cambridge; New York: Cambridge University Press.
Davies, Roy W. 1967. " 'Ratio' and 'Opinio' in Roman Military Documents." *Historia* 16: 115–118.
De Vaan, Michiel. 2008. *Etymological Dictionary of Latin and the Other Italic Languages*. Leiden: Brill.
DeWitt, Norman. 1954. *Epicurus and His Philosophy*. Minnesota: University of Minnesota Press.
Donini, Pierluigi, and Gian Franco Gianotti. 1979. *Modelli filosofici e letterari: Lucrezio, Orazio, Seneca*. Bologna: Pitagora.
Donini, Pierluigi. 1982. *Le scuole, l'anima, l'impero: La filosofia antica da Antioco a Plotino*. Torino: Rosenberg & Sellier.
Dyson, Henry. 2009. *Prolēpsis and Ennoia in the Early Stoa*. Berlin; New York: De Gruyter.
Ernout, Alfred, and Antoine Meillet. 1951. *Dictionnaire etymologique de la langue latine*. 3rd. ed. Paris: Klincksieck.
Fox, Matthew. 2007. *Cicero's Philosophy of History*. Oxford; New York: Oxford University Press.
Gigon, Olof, ed. and trans. 1988. *Marcus Tullius Cicero, Über die Ziele des menschlichen Handelns*. München; Zürich: Artemis.
Essler, Holger. 2011. *Glückselig und unsterblich: Epikureische Theologie bei Cicero und Philodem*. Basel: Schwabe Verlag.
Glidden, David K. 1985. "Epicurean 'Prolēpsis'." *OSAPh* 3: 175–217.

Griffin, Miriam T., and Brad Inwood, trans. 2010. *L. Annaeus Seneca, On Benefits.* Chicago: University of Chicago Press.

Hammerstaedt, Jürgen. 1996. "Il ruolo della πρόληψις epicurea nell'interpretazione di Epicuro, Epistula ad Herodotum 37 sg." In *Epicureismo greco e romano: Atti del Congresso Internazionale, Napoli 19–26 maggio 1993*, edited by Gabriele Giannantoni and Marcello Gigante, vol. 1: 221–237. Napoli: Bibliopolis.

Hankinson, R. J. 2003. "Stoic Epistemology." In *The Cambridge Companion to the Stoics*, edited by Brad Inwood, 59–84. Cambridge: Cambridge University Press.

Hine, Harry M., trans. 2010. *Lucius Annaeus Seneca, Natural Questions.* Chicago: University of Chicago Press.

Inwood, Brad. 2005. *Reading Seneca: Stoic Philosophy at Rome.* Oxford: New York: Oxford University Press.

Inwood, Brad, trans. 2007. *Seneca, Selected Philosophical Letters: Translation with an Introduction and Commentary.* Oxford; New York: Oxford University Press.

Jackson-McCabe, Matt A. 2004. "The Stoic Theory of Implanted Preconceptions." *Phronesis* 49: 323–347.

King, John Edward, trans. 1950. *Cicero, Tusculan Disputations.* Cambridge; London: Harvard University Press.

Lévy, Carlos. 1992. *Cicero Academicus.* Roma: École Française de Rome.

Liebich, Werner. 1954. "Ein Philodem-Zeugnis bei Ambrosius." *Philologus* 98: 116–131.

Long, Anthony A. 1991. *La filosofia ellenistica: Stoici, epicurei e scettici.* Translated by Alessandro Calzolari. Bologna: Il Mulino.

Long, Anthony, and David N. Sedley, eds. and trans. 1987. *The Hellenistic Philosophers.* 2 vols. Cambridge: Cambridge University Press.

Madvig, Johan N., ed. 1876. *M. Tullii Ciceronis De finibus bonorum et malorum libri quinque.* 3rd ed. Haunia: Gyldendal.

Malaspina, Ermanno. 1991. "L'introduzione di 'materia' nel vocabolario retorico e filosofico a Roma: Cicerone e Lucrezio." *AAT* 125: 41–64.

Manuwald, Anke. 1972. *Die Prolēpsislehre Epikurs.* Bonn: Habelt.

Marinone, Nino, ed. 1976. *Cicerone, Opere politiche e filosofiche 2: I termini estremi del bene e del male; Discussioni Tuscolane.* Torino: Utet.

Molenaar, Gaspar. 1969. "Seneca's Use of the Term 'Conscientia'." *Mnemosyne* 22: 170–180.

Morel, Pierre-Marie. 2007. "Method and Evidence: On the Epicurean Preconception." *Proceedings of the Boston Area Colloquium in Ancient Philosophy* 23: 25–48.

Moreschini, Claudio. 1979. "Osservazioni sul lessico filosofico di Cicerone." *ASNP* 9: 122–151.

Obbink, Dirk. 1992. "What All Men Believe Must Be True: Common Conceptions and 'Consensio Omnium' in Aristotle and Hellenistic Philosophy." *OSAPh* 9: 193–231.

Pease, Arthur, ed. 1958. *M. Tulli Ciceronis De natura deorum: Liber secundus et tertius.* Cambridge: Harvard University Press.

Pohlenz, Max. 1940. *Grundfragen der stoischen Philosophie.* Göttingen: Vandenhoeck & Ruprecht.

Rackham, Harris, ed. and trans. 1933. *Cicero, De Natura Deorum; Academica.* London: Heinemann.

Ramsey, John T., and David R. Shackleton Bailey, eds. and trans. 2009. *Cicero, Philippics 1–6.* Revised ed. Cambridge; London: Harvard University Press.

Reid, James, ed. 1874. *Cicero, Academica.* London: Macmillan.

Reid, James, ed. 1924. *M. Tulli Ciceronis De Finibus Bonorum et Malorum libri 1, 2.* Hildesheim: Olms.

Reinhardt, Tobias, ed. and trans. 2003. *Marcus Tullius Cicero, Topica.* Oxford: Oxford University Press.

Sandbach, Francis Henry. 1930. "Ἔννοια and Πρόληψις in the Stoic Theory of Knowledge." *CQ* 24: 44–51.
Schofield, Malcolm. 1980. "Preconception, Argument, and God." In *Doubt and Dogmatism*, edited by Malcolm Schofield, Myles Burnyeat, and Jonathan Barnes, 283–308. Oxford: Clarendon Press.
Seneca. 1928–1935. *Moral Essays.* See Basore 1928.
Seneca. 1995. *Moral and Political Essays.* See Cooper and Procopé 1995.
Seneca. 2007. *Selected Philosophical Letters.* See Inwood 2007.
Seneca. 2010. *Natural Questions.* See Hine 2010.
Seneca 2010. *On Benefits.* See Griffin and Inwood 2010.
Sharples, Robert W. 1996. *Stoics, Epicureans and Sceptics: An Introduction to Hellenistic Philosophy.* London; New York: Routledge.
Tsouna, Voula. 2007. *The Ethics of Philodemus.* Oxford: Oxford University Press.
Wildberger, Jula. 2006. *Seneca und die Stoa: Der Platz des Menschen in der Welt.* 2 vols. Berlin; New York: De Gruyter.

Did Seneca Understand Medea?
A Contribution to the Stoic Account of *Akrasia*

Jörn Müller
Julius-Maximilians-Universität Würzburg

It is a well-known phenomenon of our daily life that we do not always act according to our judgments on what would be the best or right thing to do. At least sometimes – and perhaps more often than we would like to admit – we fall prey to "weakness of will" and overturn our rational judgment in our action. One rather simple and straightforward way of explaining such behavior is to point to our irrational desires and passions as sources of motivation which are independent of our rational judgments. These irrational forces can counteract the judgment of reason and, if they are strong enough, somehow bypass or even overpower it in the end. The underlying picture is that of a mental conflict or struggle between rational and irrational powers of our soul.

This way of picturing the psychological background of weak-willed actions is deeply rooted in our philosophical tradition, stretching back at least as far Plato and Aristotle. Their explanation of *akrasia* (literally: "lack" or "loss of self-control") as the outcome of a conflict between irrational desires or passions on the one hand and reason on the other hand roughly fits the description given above.[1] However, it would be rash to assume that this was the only attitude toward weak-willed actions in ancient thought. Socrates is famous for denying the possibility of *akrasia* understood as an overpowering of our rational judgment by the desire for pleasure.[2] Opposing the Platonic and Aristotelian understanding of the phenomenon, the Stoics developed a rival account, which has been the object of increased scholarly interest over the last three decades since the seminal paper: "Did Chrysippus Understand Medea?" by Christopher Gill (to whom I pay tribute with the title of mine).[3]

---

1 For a closer analysis of the ancient discussion, including Euripides, Socrates, Plato, Aristotle, and the Stoics, see Müller 2009, 47–208.
2 Cf. Arist. *E.N.* 7.3, 1145b25–27; Ps.-Arist. *M.M.* 2.4, 1200b 25–28; X. *Mem.* 3.9.4. Aristotle obviously refers to the account given in Pl. *Prt.* 351b–358e.
3 See Gill 1983, who also contributed to this subject on several occasions in his later books and articles (1987; 1996, 216–239; 2006, 421–435; 2009), and on Stoic

That the Stoics contributed to this topic at all might come as a slight surprise if one looks at the rather scarce linguistic evidence. In the whole *Stoicorum veterum fragmenta* the technical term *akrasia* or cognates of it only turn up twice.[4] Apart from this external observation, there seem to be some internal considerations concerning Stoic psychology in general and their theory of action in particular which might prove to be an insurmountable obstacle to a Stoic reading of *akrasia* (see below, part I). Therefore, some scholars even doubted if there is conceptual space for weakness of will in Stoicism at all (e.g. Halbig 2004, 36). So, are we looking at a phantom debate which has no solid textual basis in our ancient sources?

This suggestion might be countered by pointing to the following passage from Diogenes Laertius' *Vitae philosophorum*, which deals with Chrysippus, one of the early Stoics:

> [I]n one of his works he [*sc.* Chrysippus] copied out nearly the whole of Euripides' Medea, and someone who had taken up the volume, being asked what he was reading, replied, "The Medea of Chrysippus." (D.L. 7.180, trans. Hicks)

To support one's argument by adducing characters or situations from poetry was common practice among ancient philosophers despite the critical attitude often taken toward the poets, which was also shared by the Stoics.[5] Now, especially Euripides' *Medea* was – and still is – regarded as a stellar example of *akrasia* in tragedy. Before killing her two children in order to take revenge on her husband Jason, Medea delivers a famous soliloquy in which she is torn between her desire for revenge on the one hand and her maternal feelings as well as her insight into the brutality of this course of action on the other hand (Eur. *Med.* 1021–1080). She concludes: "I understand the evils that I am going to do / But anger (*thumos*) prevails over my counsels (*bouleumata*)" (1078–1079).

This famous passage, which was later mirrored in Ovid's "video proboque meliora / deteriora sequor,"[6] was much discussed among ancient philosophers as an example of an inner conflict in which irrational passion, namely anger, finally wins out against reason.[7] The fact that Chrysippus was keen to present a description and explanation of Medea's akratic action in Stoic terms in his treatise *On the Passions* is well attested by

---

akrasia also Inwood 1985, 132–139; Gosling 1987; Price 1995, ch. 4; Joyce 1995; Guckes 2004; Boeri 2004; Gourinat 2007; Müller 2010.

4 *SVF* 3.264 and 265. Gourinat 2007 points to two further occurrences in Epictetus.
5 For a discussion of the issues involved, see Nussbaum 1993, who distinguishes two different Stoic outlooks on poetry.
6 Ov. *Met.* 7.20f.: "I see the better and acknowledge it, but I follow the worse."
7 For details of the reception of these lines in antiquity, see Dillon 1997.

Galen.[8] Apart from this, we also find a nuanced discussion of the Medea example in Epictetus.[9] The Stoic interest in this case is documented on another literary level too: Herillus wrote a *Medea* (which is lost to us) and Seneca composed a tragedy with this title.

Therefore, one promising route to approach Stoic thinking about *akrasia* is to take a closer look at one of these "case studies" of Medea. In this paper, I will try to elucidate the Stoic contribution to the ancient debate about weakness of will by analyzing Seneca's play and its central character. First, I will briefly delineate the philosophical framework in which the Medea example is discussed and describe to what extent the explanation of her behavior was a challenge to Stoicism in general (part I). In part II, Seneca's literary depiction of this case will be analyzed with the help of philosophical texts written by himself (mainly his treatise *On Anger*) and other authors (notably Galen and Plutarch). From this analysis, two different Stoic readings of *akrasia* will emerge. In the final part (III), I will summarize the overall picture of Medea as an akratic character that can be drawn from this reading of Seneca's play.[10]

I. The Stoics and Medea: Strange Bedfellows?

At first glance, there is something troubling in the idea that the Stoics used Medea as supportive evidence for their own philosophical perspective because problems immediately seem to arise for their views in two intertwined areas.[11]

[1] *Psychology*: Medea's famous lines at the end of her monologue seem to suggest that there are two different agents in the soul, which are juxtaposed in this case: irrational desire and reason. In middle Platonism this quotation was referred to in order to argue for the tripartition of the human soul which Plato first introduced in his *Republic* (book 4) and de-

---

8   Galen, *De placitis Hippocratis et Platonis*, books 4–5. For the background of this discussion, see Tieleman 2003, 17–60; Gill 1998 and 2006, 238–290.
9   Arr. *Epict.* 1.28, especially 7–10, 28; 2.17.19–22.
10 This line of argument presupposes that Seneca did at least not propagate deliberately anti-Stoic ideas in his plays. For the different positions concerning the relationship between Seneca philosophus and tragicus, see Hine 2004. I do not have a strong stake in this debate and I would like to offer what Hine calls a Stoic "diagnosis" with regard to Seneca's depiction of Medea without claiming that this is the only possible reading. As the argument will show, the portrayal of emotions in Seneca's *Medea* and in his philosophical writings seems to fit the Stoic bill quite well, but I will not argue for any strong claim that he used his tragedies as simple vehicles for his Stoic convictions.
11 For a more detailed discussion of these two points, see Müller 2009, 157–164.

veloped in his later works.[12] The inner struggle of Medea has its simplest explanation if we regard her soul as divided into different parts which have their own goals and sources of motivation, at least positing one rational and one irrational part (which in Plato's original division comprises the desiring and the spirited part). This basically bipolar psychology was – with some modifications – accepted by the older Academy as well as in Aristotle's Peripatetic school.

Now, one of the most distinctive features of Stoicism is the rejection of this kind of part-based psychology in favor of a so-called monistic model. Although the Stoics technically distinguish eight powers in the human soul (the *hēgemonikon*, the five senses, and the powers of speech and reproduction), it is clear that these other seven powers are really instances of the *hēgemonikon*, i.e. the "leading" rational capacity of the whole soul.[13] The *hēgemonikon* is the seat of reason (*logos*), and it is fundamentally involved in all psychic operations. Thus, the other powers are not – as in the Platonic scheme – independent sources of motivation which could conflict with each other or with the *hēgemonikon*. According to Stoic psychology, mental conflict cannot be accounted for by different agents in the soul but must be conceived as somehow happening within one and the same faculty, namely the *hēgemonikon*. But this seems to violate the "principle of opposites" that Plato uses in *Republic* 4 in order to justify the division of the soul into different parts: If the human being is torn between two contradictory impulses (e.g. to drink and to refrain from drinking), it cannot be one and the same psychic agent that causes this inner strife. Medea's case seems to prove exactly this because her being torn between killing and sparing her children cannot be located in one and the same psychic faculty. Hence it is not surprising that the Platonist Galen criticizes Chrysippus' use of the Medea example for having misunderstood this basic idea; instead he praises the middle Stoic Posidonius for his (alleged) renunciation of psychological monism by re-introducing Platonic part-psychology.[14] The challenge for the Stoics is this: How can they account for the split in Medea's soul within their own monistic psychology?

---

12 Cf. Alc. *Intr.* 24, p. 177: "Ὁρᾶται δέ γε ἐπὶ μὲν τῆς Μηδείας ὁ θυμὸς λογισμῷ μαχόμενος· λέγει γοῦν τό· 'Καὶ μανθάνω μὲν οἷα δρᾶν μέλλω κακά, / Θυμὸς δὲ κρείσσων τῶν ἐμῶν βουλευμάτων·' ἐπὶ δὲ τοῦ Λαΐου τὸν Χρύσιππον ἁρπάζοντος ἐπιθυμία λογισμῷ μαχομένη· λέγει γὰρ οὕτως· 'Αἲ αἲ τόδ' ἤδη θεῖον ἀνθρώποις κακόν, / Ὅταν τις εἰδῇ τἀγαθόν, χρῆται δὲ μή.'"
13 D.L. 7.110. For the unity of the soul as a basic tenet of Stoicism, see Alex. Aphr. *De An.* 2, p. 188,6–8 Bruns = SVF 2.823 (fragment LS 29A in the collection of Long and Sedley 1987).
14 For a thorough discussion of this issue, see Gill 2006, section 4.6, who questions Galen's account.

[2] *Theory of action*: Another problem with *akrasia* arises for the Stoic analysis of human action.[15] According to their basic model, actions are caused by a mental sequence made up of three elements: *phantasia – sunkatathesis – hormē*. First, the agent is confronted with an inner presentation (*phantasia*) occasioned by some antecedent sense perception. This *phantasia* already has a propositional content, e.g.: "This sweet is to be tasted." Then, it is up to the agent to give or to refuse the assent (*sunkatathesis*) to this presentation and thus to turn it into a practical judgment. After the agent has freely assented to this proposition, an impulse (*hormē*) arises to fulfill the propositional content (i.e. to taste the sweet), which is transformed into outward action if no external obstacle prevents it.

This is a very rough sketch of the causal antecedents of action, but it already shows sufficiently that it is not easy to accommodate weak-willed behavior within a Stoic framework. Let's take the case of the Euripidean Medea who confesses her knowledge that she is going to commit a terrible crime. It is certainly not far-fetched to assume that by recognizing this she assents to the proposition: "It is wrong to kill my innocent children." She even seems to recognize explicitly the wrongness of her anger when she adds afterwards that anger (*thumos*) is the source of the greatest evils for human beings,[16] which seems tantamount to assenting to the proposition: "Anger is not an appropriate motive for action." But given that Medea assents to at least one of these propositions it is not easy to see how she can proceed to kill her children at all. While assent itself is a free act of the *hēgemonikon*, the generation of impulse and its being carried out in action seems to be a straightforward causal sequence which cannot be interrupted (at least not in the internal processes of the soul). It does not seem possible to drive a wedge between assent and impulse, nor between impulse and action. But this leaves a gaping hole in the explanation of Medea's failure to follow her rational judgment, which she articulates clearly in the condemnation of her own murderous action. How is it possible at all to go against one's judgment according to this "intellectualistic" theory of action as based on the rational assent given freely by the *hēgemonikon*? This is another puzzle which every Stoic interpreter of Medea and her behavior has to solve.

Viewed from these two angles, the Stoics and Medea seem to be strange bedfellows indeed. Now, how does the professed Stoic Seneca por-

---

15 Useful overviews of the Stoic theory of action with special emphasis on its psychological background are provided by Rist 1969, ch. 14, Inwood 1985, and Annas 1992, 37–120.
16 Eur. *Med.* 1080 "ὅσπερ μεγίστων αἴτιος κακῶν βροτοῖς." The destructive nature of anger is also stressed by Jason in 446f.

tray this heroine in his play and how can this picture be related to the psychological framework just sketched?[17]

II. Seneca's Portrayal of Medea

II.1. *Dolor – Ira – Furor:* The Persistence Model of *Akrasia*

Medea's overall situation and psychic predicament is aptly described in the prologue of the play (Sen. *Med.* 1–55). She starts by invoking the gods of marriage by whom her husband Jason once swore oaths to her (1–8) and then turns for help to the furies, the goddesses who avenge crimes (8–18). She feels betrayed by her husband's impending marriage to Creusa, the daughter of King Creon, who has given Jason and Medea as well as their two children refuge in Corinth after their flight from Medea's homeland Colchis. Now Medea is threatened with further exile because of this remarriage and is thirsty for revenge on those who have inflicted pain and injustice on her. She seems to be brooding over the best course of revenge in some kind of inner dialogue in which she exhorts her own spirit (*animus*):

> Through the very guts find a path to punishment, my spirit, if you are alive, if there is any of your old energy left. [...] My pain (*dolor*) must grow more weighty: greater crimes become me now, after giving birth. Arm yourself in anger (*ira*), prepare to wreak destruction with full rage (*furore toto*). (Sen. *Med.* 40–42, 49–52)[18]

This exposition already contains the main driving forces behind Medea's murderous actions at the end of the play: *dolor – ira – furor*.[19] It is important to note how these passions are connected. Medea is severely pained by the events, above all by the remarriage of her husband, which takes place at the beginning of the play's second act.[20] She regards this primarily as an act of unfaithfulness toward herself. Jason wrongs her with this behavior,

---

17   The following discussion is very much indebted to the illuminating accounts of Seneca's *Medea* by Nussbaum (1994, 439–483; 1997) and Gill (1987; 2006, 421–435), although I do not completely agree with their reading; see below, notes 54 and 83. For a criticism of Nussbaum's influential reading, see Hine 2000, 29.
18   For the English quotations from Seneca's *Medea* and *Phaedra*, I use the translation by John G. Fitch.
19   The connection of these three elements in Medea is also alluded to by Jason in 444–446. Medea mentions them several times in her monologue (893–977), e.g. 914 (*dolor*), 916 (*ira*), 930 (*demens furor*). See also Lefèvre 1997, 75f. For a similar connection between *dolor* and *furor* in Seneca's *Phaedra*, see 99–103 and 1156–1167.
20   For pain (*dolor*) as a leitmotif in Seneca's tragedies, see Regenbogen 1930.

after all that she has done for him, which is indeed very much: She betrayed her family in helping him to get hold of the Golden Fleece, she even killed her brother to enable their flight from Colchis, and finally she staged the dismemberment of King Pelias by his own daughters so that Jason could have his revenge on him. The motive for all these cruel deeds was unequivocally her love for Jason: "How often have I spilled blood fatally – kindred blood! And yet I did no crime from anger; the cruelty came from my unhappy love" (Sen. *Med.* 134–136).

This situation is about to change radically because, from now on, Medea's own anger (*ira*), which grew out of her "unhappy love" and the pains inflicted on her, will direct her actions. The revenge itself will be carried out in a state of rage or fury (*furor*) sparked by this anger. This final turn is aptly mirrored by the description of Medea's outward appearance during the play. She visibly turns into a fury, i.e. one of the avenging goddesses, successively loosening her hair and her clothes over the various scenes, until she is presented bare-breasted, with a crown made up of serpents and with a dagger in her hand in the great incantation scene of the fourth act.[21] This matches several descriptions given by herself as well as by other characters which stress the gradual development of her state. Her anger and her fury seem to increase in the course of the play until they reach their climax in her final act of revenge, the murder of her children.[22] The overall impression is that Medea is in the gradually tightening grip of an anger which is increased step by step and finally unleashes the destructive forces of fury. She is an example of a character acting under the reign of anger; and the destructive nature of this emotion is certainly one central moral message of the play (just as in Euripides' *Medea*).[23]

A closer look reveals many parallels between Seneca's portrayal of angry Medea and his own philosophical work *On Anger* (*De ira*). I will focus on the most significant:

[1] The connection between anger (*ira*) and fury (*furor*) which Medea articulates is also stressed in *De ira*,[24] with particular emphasis on the cruel insanity which governs the outrage. Furious persons are somehow blind, even for the welfare of their own relatives, for whom it is therefore advisable to keep at a distance from them. Seneca mentions particularly

---

21 See especially Sen. *Med.* 752f., 771–774, 805–811. The chorus explicitly describes her as "bloodstained maenad" in 849.
22 Medea's outward description by others (e.g. Sen. *Med.* 382–396) can be compared to the phenomenology of anger provided by Seneca in *De ira* 1.1.3–7, which stresses the savage ugliness of this state. For Medea's development in the play, see also Kullmann 1970.
23 See above, note 16.
24 See especially *De ira* 2.36.5 and Maurach 1972, 313f., for further evidence.

that furious persons rage violently and indiscriminately even against their own loved ones.[25] This description fits the case of Medea, who does not even shrink back from murdering her own children to complete her revenge. Above all, furiously angry persons crave to harm or punish others at all costs, in order to repay the pain they have suffered,[26] even to the extent that they are ready to harm themselves substantially (*De ira* 1.1.1, 3.1.3). As Martha Nussbaum (1994, 422) expresses it aptly, "[a]nger hardens the spirit and turns it against the humanity it sees."

[2] But the fact that anger, as a "short insanity" (*De ira* 1.1.2: "brevis insania"), may end in frenzied bloodshed does not imply that anger itself is, in a sense, a mindless event which befalls the agent without any mental contribution from her part. It can only arise in human beings, where reason is present (*De ira* 1.3.4: "ubi rationi locus est"). Seneca defines it as "the desire to take vengeance for a wrong or […] the desire to punish the person by whom you reckon you were unjustly harmed."[27] Thus, in order to be angry in the sense of this definition one has to hold two opinions: [i] that one has suffered an injustice and [ii] that it is right or appropriate to take revenge for this injustice.[28] Seneca stresses that this cognitive content has to be voluntarily accepted by the agent, which means that it starts with a presentation of it to which the agent can give or withhold assent. If the agent does not subscribe to these judgments, the passion of anger will not arise. In his debate with the Peripatetics about the question as to whether anger is first and foremost triggered by an impulse (*impetus*) or by a judgment (*iudicium*), Seneca clearly opts for the cognitive alternative (*De ira* 2.1–4). He thereby stays true to the old Stoic position mainly promoted by Chrysippus according to which passions are identified with judgments (or are at least supervenient on them).[29] Without such a judgment there will be no drive (*impetus*) to take revenge. In short, anger as a passion is no blind and mindless push but always involves certain forms of rational judgment, even if this rationality is ultimately based on a false system of values like all other passions.

How "rational" is Medea's anger? It seems quite justified in the sense of judgment [i]. In fact, she has been wronged by Jason. In the exchanges with him and king Creon, Medea consistently points to her merits with

---

25 *De ira* 1.5.2, 2.36.5–6, 3.3.3.
26 In *De ira* 1.3.3 Seneca acknowledges that his understanding of anger comes, in a certain respect, close to Aristotle's definition of it as "cupiditas doloris reponendi." Cf. also *De ira* 1.5.2, 3.5.5.
27 Cf. *De ira* 1.2.3b (taken from Lactantius, *De ira dei* 17.13). Here and afterwards I use the translation of *De ira* by Robert A. Kaster.
28 This can be gathered from *De ira* 2.1.4 and 2.3.5. See Wildberger 2007, 310.
29 Cf. Gal. *P.H.P.* 4.1.16–17 and 4.2.6; D.L. 7.111 = *SVF* 3.456.

regard to saving and serving her husband. She has honored her part of the marital bargain to the extreme, even killing for him, while Jason shuns his duties toward her. This is silently recognized by Jason himself: He ought to keep his oath to her but sees a greater obligation toward his beloved children (Sen. *Med.* 431–443). Medea's recognition of this injustice is vividly described at the beginning of the second act when she hears the hymns accompanying the marriage of Jason and Creusa and can scarcely believe what she is suffering (116f.). Her husband does her injustice by despising what she did for him (120: "merita contempsit mea") and deserting her in a foreign city. The second judgment [ii], that this situation calls for revenge, follows immediately (124). While Euripides' Medea is shown to be angry and bent on revenge right from the start (because the action of the play begins only *after* the wedding has already taken place),[30] Seneca shows the psychological genesis of these emotions and their roots in Medea's recognition of how much she has been betrayed. Her anger is whipped up even more when she learns from Creon that she has not only lost her husband to another woman but that she will also be forced to leave the city for good – another keenly resented injustice inflicted on her, which increases her anger further.

The Stoics were obviously quick to criticize Medea for the value judgments constituting her passion, as Epictetus attests: "Poor woman, because she made a mistake about the most important things, she has been transformed from a human being into a poisonous snake."[31] As a consequence, she also miscalculates the values of the different courses of action open to her and opts for the wrong one. According to Epictetus, Medea's anger derives from the fact that she regards taking vengeance as more advantageous than saving her children. But in Seneca, Medea's anger is certainly not the result of a miscalculation on her part but an expression of her personality. She actively wants to identify herself with the emotions of anger and fury and addresses them several times in her internal monologues. The cognitive character of these emotions is stressed explicitly when she speaks of her "angry soul" as "decreeing" or "judging" (917f.) or of a "grief which can deliberate prudently" (155). This is also proof of the fact that Medea is not simply swept away by an irrational passion but that her mind actively embraces it. Although she addresses these emotional forces in a language reminiscent of dualism or a part-psychology in the Platonic style, there is no need to introduce a separate irrational source of

---

30 The significance of this circumstance is rightly stressed by Heldmann 1974, 164.
31 Arr. *Epict.* 1.28.8–9. For discussions of Epictetus' interpretation of Medea, see Nussbaum 1993, 142f.; Nussbaum 1994, 327f. and 447f.; Dillon 1997, 214 and 216f.; Gill 2006, 252.

motivation which overpowers her reason.³² Even when she is shaken by doubts (as in her monologue just before killing the children), we can see that she is talking of divergent inclinations of her thought or judgment and not of different internal agents, as we will see later. Seneca obviously stays within the cognitivist framework of old Stoic psychological monism in portraying Medea.

Medea certainly shows another typical symptom of anger as it is described in *De ira*, which might be called irrational. She mentally closes down to all advice from the outside and is mainly bent on considering possible options of revenge instead of questioning her initial judgment that this is the best course of action here and now.³³ But the advice given by her nurse and by Jason is mainly based on prudential considerations concerning her safety; she ignores or rejects this in accordance with her picture of herself as a heroic and mighty character, who does not fear to battle kings (527f.) and even gods (423f.) in her fury. This might strike an outward observer as a severe form of delusion (although the end of the play somehow justifies her confidence in her powers), but this attitude is based firmly on her other beliefs and judgments and is therefore at least not internally irrational.

To sum up the considerations above: Medea's anger fulfills the cognitive criteria which the old Stoics put forward in their description of passions as judgments; consequently, her actions, including her weak-willed ones, must be considered within this framework.³⁴ Seneca himself describes the generation of a passion like anger as follows:

> Now, to make plain how passions begin or grow or get carried away (*efferantur*): [1] there's initial involuntary movement – a preparation for the passion, as it were, and a kind of threatening signal; [2] there's a second movement accompanied by an expression of will not stubbornly resolved, to the effect that "I should be avenged, since I've been harmed" [...]. [3] The third movement's already out of

---

32 For a refutation of the view that Seneca falls back into psychological dualism, see Inwood 1993, who pays special attention to *De ira* 2.1–4.
33 Cf. *De ira* 1.1.2 with the description of anger as "rationi consiliisque praeclusa" and also *De ira* 1.18.1–2, stressing the "narrowing down" of attention to counter-arguments caused by anger. In Seneca's play, one may note the advice given to Medea by her nurse to hide her anger (150–154) and to calm down her passion (174f., 425f.), repeated by Jason (558f.). Medea is neither willing nor able to do any of this. For an analysis of these encounters as instances of a (failing) therapeutic discourse, see Wiener 2006, 36–46. That anger is an emotion which cannot be hidden easily is also stressed in *De ira* 3.13.1.
34 See Maurach 1972, especially 318f., who thinks that Seneca's *Medea* is meant to illustrate the genesis and development of anger and draws a number of illuminating comparisons.

control, it desires vengeance not if it's appropriate but come what may, having overthrown reason (*rationem evicit*). (Sen. *De ira* 2.4.1, trans. Kaster)[35]

Anger is structured by different movements in the soul which are indicated in brackets. While movement [1], the so-called *propatheia*, is irrelevant for our purposes here,[36] movement [2], i.e. the voluntary judgment on injustice followed by an impulse to revenge, has already been delineated above for Seneca's Medea.[37] The third kind of movement [3] is regularly used by the Stoics for their standard "argument from excess," which was directed against the Peripatetic conception of virtues as psychic powers capable of moderating the passions. Chrysippus thought that all passions are "excessive impulses" (*hormai pleonazousai*),[38] which means that they produce an impulse for action which cannot be controlled by the agent once she has given her assent. This is compared to the situation of someone running, who cannot stop at will because of the speed already reached. Put differently, once the person is in the grip of passion, she is at least temporarily unable to depart from the course of action engendered by the prevailing judgments. This state of mind, which is dominated by passions as "runaway motions" (Gal. *P.H.P* 4.5.13), is explicitly labeled "akratic" by Chrysippus:

> Such states as these are the sort that are out of control (*akrateis*), as if the men had no power over themselves but were carried away, just as those who run hard are carried along and have no control over that sort of movement. (Gal. *P.H.P.* 4.4.24, trans. de Lacy)

The truly angry person will therefore be somehow forced to seek revenge after she has consented to the corresponding judgment. This was the basis

---

35 Numbers in brackets added by me. For thorough discussions of this passage, see Inwood 1993 and Sorabji 2000, ch. 3–4. An alternative reading is provided by Graver 2007, 125–132.
36 *Propatheiai* are mostly basic physical reactions (like being startled by the sudden hissing of a snake), which even the wise man cannot avoid. Seneca does not refer to the terminology of *propatheia* explicitly but obviously has the same phenomena in mind; see the numerous examples given in *De ira* 2.2 and 2.3, and their discussion by Graver 2007, 93–101. Maurach 1972, 318f., reads the prologue in Seneca's play as a "first reaction" by Medea and reconstructs her development as a complete parallel to *De ira*. For a reading of Seneca's Medea in the light of the three phases of anger sketched above, see also Bäumer 1982, 137–160.
37 See also *De ira* 2.3.5: "Accordingly, that first mental jolt produced by the impression of an injury is no more 'anger' than the impression itself. The intentional movement (*impetus*) that follows, which has not only taken in the impression but affirmed it – that's anger, the arousal of a mind that moves willingly and deliberately toward the goal of vengeance (*concitatio animi ad ultionem voluntate et iudicio pergentis*)." (trans. Kaster).
38 For the following, see Gal. *P.H.P.* 4.2.8–18.

of Chrysippus' understanding of Medea.[39] This idea of an emotional "point of no return" is also ubiquitous in Seneca's *De ira*, e.g. when he compares anger to falling off a cliff (1.7) or to a sword that cannot be pulled back after it has been stuck in the enemy's body (2.35).

One might therefore suppose that Seneca would also include this stage [3] in the portrayal of his own Medea. And in fact, there are several hints suggesting the inability of Medea to check or rein in her emotions, first of all, the image of the bridle. The chorus comments on the violent effects of disappointed love by stating: "Blind is the fire of love when fanned by anger; it does not want to be ruled, it does not tolerate the bridle" (Sen. *Med.* 591f.); later they comment directly on the protagonist: "Medea does not know how to bridle her anger or love" (866f.).[40] This image of being unbridled is reinforced by the regular association of Medea with fire and flames which virtually consume everything and cannot be stopped easily, thus aptly depicting the inward as well as outward effects of Medea's anger. It gradually consumes her soul until it is in complete mastery of it, just as the fire caused by Medea's revenge (a poisoned gown offered as a wedding gift to Creusa) finally burns down the whole royal palace.

The lasting effect of anger is also stressed by Medea herself, who muses "how difficult it is to turn a mind from anger once it is aroused" (203f.). All exhortations by the nurse to calm down her anger and to rein in her revengeful impulse are therefore fruitless; Medea is caught in a rioting movement, a *motus efferus* (385), which comes close to the passionate "runaway states" described by Chrysippus. In *De ira*, Seneca stresses that anger literally "runs forward" against everything once the agent has given herself over to it.[41] This means that turning oneself over to a passion like anger is tantamount to losing control of oneself and one's actions. As *De ira* confirms, the angry person is *impotens sui*, "out of rational control" (1.1.2), because reason has turned into passion:

> [...] reason itself, which is entrusted with the reins, is in control only so long as it is kept separate from the passions; once it has mingled with them and become polluted, it cannot keep them in check, though it could have kept them out. Thought, once it has been shaken and dislodged from its proper footing, becomes a slave of the thing that shoves it along. [...] People who have jumped off a cliff retain no independent judgment and cannot offer resistance or slow the descent of their bodies in freefall. [...] Just so, once the mind has submitted to anger, love, and the other passions, it's not allowed to check its onrush (*impetus*): its own weight and the downward-tending nature of vices must – must – carry it along and drive it down to the depths. (Sen. *De ira* 1.7.3–4, trans. Kaster)

---

39 See Gal. *P.H.P.* 4.6.19, a view criticized by Galen in 4.2.27 and in 4.6.20–22.
40 For this imagery, see also Nussbaum 1994, 457, who also points to the image of the wave, which emphasizes the inexorability of the violence of passions.
41 *De ira* 2.3.4: "Ira non moveri tantum debet sed excurrere."

voluntary self-enslavement. There is a synchronic conflict within the mind, and reason no longer unequivocally consents to its own passionate judgments but is for the time being helpless to master itself and its former impulses. In this way, there is no need to posit conflicting parts of the soul like rational deliberations and irrational desires in order to account for Medea's internal mental conflict and her acting against reason. This reading would give support to an alternative translation of the famous lines uttered by Euripides' Medea, which has in fact been advanced by several scholars over the last few decades: "I understand the evils that I am going to do / But anger is the master of my plans (*bouleumata*)."[47]

In fact, in Euripides' play, *bouleumata* usually designate not the capacity or judgment of reason but the revenge plans of Medea. With the aid of the persistence model it is possible to make (Stoic) sense of this. Anger controls Medea's plans from the outset, and in her great monologue she realizes just this – she cannot even turn away from these plans although she now recognizes the evil character of her deed. All this fits very well the Chrysippean psychology of passions as "excessive impulses" or "runaway motions" which control our actions even if some knowledge about the badness of the performed action is present simultaneously. No wonder that Chrysippus drew so extensively on this example.

There is certainly enough evidence that this persistence model is also applicable to the protagonist of Seneca's *Medea*, especially if one takes into account the parallels with *De ira* drawn above. But there is also a different reading available, which will be sketched in the following section.

II.2. Anger versus Love: The Oscillation Model of *Akrasia*

If one compares Euripides' Medea to Seneca's, there is one striking difference: Euripides' heroine is bent on revenge against her husband right from the beginning of the play.[48] Her first revenge plan is quite straightforward and involves killing Jason and his new family; she later changes her mind, deciding that it is more effective to keep him alive and punish him by murdering his offspring.[49] The encounter between the married couple is full of accusations and counter-accusations, but the passionate bond of love does not seem to exist any longer; on Medea's side it has been completely

---

47 Eur. *Med.* 1078f. This alternative translation is vigorously defended by Diller 1966; it is also favored by Gill 1996, 223f.
48 See Steidle 1972. For an instructive comparison between Seneca's and Euripides' Medea, see Lefèvre 1997.
49 For this change of plans compare lines 374f. and 791–796 in Euripides' *Medea*.

erased by her anger toward her husband because of his betrayal of her marital relations and his unwillingness to recognize the social bonds that still exist between them.[50]

By contrast, Seneca's Medea displays rather mixed emotions toward her husband. Without doubt she is, on the one hand, angry at him because of his willingness to sacrifice her and their marriage for his own safety; on the other hand, she shies away from aiming her revenge directly at him. She even declares at the beginning of the play that the whole situation is entirely Creon's fault and that only he and his family will be punished, while "her" Jason has to stay alive at any cost (Sen. *Med.* 139–149). In her encounters with the nurse and Creon, this attitude becomes even clearer. She has not lost hope of winning Jason back and does everything to keep him at her side. When Creon confronts her with his decision to expel her from Corinth, she states three times that she is willing to leave as long as her husband accompanies her, thereby claiming him as her property, so to speak (198, 235–246, 272–275). This demand is intertwined with her repeated statements that she committed all the crimes out of love for him.

There is certainly no cold-hearted hatred toward Jason in Seneca's Medea. In her direct encounter she obviously tries to win him back, to persuade him that he is obliged to continue the flight with her, which they began together.[51] When she demands from him: "Give the fugitive back what is hers" (489), it is beyond doubt that she is referring to him. She reminds him ardently that she has sacrificed virtually everything for him (465–487, 500–503), and she is ready to stand up against Creon as well as other kings, Jason being the prize of this fight (515–527). Up to this point,

---

50 For an excellent discussion of the issues raised in the encounter between Medea and Jason in Euripides, see Gill 1996, 154–174.
51 Medea's first words in the play to Jason are: "Fugimus, Iason, fugimus" (447). The dangerous flight from Colchis, which involved her horrible deeds, is in Medea's view the foundation of their relationship. With this form of address she reminds him of this and the debt he has towards her for all the merits (*merita*) she earned out of her love for him. Therefore, it is important that she speaks in the first person plural; the singular in the English translation by Fitch ("I have fled before, Jason, I am fleeing now;" only slightly altered by Hine 2000, 447) rather obscures this point. Their unbreakable partnership in crime and guilt is also stressed in 531–537. See also her initial speech after the first chorus (line 116), where she says: "Occidimus." ("We are destroyed.") This may refer to their status as a married couple, in which case her appeal to Jason would be a ploy (since she already knows that all is over). But the plural form *fugimus* strikes me as a real last-ditch attempt to persuade him to flee together, backed up by her appeal to her homeland as her dowry, which they can return to and jointly rule, later in this speech. I owe these observations on "Occidimus" to Marcia Colish, whom I would also like to thank for her linguistic advice.

the main driving force of Medea's thought and actions is her passionate love for Jason, which still exists despite his betrayal.[52]

It is only in this conversation that her hopes of a reunion with her husband and of refueling the flame of their mutual love are finally thwarted. He is too weak and weary to continue their common fight and flight and admonishes her instead to "start thinking sensibly" (538) about other options. Although he silently recognizes his marital duty, his behavior toward her is markedly dispassionate; he just tries to calm her down as far as possible. Consequently, Medea does not only register that all traces of his former passionate love for her are obviously erased, she also no longer recognizes her beloved Jason of old, a daring adventurer, afraid of nothing, and full of vigor and spirit. Instead, she is confronted with someone who wants to settle down and live safely at any price and who fears kings and their power too much to risk anything for their former love. It is this revelation that her husband has been transformed irrevocably which turns the tables for Medea.[53] From now on, she is bent on revenge against him, and soon she perceives his most vulnerable spot, where she can hurt him deeply: his paternal love for their children (544–550). Her plan to kill Creon and Creusa is now only the overture to the true revenge on Jason himself, which will find its climax in the murder of their children. Her love for her husband has turned into anger.[54]

All this points to a deep internal conflict embedded in Medea's soul between her love for Jason and her anger, i.e, her thirst for revenge in view of the injustices inflicted on her. These emotions, although they are surely very close to each other in certain respects, can neither be fully reconciled in Medea's mind nor in her outward actions. This seems to be the reason why Medea ponders and wavers so much and so long about her revenge plans until they finally find their ultimate shape. Her love for Jason and her desperate desire to win him back effectively block the complete dominance and violent outbreak of her anger up to a certain point. Love and anger occupy her mind alternately, and this throws her into a state of indecision about which path to follow.[55] This state of mind is mirrored by several descriptions of Medea's fickleness, starting with her own observation:

---

52 The erotic character of this love is vividly described and deeply analyzed by Nussbaum 1994, ch. 12, and 1997.
53 See the convincing analysis of their relationship in Seneca's play by Maurach 1972.
54 By contrast, Nussbaum 1994 tends to downplay Medea's anger somewhat in favor of the persistence of her erotic love. But the second half of the play is in my opinion dominated by the anger which has succeeded her love. See the analysis above, in part II.1.
55 This state of indecision is rightly stressed by Steidle 1972 and Heldmann 1974, 173–175, who sees a balance of passions in the second and third act of the play.

"Perplexed and frenzied and maddened I turn one way and another" (123f.). Her nurse tells us that "she keeps running here and there (*huc et huc*) with wild movements" (385) and that her emotions are in constant change. The chorus declares: "She paces to and fro (*huc ... et illuc*)," and explains her inner predicament as follows: "Medea cannot rein in her feelings of love or anger. Now anger and love have joined their forces: what will follow?" (866–869).

Medea is obviously first pulled in different directions by these two emotions, at least until her love for Jason turns into anger.[56] The conflict of emotions which underlies Medea's erratic behavior is also mirrored in *De ira* (1.8.4–7), when Seneca states that anger can only be counteracted by another emotion (in this case: love) and not by reason.[57] According to the Stoics, the state of the passionate mind is inherently unstable, fluctuating, and "feverish" because it oscillates between incoherent sets of beliefs and judgments. In Medea's case it is the conflict of the lover and the betrayed wife that creates this incoherence because it results in contradicting judgments. Her anger dictates a revenge to her, which would surely also harm Jason and ultimately estrange him from her, while her erotic love prizes being together with him higher than anything else, even higher than her sense of dignity, which has been warped by his betrayal. Thus, one set of beliefs (anger) urges her to take revenge on him, the other one (love) to spare him at all costs.

This incoherent state of mind and the resulting indecision can now be translated into a certain model of psychic conflict which stays within the bounds of the Stoic philosophy of mind. In his *On Moral Virtue*, Plutarch discusses the difference between intemperance (*akolasia*) as a whole-hearted vice and incontinence (*akrasia*) as a state of mind to be distinguished from it because of the internal conflict which it engenders.[58] As a Platonist, he thinks that only a partitioning of the soul into rational and irrational parts can account for the internal division of the akratic agent and that the Stoics ultimately fail in their description and explanation of this phenomenon. Nevertheless, he offers one Stoic line of defense:

> But some affirm that passion is not essentially different from reason, nor is there quarreling between the two and factious strife, but only a conversion of one and

---

56 Seneca has thus united motives from Euripides (who stresses Medea's anger and revengefulness) and Ovid's twelfth *Heroid* (Medea as a lover). For the possible influence of Ovid (who also wrote a lost play about Medea) on Seneca, see Heldmann 1974, 164–177.

57 See also the more detailed discussion of this phenomenon by David H. Kaufman in this volume.

58 See Plutarch, *De virtute morali*, especially chs. 6–9. For a detailed discussion of Plutarch's views, see Gill 2006, 219–238.

the same reason to its two aspects; this escapes our notice by reason of the suddenness and swiftness of the change, for we do not perceive that it is the same part of the soul with which we naturally change to aversion, are angry and afraid, are swept along by pleasure to shameful conduct, and then, when the soul itself is being swept away, recover ourselves again. In fact, they say, desire and anger and fear and all such things are but perverse opinions and judgments, which do not arise in one certain part of the soul, but are inclinations and yieldings, assents and impulses of the whole directive faculty (*hēgemonikon*) and, in a word, certain activities which may in a moment be changed this way or that, just as the sudden assaults of children have an impetuosity and violence that is precarious and inconstant because of children's weakness. (Plu. *Virt. mor.* 7, 446f–447a; trans. Helmbold)[59]

According to this account the impression of simultaneity in our inner conflict is deceptive. The mind as a whole just shifts very rapidly between different sets of beliefs, assents, and impulses, thereby creating the false appearance of a synchronic division of mind, when in fact the mind oscillates in a diachronic movement. There are not two parts of the soul which are opposed at the same time, but one and the same mind (the *hēgemonikon*) goes back and forth in its operation. This fits at a basic level with the Stoic idea that such an oscillation is linked to an internally incoherent frame of mind which produces several passions that give rise to this indecision.[60]

Seneca's Medea seems to fill this bill right from the beginning of the play. She is alternately driven by her emotions of anger and love; very often the oscillation between them happens within a few lines. However, even after her passionate love seems to have given way to anger, her frame of mind still remains highly unstable. This is aptly mirrored by the final sequence of the play. Before murdering her children, she is torn between anger and maternal love; she addresses herself in these two different roles urging herself either to carry on with her intended crime or to desist. The rapid oscillation between these conflicting opinions and impulses as described in her soliloquy could serve as a stellar example for the phenomenon described by Plutarch. Medea is still divided and torn:

> Why do you vacillate, my spirit? Why are tears wetting my face, and anger leading me to shift in one direction, love in another? Conflicting currents whirl me from side to side. [...] So my heart wavers; anger puts mother love to flight, then mother love, anger. Give way to love, my pain. (Sen. *Med.* 937–944, trans. Fitch)

This passionate turmoil is accompanied by extensive, and rather specious, reasoning on behalf of both sides. This serves to underscore the Stoic idea that emotions and desires are not mindless blind pushes but engender a

---

59 Discussed in LS 65G. See also 441c–d = LS 61B.
60 Cf. D.L. 7.110.

belief-*cum*-reasoning which expresses conflicting facets of Medea's split personality. As Christopher Gill notes, the conflict displayed here also contains a highly relevant moral issue. Maternal or parental love counts as a paradigmatic expression of the naturalness of other-benefiting motivation; thus, we also witness the battle between a "'natural' self" (which has not been so clearly visible up to this point)[61] holding on to piety toward the children (*pietas*: cf. *Med.* 943f.) and a "passion-driven self" hungry for revenge on Jason at any cost (Gill 2009, 75). Thus, Medea's natural reason opposes her anger, and both of them occupy the mind in rapid succession, revealing at once her incoherent state of mind and delaying her outward action. In the final act of the play, Medea displays a conflict resembling the one depicted in Seneca's *Phaedra*. There, the antagonism which stretches over the whole play is from the start between Phaedra's strong passion (her love for her stepson Hippolytus) and her sense of moral shame (*pudor*). The overall effect is the same indecision as in Medea's case. Phaedra wavers constantly between a wish to commit suicide in order to preserve her dignity and her amorous desire for Hippolytus.[62] Finally, she gives in to her passion, thereby irrevocably ruining her own reputation as well as the life of her stepson, only to resort later to the suicide which was on her mind from the beginning. She obviously is another victim of incoherent and fluctuating beliefs and judgments oscillating rapidly in her mind.

The akratic conflict between reason and passion, which was stressed by the Platonists in order to defend their part-psychology, can thus be once more reinterpreted along the lines of a monistic psychology, namely as successive states of one and the same mind. This oscillation model, which accounts for internal conflicts like that of Medea and Phaedra, has been hailed by some interpreters as an overall convincing explanation of the inner struggle experienced by weak-willed agents.[63] It also fits the general Stoic idea of passions as "volatile" movements.[64] But it has to be noted that

---

61 Medea does not display much maternal feeling for her children before the final act. In fact, she seems rather disinterested in their fate.
62 For the basic conflict between *pudor* and *amor*, see especially *Phaed.* 250–254, 1159–1200.
63 See Inwood 1985, 138f.; Forschner 1995, 137f.; and Halbig 2004, 36. Long 1999, 581f. praises this model: "What we have here is a brilliant revision of the standard belief in the divided self. [...] Apparent conflict of desires, apparent conflict between reason and passion – these are the unitary mind's oscillation between pro and contra judgements. Reason is fully at work throughout, so the emotions are not due to something other than reason. They are errors of reasoning."
64 Cf. Stob. 2.7.10, vol. 2, p. 88,11f. Wachsmuth (Zeno characterizing passion as *ptoia*) = *SVF* 1.206 and 3.378 = LS 65A1.

there exists at least some tension between this and the Stoic persistence model of emotions as sketched above in part II.1.[65]

[1] It is a hallmark of the persistence model that passions are long-lasting and very violent motions of the mind from which the person in their grip cannot easily be stopped or deflected, as shown by Chrysippus' example of the runner who cannot stop at will. This is also supported by the fact that emotions are not only judgments but also physical contractions or expansions of the material *pneuma* of which the soul is made; because they are very strong, they take some time to abate.[66] Their overall character is violent excessiveness. By contrast, the oscillation model somehow presupposes that the emotions, i.e. the impulses and the judgments backing them, are inherently unstable like the "assaults of children," as Plutarch puts it in the quotation above. But if they are so "weak" after all, they are not likely to dominate the actions of a person like Medea over a longer span of time against a judgment which has changed in the meantime – and this is exactly the upshot of the explanation of conscious acts of weakness of will in the persistence model. While the oscillation model describes a diachronic structure of weak-willed behavior in which the judgment just swings around at the time of action,[67] the persistence model leaves the door open for a very strong synchronic version of clear-eyed *akrasia*.

[2] The oscillation model has to explain how it is possible that there are assents upon which no action-guiding impulses follow. Plutarch explicitly mentions that "assents and impulses" (*sunkatatheseis kai hormai*) change very rapidly, without producing immediate action. But according to the Stoic theory of action, an assent to a *phantasia hormētikē* ("impulse presentation") is always followed by an impulse which triggers the action.[68] This does not seem to be the case in the oscillation model because the hallmark of it is the wavering indecision of the agent. Thus, either there are assents without impulses,[69] or the produced impulses are not strong enough to trigger the action. One strategy to deal with this gap is to assume that passionate persons only give "weak assents" to their conflicting pre-

---

65 For a more detailed (and comparative) account of the persistence and the oscillation model of *akrasia* in Stoicism, cf. Müller 2010.
66 For the decline of passions and the problems connected with this development, see Gal. *P.H.P.* 4.7.12–17 = LS 65O.
67 Compare Socrates' analysis of weak-willed behavior in Plato's *Protagoras* (351b–358e).
68 According to Inwood 1985, 52f., the impulse is a "necessary and sufficient condition of an action."
69 This is rather unlikely because of the close connection between assent and impulse, which seems to come close to an identification. See, e.g., Stob. 2.9.7b, vol. 2, p. 88 Wachsmuth = *SVF* 3.171 = LS 65I: "Πάσας δὲ τὰς ὁρμὰς συγκαταθέσεις εἶναι." Cf. also *SVF* 1.61 and 2.980f.

sentations,[70] i.e. assents which are either not strong enough to produce impulses at all or only strong enough to produce impulses which may be blocked by competing ones. There is some evidence that already the early Stoa developed a model in which the weakness of the assent is a result of the "weakness" (*astheneia*) of the mind that gives it.[71] Because the mind itself is divided into incoherent sets of beliefs and judgments, it is not capable of giving a whole-hearted and full-blown consent; in its passionate state it is always fragmented, also with regard to the impulses which follow from the weak assents.[72] The persistence model, on the contrary, seems to assume a rather "strong" assent generated by the passions, which carries on even after the conscious judgment has already changed.

To sum up: Both models offer a way to account for weakness of will within the basic psychological framework of early Stoicism paved by Chrysippus, treating it as a problem of passion (*pathos*).[73] But the two models cannot easily be reconciled into a single coherent view of *akrasia*; at a deeper level there even seems to be a contradictory picture of the akratic agent in the grip of passion. The persistence model sees her as a more or less strong and determined – if misguided – person ruled by her emotions who carries on against all moral and rational objections to her intended actions. By contrast, the oscillation model pictures a fickle mind which is weakened and unstable because of its being constantly tossed about by an inner whirlwind of passions, while the outcome of these inner conflicts is more or less unpredictable. This general difference would also apply to the final monologue of Medea. In the persistence model, she recognizes rationally the moral dimension of the imminent atrocity and is somehow vexed by it, but anger remains the master of her plans until the end. Her internal monologue would not be an *Entscheidungsmonolog* which might lead to one or the other decision, but only a moment of brief hesitation before anger, being in the driver's seat all along, takes its final toll. The oscillation model would rather stress the openness of the situation. Because of the unstable and weak condition of Medea's mind, it is by no means pre-determined how she will act in the end; she oscillates

---

70 For explanations of the Stoic account along this line, see Joyce 1995 and Boeri 2004.
71 For this kind of weakness (*astheneia*) and its relation to akratic action, see Gal. *P.H.P.* 4.6.6–17 and Plu. *Virt. mor.* 446c. For details of this notion of "weakness," cf. Müller 2009, 179–187 and Gill 2006, 261–263.
72 See Stob. 2.7.11m, vol. 2, p. 111f. Wachsmuth = *SVF* 3.548 = LS 41G and Inwood 1985, 165: "Assent which is given in accordance with an unharmonious set of principles is bound to be weak and unstable."
73 See Gal. *P.H.P.* 4.2.19–27 and Gill 1983, 139–142.

unpredictably between contradicting as well as weak judgments, assents, and impulses.

III. Medea as an Akratic Personality

Now, how can these issues be adduced to distinguish the persistence and the oscillation model in Seneca's *Medea*? Since there elements of both models can be detected in Seneca's portrayal of Medea and her behavior throughout the play, one may surely not expect to establish a clear-cut case in favor of one of these models.[74] It is even possible that Seneca himself would not have dwelt too much on the differences of the persistence and the oscillation model of weakness of will. Certainly, a play is not the appropriate place to look for the solution to a complicated theoretical issue in Stoicism, which involves much conceptual work on notions like "assent," "impulse," or "weakness of mind." If – and this is still a big "if" – Seneca's tragedies are shaped (or at least informed) by Stoic teaching at all,[75] they are surely meant to show or to illustrate it and not to solve difficulties which are inherent in its theoretical background. But apart from these methodological and hermeneutical restrictions, I think that we can reconstruct a picture of the akratic personality from Seneca's *Medea* which provides us with some insights into his overall conception of weak-willed persons and his possible preference for one of the two models sketched above.

I would like to begin with the end, namely the killing of the children. Seneca changes the Euripidean plot at a crucial point, by separating the murder of the first from that of the second son. After having sacrificed her first child to her dead brother (which happens before Jason's arrival), Medea drags the corpse and her second son up to the roof in order to prove her criminal power to the Corinthian people by something like a public execution. She admonishes herself to fulfill her revenge, but again starts to waver considerably:

---

74 It has to be noted that in both cases Seneca's treatment of Medea does not lend itself to the hypothesis that he changed from a "monistic" Chrysippean psychology to a more "dualistic" one along the lines of Posidonius. This view is shared by Nussbaum 1994, 448–453 and Gill 2006, 423. He thinks that Senecan tragedy is "strongly informed by Chrysippean thinking about passion as internal conflict."

75 For the ongoing debate whether Senecan tragedy is exemplary of Stoic philosophy, see Gill 2006, 422f. and Hine 2004. For Seneca's attitude towards the philosophical value of poetry, see Nussbaum 1993, 126f., who judges that "Senecan drama presents Stoic psychology of passion and passional conflict with greater explicitness and clarity than any other non-Stoic poetic text."

> Why delay now, my spirit? Why hesitate? Has your powerful anger already flagged? I regret what I have done, I feel ashamed. What have I done, poor woman? (Sen. *Med.* 988–990, trans. Fitch)

Medea is obviously caught by a wave of shame that at least temporarily leads to a decline of her anger, which may also already have been satiated by the first killing. It is far from clear how she would have acted if she had remained alone. It is the appearance of Jason on the scene that refuels her anger so that it is finally strong enough to carry out the second murder:

> This was the one thing I lacked, this spectator. I think nothing has been done as yet: Such crime as I did without him was lost. (992–994, trans. Fitch)

Consequently, the final act of killing is directed at Jason in particular as the spectator of the scene: "Raise your tear-swollen eyes here, ungrateful Jason. Do you recognize your wife?" (1020f.).[76]

The appearance of Jason is obviously crucial for Medea's ability to overcome the feelings of guilt as well as the temporary "shortage" of anger, which threatens to put down her thirst for revenge. It is only on seeing him that finally she is able to go through with it. Obviously, she needs this external stimulus without which her anger would fail. Thus, the analysis of this passage tends more toward the oscillation than to the persistence model.

Throughout the whole play, it is remarkable how often Medea actively stirs her own anger in a series of passages.[77] This seems to be necessary especially in the first half of the play, where her anger is counteracted very effectively by her love for Jason; but it also happens in her final monologue in which it has to overcome her maternal love. Why is this kind of *Selbstaufreizung* ("self-excitation") necessary?[78] One might interpret it as an outward expression of her inner strength and determination. But if Seneca's Medea were as determined as her Euripidean counterpart (who effectively and silently prepares and executes her revenge plan), she would not need to convince her nurse and the chorus repeatedly of the flaring rage inside her. The overall impression is rather that she needs to convince

---

[76] This final scene, in which Medea stands on the roof while Jason watches from below, gives credit to the following analysis of Nussbaum 1994, 424: "A central element in anger is a severing of the angry person from the object of anger. In getting angry I set myself over against the one who wronged me, preparing to take pleasure in his hurt. In so doing, I usually think, 'This person is beneath me'. [...] Anger contains in this way, as Seneca says, an excessive love and exaltation of oneself (2.31)."

[77] See especially Sen. *Med.* 40–55, 140–149, 401–414.

[78] A similar behavior is shown by Phaedra in Sen. *Phaed.* 592–599. For other instances of *Selbstaufreizung* in Seneca's tragedies, see: *Her F*. 75–122; *Ag.* 108–124; *Thy.* 176–204.

herself somehow that she has the strength to persist in her anger in the face of other emotions conflicting with it.

The weakness of her personality is betrayed by herself right at the beginning of the play. She wants to return to the strength (*vigor*) of her days of old in order to find a method of revenge (40–43), but in fact, she first produces only aimless activities, as her nurse registers (382–392). The ongoing inner battle between love and anger obviously takes its toll by wearing her down, just as Jason appears to be exhausted by his conflict between loyalty for his former wife and his wish to secure the future of his children (434–443) and confesses: "I give up, worn out by troubles" (518). It is only after the conversation between husband and wife, which has the effect of cooling down Medea's erotic love for him, that she starts with the preparations for her revenge. Even then, her famous self-assertion "Now, I am Medea: My genius has grown through evils" (910), which echoes her intention expressed at the beginning to "become" Medea (171), sounds too high-pitched and therefore slightly hollow. She desperately tries to establish her own identity by cutting the bonds between herself and her life as a wife and mother, but at the time of her *Medea nunc sum* this has not truly been achieved. Despite another self-excitation of her anger (911–917), she soon realizes her hesitant attitude toward the central element of her revenge plan, the killing of her children. This is clearly expressed in her final monologue in which she changes her mind very rapidly back and forth from wifely anger to motherly love.[79] This internal struggle is quite significant concerning the strength (or rather: weakness) of her new identity. She proclaims to have left her old self behind and to have regained her strength of former days, but in the end her decision to complete the act hangs by a thread.

Therefore, one should not be misled by Medea's repeated and ferocious assertions of herself and her ever-increasing anger. At the crucial junctures of the play, she is always on the verge of collapsing. In her encounter with Jason in the third act and during the prolonged successive murder of her two children in the fifth act, she has obvious difficulties to muster the anger needed for her revenge because she is confronted with counter-emotions of erotic and maternal love. Her anger does not seem to possess the excessive and lasting quality she is eager to ascribe to her own revengeful state. It rather seems to correspond with what Seneca has to say in *On Anger* when comparing this emotion to the stability of reason:

---

[79] The sequence of oscillation is as follows: 926–932 (motherly love); 933–936 (wifely anger); 944–947 (motherly love); 948–953 (wifely anger). In 937–944 (quoted above) she stresses her being torn between these two sentiments.

> Pity has often turned anger back because, being empty and swollen, it lacks a solid core. It enjoys a violent onset, just like onshore winds and those that arise over rivers and marshes, string, but short-lived: after an initial massive assault it droops, prematurely wearied [...]. Sometimes, however, even when anger has persisted, if there are a number who have deserved to die, it stops the killing after shedding the blood of two or three. (Sen. *De ira* 1.17.4–6, trans. Kaster)[80]

Medea's anger fits this picture quite well, despite all the furious deeds it causes at the end of the play. Her attempt to establish her identity by renouncing all former bonds of love and identifying herself completely with the emotion of anger is much more fragile than it appears on the surface.[81] All this does not sit too well with the persistence model and its stress on the excessive nature of emotions in general. This approach seems much better suited to explaining the behavior of Euripides' Medea, who can whole-heartedly and plausibly declare at the end of her monologue that anger is (and has been all along) the true "master of her plans."

In my opinion, the oscillation model with its stress on a continuous internal conflict between different judgments and emotions, which causes the mind to swing around without really finding solid ground, fits Seneca's overall description of Medea as a truly akratic character much better. She resembles once again a description of Seneca's Phaedra, that "her condition is always impatient with itself and changing."[82] Seneca's Medea is not a "highly integrated and consistent character, single-mindedly focused on hatred, revenge, and violence, and reveling in her own evil motivation," who only falters and disintegrates as a person in the last act, as Christopher Gill describes her.[83] Quite to the contrary, right from the start she is whirled around by her conflicting emotions in spite of all her verbal assertions; the final scene only confirms what we see throughout the play. Medea is an inconsistent character desperately trying to establish a unified identity by focusing on her anger and her revenge plans, both of which are unstable in their build-up as well as in their execution.

But one might argue that she succeeds in "becoming Medea" in the end after having killed her second son. By murdering both of her children, she has extinguished her maternal love, and by hurling their corpses at Jason,

---

80 For the "weakness" of anger, see also *De ira* 1.20.1–5.
81 This is rightly emphasized by Henry and Walker 1967, who see a fragmentation of identity in Medea resulting in an "absence of continuous identity combined with repeated and desperate affirmation of identity existing or to come" (177). See also Schiesaro 2009, 228–235, who speaks of an "outright denial of self."
82 Sen. *Phaed.* 372–373: "semper impatiens sui / mutatur habitus."
83 Gill 2006, 424f. He regards Seneca's Phaedra as the paradigm case for a constant self-division, while he sees "a more localized phase of conflict" (432) in Medea; see also his analyses of both cases in Gill 2009. In my opinion, this underestimates the oscillation in Medea's behavior throughout the whole play.

she finally severs all familiar and loving bonds she shared with him. Now she is truly ready to leave her old human identity and head for a place "where [...] there are no gods," as Jason proclaims in the final line of the play (Sen. *Med.* 1027). Still, she has certainly not achieved a "structured self" in the Stoic sense because this would mean that her future life would be based on the right normative judgments, which she has consciously shunned in her revenge.[84] In the end, she might appear as some kind of unified self, but it is a vicious one that has left behind all morality and humanity. This portrayal corresponds to the state of brutishness (*feritas*) which Seneca describes as an ensuing result of unbridled anger in *De ira* 2.5.[85] Thus, Medea has been truly "created by her own evil deeds" (910), which were originally committed out of human passion but finally transform her into an anti-social fury beyond all feelings of mercy and compassion.

This might well be the unspoken and hidden moral of the play. There are ultimately two ways to escape from the internal turmoil and conflicts of an akratic mind: The path which Medea takes after much wavering indecision is to follow one emotion like anger right through to the end, i.e. to the dreadful deeds it causes; she leaves her state of weakness of will by ultimately becoming completely evil in a measure which transgresses all human boundaries. The opposite way is described at the end of *De ira* as "cultivating humanity."[86] This would have included the extirpation of her ruling passions of anger and erotic love by correcting the false value judgments about the world on which they are based, thus curing the incoherence of the akratic mind, which finally drives it into madness.

The Stoics were obviously interested in Medea as a truly great-minded character[87] caught in *akrasia*, who takes a horribly wrong way out of it. Instead of trying to become a Stoic sage, she turns herself into an avenging fury with all the dreadful consequences so vividly depicted in Seneca's play. Thus, she may have finally overcome the akratic division of her passionate self, but this proves to be a Pyrrhic victory.[88] This is undoubtedly a very Stoic way of "understanding" Medea.[89]

---

84 See Gill 2006 on the idea of a "structured self" based on psychophysical and ethical holism.
85 I owe this observation to Jula Wildberger. For Seneca's understanding of brutishness, see Graver 2007, 122–125.
86 See *De ira* 3.43.5: "colamus humanitatem;" a compelling reading of this motive in Seneca is provided by Nussbaum 1994, ch. 11.
87 Cf. Nussbaum 1994, 447f.
88 Cf. Maurach 1972, 312f.
89 This paper was presented at the University of Helsinki in December 2011. I would like to thank Risto Saarinen for the kind invitation and the members of the "Philosophical Psychology, Morality and Politics Research Unit" for the fruitful discussion. For a precise correction of the text I am indebted to Christine Wolf.

Bibliography

Alkinoos. 1990. *Enseignement des doctrines de Platon [= Didaskalikos]*. See Whittaker and Louis 1900.
Anderson, William S., ed. 1977. *Ovid, Metamorphoses*. Leipzig: Teubner.
Annas, Julia. 1992. *Hellenistic Philosophy of Mind*. Berkeley: University of California Press.
Aristoteles. 1894. *Ethica Nicomachea*. See Bywater 1894.
Aristoteles. 1935. *Magna Moralia*. See Susemihl 1935.
Bäumer, Änne. 1982. *Die Bestie Mensch: Senecas Aggressionstheorie, ihre philosophischen Vorstufen und ihre literarischen Auswirkungen*. Frankfurt; Bern: Peter Lang.
Boeri, Marcelo D. 2004. "The Presence of Socrates and Aristotle in the Stoic Account of Akrasia." In *Metaphysics, Soul, and Ethics in Ancient Thought: Themes from the Work of Richard Sorabji*, edited by Ricardo Salles, 383–412. Oxford: Clarendon Press.
Burnet, John, ed. 1900–1907. *Plato, Opera*. 5 vols. Oxford: Clarendon Press.
Bywater, Ingram, ed. 1894. *Aristoteles, Ethica Nicomachea*. Oxford: Clarendon Press.
De Lacy, Phillip, ed. and trans. 1978. *Galen, De placitis Hippocratis et Platonis. Libri I–V*. Corpus Medicorum Graecorum V 4.1.2. Berlin: Akademie-Verlag.
Diggle, James, ed. 1984. *Euripides, Fabulae*. Vol. 1. Oxford: Oxford University Press.
Diller, Hans. 1966. "Θυμὸς δὲ κρείσσων τῶν ἐμῶν βουλευμάτων." *Hermes* 94: 267–275.
Dillon, John. 1997. "Medea among the Philosophers." In *Medea: Essays on Medea in Myth, Literature, Philosophy, and Art*, edited by James Claus and Sarah Johnston, 211–218. Princeton: Princeton University Press.
Diogenes Laertius. 1925. *Lives of Eminent Philosophers*. See Hicks 1925.
Epictetus. 1925–1928. *The Discourses as Reported by Arrian, the Manual and Fragments*. See Oldfather 1925–1928.
Euripides. 1984. *Fabulae*. See Diggle 1984.
Fitch, John G., ed. and trans. 2002. *Seneca, Tragedies*. Vol. 1: *Hercules; Trojan Women; Phoenician Women; Medea; Phaedra*. Cambridge; London: Harvard University Press.
Forschner, Maximilian. 1995. *Die stoische Ethik: Über den Zusammenhang von Natur-, Sprach- und Moralphilosophie im altstoischen System*. 2nd ed. Darmstadt: Wissenschaftliche Buchgesellschaft.
Galen. 1978. *De placitis Hippocratis et Platonis. Libri I–V*. See De Lacy 1978.
Gill, Christopher. 1983. "Did Chrysippus Understand Medea?" *Phronesis* 28: 136–149.
Gill, Christopher. 1987. "Two Monologues of Self-Divison: Euripides, 'Medea' 1021–80 and Seneca, 'Medea' 893–977." In *Homo Viator: Essays for John Bramble*, edited by Michael Whitby, Philip Hardie, and Mary Whitby, 25–37. Bristol: Bristol Classical Press.
Gill, Christopher. 1998. "Did Galen Understand Platonic and Stoic Thinking on Emotions?" In *The Emotions in Hellenistic Philosophy*, edited by Juha Sihvola and Troels Engberg-Pedersen, 113–148. Dordrecht: Kluwer.
Gill, Christopher. 1996. *Personality in Greek Epic, Tragedy, and Philosophy: The Self in Dialogue*. Oxford: Clarendon Press.
Gill, Christopher. 2006. *The Structured Self in Hellenistic and Roman Thought*. Oxford: New York: Oxford University Press.
Gill, Christopher. 2009. "Seneca and Selfhood: Integration and Disintegration." In *Seneca and the Self*, edited by Shadi Bartsch and David Wray, 65–83. Cambridge: Cambridge University Press.
Gosling, Justin. 1987. "The Stoics and ἀκρασία." *Apeiron* 20: 179–202.

Gourinat, Jean-Baptiste. 2007. "Akrasia and Enkrateia in Ancient Stoicism: Minor Vice and Minor Virtue." In *Akrasia in Greek Philosophy: From Socrates to Plotinus*, edited by Christopher Bobonich and Pierre Destrée, 215–247. Leiden: Brill.
Graver, Margaret R. 2007. *Stoicism and Emotion*. Chicago: University of Chicago Press.
Guckes, Barbara. 2004. "Akrasia in der älteren Stoa." In *Zur Ethik der älteren Stoa*, edited by Barbara Guckes, 94–122. Göttingen: Vandenhoeck & Ruprecht.
Halbig, Christoph. 2004. "Die stoische Affektenlehre." In *Zur Ethik der älteren Stoa*, edited by Barbara Guckes, 30–68. Göttingen: Vandenhoeck & Ruprecht.
Heldmann, Konrad. 1974. *Untersuchungen zu den Tragödien Senecas*. Wiesbaden: Franz Steiner.
Helmbold, William C., ed. and trans. 1939. *Plutarch, De virtute morali*, In *Plutarch, Moralia*. Vol. 6: 15–87. Cambridge; London: Harvard University Press.
Henry, Denis, and Bessie Walker. 1967. "Loss of Identity: 'Medea superest'? A Study of Seneca's Medea." *CPh* 62: 169–181.
Hicks, Robert Drew, ed. and trans. 1925. *Diogenes Laertius, Lives of Eminent Philosophers*. 2 vols. Cambridge; London: Harvard University Press. Rpt. 1950.
Hine, Harry M, ed. and trans. 2000. *Seneca, Medea. With an Introduction, Text, Translation and Commentary*. Warminster: Aris & Phillips.
Hine, Harry M. 2004. "Interpretatio Stoica of Senecan Tragedy." In *Sénèque le tragique*, edited by Margarethe Billerbeck and Ernst A. Schmidt, 173–209. Vandœuvres-Genève: Fondation Hardt.
Inwood, Brad. 1985. *Ethics and Human Action in Early Stoicism*. Oxford: Clarendon Press.
Inwood, Brad. 1993. "Seneca and Psychological Dualism." In *Passions & Perceptions: Studies in Hellenistic Philosophy of Mind*, edited by Jacques Brunschwig and Martha C. Nussbaum, 150–183. Cambridge: Cambridge University Press.
Joyce, Richard. 1995. "Early Stoicism and Akrasia." *Phronesis* 40: 315–335.
Kaster, Robert A., and Martha C. Nussbaum, trans. 2010. *Lucius Annaeus Seneca, Anger, Mercy, Revenge*. Chicago: University of Chicago Press.
Kullmann, Wolfgang. 1970. "Medeas Entwicklung bei Seneca." In *Forschungen zur römischen Literatur: Festschrift zum 60. Geburtstag von Karl Büchner*, edited by Walter Wimmel, 158–167. Wiesbaden: Franz Steiner.
Lefèvre, Eckard. 1997. "Die Transformation der griechischen durch die römische Tragödie am Beispiel von Senecas 'Medea'." In *Tragödie: Idee und Transformation*, edited by Hellmut Flashar, 65–83. Stuttgart; Leipzig: Teubner.
Long, Anthony A. 1999. "Stoic Psychology." In *The Cambridge History of Hellenistic Philosophy*, edited by Keimpe Algra, Jonathan Barnes, Jaap Mansfeld, and Malcolm Schofield, 560–584. Cambridge: Cambridge University Press.
Long, Anthony, and David N. Sedley, eds. and trans. 1987. *The Hellenistic Philosophers*. 2 vols. Cambridge: Cambridge University Press.
Marchant, Edgar C., ed. and trans. 1923. *Xenophon, Memorabilia, Oeconomicus, Symposium, Apology*. Cambridge; London: Harvard University Press.
Maurach, Gregor. 1972. "Jason und Medea bei Seneca." In *Senecas Tragödien*, edited by Eckard Lefèvre, 292–319. Darmstadt: Wissenschaftliche Buchgesellschaft.
Müller, Jörn. 2009. *Willensschwäche in Antike und Mittelalter: Eine Problemgeschichte von Sokrates bis Johannes Duns Scotus*. Leuven: Leuven University Press.
Müller, Jörn. 2010. " 'Doch mein Zorn ist Herrscher über meine Pläne:' Willensschwäche aus der Sicht der Stoiker." In *Wille und Handlung in der Philosophie der Spätantike*, edited by Jörn Müller and Roberto Hofmeister Pich, 45–68. Berlin; New York: De Gruyter.
Nussbaum, Martha C. 1993. "Poetry and the Passions: Two Stoic views." In *Passions & Perceptions: Studies in Hellenistic Philosophy of Mind*, edited by Jacques

Brunschwig and Martha Nussbaum, 97–149. Cambridge: Cambridge University Press.
Nussbaum, Martha C. 1994. *The Therapy of Desire: Therapy and Practice in Hellenistic Ethics*. Princeton: Princeton University Press.
Nussbaum, Martha C. 1997. "Serpents in the Soul: A Reading of Seneca's Medea." In *Medea: Essays on Medea in Myth, Literature, Philosophy, and Art*, edited by James Claus and Sarah Johnston, 219–249. Princeton: Princeton University Press.
Oldfather, William Abbot, ed. and trans. 1925–1928. *Epictetus, The Discourses as Reported by Arrian, the Manual and Fragments*. 2 vols. Cambridge; London: Harvard University Press.
Ovid. 1977. *Metamorphoses*. See Anderson 1977.
Plato. 1900–1907. *Opera*. See Burnet 1900–1907.
Plutarch. 1939. *De virtute morali*. See Helmbold 1939.
Price, Anthony. 1995. *Mental Conflict*. London: Routledge.
Regenbogen, Otto. 1930. "Schmerz und Tod in den Tragödien Senecas." In *Vorträge der Bibliothek Warburg* 7: 167–218.
Rist, John. 1969. *Stoic Philosophy*. Cambridge: Cambridge University Press.
Schiesaro, Alessandro. 2009. "Seneca and the Denial of the Self." In *Seneca and the Self*, edited by Shadi Bartsch and David Wray, 221–235. Cambridge: Cambridge University Press.
Seneca. 2002. *Tragedies*. Vol. 1. See Fitch 2002.
Seneca. 2007. *De ira – Über die Wut*. See Wildberger 2007.
Seneca. 2010. *Anger, Mercy, Revenge*. See Kaster and Nussbaum 2010.
Sorabji, Richard. 2000. *Emotion and Peace of Mind: From Stoic Agitation to Christian Temptation*. Oxford; New York: Oxford University Press.
Steidle, Wolf. 1972. "Medeas Racheplan." In *Senecas Tragödien*, edited by Eckard Lefèvre, 286–291. Darmstadt: Wissenschaftliche Buchgesellschaft.
Susemihl, Franz, ed. 1935. *Aristoteles, Magna Moralia*. Reprint, Cambridge; London: Harvard University Press, 1969.
Tieleman, Teun. 2003. *Chrysippus' On Affections: Reconstruction and Interpretation*. Leiden; Boston: Brill.
Whittaker, John, ed., and Pierre Louis, trans. 1990. *Alkinoos, Enseignement des doctrines de Platon [= Didaskalikos]*. Paris: Les Belles Lettres.
Wiener, Claudia. 2006. *Stoische Doktrin in römischer Belletristik: Das Problem von Entscheidungsfreiheit und Determinismus in Senecas Tragödien und Lucans Pharsalia*. München: Saur.
Wildberger, Jula, ed. and trans. 2007. *Seneca, De ira – Über die Wut: Lateinisch/Deutsch*. Stuttgart: Reclam.
Xenophon. 1923. *Memorabilia, Oeconomicus, Symposium, Apology*. See Marchant 1923.

Seneca on Acting against Conscience

Marcia L. Colish
Yale University

According to ancient eudaimonistic ethics, once we recognize the good, we naturally seek it. Bad ethical choices stem from incorrect intellectual judgments. This theory presents a conundrum which ancient philosophy finds hard to explain: How can our moral choices conflict with what we judge to be good? The Stoics accept the eudaimonistic premise and raise the stakes. Evaluating everything correctly, the Stoic sage always acts in conformity with reason and nature. His fixed intentionality toward the good makes him incapable of moral error or backsliding. The sage has a consistently good conscience, a theme developed especially by the Roman Stoics. And, since they intellectualize the will, they face with heightened difficulty the question of how we can act against conscience. One of them, Seneca, emerges with a solution, which he upholds as compatible with the claim that the Stoic sage makes the rational law of nature the law of his own being. This paper will examine Seneca on acting against conscience in his letters and moral essays. For Seneca, conscience is the set of values alerting us to what is morally right and wrong. We acknowledge its guidance in making moral decisions. For the sage, these moral decisions always follow the advice of conscience. But Seneca is also interested in describing and explaining the condition of moral agents who act in opposition to the norms of conscience. Seneca's location in the intellectual history of the Stoic tradition, especially that of the Roman Stoa, can also be clarified by a comparison of his treatment, on this issue, with those of Epictetus and Marcus Aurelius. While all three authors are known to have drawn on philosophical sources beyond the Stoa, it is their articulation of Stoic values that will be the focus of this paper.

To the extent that other philosophical schools treat the problem of acting against conscience, they invoke *akrasia* or weakness of will, a doctrine rejected by the Stoics.[1] Whether or not they subscribe to the monopsych-

---

1   Guckes 2004, refuting Joyce 1995, who argues that Chrysippus supports *akrasia*. Guckes is supported, with a detailed doxography documenting the rejection of *akrasia* across the history of the Stoic school, by Gourinat 2007 and Müller 2009, 155–193. Also in line with Guckes' conclusion is Gosling 1987, although he holds

ism of the early Stoa, later Stoics agree that when we make bad ethical choices, having misjudged evils or matters of indifference to be goods, our will acts at full strength. And this act of will is conscious, not absent-minded or compulsive. Seneca does elaborate on the idea of weak assent.[2] In adults, weak assent reflects a sick mind that wavers indecisively between judgments and courses of action. It lacks the certitude of the sage and needs constant reminders. Another source of weak assent is developmental. It occurs in a pre-adult mind in which *oikeiōsis* has not yet matured into rational judgment and choice.

This account raises the question of how we acquire the criteria informing rational ethics in the first place, on which both the Stoics and their modern commentators are inconclusive. It is agreed that Stoic epistemology is basically empirical. Our *hēgemonikon* or ruling principle directs sensation as well as intellection, enabling us to make correct and firmly held judgments that derive initially from sense impressions. This doctrine also applies to preconceptions and common notions.[3] In theory it obviates innate or *a priori* ideas or self-evident principles. Yet, Chrysippus presents moral norms as known innately. Commenting on him, Josiah B. Gould observes, "Any assertions concerning the origins of moral goodness – or genuine knowledge about good things and bad things – can be but conjecture,"[4] a warning rarely heeded. Some scholars see Chrysippus' position as a momentary lapse in an epistemology that rules out innatism of any kind.[5] Others see moral innatism as a standard and not an aberrant Stoic view.[6] Still others accent the idea that *oikeiōsis*, with or without seminal reasons, matures into morally normative rational choice, assisted by education, observation, examples, and analogous reasoning; what is innate, in this view,

---

  that the akratic state involves the overwhelming of reason by passion, not weakness of will. Cf. Bartsch 2006, *passim* and especially 242 n. 16, who equates *akrasia* with choosing the lesser of two goods or the worse of two evils in Seneca. For the influence of *akrasia* as found in Aristotle's *Nicomachean Ethics*, see the contributions to Hoffman, Müller, and Perkams 2006; Bobonich and Destrée 2007; Hoffmann 2008; Müller 2009, 109–155, 193–208.
2 E.g. Sen. *Ep.* 95.37–41, 95.57–64, 102.28–29; *Tranq. an.* 1.4–17, 2.1–15. On weak assent, see most recently Wildberger 2006, 89–94, 98.
3 For a recent standard summary, see Frede 1999; on the epistemology of Chrysippus, see Gould 1970, 62–64.
4 Gould 1970, 170.
5 On the momentary lapse, see, for example, Sandbach 1971, 28–30; on the rejection of all innatism, see, for example, Voelke 1973, 43.
6 See, for example, Jackson-McCabe 2004; Sellars 2006, 76–78. See also Ilsetraut Hadot and Antonello Orlando in the present volume.

is a moral potential, not fully-developed moral norms.⁷ Yet another approach accents the idea that the human mind is a fragment of the divine *logos*; our inner *daimōn*, understood as a tutelary deity or simply as natural human reason or as our own best self, provides our rational moral norms, making ethical development a non-event, in the most pointed statement of this thesis.⁸

The Roman Stoics do nothing to clarify this debate, since they support all the above-mentioned theories. They certainly fly their colors as eudaimonists. As Seneca puts it, "It is impossible for anything to be good without being desirable. Thus, if virtue is desirable, and nothing is good without virtue, then every good is desirable."⁹ And, while the Stoics agree that self-knowledge is good, they elaborate in detail the daily examination of conscience. As Brad Inwood puts it, "Between Zeno and Marcus Aurelius there was no philosophy with a greater capacity to act as a guide to the conscience than Stoicism."¹⁰ This topic has drawn much comment, reflecting the fact that the Roman Stoics depict, and exemplify, self-examination in diverse ways.¹¹ Whether they commune with themselves or write to

---

7   See, for example, Voelke 1973, 61–65; Jackson-McCabe 2004; Cambiano 2001, 51–52; Inwood 2005, 207–301; Gill 2006, 157–162, 164–165, 181; Sellars 2006, 107–109; Forschner 2008.
8   For the most extended defense of this position, see Long 2002, 81–82, 101–102, 113–116, 142–172, 180, 186–188, 219–221, 225–227. Less extreme versions of this "god within" position, which accommodate it to seminal reasons or education or the force of moral example, include Edelstein 1966, 85; Rutherford 1989, 234, 237–239, 244; Kamtekar 1998; Dobbin 1998, 117–118, 188–192, 206; Algra 2007; Stephens 2007, 38–40.
9   Sen. *Ep.* 67.5: "[…] fieri non potest ut aliqua res bona quidem sit sed optabilis non sit; deinde si virtus optabilis est, nullum autem sine virtute bonum, et omne bonum optabile est." My own translation here and elsewhere in this paper unless otherwise indicated. For the scholarly consensus on Stoic eudaimonism, see Edelstein 1966, 1; Cooper 2004, 228.
10 Inwood 1999, 727.
11 Scholars have sometimes focused on the compatibility of the Stoic practice with post-classical approaches. Rabbow 1954, 132–140, 160–179, 180–189 focuses on Epictetus as the primary source for, and *comparandum* with, Christianity as exemplified in the *Spiritual Exercises* of Ignatius of Loyola. While simultaneously capitalizing on the cachet of Michel Foucault as a public intellectual and flagging his limits as an interpreter of ancient thought, P. Hadot 1995, 81–144, 179–205 also cites the influence of Stoicism on medieval monastic authors. For more recent, and largely critical, estimates of Foucault's "care of the self" as an adequate reading of Stoic practice, see, for example, Davidson 2005, 123–148; Detel 2005. On the other side of that debate, a critique of scholars who seek to apply ancient thought to Foucault is provided by Kolbet 2006, 87–88. Other scholars, avoiding such applications, who place the Stoic practice in a wider ancient context include I. Hadot 1969; I. Hadot 1986; Newman 1989; and, expanding on the theme of ethics as "lived physics" in Epictetus and Marcus Aurelius, P. Hadot 1998, *passim* and

edify others, their individual style, genre, and *Sitz im Leben* condition their approaches. Sometimes they see examination of conscience as castigating our moral failure, sometimes as approving our moral success. If the latter, they sometimes present self-esteem as its outcome, or as one of its welcome if non-essential side-effects. The Roman Stoics also propose the "premeditation of future evils" (*praemeditatio futurorum malorum*), alerting us to the problems we daily face and the principles with which to address them.[12] They invoke a range of metaphors in describing these activities. Conscience is sometimes our judge, censor, or interrogator. Sometimes it is the helmsman piloting the soul through stormy seas. Sometimes our authors use therapeutic imagery, with self-examination as an analgesic, an antibiotic, a palliative, a prophylactic, an upper, a downer, or a performance-enhancing drug.

These alternatives are rarely preclusive, even in the same text. As a Roman emperor, Marcus Aurelius gives a political gloss to the standard themes. While philosophy as a remedy against the inevitability of change and the fear of death is a commonplace, his preoccupation with these issues reflects the view from the top. Death by assassination was an occupational hazard of imperial office. And, Marcus spent half his reign defending the Danube frontier against invaders, witness to the fall of warriors in their prime. It is pointless, he says, to revel in worldly power or to seek fame, reputation, or the esteem of posterity. Citing a host of rulers, good and bad, he observes that the main condition they share is that they are all dead and

---

especially 95–96, 181, 215, 266, 274, 307–309. Accenting Stoic self-examination as therapy are Rutherford 1989, 13–21; Voelke 1993, 73–106. Focusing, unusually, on a Middle Stoic, is Gill 1993; at 352 he sees in Panaetius an element of self-crafting with a "quasi-aesthetic" appreciation of the result. In Gill 1996, 175–239 and Gill 2006, 389–391, he stresses self-examination as a means of internalizing objective, and community, values. While seconding Grimal 1978, 343–410 on the point that Seneca had a thorough grasp of Stoic physics, Cooper 2006, 43–55 argues that Seneca failed to apply it coherently to his ethics. In Cooper 2004, 346–368, he also criticizes Marcus Aurelius as presenting an incoherent "providence or atoms" physics, rendering his ethics incoherent as well. This view is challenged by Annas 2004. Perhaps the most idiosyncratic entry into recent discussions is Sorabji 2006, 178–179, 182, 191–195; while noting self-examination in the Roman Stoics, at 249, 260–261 he treats it as an intra-psychic process only in Proclus. Here, and in Sorabji 2007, 94–96, he tends to treat conscience in the Roman Stoics as self-awareness only.

12 We disagree with Wildberger 2006, 92–94, who argues that the *praemeditatio* is a prescription essentially for the sick minds subject to weak assent, not a strategy by which the sage alone confirms values he already holds firmly.

gone.[13] The absolute power the emperor wields should not tempt him: "Take care that you are not turned into a Caesar" (*mē apokaisarōthēs*); do not act the tyrant, he adjures himself.[14] Rather, recognize that your authority inspires envy, ambition, sycophancy, ingratitude, and disloyalty in the men around you. Do not display disappointment, caprice, or anger toward them, or lament the onerous nature of court intrigue and ceremonial.[15] In citing examples of virtue, Marcus bypasses standard figures in preference for his own ancestors, who shouldered these burdens and withstood these temptations.[16] Like them, he says, he must bear and forbear, not seeking sympathy or appreciation.[17] While the closest Marcus comes to a term for conscience is "right reason" (*orthos logos*), and while his entire *Meditations* can be read as an extended example of the premeditation of future evils and the examination of conscience, he specifically describes and prescribes both practices. The verb he uses in discussing daily self-examination, *exetazein*,[18] has a semantic range that includes both a commander's review of his troops, with the understanding that retribution for disciplinary infractions will be as harsh and relentless as it is summary, and a magistrate's interrogation of a suspect, with the understanding that it may entail judicial torture. Marcus reminds himself that he has the duty, and the internal capacity, to act uprightly, not just as a man but as "manly and mature, a statesman, a Roman, and a ruler."[19]

As a former slave, one of the anvils not the hammers of ancient society, Epictetus speaks as a teacher showing his students how to fortify themselves. He focuses on the temptations he thinks they will encounter, and how to judge and master them by lowering their expectations and adjusting their attitudes. He rarely alludes to his own temptations. In the morning exercise envisioning the day's problems, he includes the assessment of immediate past actions, considering how we fell short, so as to rectify or avoid our failings, an element more typical of the Stoics' nightly

---

13 Marcus Aurelius, *Ad se ipsum libri XII* 2.3, 3.2, 3.10, 4.3, 4.6, 4.19, 4.32–33, 4.48, 4.50, 5.23, 6.4, 6.15, 6.24, 6.36, 6.47, 7.6, 7.19, 7.21, 7.34, 8.3, 8.25, 8.31, 8.37, 8.44, 8.45, 9.29, 10.8, 10.27, 10.31, 11.19, 11.28, 12.27.
14 Marcus Aurelius, *Ad se ipsum* 6.30, trans. Hard 2011, 51.
15 Marcus Aurelius, *Ad se ipsum* 1.7, 1.8, 1.11, 1.16, 1.17, 2.1, 2.16, 5.1, 6.30, 7.26, 8.8, 8.9, 8.15, 9.27, 9.42, 10.9, 10.13, 11.18.
16 Marcus Aurelius, *Ad se ipsum* 1.1–4, 1.14, 1.16–17, 4.32, 6.30.
17 Marcus Aurelius, *Ad se ipsum* 1.16–17, 3.6, 6.13, 6.16, 8.8–9, 9.12, 9.30. On bear and forbear: *Ad se ipsum* 5.33.
18 Marcus Aurelius, *Ad se ipsum* 4.3, 4.25, 5.11, 5.31, 10.37, 11.1, 11.19; on right reason: *Ad se ipsum* 12.35. On self-examination, cf. van Ackeren 2011, vol. 1, pp. 212–287 and 345–347, who prefers to frame this notion as *Selbstdialog*, dialogue with oneself.
19 Marcus Aurelius, *Ad se ipsum* 3.5, trans. Hard 2011, 18.

self-examination.[20] Epictetus envisions those engaged in examination of conscience as thoroughly well-instructed; we thus use this practice to congratulate ourselves on a job well done, on dismissing matters not under our own control, on resisting obstacles to our inner freedom.[21] The virtues Epictetus accents are patience, abstinence, equanimity, and cooperation with others, virtues of private citizens, not of rulers or politicians.

While at one point he uses *conscientia* to mean simple self-awareness,[22] Seneca's handling of *praemeditatio futurorum malorum* and examination of conscience notably enriches the Roman Stoic understanding of them. He adds a major distinction to the daily forecast of problems. This exercise, he says, helps only the wise. Fools use it to excite the irrational vice of fear, to plan ahead on the fatuous assumption that present good fortune will continue, or to procrastinate, postponing what they should do today. Maxims such as "He robs present ills of their power who has envisioned their coming"[23] and "Blows foreseen strike us the more feebly"[24] sustain not fools but sages.

Seneca's earliest and fullest description of the nightly examination of conscience occurs in his *De ira*. This passage enjoys a consensus reading.[25] But there is more to be said about Seneca's treatment of examination of conscience here and elsewhere. Having dismissed the notion that anger is ever useful, he devotes most of *De ira* to advice on uprooting it. Well aware of the damage wreaked by the wrath of tyrants, his focus is not on assuaging its victims but on the negative effect of anger on those with the power to express it. After presenting both avoidance and cognitive therapies, he offers as a test of their efficacy the model of his own self-examination. He cites as his guide Sextius the Pythagorean, although elsewhere he calls Sextius a true Stoic.[26] Here is the oft-cited passage:

---

20 Epictetus, *Discourses* 4.6.34–35. On the use of *exetazein* and its cognates in the context of self-examination: Epictetus, *Enchiridion* 1.5.
21 Epictetus, *Discourses* 4.4.18. There is a strong scholarly consensus, which we share, on the importance of the theme of moral freedom in Epictetus. For a recent overview, see Dragona-Monachou 2007.
22 Sen. *Ep.* 81.21. On the use of the term *conscientia* in Seneca and previous Latin writers see Grimal 1992, 144, 158–159. This term is not included in her study of Seneca's vocabulary by Borgo 1998.
23 Sen. *Marc.* 9.5: "Aufert vim praesentibus malis qui futura prospexit."
24 Sen. *Marc.* 9.2: "quae multo ante provisa sunt languidius incurrunt."
25 See, for example, P. Hadot 1995, 81–125; on this practice in Epictetus and Marcus Aurelius, P. Hadot 1998, 95–96, 181, 266, 274, 308–309; more recently, see Reydams-Schils 2005, 10, 18–20, 98. Looking at this practice only as a form of positive self-assessment in *loci* such as *Ep.* 28.10 and *Ep.* 83.2 is Edwards 1997, 29–30. Cf. the would-be revisionism on *De ira* of Ker 2009. More dismissive of Seneca's contribution to this practice is Veyne 2003, 75–76.
26 Sen. *Ep.* 64.2.

Omnes sensus perducendi sunt ad firmitatem; natura patientes sunt, si animus illos desît corrumpere, quo cotidie ad rationem reddendam vocandus est. Faciebat hoc Sextius, ut consummato die, cum se ad nocturnam quietem recepisset, interrogaret animum suum: "Quod hodie malum tuum sanasti? Cui vitio obstitisti? Qua parte melior es?" Desinet ira et moderatior erit quae sciet sibi cotidie ad iudicem esse veniendum. Quicquam ergo pulchrius hac consuetudine excutiendi totum diem? Qualis ille somnus post recognitionem sui sequitur, quam tranquillus, quam altus ac liber, cum aut laudatus est animus aut admonitus et speculator sui censorque secretus cognovit de moribus suis! Utor hac potestate et cotidie apud me causam dico. Cum sublatum e conspectu lumen est et conticuit uxor moris iam mei conscia, totum diem meum scrutor factaque ac dicta mea remetior; nihil mihi ipse abscondo, nihil transeo. Quare enim quicquam ex erroribus meis timeam cum possim dicere [...]

All our senses should be trained to endurance. They are naturally receptive to it if the mind stops corrupting them. The mind should be summoned every day to render an account of itself. That is what Sextius used to do. At the close of each day, when he had retired to rest at night, he would ask his mind these questions: "What evil have you remedied today? What vice have you resisted? In what respect have you improved?" Your anger will abate or be reduced if the mind knows that it will have to answer each day to a judge. Can anything be finer than this practice of examining one's entire day? And, think of the sleep that follows this self-inspection, how peaceful, deep, and untroubled it is, when the mind, its own observer and internal censor, has taken stock of its behavior, whether to praise or blame. I make use of this opportunity and daily argue my own case. When the lamp has been put out and my wife, aware of my custom, falls silent, I scrutinize my whole day, recalling all my words and deeds, skimming over and hiding nothing from myself. Why should I fear any of my failings when I can say to myself [...] (Sen. *De ira* 3.36.1–3)[27]

The passage then continues. In a fictive dialogue, Seneca observes that, while he forgives himself this time, he also enjoins himself to avoid the lapses brought to light by his self-examination. These are the failings of a politician who expects to be taken seriously by other men in public life, but who is aggravated by their opposition, incivility, and failure to give him and his friends due honor.[28] In a word, this fictive self, unlike Marcus Aurelius, has not come to grips with the clash of egos, if not of policies and principles, indigenous to this habitat.

Another feature of the *De ira* passage, not often noted, is that Seneca conducts his examination of conscience in the supportive presence of his wife, not in solitude. Elsewhere he portrays himself as consulting himself by himself,[29] and advises his addressees to do likewise.[30] But he also thinks

---

27 On the background to this passage, see Fillion-Lahille 1984, *passim* and especially 2, 242, 263, 271; Harris 2001, 220–223, 229–263.
28 Sen. *De ira* 3.36.4–3.38.1.
29 Sen. *Vit. beat.* 17.3–4; *Ep.* 83.2.
30 Sen. *Brev. vit.* 10.2; *Tranq. an.* 6.1; *Ep.* 16.2; 28.10; 118.2–3.

it appropriate for friends – and friends alone – to entrust matters of conscience to each other. "There are those," he says, "who disclose whatever distresses them, which should be confided only to friends, in the hearing of just anyone. Others fear to confide matters of conscience even to their dearest friends. If they could, they would not even trust themselves, burying their secrets within."[31] Seneca certainly exchanges moral confidences with his correspondent Lucilius. Where Epictetus guides others and does not report his own self-scrutiny, and where Marcus advises himself alone, Seneca offers a range of personal and interpersonal settings for the examination of conscience. And, while *De ira* presents him confronting temptations specific to the politician's calling, his later works propose the abandonment of the forum and withdrawal into our conscience in order to meditate and to write, as a preferable form of public service.[32] Unlike Marcus, Seneca presents the contemplative life as a viable alternative to arms and the toga alike.

Whether in the active or contemplative life, the goal is to possess a good conscience. At the same time, good conscience is a means to that end. Seneca often describes and advocates this happy state. In response to the question – rhetorical or actually posed by Lucilius – whence we derive the true good, he responds: "I will tell you: from a good conscience, honorable counsels, and upright deeds, from contempt for Fortune, from a tranquil and consistent life treading a single path."[33] The Senecan sage avers, "I will do nothing on the basis of opinion, but all things for the sake of conscience;" facing death calmly, he says to himself, "I bear witness that I leave having loved a good conscience."[34] Good conscience remains our internal possession even in situations preventing its outward expression; inner intention is what counts. As with benefits extended and received with apparent invisibility, Seneca observes: "If you ask what the point of a benefit is, what it renders back, I will answer: a good conscience."[35] To be

---

31 Sen. *Ep.* 3.4: "Quidam quae tantum amicis committenda sunt obviis narrant, et in quaslibet aures quidquid illos urit exonerant; quidam rursus etiam carissimorum conscientiam reformidant et, si possent, ne sibi quidem credituri interius premunt omne secretum."
32 At greatest length in Sen. *De otio*; see also *Ep.* 8.1.
33 Sen. *Ep.* 23.7: "Dicam: ex bona conscientia, ex honestis consiliis, ex rectis actionibus, ex contemptu fortuitorum, ex placido vitae et continuo tenore unam prementis viam."
34 Sen. *Vit. beat.* 20.4: "Nihil opinionis causa, omnia conscientiae faciam;" 20.5: "testatus exibo bonam me conscientiam amasse." See also *Vit. beat.* 19.1; *Ep.* 24.12.
35 Sen. *Ben.* 4.12.4: "Eadem in beneficio ratio est: nam cum interrogaveris, respondebo: bonam conscientiam." See also *Ben.* 4.21.5. Cf. Sherman 2005, 61–63, 67–78,

sure, like virtue itself, good conscience is self-sufficient. But in addressing Nero, Seneca thinks it prudent to offer an added inducement:

> Quamuis enim recte factorum verus fructus sit fecisse nec ullum virtutum pretium dignum illis extra ipsas sit, iuvat inspicere et circumire bonam conscientiam [...], ita loqui secum: "Egone ex omnibus mortalibus placui electusque sum, qui in terris deorum vice fungerer? [...] Hodie diis inmortalibus, si a me rationem repetant, adnumerare genus humanum paratus sum."
>
> While the true fruit of good deeds is the fact of having done them and there is no reward of virtues outside of virtues themselves, it is pleasant to examine and compass a good conscience [...] and to be able to say to oneself: "Have I not, of all mortals, been favored and chosen to act on earth in place of the gods? [...] This very day, should the immortal gods require it, I stand ready to render an account for the whole human race." (Sen. *Cl.* 1.1.1–2, 4)

The other addressees in Seneca's world had neither the global moral responsibilities he assigns to Nero nor the high-profile imperial vices he tried, so thanklessly, to curb. But he is well aware that few possess a good conscience. He speaks tellingly of those who know the difference between good and evil but who balk at applying this norm to their own behavior. The fool refuses to reflect on his past failings and to castigate himself for his false values and misspent energies precisely because he knows that "all his deeds are under his own censorship."[36] In an extended comparison between ethics as the art of living and other *artes*, Seneca asserts that, while we can sin involuntarily against the liberal or mechanical arts, our moral failings are voluntary. We sin in full awareness of right and wrong. We do not misjudge or disavow these criteria but deliberately choose to exempt ourselves from them. Seneca gives a long list of examples involving the hypocritical rejection of filial, marital, personal, professional, and civic duties. Even when we behave in external conformity with these duties, we may be guilty of acting against conscience if we do so with the wrong intention and in the wrong way.[37]

---

who argues that external expression of gratitude always remains important in Seneca's analysis

36 Sen. *Vit. beat.* 10.3: "omnia acta sunt sub censura sua;" see also *Vit. beat.* 10.5.
37 Sen. *Ep.* 95.8–9, 95.37–41, 95.43–45, 95.57–64; see also *Ep.* 94.25–26. A considerable scholarly literature seeks to weigh the relative importance of will and intellect in Seneca's ethics. Zöller 2003 looks ahead to later formulations of voluntarism and intellectualism, and also tends to systematize Seneca. Conversely, Inwood 2005, 102–156 accents the multivalence of *voluntas* in Seneca and warns against anachronistic readings. Voelke 1973, 17–18, 30–49, 90–95, 131–139, 161–170, 174–179, 189–199; Dobbin 1998, 220; Bobzien 1998, 250–313; P. Hadot 1995, 84; and Veyne 2003, 64–65 argue for the primacy of the intellect over the will in Seneca. Accenting the primacy of the will over the intellect are Zöller 2003, 90–93, 130–153, 179–189, 232–254 and, reducing the self to the will, Sorabji

Seneca goes on to anatomize the earmarks and psychic consequences of bad conscience. Those who act against conscience shun the light of day.[38] They shut out others in the attempt to hide their vices:

> Rem dicam ex qua mores aestimes nostros: vix quemquam invenies qui possit aperto ostio vivere. Ianitores conscientia nostra, non superbia opposuit; sic vivimus, ut deprendi sit subito adspici. Quid autem prodest recondere se et oculos hominum auresque vitare? Bona conscientia turbam advocat, mala etiam in solitudine anxia atque sollicita est. Si honesta sunt quae facis, omnes sciant; si turpia, quid refert neminem scire cum tu scias? O te miserum si contemnis hunc testem!

> I will tell you how we can judge our morals. You will find hardly anyone who can live with his gates open. Our conscience, not our pride, has installed gatekeepers. We live in such a way that to be observed is the same as to be found out. What do we gain if we avoid the eyes and ears of others? A good conscience calls in the crowd; a bad conscience, even in solitude, is anxious and disturbed. If what you do is right, let everyone know it. If it is wrong, does it matter if no one knows it, so long as you do? How miserable you are if you disdain such a witness! (Sen. *Ep.* 43.4–5)

The jeopardy in which such people place themselves is aggravated by the knowledge that their self-delusion, shame, fear, worry, and insecurity are self-inflicted:

> Alioquin, ut scias subesse animis etiam in pessima abductis boni sensum nec ignorari turpe sed negligi: omnes peccata dissimulant et, quamvis feliciter cesserint, fructu [...] illorum utuntur, ipsa subducunt. At bona conscientia prodire vult et conspici: ipsas nequitia tenebras timet. [...] Quare? quia prima illa et maxima peccantium est poena peccasse [...] Sed nihilominus et hae illam secundae poenae premunt ac sequuntur, timere semper et expavescere et securitati diffidere; [...] hic consentiamus, mala facinora conscientia flagellari et plurimum illi tormentorum esse eo quod perpetua illam sollicitudo urget ac verberat, quod sponsoribus securitatis suae non potest credere.

> Yet, so that you may know: an awareness of the good remains in the minds even of those drawn to the worst villainy. They are not ignorant of what is wrong but neglect it. They all lie about their sins, and, if the outcome is favorable, they profit from it while hiding their sins from themselves. A good conscience wants to come forward and be seen, but wicked deeds fear even the shadows [...] Why is this the case? Because the primary and greatest punishment for wrongdoing is wrongdoing itself [...] Nonetheless, these secondary punishments follow close on the primary ones: constant fear, terror, and distrust of one's own security [...] Let us agree: evil deeds are flagellated by conscience, and their conscience suffers the greatest tor-

---

2006, 44–45, 178, 181–185. A more balanced approach characterizes Impara 1986 and Cancik 1998, 343–344.

38 Sen. *Ep.* 122.14.

ment because perpetual anxiety whips and drives them on, so that they cannot trust in any guarantees of their own safety. (Sen. *Ep.* 97.12, 14, 15)[39]

These malefactors operate in a state of conscious bad faith, acting against their own best selves and against the norms of conscience that remain embedded in their minds. They cannot escape knowledge of the truth of their situation and the fact that they have brought their own punishment upon themselves.[40]

This picture of moral agents who act against conscience still leaves open the question of how such behavior actually occurs, absent *akrasia* or weak assent. How can acting against conscience be squared with the Stoics' reigning assumptions? Seneca acknowledges that the will can be divided against itself: "Men both love and hate their vices at the same time."[41] In explaining how a good will can occupy the same psychic space as a bad will, he reframes Chrysippus' classic image of the rolling cylinder. For Chrysippus, a cylinder necessarily describes a circular motion going downhill when it is pushed. But whether or not it is pushed is a matter of contingency.[42] Seneca shift this image from physics to ethics. And, unlike Marcus Aurelius, who contrasts the cylinder's incapacity to set itself in motion with our own ability to will moral choices, Seneca yokes this metaphor to another Chrysippean example which he also changes, that of a runner who cannot come to an abrupt stop at the end of his course. Seneca also recasts this metaphor in terms of the agent's will. For Seneca, the runner cannot stop when he wants to stop not as the result of passions that overcome rational choice but as a function of his will. For, "just as one who, running downhill, cannot stop when he wills to stop, but whose body impels him onward, its momentum carrying him farther than he wills,"[43] so ingrained bad will continues to motivate, overlap with, and override both reason and good will.

In conclusion, we can gain a clear sense of the coloration Seneca brings to the topic of conscience, and acting against it, by considering his

---

39 See also *Ep.* 105.7–8.
40 Sen. *Ep.* 97.15–16.
41 Sen. *Ep.* 112.4: "Homines vitia sua et amant simul et oderunt." Noted by Voelke 1973, 172–175; Zöller 2003, 44–45; Bénatouïl 2006, 100–105, 109–112.
42 The standard classical *testimonia* are Cicero, *De fato* 42–43 and Aulus Gellius, *Noctes atticae* 7.2.11–12. An outstanding treatment of this topic is provided by Bobzien 1998. See also Graver 2007, 63–64.
43 Sen. *Ep.* 40.7: "Quemadmodum per proclive currentium non ubi visum est gradus sistitur, sed incitato corporis ponderi servit ac longius quam voluit effertur [...]" Cf. Marcus Aurelius, *Ad se ipsum* 10.33. Graver 2007, 68–70 discusses the ancient report of Chrysippus on the runner given by Galen but does not flag the difference in Seneca's handling of this theme. On this point Bénatouïl 2006, 100–105, 109–112 presents Seneca's position accurately.

treatment of a theme he shares with Epictetus and Marcus Aurelius, the idea that the world is a stage. Epictetus offers this insight in the *Enchiridion*, as related by his pupil Arrian, in a thought detached from a surrounding argument. Remember, he says, that we are actors in a play. The script and the parts assigned are the preserve of the playwright. The play may be long or short; we may be hired to play the role of a beggar, a cripple, a ruler, or a private citizen. Whatever our part and however long the play, our job is simply to perform with probity our assigned role.[44]

In his handling of this topic, Marcus Aurelius does not suppose that he might be called on to portray any character except the hero, with top billing. His performance is controlled not by the playwright but by the political official (*stratēgos*) who commissions and oversees the production. The play, and the hero's part, may have been written with five acts. But, he says, he should not complain if the magistrate rings down the curtain after three acts. Rather, as with death, whenever it comes, he should accept the play's abbreviation as a welcome reprieve from his duties.[45]

Seneca also invites us to consider this theme at the point of death. Unlike Epictetus and Marcus, his concern is not with who controls the production, the length of the play, or the possibility that we may be assigned a range of different roles. The only character we portray is ourselves, and we are also our own drama critics. Whatever the audience reception, our self-examination will judge whether we have merely attitudinized, or lied to ourselves, or portrayed ourselves authentically, truly manifesting our inner convictions.[46] For Seneca, being true to our own conscience is the ultimate test of our moral character, a test which we are fully capable of choosing to fail. His analysis of how we can act against conscience is indeed his own and stands as a perceptive contribution to the legacy of Roman Stoicism, and of ancient philosophy as such.

Bibliography

Ackeren, Marcel van. 2011. *Die Philosophie Marc Aurels*. 2 vols. Berlin; New York: De Gruyter.
Algra, Keimpe. 2007. "Epictetus and Stoic Theology." In *The Philosophy of Epictetus*, edited by Theodore Scaltsas and Andrew S. Mason, 32–55. Oxford: Oxford University Press.
Annas, Julia. 2004. "Marcus Aurelius: Ethics and Its Background." *Rhizai* 2: 103–117.

---

44 Epictetus, *Enchiridion* 17.
45 Marcus Aurelius, *Ad se ipsum* 12.36. This theme in Marcus is also noted by Giavatto 2008, 229; van Ackeren vol. 2, p. 697.
46 Sen. *Ep.* 26.5–6; see also *Ep.* 29.12.

Bartsch, Shadi. 2006. *The Mirror of the Self: Sexuality, Self-Knowledge, and the Gaze in the Early Roman Empire*. Chicago: University of Chicago Press.
Bénatouïl, Thomas. 2006. *Faire usage: La pratique du Stoïcisme*. Paris: Vrin.
Bobonich, Christopher, and Pierre Destrée, eds. 2007. *Akrasia in Greek Philosophy: From Socrates to Plotinus*. Leiden: Brill.
Bobzien, Susanne. 1998. *Determinism and Freedom in Stoic Philosophy*. Oxford: Clarendon Press.
Borgo, Antonella. 1998. *Lessico morale di Seneca*. Napoli: Loffredo.
Cambiano, Giuseppe. 2001. "Seneca e le contradizzioni del sapiens." In *Incontri con Seneca: Atti della giornata di studio, Torino, 26 ottobre 1999*, edited by Giovanna Garbarino and Italo Lana, 49–60. Bologna: Pàtron.
Cancik, Hubert. 1998. "Person and Self in Stoic Philosophy." In *Self, Soul, and Body in Religious Experience*, edited by Albert I. Baumgarten, Jan Assmann, and Gedaliahu G. Strousma, 335–346. Leiden: Brill.
Chaumartin, François-Régis, ed and trans. 2005. *Sénèque, De la clémence: Texte établi et traduit*. Paris: Les Belles Lettres.
Cooper, John M. 2004. "Stoic Autonomy." In *Knowledge, Nature, and the Good: Essays in Ancient Philosophy*, 204–246. Princeton: Princeton University Press.
Cooper, John M. 2006. "Seneca on Moral Theory and Moral Development." In *Seeing Seneca Whole: Perspectives on Philosophy, Poetry, and Politics*, edited by Katharina Volk and Gareth D. Williams, 43–55. Boston; Leiden: Brill.
Dalfen, Joachim, ed. 1979. *Marci Aurelii Antonini Ad se ipsum*. Leipzig: Teubner.
Davidson, Arnold I. 2005. "Ethics as Ascetics: Foucault, the History of Ethics, and Ancient Thought." In *The Cambridge Companion to Foucault*, edited by Gary Gutting, 123–148. 2nd ed. Cambridge: Cambridge University Press.
Detel, Wolfgang. 2005. *Foucault and Classical Antiquity: Power, Ethics, and Knowledge*, translated by David Wigg-Wolf. Cambridge: Cambridge University Press.
Dobbin, Robert F., trans. 1998. *Epictetus, Discourses Book I*. Oxford: Clarendon Press.
Dragona-Monachou, Myrto. 2007. "Epictetus on Freedom: Parallels between Epictetus and Wittgenstein." In *The Philosophy of Epictetus*, edited by Theodore Scaltsas and Andrew S. Mason, 112–135. Oxford: Oxford University Press.
Edelstein, Ludwig. 1966. *The Meaning of Stoicism*. Cambridge: Harvard University Press.
Edwards, Catharine. 1997. "Self-Scrutiny and Self-Transformation in Seneca's Letters." *G&R* 44: 23–38.
Epictetus. 1925–1928. *The Discourses as Reported by Arrian, the Manual, and Fragments*. See Oldfather 1925–1928.
Epictetus. 1998. *Discourses Book I*. See Dobbin 1998.
Fillion-Lahille, Janine. 1984. *Le De ira de Sénèque et la philosophie stoïcienne des passions*. Paris: Klincksieck.
Forschner, Maximilian. 2008. "Oikeiosis: Die stoische Theorie der Selbstaneignung." In *Stoizismus in der europäischen Philosophie, Literatur, Kunst, und Politik*, edited by Barbara Neymayr, Jochen Schmidt, and Bernhard Zimmerman. 2 vols. 1: 169–191. Berlin: De Gruyter.
Frede, Michael. 1999. "Stoic Epistemology." In *The Cambridge History of Hellenistic Philosophy*, edited by Keimpe Algra, Jonathan Barnes, Jaap Mansfeld, and Malcolm Schofield, 295–322. Cambridge: Cambridge University Press.
Giavatto, Angelo. 2008. *Interlocutore de se stesso: La dialettica di Marco Aurelio*. Hildesheim: Olms.
Gill, Christopher. 1993. "Panaetius on the Virtue of Being Yourself." In *Images and Ideologies: Self-Definition in the Hellenistic World*, edited by Anthony W. Bulloch, Erich S. Gruen, Anthony A. Long, and Andrew Stewart, 344–352. Berkeley: University of California Press.

Gill, Christopher. 1996. *Personality in Greek Epic, Tragedy, and Philosophy: The Self in Dialogue*. Oxford: Clarendon Press.
Gill, Christopher. 2006. *The Structured Self in Hellenistic and Roman Thought*. Oxford; New York: Oxford University Press.
Gosling, Justin. 1987. "The Stoics and ἀκρασία." *Apeiron* 20: 179–202.
Gould, Josiah B. 1970. *The Philosophy of Chrysippus*. Albany: SUNY Press.
Gourinat, Jean-Baptiste. 2007. "Akrasia and Enkrateia in Ancient Stoicism: Minor Vice and Minor Virtue." In *Akrasia in Greek Philosophy from Socrates to Plotinus*, edited by Christopher Bobonich and Pierre Destrée, 215–247. Boston; Leiden: Brill.
Graver, Margaret R. 2007. *Stoicism and Emotion*. Chicago: University of Chicago Press.
Grimal, Pierre. 1978. *Sénèque ou la conscience de l'Empire*, Paris: Les Belles Lettres. Rpt. 1979
Grimal. Pierre. 1992. "Le vocabulaire de l'intériorité dans l'oeuvre philosophique de Sénèque." In *Langue latine, langue de philosophie: Actes du colloque organisé par l'École française de Rome avec le concours de l'Université de Rome "La Sapienza," Rome, 17–19 mai 1990*, 141–159. Roma: École française de Rome.
Guckes, Barbara. 2004. "Akrasia in der älteren Stoa." In *Zur Ethik der älteren Stoa*, edited by Barbara Guckes, 94–122. Göttingen: Vandenhoeck & Ruprecht.
Hadot, Ilsetraut. 1969. *Seneca und die griechisch-römische Tradition der Seelenleitung*. Berlin: De Gruyter.
Hadot, Ilsetraut. 1986. "The Spiritual Guide." In *Classical and Mediterranean Spirituality: Egyptian, Greek, Roman*, edited by Arthur H. Armstrong, 436–459. New York: Crossroads.
Hadot, Pierre. 1995. *Philosophy as a Way of Life: Spiritual Exercises from Socrates to Foucault*, edited by Arnold I. Davidson, translated by Michael Chase. Oxford: Blackwell.
Hadot, Pierre. 1998. *The Inner Citadel: The Meditations of Marcus Aurelius*, translated by Michael Chase. Cambridge: Harvard University Press.
Hard, Robin, trans. 2011. *Marcus Aurelius: Meditations and Selected Correspondence*, edited by Christopher Gill. Oxford: Oxford University Press.
Harris, William V. 2001. *Restraining Rage: The Ideology of Anger Control in Classical Antiquity*. Cambridge: Harvard University Press.
Hoffmann, Tobias, ed. 2008. *Weakness of the Will from Plato to the Present*. Washington: Catholic University of America Press.
Hoffmann, Tobias, Jörn Müller, and Matthias Perkams, eds. 2006. *Das Problem der Willensschwäche in der mittelalterlichen Philosophie*. Leuven: Peeters.
Impara, Paolo. 1986. *Seneca e il mondo di volere*. Roma: Edizioni Abete.
Inwood, Brad. 1999. "Stoic Ethics." In *The Cambridge History of Hellenistic Philosophy*, ed. Keimpe Algra, Jonathan Barnes, Jaap Mansfeld, and Malcolm Schofield, 635–738. Cambridge: Cambridge University Press.
Inwood, Brad. 2005. *Reading Seneca: Stoic Philosophy at Rome*. Oxford; New York: Oxford University Press.
Jackson-McCabe. Matt. 2004. "The Stoic Theory of Implanted Preconceptions." *Phronesis* 49: 323–347.
Joyce, Richard. 1995. "Early Stoicism and Akrasia." *Phronesis* 40: 315–335.
Kamtekar, Rachana. 1998. "ΑΙΔΩΣ in Epictetus." *CPh* 93: 136–160.
Ker, James. 2009. "Seneca on Self-Examination: Rereading 'On Anger'." In *Seneca and the Self*, edited by Shadi Bartsch and David Wray, 160–187. Cambridge: Cambridge University Press.
Kolbet, Paul R. 2006. "Athanasius, the Psalms, and the Reformation of the Self." *HThR* 99: 85–101.

Long, Anthony A. 2002. *Epictetus: A Stoic and Socratic Guide to Life.* Oxford: Clarendon Press.
Marcus Aurelius. 1964. *The Meditations of Marcus Aurelius.* See Stanisford 1964.
Marcus Aurelius. 1979. *Ad se ipsum.* See Dalfen 1979.
Marcus Aurelius. 2011. *Meditations and Selected Correspondence.* See Hard 2011.
Müller, Jörn. 2009. *Willensschwäche in Antike und Mittelalter: Eine Problemgeschichte von Sokrates bis Johannes Duns Scotus.* Leuven: Leuven University Press.
Newman, Robert J. 1989. " 'Cotidie Meditare:' Theory and Practice of the 'Meditatio' in Imperial Stoicism." *ANRW* II 36.3: 1473–1517.
Oldfather, William Abbott, ed. and trans. 1925–1928. *Epictetus, The Discourses as Reported by Arrian, the Manual, and Fragments.* 2 vols. Cambridge: Harvard University Press. Rpt. 1967.
Préchac, François, ed. and trans. 1926–1929. *Sénèque, Des bienfaits.* 2 vols. Paris: Les Belles Lettres.
Rabbow, Paul. 1954. *Seelenführung: Methodik in der Antike.* München: Kösel-Verlag.
Reydams-Schils, Gretchen. 2005. *The Roman Stoics: Self, Responsibility, and Affection.* Chicago: University of Chicago Press.
Reynolds, Leighton D., ed. 1965. *L. Annaei Senecae Ad Lucilium epistulae morales.* 2 vols. Oxford: Clarendon Press.
Reynolds, Leighton D., ed. 1977. *L. Annaei Senecae Dialogorum libri duodecim.* Oxford: Clarendon Press. Rpt. with corrections 1988.
Rutherford, Richard B. 1989. *The Meditations of Marcus Aurelius: A Study.* Oxford: Clarendon Press.
Sandbach, Francis H. 1971. " 'Ennoia' and 'Prolēpsis' in the Stoic Theory of Knowledge." In *Problems in Stoicism*, edited by Anthony A. Long, 22–37. London: Athlone Press.
Sellars, John. 2006. *Stoicism.* Chesham: Acumen.
Seneca. 1926–1929. *Des bienfaits.* See Préchac, François 1926–1929.
Seneca. 1965. *Ad Lucilium epistulae morales.* See Reynolds 1965.
Seneca. 1977. *Dialogorum libri duodecim.* See Reynolds 1977.
Seneca. 2005. *De la clémence.* See Chaumartin 2005.
Sherman, Nancy. 2005. "The Look and Feel of Virtue." In *Virtue, Norm, and Objectivity: Issues in Ancient and Modern Ethics*, edited by Christopher Gill, 59–82. Oxford: Clarendon Press.
Sorabji, Richard. 2006. "Epictetus on 'Proairesis' and the Self." In *The Philosophy of Epictetus*, edited by Theodore Scaltsas and Andrew S. Mason, 87–98. Oxford: Oxford University Press.
Sorabji, Richard. 2007. *Self: Ancient and Modern Insights about Individuation, Life, and Death.* Chicago: University of Chicago Press.
Stanisford, Maxwell, trans. 1964. *The Meditations of Marcus Aurelius.* Harmondsworth: Penguin.
Stephens, William O. 2007. *Stoic Ethics: Epictetus and Happiness as Freedom.* London: Continuum.
Veyne, Paul. 2003. *Seneca: The Life of a Stoic*, translated by David Sullivan. New York: Routledge.
Voelke, André-Jean. 1973. *L'Idée de la volonté dans le stoïcisme.* Paris: PUF.
Voelke, André-Jean. 1993. *La philosophie comme thérapie de l'âme: Études de philosophie héllenistique.* Fribourg: Éditions Universitaires.
Wildberger, Jula. 2006. "Seneca and the Stoic Theory of Cognition: Some Preliminary Remarks." In *Seeing Seneca Whole: Perspectives on Philosophy, Poetry, and Politics*, edited by Katharina Volk and Gareth D. Williams, 75–102. Boston; Leiden: Brill.

Zöller, Rainer. 2003. *Die Vorstellung vom Willen in der Morallehre Senecas.* München: Saur.

Seneca on the Analysis and Therapy of Occurrent Emotions

David H. Kaufman
Transylvania University

In the *Tusculan Disputations,* Cicero distinguishes two Stoic methods of consoling people experiencing the emotion of distress, one favored by Cleanthes and the other favored by Chrysippus, both of which treat occurrent distress by arguing against one of the false beliefs correlated with it (Cic. *Tusc.* 3.76–79).[1] While Cleanthes recommends arguing against the distressed person's belief that something bad has happened to him, Chrysippus favors focusing not on that belief but rather on the distressed person's further belief that he ought to be distressed. Although Cicero introduces these methods in his discussion of how best to treat people experiencing distress, they could be applied as easily to the treatment of any emotion (*pathos*) at all.[2] For, according to the Stoics, *all* emotions depend on the impassioned person's coming to form, and hold, both the belief that something good or bad for him is present or impending, and the belief that it is, consequently, appropriate for him to be emotionally affected.[3]

In this paper, I will focus on Seneca's quite different method of consoling people experiencing especially violent emotions.[4] In *On Anger,* as

---

1 For discussion, see Graver 2002, 121–123 and 2007, 196–206 and Sorabji 2000, 175–178. – I presented an earlier version of this essay at the conference "Seneca Philosophus," which took place in Paris in May 2011. I want to thank the organizers of the conference for their invitation, and the other conference participants for their comments and suggestions. I also want to thank John Cooper, Bob Kaster, Hendrik Lorenz, Mor Segev, Christian Wildberg, and Jula Wildberger for their very helpful written comments.
2 Chrysippus explicitly extends his method of therapy to any emotion in a passage from the fourth book of his *On the Emotions* (Περὶ Παθῶν) that is preserved by Origenes, *Cels.* 8.51 = *SVF* 3.474.
3 For ancient statements of this view, see, for example, [Andronic. Rhod.] 1 = *SVF* 3.391; Cic. *Tusc.* 4.14 = *SVF* 3.393; Stob. 2.7.10b, vol. 2, p. 90 Wachsmuth = *SVF* 3.394.
4 I want to be clear that Seneca does not recommend using this method of therapy for the treatment of any occurrent emotion at all, but restricts it to the treatment of more vehement occurrent emotions that are prone to be especially harmful to oneself or those around one. For a survey of the various strategies proposed in *On*

well as in other works, Seneca argues that the only effective remedy for treating people in the grip of such emotions is to stimulate a rival emotion in them. His method of consoling people experiencing violent emotions thus differs from the belief-based approaches of Cleanthes and Chrysippus. For rather than arguing against either of the beliefs correlated with an emotion, Seneca's method overrides violent emotions by other emotions. For example, he recommends treating someone in a fit of rage by frightening him.[5]

One advantage of this method of therapy over those attributed to Cleanthes and Chrysippus is that it addresses the propensity of impassioned people, according to Stoic theory, to be inadequately responsive should they become aware of considerations speaking against their emotions. To be sure, Seneca did not invent this method of therapy, which is well attested in earlier Greek and Roman literature as well as in other philosophical works, for example, as I will discuss, in the Epicurean method of treating occurrent distress; however, he is the earliest Stoic for whom this method of therapy is attested. It is therefore possible (and, for reasons I will come to at the end of the essay, in my view quite likely) that Seneca was responsible for introducing this method of therapy into Stoic theory.

This essay is divided into three sections: In the first, I discuss Seneca's therapy of violent emotions and its basis in the classical Stoic theory of the emotions. In the second, I give an interpretation of Seneca's philosophically sophisticated analysis of anger in *On Anger* 2.4. This analysis, I argue, explains why emotions are not reason-responsive, and does so in a way that further explains the philosophical basis of his therapy of violent emotions. In the third and final section, I argue that Seneca's therapy of violent emotions should be understood as a Stoic interpretation of Epicurus' method of treating distress.

I.

In several passages Seneca argues that the *only* effective method for treating someone suffering a violent emotion is to stimulate a rival emotion in him. For example, when describing the harmful effects of fear in *Moral Epistle* 13, he writes:

Anger both for preventing people from forming emotions at all and for treating occurrent emotions, see especially Wildberger 2007, 313–316.

5 See, for example, Sen. *De ira* 1.10.1, 3.39.4, and 3.40.5. My citations from Seneca all refer to Reynolds 1965 and 1977.

Nulla autem causa vitae est, nullus miseriarum modus, si timetur quantum potest. Hic prudentia prosit, hic robore animi evidentem quoque metum respue; si minus, vitio vitium repelle, spe metum tempera.

But there is no reason for life and no limit of miseries if one fears to the degree that is possible. Here, let prudence benefit you; here, reject even a clear occasion for fear by your strength of soul. If you are unable to do this, drive away vice by vice; temper your fear by means of hope. (Sen. *Ep.* 13.12)[6]

Again, when explaining why all emotions are bad auxiliaries to reason in *On Anger*, he writes:

Ideo numquam adsumet ratio in adiutorium inprovidos et violentos impetus apud quos nihil ipsa auctoritatis habeat, quos numquam comprimere possit nisi pares illis similisque opposuerit, ut irae metum, inertiae iram, timori cupiditatem.

Therefore, reason will never take for assistance thoughtless and violent impulses, among which it would have no authority and which it would never be able to check unless it were to oppose them with impulses equal and similar to them, such as fear against anger, anger against sluggishness, and appetite against fear. (Sen. *De ira* 1.10.1)

Finally, later in *On Anger*, in distinguishing the therapy of more and less violent emotions, he writes:

[Remedium] omni arte requiem furori dabit: si vehementior erit, aut pudorem illi cui non resistat incutiet aut metum; si infirmior, sermones inferet vel gratos vel novos et cupiditate cognoscendi avocabit.

[My remedy] will give rest to rage by every means: if the rage is rather violent, it will strike it with shame or fear, which it may not resist; if it is calmer, it will apply conversations that are either pleasing or novel and will call the enraged person away by his appetite for knowledge. (Sen. *De ira* 3.39.4)

In these passages, Seneca argues that violent emotions can only be checked by rival emotions. As he explains in the second passage: "thoughtless and violent impulses" (*inprovidi et violenti impetus*) may only be checked by similarly "thoughtless and violent" impulses. Accordingly, he recommends treating fear by appetite, and anger by fear.

As we have seen, unlike the methods of emotional therapy advocated by Cleanthes and Chrysippus, Seneca's method of treating violent emotions does not directly challenge the beliefs correlated with the emotions it overrides. Indeed, the set of beliefs correlated with the emotion that someone applying this method of emotional therapy stimulates in an impassioned person most commonly conflicts *incidentally* rather than *intrinsically* with the set of beliefs correlated with the emotion it overrides:[7] that is, in

---

6   All translations from Greek or Latin are my own.
7   By *incidentally* conflicting beliefs, I mean beliefs that conflict only on account of contingent factors, external to the beliefs themselves. For example, the belief that one should live within walking distance of a café would conflict incidentally with

itself neither set of beliefs commonly gives the impassioned person reason to reconsider, let alone to abandon, the other set.⁸ For example, if one overrides someone's grief over his best friend's untimely death by stimulating an appetite in him to go to another friend's wedding reception, the set of beliefs correlated with his appetite to go to the wedding reception does not directly challenge the set of beliefs correlated with his grief. For the beliefs correlated with his appetite – namely, that attending the reception would be good for him, and that it is fitting for him to anticipate attending it eagerly – are, in themselves, silent with respect to the beliefs correlated with his grief – that his best friend's death is bad for him, and that it is fitting for him to be distressed. Accordingly, these emotions, and the beliefs correlated with them, conflict only incidentally.

More difficult are cases where in order to override an emotion one stimulates a countervailing emotion regarding the same object in the impassioned person. For example, if one treats someone who passionately desires a cup of peppermint tea by making him afraid of that cup of tea, one has, it may seem, challenged his appetite by an emotion conflicting intrinsically with it. Even in this sort of case, however, these emotions will often conflict only incidentally. For someone who passionately desires a cup of tea presumably desires it as something pleasant or thirst-quenching. By contrast, his countervailing fear is unlikely to be either of the tea's pleasant flavor or of its quenching his thirst, but rather, say, of its scalding him. Accordingly, if the tea were to cool down, the sets of beliefs correlated with these emotions, and so the two emotions themselves, would no longer conflict at all. His appetite for, and fear of, the same cup of tea, therefore, conflict incidentally, and not intrinsically.

---

    the belief that one should live within walking distance of a library if it happens that there are no available apartments nearby both a café and a library. For it is, of course, possible that both a library and a café might be within walking distance of an available apartment, in which case these beliefs would not conflict at all. By *intrinsically* conflicting beliefs, on the other hand, I mean beliefs that are internally inconsistent, and so conflict with one another independently of the attendant circumstances. For example, the belief that exercise is good conflicts intrinsically with the belief that exercise is harmful. For an ancient example of this distinction, see Arist. *E.N.* 7.3, 1146a35–1147b3. For a related contemporary discussion of the distinction between "essentially" and "accidentally" conflicting attitudes, see Arpaly 2002, 89–91, especially 89 n. 10, and Marino 2008.

8   The major exception to this rule is the therapeutic use of a sub-class of emotions, such as shame (*pudor*), circumspection (*verecundia*), and regret (*paenitentia*), which both play a positive role in moral education and are, in general, only available for the treatment of relatively decent people. As I discuss in more detail in n. 17, in their therapeutic use these emotions are commonly correlated with the belief that one's emotional behavior is itself inappropriate, and so often conflict intrinsically, rather than incidentally, with the emotions they override.

That the emotions involved in Seneca's therapy of violent emotions most commonly conflict only incidentally with one another is a serious limitation of his method. For even if one succeeds in treating someone experiencing a violent emotion by stimulating a rival emotion in him, one will often not cause him to abandon the beliefs on which his violent emotion depends.[9] Rather, the rival emotion one stimulates in an impassioned person has the effect simply of distracting him from feeling the other emotion, judged to be a worse one by the therapist.

Seneca confronts a similar difficulty in his *To My Mother Helvia: On Consolation*, where he considers the consolatory technique of distracting someone experiencing distress by taking him to a show or gladiatorial contest.

> Ludis interim aut gladiatoribus animum occupamus; at illum inter ipsa quibus avocatur spectacula levis aliqua desiderii nota subruit. Ideo melius est vincere illum [sc. dolorem] quam fallere; nam qui delusus et voluptatibus aut occupationibus abductus est resurgit et ipsa quiete impetum ad saeviendum colligit.
>
> Sometimes we occupy the mind [of the mourner] with games or gladiatorial contests; but some slight reminder of its loss among the very spectacles by which it is distracted overwhelms it. Therefore, it is better to overcome grief than to deceive it; for grief which has been beguiled and has been diverted by pleasures or activities rises again, and by this very respite gathers its impulse for raging. (Sen. *Helv.* 17.1–2)

In this passage, Seneca comments that someone whose attention has merely been diverted from his grief is very likely to resume grieving if he is faced with an impression recalling his loss. As he writes a few sentences later:

> Omnia ista ad exiguum momentum prosunt nec remedia doloris sed inpedimenta sunt.
>
> All these things are beneficial for a short time, and are not remedies but impediments of distress. (Sen. *Helv.* 17.2)[10]

---

9   This shares some affinities with Chrysippus' method of emotional therapy, which explicitly counsels against challenging the impassioned person's more fundamental belief that the object of his emotions is, in fact, good or bad. However, unlike Seneca's method of treating violent emotions, Chrysippean emotional therapy argues against the impassioned person's belief that it is appropriate for him to be emotionally affected. By contrast, as I have been arguing, Seneca's method of therapy endeavors to override an emotion without directly challenging either of the beliefs correlated with it. For Chrysippus' theory, see Cic. *Tusc.* 3.76, 79 and Origenes, *Cels.* 8.51 = *SVF* 3.474.

10 See also Seneca's description of Caligula's unsuccessful efforts to "divert" (*sevocare*) his grief over his sister's death by gambling and harming others rather than addressing the beliefs correlated with it (*Polyb.* 17.4–6).

On the other hand, the failure of Seneca's therapy of violent emotions to directly challenge the beliefs correlated with the emotions it endeavors to console helps to explain its therapeutic utility. For, as he argues in a number of texts, emotions are by nature inadequately reason-responsive, and thus unresponsive to countervailing argument.[11] For instance, in *On Anger* he writes:

> Nam si exaudit rationem sequiturque qua ducitur, iam non est ira, cuius proprium est contumacia; si vero repugnat et non ubi iussa est quiescit sed libidine ferociaque provehitur, tam inutilis animi minister est quam miles qui signum receptui neglegit. Itaque si modum adhiberi sibi patitur, alio nomine appellanda est, desit ira esse, quam effrenatam indomitamque intellego.

> For if anger listens to reason and follows where reason leads, then it is already not anger, of which obstinacy is a proper quality; if, however, it fights back and does not become quiet when it has been ordered, but is carried forward by its desire and ferocity, then it is as useless a servant of the soul as a soldier who disregards the signal for falling back. And thus, if it suffers a measure to be applied to itself, then it must be called by a different name, and it ceases to be anger, which I understand to be unrestrained and untamable. (Sen. *De ira* 1.9.2–3)

According to this passage, it is "a proper quality" (*proprium*) of anger to be unresponsive to reason. Indeed, for Seneca, if someone who is pursuing vengeance restrains himself on the basis of reason, then he is no longer angry, even if he continues to display other characteristic symptoms of anger. Moreover, by comparing an enraged person's relationship to reason with a soldier who disregards the signal for retreat, Seneca implies that an enraged person may act on the basis of his anger despite recognizing that he has reason to act differently.[12]

This lack of reason-responsiveness is not peculiar to people in the grip of anger, but is characteristic of impassioned people more generally. As Seneca writes in *Moral Epistle* 85:

> Deinde nihil interest quam magnus sit adfectus: quantuscumque est, parere nescit, consilium non accipit. Quemadmodum rationi nullum animal optemperat, non ferum, non domesticum et mite (natura enim illorum est surda suadenti), sic non sequuntur, non audiunt adfectus, quantulicumque sunt.

> It makes no difference how great an emotion is: however small it is, it does not know how to obey, it does not accept advice. Just as no animal, whether wild or tame and gentle, obeys reason (for their nature is deaf to persuasion), so too emotions, however small they are, do not follow or listen to reason. (Sen. *Ep.* 85.8)

---

11 In addition to the passages cited in the main text, see, for example, Sen. *De ira* 1.7.4 and *Helv.* 17.1.
12 That enraged people may fail to alter their behavior even if they recognize that they have reason to do so is confirmed and further explained by Seneca's tripartite analysis of the formation of anger, which I will discuss in detail in the next section (Sen. *De ira* 2.4.1).

Seneca is here fully in agreement with Chrysippus, who also held that it is constitutive of emotions to be inadequately reason-responsive.[13]

The belief-based methods of emotional therapy advocated by Cleanthes and Chrysippus therefore face a difficult task. For if emotions are partly defined by their failure to be adequately reason-responsive, then it is difficult to see what good it would do to treat them by arguing against the beliefs with which they are correlated. In the case of more violent emotions, at any rate, belief-based therapy will be ineffective and, in some instances, even harmful.[14] Seneca's method of consoling people experiencing violent emotions by a rival emotion therefore makes a great deal of sense on the basis of orthodox Stoic theory.

A significant drawback of this method of emotional therapy, however, is that it would benefit impassioned people in a far more restricted set of cases than Chrysippus' or Cleanthes' methods of emotional therapy. Indeed, since it endeavors simply to replace a harmful emotion with another harmful emotion – in Seneca's phrase, it treats "vice by vice" (*Ep.* 13.12: "vitio vitium") – it would benefit an impassioned person only when the emotion being treated is more harmful than the rival emotion introduced to counter it.[15] While all emotions are vicious according to Stoic theory, one

---

13 For the failure of emotions, according to Chrysippus, to be adequately reason-responsive, see especially his comparison of impassioned people to runners who, on account of their vehement movement, are unable to stop, or change direction, as soon as it seems best to them to do so (Gal. *P.H.P.* 4.2.15–18 = *SVF* 3.462 and 4.4.24–25 = *SVF* 3.476); see also Plu. *Virt. mor.* 450c = *SVF* 3.390 and Stob. 2.7.10a, vol. 2, p. 89 Wachsmuth = *SVF* 3.389. The best discussion of the sense in which Chrysippus takes emotions to be inadequately reason-responsive is Cooper 1998, 79–81; see also Gill 1998, 115–123, especially 117–123, and Graver 2007, 66–70.

14 For instance, in explaining his delay in writing a letter of consolation to his mother regarding his own exile, Seneca writes: "I knew that your distress should not be challenged while it was raging freshly, lest these very consolations stir it up and inflame it" (*Helv.* 1.2). See too Chrysippus' very similar comment in the fourth book of his *On the Emotions*, preserved in Origenes, *Cels.* 8.51 = *SVF* 3.474.

15 Jula Wildberger has suggested to me that this method of emotional therapy might also cause impassioned people to compare the grounds for their current emotion with that of the rival emotion one stimulates in them, and so to hold both emotions in a more circumspect, non-emotional way. This is an intriguing suggestion, but I do not think it can be Seneca's primary explanation of the efficacy of this method of emotional therapy. For, as this suggestion implies, Seneca takes it to be constitutive of emotions that one comes to form, and hold, them without exercising circumspection – on this point, see also Inwood 2005, 154–155. Thus, in forming a rival emotion, an impassioned person does not carefully consider the reasons supporting and opposing it, but forms it, like any emotion, rashly and without circumspection. It may, however, be an additional virtue of this method of therapy that someone whose emotion has been overridden by a rival emotion will be more

emotion is presumably more harmful than another by having worse consequences either for the impassioned person or for those affected by him. Thus, if an enraged person were on the verge of assaulting someone, it would probably be worth stimulating a rival emotion in him to prevent him from doing so.[16] Seneca explicitly acknowledges this limitation of this method of emotional therapy by restricting it to the treatment of a "more violent" (*vehementior*) emotion (Sen. *De ira* 3.39.4).

This limitation also explains Seneca's restricted use of this method of emotional therapy in his consolatory works.[17] For unless someone's grief prevents him from carrying out important public or private business, it is not worthwhile, according to Seneca's theory, to console him by a rival emotion. Moreover, since grief tends to be relatively long-lasting, confronting someone in mourning with a rival emotion that does not challenge his credence in the beliefs correlated with his grief – like merely distracting someone in mourning by taking him to the theater – is not an especially effective, long-term method of consolation. Seneca's reluctance to use this method in his consolatory works is, therefore, perfectly consistent with his more general endorsement of it.

---

    likely, once the overriding emotion is no longer vehement, to compare his grounds for the two competing emotions and thereby to think of them both in relative rather than absolute terms.

16 As, for instance, Augustus is said to have countered Vedius Pollio's enraged desire to cast a slave, who had accidentally broken one of his crystal glasses, into his fish pond as prey for his lampreys, by ordering all of Vedius' crystal glasses to be broken and his fish pond to be filled up (Sen. *De ira* 3.40.2–4). In summarizing this passage, Seneca comments that Augustus' method of harshly checking Vedius' anger by fear is only commendable in treating anger that is "wild, harsh, and blood-thirsty, which is now incurable, unless it has feared something greater" (*De ira* 3.40.5). For Vedius Pollio's proverbial cruelty towards his slaves, see also Pliny the Elder, *Nat.* 9.77.

17 In this essay, I focus on the role of ordinary emotions, such as anger, fear, desire, and pleasure, in Seneca's therapy of violent emotions. I should note, however, that a subclass of emotions, especially shame (*pudor*), circumspection (*verecundia*), and regret (*paenitentia*), *do* play an important role in Seneca's consolatory works, but are only available for the treatment of the emotions of relatively decent people. Unlike ordinary emotions, these emotions commonly conflict intrinsically, and not incidentally, with the emotions they override. For instance, in consoling anger by shame, one may cause the enraged person to form the belief that his enraged behavior is itself inappropriate, thereby contradicting his belief, on which the formation of his anger depends, that it is appropriate for him to eagerly pursue vengeance. For a detailed discussion of the role of this sub-class of emotions in Senecan emotional therapy, see the third chapter of my dissertation, *Love, Compassion and Other Vices: A History of the Stoic Theory of the Emotions*.

II.

Seneca's analysis of anger in *On Anger* 2.4 further explains the philosophical basis of his method of treating violent emotions. This analysis distinguishes three movements, or stages, of the formation of anger.[18] While only the third movement is full-blown anger, the other two are necessary preliminaries to the third movement.[19] I will argue that Seneca's subtle distinction between the second and third movements helps to explain why, in his view, emotions are inadequately reason-responsive despite depending fundamentally on the impassioned person's forming certain beliefs. I will begin by quoting the passage in full.

> Et ut scias quemadmodum incipiant adfectus aut crescant aut efferantur, est primus motus non voluntarius, quasi praeparatio adfectus et quaedam comminatio; alter cum voluntate non contumaci, tamquam oporteat me vindicari cum laesus sim, aut oporteat hunc poenas dare cum scelus fecerit; tertius motus est iam inpotens, qui non si oportet ulcisci vult sed utique, qui rationem evicit.

> And that you may know in what way emotions begin, grow and are carried away: the first motion is not voluntary, but is a sort of preparation for, and threat of, an emotion. The next motion is accompanied by a non-obstinate desire to the effect that it is right for me to be avenged since I have been harmed, or it is right for this man to be punished since he has committed a crime. The third motion is now out of control, and it wants to take vengeance not if it is right, but in any case – this motion has conquered reason altogether. (Sen. *De ira* 2.4.1)

The first movement in the formation of anger is a non-voluntary and largely ineliminable response to the impression of oneself or someone close to one having been unjustly injured.[20] In the second movement, one

---

18 While these movements mark distinct, diachronic stages of the genesis of an emotion, the transition from the first movement to the third need not involve any perceivable interval of time. Indeed, the formation of an emotion presumably often occurs without any perceivable gap between the emotionally-salient impression and the full-blown emotional impulse. This is supported by Seneca's frequent description of emotions as overhasty, rash assents: see, for example, *De ira* 1.18.1 and 3.2.6.

19 Some scholars have argued that the second movement is anger, and that the third movement is rather "cruelty" (*feritas*), which is described in *On Anger* 2.5: see, for instance, Fillion-Lahille 1984, 181 and, more recently, Graver 2007, 125–130. However, this interpretation is directly contradicted by Seneca's earlier claim in *On Anger* 1.9.2 that "obstinacy is a proper quality of anger" ("cuius [sc. irae] proprium est contumacia"); see also *On Anger* 2.3.4. For the second movement is, Seneca writes, "accompanied by a non-obstinate desire" ("cum voluntate non contumaci"), and thus *cannot* be full-blown anger.

20 As several texts in *De ira* tell us, the initial impression causing the first movement of anger is "the impression of injury" (*species iniuriae*). See, for instance, *De ira* 2.1.3, 2.2.2, and 2.3.5. That first movements follow unavoidably from the impression of one's having been injured is suggested by *De ira* 2.2, in which Seneca

assents to the proposition that "it is right for me to be avenged since I have been harmed," or to the similar proposition that "it is right for this man to be punished since he has committed a crime." The third and final movement differs from the second in that "it is out of control" (*impotens*), and so wants "to take vengeance not if it is right, but in any case."[21]

An important difference between the second and the third movement is that the third movement is no longer responsive to the countervailing belief that it is not right for one to be so moved.[22] As Seneca writes, while the second movement is correlated with the belief that "it is right for me to be avenged," the third movement "wants to take vengeance not if it is right, but in any case." Minimally, then, the belief that it is right to take vengeance is not correlated with the third movement.

Scholars differ, however, over the precise propositional content of the belief correlated with the third movement. For instance, Katja Vogt has argued that, in forming the third movement of anger, "the agent will assent to something like 'I have to take revenge because I have been offended'." Vogt reports that she arrives at this account by simply subtracting the notion of rightness from the beliefs correlated with the second movement (Vogt 2006, 71).

One difficulty with Vogt's interpretation is that it fails to explain why enraged people pursue vengeance "not if it is right, but in any case." For the belief that "I have to take revenge because I have been offended," while resistant to the objection that it is not right to take revenge, is open to the objection that I have not, in fact, been offended, or that I have not been offended by this person. Thus, according to Vogt's interpretation, while

---

distinguishes non-voluntary movements in response to the impression that one has been injured from full-blown anger, which one only forms by giving assent to that impression. Unlike anger, Seneca places the "first blow of the soul, which moves us after the impression of injury," among those things "which happen by a certain condition of the human lot, and so happen even to the wisest" (*De ira* 2.2.2). The strong implication is that "the first blow of the soul" (*primus ictus animi*) not only occurs without assent, but also occurs in all humans. For further support, see *De ira* 2.4.2.

21 As has often been noted, the latter phrase is very similar to Chrysippus' characterization of people suffering anger as insisting that "this [action on the basis of their emotion] is to be done in any case, even if they are mistaken, and if it is not to their advantage" (Gal. *P.H.P.* 4.6.27 = *SVF* 3.475: "καὶ ὡς τοῦτο ἐκ παντός γε τρόπου ποιητέον, καὶ εἰ διαμαρτάνουσι καὶ εἰ ἀσύμφορόν ἐστιν αὐτοῖς"). See, for example, Sorabji 2000, 61–62, with 62 n. 33.

22 This is confirmed by Seneca's distinction a couple of lines previously between someone who "has thought that he has been harmed, has wanted vengeance, but has settled down immediately when some consideration speaks against it" and anger "which leaps over reason, which drags reason with it" (*De ira* 2.3.4).

emotions are insensitive to concerns of rightness, they remain sensitive to other countervailing considerations.

Seneca is quite clear, however, that impassioned people at the apex of their emotion are inadequately responsive not only to considerations of rightness, but to countervailing considerations of whatever kind. For instance, he writes:

> Sibi enim [sc. ira] indulget et ex libidine iudicat et audire non vult et patrocinio non relinquit locum et ea tenet quae invasit et eripi sibi iudicium suum, etiam si pravum est, non sinit.
>
> For [anger] indulges itself and judges according to its desire and does not wish to listen and does not leave room for someone pleading on behalf of the defendant and holds those views which it has entered into and, even if it is wrong, does not allow its judgment to be snatched from it. (Sen. *De ira* 1.17.7)

In this passage, Seneca argues that anger is wholly unresponsive to arguments showing that it is wrong to take vengeance, irrespective of their grounds. He expresses a similar view shortly afterwards:

> Etiam si ingeritur oculis veritas, [sc. ira] amat et tuetur errorem; coargui non vult, et in male coeptis honestior illi pertinacia videtur quam paenitentia.
>
> Even if truth is brought before its eyes, [anger] loves and favors its error; it is not willing to be refuted, and when it has undertaken a base course of action, obstinacy seems more upright to it than regret. (Sen. *De ira* 1.18.2)

Presumably then, if someone in a fit of rage were faced with evidence challenging *any* of his grounds for anger – for instance, evidence showing that the person he is angry with did not in fact injure him – he would continue to be angry, and so to pursue vengeance, regardless.[23] Vogt's interpretation of the belief correlated with the third movement does not, therefore, explain why people acting on the basis of the third movement, that is of full-blown anger, do so "not if it is right, but in any case," irrespective of countervailing reasons.

On the other hand, Richard Sorabji has proposed taking the third movement to be correlated with "something like 'I must be avenged, come what may'" (Sorabji 2000, 62). His interpretation explains anger's unresponsiveness to countervailing considerations of whatever kind. However, by including the rider "come what may" in the belief correlated with the third movement, he strips the transition from the second to the third movement of much of its explanatory force. For since nothing in the second movement corresponds to the rider "come what may," it is difficult to see how, in his view, the third movement follows from the second. Sorabji's interpretation of the belief correlated with the third movement, therefore, fails to explain why enraged people form the belief correlated

---

23 See also *De ira* 1.19.1 and 3.29.2.

with the third movement. Rather, by adding "come what may" to the belief correlated with the third movement, it simply asserts that impassioned people are inadequately reason-responsive.

By contrast, I think that Seneca's tripartite analysis of the formation of anger gives an elegant explanation of why, according to Stoic theory, enraged people, as well as impassioned people more generally, are inadequately reason-responsive. In my view, the third movement is correlated with the conclusion of the beliefs involved in the second movement, stripped of any reference to the impassioned person's reasons for holding it. That is, the belief correlated with the third movement includes neither the notion of it being "right" to take vengeance, nor one's reasons for thinking it is right to take vengeance. Rather, the belief correlated with the third movement is simply "I must be avenged."

An advantage of this interpretation is that it explains why someone who holds such a belief would continue to hold it "in any case" (*utique*), irrespective of whatever countervailing reasons might be urged against it. For, in arguing against someone's belief that it is right for him to take vengeance, one presumably challenges his reasons for holding this belief; but according to the interpretation of the third movement that I have proposed, the belief correlated with someone's rage does not in fact refer to his reasons for becoming angry. That is, the occurrent belief correlated with his anger is simply "I must be avenged," and not "I must be avenged because I have been harmed" or "I must be avenged because it is right for me to be avenged." To be sure, there is a causal story involving one's forming the belief in the appropriate reasons at an earlier stage of the emotion's genesis, namely in the second movement; but the only belief correlated with the emotion itself is the conclusion of the beliefs involved in the second movement, stripped of any reference to one's reasons for holding it. There is no need, then, to take the belief correlated with the third movement to include the rider that one should continue to hold it "come what may," irrespective of countervailing reasons. For, as I have been arguing, the occurrent belief in question, "I must be avenged," is already resistant to countervailing reasons in virtue of its not being coupled with the impassioned agent's reasons for holding it.

Against the background of his analysis of anger in *On Anger* 2.4, Seneca's method of treating violent occurrent emotions by opposing them with countervailing emotions, therefore, makes better sense than the standard Stoic method of treating occurrent emotions by arguing against one or the other of the beliefs correlated with them. For if the only belief correlated with anger is "I must be avenged," then it is very difficult to see how someone would persuade an enraged person to abandon his anger by arguing against it. Rather, it would make far better sense to treat his anger by causing him to believe that he must act in a different way. Since emotions are characterized, according to the Stoics, by their ability to occupy the impassioned person's attention, thereby blinding him to countervailing considerations, a rival emotion would presumably be especially well suited for overriding a violent emotion.[24]

It remains to consider why the second movement, if unopposed, leads to the third movement. Although Seneca's discussion leaves the explanation of this transition underdetermined, it seems to me that we can make good sense of it. First, it is important to appreciate that, according to Stoic theory, the beliefs correlated with the second movement are false.[25] More particularly, the belief that "it is right for me to be avenged because I have been harmed" depends on two false beliefs: [1] The belief that I have been harmed. [2] The belief that because someone has committed a crime, he ought to be punished.

The former belief, that one has been harmed, plays an important role in Seneca's account of the genesis of anger. Indeed, Seneca takes it to be non-controversial to Stoics and non-Stoics alike that in order to become angry one must have the impression of injury (*species iniuriae*).[26]

For Seneca's criticism of this belief, it is useful to turn to his more extended discussion of injury (*iniuria*) in *De Constantia Sapientis*.

> Iniuria propositum hoc habet, aliquem malo adficere; malo autem sapientia non relinquit locum (unum enim illi malum est turpitudo, quae intrare eo ubi iam virtus honestumque est non potest); ergo, si iniuria sine malo nulla est [...], iniuria ad sapientem non pervenit.
>
> Injury has this as it aim, to affect someone with something bad. However, wisdom leaves no place for what is bad (for the only thing that is bad for it is baseness, which is not able to enter where virtue and uprightness already exist); therefore, if there is no injury without something bad [...], no injury pertains to the wise man. (Sen. *Const.* 5.3)

In this passage, Seneca argues that for people to suffer injury they must suffer something that is, in fact, bad for them. But, as he comments, according to Stoic axiology, baseness alone is bad for one; things that are conventionally taken to be bad such as death, sickness, poverty and pain are, for the Stoics, merely "dispreferred indifferents" (*apoproēgmena* in Greek, or *incommoda* in Seneca's Latin).[27] Thus, someone only suffers an

---

24 For the propensity of emotions "as they arise" to "push out" (ἐκκρούειν) even countervailing considerations that would otherwise be clear to them, see Chrysippus' explanation of the blindness of emotions, preserved in Plu. *Virt. mor* 450c = *SVF* 3.390. Tieleman 2003, 180–181 is a good, detailed discussion of this passage.
25 See Kaster in Kaster and Nussbaum 2010, 7–8 and Vogt 2006, 66–67 and 71–72.
26 *De ira* 2.1.3; see also 2.2.2 and 2.3.5.
27 For an eloquent description of the Stoic distinction between preferred and dispreferred indifferents, on the one hand, and virtue and vice, on the other, see Sen. *Ep.*

injury, and so is only harmed in the sense relevant to anger, by becoming more vicious. By contrast, the non-wise most commonly form the belief that they have been injured in response to their being "harmed" in a more colloquial sense, by, for example, someone hitting or insulting them. It follows that, in Seneca's view, both the impression of injury underlying anger and, if one assents to that impression, the consequent belief that one has been injured are nearly always false.[28]

The other belief correlated with the second movement of anger – namely, that because someone has committed a crime, he ought to be punished – directly contradicts Seneca's view that all punishment should be exclusively forward-looking. For, as Seneca writes: "He [the wise man] will always in every punishment observe this: that he may know that one punishment is applied so that it may cure evil men, another so that it may destroy them; and in both he will look not to the past, but to the future [...]."[29] Thus, in Seneca's view, it is right to punish someone only if doing so will improve either him or the larger community. That someone has harmed one, or otherwise committed a crime, is, therefore, an insufficient reason to punish him.[30]

Cumulatively, these beliefs greatly exaggerate both the injury one has suffered and the value of taking revenge for it. Thus, it seems likely that someone's overvaluation of the injury he has suffered, together with his

---

66.19–20. For the Stoic theory of indifferents, see also the passages collected with commentary in Long and Sedley 1987, 1.354–359 and, for a fuller collection of passages, *SVF* 3.117–168.

28 The only exception would be cases in which someone forms the belief that he has been harmed by being made less virtuous. However, while other people may contribute in an indirect way to someone's virtue or vice, each person is, in every case, responsible for assenting to false impressions, and so for forming the false beliefs and vicious impulses on which his vice depends. Each person is, therefore, responsible for his own virtue or vice. Thus, the only impression that one has been harmed that may be true is the impression that one has harmed oneself by acting basely; but in such cases the additional belief that it is appropriate to be excited at the prospect of taking revenge on oneself is clearly false. For ancient discussions of this sort of case, see Posidonius' objection to Chrysippus in Gal. *P.H.P.* 4.5.28, and Cic. *Tusc.* 3.77 and 4.61. For commentary, see Graver 2007, 191–211 and White 1995, 241–245.

29 Sen. *De ira* 1.19.7: "Hoc semper in omni animadversione servabit, ut sciat alteram adhiberi ut emendet malos, alteram ut tollat; in utroque non praeterita sed futura intuebitur [...]." See also *De ira* 1.6.2–4 and 1.16.2–4.

30 It is worth noting that, according to Seneca, although a person cannot, strictly speaking, *be harmed* by anyone else, another person *may harm* him – by which Seneca means that someone may act with the intention of harming him. Therefore, the belief that someone has harmed one, unlike the belief that one has been harmed, may often be true. For Seneca's discussion of this point, see especially *Const.* 7.3–8.

false belief that the people who have harmed him ought to be punished *because* they harmed him (and not because punishment would benefit either them or the larger community), may lead him to form the further belief that being avenged would be good for him. As has often been noted, this further belief plays a fundamental role in the formation of anger.[31] For, according to the Stoics, anger is not distress that one has been harmed, but rather the passionate desire for vengeance falsely conceived of as something good.[32]

Someone who forms the false beliefs correlated with the second movement of anger may, then, come to focus so excessively on taking vengeance that he no longer pays attention to his reasons for doing so or, indeed, to anything else at all, for example anything that might happen to him as a consequence. Seneca seems to have something like this in mind when he comments on the irrationality of enraged people who on account of their belief that they have been harmed act in ways that (at least according to their conception of what being harmed entails) harm themselves far worse. For instance, in describing the self-destructive anger of barbarians, he writes:

> Cum mobiles animos species iniuriae perculit, aguntur statim et qua dolor traxit ruinae modo legionibus incidunt, incompositi interriti incauti, pericula adpetentes sua; gaudent feriri et instare ferro et tela corpore urgere et per suum vulnus exire.
>
> When the impression of injury has struck their excitable minds, they are led away at once, and where their pain has dragged them, disorganized, fearless and incautious they fall on our legions in the manner of a landslide, seeking their own peril; they rejoice to be struck, urge themselves onto the sword, challenge weapons with their body and expire through a wound of their own creation. (Sen. *De ira* 3.2.6)

According to this passage, enraged people, urged on by their belief that they have been harmed unjustly, often expose themselves to, and even take pleasure in, being harmed far more severely than they were harmed by the injury they are bent on avenging.[33]

In my view, the non-voluntary first movement of anger also contributes to the transition from the second movement to the third movement. Following standard Stoic theory, Seneca is emphatic that the first movement caused by the impression of injury occurs without one's assenting to

---

31 Kaster in Kaster and Nussbaum 2010, 7–8 and Vogt 2006, 66.
32 For Stoic definitions of anger, see Sen. *De ira* 1.2.3b = Lact. *Ira* 17.13; Sen. *De ira* 2.1.4; Stob. 2.10c, vol. 2, p. 91Wachsmuth = *SVF* 3.395; D.L. 7.113 = *SVF* 3.396.
33 Along similar lines, in the very beginning of the *De ira*, Seneca describes anger as "raging with the most inhuman desire for arms, blood and torture; it is neglectful of itself provided that it may harm another, rushing onto the very weapons [of those on whom it aims to take vengeance], and is hungry for a vengeance that will draw the avenger with it" (1.1.1).

this impression and is insufficient to compel one to assent to it.[34] Thus, even the wise, who never assent to false impressions, will suffer non-voluntary first movements in response to the impression of injury.[35] If, however, a person assents to this impression, then the non-voluntary psychic and physical movements constituting the first movement – say, a quickened heart-beat and an expansion of his psychic *pneuma* – are presumably reinforced by his assent, and so contribute to the phenomenological intensity of his anger, thereby focusing his attention on taking revenge instead of his reasons for doing so. For instance, when comparing the hideous external features of enraged people to their even uglier internal state, Seneca writes:

> Qualem intus putas esse animum cuius extra imago tam foeda est? Quanto illi intra pectus terribilior vultus est, acrior spiritus, intentior impetus, rupturus se nisi eruperit!
>
> What sort of soul do you think is within, the external appearance of which is so foul? How much more terrible is the countenance within the enraged person's chest, how much sharper the breathing, how much more violent the impulse, which will burst through itself, if it does not burst forth! (Sen. *De ira* 2.35.4)

Although in this passage Seneca is describing the internal state of someone in a full-blown fit of rage, the features he describes could constitute the first movement of anger as well.[36]

Seneca thus explains the transition from the second to the third movement of anger by both the non-voluntary movements constituting the first movement and the second movement's overvaluation of actually taking vengeance. Together, these may lead someone to focus excessively on taking vengeance at the expense of remaining attentive to his reasons for wanting to do so, thereby giving rise to the third movement, occurrent anger.

III.

So far, I have argued that Seneca's works introduce a method of emotional therapy into Stoic theory that is otherwise unattested in earlier or contem-

---

34 See, for example, Sen. *De ira* 2.2.2, 2.3.1, 2.3.5, and 2.4.2. For discussion of the Stoic theory of pre-emotions (προπάθειαι), see Abel 1983 and Graver 1999 and 2007, 85–108.
35 In addition to the preceding note, see Sen. *Ep.* 99.18, *Const.* 10.3–4, and Gel. 19.1.
36 See too *De ira* 2.3.2: "For if anyone thinks that pallor and falling tears and the stirring up of obscene liquid, or deep breathing and the sudden brightening of eyes, or anything else similar to these is a sign of an emotion and a sign of the soul, he is deceived and does not understand that these are blows of the body."

porary Stoic authors,[37] but which makes very good sense on the basis of Chrysippus' theory of the emotions.[38] In particular, it gives due weight to the failure of impassioned people to be adequately reason-responsive. I now want to consider the likely origin of this method of emotional therapy. I will argue that it is best understood as a Stoic adaptation of the standard Epicurean method of treating people experiencing distress, thereby suggesting that it may be Seneca's own contribution to Stoic theory.

In the *Tusculan Disputations*, Cicero gives a brief summary of Epicurus' therapy of distress:

> Levationem autem aegritudinis in duabus rebus [sc. Epicurus] ponit, avocatione a cogitanda molestia et revocatione ad contemplandas voluptates.
>
> [Epicurus] puts the relief of distress in two things: distraction (*avocatione*) from thinking of one's misfortune, and redirection (*revocatione*) to the contemplation of pleasures. (Cic. *Tusc.* 3.32)[39]

As the similarity of the terms *avocatio* and *revocatio* suggests,[40] these methods are closely related. While *avocatio* turns a distressed person's attention away from his distress, *revocatio* redirects his attention to the contemplation of pleasure. According to Cicero, these methods are really

---

37 To my knowledge, the next source ascribing this method of emotional therapy to the Stoics is the sixth-century Platonist Olympiodorus *in Alc.* p. 37 Westerink = vol. 2, p. 54 Creuzer = *SVF* 3.489.

38 In fact, this method of emotional therapy is indirectly anticipated by a passage from Chrysippus' *On the Emotions* describing the propensity of people who suffer from "lack of psychic tension" (ἀτονία) and "weakness of soul" (ἀσθένεια ψυχῆς) to rashly abandon their countervailing dispositional and occurrent beliefs when faced with a persuasive impulsive impression (*PHP* 4.6.7–9). Chrysippus, in explaining this phenomenon, quotes a passage from Euripides' *Andromache* that describes Menelaos, after the fall of Troy, rushing at Helen in rage with his sword drawn, but forming the passionate desire to embrace her and dropping his sword as soon as he sees her breasts (*Andr.* 629–630). As in the method of emotional therapy I have been discussing, there is no question here of Menelaus *reconsidering* the case for anger when he sees Helen. Rather, his lust for her simply *overrides* his occurrent anger. While this passage does not suggest that rival emotions should ever be used to counter an emotion, it clearly allows that they are capable of doing so. I want to thank Jula Wildberger for pointing out the relevance of this passage to me.

39 Cicero's discussion in the *Tusculan Disputations* is our only direct source for Epicurus' therapy of occurrent distress; however, his report fits very well with our other evidence bearing indirectly on Epicurus' theory. See especially D.L. 10.22 = Epicur. *Frg.* 138 Usener and Plu. *Non posse suaviter vivi secundum Epicurum* 1091b = Epicur. *Frg.* 423 Usener. Other relevant passages of Cicero are *Fin.* 1.57, 2.104–106, and *Tusc.* 5.96. For discussion, see Graver 2002, 195–201.

40 The corresponding Greek terms are uncertain; Graver, following the work of Asmis and Kassel, suggests that *revocatio* translates ἐπιβολή (2001, 171). See too Kassel 1958, 31 and, especially, Asmis 1984, 124–125.

two stages of a single process of consolation, in which *avocatio* from one's distress precedes *revocatio* to the "memory of past pleasures and the anticipation of future pleasures."[41] Since *avocatio* and *revocatio* represent distinct steps of the treatment of someone in distress, they must be different in kind. *Revocatio* is not, therefore, a special kind of *avocatio*, but is rather a distinct, though complementary, stage of consolation.

A few lines later, however, Cicero, in rejecting Epicurean therapy, writes in a way that suggests *revocatio* is, in fact, the culmination of a single process of *avocatio*: "For this *revocatio*, which he [Epicurus] recommends, when he calls us away (*avocat*) from dwelling on our evils, is nothing."[42] Despite this apparent inconsistency, I believe that Cicero's account is perfectly coherent. For even if there is a difference between *avocatio* and *revocatio* in theory, there need not be any such difference in practice: that is, *avocatio* and *revocatio* may often be two aspects, rather than diachronic stages, of a single activity, separable only in account.[43] Presumably then, someone in mourning may turn his attention away from the object of his grief by redirecting his attention to the contemplation of pleasure. Of course, in other cases, *avocatio* and *revocatio* will be distinct diachronic stages of the therapy of distress. For example, someone in mourning may, first, turn his attention away from the object of his grief, and only afterwards redirect his attention to the contemplation of pleasure.

Both *avocatio* and *revocatio* also play a role in Senecan emotional therapy. For example, in the passage quoted fully on p. 113, he summarizes his strategies for treating more and less violent episodes of rage:

> [...] si infirmior, sermones inferet vel gratos vel novos et cupiditate cognoscendi avocabit.
>
> [...] if it is calmer, [my remedy] will apply conversations that are either pleasing or novel and will call the enraged person away by his appetite for knowledge. (*De ira* 3.39.4)

So far, I have focused especially on Seneca's method for treating people in the grip of violent emotions; however, in this passage, he distinguishes the proper method for treating more and less violent emotions. More particularly, he recommends treating people experiencing more violent emotions by stimulating a rival emotion in them, and treating those experiencing less violent emotions by distracting them ("avocabit") with "pleasing or novel" conversations.[44] These two methods of emotional therapy are quite similar

---

41 Cic. *Tusc.* 3.33: "praeteritarum [sc. voluptatum] memoria et spe consequentium."
42 Cic. *Tusc.* 3.35: "Nam revocatio illa, quam adfert, cum a contuendis nos malis avocat, nulla est."
43 I want to thank Geir Thorarinsson for urging this point on me in discussion.
44 I take it that "the appetite for knowledge" (*cupiditas cognoscendi*) that is stimulated by pleasing or novel conversations is not especially vivid, and so is better

to Epicurus' distinction between *avocatio* and *revocatio* – although it is worth noting that for Seneca, unlike Epicurus, they are *alternative* methods of therapy, rather than two aspects of a single therapeutic method. In particular, I propose that Seneca's method of treating more violent emotions should be understood as a Stoic interpretation of Epicurean *revocatio*.

Although, for Epicurus, the redirection from distress to the contemplation of pleasure replaces a harmful psychological state with a more pleasant and so objectively better one, if this redirection causes one to rejoice vehemently, then, from a Stoic perspective, it simply replaces one vicious emotion, distress, with another vicious emotion, pleasure (*hēdonē*). Thus, for the Stoics, Epicurean *revocatio* would be worthwhile *only* if it causes less harm than the distress it overrides. Indeed, in some cases it may even be worthwhile to override someone's intense pleasure with fear or pain. Seneca's view that one should treat not only people experiencing distress, but people experiencing violent emotions more generally by stimulating a rival emotion in them may, therefore, be understood as a Stoic adaptation of Epicurean *revocatio*.

That Seneca, in fact, had Epicurean emotional therapy in mind in developing his therapy of violent emotions is suggested by both his well-attested familiarity with Epicureanism and specific references in his works to Epicurean emotional therapy.[45] For instance, as has been widely recognized, in his consolatory works Seneca often draws on Epicurean emotional therapy, by counseling his addressees to redirect their attention from the death or exile of the person they are mourning to their pleasant memories of him.[46] A good example of this is a passage from *To Polybius: On Consolation*, in which Seneca endeavors to console Polybius over his brother's untimely death.

---

characterized as a diversion than as a full-blown emotion. At any rate, the passage strongly implies that it would be insufficient for overriding "more vehement" instances of anger. This is also supported by Sen. *Helv.* 17.1–2, which, as we saw in Section I (p. 115), argues that someone in mourning whose distress "is called away" ("avocatur") by mere "spectacles" ("spectacula") is easily called back to mourning by "some *slight* reminder of his loss" ("levis aliqua desiderii nota"). For another consolatory use of the term *avocare*, see *Polyb.* 8.3–4.

45 In addition to the passages mentioned below, a particularly clear reference to Epicurus' therapy of distress is Sen. *Ep.* 78.18.
46 For representative examples in the scholarly literature, see Abel 1967, 26–27, Grollios 1956, 52–54, Manning 1974, 79–81 and 1981, 46–48, all of whom take this feature of Senecan consolation to be indebted to Epicurean *revocatio*. For further examples from Seneca's consolatory works, see Sen. *Marc.* 3.4 and 12.1–3, *Polyb.* 10.6, and *Ep.* 99.3–5.

> Nimis angustat gaudia sua, qui eis tantummodo, quae habet ac videt, frui se putat et habuisse eadem pro nihilo ducit; cito enim nos omnis voluptas relinquit, quae fluit et transit et paene ante quam veniat aufertur. Itaque in praeteritum tempus animus mittendus est et quicquid nos umquam delectavit reducendum ac frequenti cogitatione pertractandum est: longior fideliorque est memoria voluptatum quam praesentia. Quod habuisti ergo optimum fratrem, in summis bonis pone!
>
> He makes his pleasures excessively narrow, who thinks he enjoys only those things that he has and sees, and considers having had these things to be of no value; for all pleasure leaves us quickly, and flows out and passes by and is nearly gone before it arrives. And thus, the soul must be sent into the past and whatever has delighted us must be led back and must be handled with frequent thought; the memory of pleasures is more lasting and more faithful than present pleasures. Therefore, count among your greatest goods that you had an excellent brother! (Sen. *Polyb.* 10.3)

Seneca argues that Polybius should not mourn his brother's death, but should instead be grateful for his pleasant memories of his brother's life, through which his brother will continue to benefit him. In support of this claim, Seneca argues that the memory of past pleasures is in certain respects even more satisfying than the experience of present pleasures, insofar as it is "more lasting and more faithful than present pleasures." Thus, according to this passage, so long as Polybius frequently recalls his pleasant memory of his brother, his brother will remain among his "greatest goods" ("in summis bonis"). In addition to its structural similarity to Epicurean emotional therapy, Seneca's debt to Epicurus in this passage is suggested both by its uncharacteristic emphasis on pleasure[47] and by a passage in the *On Benefits* that, in very similar language, ascribes to Epicurus the view that the memory of past pleasures is in certain respects superior to the fleeting pleasures of the present.[48]

In light of Seneca's familiarity with Epicurean *revocatio*, as well as his more general sympathetic interest in Epicureanism, it seems likely that the therapy of violent emotions he advocates is his own contribution to Stoic theory.[49] Alternatively, it is also possible that an earlier Stoic developed this method of emotional therapy, but that Seneca was attracted to it

---

47 Indeed, Seneca's claim that the pleasant memory of Polybius' brother will be among Polybius' "greatest goods" ("in summis bonis") suggests that pleasure, and not virtue, is the greatest good (*summum bonum*), which is, of course, the Epicurean, and not the Stoic, position.

48 *Ben.* 3.4.1–2; cf. *Brev. vit.* 10.2–4. For the Epicurean view that the memory of past pleasures is, in certain respects, superior to the experience of present pleasures, see also Plu. *Non posse suaviter vivi secundum Epicurum.* 1099d = Epicur. *Frg.* 436 Usener and Cic. *Fin.* 2.106.

49 Seneca's interest in Epicurus is evident throughout his *Epistulae Morales* and *Dialogi*. For discussion of his use of Epicurus, see Cooper 2004, I. Hadot 1969, 47–71, and the contribution of Wildberger in this volume.

because of its affinity to the Epicurean method of consolation. At any rate, the similarity of this method to Epicurus' therapy of distress suggests that whoever first introduced it into Stoicism referred self-consciously to Epicurean theory. Seneca's therapy of more violent emotions thus shows how a Stoic might integrate the views of other philosophical schools into Stoic theory without abandoning the basic framework of Stoicism.

IV.

In sum, in this paper I have argued that Seneca introduces a new method of emotional therapy into Stoic philosophy, which differs significantly from earlier Stoic methods of emotional therapy, but nevertheless makes very good sense on the basis of the classical Stoic theory of the emotions. I have also argued for an interpretation of Seneca's tripartite analysis of the formation of emotions, according to which his analysis helps to explain why, for the Stoics, emotions are inadequately reason-responsive despite being based fundamentally on impassioned people coming to form, and hold, certain beliefs. In the final section of the paper, I compare Seneca's therapy of violent emotions to Epicurus' therapy of distress, and argue that Seneca's therapy should be understood as a Stoic adaptation of Epicurean *revocatio*. More generally, I hope to have shown that the aspects of Seneca's theory of the emotions that I have focused on are both more innovative than has generally been recognized and, at the same time, that his innovations are based on, and perfectly consistent with, the fundamental tenets of Stoic theory. Seneca's innovations in the Stoic analysis and therapy of the emotions thus provide a model of how a later Stoic might develop Stoic theory without any hint of heterodoxy.

Bibliography

Abel, Karlhans. 1967. *Bauformen in Senecas Dialogen: Fünf Strukturanalysen: Dial. 6, 11, 12, 1 und 2*. Heidelberg: Winter.
Abel, Karlhans. 1983. "Das Propatheia-Theorem: Ein Beitrag zur stoischen Affektenlehre." *Hermes* 111: 78–97.
Arpaly, Nomy. 2003. *Unprincipled Virtue: An Inquiry into Moral Agency*. Oxford: Oxford University Press.
Asmis, Elizabeth. 1984. *Epicurus' Scientific Method*. Ithaca: Cornell University Press.
Cooper, John M. 1998. "Posidonius on Emotions." In *The Emotions in Hellenistic Philosophy*, edited by Troels Engberg-Pedersen, and Juha Sihvola, 71–112. Dordrecht: Kluwer Academic Publishers. Also in John M. Cooper. *Reason and Emotion: Essays on Ancient Moral Psychology and Ethical Theory*, 449–484. Princeton: Princeton University Press, 1999.

Cooper, John M. 2004. "Moral Theory and Moral Improvement: Marcus Aurelius." In *Knowledge, Nature, and the Good: Essays on Ancient Philosophy*, 335–368. Princeton: Princeton University Press.
De Lacy, Phillip, ed. and trans. 1978. *Galen: On the Doctrines of Plato and Hippocrates*. Berlin: Akademie-Verlag. Rpt. 1984.
Epicurus. 1887. See Usener 1887.
Fillion-Lahille, Janine. 1984. *Le De ira de Sénèque et la philosophie stoïcienne des passions*. Paris: Klincksieck.
Galen. 1978. *On the Doctrines of Plato and Hippocrates*. See De Lacy 1978.
Gill, Christopher. 1998. "Did Galen Understand Platonic and Stoic Thinking on Emotions?" In *The Emotions in Hellenistic Philosophy*, edited by Troels Engberg-Pedersen and Juha Sihvola, 113–148. Dordrecht: Kluwer Academic Publishers.
Graver, Margaret. 1999. "Philo of Alexandria and the Origins of the Stoic προπάθειαι." *Phronesis* 44: 300–325.
Graver, Margaret R. 2001. "Managing Mental Pain: Epicurus vs. Aristippus on the Pre-Rehearsal of Future Ills." *Proceedings of the Boston Area Colloquium in Ancient Philosophy* 17: 155–177.
Graver, Margaret R. 2002. *Cicero on the Emotions: Tusculan Disputations 3 and 4*. Chicago: University of Chicago Press.
Graver, Margaret R. 2007. *Stoicism and Emotion*. Chicago: University of Chicago Press.
Grollios, Constantine C. 1956. *Seneca's Ad Marciam: Tradition and Originality*. Athens: G. S. Christou and Son.
Hadot, Ilsetraut. 1969. *Seneca und die griechisch-römische Tradition der Seelenleitung*. Berlin: De Gruyter.
Inwood, Brad. 2005. "The Will in Seneca." In *Reading Seneca: Stoic Philosophy at Rome*, 132–156. Oxford: Oxford University Press.
Kassel, Rudolf. 1958. *Untersuchungen zur griechischen und römischen Konsolationsliteratur*. München: Beck.
Kaster, Robert A., and Martha C. Nussbaum, trans. 2010. *Lucius Annaeus Seneca: Anger, Mercy, Revenge*. Chicago: University of Chicago Press.
Long, Anthony A., and David N. Sedley, eds. and trans. 1987. *The Hellenistic Philosophers*. 2 vols. Cambridge: Cambridge University Press.
Manning, Charles E. 1974. "The Consolatory Tradition and Seneca's Attitude to the Emotions." *G&R* 4: 71–81.
Manning, Charles E. 1981. *On Seneca's Ad Marciam*. Leiden: Brill.
Marino, Patricia. 2008. "On Essentially Conflicting Desires." *PhilosQ* 59: 274–291.
Powell, Jonathan G. F., ed. 1995. *Cicero the Philosopher*. Oxford: Oxford University Press.
Reynolds, Leighton D., ed. 1965. *L. Annaei Senecae Ad Lucilium epistulae morales*. Oxford: Clarendon Press.
Reynolds, Leighton D., ed. 1977. *L. Annaei Senecae: Dialogorum libri duodecim*. Oxford: Clarendon Press. Rpt. with corrections 1988.
Seneca. 1965. *Ad Lucilium epistulae Morales*. See Reynolds 1965.
Seneca. 1977. *Dialogorum libri duodecim*. See Reynolds 1977.
Seneca. 2007. *De ira – Über die Wut*. See Wildberger 2007.
Seneca. 2010. *Anger, Mercy, Revenge*. See Kaster and Nussbaum 2010.
Sorabji, Richard. 2000. *Emotion and Peace of Mind: From Stoic Agitation to Christian Temptation*. Oxford; New York: Oxford University Press.
Tieleman, Teun. 2003. *Chrysippus' On Affections: Reconstruction and Interpretation*. Leiden; Boston: Brill.
Usener, Hermann, ed. 1887. *Epicurea*. Leipzig: Teubner.

Vogt, Katja M. 2006. "Anger, Present Injustice and Future Revenge in Seneca's *De Ira*." In *Seeing Seneca Whole: Perspectives on Philosophy Poetry and Politics*, edited by Katharina Volk and Gareth D. Williams, 57–74. Leiden: Brill.

White, Stephen A. 1995. "Cicero and the Therapists." In *Cicero the Philosopher*, edited by Jonathan G. F. Powell, 219–246. Oxford: Oxford University Press.

Wildberger, Jula, ed. and trans. 2007. *Seneca, De ira – Über die Wut: Lateinisch/ Deutsch*. Stuttgart: Philipp Reclam.

Double Vision and Cross-Reading in Seneca's *Epistulae Morales* and *Naturales Quaestiones*

Gareth D. Williams
Columbia University

Gaius Lucilius Iunior, Seneca's cherished friend,[1] is the addressee of a single Senecan dialogue, *De providentia*, and of those two major works, the *Epistulae morales* and the *Naturales quaestiones*; the lost *Libri moralis philosophiae* may also have been addressed to him, and possibly the *De amicitia* and *Exhortationes* as well.[2] The dating of *De providentia* is disputed in modern scholarship, but the case for its composition in the last years of Seneca's life, after his *de facto* retirement from the Neronian court in or around 62 CE, has recently been powerfully restated.[3] The *Libri moralis philosophiae*, doubtless a late work, has been plausibly dated to between October 64 and April 65;[4] and both the *Epistulae morales* and *Naturales quaestiones* clearly belong to the retirement phase in and after 62. As we shall see, no precise relative chronology for the latter two works can be established with confidence, and their chronological relationship to *De providentia* raises difficulties of its own.[5] Yet, despite these challenges, my goal in this study is to explore in an experimental way the possible thematic and therapeutic interrelationship of the *Epistulae morales* and the

---

1   For whom see PIR^2 vol. 5.1, pp. 103–104, no. 388 with Delatte 1935 and Grimal 1980; succinctly, Griffin 1992, 91 and 94 with Vottero 1989, 21–24 and now Lanzarone 2008, 18–20. – I am grateful to Jula Wildberger for her insights and advice on many points. All translations are my own.
2   See Vottero 1998a, 40–41, 63 and 75.
3   See Grilli 2000, especially 270–273, with Lanzarone 2008, 13–18, and cf. n. 5 below; the case for dating *Prov.* to Seneca's Corsican exile in 41–49 CE (for summary, Lanzarone 2008, 13 and n. 3) is now surely overridden.
4   See Vottero 1998a, 72 with n. 335; further on the problematic relation of the *Libri* to the *Epistulae morales* and *Naturales quaestiones*, section IV (p. 158) below.
5   See now Lanzarone 2008, 14–18, especially 16 (*Prov.* later than *Nat.* 2.46 but prior to *Ep.* 106). I take Book 2 to be last in the original ordering of the *Naturales quaestiones* (see p. 138 and n. 14), and *Prov.* to postdate both *Naturales quaestiones* 2 and the great majority of the *Epistulae*. Given this late dating, I exclude *Prov.* from my ensuing discussion of what I assert to be the tight contemporaneous and conceptual relationship of the *Epistulae* and *Naturales quaestiones*.

Naturales quaestiones.⁶ The developmental strategies that characterize the *Epistulae morales* in particular as a dynamic philosophical exercise have long been recognized;⁷ but to what extent is that exercise complicated, or perhaps enriched, when set alongside the *Naturales quaestiones*? To what extent can the two works be read – *are* they to be read – as complementary constructions which simultaneously, in the process of their gradual co-production, draw Lucilius along different but related, and perhaps carefully coordinated, paths of philosophical enquiry?⁸ How is our experience of either work affected by our reading of each in combination with, and in light of, the other? In comparison with the relatively neglected *Naturales quaestiones*,⁹ the *Epistulae morales* have drawn considerable attention in modern scholarship: What, perhaps, is lost in our appreciation of either work, and of their combinational meaning, through this imbalance of scholarly coverage, and through the (too) easy perception of these works as both thematically and generically discrete and separable entities?

We begin in section I below by revisiting the relative chronology of the *Epistulae morales* and *Naturales quaestiones*, in an effort to establish a foundation for my subsequent analysis of contact and cross-fertilization between the two works. In section II I offer a preliminary overview of thematic overlap and linkage across the works – what might be called "surface correlation" between them. We then turn in section III to the deeper correlation which is my main concern in this study: Seneca's cultivation of different therapeutic strategies which bear a striking resemblance to certain

---

6 I nevertheless remain acutely conscious of the dangers of underestimating the philosophical depth of the *Epistulae* in particular by focusing here primarily on the therapeutic angle; see now the important corrective offered by Inwood 2007, xvi–xviii, especially xvii: "[...] in approaching Seneca's letters philosophically, it is surely a mistake to take it for granted that the author's central motivation is to play the role of moral or 'spiritual' guide for his readers."

7 See for this approach, e.g., Maurach 1970 and Hachmann 1995.

8 My approach is in part provoked by Schafer 2011: "It is important to point out that treating the *Letters* as the self-contained story of Lucilius is potentially dangerous, since he also appears [...] as the addressee of Seneca's *Quaestiones naturales* and *De prouidentia* [...] Nonetheless, I think it both necessary and safe to restrict our study to the *Letters* alone. Necessary, because we have no way to fix the dramatic chronology of the *QNat.* and *De prouidentia* relative to the *Letters* [...] And safe, because little would be added to the picture presented in the *Letters* even if we could integrate the other two works" (38 n. 22). While the works' chronological relationship *is* clearly vexed, and while Schafer rightly stresses the need for caution, there remains scope for experimentation, I argue, from the following starting-point: what might be lost to the picture presented of Lucilius in the *Epistulae unless* we take an integrated approach at least to the *Epistulae* and *Naturales quaestiones* (to leave aside *De providentia*; cf. n. 5 above)?

9 But see now the important bibliographical survey in Hine 2009 and 2010a.

techniques of modern cognitive-behavioral therapy (CBT) and which characterize the *Epistulae morales* and *Naturales quaestiones* as related movements within his overall stream of communication with Lucilius. The unifying approach taken here to only two of Seneca's philosophical works is hardly meant to suggest that the *Epistulae morales* and *Naturales quaestiones* are disconnected from the larger ethical and therapeutic agenda extending across his prose corpus; but their chronological compatibility and their oneness of addressee confer on them, I argue, a specialness of relationship within that larger agenda. Finally, in section IV, we move beyond this vision of the *Epistulae morales* and *Naturales quaestiones* as complementary works to the proposal that the two in a sense *complete* each other as interdependent conceptual experiments; and signs of self-conscious Senecan commentary on their binary relationship are tentatively traced, in closing, to the preface to *Naturales quaestiones* 1.

Two caveats remain to be registered at this point. First, in arguing for the interrelationship of the *Epistulae morales* and *Naturales quaestiones* as complementary aspects of Seneca's larger therapeutic agenda, I seek to sketch only the outlines – the topography of the interlocking parts, as it were – of that agenda, rather than to focus in depth on the substance, functionality, and efficacy of the therapy itself. Given this emphasis on form, not content, assessment of the rationally-based value of Senecan therapy remains, at least for present purposes, a separate issue. Secondly, in weighing the relative dates, dramatic as well as actual, of the *Epistulae morales* and *Naturales quaestiones* in section I below, I accept that Seneca's *conversio ad se*, his inner turning, as portrayed in both works plausibly reflects the biographical fact of his withdrawal from the Neronian court in and after 62 CE. For present purposes, however, the relative chronology of the works that is sketched below makes no bold claim to, and no assumption about, biographical factuality beyond this withdrawal in 62. The chronology that primarily concerns us here is in any case not the real, extra-textual and now largely irrecoverable timetable of the works' literal formation but the projected chronology of the two works as loosely contemporaneous productions (I elaborate on this loose mode of contemporaneity at the end of section I below). The point is important because of my allusions later in this study to the fictionality of the *Epistulae morales*, and yet also to Senecan sincerity both in that work and in the *Naturales quaestiones*. By that fictionality I mean simply my acceptance that the *Epistulae*, at least as we have them, hardly constitute one side of a literal and real correspondence;[10] by that sincerity, I hardly mean Senecan self-revelation of a demonstrably

---

10 On this issue, see n. 13 below.

authentic, autobiographical kind, but his contrived projection of a candid, undisguised and plain-speaking self – in short, a sincere persona.

I.

The dates, dramatic or actual, of neither the *Epistulae morales* nor the *Naturales quaestiones* can be fixed precisely enough to determine the exact chronological relationship of the two works. Seneca's report in *Ep.* 91 of the destruction of Lugdunum (modern Lyon) by fire – a disaster which can be plausibly dated to the late summer or early autumn of 64 CE[11] – offers one marker for the dramatic date of the *Epistulae morales*, while various allusions to the different months and to seasonal change (December in 18.1; spring in 23.1; spring in 67.1; late June in 86.16; summer in 87.4; days growing shorter in 122.1) offer further clues. Of the two time-frames suggested by these markers, winter 62 to autumn 64 or winter 63 to autumn 64, Miriam Griffin plausibly favors the latter,[12] assigning the *Epistulae* as follows: 1–18, autumn to December 63; 19–23, December 63 to early spring 64; 24–67, early to late spring 64; 68–86, later spring to the end of June 64; 87–91, the end of July to the fire at Lugdunum; 92–122, late summer to autumn 64; 123–24, autumn 64 to before Seneca's death in April 65.[13] This scheme is tentative, caution is necessary, but to speculate further: How compatible is Griffin's scheme with what we might infer about the timeline of the *Naturales quaestiones*?

If we accept the persuasive case for an original ordering of the books of the *Naturales quaestiones* in the sequence 3, 4a, 4b, 5, 6, 7, 1 and 2,[14]

---

11 See Decourt and Lucas 1993, 43 with Viti 1997, 400–402; the fire of Seneca's letter is surely to be identified with the *clades Lugdunensis* which in Tacitus (*Ann.* 16.13.3) postdates the fire in Rome of July 64.

12 Griffin 1992, 400, finding in Abel 1967, 168: "another strong argument against the longer (62–4) chronology."

13 Griffin 1992, 400, but cf. already for this scheme Bourgery 1911, 42. Allowance is also to be made for Seneca's composition of at least two more books of *Epistulae* "after the autumn of 64, the dramatic date of the last extant ones" (Griffin, 418, citing Gel. 12.2.3). I take it that the mild winter and harsh spring of *Ep.* 23.1 belong to 63 into 64, and that the same spring of 64 is "rounding into summer" at *Ep.* 67.1 ("iam inclinatum [sc. ver] in aestatem"), albeit "often sliding back into winter weather." Elsewhere in the *Epistulae* Seneca's improbable rapidity of composition offers one argument for the letters' fictionality (on which see Griffin 1992, 416–419 and 519 with update in Schafer 2011, 34 and n. 11, 47 and n. 47); the long textual distance but short temporal space between *Ep.* 23 and 67 (both spring 64) hardly undermine the case for fictionality.

14 First proposed independently by Carmen Codoñer Merino and Harry Hine: see Codoñer Merino 1979, vol. 1, xii–xxi; Hine 1981, 6–19, especially 16–17, and

then two important temporal coordinates for the work are found in Books 6 and 7.[15] At 6.1.2 the transmitted text has it that Pompeii was devastated by an earthquake on "February 5th in the consulship of Regulus and Verginius" ("Nonis Februariis [...] Regulo et Verginio consulibus"), i.e. in the year 63 – a claim at variance with Tacitus' report (*Ann.* 15.22.2) that Pompeii was destroyed in 62. Given Seneca's insistence (6.1.2) that Campania had suffered no major earthquake prior to that described in Book 6, there cannot have been two occurrences in consecutive years, the Tacitean one in 62, the Senecan one in 63. The two accounts are reconciled, however, if the phrase *Regulo et Verginio consulibus* is adjudged an interpolation at 6.1.2 and the Senecan earthquake reassigned to 62,[16] in which case Book 6 has a *terminus post quem* of February 62. Then, in Book 7, Seneca mentions the Neronian comet of 60[17] – but he makes no allusion to that of May-July (or autumn?) 64:[18] His silence on the latter comet indicates for Book 7 a *terminus ante quem* of mid-64. In the preface to Book 3 Seneca portrays himself as newly liberated as he embarks on his daunting task of world-investigation in the *Naturales quaestiones*:

> Old age presses hard at my back and rebukes me for the years spent amid empty pursuits. But let us strive all the more, and let hard work make good the losses of my ill-spent life. Add night to day, cut back my other involvements, give up all concern for family estates that lie far from their owner; let the mind be entirely free for itself, and at the very end at least look back in contemplation of itself. (Sen. *Nat.* 3 pr. 2)

Again, caveats are in order before the authorial ego here is straightforwardly identified with the "real" Seneca in withdrawal from the Neronian court in and after 62:[19] The detachment portrayed in 3 pr. 2 conceivably portrays an idealized vision of release regardless of Seneca's biographical circumstances at the time of writing; and, as Harry Hine points out, we should in

---

1996, xxiv. For acceptance of this ordering, see, e.g., Parroni 2002, xlix; Gauly 2004, 66–67: Limburg 2007, 11–12; and Williams 2012, 13–14. For assembled bibliography on the whole question, see Hine 2010a, 28–31.

15 On these coordinates within broader discussion of the dating of the *Naturales quaestiones*, Vottero 1989, 20–21 and Gauly 2004, 21–28 with Hine 2006, 42 and n. 1 and 68–72.

16 See Hine 1984 with Vottero 1989, 178–179 and Gauly 2004, 22–24. Wallace-Hadrill 2003 nevertheless inclines to 63 for the Senecan earthquake, but see now Hine 2006, 68–72 for a judicious reevaluation of the whole question, with 62 still his cautious preference (cf. also 2010b, 194 n. 13 and 203 n. 1).

17 *Nat.* 7.6.1, 7.17.2, 7.21.3–4, 7.23.1, 7.28.3, 7.29.2–3.

18 For the former comet, Ramsey 2006, 140–146 and 2007, 181; for the latter, Ramsey 2006, 146–148 and 2007, 181.

19 See p. 137 above, and cf. Gauly 2004, 20; for the point extending to the *Epistulae*, Griffin 1992, 347: "[...] the 'you' and the 'I' of the Letters cannot always be assumed to be biographical."

any case perhaps "not be too fixated on Tacitus' account of the interview between Seneca and Nero in A.D. 62 [*Ann.* 14.52–56] as a turning point, for the change in Seneca's influence and standing in the court, and in the balance he struck between court duties and philosophy, may have been more gradual."[20] Yet if we accept that the *conversio ad se* announced in the preface to *Naturales quaestiones* 3 is biographically real (could Seneca afford to strike such a pose before a knowing Roman readership in the early 60s CE *unless* appearances at least approximated to reality?), then it remains tempting to assign *Naturales quaestiones* 3 to 62, and – given the temporal markers we have considered in Books 6 and 7 – to speculate that the work as a whole was already at an advanced stage of progress by the end of 63/early 64.

Certain topical allusions and thematic overlaps arguably shed further light on the relative chronology of the *Epistulae morales* and the *Naturales quaestiones*. In apparently calling for Lucilius to withdraw from the world (*Ep.* 8.1) and into himself (*Ep.* 7.8), Seneca would seem to apply early in the *Epistulae* a central tenet of his own new self-positioning in the preface to *Naturales quaestiones* 3.[21] In *Ep.* 14 Lucilius is already in Sicily (14.8: "When you traveled to Sicily, you crossed the straights"), installed in his new position as procurator there after years of varied military service outside Italy (cf. *Ep.* 31.9). When Seneca wrote *Naturales quaestiones* 4a the procuratorship was "recent but not brand new:"[22] If Lucilius was appointed in 62,[23] and if we hold to an original ordering of 3, 4a, 4b etc. for the *Naturales quaestiones*, Book 4a would follow Book 3 in 62/63 while also being chronologically compatible with *Ep.* 14, which Griffin's scheme locates in late 63.[24] In the proem Seneca writes as follows to Lucilius in Sicily:

> So one must flee the world and withdraw into oneself; or even withdraw from oneself. Even though we are separated by the sea, I shall try to perform this service for you: I shall take hold of you and lead you to better things. And so that you feel no loneliness, I shall join in conversation with you from here. We shall be together in the best part of ourselves [sc. in the mind]; we shall give each other advice that will not depend on the listener's expression. (Sen. *Nat.* 4a pr. 20)

For Louis Delatte, the correspondence that Seneca foreshadows here is reflected in the one-sided *Epistulae*;[25] on this (overly?) literalist line of

---

20 Hine 2006, 71; cf. 2010b, 10.
21 Further, Delatte 1935, 567.
22 Griffin 1992, 91 n. 4. For this procuratorship as in fact "not a very important post," Griffin 350 n. 2; it is facetiously styled a mere *procuratiuncula* at *Ep.* 31.9.
23 So inclines Grimal 1980, 1176; cf. Griffin 1992, 91: "probably about 62."
24 See p. 138 above; for dramatic injection in *Ep.* 14, cf. Henderson 2004, 31: "*Letter* 14 at once lives a little through Lucilius: off to Sicily."
25 Delatte 1935, 568.

argument, the collection would seem to have to be later than *Naturales quaestiones* 4a.²⁶ Then, if *Naturales quaestiones* 1 is taken to be the penultimate book of the original collection, Lucilius is given a frank assessment of his philosophical progress thus far:

> Have you escaped moral vices? You do not present a false front, you do not shape your speech to suit someone else's purpose, and your feelings are not hidden; you do not have greed, which denies to itself what it has taken from everyone else, nor luxury, which squanders money shamefully only to get it back still more shamefully, nor ambition, which will lead you to high status only through distasteful means? You have not yet achieved anything: You have escaped many evils, but not yet escaped yourself. (Sen. *Nat.* 1 pr. 6)

In this book, in effect the seventh in the extant collection, Lucilius has made limited progress and still has far to go on his continuing philosophical journey. If *Naturales quaestiones* 1 is tentatively assigned to late(r) 63, the *Epistulae* as represented in Griffin's chronological scheme have still not progressed far (*Ep.* 1–18 by December 63).²⁷ Could the blunt appraisal of Lucilius' development at *Nat.* 1 pr. 6 reflect the relative newness of Seneca's correspondence course of treatment in the *Epistulae*?

On the approach taken thus far, then, Seneca appears to have embarked on the *Naturales quaestiones* prior to the *Epistulae morales*, and both works only partially overlap in time if, on the basis of the scattered hints and clues reviewed above, we tentatively posit an arc of 62 to late 63/early 64 for the former, an arc of 63 to (at least) late 64 for the latter. In the strict sense, they hardly qualify as contemporaneous productions, gradually unfolding together over exactly the same span of time. But a looser vision of contemporaneity nevertheless vindicates the comparative approach taken to the *Epistulae morales* and the *Naturales quaestiones* in what follows. Writing of "career criticism" as "a distinct branch of [modern] literary scholarship and criticism," Philip Hardie and Helen Moore define the phenomenon thus:

---

26 But Lucilius is *already* in Sicily by *Ep.* 14 (cf. 14.8); could it be that Seneca embarked on the *Epistulae* before Lucilius departed for Sicily, and that 4a pr. 20 foreshadows the correspondence that flows only after Sicily enters the picture in *Ep.* 14? Delatte 1935, 568–570 circumvents the problem by locating Book 4a firmly in 62 – an early date that (all too) conveniently ensures that "la préface de IVa nous donne un état des relations de Sénèque avec Lucilius *antérieur à celui de la correspondance*" (570; my emphasis).

27 For Griffin's scheme, p. 138. above. On 1 pr. 6 in chronological relation to the *Epistulae*, cf. Delatte 1935, 569, noting that "la conversion de Lucilius est chose faite après la lettre 68," i.e., late spring/early summer 64 according to Griffin's scheme (on the pivotal significance of *Ep.* 68 as a marker of Lucilius' progress, cf. Schafer 2011, 38, 39).

> Instead of starting from what might be known, or claimed, about the historical life and times of an author, *career criticism takes as its starting point the totality of an author's textual output and asks how that oeuvre as a whole shapes itself*, both in its intratextual relationships (what kinds of beginnings, middles, and ends are traced in the pattern of an oeuvre), and in the claims it makes to reflect or mould extratextual conditions of production (whether located in the personal history of the author, or in the relationship of the author to political and cultural structures of power and authority). (Hardie and Moore 2010, 1; my emphasis)

In focusing on "[a]n author's sense of his or her literary career" as "traced through statements or hints, explicit or implicit, in an oeuvre that point to a developmental relationship between the individual works in the oeuvre" (2), Hardie and Moore approach the career-criticism theme with an emphasis different from my own. Whereas they prioritize authorial awareness of the career in its totality, my own focus is limited to the totality *only* of the *Epistulae morales* and the *Naturales quaestiones* – a phase demarcated within the larger Senecan career partly by extratextual conditions (his withdrawal from the Neronian court in or around 62), partly by intratextual congruence (Seneca's recurrent emphasis in both the *Epistulae morales* and the *Naturales quaestiones* on inner withdrawal and on his own decisive *conversio ad se* late in life). In effect, the two works may not be contemporaneous in the strict sense; but from the larger perspective of the post-retirement viewpoint after 62 – from a retrospect that, to adapt Hardie and Moore's phrasing, asks *how the post-62 oeuvre as a whole shapes itself* – they constitute a merged totality, a single chronological movement between, let us broadly agree, 62 and 64.

II.

What precisely is gained by a combinational reading of the *Epistulae morales* and the *Naturales quaestiones*? Both works can evidently stand alone, and they are conventionally treated separately in modern criticism: What benefit accrues from reading them with and against each other? Before we address these questions in earnest in section III below, an initial answer is supplied by the thematic commonalities that link the two works in a superficial way – commonalities of a more idiosyncratic kind than the familiar topics and emphases (e.g., Seneca on friendship, Seneca on the value of time, etc.) that recur across the Senecan prose corpus more generally. True, quite apart from their obvious differences in subject-matter, the *Epistulae morales* and the *Naturales quaestiones* also show other significant divergences, not least in Seneca's characterization of Lucilius in the two works: As Miriam Griffin points out, in *Naturales quaestiones* 4a pr. 1 Lucilius "is *ambitioni alienus*, but in *Ep.* 19–22 he has to be cured of ambition."[28] At 4a pr. 14 he is said to have rejected profitable career options to devote himself instead to literature and philosophy, but in the *Epistulae morales* he appears more driven by gain and less ready to make sacrifices for the philosophical life: "I don't yet have enough: When I've reached the desired amount, then I shall devote myself completely to philosophy" (17.5). Of course, Lucilius' shifting characterization in the *Epistulae morales* and the *Naturales quaestiones* might be attributed, at least in part, to differences of agenda and dramatic positioning in the two works. After all, Lucilius "is given a spiritual development of incredible rapidity" in the *Epistulae*,[29] a feature absent in the *Naturales quaestiones*, and one that contributes to "the synthetic quality of Lucilius' character and problems" that Griffin discerns more broadly in the *Epistulae*.[30] Yet despite these points of difference, the *Epistulae morales* and the *Naturales quaestiones* remain mutually illuminating in their special forms of "surface correlation," four of which may be sampled as follows:

[1] Before investigating the cause of the Nile's summer flooding in the main body of *Naturales quaestiones* 4a, Seneca prefaces the book with a lengthy address to Lucilius on the dangers of flattery – dangers to which he, as procurator of Sicily, is now said to be especially exposed (4a pr. 3–6). Exceptionally in the *Naturales quaestiones*, this preface immediately surprises by its likeness to the letter-form of the *Epistulae*:[31] "To judge from what you write (*quemadmodum scribis*), my excellent Lucilius, you are delighted with Sicily, and with the duties of a procuratorship that gives you time for leisure […]" (4a pr. 1). The book thus begins as if it were part of an ongoing correspondence, or as an appendix or extension to the *Epistulae morales*, even though at the end of the preface all pretense to epistolary form disappears in the transition that Seneca makes to the main body of Book 4a (4a.1.1: "[…] with you I shall investigate why the Nile floods as it does in the summer months, a topic I postponed in the previous book").[32] Why the epistolary appearance to the opening of *this* as opposed to any other book of the *Naturales quaestiones*? Perhaps the positioning of the epistolary preface is innocent enough, an affectation that Seneca simply chooses to deploy relatively early in the new work. But if we allow for a

---

28 Griffin 1992, 350 n. 3 after Gercke 1895, 326–327; cf. also 1 pr. 6 for Lucilius' apparent lack of *ambitio*.
29 Griffin 1992, 351; cf. 353. For this rapidity pointing to the fictionality of the *Epistulae*, cf. n. 13 above.
30 Griffin 1992, 350.
31 For the surprise element, Codoñer 1989, 1812; further on the epistolary aspect, Gauly 2004, 210–211 after Gross 1989, 150.
32 On this transition, Codoñer 1989, 1812; for the allusion to the previous book, cf. 3.1.2, 26.1.

shrewder intervention here, the contrasting circumstances of author and addressee, Seneca and Lucilius, in the prefaces to Books 3 and 4a suggest a more complex motive for the epistoliterarity[33] of Book 4a.

As we saw earlier (p. 139), the authorial "I" portrayed in the preface to Book 3 is that of a Seneca newly released in advancing age from the commitments and entanglements of official life; he embarks on his new project of "surveying the universe" (3 pr. 1: "mundum circumire") with an uncompromising urgency given the relatively little time he has left (cf. again 3 pr. 2: "Old age presses hard at my back and rebukes me for the years spent amid empty pursuits [...]"). Whatever his actual physical location, whether Rome, his estate at Nomentum,[34] or elsewhere, this Seneca is simultaneously in a different space, a cosmic voyager whose liberated mind (*animus*) "has sought the heights and entered the inner recesses of nature" (1 pr. 7).[35] Juxtaposed with this vision of release, the preface to Book 4a is all too confining, returning us via Lucilius' Sicilian procuratorship to the besieged life of duty (*officium*) and all "the bustle of people and events" (4a pr. 1: "turbam rerum hominumque"). The sincerity of Seneca's engagement with nature now gives way to the unnatural *in*sincerity of all the flatterers to whom Lucilius is apparently exposed on all sides in Sicily.

On this approach, the exhilaration of release in the preface to Book 3 is powerfully underscored by contrast with the suffocating atmosphere of the preface to Book 4a; and as we gradually progress with Seneca to the investigation of (e.g.) earthquakes, the winds, and remote cometary orbits later in the *Naturales quaestiones*, the epistoliterarity of Book 4a takes on a renewed significance in retrospect. After Seneca's allusions to Sicily in Book 4a, the island is mentioned only twice further in the entire *Naturales quaestiones*, at 6.8.2 and 6.30.3,[36] and no reference is made in either case to Lucilius' role there; after Book 4a, there is no further allusion to Lucilius as procurator anywhere in the 3, 4a, 4b, etc., ordering. As we look back on Lucilius in Sicily from the liberated vantage-point of Seneca's unfolding cosmic travels later in the *Naturales quaestiones*, the specifics of place, the significance of localized history (cf. 4a pr. 21–22 on the momentous military campaigns Sicily has witnessed) and Lucilius' status as procurator recede ever further into the distance, their importance reduced before our expanding, universalist viewpoint. Hence, perhaps, the notable placement of an epistolary preface at the opening of the work's *second* book: Given

---

33 Henderson's apposite term: 2004, 4, 29, 45 and 91.
34 Cf. *Ep.* 104.1; 110.1.
35 For the approach, cf. Williams 2012, especially 113–116, 289–294.
36 In addition, the adjective *Siculus* occurs in a quotation of Verg. *Aen.* 3.414–419 at 6.30.1. Down to Book 4a *Sicilia* occurs at 3.25.5 and 26.5, *Siculus* at 3.1.1 (in a quotation of Lucilius' poetry, *Frg.* 4 Courtney 1993, 348–349) and 29.7.

the way in which Seneca stretches ordinary spatial co-ordinates in the ambitious mind-travels of the *Naturales quaestiones* as a whole, the mundane mechanics of letter-exchange at ground level are pointedly left behind at an early stage in the proceedings. And, to re-invoke the contemporaneity of the *Epistulae morales* and the *Naturales quaestiones*, the jettisoning of the epistolary affectation after Book 4a symbolically distances the two works at an early separation-point, as if Seneca's ambitious world-tour in the *Naturales quaestiones* (cf. again "mundum circumire" at 3 pr. 1) presupposes a breadth of communicational reach, a cosmopolitanism, that far transcends the spatial dynamics of "ordinary" letter-dispatch and -delivery in the *Epistulae*.

[2] The *Epistulae morales* and *Naturales quaestiones* show striking overlaps of particular theme and preoccupation; the following are but three examples of a larger phenomenon. First, in *Ep*. 79 Seneca writes in these terms to Lucilius, who is still in Sicily:

> I've been awaiting a letter from you, so that you might inform me of what new information was revealed to you during your trip round Sicily, and especially that you might inform me further about Charybdis itself. [...] If you'll write to me fully on these matters, I shall then have the boldness to give you another task – also to climb Etna at my special request, [...] But let us postpone this discussion [sc. on reports that Etna was slowly diminishing in height] and inquire into the matter when you've written to tell me just how far distant the snow lies from the crater – the snow, I mean, which is so safe from the adjacent fire that it does not melt even in summer. (Sen. *Ep*. 79.1, 2, 4)

Beyond evoking "the tone of the *Nat. Quaest.*" in point of detail,[37] Seneca's interest here in Etna[38] and its snows suggestively coincides with his investigations into snow and hail in *Naturales quaestiones* 4b, his allusions to Etna and volcanology in Book 2 (2.26.4–6; 2.30.1), and his inquiries into seismology in Book 6. It is as if the two works momentarily converge in *Ep*. 79[39] before Seneca veers away from his physical probings (79.4), shifting his focus from the summit of Etna to the summit of wisdom and virtue (cf. especially 79.10–12), and thereby setting the *Epistulae* back on its main ethical course. Secondly, to dwell further on *Naturales quaestiones* 2 and 6: If the preface to Book 4a is epistolary in appearance, the concluding chapters of Books 2 and 6, both of them impassioned appeals to the familiar (Stoic) imperatives of reflection upon death (*meditatio mortis*)

---

37 Summers 1910, 271 on 79.1: "dignum est."
38 On this interest, Hyde 1916, 409–410, but his suggestion that Seneca authored the *Aetna* poem can surely be discounted; see Goodyear 1965, 56–59 and 1984, especially 348–353, with Taub 2008, 31–33, 45 and now Garani 2009, 103 n. 2.
39 Albeit *Ep*. 79, written between spring and late June 64 according to Griffin's scheme (see p. 138 above), is surely later than *Nat*. 4b, which I take to be third in the original ordering of the books (see p. 138 above and n. 14).

and the scorning of it,[40] show close affinities to many similar refrains in the *Epistulae*.[41] The ideas of course infiltrate his earlier philosophical prose,[42] but the urgency that impels Seneca *senex*, that "old man,"[43] as he contemplates life's fast approaching finish-line[44] does much to explain their marked frequency in the *Epistulae morales* and *Naturales quaestiones* in particular.

Thirdly, the *meditatio mortis* theme notably recurs in *Ep.* 91,[45] on the burning of Lugdunum in 64 CE.[46] In that letter Seneca reports to Lucilius that "our friend Liberalis[47] is now in a mood of mourning" after learning of the disaster that has befallen the city he loves (91.1). Hence the consolatory content of the letter: The techniques of consolation that Seneca describes and deploys earlier in the missive have apparently already been tried on Liberalis.[48] Basic to these techniques is that of amplification before reduction:[49] Far from trying to understate or minimize the scale of the disaster, Seneca begins by portraying it as a catastrophe of singular proportions (91.1: "sine exemplo"); many cities had hitherto been damaged by fire, he asserts, but none annihilated on the scale of Lugdunum (91.1), that place of singular distinction (91.2: "pride of Gaul"). The frequent use of intensifiers (*tam, tot, tantus* at 91.1–2), the suddenness of the disaster (91.2: "A single night elapsed between the city at its greatest and its reduction to nothing"), and evocations of the fall of Troy all contribute[50] to the dramatic inflation of an event whose magnitude in the Senecan letter finds, perhaps tellingly, no corroboration elsewhere in the historical or archaeological record.[51] After this amplification, the catastrophe is gradually "normalized" through techniques that contextualize it within an alleviating inventory of similar disasters over time, so that Lugdunum is ultimately seen to conform to the general rule that cities "stand but to fall" (91.12).

---

40 For this Senecan preoccupation, Lanzarone 2008, 186–187 on *Prov.* 2.10: "diu meditatum opus" with Noyes 1973, especially 229–232, and Armisen-Marchetti 1986, especially 189–190.
41 4.3; 24.11–14; 26.8–10; 30.5–11; 36.8; 69.6; 70.17, etc.
42 So, e.g., *De ira* 3.42.2–4; *Tranq. an.* 11.6; *Helv.* 13.2.
43 For the Seneca/*senex* play, cf. *Nat.* 3 pr. 1 – in nice contrast to his addressee, Lucilius *Iunior* (see Ker 2009, 13, 105, 153).
44 Cf. *Nat.* 3 pr. 2; *Ep.* 49.4: "admoveri lineas sentio."
45 See Armisen-Marchetti 1986, 188–189, and cf. Hadot 1969, 60 and n. 119.
46 Date: p. 138 above and n. 11.
47 Presumably the dedicatee of *De beneficiis*: see Griffin 1992, 254, 455–56 with Viti 1997, 397–399.
48 91.13: "Haec ergo atque eiusmodi solacia admoveo Liberali nostro."
49 On this technique, Armisen-Marchetti 1986, 189 and now Limburg 2007, 306–309 with Williams 2012, 215–219.
50 As Viti 1997, 404–405 well observes.
51 See Viti 1997, 403–404 with Bedon 1991.

This consolatory technique of maximization before reduction finds various Senecan parallels and variations before the *Epistulae*,[52] but the closest *comparandum* for his approach in *Ep.* 91 is found in *Naturales quaestiones* 6, on earthquakes. There, apparently writing in response to news of Pompeii's destruction by earthquake in February 62,[53] Seneca again stresses the immensity of the disaster before singularity once more gives way to multiplicity and commonality: When we begin to locate the Pompeian catastrophe in the context of so many other disasters over time, it gradually becomes rationalized, for all its traumatic effects in the moment, as but a normative aspect of seismological functionality. For present purposes, the similar consolatory techniques that Seneca deploys in response to the different catastrophes at Pompeii in 62 and Lugdunum in 64 suggest the versatility of a *modus consolandi* that could potentially find so many other applications in the face of natural disaster or personal trauma. Here is another striking convergence of the *Epistulae morales* and the *Naturales quaestiones*; or, as James Ker puts it, "[the parallel with the Pompeian earthquake] gives us every reason [...] to see the present letter [sc. *Ep.* 91] as part of the same project of collective consolation as *Natural Questions* 6."[54]

[3] After his elaborate inquiries into the causation of earthquakes in *Naturales quaestiones* 6, Seneca suddenly changes direction at 6.32.1, turning from earth-disturbance to disturbance of mind:

> So much for these explanations, Lucilius, best of men. Now to those things which serve to reassure our minds; for it's more in our interest for our minds to become braver rather than more learned. But the one doesn't come without the other. The mind gains strength only from liberal studies and from contemplating nature.

Whereas in this case Seneca balances the claims of physical investigation and theoretical learning on the one hand, mental fortification and self-improvement on the other, his imaginary interlocutor elsewhere in the *Naturales quaestiones* shows more impatience. So at 4b.13.1:

> "Why," you say, "do you so painstakingly pursue these trivialities [sc. on the nature of snow and hail], which make a person more learned, not of better character? You tell us how snow is formed, though it's far more relevant to be told by you why snow shouldn't be bought." You bid me to fight it out in court with luxury? That dispute is waged daily, and to no effect. But let us nevertheless bring the case; even if luxury is going to win, let it defeat us while we are fighting and continuing the struggle.

Again, after his long disquisition on lightning and divination in Book 2, Seneca is finally prompted by an interlocutor to offer instead a lesson that

---

52 See notably *Helv.* 1–2 with Williams 2012, 216 and n. 16.
53 Date: p. 139 above and n. 16.
54 Ker 2009, 108.

focuses not on how lightning occurs, but on dispelling our fears of its dangers (2.59.1). Seneca duly obliges: "I follow your summons: For every topic, every conversation, should contain something that serves our well-being" (2.59.2: "aliquid salutare").[55]

In these three cases Seneca varies a familiar emphasis in the *Epistulae morales*. So at *Ep.* 65.15, after reporting on a debate in which he engaged with a group of friends on causation in nature (a debate ranging over the Stoic, Aristotelian, and Platonic positions), he envisages Lucilius' response to the proceedings: "What pleasure does it give you to waste your time on these problems, which strip you of none of the emotions and rid you of none of your desires?" In this instance, Seneca vindicates his approach by insisting that physical inquiries of the sort contested by Lucilius, "as long as they are not chopped up and dispersed into such profitless refinements (*subtilitatem inutilem*), raise up and lighten the soul, which is weighed down by a heavy burden and yearns to be freed and to return to the elements of which it was once a part" (65.16). Seneca's attack on this excessive metaphysical *subtilitas* here is itself part of a wider campaign that he wages in the *Epistulae* against philosophical "quibbling about words" and "sophistical argumentation that exercises the intellect to no purpose" (45.5).[56] In contrast to philosophical *supervacua* (cf. 106.11) of this sort, or the kinds of syllogistic intricacy characterized at 117.18 ("All such matters are in the vicinity of wisdom, not in wisdom itself. But our place should be in wisdom itself"), the truer task of learning is to relate knowledge to actual conduct and to character (89.18: "ad mores"); what matters is to discuss "a subject which is useful and beneficial to us" (113.26: "aliquid utile nobis ac salutare") and to ask "how we may attain the virtues and what path will take us in their direction" (113.26).[57]

Given this insistent emphasis in the *Epistulae* on self-improvement, those moments in the *Naturales quaestiones* when Seneca is challenged to derive "something beneficial" (2.59.2: "aliquid salutare") from his physical inquiries draw us into the dominant conceptual space, as it were, of the *Epistulae*. On this approach, the *Epistulae* function as a permanent sub- or

---

55 Cf. further 1 pr. 17 ("'quid tibi' inquis 'ista proderunt?'") with Berno 2003, 146–147; 211–213; 267.
56 On "Seneca's disdain for these arguments," now Schafer 2011, 50, but for important qualification, cf. Wildberger 2006, 143–152 for Seneca's apparently shifting attitude to such *subtilitas*; and see also Cooper 2006, 49–51, especially 50: "Seneca shows a willingness [...] to blur the line between overfascination with logic, or logical fallacies, and any proper study of them; and this seems clearly to reveal an inadequate and weak grasp of the real value for the moral life of the study of logic."
57 For these and other cognate passages, Hine 1981, 439 on *Nat.* 2.59.1 with Vottero 1989, 522 n. 1 on 4b.13.1 and Gauly 2004, 111–114.

paratext for the *Naturales quaestiones*, always exerting an implicit pressure on Seneca's physical investigations to remain pertinent to the ordinary experience of living. Or, to put the point differently, the moralizing dimension in the seemingly alien territory of his meteorological researches in the *Naturales quaestiones* is itself justified and explained, even *mandated*, by the imperative of moral relevance that is laid down by the *Epistulae*.

[4] The moralizing component of the *Naturales quaestiones* is also predicated on a central tension within the work – a tension discernible elsewhere in Seneca's philosophical prose, but especially visible in the *Epistulae morales*. While the investigative instinct strives in an enlightened direction in the *Naturales quaestiones*, seeking insight into nature's mysteries (cf. 1 pr. 3), the deviants condemned in Seneca's periodic bursts of moralizing outrage[58] offer a counterweight of sorts to the uplifting momentum of the work.[59] Senecan doxography contributes importantly to this widespread tension between immersion in nature on the one hand and immersion in vice on the other. In contrast to the deviant population that is strewn across the books, the many authorities whom Seneca draws on by name and whose theories he cites constitute a counter-population of savants across the ages, a "virtual academy"[60] loosely resembling the fellowship of the wise that he commends to Lucilius in the *Epistulae*:

> Change to better associations: Live with the Catos, with Laelius, with Tubero. But if you enjoy living with Greeks also, spend time with Socrates and with Zeno: [...] Live with Chrysippus, with Posidonius [...] (Sen. *Ep.* 104.21–22)[61]

Just as the deviants of the *Naturales quaestiones* constantly challenge our philosophical progress, as if a contagion always threatening to infect the vulnerable, so the crowd (*turba, multitudo, populus*, etc.)[62] in the *Epistulae* functions as a permanent source of danger: "To consort with the crowd is harmful; there is no one who doesn't make some vice attractive to us, or stamp it upon us, or taint us unconsciously with it."[63] Here the two works meet again: The deviants of the *Naturales quaestiones* are an implicit,

---

58 Cf. 3.17–18, 4b.13, 5.18, 7.31–32, 1.16.
59 For the approach, Williams 2012, 11–12, 55–56 and 87–89.
60 Hine 2006, 58.
61 For this keeping of company across the ages, all epochs open to the mind (*Ep.* 102.22), Wildberger 2006, 131–132 with 669 n. 669 and 671 n. 676. See also Wildberger 2010 for the elevated vision and "Big Talk" of 102.21–22 in tension with, and yet ultimately complementary to, syllogistic exactness and nicety of the sort portrayed in 120.20 (Wildberger interestingly relates the two tendencies to different aspects of Seneca's authorial self).
62 See on Seneca's "variations [...] to describe the general multitude" Richardson-Hay 2006, 253 on *Ep.* 7.2.
63 *Ep.* 7.2; cf. 32.2; 94.53–54; 103.1–2; 123.8–12. On "the motif of the 'crowd'," Reydams-Schils 2005, 111–113.

albeit larger-than-life, presence in the *turba* haunting the *Epistulae*, while the background noise that the cacophonous *turba* contributes to the *Epistulae* is matched by the equal importance of sound-effect in the *Naturales quaestiones*.[64] In the *Epistulae* Seneca exposes us to the racket of the bathhouse (*Ep*. 56.1), the racetrack (80.2: *stadium*), the games (83.7: *circenses*), the urban workshops (90.19), and so on: In the midst of this tumult, which is seemingly so antithetical to quiet contemplation (cf. 56.1), he portrays himself as impervious to the nuisance (56.3), his concentration firmly focused; for external noise makes no impact so long as reason (*ratio*) engenders quiet within the self (56.5–6). So in the *Naturales quaestiones* the world is engulfed by cataclysm (3.27–30), cloudbursts and whirlwinds rage (5.12–13), thunder explodes and lightning-bolts crash forth (2.17–20, 27–28), entrapped air roars underground (6.14–15, 17–18), and whole regions are split asunder by earthquake (6.30.2); yet *ratio* brings fortification against this intimidating cacophony (cf. 6.32.4), just as it counters all the tumult of the *Epistulae*. Here we find an alternative mode of amplification before reduction: Their prevailing soundtracks may differ, one more urban than the other, but both works are nevertheless closely related in promoting indifference to the vast noisiness which they simultaneously generate.

III.

Beyond these points of "surface correlation," the *Epistulae morales* and *Naturales quaestiones* are mutually implicating at a more fundamental level through the different but related therapeutic strategies that they deploy. For present purposes, the relatedness of these strategies is conveniently introduced through the loose but telling analogy supplied by modern cognitive-behavioral therapy (CBT). The behavioral and cognitive aspects of CBT are delineated as follows by Aaron Beck, one of the pioneering figures of CBT:

> Many of the techniques used by behavior therapists are aimed at the patient's overt behavior. He is directed to be more active, to approach situations he fears, and to be more assertive. Insofar as the patient's overt behavior is the target of the therapeutic maneuvers, *these methods could be labeled "behavioral"*. When the mode of action is analyzed, however, it is usefully explained in cognitive terms; that is, *its success depends on modifying the patient's interpretations of reality, his attitudes, and his expectations*. For lasting change to occur, the patient either

---

64 On the relative noisiness of the two works, already Vottero 1998b, especially 293–296.

corrects faulty concepts or acquires new concepts or techniques in areas in which he is deficient. (Beck 1976, 325–326; my emphasis)

The parallels to be drawn between these cognitive-behavioral elements and the therapeutic capacities of Hellenistic philosophy have long been recognized,[65] albeit with the qualification that

> such parallels do not necessarily reflect direct causal links. Of course CBT is embedded within a tradition of Western thought that has been influenced by a variety of broad intellectual developments, including the Hellenistic philosophies, the teachings of the Medieval Church, the Enlightenment, and so on. But this is a far cry from asserting that a specific historical philosophy underlies a specific modern school of psychotherapy. (Herbert 2004, 53)

Allowance also has to be made for the fact that the modern mental-health professions find no close analogue in antiquity.[66] And yet, duly cautioned, we nevertheless find striking similarities between CBT and Stoicism in particular,[67] especially in their "shared emphasis upon cognition (ideas, judgements, opinions, etc.) as both the cause and cure of emotional disturbance."[68] In his *The Philosophy of Cognitive-Behavioural Therapy (CBT): Stoic Philosophy as Rational and Cognitive Psychotherapy* (London, 2010), Donald Robertson usefully separates out key aspects of Stoic therapeutic technique, devoting chapters 7 to 13 of "Part II: The Stoic Armamentarium" to "Contemplation of the ideal sage" (135–150), "Stoic mindfulness of the 'here and now'" (151–168), "Self-analysis and disputation" (169–191), "Autosuggestion, premeditation, and retrospection" (193–206), "*Praemeditatio malorum* and mental rehearsal" (207–225), "Stoic fatalism, determinism, and acceptance" (227–247) and, finally, "The view from above and Stoic metaphysics" (249–259). In each case, Robertson directly compares CBT practice. For the ideal sage as role-model, for example, he cites the modern technique of "modeling" (148–149), which A. A. Lazarus conveniently defines thus: "Basically, modeling consists of learning by observation. The therapist serves as a model or provides

---

65 See, e.g., Montgomery 1993; Still and Dryden 1999; Reiss 2003; McGlinchey 2004; Moore Brookshire 2007; Robertson 2010, especially 39–49; and Olligschläger 2011. From the Classical side, essential foundations on which to base comparison with modern therapeutic approaches are laid by Foucault 1986; Nussbaum 1994; Hadot 1995 and 2002, 91–233; and Sorabji 2000.
66 See Gill 1985, especially 308: "[…] there is no class of persons whose profession corresponds exactly to that of modern psychiatrists and psychotherapists. To identify the nearest equivalents to modern psychotherapy, we need to look at the borders of certain ancient areas, the borders of religion and medicine, on the one hand, and of medicine and philosophy, on the other."
67 See, e.g., Montgomery 1993; Still and Dryden 1999; McGlinchey 2004; Moore Brookshire 2007; and especially Robertson 2005 and 2010.
68 Robertson 2010, 7; cf. 73–74.

[another] role model for a particular behavior the client is encouraged to imitate" (247). For Stoic attentiveness to the here and now, Robertson compares the "range of [CBT] interventions based upon 'mindfulness' meditation practices, particularly in the treatment of depression" (151). But while these chapters solidly reinforce the case that the Stoics practiced "just about every technique and method in the CBT arsenal,"[69] our immediate interest in Robertson's argument lies not just in its substance, but also in its arrangement.

In devoting a separate chapter to the view from above,[70] Robertson compares the Stoic application of this idea to modern "visualization technique," then to the technique of "enlarging perspective," and also to that of "distancing," whereby "the client alters their [sic] perspective on their current situation and thoughts in order to re-evaluate them more objectively, 'from a distance'."[71] In the context of "Part II: The Stoic Armamentarium", this section, chapter 13, is positioned as only one of a battery of techniques, all of which are available to patient and practitioner according to the idiosyncrasies of the case, the stage of the treatment, or the requirements of the moment. If at this point we turn to Seneca, the view from above is especially prominent in one particular work of his, the *Naturales quaestiones*. True, the general idea is manifested across his oeuvre, as when he writes to his mother, Helvia, from exile on Corsica, consoling her with the vision of his liberated *animus* breaking through the ramparts of the sky: It "delights in the most beautiful sight of things divine" as, "mindful of its own immortality, it moves freely over all that has been and will be in every age across time" (*Helv.* 20.2); from this enlightened perspective, the argument goes, Seneca's exile can count as no hardship. Later, in his discourse on causation in nature in *Ep.* 65, Seneca vindicates his meditation on such questions by asserting that they "raise up and lighten the soul" (65.16).[72] His subsequent vision of release from the body and of contemplation of the universe in 16–22 temporarily activates the view from above, only for him to narrow his vision by dutifully returning to his original topic before he draws the letter to its close.[73]

Occasional appearances in other works, then; but the view from above permanently and fundamentally conditions Seneca's self-presentation in the *Naturales quaestiones*. On the 3, 4a, 4b, etc. ordering of the work, the

---

69 So Ferraiolo 2011, 242.
70 On this "perennial motif in ancient philosophic writing," Rutherford 1989, 155–161 with Hadot 1995, 238–250.
71 Robertson 2010, 250, 256.
72 Cf. p. 148 above.
73 *Ep.* 65.23: "Ut ad propositum revertar [...]." For further evocations of the view from above, see, e.g., *Marc.* 18.2–8; *De otio* 5.5–6; *Helv.* 8.5–6.

view from above is first manifested, as we saw earlier (p. 139), in the cosmic consciousness with which Seneca embarks on his world-tour in the preface to Book 3, as if a newly liberated convert from all the distractions of the preoccupied life. It is from *this* sublime perspective, this new attunement to the rhythms of cosmic rather than localized time, that Seneca can gaze intently upon the vast cataclysm that ends one world-cycle in 3.27–30 and recount the details of its destructiveness as if in "real" time.[74] After the stifling vision of Lucilius in Sicily in the preface to Book 4a, flatterers all around him, Seneca's tour of the Nile in 4a.2 reasserts the free-traveling, cosmic viewpoint – a perspective then sustained in (e.g.) his seemingly timeless evocation in 5.18 of an age before the rapacious excesses of navigation corrupted nature's providential gift of the winds to mankind; in the mind's eye with which he confidently conducts his subterranean enquiries into the cause(s) of earthquake in Book 6; in his mind-travels to the limits of remote cometary orbits in Book 7;[75] and in the access that the unencumbered *animus* gains to the universal totality at 1 pr. 11: "There are vast spaces up above, which the mind is allowed to occupy only if it retains as little as possible of the body, if it has wiped away all impurity and it flashes forth unencumbered and light, and self-contained."

This Senecan self-positioning has at least four important consequences for the inter-relationship of the *Epistulae morales* and *Naturales quaestiones*. First, Seneca hardly claims to be a Stoic sage[76] – but our experience of his self-projection in the *Naturales quaestiones* nevertheless adds an important shading to his persona at the start of the *Epistulae*.

> "[Continue to] act (*fac*) thus, my dear Lucilius – claim yourself for yourself, and gather and protect your time, which until now was either being forced from you or snatched away, or was merely slipping from your grasp. [...] Therefore, Lucilius, do (*fac*) what you write that you are doing (*facere*): hold every hour in your grasp" (*Ep.* 1.1, 2).[77]

Seneca's call to action here becomes all the more compelling when we recognize that he acts as he speaks: In claiming himself for himself in the preface to *Naturales quaestiones* 3, in taking action (cf. 3 pr. 3, 4: "faciet [sc. animus]" and "faciamus") and in doing all he can to make up for lost

---

74 Further, Williams 2012, 110–116.
75 Cf. 7.22.1: "I do not agree with our Stoics; for I do not consider a comet to be a sudden fire, but one of the eternal works of nature;" 7.27.6: "Nature does not often display comets. She has assigned them a different place, a different timetable, and movements unlike those of the other planets [...]"
76 Cf. *Helv.* 5.2; *Ep.* 8.2–3; 27.1; 45.3–5; 52.3; 57.3; 68.8–9.
77 See now Schafer 2011, 36 for *fac/facere* implicated in the "dramatic reading" mode which "offers a way for us to read Seneca as he tells us to read him: interactively, creatively."

time (3 pr. 1–4), he underwrites his admonitions to Lucilius in *Ep.* 1 by applying them to transforming effect in his own case in the contemporaneous story-line of the *Naturales quaestiones*.

Secondly, and to develop this first point: The cosmic consciousness on display in the *Naturales quaestiones* offers important reassurance as we follow Seneca from one episode of worldliness to the next in the *Epistulae* – from his potentially contaminating visit to the games in *Ep.* 7,[78] for example, to his reflections on aging in *Ep.* 12 and beyond,[79] from his various bouts of ill health [80] to the discomforts of travel,[81] or from his practical advising of Lucilius[82] to hard assessment of his own philosophical frailties, for example at 27.1: "No, I'm not so shameless as to undertake treatments for others when I'm ill myself." If in the *Epistulae* Seneca implicates himself with Lucilius in the dramatized struggle for self-improvement, that picture of vulnerability and development is offset by the cosmic consciousness of the *Naturales quaestiones*. But how *then* to reconcile the different stages of philosophical maturation on display in these two contemporaneous works? Despite the seeming incongruity between Seneca as philosophical progressive in the one work, Seneca as cosmic voyager in the other, there is another way: Read in conjunction, the two works prioritize different but complementary aspects of the overall philosophical mission, with the *Epistulae* broadly focusing on process, the *Naturales quaestiones* on arrival at cosmic consciousness. The works' contemporaneity here acquires a new connotation: In combinational reading with and against each other, the hard philosophical exertions of the *Epistulae* find their culmination or reward in the cosmic consciousness of the *Naturales quaestiones*; yet the serenity of the cosmic viewpoint in the *Naturales quaestiones* is qualified by the stress which Seneca places in the *Epistulae* on the need for ongoing effort and unceasing self-scrutiny – that basic scaffolding, if you will, for higher philosophical construction in the *Naturales quaestiones*.[83]

Thirdly, important attention has been drawn in recent scholarship to the relative spatial positionings of author and addressee at different points

---

78 Cf. 32.2; 94.53–54; 103.1–2; etc.
79 Cf. 26.1–7; 70.1–2; 76.1–5; etc.
80 Cf. 54.1–3; 61.1; 65.1; 67.2
81 Cf. 53.1–5; 55.1–2; 57.1–3; 84.1
82 Cf. 35.1; 44.1; 71.1; 88.1; etc.
83 This is not to deny, of course, that the cosmic dimension is glimpsed in the *Epistulae morales* (e.g., 8.5; 23.6; 65.16–22; 120.13–16), and that something of the tension that I posit between the divergent pulls of the *Epistulae* and *Naturales quaestiones* respectively can be discerned independently in both works. But the tension generated by the works *in combination* vastly outsizes, I argue, these individualized manifestations of the phenomenon.

in their correspondence in the *Epistulae*.[84] When in *Ep.* 51, for example, Seneca is on his travels, writing from Campania (cf. 49.1) to Lucilius in Sicily, that scene-change immediately shifts the terms of their epistolary and philosophical engagement as new physical context (e.g., Baiae in *Ep.* 51) bears on letter-content. But if the basic spatial dynamics of the *Epistulae* run from points A to B, from epistolary point of origin to place of destination, the *Naturales quaestiones* stretch the physical coordinates of his correspondence with Lucilius by adding a point C: As if writing from the sublime perspective of the view from above, Seneca begins from a starting-position in the *Naturales quaestiones* far removed from the localizations of place in the *Epistulae*. Through letter-exchange with Lucilius Seneca claims to create the illusion of presence despite absence, conversation despite separation.[85] But whereas distance is overcome in the *Epistulae*, in the *Naturales quaestiones* it is in a way insurmountable, the life-trajectories of Seneca and Lucilius so different: While Lucilius makes his way in the world as procurator of Sicily, Seneca turns his back on official life in the preface to *Naturales quaestiones* 3; whereas Lucilius will hopefully find time for study despite his official duties (cf. 4a pr. 1), Seneca devotes himself exclusively to his new project in the *Naturales quaestiones*, his mind entirely free for itself (3 pr. 2: "sibi totus animus vacet"). Read in combination, the two works thus apply opposite but complementary strategies: While the *Epistulae* nurture proximity and contact between Lucilius and Seneca, the *Naturales quaestiones* highlight the distance resulting from contrasting world-outlooks; whereas Lucilius and Seneca are fellow travelers in the *Epistulae*, Seneca as solo cosmic voyager delivers a more unilateral lesson-by-example in the *Naturales quaestiones*; and while the narrative flow of the *Epistulae* captures the day-to-day oscillations of philosophical development through sudden changes of direction from one letter to the next, through shifts of theme and through variations in letter-size, the flow of the *Naturales quaestiones* is more austere and regularized, one-sided rather than co-operational – more lecture than admonition. If Lucilius is pictured as reading the one work without the other, the tension of combinational reading is instantly lost, the benefits of cross-meaning wasted; he may still gain from Senecan wisdom, but he reads only one side of a two-sided story.[86]

---

84 See Henderson 2004, 32–39, especially 32–33.
85 Cf. *Ep.* 67.2; 75.1–2. For the familiar notion of the letter as *colloquium*, Thraede 1970, 51–55.
86 The objection might yet be made that, in the *Naturales quaestiones*, Seneca *does* stress togetherness with Lucilius despite their physical separation. To cite 4a pr. 20 once more (cf. p. 140 above): "And so that you feel no loneliness, I shall join in conversation with you from here. We shall be together in the best part of ourselves

Fourthly (and partly to revisit the first point above, on p. 151f.), Seneca's *conversio ad se* in the preface to *Naturales quaestiones* 3 takes on added interest in light of the following remarks of Donald Robertson:

> The modern *industrialization* of psychotherapy, the division of the therapist's labour, has compartmentalized it in a manner that is bound to cause certain contradictions. What was once a lifestyle and calling, a vocation in the true sense of the word, has now largely been degraded into a mere "job." By nature, however, we do *not* merely study the cure of human suffering in order to alleviate it, but also to understand and transform *ourselves* and our relationship with life itself. Perhaps, as the ancients seemed to believe, the philosopher-therapist must first transform his *own* way of life, making it a living example of his views, in order to be able to help others. (Robertson 2010, xxvi; his emphasis)

Against this background, the self-transformation enacted by Seneca casts his therapeutic involvement with Lucilius in the *Epistulae morales* and *Naturales quaestiones* as no disinterested intervention on the part of a career practitioner, but as an extension of his own lifestyle and calling; his account of that self-transformation also functions as a pledge of sincerity that endorses and authenticates the living example of himself on offer to Lucilius in the *Epistulae* in particular. Later in the preface to *Naturales quaestiones* 3 he dwells in sermon-like fashion on the question "Quid est

---

[sc. in the mind]; we shall give each other advice that will not depend on the listener's expression." But we have already observed the epistolary credentials of the preface to Book 4a (see pp. 143-145 above). As part of that preface, could it be that Seneca's emphasis on togetherness despite absence in 4a pr. 20 is to be read as an essentially *epistolary* gesture, with appropriate parallels within the *Epistulae* themselves (cf. again 67.2; 75.1–2) – a gesture out of keeping with the distancing dynamic that evolves as the *Naturales quaestiones* progresses? After all, in the preface to Book 1 (which I take to be penultimate in the original ordering of the books; cf. p. 138 above and n. 14) Seneca continues to address Lucilius with customary affection (1 pr. 1: "In my opinion, Lucilius, best of men [...]"), but he makes no mention there of the closeness-by-letter anticipated at 4a pr. 20. On the contrary, Seneca portrays his own detachment from life at ground level, so to speak (cf. 1 pr. 5: "What a contemptible thing man is, unless he rises above his human concerns!;" 6: "The virtue to which we aspire [...] unchains the mind and readies it for comprehension of the celestial, and makes it worthy of entering into association with god") – a perspective from which he dispassionately weighs Lucilius' limited philosophical progress thus far against the challenges that yet await him (cf. 1 pr. 6: "You have not yet achieved anything: you have escaped many evils, but not yet escaped yourself"). Cosmic detachment in the *Naturales quaestiones* is in this instance conveyed and confirmed by the movement from the (epistolary) forecast of presence despite absence at 4a pr. 20 to Seneca's remoter self-positioning in the preface to Book 1. The meeting of minds in 4a pr. 20 ("erimus una qua parte optimi sumus") gives way at 1 pr. 14 to preoccupation instead with *divine* mind: "What then is the difference between god's nature and our own? The mind is the better part of us (*nostri melior pars animus est*); but in god there is nothing apart from mind."

praecipuum?" ("What is important?"), serially repeating the phrase to mantra-like effect in 10–16. What is important? The wide-ranging answers that he gives ("To be able to endure adversity with a glad mind," "A mind bold and defiant in the face of calamity," "Lifting your spirits high above chance events," etc.) all coalesce around the formation of a resilient core self – even a programmatic vision of self-formation which casts the preface of Book 3 as a worthy introduction of sorts not just to the *Naturales quaestiones* alone, but also to the combinational therapy offered by the *Epistulae morales* and *Naturales quaestiones* in tandem.

If we at last return to the seven chapters which Robertson includes in his "Part II: The Stoic Armamentarium," and if we accept that the view from above fundamentally conditions Seneca's (and our) world-outlook in the *Naturales quaestiones*, then we can finally press a long promising analogy with Robertson's volume: Just as the view from above is featured in Robertson's chapter 13 as but one of many cognitive-behavioral techniques that are available to the therapist (techniques surveyed in the collectivity of chapters 7 to 13 as a whole), so the view from above gives the *Naturales quaestiones* a distinctive identity and function within the larger therapeutic armory assembled across Seneca's philosophical works; like Robertson's chapter 13, the *Naturales quaestiones* constitutes one specialist chapter within Seneca's overall therapeutic repertoire. Moreover, as Robertson's multiple allusions to the *Epistulae morales* in his chapters 7–13 attest, that work shows striking overlaps with many aspects of modern CBT technique. This practical dimension is supported by the quotidian tenor of the *Epistulae*, many of which begin with a topical allusion to everyday life before Seneca steers the proceedings in a philosophical direction; even though the letters appear hermetically sealed from life in one way,[87] his use of everyday diction, his focus on daily vicissitudes and vulnerabilities, and the sense of fragmentation and of piecemeal progress as we move from one letter to the next all contribute to the "real-life" atmospherics of the collection. In this respect, the world of the *Epistulae* is focalized, we might say, through the view from below. In the collectivity of the *Epistulae morales* on the one hand and the *Naturales quaestiones* on the other, the views from below and above thus collide and collude with each other. As we follow Seneca's reflections to Lucilius in the *Epistulae* on, e.g., the circumstances in which suicide is justified[88] or on the trials and benefits of aging,[89] on friendship[90] or on the nature of virtue,[91] a path

---

[87] So Henderson 2004, 6: "Referential moments are shockingly rare, as names, locales, dates, and events are either repressed or repeatedly, emphatically, *anonymized*" (his emphasis).
[88] Cf. 17.9; 58.33–36; 98.16.
[89] Cf. 12.4–6; 30.2; 68.13; 108.28.

is delineated *through* life; transported to the view from above in the *Naturales quaestiones* and looking down on all the pettiness beneath (cf. 1 pr. 6–13), we find detachment *from* ordinary life; and yet the tension between the two approaches, above and below, down-to-earth and cosmically removed, validates each within the binary approach that Seneca takes towards Lucilius as the double-duty addressee of the *Ep.–Nat.* ensemble.[92]

IV.

From contemporaneous texts attention now turns to Lucilius as the simultaneous addressee of the *Epistulae morales* and *Naturales quaestiones*, and to the oscillating effect of switching between the different therapeutic trajectories of the two works. On this approach, Lucilius (or, by extension, the general reader) is to be pictured withdrawing from the cosmic breadth of the *Naturales quaestiones* to the micro-level of the given event or topic that motivates this letter or that; he then expands outwards from the epistolary moment towards the cosmic reach of the *Naturales quaestiones* before, we anticipate, he returns once more in alternating fashion to the view from below in the *Epistulae*. In this respect the two works might loosely be said to complete each other – even though the fact that the lost *Libri moralis philosophiae* was also addressed to Lucilius in Seneca's last years[93] obviously qualifies any attempt to delineate a special relationship between only two of what was at least a triad of late works to this one addressee.[94] At the risk of speculating further, however, the oscillation-effect described above is complicated by a feature of the *Epistulae* well illuminated by Gianpiero Rosati.[95]

In contrast to the dimensions of a treatise proper, Seneca's letter-format in the *Epistulae* tends to touch on topics rather than handling them fully. So in his explanation in *Ep.* 106.1–3 of why he is late to reply to Lucilius' recent missive:

> So you want to know why I didn't answer your letter sooner? The matter about which you made your inquiry was being gathered into the overall scheme of my

---

90   Cf. 9.5–12; 35.1; 78.4; 81.12.
91   Cf. 66 *passim*; 76.10; 16–17; 79.13–18; 115.6–7.
92   Again (cf. n. 83 above), I stress general tendency and hardly dispute that shades of the view from above are detectable at points in the *Epistulae* (e.g., 65.16–22), the view from below discernible in the *Naturales quaestiones*, most obviously in Seneca's sporadic tirades against vice in 3.17–18, 5.18, 1.16; etc.
93   See p. 135 above.
94   See further on this point p. 161, below.
95   Rosati 1981, especially 11–15.

volume (*in contextum operis mei*). For you know that I want to cover the whole of moral philosophy and to settle all the problems related to it. I therefore hesitated as to whether I should make you wait until the proper occasion for this topic came along, or pronounce judgment out of sequence; but it seemed more considerate not to keep waiting one who has come so far.[96] And so I'll take this topic out of the proper sequence of connected subject-matter, and I shall also send you, without waiting for you to ask me, whatever has to do with questions of this kind.[97]

Far from aspiring to systematic completeness on a given theme, the *Epistulae* focus more on the particular point or the single strand of argument; progress towards wisdom proceeds, at least in the early stages, by small steps and modest advances, as in Seneca's advice to Lucilius at *Ep.* 108.1–2 on how to regulate his burning enthusiasm for learning ("ista cupiditas discendi, qua flagrare te video"):

> Entire subjects are not to be randomly gathered in nor greedily seized upon; knowledge of the whole will be attained by studying the parts (*per partes pervenietur ad totum*).

The aphorisms with which he concludes many of the early *Epistulae* well emblematize this fragmentariness of the epistolary learning experience.[98] As Rosati observes, many of the later *Epistulae* are extended in scale and treatise-like in their dimensions and form of argumentation,[99] their greater length suggesting the growth of intellectual ambition as Lucilius' philosophical progress advances; but the basic equation between epistolary form and piecemeal learning, especially in the early *Epistulae*, stands despite this later development.

If we accept this tension between letter and treatise, the combinational relationship of the *Epistulae morales* and *Naturales quaestiones* takes on a new complexion. To re-articulate the dynamic which Rosati discerns between "the different phases of the process of *Seelenleitung* and the characteristics that the letter takes on in the course of Seneca's correspondence:"[100] The tension that Rosati identifies *within* the *Epistulae* between fragmented partiality on the one hand, treatise-like elaboration on the other, is now transferable to the macro-relationship between the "piecemeal" *Epistulae* on the one hand, the treatise-like *Naturales quaestiones* on the other. As he moves from one to another, or between one and the other, Lucilius is simultaneously exposed to the two different but complementary instructional units of fragment and treatise, part and whole.

---

96 I.e., "a retrospective assessment of Lucilius' development as a philosopher" (Inwood 2007, 262).
97 Cited by Rosati 1981, 11.
98 On this point, Rosati 1981, 13.
99 Rosati 1981, 15. Cf. already Bourgery 1911, 54 on *Ep.* 88–124 as (very broadly speaking) "véritables traités."
100 Rosati 1981, 15.

Those different entities are suggestively implicated in the distinction that Seneca draws late in the *Naturales quaestiones* between ethics and physics (with a particular focus on the theological branch of physics):

> Quantum inter philosophiam interest, Lucili virorum optime, et ceteras artes, tantum interesse existimo in ipsa philosophia *inter illam partem quae ad homines et hanc quae ad deos pertinet*. Altior est haec et animosior; multum permisit sibi; non fuit oculis contenta: maius esse quiddam suspicata est ac pulchrius quod extra conspectum natura posuisset. Denique tantum inter duas interest quantum inter deum et hominem: *altera docet quid in terris agendum sit, altera quid agatur in caelo*; altera errores nostros discutit et lumen admovet quo discernantur ambigua vitae, altera multum supra hanc in qua volutamur caliginem excedit, et e tenebris ereptos perducit illo unde lucet.
>
> In my estimation, Lucilius, best of men, the difference between philosophy and the other fields of study is matched in philosophy itself by the equally great difference *between the branch which deals with humans and that which deals with the gods*. The latter is loftier and more noble; it gives itself much freedom; it is not satisfied with what is seen with the eyes; it suspects that there is something greater and more beautiful that nature has placed beyond our vision. In short, there is as much difference between the two branches as there is between god and man: *The one branch teaches what ought to be done on earth, the other what is done in the heavens.* The one dispels our errors and applies a light by which the uncertainties of life may be clearly discerned; the other rises far above the darkness in which we wallow, and, snatching us from shadows, it leads us to the very source of illumination. (Sen. *Nat.* 1 pr. 1–2)

If we accept that *Naturales quaestiones* 1 was composed in late(r) 63, when Seneca was in the early stages of the *Epistulae morales*,[101] can we avoid detecting in his above remarks a loosely drawn template for seeing the *Epistulae* and *Naturales quaestiones* in combination? For all his focus on the intermediate region of meteorological phenomena (*sublimia*) in the *Naturales quaestiones*, above earthly phenomena (*terrena*) but below the region of the heavenly bodies (*caelestia*; cf. 2.1.1–2), Seneca's cultivation of the cosmic viewpoint strives in a celestial direction above *sublimia* – a striving perhaps pictured most graphically not just in his vision of cosmic emancipation in the prefaces to Books 3 and 1, but also in his endorsement in Book 7 of comets as planets moving in unknown orbits beyond the zodiac (cf. 7.22–27). In this respect, the distinction drawn above between mortals and gods ("ad homines," "ad deos"), heavens and earth ("quid *in terris* agendum sit [...] quid agatur *in caelo*"), has important paradigmatic implications for the *Epistulae morales* and *Naturales quaestiones*. If the former may be said to confront "our errors and apply a light by which the uncertainties of life may be clearly discerned," the latter, by invoking the

---

[101] 1–18 by the end of 63, at least according to Griffin's scheme, for which p. 138 above.

clarity of the cosmic viewpoint, raises us "far above the darkness in which we wallow," guiding us towards true illumination. If the one work is rooted *in terris*, in the other Seneca portrays the restless *animus* finding release as if from its earthly chains ("velut vinculis liberatus") and seeking to return to its origins in the *regio caelestis* (1 pr. 12, 13). In effect, can we detect in the contrast between *in terris* and *in caelo* at 1 pr. 1–2 a tacit allusion to the dyad of the *Epistulae* and *Naturales quaestiones*? And can we also find there a hint of Seneca's own oblique theorization of the relationship between the two works?

Of course, the loss of the *Libri moralis philosophiae* complicates this interpretation of the sphere of Senecan self-reference in *Nat.* 1 pr. 1–2: a third referent is not easily accommodated in the binary structure of that passage – unless, that is, we tentatively group the *Libri moralis philosophiae* with the *Epistulae morales* as works pertaining *ad homines* while the *Naturales quaestiones* strive predominantly to elevate us "above the darkness in which we wallow." Uncertainty thus remains, but in the absence of this possibly (but not *necessarily*) influential third party, and at the risk of overstating the special relationship that I posit between the *Epistulae morales* and *Naturales quaestiones*, I revert to my primary claim in this study: When those two works are read with and against each other, each acquires a significance – a meaning generated through the tension of comparison and difference – that is too easily lost in separate reading. Important attention has been drawn in recent scholarship to the limitations and challenges involved in treating only selections of the *Epistulae*, whether in commentary-format or in more discursive contexts.[102] A different but related problem arises, I propose, in the case of the *Epistulae morales* and *Naturales quaestiones*: *Not* to read them with and against each other is itself to impose a selectivity of vision and approach which, I argue, detracts from the therapeutic meaning and function of both works.

Bibliography

Abel, Karlhans. 1967. *Bauformen in Senecas Dialogen: Fünf Strukturanalysen: dial. 6, 11, 12, 1 und 2*. Heidelberg: Winter.
Armisen-Marchetti, Mireille. 1986. "Imagination et méditation chez Sénèque: l'exemple de la praemeditatio." *REL* 64: 185–195.
Beck, Aaron T. 1976. *Cognitive Therapy and the Emotional Disorders*. New York: International Universities Press.

---

102 See, e.g., Inwood 2007, xxi–xxiii.

Bedon, Robert. 1991. "Sénèque, Ad Lucilium, 91: L'incendie de 64 à Lyon: Exploitation littéraire et réalité." In *Présence de Sénèque*, edited by Raymond Chevallier and Rémy Poignault, 45–61. Paris: J. Touzot.
Berno, Francesca Romana. 2003. *Lo specchio, il vizio e la virtù: Studio sulle Naturales Quaestiones di Seneca*. Bologna: Pàtron.
Bourgery, Abel. 1911. "Les Lettres à Lucilius sont-elles de vraies lettres?" *RPh* 35: 40–55.
Codoñer (Merino), Carmen, ed. and trans. 1979. *L. Annaei Senecae Naturales Quaestiones*. 2 vols. Madrid: Consejo Superior de Investigaciones Científicas.
Codoñer (Merino), Carmen. 1989. "La physique de Sénèque: Ordonnance et structure des Naturales Quaestiones." *ANRW* II 36.3: 1779–1822.
Cooper, John M. 2006. "Seneca on Moral Theory and Moral Improvement." In *Seeing Seneca Whole: Perspectives on Philosophy, Poetry and Politics*, edited by Katharina Volk and Gareth D. Williams, 43–55. Leiden; Boston: Brill.
Courtney, Edward, ed. 1993. *The Fragmentary Latin Poets*. Oxford: Clarendon Press.
Decourt, Jean-Claude, and Gérard Lucas. 1993. *Lyon dans les textes grecs et latins: La géographie et l'histoire de Lugdunum, de la fondation de la colonie (43 avant J.-C.) à l'occupation burgonde (460 après J.-C.)*. Lyon; Paris: F.U.-Maison de l'Orient; Diffusion de Boccard.
Delatte, Louis. 1935. "Lucilius, l'ami de Sénèque." *LEC* 4: 367–385, 546–590.
Ferraiolo, William. 2011. Review of *The Philosophy of Cognitive-Behavioural Therapy (CBT): Stoic Philosophy as Rational and Cognitive Psychotherapy*, by Donald Robertson. *Journal of Value Inquiry* 45: 239–243.
Foucault, Michel. 1986. *The Care of the Self: The History of Sexuality*. Vol. 3, translated by R. Hurley. New York: Vintage Books.
Garani, Myrto. 2009. "Going with the Wind: Visualizing Volcanic Eruptions in the Pseudo-Vergilian Aetna." *BICS* 52: 103–121.
Gauly, Bardo M. 2004. *Senecas Naturales Quaestiones: Naturphilosophie für die römische Kaiserzeit*. München: Beck.
Gercke, Alfred. 1895. *Seneca-Studien*. Leipzig: Teubner = *Jahrbücher für klassische Philologie*, Suppl. 22 (1896): 1–334.
Gill, Christopher. 1985. "Ancient Psychotherapy." *JHI* 46: 307–325.
Goodyear, Francis R. D., ed. 1965. *Incerti Auctoris Aetna*. Cambridge: Cambridge University Press.
Goodyear, Francis R. D. 1984. "The Aetna: Thought, Antecedents, and Style." *ANRW* II 32.1: 344–363.
Griffin, Miriam T. 1992. *Seneca: A Philosopher in Politics*. 2nd ed. Oxford: Clarendon Press.
Grilli, Alberto. 2000. "Problemi del De prouidentia." In *Seneca e il suo tempo: Atti del Convegno internazionale di Roma-Cassino 11–14 novembre 1998*, edited by Piergiorgio Parroni, 261–273. Roma: Salerno Editrice.
Grimal, Pierre. 1980. "Lucilius en Sicile." In *Φιλίας χάριν: Miscellanea di studi classici in onore di Eugenio Manni*, edited by M. José Fontana, Maria Teresa Piraino, and F. Paolo Rizzo, vol. 4: 1173–1187. Roma: Bretschneider.
Gross, Nikolaus. 1989. *Senecas Naturales Quaestiones: Komposition, naturphilosophische Aussagen und ihre Quellen*. Stuttgart: Steiner.
Hachmann, Erwin. 1995. *Die Führung des Lesers in Senecas "Epistulae morales."* Münster: Aschendorff.
Hadot, Ilsetraut. 1969. *Seneca und die griechisch-römische Tradition der Seelenleitung*. Berlin: De Gruyter.

Hadot, Pierre. 1995. *Philosophy as a Way of Life: Spiritual Exercises from Socrates to Foucault* edited by Arnold I. Davidson, translated by Michael Chase. Oxford: Blackwell.
Hadot, Pierre. 2002. *What is Ancient Philosophy?*, translated by Michael Chase. Cambridge; London: Harvard University Press.
Hardie, Philip, and Helen Moore, eds. 2010. *Classical Literary Careers and Their Reception*. Cambridge: Cambridge University Press.
Henderson, John. 2004. *Morals and Villas in Seneca's Letters: Places to Dwell*. Cambridge: Cambridge University Press.
Herbert, James M. 2004. "Connections Between Ancient Philosophies and Modern Psychotherapies: Correlation Doesn't Necessarily Prove Causation." *The Behavior Therapist* 27: 53–54.
Hine, Harry M., ed. 1981. *An Edition with Commentary of Seneca, Natural Questions, Book 2*. New York: Arno Press.
Hine, Harry M. 1984. "The Date of the Campanian Earthquake: A.D. 62 or A.D. 63, or Both?" *AC* 53: 266–269.
Hine, Harry M., ed. 1996. *L. Annaei Senecae Naturalium Quaestionum Libri*. Stuttgart; Leipzig: Teubner.
Hine, Harry M. 2006. "Rome, the Cosmos, and the Emperor in Seneca's Natural Questions." *JRS* 96: 42–72.
Hine, Harry M. 2009. "Seneca's Naturales Quaestiones 1960–2005 (Part 1)." *Lustrum* 51: 253–329.
Hine, Harry M. 2010a. "Seneca's Naturales Quaestiones 1960–2005 (Part 2) – with Addenda Covering 2006." *Lustrum* 52: 7–160.
Hine, Harry M., trans. 2010b. *Lucius Annaeus Seneca, Natural Questions*. Chicago; London; University of Chicago Press.
Hyde, Walter W. 1916. "The Volcanic History of Etna." *Geographical Review* 1, 401–418.
Inwood, Brad, trans. 2007. *Seneca, Selected Philosophical Letters: Translation with an Introduction and Commentary*. Oxford; New York: Oxford University Press.
Ker, James. 2009. *The Deaths of Seneca*. Oxford; New York: Oxford University Press.
Lanzarone, Nicola, ed. 2008. *L. Annaei Senecae Dialogorum Liber 1 De Prouidentia*. Firenze: Le Monnier.
Lazarus, Arnold A. 1981. *The Practice of Multimodal Therapy: Systematic, Comprehensive, and Effective Psychotherapy*. New York: McGraw-Hill.
Limburg, Florence J. G. 2007. *'Aliquid ad Mores': The Prefaces and Epilogues of Seneca's Naturales Quaestiones*. PhD diss., University of Leiden.
Maurach, Gregor. 1970. *Der Bau von Senecas Epistulae Morales*. Heidelberg: Winter.
McGlinchey, Joseph B. 2004. "On Hellenistic Philosophy and its Relevance to Contemporary CBT: A Response to Reiss (2003)." *The Behavior Therapist* 27: 51–52.
Montgomery, Robert W. 1993. "The Ancient Origins of Cognitive Therapy: The Reemergence of Stoicism." *Journal of Cognitive Psychotherapy* 7: 5–19.
Moore Brookshire, Sarah A. 2007. "Utilizing Stoic Philosophy to Improve Cognitive Behavioral Therapy." *NC Perspectives* 1: 30–36.
Noyes, Russell. 1973. "Seneca on Death." *Journal of Religion and Health* 12: 223–240.
Nussbaum, Martha C. 1994. *The Therapy of Desire: Theory and Practice in Hellenistic Ethics*. Princeton: Princeton University Press.
Olligschläger, Uwe J. *Die Gesundheit der Seele: Sokrates – Seneca – Epiktet: Antikes Denken, moderne kognitive Psychotherapie und die Biochemie unserer Gedanken*. Berlin; Münster: Lit.

Parroni, Piergiorgio, ed. and trans. 2002. *Seneca, Ricerche sulla natura*. Milan: Mondadori.
Ramsey, John T. 2006. *A Descriptive Catalogue of Greco-Roman Comets from 500 B.C. to A.D. 400*. Iowa City: Classics Dept., University of Iowa.
Ramsey, John T. 2007. "A Catalogue of Greco-Roman Comets from 500 B.C. to A.D. 400." *JHA* 28: 175–197.
Reiss, Steven. 2003. "Epicurus: the First Rational-Emotive Therapist." *The Behavior Therapist* 26: 405–406.
Reydams-Schils, Gretchen. 2005. *The Roman Stoics: Self, Responsibility, and Affection*. Chicago; London: University of Chicago Press.
Richardson-Hay, Christine 2006. *First Lessons: Book 1 of Seneca's "Epistulae Morales" – A Commentary*. Bern et al.: Peter Lang.
Robertson, Donald. 2005. "Stoicism: A Lurking Presence." *Counselling & Psychotherapy Journal* 16: 35–40.
Robertson, Donald. 2010. *The Philosophy of Cognitive-Behavioural Therapy (CBT): Stoic Philosophy as Rational and Cognitive Psychotherapy*. London: Karnac.
Rosati, Gianpiero. 1981. "Seneca sulla lettera filosofica: Un genere letterario nel cammino verso la saggezza." *Maia* 33: 3–15.
Rutherford, Richard B. 1989. *The Meditations of Marcus Aurelius: A Study*. Oxford; New York: Clarendon Press; Oxford University Press.
Schafer, John. 2011. "Seneca's 'Epistulae Morales' as Dramatized Education." *CPh* 106: 32–52.
Seneca. 1910. *Select Letters*. See Summers 1910.
Seneca. 1979. *Naturales Quaestiones*. See Codoñer 1979.
Seneca. 1989. *Questioni Naturali*. See Vottero 1989.
Seneca. 1996. *Naturalium Quaestionum Libri*. See Hine 1996.
Seneca. 1998. *I frammenti*. See Vottero 1998.
Seneca. 2002. *Ricerche sulla natura*. See Parroni 2002.
Seneca. 2007. *Selected Philosophical Letters*. See Inwood 2007.
Seneca. 2010. *Natural Questions*. See Hine 2010b.
Sorabji, Richard. 2000. *Emotion and Peace of Mind: From Stoic Agitation to Christian Temptation*. Oxford; New York: Oxford University Press.
Still, Arthur, and Windy Dryden. 1999. "The Place of Rationality in Stoicism and REBT." *Journal of Rational-Emotive & Cognitive-Behavior Therapy* 17: 143–164.
Summers, Walter C., ed. 1910. *Select Letters of Seneca: Edited with Introduction and Explanatory Notes*. London: Macmillan.
Taub, Liba Chaia. 2008. *Aetna and the Moon: Explaining Nature in Ancient Greece and Rome*. Corvallis: Oregon State University Press.
Thraede, Klaus. 1970. *Grundzüge griechisch-römischer Brieftopik*. München: Beck.
Viti, Anastasia. 1997. "Seneca, Ep. 91: Liberale e l'incendio di Lione." *Paideia* 52: 397–406.
Vottero, Dionigi, ed. and trans. 1989. *Questioni Naturali di Lucio Anneo Seneca*. Torino: UTET.
Vottero, Dionigi, ed. and trans. 1998a. *L. Anneo Seneca: I frammenti*. Bologna: Pàtron.
Vottero, Dionigi. 1998b. "Seneca e la natura." In *L'uomo antico e la natura: Atti del Convegno nazionale di studi, Torino 28–29–30 aprile 1997*, edited by Renato Uglione, 291–303. Torino: Celid.
Wallace-Hadrill, Andrew. 2003. "Seneca and the Pompeian Earthquake." In *Seneca uomo politico e l'età di Claudio e di Nerone: Atti del Convegno internazionale (Capri 25–27 marzo 1999)*, edited by Arturo De Vivo and Elio Lo Cascio, 177–191. Bari: Edipuglia.

Wildberger, Jula. 2006. *Seneca und die Stoa: Der Platz des Menschen in der Welt.* 2 vols. Berlin; New York: De Gruyter.
Wildberger, Jula. 2010. " 'Praebebam enim me facilem opinionibus magnorum uirorum:' Platonic Readings in Seneca Ep. 102." In *Aristotle and the Stoics Reading Plato*, edited by Verity Harte, Mary M. McCabe, Robert A. Sharples, and Ann Sheppard, 205–232. London: Institute of Classical Studies.
Williams, Gareth D. 2012. *The Cosmic Viewpoint: A Study of Seneca's Natural Questions.* Oxford: Oxford University Press.

Freedom in Seneca: Some Reflections on the Relationship between Philosophy and Politics, Public and Private Life

Rita Degl'Innocenti Pierini
Università degli Studi di Firenze

> Que le mot de liberté soit l'un des plus obscurs qui soient, personne n'en doute. [...] La liberté, que l'on conçoit communément comme une source de spontanéité et de vie, comme la manifestation même de la vie, se révèle, à l'expérience, comme inséparable de la mort.
>
> Pierre Grimal, *Les erreurs de la liberté*, Paris 1989

This essay will be concerned with exploring only a few of the many senses in which freedom is evoked in Seneca's philosophical work and does not aspire to offer a complete discussion of this very complex subject. In particular, my discussion will focus on some distinctive images[1] and on those key personages who, in my opinion, embody Seneca's idea of freedom best.

My reflections on freedom in Seneca take their origin from a well-known passage in *De brevitate vitae*, chapter five, the famously unflattering portrait that Seneca dedicates to Cicero. It develops and is based on the presupposition of a concept of freedom profoundly different from Cicero's own. As its starting point Seneca takes the renowned and problematic term *semiliber*, "half a prisoner," as John Basore translates, or more precisely, "half free," which Cicero had attributed to himself, but which the Stoic philosopher judged unworthy of a *sapiens*, or "a wise man:"

> M. Cicero inter Catilinas Clodios iactatus Pompeiosque et Crassos, partim manifestos inimicos, partim dubios amicos, dum fluctuatur cum re publica et illam pessum euntem tenet, novissime abductus, nec secundis rebus quietus nec adversarum patiens, quotiens illum ipsum consulatum suum non sine causa sed sine fine laudatum detestatur! 2 Quam flebiles voces exprimit in quadam ad Atticum epistula iam

---

[1] On the importance of metaphors in Seneca, see Armisen-Marchetti 1989; Bartsch 2009, 216–217.

> victo patre Pompeio, adhuc filio in Hispania fracta arma refovente! "Quid agam" inquit "hic quaeris? moror in Tusculano meo semiliber." Alia deinceps adicit quibus et priorem aetatem complorat et de praesenti queritur et de futura desperat. 3 Semiliberum se dixit Cicero: at mehercules numquam sapiens in tam humile nomen procedet, numquam semiliber erit, integrae semper libertatis et solidae, solutus et sui iuris et altior ceteris. Quid enim supra eum potest esse qui supra fortunam est?
>
> Marcus Cicero, long flung among men like Catiline and Clodius and Pompey and Crassus, some open enemies, others doubtful friends, as he is tossed to and fro along with the state and seeks to keep it from destruction, to be at last swept away, unable as he was to be restful in prosperity or patient in adversity —how many times does he curse that very consulship of his, which he had lauded without end, though not without reason! 2 How tearful the words he uses in a letter written to Atticus, when Pompey the elder had been conquered, and the son was still trying to restore his shattered arms in Spain! "Do you ask," he said, "what I am doing here? I am lingering in my Tusculan villa half a prisoner." He then proceeds to other statements, in which he bewails his former life and complains of the present and despairs of the future. 3 Cicero said that he was "half a prisoner." But, in very truth, never will the wise man resort to so lowly a term, never will he be half a prisoner – he who always possesses an undiminished and stable liberty, being free and his own master and towering over all others. For what can possibly be above him who is above fortune? (Sen. *Brev. vit.* 5.1–3)[2]

Here, Cicero is clearly not described as a Stoic wise man, but almost as its exact opposite, owing to his uncertainties, his "lack of consistency" (*inconstantia*), which seems to Seneca to clash with freedom of conscience, the only quality that is fitting for the moral stature of a philosopher. Cicero's political activity, which is deeply influenced by the complex, problematic reality of the contemporary political situation, is misinterpreted in favor of an abstract concept of freedom, which for the Stoic Seneca is truly monolithic and cannot be watered down or subject to compromises.[3] "Tossed to and fro along with the state" (*Brev. vit.* 5.1), desperately trying to prevent its destruction, Cicero is overwhelmed in the end, and for Seneca he appears to embody the role of an anti-*sapiens*. Seneca describes him as carried away by his destiny, rather than in control of it: He is like Thyestes, the protagonist in Seneca's tragedy of the same name, who is obsessed by fear and expresses his irrational condition with similar metaphorical imagery in this manner: "And other-whither than I strive to go am I borne

---

2   Here and subsequently, the translations of the *Dialogi*, *De beneficiis*, and *De clementia* are by Basore 1928–1935, with some minor changes.
3   On freedom in Rome, see for example Wirszubski 1950; Hammond 1963; Lana 1973; Roller 2001. For freedom in Seneca, see in particular Traina 1987; Traina 2000, 9–13; Garbarino 2001; Codoñer 2003, 60–68; Inwood 2005, 302–321; Edwards 2009, 139–159; Ker 2009, 248–257.

away in thrall. Just so a ship, urged on by oar and sail, the tide, resisting both oar and sail, bears back."[4]

Furthermore, the accusation concerning Cicero's lack of consistency appears to be the fruit of reflections that were traditional in the imperial schools of rhetoric, seeing that we find the following remark of the orator Julius Bassus in a *Controversy* reported by Seneca the rhetorician, the father of the philosopher: "No-one is faultless: Cato lacked moderation, Cicero firmness, Sulla clemency."[5] The same idea returns again in the sixth Senecan *Suasoria*, entitled "Cicero deliberates whether to beg Antony's pardon," where the historian Titus Livy underlines that "of all disasters he faced none but his death as becomes a man."[6] In the same *Suasoria*, Asinius Pollio, who remained for his whole life a fierce opponent of Cicero's reputation, allows himself an exclamation which, with patent irony, alludes to Cicero's lack of balance: "Would that he could have shown more temperateness in prosperity, more stoutness in adversity!"[7] This is an affirmation not unlike the remark in the passage quoted above, that Cicero was "unable [...] to be restful in prosperity or patient in adversity."[8] The criticism of Asinius Pollio and that of Seneca the philosopher appear all the more biting, and unjust, if we consider that it is almost a literal repetition of one of Cicero's own claims. In *De officiis*, he had praised "a well-balanced mind" (*aequabilitas*) in the following words: "But it is a fine thing to keep an unruffled temper, an unchanging mien, and the same cast of countenance in every condition of life."[9]

Before going on with our examination of *Brev. vit.* 5, it may be appropriate to dwell briefly on the quotation from Cicero's letter in which the term *semiliber* appears, since it is the hub of Seneca's critical argument. In the form in which it is quoted by the philosopher, the epistle is not included in the corpus of Cicero's extant letters. There are thus two possible

---

4 Sen. *Thy.* 437–439: "Alioque quam quo nitor abductus feror. / Sic concitatam remige et velo ratem / aestus resistens remigi et velo refert." Translations of Seneca's plays are quoted from F. J. Miller 1917–1919. Schiesaro 2003, 108 sees in the character of Thyestes an "opposition between rational understanding and emotional foreboding;" see also 147–151.
5 Sen. *Contr.* 2.4.4: "Nemo sine vitio est: in Catone <deerat> moderatio, in Cicerone constantia, in Sulla clementia." Quotations from works of Seneca the Rhetor and translations are taken from Winterbottom 1974. More about these Senecan texts in Degl'Innocenti Pierini 2003.
6 Sen. *Suas.* 6.22: "omnium adversorum nihil ut viro dignum erat tulit praeter mortem."
7 Sen. *Suas.* 6.24: "Utinam moderatius secundas res et fortius adversas ferre potuisset!"
8 Sen. *Brev. vit.* 5.1: "nec secundis rebus quietus nec adversarum patiens."
9 Cic. *Off.* 1.90, trans. W. Miller: "Nam ut adversas res, sic secundas immoderate ferre levitatis est, praeclaraque est aequabilitas in omni vita."

solutions:[10] either to emend *ad Atticum* to *ad Axium*, as Justus Lipsius had suggested, and thus to imagine a fragment of a lost letter, or to hypothesize a free quotation, from memory, of *Att.* 13.31.3, a letter written at Cicero's estate near Tusculum on 28 May in 45 BCE. In that letter Cicero uses the plural form *semiliberi* to describe his own condition, but in a conceptually different context: "For pity's sake let us chuck all this nonsense, and be half free at any rate. That we shall manage by holding our tongues and lying low."[11] The second hypothesis appears more convincing to me:[12] Seneca remembered the word *semiliberi* that he had read in *Att.* 13.31.3, which Cicero had applied to himself in the tough years between the battles of Pharsalus and Munda (48–45 BC), in a period of particularly distressing political uncertainty, and then recontextualized it, giving it a different, new interpretation and generalizing deliberately. It also seems appropriate to underline that in the above-quoted letter, Cicero connects his condition of half-freedom to two attitudes exemplified by the instrumental expression *tacendo et latendo* ("by holding our tongues and lying low"), both of which allude to an escape from involvement and activity: The sense of Cicero's *latere*[13] in this context may have been partly recovered by the verb *moror* found in Seneca, which implies a "non-life," a "remaining alive," as we read in Seneca *Ep.* 93.3 with reference to the death of an octogenarian: "A person like him has not lived; he has merely tarried awhile in life."[14] Cicero is portrayed like Vatia, who is described in *Ep.* 55.3–4 as "famed for nothing else than his life of leisure" and of whom Seneca observes: "But what he knew was how to hide, not how to live,"[15] promptly pointing out that this attitude was equivalent to a death-in-life, and not philosophical leisure (*otium*).

Furthermore, the words that Seneca puts into the mouth of Cicero in his rewriting of the presumed letter to Atticus are defined as plaintive, unmanly words (*flebiles voces*), such as those pronounced by a tragic charac-

---

10 There is no foundation for the hypothesis of Nicholson (1998, 70) that Seneca is repeating a quotation from a lost book of Varro's *De lingua latina*: Nicholson does not even try to explain why Seneca, so hostile to grammarians, should take quotations from a grammarian like Varro.
11 Cic. *Att.* 13.31.3, no. 302 Shackleton Bailey, whose translation I quote: "Obsecro, abiciamus ista et semiliberi saltem simus; quod adsequemur et tacendo et latendo."
12 I follow here some arguments proposed by Traina 1982 in his commentary on *De brevitate vitae*. See also Setaioli 2003, 59.
13 Compare my essay *Vivi nascosto* in Degl'Innocenti Pierini 1999, 81–107.
14 Sen. *Ep.* 93.3: "Non vixit enim ille sed in vita moratus est." Here and subsequently, the translations of Seneca's *Epistulae morales* are by Gummere 1917–1925. See Berno 2006, 198 with reference to Sen. *Ep.* 55.4.
15 Sen. *Ep.* 55.3: "nulla alia re quam otio notus;" 55.4: "At ille latere sciebat, non vivere."

ter like Philoctetes in a well-known passage from the tragedy of the same name by Accius,[16] which Cicero quoted, not by chance, I believe, in *Tusc.* 2.33 (see also 2.94–95), in a context in which he clearly considered such lamentations to be unworthy of a hero (*vir fortis*): Here, too, this might be a subtle, treacherous backlash against the Cicero of the *Tusculanae disputationes*, a work which appears to be not very distant from Stoicism.[17]

With his merciless analysis of this letter by Cicero, Seneca extends a shadow of contempt over the whole of the last part of Cicero's life, presenting him as bewailing his past, complaining about the present, and without hope for the future. It is clear that Seneca is not interested in a historical or political evaluation of Cicero's achievements. But behind the failure of Cicero's public life as an *occupatus*, a busy man without time to spare (we should not forget the context of the dialogue), and thus behind his negative example we can implicitly perceive the positive model of the sponsor of all Stoic values, that is to say, Cato, the champion of the final choice, and thus of freedom.[18] In Seneca's mind Cicero is contrasted with an ideal Stoic wise man who corresponds to what we read of Cato in *Const.* 2.2; to some extent, this portrait is the positive mirror image to the negative picture of Cicero, inasmuch as it is based on a similar image about the fall of the Roman republic:

> Adversus vitia civitatis degenerantis et pessum sua mole sidentis stetit solus et cadentem rem publicam, quantum modo una retrahi manu poterat, tenuit, donec abstractus comitem se diu sustentatae ruinae dedit simulque extincta sunt quae nefas erat dividi; *neque enim Cato post libertatem vixit nec libertas post Catonem.*
>
> He stood alone against the vices of a degenerate state that was sinking to destruction beneath its very weight, and he stayed the fall of the republic to the utmost that one man's hand could do to draw it back, until at last he was himself withdrawn and shared the downfall which he had so long averted and the two whom heaven willed should never part were blotted out together. *For Cato did not survive freedom, nor freedom Cato.* (Sen. *Const.* 2.2, trans. Basore)[19]

16　Acc. *trag.* 549–551 Ribbeck: "in tecto umido, / quod eiulatu, questu, gemitu, fremitibus / resonando mutum flebilis voces refert" – "in shelter damp, which, dumb thing though it is, repeats my cries, tearful, re-echoing with wails and plaints, with moans and groans" (trans. Warmington). On the context of the fragment, see Degl'Innocenti Pierini 2007, 158–159.
17　I take the liberty of referring readers to my arguments in Degl'Innocenti Pierini 2008, *passim.*
18　On Cato in Seneca, see Pecchiura 1965, Isnardi Parente 2000, and n. 47 below.
19　Here we have the image of the "precipitous collapse" of the state, which is quite common (see, for example, Cic. *Sull.* 87: "rei publicae praecipitanti subveni;" Liv. 22.12.11: "ad rem publicam praecipitandam;" Vell. 2.48.6: "in re publica […] certe non praecipitata"). The familiar image of the collapsing state appears here intertwined with a nautical metaphor since *pessum* is often used in contexts pertaining to waters and the sea. Another such illogical accumulation of diverse imagery can

As I would suggest, Cato is depicted as someone very similar to a helmsman trying to hold steady (*tenere*) the rudder of the foundering ship of state.[20] Cicero was swept away (*Brev. vit.* 5.1), but Cato retains his ideal image, according to Seneca, because he voluntarily associates himself with the collapse[21] and in dying with the Roman republic avoids an irreparable and eternal blame. As a perfect Stoic, he recognizes and collaborates with his destiny in his choice of suicide,[22] which thus coincides perfectly with freedom. On the contrary, Cicero is presented in *De brevitate vitae* as oscillating between different inclinations: He allows himself to be transported, as it were, by events and thus shows a lack of consistency, the greatest virtue of the Stoic wise man.[23] Above all, he could appear to be incapable of freely choosing death. Even if he faces up to it with great fortitude, he does not anticipate it and so misses the opportunity to redeem all the inconsistencies of his existence by committing suicide. Seneca's position on suicide does not correspond completely with the Stoic doctrine, which allows it under certain circumstances but does not appear to exalt it

---

be observed in *Prov.* 5.9, where life is first described as a trip by land and then simultaneously as a sea voyage. It is highly significant that these are the only two occurences of *pessum* in a figurative meaning. In its primary sense it occurs in *Nat.* 3.25.5 and 7, in both cases in relation to waters, and, for example, also in Lucretius' (6.588–591) to describe the collapse of buildings combined with the submersion of cities during an earthquake: "Multaque praeterea ceciderunt moenia magnis / motibus in terris et multae per mare pessum / subsedere suis pariter cum civibus urbes." For the idea of the sinking ship of state, compare also Flor. *Epit.* 1.47.8: "Illae opes atque divitiae adfixere saeculi mores, mersamque vitiis suis quasi sentina rem publicam pessum dedere," while the recurrence of the same vocabulary *pessum*, *sidere*, and *tenere* to refer to something sinking but held afloat for a time in Lucan (3.674–675: "In pugnam fregere rates. Sidentia pessum / corpora caesa tenent [...]") confirms my suggestion that *Const.* 2.2 is supposed to evoke a similar idea as well.

20 Note the metaphorical use of expressions such as *tenere cursum* (Sen. *Prov.* 5.9; *Ep.* 14.8 and 85.31) or, even closer, *tenere clavum* at Sen. *Marc.* 6.3. – The parallel of the politician's destiny with the state is already present in Cicero; see, e.g., with reference to the Ciceronian exile, *Red. sen.* 36: "in rem publicam sum pariter cum re publica restitutus;" for Crassus, *De orat.* 3.10: "ut ille, qui haec non vidit, et vixisse cum re publica pariter et cum illa simul extinctus esse videatur."
21 We find a similar image in Aufidius Bassus, quoted at Sen. *Suas.* 6.23: "Sic M. Cicero decessit, vir natus ad rei publicae salutem, quae diu defensa et administrata in senectute demum e manibus eius elabitur" – "So died Cicero, a man born to save the state. Long did he defend and administer it; then in his old age it finally slipped from his grasp, shattered by this personal mistake."
22 See *Ep.* 54.7.
23 See *Ep.* 104.30: "Nemo mutatum Catonem totiens mutata re publica vidit: eundem se in omni statu praestitit" – "No one ever saw Cato change, no matter how often the state changed: he kept himself the same in all circumstances."

as an affirmation of freedom.[24] This is a conceptual elaboration, therefore, that seems to find its origin and its vindication in recent Roman history and its martyr, Cato. It is the freedom of an individual conscience, pure and inviolable, which is fulfilled and recognized in the exemplary story of Cato, but also in that of Socrates and, in the particular context of *Epistle* 70, in the many examples featuring even lowly slaves capable of rising to the challenge of a glorious end.

With respect to Cicero, Seneca the philosopher takes a different position from that of many declaimers and rhetoricians recalled in the work of his father. There the concept of *libertas* often appears in connection with Cicero's firm opposition to Antony, and his death is equated with manly strength. Quintus Haterius, who is quoted in the two *Suasoriae* (6 and 7) dedicated to Cicero, sketches the conflict between Antony and Cicero with incisive statements referring to the concept of freedom,[25] for example at *Suas.* 6.1: "Let posterity know that if the state was capable of being Antony's slave, Cicero was not."[26] At the beginning of the seventh *Suasoria* we read: "I should advise you, Cicero, to rate your life high if freedom held its proper place in a free community, if our necks were not the sport of our countrymen's swords. As it is, Antony is promising you your life – so you may be sure that nothing is preferable to death."[27]

Consistency and freedom may coincide if the wise man takes the route that, according to Seneca, is the only one still open to him after Pharsalus: the recourse to suicide. As regards the position of the Stoics[28] and the debate that was undoubtedly prompted by their school, it is, in my opinion, important to remember the epigrammatic statement by which Lucan makes Cato reflect on the death of Pompey in *Phars.* 9.211–212: "Best gift of all /

---

24 See the commentary of Lanzarone 2008 on this passage, with an ample bibliography; Scarpat 2007, 16–19.
25 Also in the words of Cestius Pius in *Suas.* 7.3, we read an invitation to Cicero to choose death and to claim his freedom from Antony: "What has become of that revered phrase of yours: 'For to die is the end granted by nature, not a punishment'? Are *you* the only man who does not realise its obvious truth? You may think you have persuaded Antony. Claim your freedom, rather, and let your enemy have one crime the more; die – and make Antony the guiltier" – "Ubi est sacra illa vox tua: 'mori enim naturae finis est, non poena'? Hoc tibi uni non liquet? At videris Antonio persuasisse. Adsere te potius libertati et unum crimen inimico adice: fac moriendo Antonium nocentiorem."
26 "Sciant posteri potuisse Antonio servire rem publicam, non potuisse Ciceronem."
27 Sen. *Suas.* 7.1: "Hortarer te, Cicero, ut vitam magni aestimares si libertas suum haberet in civitate locum, si suum in libertate eloquentia, si non civili ense cervicibus luderetur; nunc, ut scias nihil esse melius quam mori, vitam tibi Antonius promittit."
28 See Colish 1985, vol. 1, p. 49–51.

The knowledge how to die; next, death compelled,"[29] in words that are similar to those of Seneca in *Ep.* 45.5: "Have we leisure enough for this? Do we already know how to live, or die?"[30] In this connection, it is impossible to disagree with Syme, when he acutely observes that "Seneca did his best to convert Cato from a politician into a sage" (1958, vol 2, p. 557 n. 5). There is a clear lack of understanding in Seneca for a concept of freedom that is not abstract but fulfilled in certain political and social conditions: Seneca idealizes the absolute freedom of the Stoics, which Cicero tries to clarify and define[31] in the fifth of the *Stoic Paradoxes*, where we read: "For what is freedom? The power to live as you will. Who then lives as he wills except one who follows noble things?"[32]

Cicero himself, on the contrary, seems to bend the rigor of Stoic dogma to the requirements of the contemporary political elite even in *De officiis*, a work which is pervaded with Stoicism. He adjusts moral stringency to the needs of the times, *tranquillitas* and *dignitas*, and proposes various possible options, in the illusionary attempt to find a difficult, but feasible, equilibrium. The Stoic philosopher judges this attempt unworthy of the intellectual stature of a wise man, who should not be lured by unworthy alternatives but rather glory in the fact that he is "towering over all others" (*Brev. vit.* 5.3: "altior ceteris"), superior not to other individuals, but to the things that are "other" than himself, extraneous and indifferent, so that finally he will be "above fortune" ("supra fortunam"). He should be proud of defeating fortune, and for this reason, he should not feel weighed down in any way: Freedom is thus an inner resource that contributes to the self-sufficiency of the wise man,[33] as we read in *Const.* 19.2: "But not to put up with anything is not liberty; we deceive ourselves. Liberty is having a mind that rises above injury, that makes itself the only source from which its pleasures spring, that separates itself from all external things."[34] While

---

29 "Scire mori sors prima viris, sed proxima cogi" (trans. Ridley).
30 "Tantum nobis vacat? iam vivere, iam mori scimus."
31 Observations on this subject in Wirszubski 1950, 19. On will power and freedom in Stoicism, see Wildberger 2006, vol. 1, pp. 338–351.
32 Cic. *Parad.* 5.34, trans. Rackham: "Quid est enim libertas? Potestas vivendi, ut velis. Quis igitur vivit, ut volt, nisi qui recta sequitur [...]?"
33 Thus Traina 1987, 50.
34 "Non est autem libertas nihil pati, fallimur: libertas est animum superponere iniuriis et eum facere se ex quo solo sibi gaudenda veniant, exteriora diducere a se." See also *Ep.* 51.9: "Libertas proposita est: ad hoc praemium laboratur. Quae sit libertas quaeris? Nulli rei servire, nulli necessitati, nullis casibus, fortunam in aequum deducere" – "I have set freedom before my eyes; and I am striving for that reward. And what is freedom, you ask? It means not being a slave to any circumstance, to any constraint, to any chance; it means compelling Fortune to enter the lists on equal terms."

for Seneca *libertas* must be *integra* and *solida* (see above, *Brev. vit.* 5), the wise man, in turn, is "free from constraints" (*solutus*), in the sense that he is not forced to undergo any conditioning by passions or by earthly, temporary laws, and is thus "not subject to the laws of a state" (*legibus solutus*)" but truly master of himself, that is *sui iuris*[35] or "self-ruled," protected by a higher, abstract universal right, which does not coincide with the law of the Roman republic. The expression *sui iuris* must have sounded revolutionary to a Roman, shifting the perspective from the enjoyment of rights within the environment of a state to freedom as the right to complete and independent mastery of oneself, for we must not forget that in Roman law, *sui iuris* opposed the freeborn to the slave, who is always *in potestate* and, consequently, *alieni iuris*.[36] Indeed, in belonging only to himself, the wise man of the imperial age clearly demonstrates what Seneca states in *Ep.* 75.18,[37] that is to say, what *absoluta libertas* consists in: "It means not fearing either men or gods; it means not craving wickedness or excess; it means possessing supreme power over oneself. And it is a priceless good to be master of oneself."[38] This *sui iuris* sage finds a perfect representation also in a speech of the character "Seneca" in the play *Octavia* written by an anonymous first-century playwright and admirer of the philosopher. "Seneca" narrates that once, during his Corsican exile, he enjoyed a freedom without limits and was thus fully master of himself: "I was happier hiding on the cliffs of Corsica's sea far from envy's stings, where my free and autonomous spirit had leisure for reflection and study."[39]

The philosopher in exile is represented by the author of *Octavia* in a state of "perfect" freedom, like that of the soul which is freed from the body and finally reaches a suitable condition to express its true essence. Thus we read about the soul of the dead brother of the freedman Polybius in the consolation written for him from Corsica: "If, however, the dead do retain some feeling, at this moment my brother's soul, released, as it were, from its long imprisonment, exults to be at last its own lord and master, enjoys the spectacle of Nature, and from its higher place looks down upon all human things, while upon things divine, the explanation of which it had

---

35 On *sui iuris*, see Traina 1987, 12 and 52f.; Lotito 2001, 155f.
36 Wirszubski 1950, 8; see also Roller 2001, 223 n. 17.
37 I quote from Traina 2000, 10.
38 "Non homines timere, non deos; nec turpia velle nec nimia; in se ipsum habere maximam potestatem: inaestimabile bonum est suum fieri."
39 *Oct.* 381–384, trans. Boyle: "Melius latebam procul ab invidiae malis / remotus inter Corsici rupes maris, / ubi liber animus et sui iuris mihi / semper vacabat studia recolenti mea." See Boyle 2008, 171, on lines 381–390: "An idealizing description of Seneca's exile on Corsica 41–49 CE, which serves (among other things) to identify the speaker immediately for the audience."

so long sought in vain, it gazes with a nearer vision,"[40] and also in a passage at *Ben.* 3.20.1, which reveals Platonic undertones, at least on the terminological level: "Only the body is at the mercy and disposal of a master; but the mind is its own master, and is so free and unshackled that not even this prison of the body, in which it is confined, can restrain it from using its own powers."[41] Who is truly free, then, for Seneca? The wise man is the answer that comes naturally, but we must also add that the Senecan wise man seems to acquire this attribute of true freedom once he is free from the daily commitments of political life (as with, for example, Oedipus and Creon in the Seneca's *Oedipus*)[42] or, definitively, once he is freed from the body in the final choice to die.

In the absence of political freedom, suicide may be a highly political act, in that it confirms freedom also as a collective value. Precisely in its voluntary, individual dimension suicide may therefore be said to represent for Seneca a sublimation of freedom, both on the philosophical and the political level: I would not at all interpret the frequency of the motif of suicide in Seneca's works as a sign of pessimism,[43] seeing that, as has been said, it represents true freedom, which consists in the acceptance of one's own individual destiny and, at the same time, in recognizing oneself as part of a higher order and in obeying God, who is also fate.[44] Indeed, suicide, seen as contempt for death,[45] is ultimately a highly comforting moment, and, no less than a death at the right time, it offers a sure way out, since it makes it possible to reach the immortality of true glory in a perfectly consistent manner. Suicide offers to the individual the opportunity to be the arbiter of his own destiny, just like a god, as we read in a chorus of the *Agamemnon*: He who does not yield to the "sweet evil" (589: "dulce malum") of a pernicious attachment to life (590: "vitae dirus amor"), he who despises the gods and death, he who dares to put an end to his life, "a

---

40 Sen. *Polyb.* 9.3: "Si est aliquis defunctis sensus, nunc animus fratris mei velut ex diutino carcere emissus, tandem sui iuris et arbitrii, gestit et rerum naturae spectaculo fruitur et humana omnia ex loco superiore despicit, divina vero, quorum rationem tam diu frustra quaesierat, propius intuetur."
41 "Corpora obnoxia sunt et adscripta dominis, mens quidem sui iuris, quae adeo libera et vaga est, ut ne ab hoc quidem carcere cui inclusa est teneri queat quo minus inpetu suo utatur."
42 Sen. *Oed.* 13: "curis solutus exul," 687: "solutus onere regio." On this interpretation of Seneca's *Oedipus*, see Degl'Innocenti Pierini 2012, 89–93.
43 See instead Hill 2004, 145–147. On suicide as a form of healing, see Tommaso Gazzarri's contribution to this volume.
44 "Praebere se fato" of Sen. *Prov.* 5.8 corresponds to "deo parere libertas est" in Sen. *Vit. beat.* 15.7. See Mazzoli 1984, 961–963.
45 On *liber* in tragedies, see Garbarino 2001, 44f. n. 65.

match for kings, a match for the high gods will he be."[46] This was the case with Cato,[47] who is, for Seneca, "that hero, who was born no less for personal than for political freedom" (*Marc.* 20.6) and for whom the most profound, innermost meaning of his personality coincides with the personification of freedom itself, as we have read in the *De constantia sapientis* and as is echoed in *Ep.* 95.72, which evokes "that last and bravest wound of Cato's, through which freedom breathed her last."[48] Even his political activity and the glory that derives from it appear to be completely equated with the substance of his final gesture, as we read in *Ep.* 13.14: "Wrench from Cato's hand his sword, the vindicator of liberty, and you deprive him of the greatest share of his glory." The passages connecting Cato and freedom are almost always formulated in the most vivid and concise expressions of Seneca's repertoire, including figures of speech such as personification (as in *Const.* 2.2), which is natural for the Romans, who venerated freedom as the goddess Libertas and even dedicated a temple to her.[49] Another stylistic device in these contexts is Seneca's use of rhetorical questions serving as slogans that entrust the effectiveness of communication to the force of the word. The complexity of history with its multiple aspects and its doubts is moved to the background, and so the exemplary role of Cato may be simply defined as "the living image of all the virtues" (*Tranq. an.* 16.1: "virtutium viva imago").

Among the numerous significant passages connecting the Senecan myth of Cato with the theme of freedom, I would like to quote one in which the exquisite incisiveness of the imagery is striking. This is a famous passage from *De providentia* 2.9–10, where, to use the words of Mazzoli, the philosopher "mette in scena"[50] Cato Uticensis, and makes him express his refusal of any compromise with Caesar, the despot, in the name of freedom: "Although, said he, all the world has fallen under one man's

---

46 Sen. *Ag.* 609: "Par ille regi, par superis erit." See Narducci 2002, 391–395.
47 There is an excellent discussion of the figure of Cato in Seneca in Narducci 2002, 375–383. I agree whole-heartedly with his observation, on p. 381, that tyranny becomes an occasion to discover true freedom and the truly civic value of Cato's virtue and that the reasons for his political battle sometimes tend to pass into the background. The historical failure appears to be more than redeemed by the triumphal victory over every external power obtained through death. On the figure of Cato and the idea of fighting the fear of death, see Edwards 2007, 97–112.
48 "Catonis illud ultimum ac fortissimum vulnus per quod libertas emisit animam."
49 Suffice it to mention the well-known episode of Cicero's house, destroyed by Clodius during his exile, on the site of which a temple of Libertas was constructed (see for example Cic. *Dom.* 108: "Ista tua pulchra Libertas deos penatis et familiaris meos lares expulit;" Allen 1944).
50 Mazzoli 2000, 255f. insists, appropriately, on the spectacular character of the scene.

sway, although Caesar's legions guard the land, his fleets the sea, and Caesar's troops beset the city gates, yet Cato has a way of escape; with one single hand he will open a wide path to freedom."[51] From my point of view what seems to be particularly important is, on the one hand, the fighting spirit of Cato, which has as his battlefield his body and, on the other hand, the image of suicide as a road to freedom.[52] The latter is a leitmotif extremely common in Seneca, which takes various forms[53] and seems to have accompanied the philosopher for the whole of his life: Cato's path to death could seem equivalent to a journey to wisdom, and freedom is in a certain sense the most tangible reward, as is the glory to which the individual can aspire.[54] Both the ideological presuppositions and the flagrant exhibition of ethical agonism are already present in a passage of *De ira* 3.15.4,[55] which

---

51 " 'Licet' inquit 'omnia in unius dicionem concesserint, custodiantur legionibus terrae, classibus maria, Caesarianus portas miles obsideat, Cato qua exeat habet: una manu latam libertati viam faciet.' " Cato's speech continues as follows: "Ferrum istud, etiam civili bello purum et innoxium, bonas tandem ac nobìles edet operas: libertatem quam patriae non potuit Catoni dabit. Aggredere, anime, diu meditatum opus, eripe te rebus humanis. Iam Petreius et Iuba concucurrerunt iacentque alter alterius manu caesi, fortis et egregia fati conventio, sed quae non deceat magnitudinem nostram: tam turpe est Catoni mortem ab ullo petere quam vitam" – "This sword, unstained and blameless even in civil war, shall at last do good and noble service: the freedom which it could not give to his country it shall give to Cato! Essay, my soul, the task long planned; deliver yourself from human affairs. Already Petreius and Juba have met and lie fallen, each slain by the other's hand. Their compact with Fate was brave and noble, but for my greatness such would be unfit. For Cato it were as ignoble to beg death from any man as to beg life." The metaphor of the journey returns subsequently in similar terms in 6.7: "Prono animam loco posui: †trahitur† adtendite modo et videbitis quam brevis ad libertatem et quam expedita ducat via" – "I have set life on a downward slope: if it is prolonged, only observe and you will see what a short and easy path leads to the freedom."
52 Armisen-Marchetti 1989, 87–88.
53 See Wildberger 2006, vol. 1, p. 293.
54 So Tacitus may speak of an ostentatious death, as in the *Agricola* 41: "mors ambitiosa;" see Edwards 2007, 125.
55 "Quocumque respexeris, ibi malorum finis est. Vides illum praecipitem locum? illac ad libertatem descenditur. Vides illud mare, illud flumen, illum puteum? libertas illic in imo sedet. Vides illam arborem breuem retorridam infelicem? pendet inde libertas. Vides iugulum tuum, guttur tuum, cor tuum? effugia servitutis sunt. Nimis tibi operosos exitus monstro et multum animi ac roboris exigentes? Quaeris quod sit ad libertatem iter? quaelibet in corpore tuo vena" – "In whatever direction you may turn your eyes, there lies the means to end our woes. See you that precipice? Down that is the way to liberty. See you that sea, that river, that well? There sits liberty – at the bottom. See you that tree, stunted, blighted, and barren? Yet from its branches hangs liberty. See you that throat of yours, your gullet, your heart? They are ways of escape from servitude. Are the ways of egress

blends the imagery of philosophy and the *topoi* of tragedy. A detailed catalog of suicidal intentions and scenarios of death expands and amplifies the traditional listing of tragedy (for example:[56] rock, rope, and sword), finally reducing it to the throbbing vein as the minimal[57] but highly effective path to freedom. A strongly anti-tyrannical voice characterizes this part of *De ira*, given that the words belong to an exhortation to manly resistance directed at victims of the despotic wrath of Persian kings and introduced by the premise that (15.3) the aim of the philosopher is to demonstrate ("ostendemus") that in any kind of servitude the way lies open to freedom. This last motif appears in similar terms also in the *Consolatio ad Marciam*, a work that is characterized by the leitmotif of suicide. The voluntary death of Marcia's father Cremutius Cordus, "a man free in thought, in purpose, and in act,"[58] is, right from the opening words of the philosopher, compared to an open route of escape from servitude (1.2: "illam unam patere servitutis fugam"), the only way that Cremutius could take to escape from Sejanus and his brigands. The theme is exalted again in chapter 20, where the voluntary death of Marcia's father is seen as the only feasible course of action in the face of the sadism of the tyrant and in the face of a hell-on-earth represented by the tortures inflicted by an oppressive power. Here too, true freedom takes the paradoxical form of a conscious step taken toward death, which, in a context so deeply marked by recent history, assumes all the appearance of liberation from intolerable slavery.[59]

I show you too toilsome, do they require too much courage and strength? Do you ask what is the highway to liberty? Any vein in your body!"

56 See also Sen. *Ep.* 70.12: "In nulla re magis quam in morte morem animo gerere debemus. Exeat qua impetum cepit: sive ferrum appetit sive laqueum sive aliquam potionem venas occupantem, pergat et vincula servitutis abrumpat" – "There is no occasion when the soul should be humoured more than at the moment of death. Let the soul depart as it feels itself impelled to go; whether it seeks the sword, or the halter, or some draught that attacks the veins, let it proceed and burst the bonds of its slavery." This three-fold tragic choice is the object also of parody, from Aristophanes to Lucilius *Frg.* 601 Marx ("suspendat se an in gladium incumbat, ne caelum bibat") and Petronius 94.8–11; see Degl'Innocenti Pierini 2012, 107.

57 This motif also returns in Sen. *Ep.* 70.16: "Non opus est vasto vulnere dividere praecordia: scalpello aperitur ad illam magnam libertatem via et puncto securitas constat" – "If you would pierce your heart, a gaping wound is not necessary – a lancet will open the way to that great freedom, and tranquillity can be purchased at the cost of a pin-prick."–

58 Sen. *Marc.* 1.3: "homo ingenio animo manu liber."

59 See also *Marc.* 20.3: "Non est molestum servire ubi, si dominii pertaesum est, licet uno gradu ad libertatem transire. Caram te, vita, beneficio mortis habeo!" – "Slavery is no hardship when, if a man wearies of the yoke, by a single step he may pass to freedom. O life, by the favour of death I hold you dear!"

Far from being equated with the freedom offered by the political life or by the exercise of rights, or even with the *libertas senatoria*, the freedom of a senator (to the best of my knowledge, there is no passage in Seneca linking Senate and freedom),[60] Seneca's idea of freedom does not seem to undergo any evolution or deviation, as the passage from *De brevitate vitae* 5, from which we started, clearly seems to indicate. The reflection on past history also leads the philosopher not to underestimate the practical management of this "resource" at difficult moments in the life of the Roman state: To him, the choice of suicide constantly appears as a possible route, available to avoid wrong compromises, and to protect from harm the integrity of an inalienable good, to the point that, as Italo Lana quite rightly states, sometimes rather than speaking of freedom in Seneca, we should speak of liberation.[61]

At this point, I believe, we must ask what space the concept of freedom occupies in Seneca's political treatise *De clementia*. In this work the concept is afforded only marginal attention. The word *libertas* occurs five times, of which only two occurrences are of a certain importance for understanding the meaning in perspective: In the concise face-to-face dialogue between the intellectual and the sovereign. Freedom is presented as a tangible good, a good that the emperor can donate, as in 1.1.2 in the words of Nero, the "arbiter of life and death for the nations," when he places the emphasis on the fact that "what nations shall be utterly destroyed, which banished, which shall receive the gift of liberty, which have it taken from them, what kings shall become slaves and whose heads shall be crowned with royal honour, what cities shall fall and which shall rise, this it is mine to decree"[62] and, above all, in 1.1.8, where the philosopher maintains that "before their eyes hovers the fairest vision of a state which lacks no element of complete liberty except the license of self-destruction,"[63] by which Seneca means that uncontrolled freedom (*licentia*) which, in *Ep.* 104.28, with reference to the Athens of Socrates, he describes as more cruel than wars and tyrants ("in libertate bellis ac tyrannis saeviore"). The freedom under the rule of the emperor (*principatus*) is guaranteed by the coercive and mitigating activity of the emperor (*princeps*) toward the people, who are seen in the first chapter of the work as a "vast throng – discordant, factious, and unruly, ready to run riot alike for the destruction of others and

---

60 On *libertas senatoria*, see Wirszubski 1950, 130.
61 Lana 1973, 108–110. See also Setaioli 2014, 255–256. On the idea of suicide as a form of self-healing see the contribution by Tommaso Gazzarri in this volume.
62 *Cl.* 1.1.2: "princeps vitae necisque gentibus arbiter;" "quibus [sc. nationibus] libertatem dari, quibus eripi, mea iuris dictio est."
63 *Cl.* 1.1.8: "Obversatur oculis laetissima forma rei publicae, cui ad summam libertatem nihil deest nisi pereundi licentia."

itself"[64] and therefore the most irrational element that can be imagined, which consequently needs the restraint of the most rational virtue of an emperor, *clementia*. Also in this case, it is not difficult to observe that the imperial political struggle is based on autocracy,[65] and that Seneca offers a prelude to the Tacitus of *Agricola* 3.1, who exalts the action of Nerva as capable of amalgamating *principatus* and freedom, which were incompatible before ("res olim dissociabilis").[66]

In Seneca's *De clementia* the enlightened *princeps*, who guarantees the freedom of individuals, is however called to exercise control over his own prerogatives, which consists in limiting, paradoxically, his own freedom of speech and in being aware that true slavery (*servitus*) is not that of his subjects but that of the sovereign with respect to the task assigned to him by the gods, with whom he shares the same hard necessity (*necessitas*). This is an important conceptual intersection, which involves the Hellenistic theory of the noble slavery of kings (*endoxos douleia, nobilis servitus*)[67] and which is based on the leitmotif of restricted freedom to act (*non licere*).[68] Thus Seneca portrays in *Cl*. 1.8.1 the surprise of the young emperor Nero who regards it as a serious matter that "kings are not allowed that freedom of speech which the most humble citizens possess,"[69] and the *princeps* is almost unexpectedly opposed not to Seneca as a severe teacher of morals but to a private citizen, who describes himself as free to move around through the city according to his whim: "How many things there are which you may not do, which we, thanks to you, may do! It is possible for me to walk alone without fear in any part of the city I please,

---

64 *Cl*. 1.1.1: "hanc immensam multitudinem discordem, seditiosam, impotentem, in perniciem alienam suamque pariter exsultaturam, si hoc iugum fregerit."
65 On the individualism of imperial power, see D'Ippolito 2003, 17.
66 On the well-known formula and the relationship of these elements in the early imperial age, see Hammond 1963.
67 The reading of the manuscripts (*nobis esse* O, *esse nobis* A) was emended to *nobilem* by Wilamowitz 1902, 307 on the basis of Ael. *V.H.* 2.20, where Antigonus Gonatas speaks of *endoxos douleia* in connection with the monarch's task. (This text was accepted and defended by Malaspina 2001, *ad loc.*) On the relationship between Antigonus and Stoicism, see Volkmann 1967, 155f.; Adam 1970, 27f.
68 The same idea appears already in Sen. *Polyb.* 7.2: "Caesari quoque ipsi, cui omnia licent, propter hoc ipsum multa non licent" – "Even Caesar himself, who may do all things, may not do many things for the very same reason."
69 See also *Cl*. 1.7.4: "Regi vociferatio quoque verborumque intemperantia non ex maiestate est" – "In a king, even loud speech and unbridled words ill accord with his majesty."

though no companion attends me, though I have no sword at my house, none at my side."⁷⁰

Even though he is addressing Nero here, Seneca comes close to a tone that is typical of diatribe directness, partly because the freedom of speech seems to evoke almost the impudence embraced by a Cynic; it is only a momentary, but in my opinion significant, flash of frankness, and this is confirmed also by a clear consonance with a famous passage of the *Satires* of Horace (1.6.110–115), in which the poet describes his solitary, free movements through the streets of Rome, contrasting himself with those who, for reasons of representation and power, are always accompanied by a large retinue.⁷¹ Equally illuminating in this sense is a passage of the sixth oration by Dio Chrysostom, entitled *Diogenes, or On Tyranny*,⁷² which is characterized by the marked opposition between the life of the Persian king and that of the exile, Diogenes of Sinope, who describes himself in terms very similar to those of Seneca: "I, however," says Diogenes, "walk (*badizō*) by night wherever I will, and travel by day unattended, and I am not afraid to go even through an army if need be, without the herald's staff, yea, and amid brigands" (D.Chr. 6.60).⁷³ As we can see also from this very short quotation, the opposition between the despot and the Cynic Diogenes is extremely clear.⁷⁴ This pattern of opposition, probably as a heritage of an anti-tyrannical, libertarian tradition derived from the Cynics, emerges in Seneca too. All the same it is amply outweighed by an attitude that seeks multiple mediations through the Stoic, and Roman, doctrine of the state as a living organism, of which the emperor is the spirit (*spiritus*) and mind (*ratio*) that prevents the countless masses (*immensa multitudo*) of the

---

70 *Cl.* 1.8.2: "Quam multa tibi non licent, quae nobis beneficio tuo licent! Possum in qualibet parte urbis solus incedere sine timore, quamvis nullus sequatur comes, nullus sit domi, nullus ad latus gladius."
71 A more detailed discussion is given in Degl'Innocenti Pierini 1990, 249f.
72 See Malaspina 2001 on this passage. The translations of Dio's Discourses are quoted from Cohoon 1932.
73 It is worthwhile underlining that the whole speech presents significant points of contact with arguments present in *De clementia*. Suffice it to point out for my purposes what we read in § 40, where Diogenes maintains that "Still, all human ills admit of this one consolation, they may possibly come to an end. The prisoner in chains expects some time to be set free; it is not impossible for the exile to return to his home; and he who is sick can hope until the end comes for recovery. But the tyrant may not escape his condition; no, he cannot even so much as pray except it be for something else."
74 Desideri 1978, 201f. comments on this prominent opposition between the despot and the Cynic Diogenes, observing that social pessimism is implicit in the collapse of a pattern of political organization. There exist only the two figures of the intellectual and the despot, who are opposed in the social void of an ideal confrontation, the outcome of which may be taken for granted.

empire from rushing to their own ruin,[75] and includes in itself a paternalistic vision of imperial power that makes it possible that even the freedom and the safety of the individual is defined as a favor graciously donated by the emperor to his subjects (see above, p. 181f., on *Cl.* 1.8.2).

The accentuated comparison of the first part of Seneca's political treatise, which sees the philosopher-advisor and the *princeps* interacting in a close, face-to-face dialogue, in an almost theatrical *mise-en-scène*,[76] seems to have been continued in the famous parting dialogue between the advisor and Nero which we read in Tacitus *Ann.* 14.53f. Also from the formal point of view, we find significant traces of Tacitus' reception of Seneca's work. In the role-playing that has its origin in the negative evolution of the relations with the *princeps*, the amazement that characterized the beginning of Nero's speech[77] in *De Clementia*, is here attributed to the philosopher: "Is it I, born in the station of a simple knight and a provincial, who am numbered with the magnates of the realm?"[78] Seneca asks rhetorically in Tacitus. Here too the gratitude of the *princeps* is presented as the reason for the changed conditions of the philosopher, but there is no doubt that similar metaphors and images, like that of brightness (*fulgor*) for example,[79] are strained to take on a different meaning. In Tacitus they underline the oppression by a power of which the philosopher now wants to be free, a desire which leads him to exclaim: "Where is that spirit which found contentment in mediocrity?"[80] Tacitus perceptively detects one of the fundamental motifs of Seneca's thought, the demonization of the power of money that is manifested in the disgust for possessing only in order to possess: Seneca's unhampered walk around Rome in *De clementia* is transformed in the Tacitean context into a rich landowner's solemn inspection of his possessions, which he has seen rapidly growing around him, and which he now with surprised disappointment sees as something extraneous to him: "Is this the man who is building up his garden terraces, who paces grandly through these suburban parks, and revels in the affluence of such

---

75 *Cl.* 1.3.5: "In the same way this vast throng, encircling the life of one man, is ruled by his spirit, guided by his reason, and would crush and cripple itself with its own power if it were not upheld by wisdom."
76 So comments Mazzoli 2003, 123 138; see in particular 131.
77 Only a mention in the commentary of Köstermann *ad loc.*
78 "Egone, equestri et provinciali loco ortus, proceribus civitatis adnumeror? inter nobiles et longa <de>cora praeferentes novitas mea enituit? ubi est animus ille modicis contentus?"
79 See, e.g,. Tac. *Ann.* 14.54: "Nec me in paupertatem ipse detrudam, sed traditis quorum fulgore praestringor, quod temporis hortorum aut villarum curae seponitur in animum revocabo;" Sen. *Ep.* 94.58: "Vis scire quam falsus oculos tuos deciperit fulgor?" Translations of Tacitus are taken from Jackson 1937.
80 "Ubi est animus ille modicis contentus?"

broad lands and such widely-spread investments?"[81] In the dialogue with the *princeps* in Tacitus, there is no room for the word "freedom," but it is clear that through his refusal of the *res*, the riches accumulated, Tacitus' Seneca is implicitly represented as a man in search of freedom from the indifferent things (*adiaphora*)[82] and the vain occupations, which they inevitably involve, indeed, in search of liberation from these, or at least of the beginning of this rediscovered route to true wisdom.

Bibliography

Adam, Traute. 1970. *Clementia Principis: Der Einfluss hellenistische Fürstenspiegel auf den Versuch einer rechtlichen Fundierung des Principats durch Seneca*. Stuttgart: Klett.
Allen, Walter. 1944: "Cicero's House and Libertas." *TAPhA* 75: 1–9.
Armisen-Marchetti, Mireille. 1989. *Sapientiae facies: Étude sur les images de Sénèque*. Paris: Les Belles Lettres.
Bartsch, Shadi. 2009. "Senecan Metaphor and Stoic Self-Instruction." In *Seneca and the Self*, edited by Shadi Bartsch and David Wray, 188–217. Cambridge: Cambridge University Press.
Basore, John W., ed. and trans. 1928–1935. *Seneca, Moral Essays*. 3 vols. London; New York: Heinemann; Putnam.
Bellincioni, Maria, ed. and trans. 1979. *Lucio Anneo Seneca, Lettere a Lucilio, Libro XV: Le lettere 94 e 95*. Brescia: Paideia Editrice.
Bellincioni, Maria. 1984. *Potere ed etica in Seneca: Clementia e voluntas amica*. Brescia: Paideia Editrice.
Berno, Francesca Romana. 2006. *L. Anneo Seneca, Lettere a Lucilio libro VI: Le lettere 53–57*. Bologna: Pàtron.
Boyle, Anthony James, ed. and trans. 2008. *Octavia: Attributed to Seneca: Edited with Introduction, Translation, and Commentary*. Oxford: Clarendon Press.
Cicero. 1919. *De Officiis*. See Miller 1913.
Cicero. 1948. *De oratore; De fato; Paradoxa Stoicorum; De partitione oratoria*. See Rackham 1948.
Cicero. 1999. *Letters to Atticus*. See Shackleton Bailey 1999.
Codoñer, Carmen. 2003. "La expresión del poder en Seneca." In *Seneca uomo politico e l'età di Claudio e di Nerone: Atti del Convegno internazionale Capri 25–27 marzo 1999*, edited by Arturo De Vivo and Elio Lo Cascio, 55–88. Bari: Edipuglia.
Cohoon, James W., trans. 1932. *Dio Chrysostom, Discourses 1–11*. London; Cambridge: Heinemann; Harvard University Press.
Colish, Marcia L. 1985. *The Stoic Tradition from Antiquity to the Early Middle Ages*. 2 vols. Leiden: Brill.
Degl'Innocenti Pierini, Rita. 1990. *Tra Ovidio e Seneca*. Bologna: Pàtron.
Degl'Innocenti Pierini, Rita. 1999. *Tra filosofia e poesia: Studi su Seneca e dintorni*. Bologna: Pàtron.

---

81 "Talis hortos extruit et per haec suburbana incedit et tantis agrorum spatiis, tam lato faenore exuberat?"
82 On *adiaphora* in Stoicism, see Inwood 1985, 197–201; Fortenbaugh 1983, 15–18.

Degl'Innocenti Pierini, Rita. 2003. "Cicerone nella prima età imperiale: Luci ed ombre su un martire della repubblica." In *Aspetti della fortuna di Cicerone nella cultura latina: Atti del III Symposium Ciceronianum Arpinas (Arpino 10 maggio 2002)*, edited by Emanuele Narducci, 3–54. Firenze: Le Monnier.

Degl'Innocenti Pierini, Rita. 2006. "I naufragi degli altri: Cicerone e gli otia del 59 nella testimonianza dell'epistolario." In *"Concentus ex dissonis:" Scritti in onore di Aldo Setaioli*, edited by Carlo Santini, Loriano Zurli, and Luca Cardinali, 535–548. Napoli: Edizioni Scientifiche Italiane.

Degl'Innocenti Pierini, Rita. 2007. "Per voce sola: L'eloquente retorica del silenzio e dell'incomunicabilità nell'esilio antico (e moderno)." *Aevum(ant)* 7: 179–193.

Degl'Innocenti Pierini, Rita. 2008. "La tragedia nelle Tuscolane di Cicerone tra esemplarità e terapia: Riflessioni in margine agli Inferi a teatro." In *La riflessione sul teatro nella cultura romana: Atti del Convegno internazionale (Milano 10–12 maggio 2006)*, edited by Giuseppe Aricò and Mario Rivoltella, 41–64. Milano: Vita e pensiero.

Degl'Innocenti Pierini, Rita. 2012. "Scenari romani per un mito greco: l'Oedipus di Seneca." In *Edipo Classico e Contemporaneo*, edited by Francesco Citti and Alessandro Iannucci, 89–114. Hildesheim: Olms.

Desideri, Paolo. 1978. *Dione di Prusa: Un intellettuale greco nell'impero romano*. Messina; Firenze: D'Anna.

Dio Chrysostom. 1932. *Discourses 1–11*. See Cohoon 1932.

D'Ippolito, Federico. 2003. "Etica e stato in età giulio-claudia." In *Seneca uomo politico e l'età di Claudio e di Nerone: Atti del Convegno internazionale Capri 25–27 marzo 1999*, edited by Arturo De Vivo and Elio Lo Cascio, 9–35. Bari: Edipuglia.

Edwards, Catharine. 2007. *Death in Ancient Rome*. New Haven: Yale University Press.

Edwards, Catharine. 2009. "Free Yourself! Slavery, Freedom and the Self in Seneca's Letters." In *Seneca and the Self*, edited by Shadi Bartsch and David Wray, 139–159. Cambridge: Cambridge University Press.

Fortenbaugh, William W. 1983. *On Stoic and Peripatetic Ethics: The Work of Arius Didymus*. New Brunswick; London: Transaction.

Garbarino, Giovanna. 2001. "Necessità e libertà in Seneca tragico." In *Incontri con Seneca: Atti della giornata di studio Torino, 26 ottobre 1999*, edited by Giovanna Garbarino and Italo Lana, 29–48. Bologna: Pàtron.

Goar, Robert. 1987. *The Legend of Cato Uticensis from the First Century B.C. to the Fifth Century A.D.* Bruxelles: Latomus.

Griffin, Miriam T. 1992. *Seneca: A Philosopher in Politics*. 2nd ed. Oxford: Clarendon Press.

Grimal, Pierre. 1978. *Sénèque ou la conscience de l'Empire*. Paris: Les Belles Lettres.

Grimal, Pierre. 1989. *Les erreurs de la liberté*. Paris: Les Belles Lettres.

Gummere, Richard M., ed. and trans. 1917–1925. *Seneca, Ad Lucilium epistulae morales*. 3 vols. London; Cambridge: Heinemann; Harvard University Press.

Hammond, Mason. 1963. " 'Res Olim Dissociabiles: Principatus ac Libertas:' Liberty under the Early Roman Empire." *HSPh* 67: 93–113.

Hill, Timothy. 2004. *Ambitiosa Mors: Suicide and Self in Roman Thought and Literature*. London; New York: Routledge.

Inwood, Brad. 1985. *Ethics and Human Action in Early Stoicism*. Oxford: Clarendon Press.

Inwood, Brad. 2005. *Reading Seneca: Stoic Philosophy at Rome*. Oxford: Clarendon Press.

Isnardi Parente, Margherita. 2000. "Socrate e Catone in Seneca: Il filosofo e il politico." In *Seneca e il suo tempo: Atti del Convegno internazionale di Roma-Cassino*

11–14 Novembre 1998, edited by Piergiorgio Parroni, 215–225. Roma: Salerno Editrice.
Jackson, John, ed. and trans. 1937. *Tacitus, The Annals: Books 13–16*. London; Cambridge: Heinemann; Harvard University Press.
Ker, James. 2009. *The Deaths of Seneca*. Oxford; New York: Oxford University Press.
Köstermann, Erich. 1963–1968. *Tacitus, Annalen*. Heidelberg: Winter.
Lana, Italo. 1973. "La libertà nel mondo antico." In *Studi sul pensiero politico classico*, 17–39. Napoli: Guida.
Lanzarone, Nicola, ed. 2008. *Senecae Dialogorum liber I De providentia*. Firenze: Le Monnier.
Lotito, Gianfranco. 2001. *Suum esse: Forme dell'interiorità senecana*. Bologna: Pàtron.
Lucan. 1905. *The Pharsalia*. See Ridley 1905.
Malaspina, Ermanno, ed. 2001. *L. Annaei Senecae De clementia libri duo*. Alessandria: Edizioni dell'Orso.
Mazzoli, Giancarlo. 1984. "Il problema religioso in Seneca." *RSI* 96: 953–999.
Mazzoli, Giancarlo. 2000. "Le 'voci' dei Dialoghi di Seneca." In *Seneca e il suo tempo: Atti del Convegno int. di Roma-Cassino 11–14 novembre 1998*, edited by Piergiorgio Parroni, 249–260. Roma: Salerno Editrice.
Mazzoli, Giancarlo. 2003. "Lo spettacolo del potere nel De clementia di Seneca." In *Intellettuali e potere nel mondo antico: Atti del Convegno nazionale di studi (Torino 22–23–24 aprile 2002)*, edited by Renato Uglione, 123–138. Alessandria: Edizioni dell'Orso.
Migliario, Elvira. 2007. *Retorica e storia: Una lettura delle Suasoriae di Seneca padre*. Bari: Edipuglia.
Miller, Frank Justus, ed. and trans.. 1917–1919. *Seneca's Tragedies*. 2 vols. London; New York: Heinemann; G. P. Putnam's Sons
Miller, Walter, ed. and trans. 1913. *Cicero, De Officiis*. London; Cambridge: Heinemann; Harvard University Press.
Narducci, Emanuele. 2002. *Lucano: Un'epica contro l'impero: Interpretazione della "Pharsalia."* Roma; Bari: Laterza.
Nicholson, John. 1998. "The Survival of Cicero's Letters." In *Studies in Latin Literature and Roman History IX*, edited by Carl Deroux, 63–105. Bruxelles: Latomus.
Pecchiura, Paolo. 1965. *La figura di Catone Uticense nella letteratura latina*. Torino: Giappichelli.
Rackham, Harris, ed. and trans. 1948. *Cicero, De oratore; De fato; Paradoxa Stoicorum; De partitione oratoria*. London; Cambridge: Heinemann; Harvard University Press.
Ridley, Edward, trans. *The Pharsalia of Lucan*. London: Longmans, Green, and Co. 1905.
Roller, Matthew. 2001. *Constructing Autocracy: Aristocrats and Emperors in Julio-Claudian Rome*. Princeton: Princeton University Press.
Scarpat, Giuseppe. 2007. *Seneca: Anticipare la morte o attenderla: La lettera 70 a Lucilio*. Brescia: Paideia.
Schiesaro, Alessandro. 2003. *The Passions in Play: Thyestes and the Dynamics of Senecan Drama*. Cambridge: Cambridge University Press.
Seneca. 1917–1919. *Tragedies*. See Miller 1917–1919.
Seneca. 1917–1925. *Ad Lucilium epistulae morales*. See Gummere 1917–1925.
Seneca. 1928–1935. *Moral Essays*. See Basore 1928–1935.
Seneca. 1982. *La brevità della vita*. See Traina 1982.
Seneca. 2001. *De clementia*. See Malaspina 2001.
Seneca. 2003. *De otio; De brevitate vitae*. See Williams 2003.
Seneca. 2008. *Dialogorum liber I De providentia*. See Lanzarone 2008.
[Seneca]. 2008. *Octavia*. See Boyle 2008.

Seneca the Elder. 1974. *Declamations*. See Winterbottom 1974.
Setaioli, Aldo. 2003. "Seneca e Cicerone." In *Aspetti della fortuna di Cicerone nella cultura latina: Atti del III Symposium Ciceronianum Arpinas (Arpino 10 maggio 2002)*, edited by Emmanuele Narducci, 55–77. Firenze: Le Monnier.
Setaioli, Aldo. 2014. "Philosophy as Therapy, Self-Transformation and 'Lebensform'." In *Brill's Companion to Seneca: Philosopher and Dramatist*, edited by Gregor Damschen and Andreas Heil, 239–256. Leiden; Boston: Brill.
Shackleton Bailey, David Roy. 1999. *Cicero, Letters to Atticus*. Vol. 4. Cambridge; London: Harvard University Press.
Syme, Ronald. 1958. *Tacitus*. 2 vols. Oxford: Clarendon Press.
Tacitus. 1937. *The Annals: Books 13–16*. See Jackson 1937.
Traina, Alfonso, ed. and trans. 1982. *Seneca, La brevità della vita*. 3rd ed. Torino: Loescher.
Traina, Alfonso. 1987. *Lo stile "drammatico" del filosofo Seneca*. 4th ed. Bologna: Pàtron.
Traina, Alfonso. 2000. "Introduzione a Seneca." In *Seneca: Letture critiche*. 2nd ed. Milano: Mursia.
Volkmann, Hans. 1967. "Die Basileia als ἔνδοξος δουλεία: Ein Beitrag zur Wortgeschichte der Duleia." *Historia* 16: 155–161.
Warmington, Eric Herbert, ed. and trans. *Remains of Old Latin*. Vol. 2: *Livius Andronicus; Naevius; Pacuvius; Accius*. London; Cambridge: Heineman; Harvard University Press.
Wilamowitz-Möllendorff, Ulrich von. 1902. "Lesefruechte." *Hermes* 37: 302–314.
Wildberger, Jula. 2006. *Seneca und die Stoa: Der Platz des Menschen in der Welt*. 2 vols. Berlin; New York: De Gruyter.
Williams, Gareth D. 2003. *Seneca, De otio; De brevitate vitae*. Cambridge: Cambridge University Press.
Winterbottom, Michael, ed. and trans. 1974. *The Elder Seneca, Declamations in Two Volumes*. 2 vols. London; Cambridge: Heinemann; Harvard University Press.
Wirszubski, Chaim. 1950. *Libertas as a Political Idea at Rome During the Late Republic and Early Principate*. Cambridge: Cambridge University Press.

Torture in Seneca's Philosophical Works: Between Justification and Condemnation

Jean-Christophe Courtil
Université de Toulouse II-Le Mirail

The mutilated body is a significant theme frequently encountered in Seneca's tragedies. This topic has received much attention and has often been considered as their main characteristic.[1] However, as there are more than two hundred and fifty allusions to torture[2] – an intentional mutilation of a body – in Seneca's extant philosophical works,[3] it clearly appears that this theme, far from being peculiar to the tragedies, is a central issue in Seneca's thought.

Regarding the tragedies, there have been only literary explanations for the motif of torture. The first of these explanations postulates an influence of education on Seneca's works. Indeed, Roman declamation expresses a very peculiar taste for cruel stories and specifically for torture scenes.[4] Nevertheless, even if the rhetorical influence on Seneca's style is obvious, literary reasons cannot be the only explanation for the numerous references to a motif. The second explanation refers to stylistic tastes in the Early Empire. Many scholars have noted that works of post-Augustan literature express an obvious taste for descriptions of gory scenes, with an emphasis on gruesome details. They have deduced that at that time there must have existed an aesthetic of horror, which was also described as "mannerism,"[5] "baroque"[6] or "expressionism."[7] However, it is hard to conceive the creation of frightening images of torture scenes as an end in itself, that is to

---

1   See, e.g., Regenbogen 1930; Pasche 1976, 1 and 41; Hallak 1985; Most 1992, 391–419; Schiesaro 2003, 20–21; Tarrant 2006, 5. – I am very grateful to Christelle-Rébecca Fairise and Joshua Parks for their amiable and efficient help in translating this paper.
2   I have taken into account all the passages in which an instrument or method of torture is mentioned.
3   I mean the *Dialogues*, *Letters*, *Quaestiones Naturales*, and prose fragments.
4   See Most 1992; Van Mal Maeder 2007, 81. On the influence of rhetoric on Seneca's works, see Setaioli 1985, 814–817; Traina 1987, 25–41.
5   Wanke 1964; Burck 1971.
6   Segal 1984, 311–325; André 1989, 1766.
7   Berti 2007, 329–340.

say, as a literary performance which is a feature of mannerism. The third explanation is that Seneca himself had a "peculiar taste" and an "obsession"[8] with gruesome images. The idea that Seneca, grimly fascinated by horror, depicted scenes of mutilations with great pleasure became a commonplace critical approach.[9] But the quasi-anatomical descriptions of battle wounds are traditional in classical literature. They are also a *topos* of epic poetry, which goes back to Homer and can be found in Vergil[10] and Ovid as well as in Roman theater.[11] None of these stylistic or biographical explanations, which are only based on the tragic corpus and not on the philosophical œuvre, is sufficient to explain the omnipresence of torture in a set of works which are above all a display of Stoic philosophy.

Yet, there are almost no studies about conceptions of torture in the large bibliography dealing with Seneca's thought. In the present article it will be shown that, beyond socio-historical and literary reasons, the clear emphasis on the tortured body is first of all a consequence of the author's political and philosophical system of thought. This philosophical perspective will allow us to define Seneca's position on torture as lying between justification and condemnation. Stoicism was often perceived as the school of thought which, before the rise of Christianity, softened cruelty in violent acts with a new concern for other human beings (*humanitas*).[12] However, I will show that Seneca expresses a nuanced view on the matter which is far from a firm condemnation. I will then try to demonstrate that in Seneca's works physical punishment can also appear as something that is put to productive use.

I. The Torture Motif in Seneca's Philosophical Works

In Seneca's philosophical works we find a great variety of different forms of torments, not only regarding the means used and the kinds of injuries inflicted but also regarding the body parts concerned. It is a remarkable catalog of *modi operandi*, which runs the gamut from more traditional forms of torture to those more elaborately devised. The torture most

---

8   Favez 1947, 158. See also Cupaiuolo 1973, 39; Hallak 1985, 4; Segal 1983, 186–187; Most 1992, 400.
9   See, e.g., Bayet 1965, 328. On this commonplace, see Aygon 2004, 120.
10 See Heuzé 1985, chapter 2, and e.g., Vergil, *A*. 9.698–701.
11 For the torture motif in Roman theater, see, e.g., Pl. *As*. 481; *Mil*. 502, 511; Ter. *Ad*. 313; *An*. 622, 786.
12 On Seneca's *humanitas*, see Boyancé 1965, 231–245; Sørensen 1984; Bauman 2000, 79–82; Bradley 2008, 345.

frequently evoked is flagellation,[13] performed with the *flagella* or *verbera*, whips destined to chastise slaves, for whom this punishment was reserved in theory.[14] Fire was also a very common means of torture applied in various fashions, e.g., the branding of a fugitive or thieving slave[15] or the application of burning objects to the skin,[16] which most of the time were red-hot iron blades, so-called *laminae*. Another form of fire torture was cremation (*crematio*),[17] sometimes dramatically performed in order to emphasize the infamy of the condemned. According to Seneca's descriptions, the victim of a *crematio* was half-buried in a pit surrounded by flames[18] or clothed in the *tunica molesta*,[19] a shirt woven from and soaked in flammable materials. Death on the cross,[20] also called *servile supplicium* ("a punishment for slaves")[21] because of its infamous nature, was normally applied only to slaves and foreigners.[22] Seneca frequently refers to the cross[23] as the emblematic instrument of torture, and occasionally as a metonymy for those instruments in general.[24] Its vertical part, the *stipes*,

---

13 Sen. *Marc.* 20.3; *De ira* 1.16.5, 3.19.1; *Ep.* 24.14; 85.27. See Daremberg and Saglio 1877–1919, s.v. *flagellum*, vol. 2, p. 1152–1156.
14 See Mommsen 1907, vol. 3, p. 322; Ermann 2000.
15 Sen. *De ira* 3.3.6: "inscriptiones frontis" – "the branding of foreheads;" *Ep.* 4.4. All English translations of the *Dialogi*, *De beneficiis*, and *De clementia* are quoted from Basore 1928–1935, translations of the *Epistulae morales* from Gummere 1917–1925.
16 Sen. *Ep.* 7.5; 78.19; *Frg.* 96 Vottero, 124 Haase. See also Cic. *Ver.* 5.63; Hor. *Ep.* 1.15.36; Quint. *Decl.* 18.11.15 and 19.15. See Daremberg and Saglio 1877–1919, s.v. *quaestio*, vol. 4, p. 797.
17 Sen. *Marc.* 17.5; *De ira* 3.3.6, 3.19.1, 3.19.2; *Ben.* 4.21.6, 7.19.8; *Cl.* 2.4.1; *Ep.* 14.4; 24.13; 66.18; 67.3; 78.19; 85.26; 88.29; *Nat.* 4a pr. 17. On *crematio*, see Cantarella 1991, 112. It should be noted that it is sometimes difficult to distinguish among the occurrences of *ignis* those referring to *crematio* from those referring to the use of the *laminae*. According to Daremberg and Saglio 1877–1919 (s.v. *quaestio*, vol. 7, p. 797), *laminae* and *ignis* refer to the same *modus operandi*.
18 Sen. *De ira* 3.3.6: "circumdati defossis corporibus ignes" – "fires encircling living bodies implanted in the ground.".
19 Sen. *Ep.* 14.5: "illam tunicam alimentis ignium et illitam et textam" – "the terrible shirt smeared and interwoven with inflammable materials." See also Mart. *Ep.* 4.86.8; 10.25.5–6; Juv. 8.235.
20 See Daremberg and Saglio 1877–1919, s.v. *crux*, vol. 2, p. 1573–1575; Hengel 1977; Parente 1979; Briquel 1980; Zugibe 1984; Jaume 2008.
21 Cic. *Clu.* 66; *Phil.* 1.2.
22 Pl. *Mil.* 372; *Bac.* 362; Cic. *Clu.* 187; Caes. *B. Hisp.* 20.5; Hor. *S.* 1.3.80–81; Liv. 3.8.10, 22.23, 22.33.2, 24.14.7, 30.44.13; Tac. *Hist.* 4.3, 4.11; Juv. 6.219–223; Dio Cassius 49.12. See Mommsen 1907, vol. 3, p. 255.
23 Sen. *Marc.* 20.3; *De ira* 1.2.2 and 3.3.6; *Cl.* 1.23.1 and 1.26.1; *Brev. vit.* 19.3; *Prov.* 3.10; *Ep.* 14.5; 98.12; 101.12; 101.14.
24 *Cruces* is also used as a synonym of the generic terms *machina* or *instrumenta*: Sen. *Marc.* 20.3; *Ep.* 98.12 (for Regulus, who was not crucified).

could also be used for impalement,[25] in which case it was called the "sharp" or "pointed cross" (*acuta crux*).[26] Another form of torture often evoked by Seneca is being drawn and quartered, usually upon the rack (*eculeus*[27] or, by metonymy, *fidicula*[28]), a torment which was mainly used for interrogating slaves.[29] Torture could also include animals. The most well-known of these torments is the *damnatio ad bestias* ("condemnation to beasts"),[30] a punishment that consisted in being mauled to death by wild animals in the arena.[31] It was reserved for enslaved men or robbers as a more severe form of the death penalty. Another punishment which made use of animals was the well-known *culleus*[32] reserved for parricides.[33] The guilty offender was sewn into a leather sack hermetically sealed with pitch into which various animals had been introduced[34] and then thrown into the nearest river or directly into the sea. Seneca also mentions the punishment practiced by Publius Vedius Pollio, a very wealthy friend of Augustus notorious for his proverbial cruelty towards his slaves,[35] who had his clumsy servants devoured by huge moray eels, which he kept expressly for this purpose. Finally, Seneca counts among the different forms of torture also imprisonment under extreme and particularly excruciating conditions.[36] Besides these torments actually used by the Romans, to which

---

25 In Seneca's work, the word *stipes* always refers to the pale: *Marc.* 20.3; *Ep.* 14.5.
26 Sen. *Ep.* 101.10 and 11.
27 Sen. *De ira* 3.3.6 and 3.19.1; *Ben.* 4.21.6; *Cl.* 1.13.2; *Ep.* 14.5; 24.14; 66.18; 67.3; 71.21; 78.14; 78.19. See Daremberg and Saglio 1877–1919, s.v. *equuleus*, vol. 2, p. 794.
28 Sen. *Marc.* 20.3; *De ira* 3.3.6 and 3.19.1. See Daremberg and Saglio 1877–1919, s.v. *fidicula*, vol. 2, p. 117.
29 Cic. *Mil.* 21.57: "Facti enim in eculeo quaestio est [...]" – "It is facts that are extorted upon the rack [...]" (trans. Watts).
30 Sen. *De ira* 3.3.6; *Cl.* 1.18.2 and 2.6.2; *Brev. vit.* 13.6; *Ep.* 7.3–5; 14.4. See also Cic. *Pis.* 89; Suet. *Cal.* 27.
31 Sen. *Brev. vit.* 13.6: "elephantorum duodeviginti" – "eighteen elephants;" *Ep.* 7.4: "leonibus et ursis" – "to the lions and the bears."
32 Sen. *De ira* 1.16.5; *Cl.* 1.15.7 and 1.23.1.
33 See Mommsen 1907, vol. 2, p. 324; Briquel 1980, 87–107. See also Just. *Dig. fr.* 1.9, *Ad Leg. Pomp. de Parricid.* 48.9.
34 Seneca alludes to the presence of snakes in *Cl.* 1.15.7: "non culleum, non serpentes [...] decrevit" – "His sentence was not the sack, nor serpents," just as in Juv. 8.212–214: "cuius [sc. Neronis] supplicio non debuit una parari / simia, nec serpens unus, nec culleus unus;" Quint. *Decl.* 17.9; Sen. *Con.* 5.4: "imaginabar mihi culleum, serpentis;" Just. *Dig.* 48.9.9.
35 *De ira* 3.40.2 and 3.40.4; *Cl.* 1.18.2. See also Plin. *Nat.* 9.77 and 9.167; Dio Cassius 54.23.2–4.
36 Sen. *De ira* 3.17.3: "in cavea velut novum aliquod animal et invisitatum [...] squalor et illuvies corporis in stercore suo destituti" – "in a cage as if he were some strange and unknown animal [...] starvation and squalor and the filth of a body left

others could be added – too many to be enumerated – there are also those that are part of legendary *exempla*: mythic, hyperbolic, and imaginary forms of torture, such as the famous bed in which Procrustes,[37] the Attic brigand and son of Neptune, forcefully mutilated his victims by shortening or stretching their limbs, or Phalaris' bronze bull,[38] in which the one to be tortured was enclosed and then roasted alive.

Two elements are common to all of these practices: the desire to inflict pain and their application, in theory, only to slaves and foreigners. Torture is the voluntary causation of physiological stress to make an individual – a slave or foreigner – suffer sharp pain for a specific purpose. While there is always the desire to inflict suffering, there can be three different motives for this desire: to make someone suffer for the pleasure that one derives from his suffering, out of anger, vengeance, or sadism (*crudelitas*); to make someone suffer a long and painful death in order to punish a crime with a painful bodily wound or a mutilation, on the basis of a sentence permitting the retributive act (*supplicium*); to make someone suffer in order to overpower his personal strength of will and force him to say what he refuses to reveal (*quaestio*). Torture can be the application of either a private and domestic punishment or a public one. The former is decided in an arbitrary manner by the master who wishes to punish a slave; the latter is usually decreed[39] by the tyrant and involves a political dimension.

Seneca's philosophical work contains two hundred and fifty-nine references to torture in a very large variety of situations and in many different forms. This number contrasts with only thirty-one in the tragedies. The tragedies therefore do not have a monopoly on the description of the brutalized body, as many have asserted.[40] It should be noted that, in the *Dialogi*, seventy references of one hundred and thirty-four come from *De ira* and twenty-six from *De clementia*, texts that particularly relate the mutilation of the body to these two notions: anger (*ira*) and mercy (*clementia*). The massive presence of the torture motif in these philosophical treatises also indicates its role as a departure point for a political and philosophical reflection.

---

to wallow in its own dung," 3.17.4: "angustiae loci" – "the narrowness of his quarters," 3.32.2: "fames" – "starvation;" *Prov*. 3.9; *Ep*. 70.6: "in caveam coniectus esset a tyranno et tamquam ferum aliquod animal aleretur" –"[…] was thrown into a cage by his tyrant, and fed there like some wild animal."

37 Sen. *Cl*. 2.14.1.
38 Sen. *Ben*. 7.19.8; *Ep*. 66.18.
39 In *De ira* 1.6.3, the magistrate inflicts the torture.
40 See n. 1.

II. The Socio-Political Dimension of Torture

II.1. Torture as a Symbol of Tyranny

Seneca's political condemnation of torture deals foremost with the broadening of its application to free men by a tyrannical regime. In Rome, torture as a consequence of a master's absolute power had at all times been reserved for slaves.[41] But the advent of the Empire saw the gradual demise of this basic principle of Roman legislation.[42] The punishment became an instrument of the state's defense: With the introduction of the *crimen maiestatis*, a legal procedure punishing an offence against the Emperor,[43] no one was exempt from torture. The use of flagellation was, for Seneca, indicative of this change.[44] Seneca evokes the fact that this very punishment was applied even to the Roman *equites* (members of the equestrian order) and to the senators whom Caligula had whipped:

> Modo C. Caesar Sex. Papinium, cui pater erat consularis, Betilienum Bassum quaestorem suum, procuratoris sui filium, aliosque et senatores et equites Romanos uno die flagellis cecidit, torsit […]
>
> Only recently Gaius Caesar slashed with the scourge and tortured Sextus Papinius, whose father had been consul, and Betilienus Bassus, his own quaestor and the son of his procurator, and others, both Roman senators and knights, all in one day […]" (Sen. *De ira* 3.18.3, trans. Basore).

Seneca vehemently opposes the idea that this punishment traditionally reserved for slaves[45] be applied to people of quality, to whom he refers by their social status first of all: a consul's son, a *quaestor*, and other senators and Roman *equites*, grouped together in an anonymous fashion based on the treatment reserved for them. Later on, Seneca underlines his indignation by emphasizing the contradiction between the social status of a slave and that of the senators, who were theoretically exempt from torture but were treated "as worthless slaves:"

> Magnam rem! si tres senatores quasi nequam mancipia inter verbera et flammas divisit homo qui de toto senatu trucidando cogitabat, qui optabat ut populus Romanus unam cervicem haberet […]
>
> A great matter, truly! Because three senators, as if no better than worthless slaves, were mangled by whip and flame at the behest of a man who contemplated mur-

---

41 See Pl. *Mos.* 991; Cic. *Ver.* 3.23 and 5.62; *Part.* 34.113; *Phil.* 11.2–3; [Quint.] *Decl. maior* 7: "Liberum hominem torqueri ne liceat." See also Daremberg and Saglio 1877–1919, vol. 4, p. 797; Mommsen 1907, vol. 2, p. 80.
42 See *Der Kleine Pauly* 1975, vol. 5, p. 888; Just. *Dig.* 9.41.1a.196.
43 See Mommsen 1907, vol. 2, p. 233.
44 See also Suet. *Cl.* 34; *Nero* 49; Gel. 17.21–24.
45 See Mommsen 1907, vol. 3, p. 322.

dering the whole senate, a man who used to wish that the Roman people had only one neck [...] (Sen. *De ira* 3.19.2, trans. Basore).

This kind of practice is strongly denounced by Seneca, whose view that to offend a senator is to offend the entire senate and thus all citizens is indicated by the progressive succession senators – the whole senate – the Roman people ("senatores [...] toto senatu [...] populus Romanus"). The rack was also, in theory, only applied to slaves who were undergoing interrogation. But it is present along with the whip in the list of torture instruments used by Caligula on senators.[46] Seneca states that Claudius also inflicted torture on free citizens, and even on those of the highest positions.[47] Even though, according to Dio Cassius,[48] this emperor had given his word at the time of his coronation that he would not submit citizens to torture, he demonstrated a particularly ferocious ardor when punishing parricides.[49] However, we know from Tacitus and Suetonius that Nero also resorted to this practice after the *quinquennium Neronis* (the first five years of Nero's reign).[50] It seems that Seneca, by recalling the punishments meted out by his cruel predecessors, tried to convince Nero not to use political torture.

Torture, especially that of free men, is in Seneca's works thus clearly linked to the tyrant, whose cruelty is a *topos* of Roman declamation.[51] Seneca often cites the example of Phalaris,[52] the tyrant of Agrigentum, whose perversity had become the archetype of tyrannical behavior,[53] and the example of Busiris, the legendary king of Egypt, another traditional paradigm of cruelty.[54] In Seneca's prose, tyrants who are avid torturers abound: On the one hand, there were legendary or semi-legendary ones

---

46 Sen. *De ira* 3.19.1: "Ceciderat flagellis senatores [...]" – "He had scourged senators [...]."
47 See also Tac. *Ann.* 11.22.
48 Dio Cassius, 60.24.
49 Sen. *Cl.* 1.23.1: "Pater tuus plures intra quinquennium culleo insuit quam omnibus saeculis insutos accepimus." – "Your father within five years had more men sewed up in the sack than, by all accounts, there had been victims of the sack throughout all time;" Suet. *Cl.* 34.1.
50 Tac. *Ann.* 15.56; Suet. *Nero* 15.44.
51 Sen. *Con.* 1.6, 1.7, 2.5, 3.6, 4.7, 5.8, 7.6, 9.4. See Van Mal-Maeder 2007, 74.
52 Sen. *De ira* 2.5.1; *Tranq. an.* 14.4; *Cl.* 2.4.3; *Ben.* 7.19.5 and 7.19.7; *Ep.* 66.18. See Halm-Tisserant 1998, 62–63.
53 Pindar, *P.* 1.95–98; Plb. *Frg.* 12.5; D.S. 13.90.4; 19.108.71; Cicero: 17 references; Hyg. *Fab.* 257; Liv. 33.73; Prop. *Eleg.* 2.25.11; Ov. *Ars* 1.653; *Ib.* 437; *Tr.* 3.11.51; 5.1.53; V. Max. 3.3, 9.2; Plin. *Nat.* 7.200, 34.89; Quint. *Inst.* 8.6; Juv. 6.614; 8.80.
54 Sen. *Cl.* 2.4.1. See also Apollod. 2.116–117; Cic. *Rep.* 3.15; Verg. *G.* 3.5; Hyg. *Fab.* 31 and 56; Ov. *Met.* 9.183–84; *Ars* 1.645–650; *Pont.* 3.6.41; *Tr.* 3.11.39; Quint. *Inst.* 2.17.

from foreign countries such as Phalaris and Busiris, but also the tyrants Hippias of Athens and Dionysius of Syracuse, the kings of Macedonia such as Alexander the Great and Lysimachus, and a Persian satrap.[55] On the other hand, there were those closer in time and space to Seneca and his contemporary readers, such as Sulla and, above all, Caligula and Claudius, two emperors of the Julio-Claudian dynasty.[56] The mention of the legendary figures using torture implicitly attributes to the Roman emperors the same barbarism as that of the foreign tyrants, whose cruelty was proverbial.[57] Furthermore, several passages associate Caligula explicitly with some of these tyrants: Seneca calls him "that Phalaris"[58] and describes him as a potential satrap.[59] For Seneca, the tyrant is not directly defined by his political power, but by his cruelty (*crudelitas*) and the blood (*cruor*) of citizens he sheds, a motif systematically present whenever the tyrant is mentioned:[60]

> Si vero sanguine humano non tantum gaudet, sed pascitur, sed et suppliciis omnium aetatium crudelitatem insatiabilem exercet [...] si arx eius cruore semper recenti madet [...]
>
> If, however, he not only delights in human blood, but feeds upon it; if also he exercises his insatiable cruelty in the torture of persons of all ages [...] if his castle is always wet with freshly shed blood [...] (Sen. *Ben.* 7.19.8, trans. Basore).

The torture that the tyrant favors is generally very gory, involving atrocious mutilations or animals, which are the symbolic reflection of the

---

55 Hippias: Sen. *De ira* 2.23.1; Dionysius: Sen. *Marc.* 17.5; Alexander: Sen. *De ira* 3.17.2; *Cl.* 1.25.1; Lysimachus: Sen. *De ira* 3.17.3; *Ep.* 70.6; Persian satrap: Sen. *De ira* 3.20.1.
56 Sulla: Sen. *De ira* 3.18.1; Caligula: Sen. *De ira* 3.18.1 and 3.19.1–4; *Nat.* 4a pr. 17; Claudius: Sen. *Cl.* 1.23.1.
57 See *De ira* 3.18.1: "Utinam ista saevitia intra peregrina exempla mansisset nec in Romanos mores cum aliis adventiciis vitiis etiam suppliciorum irarumque barbaria transisset!" – "Would to heaven that the examples of such cruelty had been confined to foreigners, and that along with other vices from abroad the barbarity of torture and such venting of anger had not been imported into the practices of Romans!"
58 Sen. *Tranq. an.* 14.4: "Phalaris ille."
59 Sen. *Ben.* 2.12.2.
60 Sen. *Marc.* 22.5 (Seianus); *De ira* 2.5.4 (Hannibal); *Tranq. an.* 14.3; *Cl.* 1.1.3, 1.7.3, 1.11.1; *Brev. vit.* 4.5 (Augustus in his youth); *Prov.* 3.7; *Ben.* 5.16.3 (Sulla); *Brev. vit.* 13.7 (Pompey); *Ep.* 83.25 (Anthony). See also Malaspina 2001, 321 and compare Plato, *R.* 8.565e; Sen. *Cl.* 1.12.2: "[...] quis tamen umquam tyrannus tam avide humanum sanguinem bibit quam ille [sc. Sulla] [...]?" – "[...] yet what tyrant ever drank so greedily of human blood as he [...]?"; *Ben.* 4.31.2: "Caium Caesarem [...] hominem humani sanguinis avidissimum" – "Gaius Caesar [...] a man so greedy of human blood."

tyrant's own ferocity.[61] The most emblematic tyrant characterized by such cruelty and the one most often referred to is Caligula. The frequent lists of torments in Seneca's works very often concern this emperor.[62] They contribute to a picture of sadistic cruelty as it is also found in his tragedies.[63] The tyrant thus becomes a veritable torturer, whose mere apparition constitutes torture.[64]

Seneca uses a certain number of traditionally tyrannical figures, but he especially stresses the cruelty of Nero's predecessors, examples from the recent past, in order to reflect on tyrannical cruelty: It is not a disinterested depiction of cruelty, but a warning against the possibility that the political system under which he lives may develop into tyranny.

II.2. Reason and Punishment: On the Productive Use of Suffering

The purpose of Seneca's political discourse in *De clementia* is not so much to condemn the use of torture but to persuade the emperor not to resort to it. Seneca presents the virtue of clemency, "moderation of a soul in the power of punishment,"[65] as an indication of a good ruler's inner quality. This ruler is for his subjects a loving and merciful father, whereas the bad ruler is a cruel father who severely punishes his children.[66] He is also the head of a large social body of which the citizens are members.[67] These two images, used several times by Seneca, clearly show that the emperor above

---

61   Mutilation: Sen. *De ira* 3.17.3: Lysimachus orders to cut off his friend Telesphorus' nose and ears; 3.18.1: Sulla orders to break legs, to put eyes out, to cut off the tongue and hands; 3.20.1: The Persian satrap orders to cut off the noses of an entire people. – Animals: Sen. *De ira* 3.17.2: Alexander's lion; *Cl.* 1.23.1: Claudius' sack full of snakes; *Ep.* 66.18: Phalaris' bronze bull.
62   Sen. *De ira* 3.18.1 and 3.19.1; *Brev. vit.* 18.6; *Nat.* 4a pr. 17.
63   Sen. *Ag.* 44–48: Thyestes; 988–997: Aegisthus; *Thy.* 720–775: Atreus.
64   Sen. *De ira* 3.19.1: "Torserat per omnia quae in rerum natura tristissima sunt, fidiculis talaribus, eculeo igne vultu suo" – "He [sc. Caligula] had tortured them by every unhappy device in existence, by the cord, by knotted bones, by the rack, by fire, by his own countenance."
65   Sen. *Cl.* 2.3.1: "Clementia est temperantia animi in potestate ulciscendi [...]."
66   Sen. *Cl.* 1.10.3 and 1.16.3: "Nonne pessimus pater videbitur qui adsiduis plagis liberos etiam ex levissimis causis compescet?" – "Will he not seem the worst sort of father who controls his children by constant whippings for even the most trifling offences?"
67   Sen. *Cl.* 1.5.1: "Nam si [...] tu animus rei publicae tuae es, illa corpus tuum, vides, ut puto, quam necessaria sit clementia: tibi enim parcis, cum videris alteri parcere" – "For if [...] you are the soul of the state and the state your body, you see, I think, how requisite is mercy; for you are merciful to yourself when you are seemingly merciful to another;" *De ira* 2.31.7; *Ep.* 95.52.

all must display benevolence towards his fellow citizens, since they are parts of a whole. To be violent towards them is for him to be violent towards himself. If the ruler must be merciful, it is primarily because it is in his own interest to assure political stability and to protect his power from the revolts that are necessarily provoked by cruelty.[68] This idea is very clearly found in a different context in *De ira*, with the image of a blow to the face that is not without risk for the attacker.[69] Besides, the multiplication of torments is as embarrassing for the ruler as the multiplication of burials for the physician,[70] for it shows everyone the frequency of offences committed and thus the possibility of unlawful conduct under a regime that cannot prevent it.[71] According to this political pragmatism, it is necessary to limit the use of torture as much as possible in order not to encourage criminality.

However, this political ideology, if it limits punishment, does not altogether exclude its practice. Seneca sometimes justifies the use of violence on the part of the ruler towards his subjects. To elucidate this apparent contradiction it is necessary to examine the purpose that Seneca attributes to corporal punishment. He considers physical suffering during punishment as sometimes necessary, when it leads to the correction of depraved characters:

> "Quid ergo? Non aliquando castigatio necessaria est?" Quidni? Sed haec sincera, cum ratione; non enim nocet sed medetur specie nocendi. Quemadmodum quaedam hastilia detorta ut corrigamus adurimus et adactis cuneis non ut frangamus sed ut explicemus elidimus, sic ingenia vitio prava dolore corporis animique corrigimus.
>
> "What then?" you say; "is not correction sometimes necessary?" Of course it is; but with discretion, not with anger. For it will not hurt, but will heal under the guise of hurting. As we apply the flame to certain spearshafts when they are

---

68 Sen. *De ira* 2.11.4; *Cl.* 1.15.1: the counter-example of Tricho; 1.16.3: that of the brutal centurion; 2.2.2: the famous sentence "Oderint dum metuant" ("Let them hate if only they fear") is considered "detestabilis" by Seneca. See Malaspina 2001, 325.
69 Sen. *De ira* 3.28.3: "Saepe nimia vis caedentis aut articulum loco movit aut nervum in iis quos fregerat dentibus fixit; multos iracundia mancos, multos debiles fecit [...]" – "But too great violence in the striker has often dislocated a joint, or left a sinew fastened in the very teeth it had broken. Anger has left many a man crippled, many disabled [...]."
70 Sen. *Cl.* 1.24.1: "Non minus principi turpia sunt multa supplicia quam medico multa funera" – "Numerous executions are not less discreditable to a prince than are numerous funerals to a physician."
71 Sen. *Cl.* 1.23.1: "Praeterea videbis ea saepe committi quae saepe vindicantur. [...] illis facinus poena monstravit" – "You will notice, besides, that the sins repeatedly punished are the sins repeatedly committed. [...] punishment showed children the way to the deed."

crooked in order to straighten them, and compress them by driving in wedges, not to crush them, but to take out their kinks, so through pain applied to body and mind we reform the natures of men that are distorted by vice. (Sen. *De ira* 1.6.1, trans. Basore)

Seneca uses the image of curved spear-shafts which must be placed in a fire and pressed between the wedges of a vise, not to break but to straighten them, an image which recalls the torment of the boot (*talaria*). The double opposition, each time enhanced by the conjunctions *non* and *sed* ("not ... but"), puts forth the two possible purposes of the punishment, one of which, simply to cause suffering, has to be rejected, whereas the other, correction or cure, gives the punishment its true meaning. Only in this latter case, and only with this objective, is the recourse to physical punishment justifiable, for the pain becomes "useful,"[72] not only for the rehabilitation of the guilty but also for the state, insofar as the suffering of the tortured is an example ("documentum") of the necessity not to commit crimes.[73] The bad ruler, on the contrary, will torture not to correct but to quench his blood thirst, as a game or simply to follow his whim.[74]

Like the term *mederi* ("to heal") in *De ira* 1.6.1, the therapeutic image is used many times to indicate that the punishment serves to cure the guilty but not to kill him, leave him ugly scars, or make him the victim of ex-

---

[72] Sen. *De ira* 2.27.3: "iudices, quorum castigatio sic accipienda est quomodo scalpellum et abstinentia et alia quae profutura torquent" – "judges, and we ought to submit to the chastening they give in the same spirit in which we submit to the surgeon's knife, a regimen of diet, and other things which cause suffering that they may bring profit."

[73] Sen. *De ira* 1.6.4: "hic [sc. iudex] damnatos cum dedecore et traductione vita exigit, non quia delectetur ullius poena – procul est enim a sapiente tam inhumana feritas – sed ut documentum omnium sint, et quia vivi noluerunt prodesse, morte certe eorum res publica utatur" – "[...] the other forcibly expels the condemned from life, covered with disgrace and public ignominy, not because he takes pleasure in the punishment of anyone (for the wise man is far from such inhuman ferocity) but that they may prove a warning to all, and, since they were unwilling to be useful while alive, that in death at any rate they may be of service to the state." See also Plato, *Grg.* 525b; *Lg.* 854e, 862e, 934b; Cels. pr. 26: [According to the Empirical School] "neque esse crudele, sicut plerique proponunt, hominum nocentium et horum quoque paucorum suppliciis remedia populis innocentibus saeculorum omnium quaeri" – "Nor is it, as most people say, cruel that in the execution of criminals, and but a few of them, we should seek remedies for innocent people of all future ages" (trans. Spencer).

[74] Sen. *De ira* 3.18.3: "[Caligula] torsit non quaestionis sed animi causa" – "tortured [...] not to extract information but for amusement;" *Ep.* 95.33: "Homo, sacra res homini, iam per lusum ac iocum occiditur" – "Man, an object of reverence in the eyes of man, is now slaughtered for jest and sport."

cessive bloodletting.⁷⁵ The painful punishment must not be systematically applied but only to those individuals, the "curables," for whom it works, while it is useless for incurable cases.⁷⁶ As the physician must adapt his treatment to the gravity of the illness, so the ruler must choose the punishment which will permit a better correction of the guilty⁷⁷ and not the one which will make him suffer the most. The physical punishment in itself is not criticized, but its motivation must be exempt from any angry passion and must be founded in reason only, in the interest of the culprit himself and of society.⁷⁸ While torture whose only goal is to make the patient suffer and to satisfy the cruelty of its author is to be avoided, the physical punishment applied in accordance with reason and with the goal of correcting the victim's character is necessary and perfectly justified.⁷⁹

Seneca's position concerning the state's use of torture is thus largely influenced by his political pragmatism, which explains two ideas that at first sight might appear contradictory: on the one hand, a warning against violence which only incites revolt among the ruler's subjects and, on the other hand, an advice to chastise severely the bad elements. With this view,

---

75 Sen. *Cl.* 1.17.2: "Mali medici est desperare, ne curet […] agat princeps curam non tantum salutis, sed etiam honestae cicatricis" – "It is a poor physician that lacks faith in his ability to cure […] the aim of the prince should be not merely to restore the health, but also to leave no ugly scar;" 1.5.1: "Parcendum itaque est etiam improbandis civibus non aliter quam membris languentibus et, si quando misso sanguine opus est, sustinenda est <manus>, ne ultra quam necesse sit incidat" – "And so even reprobate citizens should have mercy as being the weak members of the body, and if there should ever be need to let blood, the hand must be held under control to keep it from cutting deeper than may be necessary." – The parallel between surgery and torture, which share much of their instruments, seems to have been a commonplace. See, e.g., the expression "ferro et igne," which may refer to both fields (to torture: Ov. *Am.* 1.14.25; Sen. *Ep.* 7.4; Plin. *Nat.* 2.157, 16.71; Quint. *Inst.* 6.1.18; Suet. *Iul.* 75.3; to surgery: Plato, *Grg.* 456b, 479a, 480c, 522a; Larg. ep. 2; Sen. *Prov.* 3.2; Aret. *De caus. et sign. diut. morb.* 1.1; Plin. *Nat.* 29.13) and the word *ferramenta*, which may designate the instruments of torture (Sen. *Cl.* 1.13.2) or those of the surgeon (Sen. *Ep.* 95.18).
76 Sen. *Cl.* 1.2.2.
77 Sen. *De ira* 1.16.4: "[…] pro cuiusque morbo medicina quaeratur, hunc sanet verecundia, hunc peregrinatio, hunc dolor, hunc egestas, hunc ferrum" – "[…] for each man's malady the proper treatment should be sought; let this one be restored by his own self-respect, this one by a sojourn abroad, this one by pain, this one by poverty, this one by the sword!"
78 Sen. *De ira* 1.15.2: "Nec ira sed ratio est a sanis inutilia secernere" – "Yet it is not anger, but reason that separates the harmful from the sound," 1.16.5: "[…] iubebo non iratus sed severus […] sine ira eo vultu animoque ero […]" – "[…] not with anger, but with sternness, I shall order […] I shall have no trace of anger […]."
79 See André 1979, 278–297.

Seneca is in perfect agreement with the Stoic doctrine on punishment.[80] Punishment serves to educate the guilty and is necessary. All pity (*misericordia*) would be weakness; all excess, cruelty (*crudelitas*). These two passions prevent one from arriving at a fair sentence, the one falling short of justice, the other surpassing it. Thus, the application of the sentence must be governed at the same time by severity (*severitas*) and by clemency (*clementia*).[81] Complementing each other, these two converge to avoid excesses and to impose the just punishment, with moderation and conforming to the gravity of the crime as well as in accordance with reason and justice.

Seneca does not condemn the practice of physical punishment in general but defines the field for its reasonable practice. This theory is transferred, to a certain extent, from the level of the state to that of the home (*domus*), where the master of the house (*dominus*) must keep a balance between clemency and severity in his attitude towards his slaves.[82] Seneca does not tolerate the torture of free men at all,[83] but only limits the torture applied to slaves, by promoting more justice and moderation in accordance with the Stoic concept of *humanitas*, but also in part for pragmatic reasons, to maintain slaves under the boot of their masters. Indeed, this limitation also leads to *utilitas* ("utility"),[84] the necessity to conserve power over slaves, while preventing the hatred[85] and revolts which could be provoked by physical punishments of an excessive cruelty.[86] To the proverbial doctrine "You have as many enemies as you have slaves," Seneca answers in *Letter* 47: "They are not enemies when we acquire them; we make them enemies."[87]

However, Seneca congratulates Lucilius for only verbally chastising his slaves: Only animals are to be corrected by blows.[88] In reality, it is not the principle of punishment that Seneca condemns, but the excess of the agonies inflicted by mere cruelty. He cries out against the owners who treat

---

80 Stob. 2.7.11d, vol. 2, p. 95 Wachsmuth = *SVF* 3.640: "Φασὶ μηδὲ συγγνώμην ἔχειν <μηδενὶ τὸν νοῦν ἔχοντα>" – "They say that the wise man does not feel pity for anyone."
81 See Sen. *Cl.* 2.4.1; *De ira* 1.16.5.
82 On the question of Seneca's attitude to slaves, see Griffin 1976; André 1979; Bradley 2008.
83 See also Plu. *De puerorum educatione* 12.
84 See Cic. *Off.* 3.89.
85 Sen. *Cl.* 1.18.2: "Quis non Vedium Pollionem peius oderat quam servi sui [...]?" – "Who did not hate Vedius Pollio even more than his own slaves did [...]?"
86 Sen. *Ep.* 47.4. See Bradley 2008, 335–347.
87 Sen. *Ep.* 47.5: "Quot servi, tot hostes;" "non habemus illos hostes, sed facimus.".
88 Sen. *Ep.* 47.19: "Rectissime ergo facere te iudico quod timeri a servis tuis non vis, quod verborum castigatione uteris: verberibus muta admonentur" – "So I hold you are entirely right in not wishing to be feared by your slaves, and in lashing them merely with the tongue; only dumb animals need the thong."

their slaves "not as if they were men, but beasts of burden."[89] As opposed to animals, which lack reason (*muta*), slaves, who are human and therefore gifted with *ratio*,[90] must be treated like rational beings.

III. Torture an Act against Nature

Even more than a political issue, torture is above all a target for moral condemnation. According to the Stoic school, characterized by "kindness and gentleness,"[91] "man <is> a social being born for the good of the community"[92] because he shares with his fellow men the divine *logos*, reason. This community engenders in man a natural feeling of respect and empathy, and renders "man a sacred thing for man."[93] In light of this shared humanity, he owes respect to all men, to a slave as well as a free man and to the good as well as the bad.[94] Therefore, clemency is the "most human" virtue: "[...] no one of all the virtues is more seemly for a man, since none is more human [...]."[95] Far from being a tautology, this sentence underlines the fact that what is peculiar to man is to behave as a man, that is to say, to be marked by humanity. Here the author plays on a double meaning of the adjective *humanus*, which means "that which is peculiar to the nature of man," but also describes "those who have the qualities of a man worthy of this name," that is to say, goodness and kindness. Cruelty, on the other hand, is the basest and most bestial vice.[96] To be cruel, to take pleasure in

---

89 Sen. *Ep.* 47.5: "ne tamquam hominibus quidem, sed tamquam iumentis."
90 Sen. *De ira* 1.6.1.
91 Sen. *Cl.* 2.5.3: "Sed nulla secta benignior leniorque est, nulla amantior hominum [...]" – "But the fact is, no school is more kindly and gentle, none more full of love to man and more concerned for the common good [...]."
92 Sen. *Cl.* 1.3.1; *De ira* 2.31.7: "Ut omnia inter se membra consentiunt quia singula servari totius interest, ita homines singulis parcent, quia ad coetum geniti sunt, salva autem esse societas nisi custodia et amore partium non potest" – "As all the members of the body are in harmony one with another because it is to the advantage of the whole that the individual members be unharmed, so mankind should spare the individual man, because all are born for a life of fellowship, and society can be kept unharmed only by the mutual protection and love of its parts;" *Ben.* 7.1.7.
93 Sen. *Ep.* 95.3: "Homo, sacra res homini."
94 Sen. *De ira* 2.31.7; *Cl.* 1.18.1. See also Cic. *Off.* 1.149.
95 Sen. *Cl.* 1.3.2: "Nullam ex omnibus virtutibus homini magis convenire, cum sit nulla humanior [...]."
96 Sen. *De ira* 2.31.6: "foedam esse et execrabilem vim nocendi et alienissimam homini" – "[...] the power of injury is vile and detestable and most unnatural for man [...];" *Cl.* 1.25.1: "Crudelitas minime humanum malum est [...] ferina ista rabies est sanguine gaudere ac vulneribus [...]" – "Cruelty is an evil thing befitting

the suffering of human beings, and ceaselessly to create more sophisticated means[97] to cause pain is inhuman and contrary to the rational nature of man, which demands the protection of fellow men. The criticism is extremely harsh because the Stoic ideal is precisely "to live according to nature."[98] If man strays from the path which nature has set out for him, the path of reason, it is because he falls prey to the passion of anger (*ira*). It is significant that the greatest number of references to torture is found in *De ira*, because torture is intrinsically linked to angry passion[99] and to cruelty (*crudelitas*), which is the consequence and the visible manifestation of anger. That is why Seneca often uses the image of torture to refer to other practices that stray from the path which nature has set out for man: It is against nature for a man to "torture" his voice, or even to "torture" his body by doing sports, sunbathing, removing hair, taking hot baths, or not washing at all.[100]

The practice of torture is against the nature of man and consequently leads to a dehumanization of the torturer as much as of the victim and even of the one who attends the public spectacle of the punishment. Most philosophers agreed that there was a fundamental difference between human beings and animals.[101] For the Stoics, only men share divine reason and profit from the community with God.[102] But torture blurs this natural distinction. First of all, some torture relies precisely on the dehumanization of the victim: The mutilations which disfigure or physically impair, or the punishments that animalize, such as the combat against beasts, captivity in a cage, and the complete deprivation of hygiene and privacy.[103] In the *damnationes ad bestias*, in particular, everything is done to animalize the condemned, to the point of sometimes making them wear animal skins.[104] As for dismemberment, it refers in a general manner to the treatment of an

---

    least of all man [...] to take delight in blood and wounds [...] is the madness of a wild beast [...]."
97 Sen. *De ira* 2.31.6; *Cl.* 1.25.2.
98 E.g. Sen. *Vit. beat.* 3.3.
99 Sen. *De ira* 1.1.1: "doloris armorum, sanguinis suppliciorum minime humana furens cupiditate" – "with a most inhuman lust for weapons, blood, and punishment," 1.2.2–3.
100 Voice: Sen. *Brev. vit.* 12.4; sports: *Ep.* 56.1; sunbathing: *Ep.* 86.11; depilation: *Ep.* 56.2; hot baths: *Ep.* 86.10; not washing: *Ep.* 5.4.
101 See, e.g., Plato, *Plt.* 271e, unlike the Cynics and the Epicureans (Most 1992, 403).
102 Sext. Emp. *Math.* 9.88 = *SVF* 1.529; Sext. Emp. *Math.* 8.275 = *SVF* 2.223.
103 The mutilations which disfigure: Sen. *De ira* 3.17.3, 3.20.1, 3.28.3; *Prov.* 3.9; *Ep.* 101.11; the combat against beasts: *De ira* 3.3.6; *Cl.* 1.18.2; *Brev. vit.* 13.6; *Ep.* 7.4; 14.4; the captivity in a cage and the complete deprivation of hygiene and privacy: *De ira* 3.17.3; *Ep.* 70.6.
104 Tac. *Ann.* 15.44.

animal which is carved into pieces before being cooked and eaten.[105] For a Stoic, such a transgression of the division between rational men and irrational animals could only provoke indignation.[106] Furthermore, the torturer himself, as an instrument of bestial cruelty, forfeits all human character. Dionysius, who enclosed Telesphorus in a cage like an animal after having him disfigured, is just like an animal because his bestial behavior dehumanizes him in turn.[107] Similarly, Seneca describes how a tyrant threw his tortured victims to his men "as if to wild animals."[108] It is interesting to note the antonymic juxtaposition "bestiis homines," which underlines the animalization of the torturer precisely because his victim is a man. But Seneca warns above all against the risk that spectators of torture find themselves contaminated by cruelty. Indeed, he had himself experienced this contagion[109] when attending an execution of men condemned *ad bestias*, a spectacle which teaches cruelty and from which he came back "more cruel, less human."[110] For Seneca, the vice penetrates the spectator because of the pleasure, which renders him less human and turns him into a beast as ferocious as those he sees devouring the condemned.[111] Indeed, the public attending such spectacles approves of the cruelty in which they originate and becomes itself responsible for it.

---

105 See, e.g., Hom. *Il*. 1.459–469, 2.422–432, 9.206–217; *Od*. 3.448–473; Sen. *Thy*. 755–770. See also Detienne and Vernant 1979; Most 1992, 403.

106 Sen. *De ira* 2.31.6: "Pudebit cum animalibus permutasse mores!" – "We shall blush to have exchanged characters with the beasts!"

107 Sen. *De ira* 3.17.4: "Tamen, cum dissimillimus esset homini qui illa patiebatur, dissimilior erat qui faciebat" – "Yet, while he who suffered these things was utterly unlike a human being, he who inflicted them was still less like one."

108 Sen. *Cl*. 1.13.2: "quibus in tormentis ut eculeo et ferramentis ad mortem paratis utitur, quibus non aliter quam bestiis homines obiectat" – "whom he uses, like the rack and the axe, as instruments of torture and death, to whom he flings men as he would to wild beasts."

109 Sen. *Ep*. 7.5: "docetis esse crudelem" – "you are teaching cruelty.".

110 Sen. *Ep*. 7.3: "immo vero [sc. redeo] crudelior et inhumanior, quia inter homines fui. [...] mera homicidia sunt" – "even more cruel and inhuman, because I have been among human beings. [...] it is pure murder."

111 Sen. *Ep*. 7.4: "Mane leonibus et ursis homines, meridie spectatoribus suis obiciuntur" – "In the morning they throw men to the lions and the bears; at noon, they throw them to the spectators." We can find the same concern for the moral welfare of the spectators in Plutarch. According to him, the public accustomed to the sight of blood and injuries becomes bestial (*De sollertia animalium* 959d).

IV. Conclusion

The socio-political context of the Early Empire, which saw a broadening of the application of torture, raised the question of its place in Roman society. On the one hand, torture, a symbol of tyranny, is used by Seneca in an effort to dissuade the emperor from resorting to cruelty in the application of punishments. On the other, physical punishment, as a guarantee of political stability and instrument for the betterment of man, is considered useful for society. The apparent contradiction between these two positions finds its resolution at a philosophical level. It is the excesses of torture, its motivation, and not the actual existence of physical punishment, that Seneca denounces. For him, torture can be justified when it results from reason and has the purpose of correcting the wrongdoer. But as a result of anger or cruelty, it is reprehensible and to be rejected. Thus, the axiological plan passes over the question of the condemnation of torture: It is in itself an "indifferent," while its motivation is not, since it can come either from reason or from angry passion. Seneca's political and ethical views about torture thus join in a coherent system. The reluctant use of torture is not the simple expression of behavior guided by concern for practical utility (*utilitas*), by which the ruler would spare the citizens or slaves in order to be loved and obeyed, nor even only a manifestation of *humanitas*, a concern for others that urges one to treat one's fellow with kindness. The Senecan conception of torture lies above all in the need to submit the punishment to the judgment of reason in order to impose a just sentence, neither more nor less. *Humanitas* lies only in the will to treat slaves like any other individual, with the same clemency but also with the same severity. It is true that Seneca does not question the civil laws, but he also affirms the superiority of moral law, which is what is really at stake and which makes torture an act contrary to reason that shows "what an utter monster a man is when he is enraged against a fellow-man."[112]

Bibliography

André, Jean-Marie. 1979. "Sénèque et la peine de mort." *REL* 57: 278–297.
André, Jean-Marie. 1989. "Sénèque: 'De brevitate vitae,' 'De constantia sapientis,' 'De tranquillitate animi,' 'De otio'." *ANRW* II 36.3: 1724–1778.
Armisen-Marchetti, Mireille. 1989. *Sapientiae facies: Étude sur les images de Sénèque*. Paris: Les Belles Lettres.
Auguet, Roland. 1970. *Cruauté et civilisation: Les jeux romains*. Paris: Flammarion.

---

112 Sen. *De ira* 3.3.2: "quantum monstri sit homo in hominem furens."

Aygon, Jean-Pierre. 2004. *Pictor in fabula: L'ecphrasis-descriptio dans les tragédies de Sénèque*. Bruxelles: Latomus.
Ballengee, Jennifer. 2009. *The Wound and the Witness: The Rhetoric of Torture*. Albany: State University of New York Press.
Basore, John W., ed. and trans. 1928–1935. *Seneca, Moral Essays*. 3 vols. London; New York: Heinemann; Putnam.
Bauman, Richard. 2000. *Human Rights in Ancient Rome*. London; New York: Routledge.
Bayet, Jean. 1965. *Littérature latine*. Paris: Armand Colin.
Berti, Emanuele. 2007. *Scholasticorum studia: Seneca il Vecchio e la cultura retorica e letteraria della prima età imperiale*. Pisa: Giardini.
Boyancé, Pierre. 1965. "L'humanisme de Sénèque." In *Actas del Congreso Internacional de Filosofía en conmemoración de Séneca en el XIX centenario de su muerte*, 231–245. Madrid: Libreria Editorial Augustinus.
Bradley, Keith R. 1984. *Slaves and Masters in the Roman Empire: A Study in Social Control*. Bruxelles: Latomus.
Bradley, Keith R. 2008. "Seneca and Slavery." In *Seneca*, edited by John G. Fitch, 335–347. Oxford: Oxford University Press.
Briquel, Dominique. 1980. "Sur le mode d'exécution en cas de parricide et en cas de 'perduellio'." *MEFRA* 1/92: 87–107.
Burck, Erich. 1971. *Von römischen Manierismus: Von der Dichtung der frühen römischen Kaiserzeit*. Darmstadt: Wissenschaftliche Buchgesellschaft.
Bushala, Eugene W. 1968. "Torture of Non-Citizens in Homicide Investigations." *GRBS* 9: 61–68.
Cantarella, Eva. 1991. *I supplizi capitali in Grecia e a Roma*. Milano: Rizzoli.
Celsus. 1935. *On Medicine*. See Spencer 1935.
Cicero. 1931. *The Speeches*. See Watts 1931.
Cupaiuolo, Fabio. 1973. *Itinerario della poesia latina nel I secolo dell'impero*. Napoli: Società Editrice Napoletana.
Daremberg, Charles, and Edmond Saglio, eds. 1877–1919. *Dictionnaire des antiquités grecques et romaines*. Paris: Hachette.
Detienne, Marcel, and Jean-Pierre Vernant, eds. 1979. *La cuisine du sacrifice en pays grec*. Paris: Gallimard.
Durand, Bernard, ed. 2002. *La torture judiciaire: Approches historiques et juridiques*. Lille: Centre d'Histoire Judiciaire.
Ermann, Joachim. 2000. "Die Folterung Freier im römischen Strafprozeß der Kaiserzeit bis Antonius Pius." *ZRG* 117: 424–431.
Favez, Charles. 1947. "Le pessimisme de Sénèque." *REL* 25: 158–163.
Fuhrmann, Manfred. 1968. "Die Funktion grausiger und ekelhafter Motive in der lateinischen Dichtung." In *Die nicht mehr schönen Künste: Grenzphänomene des Ästhetischen*, edited by Hans R. Jauss, 23–66. München: Fink.
Griffin, Miriam T. 1992. *Seneca: A Philosopher in Politics*. 2nd ed. Oxford: Clarendon Press.
Gummere, Richard M., ed. and trans. 1917–1925. *Seneca, Ad Lucilium epistulae morales*. 3 vols. London; Cambridge: Heinemann; Harvard University Press.
Hallak, Laurence. 1985. "L'horreur physique dans les tragédies de Sénèque: Étude rhétorique et poétique." PhD dissertation, University of Geneva.
Halm-Tisserant, Monique. 1998. *Réalités et imaginaire des supplices en Grèce ancienne*. Paris: Les Belles Lettres.
Helbing, Franz. 1902. *Die Tortur: Geschichte der Folter im Kriminalverfahren aller Völker und Zeiten*. Berlin: Gnadenfeld.
Hengel, Martin. 1977. *Crucifixion in the Ancient World*. Philadelphia: Fortress Press.

Heuzé, Philippe. 1985. *L'image du corps dans l'œuvre de Virgile*. Roma: École Française.
Jaume, Jacques. 2008. "La crucifixion: Étude anatomique d'un supplice antique." *Archaeologia* 441: 64–69.
Malaspina, Ermanno, ed. 2001. *L. Annaei Senecae De clementia libri duo*. Alessandria: Edizioni dell'Orso.
McMullen, Robert. 1986. "Judicial Savagery in the Roman Empire." *Chiron* 16: 147–166.
Mommsen, Theodor. 1907. *Le droit pénal romain*. Paris: Fontemoing.
Most, Glenn W. 1992. " 'Disiecti membra poetae:' The Rhetoric of Dismemberment in Neronian Poetry." In *Innovations of Antiquity*, edited by Ralph Hexter and Daniel Selden, 391–419. London; New York: Routledge.
Parente, Fausto. 1979. "*Patibulum, crux, furca*." *RIFC* 107: 369–378.
Pasche, Micheline. 1976. "Les scènes d'horreur chez Sénèque et les poètes épiques du 1er siècle après J.-C." PhD dissertation, University of Geneva.
Prost, François. 2004. *Les théories hellénistiques de la douleur*. Louvain; Paris; Dudley: Peeters.
Regenbogen, Otto. 1930. "Schmerz und Tod in den Tragödien Senecas." *Vorträge der Bibliothek Warburg* 7: 167–218.
Riess, Werner. 2002. "Die historische Entwicklung der römischen Folter- und Hinrichtungspraxis in kulturvergleichender Perspektive." *Historia* 51: 206–226.
Schiesaro, Alessandro. 2003. *The Passions in Play: Thyestes and the Dynamics of Senecan Drama*. Cambridge: Cambridge University Press.
Segal, Charles. 1983. "Boundary Violation and the Landscape of the Self in Senecan Tragedy." *A&A* 29: 172–187.
Segal, Charles. 1984. "Senecan Baroque: The Death of Hippolytus in Seneca, Ovid, and Euripides." *TAPhA* 114: 311–325.
Seneca. 1917–1925. *Ad Lucilium epistulae morales*. See Gummere 1917–1925.
Seneca. 1928–1935. *Moral Essays*. See Basore 1928–1935.
Seneca. 2001. *De clementia*. See Malaspina 2001.
Setaioli, Aldo. 1985. "Seneca e lo stile." *ANRW* II 32.3: 776–858.
Sørensen, Villy. 1984. *Seneca: The Humanist at the Court of Nero*. Chicago: University of Chicago Press.
Spencer, Walter George, ed. and trans. 1935. *Celsus, On Medicine in Three Volumes*. Vol. 1: Books 1–4. London; Cambridge: Heinemann; Harvard University Press
Tarrant, Richard J. 2006. "Seeing Seneca Whole?" In *Seeing Seneca Whole: Perspectives on Philosophy, Poetry and Politics*, edited by Katharina Volk and Gareth D. Williams, 1–18. Leiden; Boston: Brill.
Traina, Alfonso. 1987. *Lo stile "drammatico" del filosofo Seneca*. 4th ed. Bologna: Pàtron.
Van Mal Maeder, Danielle. 2007. *La fiction des déclamations*. Leiden; Boston: Brill.
Wanke, Christiane. 1964. *Seneca, Lucan, Corneille: Studien zum Manierismus der römischen Kaiserzeit und der französischen Klassik*. Heidelberg: Winter.
Watts, Nevile H., ed. and trans. 1931. *Cicero, The Speeches: Pro T. Annio Milone; In L. Calpurnium Pisonem; Pro M. Aemilio Scauro; Pro M. Fonteio; Pro C. Rabirio Deitaro; Pro M. Marcello; Pro Q. Ligario; Pro Rege Deiotaro*. London; Cambridge: Heinemann; Harvard University Press.
Zugibe, Frederick T. 1984. "Death by Crucifixion." *Canadian Society of Forensic Science* 17/1: 1–13.

Gender-Based Differential Morbidity and Moral Teaching in Seneca's *Epistulae morales*

Tommaso Gazzarri
The University of Memphis

In *Ep.* 95 Seneca develops a series of analogies centered on food and diet. He does so resorting to his medical lore and, more specifically, to his gynecological opinions. Thus it is not simply food that is the semantic backbone of Seneca's tropes but rather an articulate theory of the relations between food, medicine, and the observation of sick female bodies. The relation between food and medicine should not come as a surprise; diet was a fundamental component of ancient medicine. The Hippocratic corpus contains innumerable references to it, and already in the first century BCE in Rome, Asclepiades of Bithynia developed much of his therapeutic approach on diet.[1]

Although food and sex imagery are traditional components of the Roman satirical repertoire, in *Ep.* 95.15–23 Seneca combines them in an original way in order to show how pathologies caused by eating the wrong food can be gender-coded. The trajectory he outlines consists in a climactic series of interconnected ethical and physical degenerations of women. By comparing both satirical texts targeting female sexual deviations and ancient medical treatises dealing with gynecological conditions, I will show how, under the traditional motif of the "misuse of food," there lies a specific rhetorical strategy that allows Seneca to conduct his philosophical preaching from multiple angles: Food and medical tropes can be used to signify an immoral world of misguided motivations, which is just as sick and mixed-up as its sexual and culinary appetites are all askew.

Finally, attention to the motif of health and behavior related to it in other letters will show how, within this gender-coded perspective, suicide can be considered a sign of the virtuous male's mental fitness, with the logically coherent yet emotionally baffling consequence that death appears as a manifestation of health.

---

[1] Rawson 1982, 358–370.

Twisted Diets and Never-Seen-Before Illnesses

Starting from paragraph 14, Seneca outlines a history of the development of medicine. He shows that there is a general tendency for things to become increasingly complicated and, as a consequence, for medicine to follow suit:

> Nondum in tantum nequitia surrexerat nec tam late se sparserat. Poterant vitiis simplicibus obstare remedia simplicia. Nunc necesse est tanto operosiora esse munimenta quanto vehementiora sunt quibus petimur. 15 Medicina quondam paucarum fuit scientia herbarum quibus sisteretur fluens sanguis, vulnera coirent; paulatim deinde in hanc pervenit tam multiplicem varietatem. Nec est mirum tunc illam minus negotii habuisse firmis adhuc solidisque corporibus et facili cibo nec per artem voluptatemque corrupto: qui postquam coepit non ad tollendam sed ad inritandam famem quaeri et inventae sunt mille conditurae quibus aviditas excitaretur, quae desiderantibus alimenta erant onera sunt plenis.

> Wickedness had not risen to such height or spread itself so far abroad: simple remedies could resist simple failings. Now inevitably our defenses have to be so much more laborious because the forces attacking us are so much more violent. 15 Medicine was once the knowledge of a few plants to staunch flowing blood and knit wounds together: after that it gradually reached this manifold variety. It is not surprising that it had less business when human bodies were sturdy and solid, with a simple diet not corrupted by artifice and pleasure; after men began to seek out food not to remove hunger but to provoke it, and a thousand seasonings were discovered to stimulate greed, foods that were nourishment for those who craved them became a burden once they were sated. (Sen. *Ep.* 95.14–15, trans. Fantham)

Food is conceived as a weight for the stomach rather than nourishment (cf. *Ep.* 84.6). Medicine was initially simple, "the knowledge of a few plants" but, over time, it has become more and more complex and "gradually reached this manifold variety." The reason for this process is a change in the nature of human bodies that were initially sturdy and solid and that have become sick on account of the degeneration of eating habits. Medicine has changed, because bodies themselves underwent a process of degeneration. A few lines later, at *Ep.* 95.17, Seneca presents a list of various exotic illnesses, and it is hard to resist the temptation to compare this description with topical banquet descriptions detailing the menue served at the table of the rich and wealthy. It is a *satura lanx*, a dish made up of many delicacies, but these delicacies are illnesses and not dainties:

> Quid capitis vertigines dicam? Quid oculorum auriumque tormenta et cerebri exaestuantis verminationes et omnia per quae exoneramur internis ulceribus adfecta? Numerabilia praeterea febrium genera, aliarum impetu saevientium, aliarum tenui peste repentium, aliarum cum horrore et multa membrorum quassatione venientium?

> Need I mention dizziness in the head? Or the tortures of eyes and ears and the pricking of a seething brain, and all the parts which serve to excrete afflicted with

internal ulcers? Besides there are countless varieties of fever, some raging in their attacks, others insinuating with a subtle sickness, and others that come with shuddering and extended shaking of the limbs. (Sen. *Ep.* 95.17, trans. Fantham)

The following paragraph restates the idea by adopting a reversed perspective. If the present bad diet produces weak bodies, then it is reasonable to assume that the ancients had healthier bodies because their food was simple. Seneca closes this passage with a statement that could not be more explicit in connecting the variety of courses now feasted on with the variety of new pathologies:

> Quid alios referam innumerabiles morbos, supplicia luxuriae? immunes erant ab istis malis qui nondum se deliciis solverant, qui sibi imperabant, sibi ministrabant. Corpora opere ac vero labore durabant aut cursu defatigati aut venatu aut tellure versanda. Excipiebat illos cibus qui nisi esurientibus placere non posset. Itaque nihil opus erat tam magna medicorum supellectile nec tot ferramentis atque pyxidibus. Simplex erat ex causa simplici valetudo: multos morbos multa fericula fecerunt.
>
> Need I mention countless other diseases, the punishments of luxury? Men who had not yet weakened themselves with pampering were immune to these woes, men who controlled themselves and tended their own needs. They hardened their bodies with toil and real effort, worn out either with racing or hunting or tilling the earth; food sustained them which could only please really hungry men. So there was no need for such a mighty pharmacopoeia, or so many instruments or jars. Their health was simple, and from a simple source; it was many dishes that made many sicknesses. (Sen. *Ep.* 95.18, trans. Fantham)

The connection is stressed again a few lines later:

> Nec mirum quod inconstans variusque ex discordi cibo morbus est et illa ex contrariis naturae partibus in eundem conpulsa <ventrem> redundant. Inde tam multo aegrotamus genere quam vivimus.
>
> It is not surprising that the sickness from this inharmonious food is intermittent and variable, and when those ingredients from opposed parts of nature are forced into the same stomach they overflow. This is why we are sick in as new a fashion as our life is newfangled. (Sen. *Ep.* 95.19, trans. Fantham)

The verb *vivere* ("to live") at the end of the quote must be taken almost as "to eat." Seneca restates the idea yet another time in the same epistle: "You will not be surprised by diseases beyond counting; just count the cooks."[2]

In *Ep.* 95.15–18 Seneca makes a connection between food and illness and, at the same time, evokes the moralistic *topos* of the good old times symbolizing positive values, while the present days epitomize a sick and compromised lifestyle. Seneca tackles this rather traditional idea by resorting to medicine. The degeneration of his contemporaries' health results from the degeneration of their diet, and modern vices are represented as

---

2   Sen. *Ep.* 95.23, trans. Fantham.

pathologies, the direct result of a bad diet. Since the ailments produced by such a diet are unnatural, medical science cannot cure them.

Culinary Perversions and Perveted Sexual Appetites

Seneca's conception of the relationship between food and health, as it is stated expressly in *Ep.* 95.20, is also conditioned by cultural assumptions about gender, which are at odds with Stoic views about the capacity of both men and women to attain virtue. Here is how he envisions the issue for women:

> Maximus ille medicorum et huius scientiae conditor feminis nec capillos defluere dixit nec pedes laborare: atqui et capillis destituuntur et pedibus aegrae sunt. Non mutata feminarum natura sed victa est: nam cum virorum licentiam aequaverint, corporum quoque virilium incommoda aequarunt. 21 Non minus pervigilant, non minus potant, et oleo et mero viros provocant; aeque invitis ingesta visceribus per os reddunt et vinum omne vomitu remetiuntur; aeque nivem rodunt, solacium stomachi aestuantis. Libidine vero ne maribus quidem cedunt: pati natae (di illas deaeque male perdant!) adeo perversum commentae genus inpudicitiae viros ineunt. Quid ergo mirandum est maximum medicorum ac naturae peritissimum in mendacio prendi, cum tot feminae podagricae calvaeque sint? Beneficium sexus sui vitiis perdiderunt et, quia feminam exuerant, damnatae sunt morbis virilibus.

> The greatest of doctors and founder of this science said women did not lose their hair or suffer from gout; but now they go bald and are sick in the feet. The nature of women has not changed, but has been overwhelmed; for in matching the licence of men they have also matched the afflictions of male bodies. 21 They stay up all night no less than men, they drink no less, they challenge the men in both oil and wine; they throw up food heaped on to their unwilling organs and return all their wine in vomiting; they nibble snow as much as men, as comfort for a feverish stomach. They don't even give way to men in lust; born to be penetrated (may the gods and goddesses curse them!), they have dreamed up such a perverted kind of indecency that they penetrate men. So why should we be surprised that the greatest of doctors, most expert in nature, was caught making a false statement when there are so many bald and gouty women? They have destroyed the advantage of their sex by their vices, and because they have cast off their womanhood they have been condemned to the ailments of men. (Sen. *Ep.* 95.20–21, trans. Fantham)

Seneca describes the occurrence of what he regards as masculine pathologies among women: They lose their hair and suffer from gout. To indicate that this happens against the natural order of things he refers to the authority of Hippocrates, according to whom "women did not lose their hair or suffer from gout," a tenet also attested in parallel sources.[3] As we

---

3   See, in the Corpus Hippocraticum, *Aph.* 6.28–29: "Εὐνοῦχοι οὐ ποδαγριῶσιν, οὐδὲ φαλακροὶ γίνονται. Γυνὴ οὐ ποδαγριᾷ, ἢν μὴ τὰ καταμήνια αὐτέῃ ἐκλίπῃ" –

see in the quoted passage, Seneca argues that these atypical symptoms result from women's abandonment of their female nature and engagement in behaviors gendered as male, behaviors that are unhealthy even for men. Thus, they contract masculine complaints. Seneca points out that women use snow to cool drinks (wine in particular),[4] that they consume excessive

---

"Eunuchs do not take the gout, nor become bald. A woman does not take the gout, unless her menses be stopped" (trans. Adams). Some similar observations on baldness are presented by Aristotle at *G.A.* 784a: "Καὶ αἱ γυναῖκες οὐ φαλακροῦνται· παραπλησία γὰρ ἡ φύσις τῇ τῶν παιδίων· ἄγονα γὰρ σπερματικῆς ἐκκρίσεως ἀμφότερα. καὶ εὐνοῦχος οὐ γίγνεται φαλακρὸς διὰ τὸ εἰς τὸ θῆλυ μεταβάλλειν. Καὶ τὰς ὑστερογενεῖς τρίχας ἢ οὐ φύουσιν ἢ ἀποβάλλουσιν, ἂν τύχωσιν ἔχοντες οἱ εὐνοῦχοι, πλὴν τῆς ἥβης· καὶ γὰρ αἱ γυναῖκες τὰς μὲν οὐκ ἔχουσι τὰς δ' ἐπὶ τῇ ἥβῃ φύουσιν. Ἡ δὲ πήρωσις αὕτη ἐκ τοῦ ἄρρενος εἰς τὸ θῆλυ μεταβολή ἐστιν" – "Women do not go bald because their nature is similar to that of children: both are incapable of producing seminal secretion. Eunuchs, too, do not go bald, because of their transition into the female state, and the hair that comes at a later stage they fail to grow at all, or if they already have it, they lose it, except for the pubic hair: similarly women do not have the later hair. This deformity constitutes a change from the male state to the female" (trans. Peck). Among the Latins see Celsus 4.31.1: "Ea [sc. *podagra* and *chiragra*] raro vel castratos vel pueros ante feminae coitum vel mulieres, nisi quibus menstrua suppressa sunt, tentant" – "These seldom attack eunuchs or boys before coition with a woman, or women except those in whom menses have become suppressed" (trans. Spencer); see Bellincioni 1979, 253. – Ov. *Am.* 1.14 is entirely devoted to the theme of a woman who has become bald after using some unhealthy substance to color her hair; already in Ovid a link is suggested between female baldness and the corrupted spirit of the times (although the tone of the poem is more relaxed and, unlike Seneca, Ovid is not inclined towards harsh moral preaching). As far as gout is concerned, the English term, derived from Latin *gutta* ("drop"), translates the Greek concept of *rheuma*, the descent of body fluids creating an accumulation and thus producing rheumatic pain on account of the congestion and obstruction of the joints. This condition was believed to be the result of sexual excesses and abuse of wine combined with too rich a diet. Hence the motto "Bacchus pater, Venus mater, et Ira obstetrix arthritidis" – "Bacchus is arthritis' father, Venus its mother, Rage its midwife." See Copeman 1964, 21–37; Porter and Rousseau 1998, 13–22; Nriagu 1983, 660–663. For the theory that the appearance of gout in Roman women may have depended on their increasing consumption of lead-poisoned wine, see Wedeen 1984, 75–76.

4 According to an archaic Roman custom (see, e.g., Plin. *Nat.* 14,89–90), women found guilty of drinking wine were punished or even put to death. Various hypotheses have been proposed to explain the reason for this prohibition. It has been argued that wine was regarded to contain a principle not different from masculine semen, so that women, by drinking it, would have somehow compromised the purity of lineage (Noailles 1984, 8–15). Another possible reason for this rigid rule could have been the fact that wine was considered an abortive substance, as we read in Durry 1955. According to Piccaluga's hypothesis (1964), it was feared that a specific type of wine, the so called *temetum*, normally used in sacrifices and for vatication, would lead them to a complete loss of control if consumed by women, and a similar conclusion is proposed by Minieri 1982. Fundamental for its clarity

quantities of food, and that they regularly throw up when they are no longer able to retain it.

This abuse shifts the focus to the female stomach, away from the ancient utero-centric conception of the female body and what its health requires, a tradition which the Roman Stoics did not reject.[5] Seneca substitutes the female stomach for the uterus[6] and inverts the life-giving functions of these organs. We eat to sustain life, and the womb assures the perpetuation of life in the next generation. But, for the women of *Ep.* 95, vomiting of food replaces the act of giving birth. Completely deprived of its principal generative function, the female body is conquered by vice. This is the idea Seneca conveys by saying that feminine nature is not changed but overcome (*Ep.* 95.20).

Such a conservative vision of female anatomy and its consequences for the construction of the female role within family life and society are in line with Seneca's stand on this moot issue. Despite embracing at least some of the ideas on sexual equality that Roman Stoicism, and in particular Musonius, had brought forth, Seneca's position is far more moderate than that of Epictetus' illustrious master. While Seneca makes an overture to the potential ability of women to attain virtue,[7] he simultaneously avers that their nature is weaker than that of men.[8] Furthermore, when epitomizing

---

and philological acumen is Timpanaro 1987. More recent contributions are Bettini 1995 and MacGregor 1999.

5 The Stoics introduce the new idea that both the male and the female parent contribute to the *pneuma* ("vital breath") of the child, with the woman playing an active role rather than being only the passive agent, cf. Aët. 5.13.3 = *SVF* 2.752 and Reydams-Schils 2005, 123–125. Yet female health and biology continue to be addressed within the framework of their reproductive biological tasks, and procreation remains the central purpose of marriage. Female health still falls solely under the heading of gynecology, and by drawing a sharp line between masculine and feminine pathologies in *Ep.* 95, Seneca fully embraces this rather traditional perspective. Furthermore, as Reydams-Schils points out, even within the Stoic system, variously shaded views on the matter coexisted, and some of them were very conservative, e.g., Sphaerus' theory that the female sperm's infertility is due to its substantial lack of tension, by which it is inferior in natural quality to the male semen. On the various theoretical approaches concerning semen, see Föllinger 1996, 256–261.

6 See Sissa 1992, 9–60. Sissa stresses the ambivalence of the Greek term *gastēr*, which indicates an empty space that can be filled, thus suggesting at once both eating and conceiving. Similarly, *stoma* ("the swallowing opening") can allude both to the mouth receiving food and to the vagina being penetrated by the penis.

7 See *Marc.* 16.1, where Seneca attacks the stereotype of nature treating women less generously than men.

8 In *Const.* 1.1 he bluntly declares that females are born to obey, while males ought to command.

female virtue in one word, Seneca chooses *pudicitia*,[9] a term which refers to the virtues of modesty and chastity and the concomitant conduct expected from women. While he encourages women to pursue Stoic virtue, Seneca stresses female *pudicitia*, reflecting the gender-specific limits which he thinks they should observe while seeking it.

The transition from the misuse of food to sexual degeneration becomes even more explicit in *Ep.* 95.20–21. With a traditional trait of misogynistic invective (Seneca wishes that the gods and the goddesses may confound them), he describes the sickness of women's sexual acts. They have invented a way to penetrate their male partners. Seneca tropes this sexual perversion as a descent from culture to animal behavior.[10] If we heed Gourévitch's[11] fascination with the assonance of *cruditas* ("rawness" of foods) and *crudelitas* ("cruelty" of wild beasts), sex and food here coalesce. Not only do degenerate women vomit undigested food, they are also guilty of sub-human sexual practices. Departing from their traditionally ascribed sexual and reproductive duties, they subvert their natural gender roles. This passage is a masterfully constructed invective, designed to excite the revulsion of the reader, who is supposed to imagine a woman making use of an artificial penis.[12] This description is framed by references to baldness

---

9   See *Helv.* 16.3 and 19.6, and n. 36 below.
10 Such is the semantic field of the verb *inire*, which is often used in references to breeding animals, see *ThLL* 7, s.v., col. 1296. Admittedly it would have been impossible for Seneca to utilize a more specific term since what we have here is a man being anally penetrated by a woman or, if we want to revert the perspective, a woman artificially penetrating a man. The verbal forms canonically used for anal penetration are *pedicare* for the insertive partner and *cevere* for the receptive one (but only if the penetrative agent is a man), cf. Adams 1982, 123–125, 136–138 and Williams 2010, 178. Thus while the use of verb *inire* could imply a regression of women's sexual acts to an animal condition, we must also contemplate the much simpler idea that the selection of the disparaging verb might depend on the lack of alternative options.
11 See Gourévitch 1974, 320–322. From an anthropological point of view, Lévi-Strauss 1965 showed how the so-called "culinary triangle" (raw, cooked, and rotted food) functions as a universal pattern for the mythological organization of culture. For the cultural significance of food in Rome, see Gowers 1993, 1–49.
12 Seneca alludes to the *olisbos*, otherwise known as *penis coriaceus*; cf. Ar. *Lys.* 107–110: "Ἀλλ' οὐδὲ μοιχοῦ καταλέλειπται φεψάλυξ. / Ἐξ οὗ γὰρ ἡμᾶς προὔδοσαν Μιλήσιοι, / οὐκ εἶδον οὐδ' ὄλισβον ὀκτωδάκτυλον, / ὃς ἦν ἂν ἡμῖν σκυτίνη 'πικουρία" – "And not the slightest glitter of a lover! / and since Milesians betrayed us, I've not seen / the image of a single eight-finger *olisbos* / to be a leather consolation to us" (trans. Lindsay, modified). Concerning the passage in *Ep.* 95, see Flemming 2000, 369: "Now women not only party as hard as men [...] but they have abandoned the sexual passivity which is their birthright in favor of the active, male sexual role. Hence they now suffer from men's diseases." See also Kutzko 2008, 443–452, who registers the presence of a joke associating bodily

and gout, the two symptoms of affecting women, which are located at the very beginning of the tirade and at its conclusion.

The literary representation of women playing the part of males is not Seneca's invention. This scene seems to be molded according to typical descriptions of the *tribas*, the lesbian masculine woman par excellence.[13] The generation of satirists immediately following Seneca provides remarkable literary samples of these women. Martial's and Juvenal's texts reveal a repertoire of cultural representations deriving from older traditions, coeval with and even preceding Seneca.[14] Assessing the main features of these representations will help evaluate how Seneca innovates and distances himself from the traditional models. Martial presents the unmerciful portrayal of a certain Bassa: She is described as a "fornicator," whose "monstrous organ feigns masculinity."[15] The activities of another such woman, Philaenis, are couched in terms intended to shock Martial's readers. From the very first line he labels her as *tribas*, and he clearly says that she sodomizes boys, works out in the gym, lifting weights, and devours enormous quantities of food.[16] These satirical texts show the existence of a well-defined character. Both our satirists and Seneca must have drawn their inspiration from a wide array of typified situations, which may also serve as testimony for real life practices if one discounts the genre-specific exaggerations. The figure of the *tribas* was largely known, prob-

---

odor, sexually transmittable diseases, and gout already in Catullus. From an anthropological point of view, Sissa 2003, 17–64 distinguishes the concave space representing the specific figuration of the female desire, while the masculine erotic universe, through the evidence of the erection, externalizes sexual attraction. An artificial penis utilized by a woman would violate such an order of things.

13 This is a wordy attempt to explain what the term *tribas* signifies. The difficulty lies in the differences between modern and ancient, in particular Roman, gender categories. It is debated whether *tribades* should be considered as the female counterpart of *cinaedi*, that is males that are described as soft, effeminate, and anally receptive. Richlin 1993 maintains that *cinaedi* were the homosexuals (*ante litteram*) of Roman society and, as such, despised. Thus the correct understanding of both *tribas* and *cinaedus* may lead to the acknowledgement of the existence of a form of "homosexuality" or better of a "homosexual subculture" in ancient Rome.

14 See Boehringer 2007, 261–331.

15 Mart. 1.90.6–8: "At tu, pro facinus, Bassa, fututor eras. / Inter se geminos audes committere cunnos / mentiturque virum prodigiosa Venus" – "But Bassa, for shame, you were a fornicator. You dare to join two cunts and your monstrous organ feigns masculinity" (trans. Shackleton Bailey).

16 Mart. 7.67.13–17: "Post haec omnia cum libidinatur / non fellat (putat hoc parum virile), / sed plane medias vorat puellas. / Di mentem tibi dent tuam, Philaeni, / cunnum lingere quae putas virile" – "When after all she gets down to sex, she does not suck men (she thinks that not virile enough), but absolutely devours girl's middles. May the god give you your present mind, Philaenis, who think it virile to lick a cunt" (trans. Shackleton Bailey).

lematized, and scorned. Yet it is remarkable that, among the various paradigms, Seneca chooses the woman penetrating males instead of the womanizer-*tribas* exemplified by Martial's Bassa. This confirms that Seneca's preoccupation is not simply in keeping with a traditional repertoire on the degeneration of customs; it reveals, once more, that his ideology concerning women is rather conservative: For him, women are passive creatures, and their normative gender role is oriented towards procreation. Penetrating men is even more of an inversion than penetrating women, insofar as the natural roles of man and woman in the procreative act are both reversed. As Williams (2010, 239) frames it: "What is particularly striking in Seneca's brief tirade is that he makes no mention of sexual relations *between* women. What arouses his indignation is that these women penetrate, and the fact that they penetrate men is especially shocking, as it upends the normative distribution of sexual roles."

Perverted Behaviors and Gynecological Conditions

While the female behavior Seneca relates as a monstrosity in *Ep.* 95 inspires his ethical criticism and social reproach, he also wants to interpret it medically. It is true that modern no less than ancient medicine recognizes differential morbidity based on gender.[17] From this perspective, Seneca's argument can be seen as both drawing on and departing from views of the female body and of female health inherited from ancient philosophers and medical writers.[18] Already Plato presents the female body as inferior to the male and women as inferior to men. The *locus classicus* for such assumptions is the fifth book of the *Republic* (449a–457c), e.g. at 455d:

> Ἀληθῆ, ἔφη, λέγεις, ὅτι πολὺ κρατεῖται ἐν ἅπασιν ὡς ἔπος εἰπεῖν τὸ γένος τοῦ γένους. Γυναῖκες μέντοι πολλαὶ πολλῶν ἀνδρῶν βελτίους εἰς πολλά· τὸ δὲ ὅλον ἔχει ὡς σὺ λέγεις.

> "You are right, he said, that the one sex [female] is far surpassed by the other [male] in everything, one may say. Many women, it is true, are better than many men in many things, but broadly speaking, it is as you say." (trans. Shorey)

---

17 See Gourévitch 1995, in particular 152: "It is important to distinguish clearly between the problem of specifically feminine (or masculine) states, and that of differential morbidity according to sex, recognized at least since Hippocratic times, and attributed as much to the partially different nature of men and women (biological factors), as to their different lifestyles: more active and oriented towards the outside world for men, more domestic and quieter for women (social factors). This sex-linked morbidity is connected with far more than the genital region." See also Manuli 1983, 147–204 and Sissa 1983, 81–145.
18 Hanson and Flemming 2005; Cantarella 1981; De Filippis Cappai 1993, 177–225.

Female inferiority reoccurs even in Plato's theory of metempsychosis. A woman, he avers, is the lower reincarnation of a previously masculine soul, who was not able to live his past life in keeping with virile virtues. The female body functions as the epitome of the worst possible physical abode for a human soul before it descends into animal form:[19]

> Τῇδ' οὖν τὸ τοιοῦτον ἔστω λεγόμενον· τῶν γενομένων ἀνδρῶν ὅσοι δειλοὶ καὶ τὸν βίον ἀδίκως διῆλθον, κατὰ λόγον τὸν εἰκότα γυναῖκες μετεφύοντο ἐν τῇ δευτέρᾳ γενέσει.
>
> According to the probable account, all those creatures generated as men who proved themselves cowardly and spent their lives in wrong-doing were transformed, at their second incarnation, into women. (Pl. *Ti.* 90e, trans. Lamb)

According to Aristotle (*P.A.* 2.7, 653a28–29), men and women belong to the same *genos* ("kind"), but women are weaker and possess smaller brains; therefore, he maintains, they are inferior to men. This conception was broadly diffused in the Roman world. Pliny the Elder, for instance, fully endorses it.[20] The Hippocratic tradition holds that weaker paternal sperm accounts for the conception of female rather than male offspring.[21] Women are therefore imperfect by definition. It is by unimpeded menstruation, heterosexual intercourse, pregnancy, and childbirth that women can maintain and recover their health.[22]

---

19   On the inferiority of women according to Plato, see Föllinger 1996, 85–90 and Blair 2012, 1–16. For the direct consequences of such an ideology on Athenian women's lives, see Pomeroy 1975, 58–75.

20   Plin. *Nat.* 11.133: "Cerebrum omnia habent animalia quae sanguinem, etiam in mari quae mollia appellavimus, quamvis careant sanguine, ut polypus. Sed homo portione maximum et umidissimum omniumque viscerum frigidissimum, duabus supra subterque membranis velatum, quarum alterutram rumpi mortiferum est. Cetero viri quam feminae maius" – "All blooded animals have a brain, and so also have the sea-creatures that we have designated the soft species, although they are bloodless, for instance the polypus. Man however has the largest brain in proportion to his size and the most moist one, and it is the coldest of all his organs; it is wrapped in two membranes above and below, the fracture of either of which is fatal. For the rest, a man's brain is larger than a woman's" (trans. Rackham).

21   According to the teachings of the school, both males and females possessed semen, of which the one of the male was the stronger. The sex of the fetus was determined by the quantity of each kind of semen. A greater quantity of stronger semen would produce a male; a greater abundance of weak semen, on the other hand, would lead to the generation of a female.

22   Hanson and Flemming 2005, 308 outline this utero-centric conception: "Female flesh was soft, porous and the polar opposite of the male. The pubescent girl was masculinate, but menarche and coitus initiated the process of breaking down her dense flesh and opening her closed body; pregnancy completed the transformation. The ability to generate, or more accurately to bear the husband's children, was the measure of a woman's value, and the very health of her body was thought to depend completely on her reproductive duty, and on the phallic role played by the

Two passages in particular illuminate the complexity of the gendered troping we observe in *Ep.* 95 and its relation to ancient medical lore. According to Aristotle, the inability of women to produce the same genetic materials as men derives from the differential ways in which men and women assimilate food. In the masculine body food finds enough warmth to turn into blood and then into sperm, while in the feminine body the second step of this process does not take place on account of the innate coldness of the feminine organism. What is produced instead is menstrual blood.[23]

Another medical anomaly is reported in the Hippocratic *Epidemica*: the death of a female patient, Phaëtusa. After her husband went into exile, she stopped menstruating and grew a beard; the doctors did not find a therapy to restore her menses:

Ἐν Ἀβδήροις Φαέθουσα ἡ Πυθέου γυνὴ οἰκουρὸς, ἐπίτοκος ἐοῦσα τοῦ ἔμπροσθεν χρόνου, τοῦ δὲ ἀνδρὸς αὐτῆς φυγόντος, τὰ γυναικεῖα ἀπελήφθη χρόνον πουλύν· μετὰ δὲ, ἐς ἄρθρα πόνοι καὶ ἐρυθήματα· τούτων δὲ ξυμβάντων, τό τε σῶμα ἠνδρώθη, καὶ ἐδασύνθη πάντα, καὶ πώγωνα ἔφυσε, καὶ φωνὴ τρηχέη ἐγενήθη, καὶ πάντα πραγματευσαμένων ἡμῶν ὅσα ἦν πρὸς τὸ τὰ γυναικεῖα κατασπάσαι, οὐκ ἦλθεν, ἀλλ' ἀπέθανεν, οὐ πουλὺν μετέπειτα χρόνον βιώσασα.

In Abdera Phaëtusa, the wife of Pytheas, who kept at home, having borne children in the preceding time, when her husband was exiled, stopped menstruating for a long time. Afterwards pains and reddening in the joints. When that happened her body was masculinized and grew hairy all over, she grew a beard, her voice became harsh, and though we did everything we could to bring forth menses, they did not come, but she died after surviving a short time. (*Epid.* 6.8.32, trans. Smith)[24]

---

male. A woman who would not be penetrated regularly, or who could not give birth to children, was considered sick tout court. The masculine body penetrating the feminine was an indispensable element for the health of the latter."

23 "Ἔοικε δὲ καὶ τὴν μορφὴν γυναικὶ παῖς, καὶ ἔστιν ἡ γυνὴ ὥσπερ ἄρρεν ἄγονον· ἀδυναμίᾳ γάρ τινι τὸ θῆλύ ἐστι τῷ μὴ δύνασθαι πέττειν ἐκ τῆς τροφῆς σπέρμα τῆς ὑστάτης (τοῦτο δ' ἐστὶν ἢ αἷμα ἢ τὸ ἀνάλογον ἐν τοῖς ἀναίμοις) διὰ ψυχρότητα τῆς φύσεως. ὥσπερ οὖν ἐν ταῖς κοιλίαις διὰ τὴν ἀπεψίαν γίγνεται διάρροια οὕτως ἐν ταῖς φλεψὶν αἵ τ' ἄλλαι αἱμορροΐδες καὶ αἱ τῶν καταμηνίων· καὶγὰρ αὕτη αἱμορροΐς ἐστιν, ἀλλ' ἐκεῖναι μὲν διὰ νόσον αὕτη δὲ φυσική" – "Further a boy actually resembles a woman in physique, and a woman is as it were an infertile male; the female, in fact, is female on account of inability of a sort, viz., it lacks the power to concoct semen out of the final state of the nourishment (this is either blood, or its counterpart in bloodless animals) because of the coldness of its nature. Thus, just as lack of concoction produces in the bowels diarrhoea, so in the blood-vessels it produces discharge of blood of various sorts, and especially the menstrual discharge (which has to be classes as a discharge of blood, though it is a natural discharge, and the rest are morbid ones)" (Arist. *G.A,* 728a17–25, trans. Peck).

24 On the same note, a beard is considered the ultimate sign of masculinity as pointed out by Epictetus (Arr. *Epict.* 1.16.10), so much so that the philosopher may well prefer death to having his beard shaved (Arr. *Epict.* 1.2.29).

In this example the pathology affecting the regularity of the menstrual cycle causes the growth of facial and body hair specific to men.

As for gout, which Seneca includes with baldness among the newly sprouting pathologies affecting masculinized women, it is remarkable that menstrual blood was considered a cure for it[25] (as for many other pathologies).[26] This fact again underscores the importance attributed to the reproductive functions for assuring the health of women.

Comparing the positions of Plato, Aristotle, and the Hippocratic author just discussed, we can see where Seneca agrees and disagrees with them in *Ep.* 95. He agrees that women have natural and conventional sexual roles,

---

25 Plin. *Nat.* 28.82: "Multi vero inesse etiam remedia tanto malo: podagris inlini, strumas et parotidas et panos, sacros ignes, furunculos, epiphoras tractatu mulierum earum leniri" – "Many however say that even this great plague is remedial; that it makes a liniment for gout, and that by her touch a woman in this state relieves scrofula, parotid tumors, superficial abscesses, erysipelas, boils and eye-fluxes" (trans. Jones).

26 It was believed that regular menstruation assured the expulsion from the body of substances otherwise excreted or eliminated through urination. Feces and urine are, of course, common to males and females. But while males "grew out" the products of their waste concoction in the form of beard, body hair, and other hair that is cut or naturally lost, women did not need to lose hair because these very substances were already eliminated through menstrual blood. This was offered as a physiological explanation why women did not get bald and why menstruation and hair loss were biologically incompatible. According to ancient medicine, loss of hair worked for males in a fundamentally similar way as menstruation for women. Furthermore, the ancients thought that, given the lower temperature of the female head, the balding process was not favored in the first place. Aristotle posited these theories, e.g., in *G.A.* 727a16–19: "Ἔτι δὲ οὔτε φλεβώδεις ὁμοίως γλαφυρώτερά τε καὶ λειότερα τὰ θήλεα τῶν ἀρρένων ἐστὶ διὰ τὸ συνεκκρίνεσθαι τὴν εἰς ταῦτα περίττωσιν ἐν τοῖς καταμηνίοις" – "Again, their blood-vessels are not so prominent as those of males: and females are more neatly made and smoother than males, because the residue which goes to produce those characteristics in males is in females discharged together with the menstrual fluid" (trans. Peck). Cf. also *G.A.* 783b33–784a12: "ὥστ' ἄν τις ἀναλογίσηται ὅτι αὐτός τε ὀλιγόθερμος ὁ ἐγκέφαλος, ἔτι δ' ἀναγκαῖον τὸ πέριξ δέρμα τοιοῦτον εἶναι μᾶλλον, καὶ τούτου τὴν τῶν τριχῶν φύσιν ὅσῳ πλεῖστον ἀφέστηκεν, εὐλόγως ἂν δόξειε τοῖς σπερματικοῖς περὶ ταύτην τὴν ἡλικίαν συμβαίνειν φαλακροῦσθαι. διὰ τὴν αὐτὴν δ' αἰτίαν καὶ τῆς κεφαλῆς τὸ πρόσθιον μόνον γίγνονται φαλακροὶ καὶ τῶν ζῴων οἱ ἄνθρωποι μόνοι – τὸ μὲν πρόσθιον ὅτι ἐνταῦθα ὁ ἐγκέφαλος, τῶν δὲ ζῴων μόνον ὅτι πολὺ πλεῖστον ἔχει ἐγκέφαλον καὶ μάλιστα ὑγρὸν ὁ ἄνθρωπος" – "So that is you reckon up that the brain itself has very little heat, that the skin surrounding it must of necessity have even less, and that the hair, being the furthest off of the three, must have even less still, you will expect persons who are plentiful in semen to go bald at about this time of life. And it is owing to the same cause that it is on the front part of the head only that human beings go bald, and that they are the only animals that do so at all: i.e., They go bald in front because the brain is there, and they alone do not go bald" (trans. Peck).

which include limitations not shared by men. He also sees the disruptions of normal, and normative, female functions and activities as the causes of illnesses suffered by women, including complaints and conditions typical of or gender-specific to men. But Seneca also departs from these traditions in his account of bald, gouty, and sexually perverse women. The weaknesses that Plato and Aristotle ascribe to women are generic. They are inborn and permanent. No one can change them. In the Hippocratic case, the cause of the patient's maladies is a supervening gynecological dysfunction, one from which she did not previously suffer. In neither of these models do the women involved bring their medical problems and deficiencies upon themselves. By contrast, the female behaviors leading to the outcomes which Seneca so roundly condemns in *Ep.* 95 are fully voluntary. The women in question choose to misuse food, they choose to participate in prototypical masculine pursuits, and they choose to engage in perverse sexual activities. The masculinizing ills which they suffer are thus self-inflicted. Seneca does not say whether these conditions can be reversed if depraved women undergo moral catharsis and reform. But it is evident that his goal, and his achievement, is to moralize ancient philosophical and medical gender theory, by connecting the described pathologies to voluntary ethical choices, choices which lie within the power of all moral agents, female and male alike.

Healthy Suicidal Males

In *Ep.* 95 Seneca presents a long tirade on women in which he connects their moral perversions to the outburst of never-seen-before illnesses. The entire reasoning hinges on well-defined gender assumptions that are invoked in his adaptation of Platonic, Aristotelian, and Hippocratic lore. It goes without saying that this passage is a *pars destruens* within Seneca's preaching. The women of *Ep.* 95 are examples of moral corruption. One of Seneca's strategies as an ethicist is to make a two-part argument. He couples the discouragement of vice by showing its practitioners as repulsive with the encouragement of virtue by showing its practitioners as admirable. The moral ideal which he contrasts with the women of *Ep.* 95 is found elsewhere in his works, and it is also gender-specific. His most laudable paradigms of virtue are all male. Their use of food plays no role in Seneca's depiction of them, but he does appeal to the medical lexicon.

Seneca's exemplary men, above all Cato of Utica, the Roman Socrates,[27] and Socrates himself, manifest their moral health, and the moral

---

27 On this topic see Isnardi Parente 2000.

autonomy of the Stoic sage in a death which they freely administer to themselves. Seneca's *Ep.* 24 recalls Cato's decision to protest the death of the Roman Republic at the hands of Julius Caesar by abandoning his own life, choosing to fall on his sword rather than live under a tyrant. What is more, Cato acts as his own surgeon in Seneca's description of him. With his own hands he opens his wound, precipitating his death. By forcing the death of his mortal body, he gains immortal honor and reputation. The phrase used by Seneca, "he thrust his hands into the wound,"[28] is drawn from the surgical vocabulary and thus reinforces the appeal to medical imagery found here and elsewhere in his works.[29]

Among the many challenges that men undergo during their lives Seneca includes the pain produced by harsh surgical practices (*Ep.* 67.3). Right after this, he mentions some examples of virtuous men who faced their death without fear. Once again Socrates and Cato are associated (*Ep.* 67.7). Unlike the gouty women denounced as an incurable "monstrosity" (*monstrum*) on account of their unnatural gender roles, Socrates and Cato comply with male standards of conduct. They act like doctors curing themselves (the former drinking a potion, a self-administered poisoned cup,[30] the latter, as noted, performing fatal surgery on himself).[31] These medical images are clearly constructed around a paradox. The result of the therapy is death, which is for both men a means to "health," understood as the preservation of freedom. Thus, Socrates and Cato are not only examples of virtue; their actions also represent the right functioning of a body in

---

28 Sen. *Ep.* 24.6–8: "Inpressit deinde mortiferum corpori vulnus. Quo obligato a medicis cum minus sanguinis haberet, minus virium, animi idem, iam non tantum Caesari sed sibi iratus nudas in vulnus manus egit et generosum illum contemptoremque omnis potentiae spiritum non emisit, sed eiecit" – "Then he inflicted a mortal wound on his body, and when he was bound up by the doctors, leaving him less blood and less strength but the same spirit, he was angry not just with Caesar but with himself and thrust his hands into the wound and cast out, rather than released, that noble spirit despising all power" (trans. Fantham).

29 For a similar image see *Marc.* 22.3: "To this add fires and falling houses, and shipwrecks and the agonies from surgeons as they pluck bones from the living body, and thrust their whole hands deep into the bowels, and treat the private parts at the cost of infinite pain. And besides all these there is exile – surely your son was not more blameless than Rutilius! – and the prison – surely he was not wiser than Socrates! – and the suicide's dagger, piercing the heart – surely he was not more holy than Cato!" (trans. Basore).

30 *Ep.* 67.7: "calix venenatus." It is remarkable that according to Tac. *Ann.* 15.64, Seneca tried to commit suicide by drinking the *cicuta* like Socrates when the time came to end his life. Only later, when the poison did not produce a mortal effect, did he resort to slashing his wrists. On the philosophical connotation and reception of Seneca's suicide, see Ker 2009.

31 *Ep.* 67.6: "Catonis scissum manu sua vulnus."

accordance with a set of moral qualities that are distinctive of the gender to which that body belongs. The virtuous man, as a male, must be ready to sacrifice his life.[32]

Ep. 70 offers yet another instance of this mechanism and of the centrality of suicide as the culmination of moral health. At *Ep.* 70.15 Seneca presents death not as the tragic outcome of an illness but rather as an opportunity to achieve freedom: "Should I wait for either the cruelty of a disease or a man, when I can escape the crowd of tortures and shake off hostile attack?" Paragraph 16 promptly introduces surgical imagery for suicide: "You often let blood in order to relieve the pressure pains of headache: a vein is tapped to ease the body. You don't need to sever your breast with a gaping wound; the path to great liberty is opened with a scalpel, and safety in found in a puncture" (here and above, trans. Fantham). The technical term *scalpellum* designates the surgeon's lancet, but again paradoxically, for the male the lancet is not indispensable. It is far more important for him to find the courage, when the time comes, to use whatever is within reach, as if it were a scalpel.[33] Death is an act of virtue troped as a form of surgery. Ethical and medical motifs once more coalesce.

In conclusion: In his *Epistles*, and *Ep.* 95 in particular, Seneca overlaps three layers of imagery (food, medicine, and sex) as a vehicle for his moral preaching. What emerges in *Ep.* 95 is a gender-coded way of constructing female anatomy and behavior that is ideologically charged. Though Seneca maintains that women are not unable to pursue a path of moral improvement,[34] the rhetorical strategy that he adopts reveals a more traditional perspective, according to which women are, first of all, sexual beings. They are, ideally, wives and mothers.[35]

---

32 See Isnardi Parente 2000, 217–218: "Sono due figure [*sc.* Socrates and Cato] di saggi che hanno veramente compiuto, e concluso, la loro vita con la morte, non una morte qualsiasi; due figure che, valutate togliendo la loro morte, perderebbero gran parte della loro vitalità. Al filosofo corrisponde il politico, secondo una lunga tradizione di pensiero che già Platone ha ereditato; e all'uno e all'altro la morte è essenziale a conclusione della vita. Senza la morte, quella morte, il valore di quanto essi hanno detto si vanificherebbe." For the theme of suicide in Roman society and culture, see, e.g., Bayet 1922; Veyne 1981; and Grisé 1982.

33 In *Ep.* 70.20–21 Seneca describes the scene of a German gladiator choking himself to death with a toilet sponge otherwise utilized for anal cleansing (so much the man abhorred his life of slavery).

34 At least he does so in *Marc.* 16.1, where he clearly says that women have equal capacity for virtuous actions and that they can endure pain and struggles like men if they were trained to do so.

35 Cf. Favez 1938; Manning 1973; Loretto 1977; Francia Somalo 1995; and more recently Torre 2000 and Reydams-Schils 2005, 115–176 . While Favez points out the different positions of Seneca on the subject and labels them as incoherent, Manning concludes that precisely on the basis of the many Senecan passages

Despite his acknowledgment of the Stoic claim that many kinds of people are capable of virtue, his chosen models of its highest attainments are adult males in public life. The examples which they provide are the positive antitheses of the vicious women of *Ep.* 95. Seneca is well aware that vicious behavior in men can be inhuman and utterly despicable; the public and private spheres which men inhabit, and the powers they wield, multiply their opportunities for wrongdoing, and their ability to harm others. For both sexes, vice results from abandoning the rule of life in accordance with nature.[36] However, while the gluttonous and sexually deviant women of *Ep.* 95 act like men, Seneca depicts the consequences which they suffer as worse than those of the men whose excess and self-indulgence in the banquet-hall they imitate. In that setting, the same vices are more reprehensible in women than in men, and their alleged medical consequences for women are as onerous as they are bizarre.

Aspects of ancient gender theory which inform Seneca's views on the natural weakness of women undergo an ethical reformulation in his hands. He places the full responsibility for their unusual ailments on the women who voluntarily disdain their proper gender roles. The sick female bodies that result, in turn, signal the larger concern in which Seneca situates them, the decline of society from an earlier, better state to the morally sick society he laments in his own time.

---

where women are seen as negative, we ought to reshape our idea of a substantially positive and almost "feminist" approach *ante litteram* on the part of the Stoics. Loretto presents Seneca as a follower of the Stoic school, who therefore asserts the equality of sexes but, at the same time, uses images that contradict the egalitarian view for pedagogical or rhetorical reasons. Francia Somalo chooses a more cautions position, outlining what is in my opinion the most convincing description of the problem (68): "Creemos que puede decirse que también para Séneca ambos sexos eran moralmente iguales, pero difieren en una serie de rasgos de los que todos eran secundarios, excepto la incompetencia intelectual, filosófica, que, si non se subsana, la incapacita para una responsabilidad plena. Cosa que no equivale, claro, a sostener que fuera un activo feminista precisamente." Both Torre and Reydams-Schils tackle the moot issue of women's (potential and actual) roles in Seneca's works by taking into consideration the specific dynamics of marriage and parenthood. Within this perspective, Seneca constantly grapples, on the one hand, with the necessity of making women active agents of family life (with family being the fundamental cell of society, where the process of *oikeiōsis* is first experienced and propelled) and, on the other, with the constant necessity of stressing that women are weaker by nature. If finding the real wise man is a rare and almost exceptional event, then the occurrence of a wise woman is even more unlikely.

36 Men and women must always pursue virtue in gender-specific ways: the former by seeking glory (*gloria*), the latter chastity and modesty (*pudicitia*); cf. *De Matrimonio* 78–79 Haase, 50 Vottero, where the *gloria* that men ought to achieve encompasses politics, rhetoric and war.

Bibliography

Adams, Charles D., trans. 1868. *Hippocrates, The Genuine Works of Hippocrates*. New York: Dover.
Adams, James N. 1982. *The Latin Sexual Vocabulary*. Baltimore: Johns Hopkins University Press.
Aristophanes. 1925. *Lysistrata*. See Lindsay 1925.
Aristoteles. 1942. *Generation of Animals*. See Peck 1942.
Bayet, Albert. 1922. *Le suicide et la morale*. Paris: Alcan.
Basore, John W., ed. and trans. 1935. *Seneca, Moral Essays*. Vol. 3. London; New York: Heinemann; Putnam.
Bellincioni, Maria, ed. and trans. 1979. *Lucio Anneo Seneca, Lettere a Lucilio: Libro XV: Le lettere 94 e 95*. Brescia: Paideia.
Bettini, Maurizio. 1995. "In Vino Stuprum." In *In Vino Veritas*, edited by Oswyn Murray and Manuela Tecusan, 224–235. London: British School at Rome.
Blair, Elena. 2012. *Plato's Dialectic on Woman: Equal, Therefore Inferior*. London; New York: Routledge.
Boehringer, Sandra. 2007. *L'homosexualité féminine dans l'Antiquité grecque et romaine*. Paris: Les Belles Lettres.
Cantarella, Eva. 1981. *L'ambiguo malanno*. Roma: Editori Riuniti.
Celsus. 1935. *On Medicine*. See Spencer 1935.
Copeman, William S. 1964. *A Short History of the Gout and the Rheumatic Diseases*. Berkeley; Los Angeles: University of California Press.
De Filippis Cappai, Chiara. 1993. *Medici e medicina a Roma*. Torino: Tirrenia Stampatori.
Durry, Marcel. 1955. "Les femmes et le vin." *REL* 33: 108–113.
Fantham, Elaine, trans. 2010. *Seneca: Selected Letters*. Oxford: Oxford University Press.
Favez, Charles. 1938. "Les opinions de Sénèque sur la femme." *REL* 16: 335–345.
Flemming, Rebecca. 2000. *Medicine and the Making of Roman Women: Gender, Nature, and Authority from Celsus to Galen*. Oxford: Oxford University Press.
Föllinger, Sabine. 1996. *Differenz und Gleichheit: Das Geschlechterverhältnis in der Sicht griechischer Philosophen des 4. bis 1. Jahrhunderts v. Chr*. Stuttgart: Franz Steiner.
Francia Somalo, Rosa. 1995. "Séneca y la posición estoica sobre la mujer." In *Comportamientos antagónicos de las mujeres en el mundo antiguo*, edited by María D. Verdejo Sánchez, 53–68. Málaga: Universidad de Málaga.
Gourévitch, Danielle. 1974. "Le menu de l'homme libre: Recherches sur l'alimentation et la digestion dans les oeuvres en prose de Sénèque le philosophe." In *Mélanges de philosophie, de littérature et d'histoire ancienne offerts à Pierre Boyancé*, 311–344. Rome: École Française de Rome.
Gourévitch, Danielle. 1995. "Women Who Suffer from a Man's Disease: The example of Satyriasis and the Debate on Affections Specific to the Sexes." In *Women in Antiquity: New Assessments*, edited by Richard Hawley and Barbara Lewick, 149–165. London; New York: Routledge.
Gowers, Emily. 1993. *The Loaded Table: Representations of Food in Roman Literature*. Oxford: Oxford University Press.
Grisé, Yolande. 1982. *Le suicide dans la Rome antique*. Montreal; Paris: Les Belles Lettres.
Hanson, Ann E., and Rebecca Flemming. 2005. "Frau" and "Frauenheilkunde." In *Antike Medizin: Ein Lexikon*, edited by Karl-Heinz Leven, 308–313. München: Beck.
Hippocrates. 1868. *The Genuine Works of Hippocrates*. See Adams 1868.

Hippocrates. 1994. *Epidemics: Book 2,4–7*. See Smith 1994.
Isnardi Parente, Margherita. 2000. "Socrate e Catone in Seneca: Il filosofo e il politico." In *Seneca e il suo tempo: Atti del Convegno internazionale di Roma-Cassino, 11–14 novembre 1998*, edited by Piergiorgio Parroni, 215–225. Roma: Salerno Editrice.
Jones, William H. S., ed. and trans. 1963. *Pliny, Natural History in Ten Volumes*. Vol. 8. *Books XVIII–XXXII*. London; Cambridge: Heinemann; Harvard University Press.
Ker, James. 2009. *The Deaths of Seneca*. Oxford; New York: Oxford University Press.
Kutzko, David. 2008. "Catullus 69 and 71: Goat, Gout, and Venereal Disease." *CW* 101: 443–452.
Lamb, William R. M., ed. and trans. 1925. *Plato in Twelve Volumes*. Vol. 9. London; Cambridge: Heinemann; Harvard University Press.
Lévi-Strauss, Claude. 1965. "Le triangle culinaire." *L'Arc* 26: 19–29.
Lindsay, Jack, trans. 1925. *Aristophanes, Lysistrata*. Sydney: Francfolico Press.
Loretto, Franz. 1977. "Das Bild der Frau in Senecas philosophischen Schriften." *ZAnt* 27: 119–128.
MacGregor, Arthur. 1999. "Wine, Women, and What? Some Vices in Seneca's 'De Ira'." In *Veritatis Amicitiaeque Causa: Essays in Honor of Anna Lydia Motto and John R. Clark*, edited by Shannon N. Byrne and Edmund P. Cueva, 129–145. Wauconda: Bolchazy-Carducci.
Manning, Charles E. 1973. "Seneca and the Stoics on the Equality of the Sexes." *Mnemosyne* 26: 170–177.
Manuli, Paola. 1983. "Donne mascoline, femmine sterili, vergini perpetue: La ginecologia greca tra Ippocrate e Sorano." In *Madre materia: Sociologia e biologia della donna greca*, edited by Silvia Campese, Giulia Sissa, and Paola Manuli, 147–204. Torino: Boringhieri.
Martial. 1993. *Epigrams*. See Shackleton Bailey 1993.
Minieri, Luciano. 1982. "Vini usus feminis ignotus." *Labeo* 28: 150–163.
Noailles, Pierre. 1984. *Fas et ius: Études de droit romain*. Paris: Les Belles Lettres.
Nriagu, Jerome O. 1983. "Saturnine Gout among Roman Aristocrats." *New England Journal of Medicine* 308: 660–663.
Peck, Arthur L., ed. and trans. 1942. *Aristotle, Generation of Animals*. London; Cambridge: Heinemann; Harvard University Press.
Piccaluga, Giulia. 1964. "Bona Dea: Due contributi alla storia del suo culto." *SMSR* 35: 195–237.
Plato. 1925. *Plato in Twelve Volumes*. Vol. 9. See Lamb 1925.
Plato. 1930. *The Republic in Two Volumes*. Vol. 1. See Shorey 1930.
Pliny. 1950. *Natural History in Ten Volumes. Books VIII–XI*. See Rackham 1950.
Pliny. 1963. *Natural History in Ten Volumes. Books XVIII–XXXII*. See Jones 1963.
Pomeroy, Sarah B. 1975. *Goddesses, Whores, Wives, and Slaves: Women in Classical Antiquity*. New York: Schocken.
Porter, Roy, and George S. Rousseau. 1998. *Gout: The Patrician Malady*. New Haven and London: Yale University Press.
Rackham, Harris, ed. and trans. 1950. *Pliny, Natural History in Ten Volumes*. Vol. 3. *Libri VIII–XI*. London; Cambridge: Heinemann; Harvard University Press.
Rawson, Elizabeth. 1982. "The Life and Death of Asclepiades of Bithynia." *CQ* 32: 358–370.
Reydams-Schils, Gretchen. 2005. *The Roman Stoics: Self, Responsibility, and Affection*. Chicago: University of Chicago Press.
Richlin, Amy. 1993. "Not Before Homosexuality: The Materiality of the Cinaedus and the Roman Law against Love Between Men." *JHSex* 3: 523–573.
Seneca. 1935. *Moral Essays*. Vol. 3. See Basore 1935.

Seneca. 1979. *Lettere a Lucilio: Libro XV: Le lettere 94 e 95* See Bellincioni 1979.
Seneca. 2010. *Selected Letters.* See Fantham 2010.
Shackleton Bailey, David R., ed. and trans. 1993. *Martial, Epigrams.* 2 vols. Cambridge: Harvard University Press.
Shorey, Paul, ed. and trans. 1930. *Plato, The Republic in Two Volumes.* Vol. 1. *Books 1–5.* London; Cambridge: Heinemann; Harvard University Press.
Sissa, Giulia. 1983. "Il corpo della donna: Lineamenti di una ginecologia filosofica." In *Madre materia: Sociologia e biologia della donna greca*, edited by Silvia Campese, Giulia Sissa, and Paola Manuli, 81–145. Torino: Boringhieri.
Sissa, Giulia. 1992. *La verginità in Grecia.* Roma: Laterza (translation of *Le corps virginal: La viginité feminine en Grèce ancienne.* Paris: J. Vrin, 1987).
Sissa, Giulia. 2003. *Eros Tiranno: Sessualità e sensualità nel mondo Antico.* Roma: Laterza.
Smith, Wesley D., ed. and trans. 1994. *Hippocrates.* Vol. 7: *Epidemics: Book 2,4–7.* Cambridge: Harvard University Press.
Spencer, Walter G., ed. and trans. 1935. *Celsus, On Medicine.* Vol. 1. London; Cambridge: Heinemann; Harvard University Press.
Timpanaro, Sebastiano. 1987. "Il ius osculi e un passo di Frontone." *Maia* 39: 201–211.
Torre, Chiara. 2000. *Il matrimonio del sapiens: Ricerche sul "De Matrimonio" di Seneca.* Genova: Università di Genova.
Veyne, Paul. 1981. "Suicide, fisc, esclavage, capital et droit romain." *Latomus* 40: 217–268.
Wedeen, Richard P. 1984. *Poison in the Pot: The Legacy of Lead.* Carbondale: Southern Illinois University Press.
Williams, Craig A. 2010. *Roman Homosexuality.* 2nd ed. Oxford: Oxford University Press.

My Family Tree Goes Back to the Romans: Seneca's Approach to the Family in the *Epistulae Morales*

Elizabeth Gloyn
Royal Holloway, University of London

Seneca's *Epistulae Morales* operate primarily as an exercise in individual moral development. The letters seek to guide the reader through a process of deliberate ethical education that revolves around a focus on the self.[1] Part of that process is to remove all external baggage from the aspiring Stoic pupil so that he has no distractions as he begins to reorient his core values and beliefs towards virtue. Yet despite the corpus' prioritization of the self, careful study of the letters reveals a number of assumptions made about other subjects and the Stoic attitude to them. This is especially true of the family, a topic which has thus far received comparatively little attention in the scholarly literature on ancient philosophy and Stoicism in particular. In this chapter, I argue that Seneca's treatment of the family in the *Epistulae Morales* illuminates how the letters function as a systematically organized collection and serves as a microcosmic view of the collection's approach to wider philosophical issues.[2] He initially strips away all refer-

---

1   Most scholarship on the *Epistulae Morales* is happy to accept the collection's emphasis on self and interior concerns. Henderson 2004, 1–6 goes further, postulating that part of this interiority involves removing all extraneous references to external objects. (He does not explicitly refer to the family, but it must be included as part of the totality of things he believes the Stoic disciple needs to expunge.) I take his conclusions in a different direction and apply them instead to the presence of the family in the collection. – This chapter is a compressed version of the final chapter of my 2011 Ph.D. thesis. I thank Leah Kronenberg, Malcolm Schofield, Serena Connolly and Alan Code for their support as the members of my dissertation committee. Caroline Bishop, Lauren Donovan, Isabel Köster, and Darcy Krasne also offered indispensable advice during process of writing and revision. Jula Wildberger and Marcia Colish provided significant guidance during preparation for publication.
2   There has been much work on how the *Epistulae Morales* function as a sequence and as letters. Inwood summarizes the academic *communis opinio* when he says that "Seneca's letters in their present form, whatever their relationship might have been to a real correspondence, are creations of the writer's craft" (2007a, xii).

ences to the concept of "family," even cautionary ones; as the reader progresses through the collection and has absorbed enough Stoic doctrine to approach the subject rationally, Seneca slowly reintroduces the family, both conceptual and actual, into the conversation of the letters. The reader becomes inoculated against his family's potential dangers by its removal and gradual reintroduction; this process allows the family to take its proper place in the structure of the aspiring Stoic's ethical thought.

The major themes of the *Epistulae Morales*, such as how to cope with the fear of death, recalibrating one's desires so as to want little rather than luxury, and adapting to the vicissitudes of Fortune, revolve around the individual rather than the collective.[3] Edwards argues that Seneca's letters are part of "a tendency within Stoic thought to focus on the interior disposition of the individual" (1997, 36). This emphasis on what Edwards calls "the urge to self-scrutiny and self-transformation" explains the lack of interest in the environment of the letter writer and the letter reader, both in terms of objects and other people. In a work obsessed with the individual, lengthy disquisitions on how to engage with others would be out of place; for advice on interpersonal relations, we would turn to *De Ira* or *De Beneficiis*.

But the letters have something to say about the family, even if it does not form a central part of the discussion. The Latin word *familia* does not mean the same as the English word "family." One way of understanding *familia* is through its definition in Roman law; it could also be defined as

---

Richardson-Hay 2006 has recently analyzed the thematic unity of book one of the *Epistulae Morales*; in this she continues the trend set by Cancik 1967 and Maurach 1970 of seeing the letters as a deliberately constructed work with an underlying conceptual framework that it is possible to recover. Cancik-Lindemaier argues that the letters are a fictional literary work (1998, 102). Grimal makes the case for a three-year-long genuine correspondence between summer 62 CE and 65 CE (1978, 155–164). Mazzoli 1989 suggests that Seneca took a genuine correspondence and edited it to make it appropriate for publication, removing all irrelevancies and creating thematic unity where necessary. Graver, however, counters this by arguing that "to posit editorial revisions of such an extent" means that scholars "turn the editor into the creator of a new, essentially literary work," and concludes that the *Epistulae Morales* are aimed "not at Lucilius but at that wider public which Seneca knew well and for which he had often written before" (1996, 24). On the date of the work, its structure, and the question of the reality or fictitiousness of the authorial self, see also the contributions of Williams, Graver, Cermatori, and Wildberger in this volume.

3   For a non-exhaustive selection of letters dealing with the fear of death, see *Letters* 4, 12 and 54; for adapting to want little rather than a lot, see *Letters* 5, 8 and 17; for accepting fate, see *Letters* 9, 13 and 16. Bartsch and Wray 2009 is an example of the current academic interest in this subject; many of the twelve essays on the question of Seneca and the self focus on the *Epistulae Morales*.

those under control of the *paterfamilias*, the oldest and most senior male.⁴ The latter definition included the slaves belonging to a household as well as those biologically related to each other through the male line. Indeed, *familia* could refer specifically to the slaves alone. Romans also identified themselves as members of a clan (*gens*), which invoked both historical and ethnic associations. A Roman thinking about "his family" could thus be considering his biological family, the people who lived in the same house, the people who belong to the same *gens*, or those whom the law defined as legally forming his family. However, I am interested in Seneca's philosophical ideas about living ethically within a biological family, not in attempting to recreate the lived cultural system of familial relationships from Seneca's texts in the way one might use legal texts or inscriptions. In this context, *Letter* 121 provides one of the fundamental texts on *oikeiōsis*, the process through which one begins to see the interests of others as one's own and in which the family plays a central role.⁵ Moreover, the families who appear in the letters exist in the messy, confusing sphere of the real world rather than an isolated philosophical utopia; the letters' focus of the individual *qua* individual enables consideration of how one might best negotiate the complex situations encountered in the real world. While in the *Epistulae Morales* Seneca concentrates first and foremost on the relationship one must have to oneself in order to begin the pursuit of virtue, the latter stages of the corpus only hint at the next step – the development of the connections we have with our parents, spouses, and children. The overall preoccupations of the *Epistulae Morales* require the family to play

---

4   For more on the etymological problems of *familia*, see Milnor 2005, 19. Gardner 1998 explores the concept of the *familia*, as the Romans defined it, in both law and every-day life. Saller 1984 has shown that the legal definition of *familia* encompasses only those blood relatives who are agnates, or related through the male line, and not cognates, or relatives through the female line. For more on the Roman family, see George 2005, Rawson and Weaver 1997, Dixon 1992, Bradley 1991a and 1991b, and Rawson 1986.

5   This process enables one's sense of self to expand out from an individual's perspective to embrace the entirety of humanity, via the intermediate step of assimilating one's family's interests to oneself. The fundamental primary Stoic texts that discuss *oikeiōsis* are D.L. 7.85–86, Cic. *Fin.* 3.16–25, Sen. *Ep.* 121, and Hierocles' discussion, found at Stobaeus 4.27.23, vol. 4, pp. 671–673 Hense = LS 57G. LS 57 is a collection of these passages. The surviving portions of Hierocles' *Elements of Ethics*, which focus specifically on the evidence animals provide for *oikeiōsis*, is available with translation and accompanying commentary in Ramelli and Konstan 2009, 2–62. This text shows close parallels to Seneca's discussion in *Letter* 121. See Inwood 1999, 677 n. 8 for the issues involved in translating *oikeiōsis* accurately. I will always refer to letters from the *Epistulae Morales* as *Letter* X, rather than *Epistula* X, in what follows.

a comparatively minor role in the corpus; nevertheless, as we will see, the family has a potential role in the moral formation of the aspiring sage.

In this paper, I attempt to respect the nature of the *Epistulae Morales* as a letter collection. They are designed to be read as letters, received in the set sequence in which they are presented;[6] the recipient of the letters would know the content of those already received and would be ignorant of those yet to come.[7] Retracing the path of the first-time reader of the corpus, it becomes clear that Seneca develops his treatment of the family as the collection progresses, refining and further complicating his presentation over time. As the corpus is so large, some selectivity is inevitable; here I concentrate on the passages which most significantly demonstrate the progression of the concepts Seneca explores and substantiate my argument that he adopts a unified and developmental approach to the family throughout the collection.[8]

I. The Initiation

The first twelve letters of the *Epistulae Morales* make a programmatic statement about the purpose of the collection and what the reader is letting himself in for. As Cancik puts it, the first book is conceived as the entrance to the work as a whole (1967, 4); successful passage through this initiation ritual shows the requisite dedication to the cause.[9] Henderson takes this idea to its logical conclusion:

---

6 Inwood 2007a, xiii–xv addresses the question of how complete our extant collection is. It is tempting to think that the surviving 124 letters in twenty books represents the full corpus, but Aulus Gellius quotes from a letter on style which came in book 22 (12.2), implying that the manuscript tradition has lost a significant chunk of the collection. Wildberger argues in this volume that *Letter* 124 may have been the intended closure of the collection.

7 When I refer to the effect upon Lucilius of reading a particular letter, it should be understood that I also refer to the effect upon any contemporary Roman reader who might have read these letters upon their publication.

8 In what I omit, there is nothing that would contradict this developmental reading. Seneca makes many passing references to familial relationships which I will mostly omit from my discussion; they are normally very brief and used for illustrative purposes. As an example, I omit a reference to a girl giving birth in *Letter* 24.14, where Seneca compares her endurance of birth-pangs to a gouty complainer or some glutton with an upset stomach. Although the girl will become a mother, her status as such has nothing to do with her inclusion as an illustration of brave suffering.

9 The introductory function of the first twelve letters is also explored by Maurach 1970, who argues that *Letter* 12 is not in fact structurally part of the first book but instead acts as a bridge between *Letters* 11 and 13; Richardson-Hay 2006, 30

present a good potted anecdote about the principles that apply to the family and that he will expand in later letters; a family is a good thing to have, but its loss does not equate to the loss of virtue. Losses like those experienced by Stilbo are not unfelt, but Seneca shows that the wise man, like Stilbo, will not be uprooted from virtue because of them.

The immediately preceding passage reinforces this message by explaining how the Stoic sage will balance his self-sufficiency with the normal pleasurable activities of a human being:

> Quamdiu quidem illi licet suo arbitrio res suas ordinare, se contentus est et ducit uxorem; se contentus <est> et liberos tollit; se contentus est et tamen non viveret si foret sine homine victurus. Ad amicitiam fert illum nulla utilitas sua, sed naturalis inritatio.
>
> As long as he [sc. the wise man] may order his own affairs through his own judgment, he is content in himself, and marries a wife; he is content in himself, and raises children; he is content in himself, and yet would not live if he were to live without a human being. No personal benefit brings him to friendship, but a natural stimulus. (Sen. *Ep.* 9.17)

Seneca sees no conflict between the sage's self-sufficiency and following one's natural desires, so long as these decisions are guided by his own fully rational judgment (*arbitrium*) rather than the irrational passions of non-sages. As the Stoics equated living in accordance with nature with living virtuously and friendship, marriage, and procreation are all considered natural (*naturalis*), the sage may decide to start a family if the circumstances are appropriate and he feels the desire to do so. But this is uncontroversial; it is the logic behind the sage's *engagement* with his family once he has created one that I hope to unpick. While this passage suggests that the sage cannot live without other people, it also suggests that the normal rhythms of life will shape that engagement; death, alongside birth and marriage, forms part of the natural pattern which Seneca invokes here.

One might argue that Seneca's comment that it is impossible for the sage to live without humanity appears to undermine the radical self-sufficiency that elsewhere suffuses descriptions of the wise man. However, the Stoic attitude to suicide helps explain this contradiction. There are certain circumstances under which it is acceptable for a sage to decide to end his own life, for instance if he is incurably ill or living under a tyrant. It is possible for him to make this choice while still being content in himself because all that is required for him to be in this state is his reason. It is *only* acceptable for a sage to make such a decision consciously because only a sage is fully in control of his reason and thus capable of correctly judging whether committing suicide would be the rational thing to do under any given set of circumstances.[15] We can now make sense of Seneca's assertion that "he is content in himself, and yet would not live if he were to live without a human being." The implication behind "would not live" is that living without human contact would be one of the circumstances in which Seneca believes the choice of suicide could be rationally justified. We may surmise that the wife and child Seneca has just said a sage may choose to take may be one of the subcategories of "human being" without whom the sage may choose not to live. Should the sage lose his family, then, it is *possible* for suicide to be the rational response – but, as the example of Stilbo shows, it does not become the *inevitable* response.

One can be self-sufficient and obey natural imperatives that involve interactions with other people. So long as these relationships are governed by reason, their loss will not disturb the sage's equanimity; his mental balance depends on maintaining his independence from these indifferents. Family and friends serve the same purpose; the sage obtains both for natural reasons and does not locate his virtue in either. They give him space to demonstrate his virtue (as Seneca specifically says of friends at *Ep.* 9.8), but do not define it. But we are still in the first letters, the initial crossing into Stoicism. Of course the reader cannot think of the family as anything but completely external to virtue; to talk of the sort of environment that nurtures virtue risks placing responsibility for developing virtue on something outside the individual. Lucilius must undertake this journey entirely on his own.

II. Advance Warning

The family disappears from the letters until the sequence of *Letters* 31, 32 and 33. These letters instruct Lucilius in the best way to guarantee his

---

[15] Cato, the Stoic speaker in Cicero's *De Finibus*, says that "For the man for whom there are more things which are according to nature, it is his duty to remain in life; however, for him for whom either there are or it appears there will be more things contrary to nature, it is his duty to depart from life" (3.60: "in quo enim plura sunt quae secundum naturam sunt, huius officium est in vita manere; in quo autem aut sunt plura contraria aut fore videntur, huius officium est de vita excedere"). He explains that this is why it is possible for the wise man to commit suicide despite his being happy, for virtue does not necessarily require him to live (3.61). In his representation of Cato as a sage-like figure, Lucan attributes his choice to marry and raise children to his desire to serve the state rather than his own personal interests (*Pharsalia* 2.380–395). Diogenes Laertius also mentions that the wise man may commit suicide for the sake of his country or his friends, or because he is experiencing very harsh physical pain, has been maimed, or is suffering an incurable disease (D.L. 7.130).

progress – and his family is not necessary for that journey. Close examination of the sequence shows that these are more than casual references to the family. Seneca has something significant to say here about the relationship between being an ethically responsible individual and one's interaction with one's parents, and focuses on this very specific relationship. The scene is set in *Letter* 31. Seneca warns Lucilius to stop up his ears with wax, as Ulysses used it for his companions, because of the siren songs sung by those around him:

> Illa vox quae timebatur erat blanda, non tamen publica: at haec quae timenda est non ex uno scopulo sed ex omni terrarum parte circumsonat. Praetervehere itaque non unum locum insidiosa voluptate suspectum, sed omnes urbes. Surdum te amantissimis tuis praesta: bono animo mala precantur. Et si esse vis felix, deos ora ne quid tibi ex his quae optantur eveniat.

> That voice which used to be feared was charming although not public – but this one which must be feared resounds not from a single rock but from every part of the world. Therefore, sail past not just one place doubtful with treacherous pleasure but all cities. Make yourself deaf to those who are most affectionate: they pray for evils with good intention. And if you want to be lucky, beg the gods that none of those things that they wish for befalls you. (Sen. *Ep.* 31.2)

The letter at this point does not explicitly identify the people who most love Lucilius, but makes it clear that their fond prayers do not desire anything that is truly good. Seneca then discusses how work can and cannot be good, and then makes it clear to whose prayers he previously referred:

> Non est ergo quod ex illo <voto> vetere parentum tuorum eligas quid contingere tibi velis, quid optes; et in totum iam per maxima acto viro turpe est etiamnunc deos fatigare.

> Therefore there is no reason why you should select what you wish to happen to you or what you wish for from that old prayer of your parents; and in general, already it is shameful for a man who has come through the greatest things still to exhaust the gods. (Sen. *Ep.* 31.5)

Lucilius' parents were misguided in their prayers. All Lucilius needs to do is make himself happy, through his own effort rather than the wishes of others; he will not get any extra satisfaction from chasing after external successes like glory or honor. The letter continues to explain that the knowledge of things (*rerum scientia*) is truly good and the lack of knowledge of things (*rerum imperitia*) is truly bad (31.6); the wise man's grasp of true knowledge validates his choices in whatever situation he finds himself and thus ensures his happiness. Seneca exhorts Lucilius to work towards possession of knowledge alone, and cheerfully reminds him that he will not need to travel through such harsh terrain as he did for the reward of his little procuratorship (31.9: "procuratiunculae pretio"); he thus suggests that there are other things besides a political career upon which Lucilius should concentrate his mind. The letter closes by reminding Lucilius that the soul makes the difference and that the soul does not care whether it lives inside a knight, a freedman, or a slave; the physical container is irrelevant to the mind within (31.10).

Two important themes emerge from this letter that will reappear both in the collection as a whole and in the subsequent letter. The first theme is the well-meaning error of parents, or indeed the people who love you most (31.2: "amantissimis tuis"), who do not want what is best for you. They do not actively set out to harm you, but their aims and desires for you are founded on what society judges as desirable rather than knowledge of what is and is not truly good. The parents' desires do not spring from deliberate malice, but from lack of the knowledge that Seneca identifies as key to the wise man's identity. In the world of the *Epistulae Morales*, where the emphasis is on the individual's responsibility for himself, the wise man cannot rely on his family to direct his steps. At this stage in the *Epistulae Morales*, Seneca does not ask Lucilius to withdraw from his family completely, but he makes a compelling case that the serious Stoic disciple must ultimately rely on his own inner drive towards virtue, and not on the comfort he may derive from his family.

The second theme that emerges from *Letter* 31 highlights the relative *lack* of importance that the family has for Lucilius. This comes only at the letter's close, when Seneca reminds us at 31.11 that a soul which is "upright, good, and great" ("rectus, bonus, magnus") can descend into anyone, whether a knight, a freedman, or a slave. These are just names arising from ambition or injury.[16] They have no impact on the substance of a man's soul. The point here is subtle but anticipates a concept of the family to which Seneca will shortly return; ancestry is irrelevant for the pursuit of virtue. Here, Seneca makes the point in terms of status, but the status of knight and slave were hereditary. *Libertinus* is somewhat more problematic, as it can refer to a freedman or the son of a freedman, although the former meaning is more common.[17] That said, the basic idea is still clear: A man's ability to possess virtue is unconnected to his social status. The tricolon of possible bodies for the good soul ostensibly frames that irrelevance in terms of being free, once having known slavery, and being enslaved; more subtly, it reinforces the lack of importance the hereditary status of knighthood confers upon the knight and thus undermines the importance of that political status for the aspiring sage.

---

16 Sen. *Ep.* 31.11: "nomina ex ambitione aut ex iniuria nata."
17 For examples of the former use, see Quint. *Inst.* 5.10.60; Pl. *Poen.* 832; Cic. *De Orat.* 1.38; and Suet. *Aug.* 74. For examples of the latter use, see Suet. *Cl.* 24 and Isid. *Orig.* 9.4.47. The *OLD* s.v. *libertinus* 2 gives "a member of the class of freedmen, a freedman" as the primary meaning, with "the son of a freedman" as a dependent definition.

Letter 32 is shorter and once more rejects the prayers of Lucilius' parents:

> Optaverunt itaque tibi alia parentes tui; sed ego contra omnium tibi eorum contemptum opto quorum illi copiam. Vota illorum multos compilant ut te locupletent; quidquid ad te transferunt alicui detrahendum est.
>
> And so your parents wished other things for you; but I wish you to have scorn for all those things whose abundance they desired. Their prayers pillage many to enrich you. Whatever they hand over to you must be taken away from someone else. (Sen. *Ep.* 32.4)

The letter concludes with Seneca's wish that Lucilius would stop wandering and come to rest, understanding that all true goods are within our possession. This final section revisits the themes of *Letter* 31 and emphasizes that Seneca wishes Lucilius to progress towards this goal. The juxtaposition of the wishes of Lucilius' parents with those of Seneca marks out the difference between the two viewpoints more starkly than *Letter* 31. Seneca's better-informed aspirations for Lucilius surpass his parents' conventional wishes. Indeed, Seneca's exhortation that Lucilius avoid keeping company with people who are different from himself and want different things,[18] in tandem with this warning about misguided parents, reads as a further recommendation to withdraw from one's biological family lest they provide erroneous direction. Seneca knows precisely what is good for Lucilius and thus serves as a better companion on the road to virtue than the well-intentioned but ill-advised family provided by fate.[19]

Letter 33, following in the footsteps of this *caveat* against misguided familial influence, does not mention the family directly but is a well-recognized moment of transition in the collection. *Letter* 32 omitted the by now customary Epicurean tagline, and Lucilius has written to complain. Seneca responds that the time to use such potted wisdom is past and that Lucilius will never achieve virtue by memorizing phrases, no matter from whom they are taken. Seneca closes his argument by asserting that those who rely on the words of great men never attain their own mental independence.[20] *Tutela*, the term used in this context, is a loaded word. Fatherless minors who had not yet reached the legal age of maturity had to be under the control of a guardian (*tutor*), and women were judged to need the *tutela*

---

18 Sen. *Ep.* 32.2: "non conversari dissimilibus et diversa cupientibus."
19 *Letter* 32 bases its assumptions about the bad influence of the family on the Stoic theory of perversion or *diastrophē*, which argues that all humans risk being drawn away from what was natural and good by external influences; one of the main factors in this process is "the echoing voices of the many" (*katēchēsis tōn pollōn*). For further discussion, see Donini 1999, 708–709.
20 Sen. *Ep.* 33.10: "qui numquam tutelae suae fiunt."

mulierum.²¹ The word carries overtones both of the legal process needed to obtain independence and the familial basis on which this rested; a tutor would usually be a senior male relative from the tutee's agnatic family. Only young men whose fathers had died required tutors under the system of *tutela*, and only until they reached the age of fourteen, at which point they passed into the protection of a *curator* until they were considered capable of transacting their own business by the age of twenty-five.²² Not to gain one's own intellectual *tutela*, then, and to rely on the guidance of others to gain virtue, is framed in terms of a young man obtaining legal independence under Roman law – it is to have the potential to obtain full power over one's own actions, but to never gain full autonomy.²³ The serious Stoic disciple must distance himself from the influence of his biological family if he ever hopes to understand truth, just as he must move beyond blindly following the words of his philosophical predecessors and begin to see them as guides rather than masters.²⁴

III. What Is a Family?

The next section of the *Epistulae Morales* that deals with the family subtly questions *what* the family is and what kinds of inheritance Lucilius should

---

21 All children who were *sui iuris* and *impubes*, i.e. fatherless and below the legal age of puberty, required a *tutor impuberis*. Boys were considered legally mature at fourteen, at which point they became legally independent. Girls reached puberty at twelve, but then required a guardian to provide *tutela mulierum*. In 9 CE Augustus' Papian-Poppaean Law released free women with three children and freedwomen with four children from the need of *tutela*. For more on *tutela* and guardianship, see Gardner 1986, 5–29 and Borkowski and du Plessis 2005, 139–147.

22 Roman law recognized that young men were still vulnerable and so established the *cura minorum* to provide a guardian for young men who had reached puberty but were still under twenty-five; see Evans Grubbs 2002, 23. Of course, a young man whose father had *not* died and had not emancipated him would have continued to be under his father's legal control, which *tutela impuberis* was intended to replace, until his father died or emancipated him.

23 A similar idea is expressed at *Ep.* 4.2: Seneca reminds Lucilius of his joy in putting on the *toga virilis* and joining the men, and invites him to consider how much more joy he will experience in putting aside a childish mind and being enrolled among men by philosophy. This theme intertwines with that identified by Edwards 2009, 154–155, namely the articulation of control over oneself in terms of the difference between a slave and a free man. On this point, compare also the contribution of Degl'Innocenti Pierini in this volume. The idea of freedom, of course, is not the same as being able to do whatever one wishes to do, but the ability to acquiesce in whatever Fortune has allotted us; see Wildberger 2006, 340–341.

24 Sen. *Ep.* 33.11: "veritas;" "non domini nostri sed duces."

be concerned with.²⁵ These passages look at a different type of familial relationship to the one explored in the earlier letters, where Seneca was interested in the relationship between the Stoic disciple and his biological family. Beginning at *Letter* 44, the horizon expands to incorporate a wider concept of family and different issues. For the time being, Seneca puts aside the discussion on how to interact with one's parents and turns to the social question of how a family is defined. This examination expands out from the microscopic level of one-on-one relationships and asks how families function in the wider community.

Letter 44 develops the theme of *Letter* 31, that pedigree is irrelevant to philosophy. Lucilius has complained that he is small and insignificant (44.1: "pusillum"), but Seneca loses patience. Everyone can attain a good mind,²⁶ so Lucilius worries fruitlessly about his ancestors. Other philosophers have not been of noble descent:

> Patricius Socrates non fuit; Cleanthes aquam traxit et rigando horto locavit manus; Platonem non accepit nobilem philosophia sed fecit: quid est quare desperes his te posse fieri parem? Omnes hi maiores tui sunt, si te illis geris dignum; geres autem, si hoc protinus tibi ipse persuaseris, a nullo te nobilitate superari.
>
> Socrates was not of patrician rank. Cleanthes drew water and hired himself out to water a garden. Philosophy did not receive Plato noble but made him so. Why then should you despair of becoming equal to these men? All these are your ancestors if you behave in a way that is worthy of them; but you will bear yourself so if you immediately persuade yourself of this, that you are surpassed by nobody in nobility. (Sen. *Ep.* 44.3)

Seneca invites Lucilius to redraw the boundaries of the family, replacing his imperfect relations with a group of idealized philosophers. Socrates, Cleanthes, and Plato all became noble through philosophy rather than their inherited status and thus form a worthy group for Lucilius to take as his ancestors – presumably in place of a traditional Roman family tree. Seneca repeatedly emphasizes the motif that all human beings come from a common ancestor (44.4), so in some ways it is a legitimate tactic for Lucilius to choose the people whom he wishes to claim as his relatives.²⁷ But again, Seneca counsels Lucilius about the importance of relying on his own merits rather than those of his forebears:

---

25 For a discussion of the difference between various Latin words for family, and the sort of family that I believe Seneca refers to here, see pages 230f. above.
26 Sen. *Ep.* 44.2: "bona mens omnibus patet."
27 Seneca expresses a similar idea in *Brev. vit.* 15.3, where he says that while we cannot choose our parents, we can choose whose children we will be; he describes the philosophical schools as families of the most noble characters ("nobilissimorum ingeniorum familiae"). That Seneca thought of philosophical schools in familial terms is clear from a passage in the *Naturales Quaestiones* (7.32.2), which refers to families of philosophers that perish without successors.

> Non facit nobilem atrium plenum fumosis imaginibus; nemo in nostram gloriam vixit nec quod ante nos fuit nostrum est.
>
> A hall full of smoky images does not make a man noble. Nobody lived for our glory nor is that which came before us ours. (Sen. *Ep.* 44.5)

The "smoky images" of the aristocrat's main hall would have been a familiar sight to Lucilius from his day-to-day life. Admittedly, the rise of the principate meant that the *imagines* no longer held the political force they had had during the Republic; then, they "served as constant and powerful advertisements of a family's achievements and eminence" (Flower 1996, 65). However, the *imagines* remained a potent symbol of past political power and reinforced the social hierarchies which their owners sought to sustain under the principate.[28]

Yet Seneca dismisses these compelling objects as irrelevant to the pursuit of nobility, or at least, nobility as defined by virtue.[29] He advises the aspiring Stoic to discard the traditional trappings of the family. Building on the rejection of Lucilius' parents' prayers in *Letter* 32, he goes further and suggests a whole range of philosophical ancestors for Lucilius to appropriate in place of his deficient 'normal' family. The central point of the letter is that Lucilius need not worry about being *pusillus*, because philosophy is not concerned about that sort of thing. Lucilius' social status provides no hindrance, or indeed any help, for his pursuit of virtue. This is presumably a sore spot for Lucilius as personified in the letters since Seneca dwells on his specific complaints about both nature and fortune treating him grudgingly (44.1: "naturam prius, deinde fortunam") before scolding him for his preoccupation with irrelevant matters. But Seneca does not take away the comfort Lucilius receives (or wishes he could receive) from his ancestors. Rather, he shows Lucilius how he could fashion his *own* ancestral identity, creating his own family of philosophers to whom he may turn for inspiration – remembering, of course, that they are his leaders, not his masters.

Letter 44 blurs the border between Lucilius as addressee and the general reader as addressee through its discussion of familial prestige. The beginning of the letter is firmly rooted in Lucilius' personal grievances, and Seneca sets out to remonstrate with him. Yet the letter swings from the

---

[28] This letter was composed before the great fire in 64 CE, "which destroyed most of the old aristocratic homes together with their traditional decorations" (Flower 1996, 259). For more on the general history of the *imagines* under the Republic and empire, see Flower 1996.

[29] The dismissal of the "imagines" as a way to judge character is a standard rhetorical commonplace (e.g. Cic. *Pis.* 1; Hor. *S.* 1.12–17), but here Seneca reframes it within a Stoic context. Indeed, one of the famous Stoic paradoxes stated that only wise men could be kings, providing a precedent for Seneca's redefinition of nobility.

personal to the abstract, abandoning the concrete particulars of Lucilius' complaints. When he mentions the *imagines* in the hall, Seneca does not personalize those *imagines*; he does not say "the image of so-and-so, who won this campaign and that political office, will not make you noble, Lucilius." Instead, the impersonality of the image enables the reader to picture any house with such a smoky corner – even his own. One might object that a moment of specificity returns when Seneca asks the reader to imagine that he is a freedman rather than a Roman knight,[30] but even here, there is space for the senator to think "and rather than a senator too." Seneca's advice about reconstructing one's family to include philosophers is sufficiently general for every reader to implement.

Soon after this letter, Seneca's own family surfaces in the *Epistulae Morales* for the first time, in an unexpected way that reinforces Seneca's decision to modify how Lucilius and the reader should define the family. At the beginning of *Letter* 50, Seneca offers Lucilius an illustration of his point that we are blind to our own faults. He tells the story of Harpaste, a household fool (*fatua*), who has recently gone blind:

> Harpasten, uxoris meae fatuam, scis hereditarium onus in domo mea remansisse. Ipse enim aversissimus ab istis prodigiis sum; si quando fatuo delectari volo, non est mihi longe quaerendus: me rideo. Haec fatua subito desiit videre. Incredibilem rem tibi narro, sed veram: nescit esse se caecam; subinde paedagogum suum rogat ut migret, ait domum tenebricosam esse.
>
> You know Harpaste, my wife's fool, has remained in my house, an inherited burden. Myself, I am especially hostile to these sorts of monstrosities. If I ever wish to be entertained by a fool, I do not have to look far – I laugh at myself. Anyway, this fool suddenly stopped seeing. I tell you an incredible but true fact – she does not know she is blind. She repeatedly asks her guardian to move. She says that the house is dark. (Sen. *Ep.* 50.2)

Harpaste illustrates our own inability to understand that we may be greedy or lustful, but at least she realizes she must rely on a guide, something which those with moral blindness fail to grasp. The letter closes with the reassurance that once the mind has begun to take its philosophical medicine and look at its own faults, virtue will make the process both wholesome and sweet (50.9: "salutaris et dulcis"). In this letter, in a very discreet way, Seneca makes the first mention of his *own* family. Harpaste is not in the household because Seneca wants her there – he himself is most ill-disposed towards the concept of fools, although he is kind to Harpaste herself. She is there because she was the fool of Seneca's wife (50.2: "uxoris meae fatuam").

---

30 Sen. *Ep.* 44.6: "puta itaque te non equitem Romanum esse sed libertinum."

This brief phrase both tantalizes and frustrates the reader.[31] On the one hand, finally here is a sign that Seneca does not live in isolation. He has a wife, he has a family, and potentially inhabits normal society.[32] On the other hand, his wife appears only fleetingly. She happens to own the *fatua* whom Seneca uses as an example and is not a willing owner herself. Seneca makes it clear that Harpaste only belongs to his household because of a legacy (presumably to his wife), which is a burden rather than a gift.[33] Although the concept of an inheritance immediately points to the wider social context within which Seneca, or at least his wife, moves, Seneca does not explain who would leave his wife such an ill-suited gift or why his wife feels obliged to keep Harpaste rather than selling her.[34] Paulina appears as the owner of the person about whom Seneca *really* wants to talk.

Paulina remains anonymous while Harpaste is named in an inversion of social convention. Seneca gives the dignity of identity to a slave whom he openly detests, but does not bring his wife into the narrative in the same way. If the passage occurred in a work addressed to a public audience, such as a legal speech, where retaining Paulina's anonymity would have been more respectful, I would not highlight this omission. Similarly, were this one letter among many where Paulina had appeared, with her name, and participated in scenes of domestic life as recorded by Cicero and Pliny,

---

31 I mean here the reader who is *not* Lucilius; presumably Lucilius would be aware of the composition of Seneca's household.
32 Details of Seneca's political life never appear in the *Epistulae Morales*, despite Seneca's obvious comfort with discussing political matters; Nero, too, is strikingly absent. If, out of the Senecan corpus, only the *Epistulae Morales* had survived, we would have very little grounds to connect the author to the Neronian adviser recorded in Tacitus.
33 Sen. *Ep.* 50.2: "hereditarium onus." – The alternative reading of this passage is that the wife in question is not Paulina but Seneca's first, deceased wife. It is impossible to judge whether Seneca had been married before Paulina; for a discussion of the evidence, see Griffin 1992, 57–59. However, given that Paulina is named as Seneca's wife later in the collection, it feels out of place to read the word "uxor" without some qualifying adjective like "prima" as a reference to Seneca's first wife. It was not unusual to refer to one's wife in correspondence without giving her name; see Claassen 1996, 214–215 for an analysis of Cicero's mentions of Terentia.
34 It was possible, in a bequest, to forbid the sale of whatever was being left to the legatee. *Digest* 34.2.16 refers to a woman who charged her heir not to sell her jewelry, gold, silver, or clothing, but to keep the property for her daughter. It was also possible in a bequest to forbid that a slave should be manumitted; the will of Dasumius (*CIL* VI.10229), for instance, stipulates that the legatee's maternal aunt should not free Paederotes and Menecrates but keep them in the same jobs that he gave them.

perhaps this passage would arouse no comment.[35] But the *Epistulae Morales* do not provide an equivalent of Cicero's chatty tone to Atticus, memorably dropping in a mention of Terentia's rheumatism at the close of a letter that has covered Cicero's grief at the loss of a cousin, the marital problems between Atticus' sister and Cicero's brother, and Cicero's management of Atticus' business in his absence (Cic. *Att.* 1.5).[36] Instead, Seneca's first explicit mention of his home life in the letters shows us a freak from whom he feels alienated and an invisible wife who is responsible for this monstrosity. Granted, Seneca shows some consideration towards Harpaste. Despite his revulsion, he does not mock her blindness or whatever physical or mental affliction makes her a fool. However, this rare glimpse that Seneca permits us into his personal life implies that he does not wish Lucilius to rely on the comforts of domestic bliss any more than on the prestige of his biological ancestors.

IV. Gradual Inoculation

At this stage in the *Epistulae Morales*, other themes concerned with the individual dominate the collection. Nonetheless, specific mentions of the family continue to appear and explore both the intimate relationships and wider social dimensions of the family that the letters have already touched on. I offer a few examples to demonstrate how Seneca develops the ideas he has established earlier in the letters. However, he also begins to incor-

---

35 The closest we get to a Ciceronian vignette in the Senecan corpus comes at *De Ira* 3.36, where Seneca describes his evening *meditatio* over the day's events, and comments on his wife's sympathetic understanding of the practice. However, the passage does not name his wife; see note 33**Error! Bookmark not defined.**.

36 Of the 426 letters in the Atticus correspondence, not all of which are authored by Cicero, Terentia is mentioned 49 times, either by name or indirectly, and Tullia 48 times. For a comprehensive overview of the lives of the women in Cicero's letters, see Treggiari 2007. Grebe 2003 analyzes the letters Cicero sent to Terentia from exile. The domestic aspect in Pliny the Younger is particularly marked; Carlon suggests that all the female addressees in the collection were probably his relatives by marriage (2009, 76). These women also appear in letters which are not addressed to them; for instance, he mentions his wife Calpurnia, although not always by name, in letters to Calpurnius Fabatus, her grandfather (*Ep.* 4.1, *Ep.* 8.10); Calpurnia Hispulla, her aunt (*Ep.* 4.19, *Ep.* 8.11); Pontius Allifanus (*Ep.* 5.14); Maximus (*Ep.* 8.19); Fuscus Salinator (*Ep.* 9.36); and even the emperor Trajan (*Ep.* 10.120). Carlon has argued that "no study of women in Pliny would be complete without consideration of his presentation of ideal wives," suggesting that the domestic sphere is key to understanding Pliny's epistolary self-presentation (2009, 16).

porate positive familial associations, provided they appear in a suitably protected context.

The overall unifying theme of *Letter* 66's fifty-three sections is a discussion of virtue and its relationship to goods; it ultimately concludes that there is no good without virtue and that virtue makes everything that partakes in it equally good.[37] This wide brief allows the letter to allude to many varied topics, and it eventually refers to how a parent relates to a child:

> Num quis tam iniquam censuram inter suos agit ut sanum filium quam aegrum magis diligat, procerumve et excelsum quam brevem aut modicum?
>
> Surely no one would make such an unjust appraisal of his own children as to love a healthy son more than a sick son, or a tall and nobly built son more than a short or average-sized one? (Sen. *Ep.* 66.26)

In the previous section, Seneca lampooned the man who maintains friendship with one of two equally virtuous men on the basis of which one is better dressed; this passage extends the point, illustrating that parents love their children equally and not on the basis of irrelevant things like health or height. This affectionate impulse arises naturally, and Seneca makes the follow-up comment that wild animals do not distinguish between their offspring. The point of all of this is to reinforce that virtue, too, loves her offspring equally:

> Quorsus haec pertinent? ut scias virtutem omnia opera velut fetus suos isdem oculis intueri, aeque indulgere omnibus, et quidem inpensius laborantibus, quoniam quidem etiam parentium amor magis in ea quorum miseretur inclinat.
>
> What is the point of these examples? So that you might know that virtue looks at all her works like her young with the same eyes, is tender to them all equally and in fact more lavishly to those who suffer; after all, even the love of parents turns more to those for whom it has compassion. (Sen. *Ep.* 66.27)

The use of the deliberately biological phrase "fetus suos" ("her young"), strikingly foregrounds the procreative aspect of virtue, and strengthens the parallel with the man who does not prefer his healthy son over his sick son or his tall son over his short son. The continuation of the biological image, and the consequent personification of virtue, must be deliberate.[38] The examples of the sick and healthy son and the wild beasts gradually lead to the image of virtue as the ideal parent who loves all her offspring equally. Of course, Seneca's contemporaries could have argued that a healthy son was preferable to a sick son for personal and political advancement, but

---

37 Hachmann 2006 and Inwood 2007a, 155–181 provide detailed discussion and commentary for this letter.
38 Hachmann 2006, 205 suggests that this image ultimately comes from Diotima's speech in Pl. *Smp.* 207a5–212c3, specifically the comparison between the results of virtue and biological children.

Lucilius is considered sufficiently advanced in his philosophical education that he will not make that sort of mistake.[39]

In this passage Seneca returns to the idea of the family as a natural phenomenon for the first time after he had briefly deployed it in *Letter* 9. The wide-ranging letter in which it occurs is placed just after the midpoint of the extant collection, sixty-sixth in the surviving series of a hundred and twenty four. Before Seneca presents an unequivocally positive image of the family, and provides this image of how family relations can mirror our relationship to virtue, he wants Lucilius to have made his way through not only the sixty-five letters that come before this passage, but also the twenty-five sections meditating on virtue before it, and supposes he will finish the twenty-six sections that follow.

The reader only encounters this image when it is safely insulated, both by the collection and by the letter which enfolds it; the process of Stoic doctrinal formation leads the reader to concentrate on what this means for his relationship with virtue rather than becoming distracted by the secondary matter of the family in itself. That said, Seneca still emphasizes the attitude of virtue towards its *opera* ("works," presumably a reference to virtuous deeds) as if these *opera* were offspring, thus suggesting that it models ideal parenting behavior; indeed, the passage goes on to note that *even* imperfect parents manage to replicate this attitude to some extent. Presumably the counterpoint to this is that we should imitate virtue and try, as parents, to treat our children on the basis of their inner virtue rather than their external qualities. This remains a secondary message; Seneca wishes to engage the reader's mind with the question of virtue and its functions rather than to digress into the subject of familial ethics.

Family takes on an unexpected particularity in *Letter* 70, where Seneca reports the suicide of Drusus Libo.[40] *Letter* 70 primarily concerns itself at some length with the proper time to die. Seneca illustrates his point with a naval metaphor. If life is a voyage, and death the final port, the man who reaches it swiftly has no more to complain about than a sailor who has had a swift passage (70.3). It is not always correct to cling to life – one must not just live but must live *well*.[41] Naturally this observation leads into a

---

39 Inwood 2007a, 171–172 argues that Seneca here suggests a "kind of compensatory pity for the weaker offspring" to account for the phenomenon that parents sometimes do feel an affective difference in their emotions for their children. However, I am not convinced that the actual language of the parental example Seneca uses supports this interpretation.
40 Reydams-Schils 2005, 45–52 gives a general overview of the Roman Stoics' opinions about suicide and which factors besides oneself should be taken into account when considering it.
41 Sen. *Ep.* 70.4: "non enim vivere bonum est, sed bene vivere."

discussion of the circumstances under which it is appropriate to end one's own life, and that examination introduces the anecdote about Libo's suicide:

> Scribonia, gravis femina, amita Drusi Libonis fuit, adulescentis tam stolidi quam nobilis, maiora sperantis quam illo saeculo quisquam sperare poterat aut ipse ullo. Cum aeger a senatu in lectica relatus esset non sane frequentibus exsequîs (omnes enim necessarii deseruerant impie iam non reum sed funus), habere coepit consilium utrum consciceret mortem an exspectaret. Cui Scribonia "Quid te" inquit "delectat alienum negotium agere?" Non persuasit illi: manus sibi attulit, nec sine causa. Nam post diem tertium aut quartum inimici moriturus arbitrio si vivit, alienum negotium agit.

> Scribonia, a severe woman, was the aunt of Drusus Libo, a young man as dim as he was noble, who was hoping for greater things than anyone could hope for in that age – or indeed than *he* could in *any* age. When he was carried away unwell from the senate in a litter, certainly not with many mourners (all his close connections impiously had deserted him now that he was not a defendant but a dead man), he began to hold a council on whether he should anticipate or await death. Scribonia said to him: "What pleasure does it give you to do another man's business?" She did not persuade him; he laid hands upon himself, and not without justification. For if a man about to die in three or four days by his enemy's decision continues to live, he does another man's business. (Sen. *Ep.* 70.10)

The familial frame is arguably superfluous here, as the point of the anecdote lies in Libo's choice to die before Tiberius makes the decision for him. Seneca introduces the anecdote through Scribonia, marking her out very deliberately as Libo's aunt, although the anecdote which he wishes to tell is actually about the nephew. Libo, under prosecution for conspiring against Tiberius, decides to commit suicide against the advice of Scribonia. Yet Libo's decision to ignore his aunt and commit suicide wins Seneca's approval. There was no point in continuing to live when he lived at another man's pleasure rather than his own.

The question, then, is why Seneca decided to include the assertive and severe Scribonia in the narrative at all, as the anecdote works just as well without her. The answer lies in Scribonia's advice and Libo's decision to ignore it. Indeed, in some ways Scribonia is the antithesis of Arria, who encouraged her husband to commit suicide by stabbing herself first and handing him the dagger with the cheerful words: "It doesn't hurt, Paetus."[42] Where Pliny makes Arria the embodiment of good Stoic womanhood, Scribonia reflects the social mores of the unphilosophical world at Rome. The key to interpreting her inclusion comes from the theme introduced in *Letter* 31, that those who love us do not always wish what is best for us. Seneca presents a worked example of a real-life

---

42 Plin. *Ep.* 3.16.13: "Paete, non dolet." This incident took place under the reign of Claudius in 42 CE, and it is thus probable that Seneca was aware of it.

situation where the wishes of a close relative were not in the best interests of the individual. Thankfully, Libo recognized this and followed his own rational judgment. Despite Scribonia's qualifications as a morally respectable woman ("gravis femina"), she does not determine the appropriate course of action. In the context of Seneca's thought, Libo made the correct judgment and chose to leave life freely; his aunt's desires would have deprived him of that choice.

Letter 78 gives us the second glimpse into Seneca's own family in the collection. After a sequence of letters continuing to consider the nature of suicide, Seneca begins by consoling Lucilius on his frequent catarrh and fevers (78.1: "destillationibus crebris ac febriculis"). Seneca himself suffered from similar symptoms in his youth, and at first bore them bravely.

> Deinde succubui et eo perductus sum ut ipse destillarem, ad summam maciem deductus. Saepe impetum cepi abrumpendae vitae: patris me indulgentissimi senectus retinuit. Cogitavi enim non quam fortiter ego mori possem, sed quam ille fortiter desiderare non posset. Itaque imperavi mihi ut viverem; aliquando enim et vivere fortiter facere est.

> Then I succumbed, and was brought to the point that I myself was wasting away, reduced to utmost emaciation. I often entertained the impulse to break off my life; the old age of my most tender father restrained me. For I thought not about how bravely I could die, but how little he would have been able to miss me bravely. And so I ordered myself to live. Sometimes even to live is to act bravely. (Sen. *Ep.* 78.1–2)

Sometimes it is braver, and more proper, to suffer through a difficult situation rather than to end one's life. The letter explains that it was Seneca's philosophical studies, the work of the mind, that gave him the comfort he needed to persevere and so continues to discuss the benefits of properly directed mental activity as a general-purpose cure. But the beginning of the letter presents Seneca's father for the first time in the collection, in connection with a particular choice about suicide. The closest parallel in the preceding *Epistulae Morales* is the story of Libo Drusus and his aunt Scribonia from *Letter* 70. If that incident offered a template for how to behave in these situations, Seneca himself is at fault for paying attention to concerns for his father instead of ignoring them. However, the situations are not comparable. Libo was under a likely sentence of death from Tiberius; Seneca is held hostage by his own body, not the power of another man. Libo is fairly certain that the sentence of death will come within a couple of days; Seneca knows that he may, eventually, recover. Libo, at least as far as the anecdote is concerned, has no family dependent upon him, and Scribonia makes no appeal to obligations he has to others; Seneca views his responsibility to his father as a significant factor in his decision not to commit suicide. Scribonia speaks directly to Libo to give him her misguided advice; Seneca the Elder remains a silent but significant presence in his son's deliberations.

Whether Seneca *actually* had this conversation with himself during a period of extreme illness is immaterial.[43] The memory is included because it again shows the family in a positive light, where a son incorporates his concern for his father into a rational decision not to commit suicide. Seneca does not object to taking one's family into consideration; it follows that the family can play an important role in an individual's life. If families were dispensable and to be disregarded, Seneca would not have taken his father into account at all when making his decision. Instead, he paints a touching image of the grief he knows his father will suffer at his loss, making a convincing case for sparing Seneca the Elder the emotional pain of his suicide. The contrast between his decision and Libo's rests on the fact that nobody offers Seneca advice. He makes up his own mind, whereas Libo disregards his aunt's unwise counsel.[44] Families, then, can be a good and important part of our lives, but we must not be misled by their ill-informed guidance into ignoring our own reason.

Seneca only reveals his positive relationship with his father when the reader has been sufficiently inoculated against drawing the wrong conclusion from such a display. Libo's story illustrates the point that family members do not give infallible advice in matters of suicide; Seneca's story shows that this does not mean the family should be completely excluded from such deliberations. These people who will be affected by one's decision must be sensibly taken into account. After all, the Stoic wise man is not inhuman. He would not make a decision to kill himself without considering the impact on his wife, children, parents, and friends, because that would be against his nature as a human being.

Now that the reader is further along the *Epistulae Morales*' developmental path, examples that would have been dangerous at the beginning of

---

43 As Edwards comments, "however much we may want to interpret such remarks as rare glimpses into the personal experience of one of Neronian Rome's most complex characters, even these few plausible details are hardly to be trusted" (1997, 23). Griffin notes the problem that "the surviving prose works [...] tell us little about Seneca's external life or about the people and events that formed its setting" (1992, 1), but does her best to construct as detailed a history of Seneca's life as possible from the fragments. In her discussion she assumes that comments of this sort in the *Epistulae Morales* are based on at least a grain of truth. Inwood also cautions that "the not infrequent notion that the Seneca we know from the letters is the man himself should not be accepted uncritically" (2007b, 137). See also above, n. 2.

44 Of course, in reality Seneca the Elder did offer his three sons a considerable amount of advice through writing the *Controversiae* and *Suasoriae* for them as oratorical guides.

the journey have become safe to read. But Seneca is careful always to provide a reminder of the dangers associated with the family, lest the aspiring Stoic disciple wander in the wrong direction.

V. Teaching with Precepts

At this stage, the *Epistulae Morales* reach a turning point in Seneca's portrayal of the family. Now that the reader has been carefully immunized against familial examples, such examples begin to occur more frequently. *Letters* 94 and 95 discuss questions of education, what should be taught to children and how to teach them. These pedagogical issues tie into wider questions of how one should approach ethical education and of the family as a place where that education takes place. Working out how the two strands interact provides further insight into how Stoicism and the family should operate at this more rarefied level. The reappearance of familial matters suggests that by now Lucilius should have absorbed enough Stoic theory to process these issues properly. The fact that these references come in an explicit discussion of education reflects on Lucilius' own educational progress through the *Epistulae Morales* and his new ability to tackle these previously dangerous subjects.

Letters 94 and 95 form a pair of complementary views on the value of education through precepts.[45] *Letter* 94 lays out at some length the arguments of people like Aristo, who claim that attempting to teach philosophy by precepts is at best meaningless and at worst actively harmful, and then demolishes them point by point.[46] *Letter* 95 argues that while precepts have curative properties, in and of themselves they are not enough to bring someone to virtue. Both letters use evidence drawn from familial contexts to make their point, and so suggest that moral education is in some ways irreversibly connected to our relatives.

The structure of *Letter* 94 is slightly confusing, as Seneca first lays out the objections to precepts, only to refute them. However, his first move *in propria persona* as the letter opens is to establish what precepts are and what purpose they serve; he does this with a familial example. Precepts tell

---

[45] Schafer 2009 provides a thoughtful study of these letters and their implications for the didactic program of the *Epistulae Morales* as a whole. He concludes that *Letters* 94 and 95 defend and explain Seneca's philosophical pedagogy, and demonstrate the controlled artistry that helps structure and reinforce the whole collection. Hadot 1969 and Bellincioni 1979 also emphasize the pedagogical importance of these two letters.

[46] The debate on the best pedagogical approach was a lively one. For more discussion of the arguments involved, see Kidd 1978 and 1988, 646–651.

a husband how to behave towards his wife or a father how to treat his children, as well as instructing a master how to treat his slaves (94.1).[47] Seneca then adopts the persona of Aristo to argue that precepts are pointless, as the wise man should learn how to live well full stop; that final goal automatically includes behaving correctly towards one's wife and children (94.3). Seneca continues through Aristo to present a lengthy criticism of precepts, which specifically targets those who claim to offer advice to the married:

> In matrimonio praecipies quomodo vivat cum uxore aliquis quam virginem duxit, quomodo cum ea quae alicuius ante matrimonium experta est, quemadmodum cum locuplete, quemadmodum cum indotata. An non putas aliquid esse discriminis inter sterilem et fecundam, inter provectiorem et puellam, inter matrem et novercam? Omnis species conplecti non possumus: atqui singulae propria exigunt, leges autem philosophiae breves sunt et omnia alligant.
>
> In marriage, you will advise in what way a man should live with a wife whom he married as a virgin, in what way with her who has prior experience of another marriage, in what manner he should live with a wealthy wife, and with one without a dowry. Or do you not think there is some difference between the barren and the fertile woman, between the more mature woman and the young girl, between the mother and the step-mother? We cannot include all the specific types, but each one demands its own particulars; yet the laws of philosophy are brief and unite everything. (Sen. *Ep.* 94.15)

With this obvious *reductio ad absurdum*, Aristo shows that attempting to provide precepts for each and every situation is an endless task, and indeed a fruitless one. General statements about how married people should behave are useless because of the differences in what constitutes a "married couple." Trying to provide precepts for all types of married couples is equally useless, as the task would be never-ending, and philosophy should have discrete boundaries. Wisdom, not precepts, should answer questions about proper conduct. Seneca's choice of marital advice as the particular target for Aristo's attack shows that marriage remains an important locus for ethical behavior – but, the interlocutor argues, the disciple will not find the key to correct conduct in precepts.

Seneca then returns to his own persona to refute Aristo's arguments, and also returns to the marital theme. He explains that the point of advice and precepts is not to create a cure but to state the obvious; it reminds us of what we already know (94.25). He agrees with Aristo that universal precepts cannot help us in our individual circumstances, but believes they have value in offering a broad framework of moral rules of thumb. They offer "entrenched but modifiable general rules prescribing appropriate

---

47 This follows the conception of the component parts of the household found in Arist. *Pol.* 1.3, 1253b.

actions as a framework for their thinking" to imperfect moral agents (Inwood 2005, 111). Seneca then lists examples of situations where we know we are doing the wrong thing, yet do it anyway. In this case, Seneca uses the example of adultery as always unacceptable; he describes broad behaviors rather than particularized individuals as his interlocutor does:

> Scis inprobum esse qui ab uxore pudicitiam exigit, ipse alienarum corruptor uxorum; scis ut illi nil cum adultero, sic tibi nil esse debere cum paelice, et non facis.
>
> You know that the man who exacts *pudicitia*[48] from his wife while being the corruptor of the wives of others is morally unsound; you know that just as there should be nothing between your wife and a lover, there should be nothing between you and a mistress, and you do not act accordingly. (Sen. *Ep.* 94.26)

Seneca returns to marriage to show the kind of preceptual advice that *would* actually be useful, in that people need reminding that infidelity is bad for both men and women. To be effective, precepts have to provide broad *aide-mémoires* about conduct. His argument that precepts *can* provide us with helpful moral advice in this way, and thus guide our decision-making, implies that there are some fixed standards of moral behavior. In this case, as a rule of thumb, within a marriage infidelity by either partner is *never* acceptable, regardless of the individual natures of the partners.[49] The ethics of this particular situation imply that while the dynamics of individual relationships may vary, some overarching rules apply to all marriages. Precepts work by reminding us of this kind of generalized guidance; his choice of example demonstrates that Seneca believes one of the questions for which precepts can be useful is how to live well with one's family.

Of course, the utility of precepts depends on the person who is offering them. Seneca goes on to explain that not all precepts are worth paying attention to. We need someone to act as our preceptor who can speak against the precepts of the world at large.[50] We are surrounded by people who give us false advice:

---

48 I leave the word *pudicitia* deliberately untranslated, as there is no adequate English word to encompass the concept that the Latin expresses. The possible choices (e.g. shamefacedness, modesty, and chastity) are loaded with our own ideological burdens, especially "chastity." Langlands 2006, 29–37 discusses the issue further.

49 I say "as a rule of thumb" because Stoic ethics does allow for exceptional situations where the rational action may in fact be what is unacceptable 99.99% of the time. Inwood 2005, 95–131 provides an excellent discussion of the role of rules, precepts, and decrees in Stoic decision-making, and how these provide a flexible framework for moral reasoning.

50 Sen. *Ep.* 94.52: "Interim omissis argumentis nonne apparet opus esse nobis aliquo advocato qui contra populi praecepta praecipiat?"

> Non licet, inquam, ire recta via; trahunt in pravum parentes, trahunt servi. Nemo errat uni sibi, sed dementiam spargit in proximos accipitque invicem.
>
> I say, it is not permitted to walk a straight path. Our parents, our slaves drag us in a crooked direction. No one goes astray on his own, but sprinkles his insanity on those closest to him and receives it in his turn. (Sen. *Ep.* 94.54)

Once again, parents are among a number of people who give us bad advice through their ignorance of virtue, and slaves are just as guilty of offering false moral guidance. The juxtaposition of the two raises interesting questions about the parent-child and master-slave relationship, but suffice it to say that anyone with whom we interact could lead us into the wrong behaviors if we do not carefully judge the precepts they offer us. Seneca goes on to offer the solution that Nature be our guardian. She does not reconcile us with any vice, and only produces health and freedom in us (94.56). Nature, our ultimate parent, can be trusted to give us wise and true advice; our biological parents cannot. This reminder of the theme that Seneca developed so much in the earlier letters protects the reader from mistaking the concerns that loved ones have for us for the true path to virtue. Even the devotee who has made it thus far through the *Epistulae Morales* still has to be reminded lest he deviate from his true course.

Letter 95 continues to use familial themes as part of the wider discourse on preceptual education, although the first mention of families in the letter is less serious. Acknowledging that *Letter* 94 was rather lengthy, taking seventy-four sections to make its point, Seneca says that Lucilius has only himself to blame if, after reading *Letter* 95, he starts to feel like a husband whose wife is torturing him.[51] This is a standard *topos* in Latin literature, but Seneca puts himself in the position of the wife and casts Lucilius as the harried husband. Seneca uses this negative image of a familial relationship to describe his relationship with Lucilius in a way that undercuts the supportive relationship the letters try to create between friends aspiring to philosophy together. Seneca pairs the image of the henpecked husband with the man harassed by his own riches and those burdened by the honors they worked so hard to gain (95.3). These are all

---

51 Sen. *Ep.* 95.3: "Ego me omissa misericordia vindicabo et tibi ingentem epistulam inpingam, quam tu si invitus leges, dicito 'ego mihi hoc contraxi,' teque inter illos numera quos uxor magno ducta ambitu torquet, inter illos quos divitiae per summum adquisitae sudorem male habent, inter illos quos honores nulla non arte atque opera petiti discruciant, et ceteros malorum suorum compotes" – "I will avenge myself with all pity laid aside, and thrust a huge letter upon you; if you read it unwillingly, say 'I brought this upon myself,' and consider yourself among those men whose wives, married with great ambition, torture them; among those, whose riches, acquired through much sweat, treat them badly; among those, whose honors sought by a great deal of skill and labor torture them, and others who have obtained their own misfortunes."

examples of difficulties people bring upon themselves; in this context, a wife is a self-inflicted source of suffering, but then so potentially is Lucilius' request that Seneca explain whether precepts on their own are sufficient to gain virtue. Hopefully, Lucilius will gain more from this letter than a scolding, and hopefully a husband may get more out of his relationship with his wife than antagonism. The negative image suggests what *could* happen, but not what *should* happen.

This idea that what *should* happen does not always happen reappears later, in a similar way to *Letter* 94. A man may know that keeping a concubine is an insult to his wife, but he does it anyway (95.37). This is the final example in a list of things people know they should not do but do anyway because of our incorrect understanding of what we should admire and what we should fear (95.37: "falsa admiratio et falsa formido"); only when we have the correct understanding about what is truly to be admired and feared will we stop doing things we rationally know we should not do. Precepts provide no help in removing those false conceptions. The aspiring Stoic must work to remove them first so that they do not stand in the way of effective application of the precepts which "flow from" the "Stoic physical principles (holism, rational teleology, a part-whole understanding of the cosmos)" and "the natural foundation of human sociability," which lie at the heart of the Stoic understanding of how the universe functions (Inwood 2005, 122).

The passage provides the key to why references to the family are so thin on the ground in the *Epistulae Morales*. There is no *point* in discussing how to relate to one's family until the fundamental barriers to those relationships have been removed:

> Nihil ergo proderit dare praecepta nisi prius amoveris obstatura praeceptis, non magis quam proderit arma in conspectu posuisse propiusque admovisse nisi usurae manus expediuntur. Ut ad praecepta quae damus possit animus ire, solvendus est.

> Therefore it will be of no benefit to give precepts unless first you have removed the things that will stand in the way of precepts, no more than it will be of benefit to place weapons within sight and to move them closer unless the hands are set free for using them. For the mind to be able to go to the precepts which we give, it must be set free. (Sen. *Ep.* 95.38)

References to the family have been omitted from the *Epistulae Morales* for the reader's own safety. Just as approaching an enemy with weapons nearby but no hands free to use them would result in severe injury at best and outright slaughter at worst, approaching dangerous moral ground with an understanding of the ethical tools at one's disposal but unable to use them can only harm the person traveling towards virtue. The *Epistulae Morales* strip away these external dangers until the reader has gotten his hands free by reorienting his inner moral landscape. He now has come some way towards eradicating his false ideas about what is good and bad in the world, and so can begin cautiously to approach the enemy.

Similarly, Seneca mentions Marcus Brutus' work *On Duties*, which provides precepts concerning parents, children, and siblings. But, says Seneca, it will be no good unless a person has something to refer back to, an underlying principle in accordance with which to act (95.45). There is no benefit in having precepts until the foundations of virtue are in place which enable an individual to apply them properly. Seneca's deliberate elision of the family from the first part of the collection, followed by a slow and sparing reintroduction towards the end, springs from an approach to philosophical education that believes it is vital to get the basics firmly in place before approaching more significant challenges. This lengthy initial stage of education means that the family's gradual introduction begins late in the collection, and so the family never achieves a substantial presence in the letters.

VI. Seneca Gets Personal

As the end of the extant collection approaches, Seneca seems to relax a little. Now that Lucilius has a good grasp of the basic tenets of Stoic philosophy, more detailed accounts of people and Seneca's relationship to them begin to appear. We have seen two references to Seneca's own family, a one-word allusion to his wife in *Letter* 50 and a brief mention of his father in *Letter* 78. Suddenly, in the last thirty or so letters, specific mentions of relationships with families, complete with context, occur four times – astonishingly frequent for the *Epistulae Morales*, despite the collection's statistically small size. Now that the reader has been primed for specifics, he is given specifics, in the hope that he will process them correctly and extract their meaning.

Letter 99 also engages with a specific moment, more than earlier letters did, although the presentation of this particular missive has created some difficulties in its interpretation. Rather than a normal letter, Seneca sends on to Lucilius another letter he wrote to Marullus following the death of his son. The tone of the enclosed correspondence opens with a harsh order for Marullus to prepare himself to receive reproaches instead of comfort (99.2: "Solacia expectas? convicia accipe"). However, to take this as evidence for Stoic heartlessness misses several important points about the wider context in which the text is presented.[52]

---

[52] It is not impossible for the sage to experience grief at the loss of a loved one, but that grief will not be categorized as a *pathos* or irrational emotion. The sage's state

First, the introduction of the letter, where Seneca explains the circumstances under which he wrote to Marullus, makes it clear that it is not grief *per se* that he wishes to rebuke but indulgent grief:

> Adflicto enim et magnum vulnus male ferenti paulisper cedendum est; exsatiet se aut certe primum impetum effundat: hi qui sibi lugere sumpserunt protinus castigentur et discant quasdam etiam lacrimarum ineptias esse.
>
> One must yield for a little while to someone afflicted by a serious wound and bearing it badly; let him satisfy himself or certainly vent the first impulse; those who have taken it upon themselves to grieve should be chastised immediately and learn that there are certain follies even in tears. (Sen. *Ep.* 99.1)

Seneca upbraids Marullus not for mourning his son, but for deliberately engaging in grief;[53] the letter later, at 99,16 criticizes the "display of grief" (*ostentatio doloris*), suggesting that there is a performative element to Marullus' behavior which Seneca finds inappropriate.[54] The location of the letter in the collection also matters. Immediately before this, in *Letter* 98, as part of a discussion of indifferents, Seneca says that a man needs to realize that his wife, children, and property are not going to be his always so that he can avoid becoming miserable when losing them (98.5). Seneca advised Lucilius to prepare for the loss of *things* at the very beginning of the collection (18.5), but the loss of *people* is more difficult to handle.

The letter to Marullus stands in stark contrast to the account of the death of Bassus back in *Letter* 30. The subject matter provides an immediate contrast: Seneca frequently refers to him as "our friend Bassus" (e.g. 30.3: "Bassus noster"), thus prioritizing the discussion of friendship in the letter collection over family matters. Although Bassus prepared himself for death from old age, he seemed to do so in a complete vacuum. Seneca spoke of Bassus' healthy mind despite his body giving up although he tried to hold it together; he did not mention Bassus' family or his dependents, or indeed any negative effect that Bassus' death might have on anyone but Bassus. His only company comes from his visitors, of whom Seneca is one and with whom he talks freely about death (30.5). In fact, Seneca emphasizes how much of a *positive* experience visiting Bassus has been, in terms of teaching him not to fear death. Finally, Bassus does not actually die in

---

of *apatheia* does not require the extirpation of everything that we would recognize as an emotive response; see, for instance, Seneca's description of a wise man weeping at a funeral in *Ep.* 99.20–21. Graver 2007, 86–108 discusses this distinction further.

53 Seneca speaks of anger as being similarly difficult to control when it first arises (*De ira* 3.39.2). See David Kaufman's article in this volume for a discussion of how to address the passions when reason cannot be applied.

54 This approach is in keeping with the Stoic idea that death is not an evil and that grief should not be drawn out; Seneca presents similar ideas in his consolations to Marcia and Polybius.

Letter 30. We only see him approaching his death rationally and without fear.

The letter to Marullus builds on the approach to death that the *Epistulae Morales* have taken so far. Like much else in the collection, it is introduced gradually. Although abstract references to death occur in the very first letter and examples of good deaths (including that of Cato) appear as early as *Letter* 24, Seneca holds back from discussing deaths of people he and Lucilius know. The first instance occurs in *Letter* 63, which consoles Lucilius on the death of his friend Flaccus but instructs him to grieve appropriately;[55] *Letter* 70 includes examples of men who commit suicide when faced with the arena; and *Letter* 77 describes in detail the suicide of Tullius Marcellinus. As Wilson notes, *Letter* 99 "revisits the theme of grief broached in *Letter* 63 but with this disconcerting departure: it turns back on itself to question the value of some forms of consolation as well" (1997, 50); it also is the first time that the collection addresses how one should mourn for a family member instead of a friend.[56] Now, at this stage in the letters the reader can face the realities of what it means to treat a member of one's family as an indifferent – not to lose concern and care for them entirely but to moderate grief by remembering that they did not belong to you. Further, the relationship in *Letter* 99 is between parent and child; Marullus gives in to his grief because that is the automatic inclination of a parent who is not a sage. The tough advice that Seneca has to give him needs to be heard by all parents so that they may be ready for this situation if they have the misfortune to encounter it. By this stage in the *Epistulae Morales*, the reader knows that interpersonal relationships matter, but also that the family is ultimately a gift of fate that can readily be taken away. That build-up makes the tone of this letter less brusque than Wilson suggests.

The details of Marullus' situation soon give way to more general advice. A specific family provides the stage upon which to examine the working out of ethical problems on the microcosmic scale, with the discussion then expanding to the case's macrocosmic implications. Wilson notes that Seneca uses "a sophisticated rhetorical technique whereby the discussion oscillates between examining grief on an abstract and on a

---

55 Sen. *Ep.* 63.1: "plus tamen aequo dolere te nolo."
56 *Letter* 98.9 mentions Metrodorus' letter to his sister consoling her on the loss of her son, but uses a sentence from it to launch a discussion of how all our goods are mortal rather than considering how best to mourn a child. The letter also puts this particular death in a wider social context; Seneca asks Marullus how he would have coped with the death of a friend, the greatest of all injuries (99.3: "damnorum omnium maximum"), if his reaction to the death of an infant of unknown qualities is so extreme.

personal level" (1997, 51), refusing to engage with the specifics of Marullus' loss except in very restricted circumstances. This generalization of themes means that Seneca can make his advice applicable to *any* reader, not just Marullus or someone in his situation. It also applies the general advice given in *Letter* 98 about how to cope with losing indifferents to a real-life case study. Applying these ideas is not easy. Losing a child genuinely hurts. Yet a man with a correct understanding of what is and is not important will not be adrift in grief. Instead, he will take pleasure in the memory of what has been lost (99.11). Seneca does not ask Marullus to be negligent or heedless of his loss. Rather, he wants him to put his bereavement in perspective, through the Stoic theory of indifferents, so that he may stop his obsession with grief and enjoy the memories of his son. As Henderson notes, the letter seems to prepare Lucilius for a similar fate, "rallying him against any loss *he* may [soon?] suffer" (2004, 43). In Marullus, Seneca presents a test case of how to analyze an individual situation and produce such broad advice. The reader may then concentrate on his own specific circumstances and apply that advice as appropriate, but the transition between the general and specific occurs through the mediation of personal relationships.

In *Letter* 104, Seneca writes about his wife Paulina's tender concern for him as he departs for his villa at Nomentum and poignantly describes how her care for him revitalizes his own zest for life. The opening of the letter suggests a close and intimate relationship, in which their actions towards each other are motivated by love:

> Hoc ego Paulinae meae dixi, quae mihi valetudinem meam commendat. Nam cum sciam spiritum illius in meo verti, incipio, ut illi consulam, mihi consulere. [...] Itaque quoniam ego ab illa non inpetro ut me fortius amet, <a me> inpetrat illa ut me diligentius amem.

> I said this to my Paulina, who commends my health to me. For since I know that her breath depends upon mine, I am beginning to take care of myself in order to take care of her. [...] Accordingly, since I cannot get her to love me more bravely, she gets me to love myself more attentively. (Sen. *Ep.* 104.2)

The relationship appears to give him pleasure, since he comments that nothing is sweeter than to be so dear to one's wife that one begins to become dearer to oneself (104.6). He also mentions the example of his brother Gallio, who left Achaia when he came down with a fever because it came from the location rather than the body (104.1). Seneca nowhere else mentions two members of his family in the same letter at the same time.[57] The letter continues by relating the improvement in Seneca's health when

---

[57] This is also the only internal evidence of Paulina's name in Seneca. Her name is recorded in Tacitus' account of Seneca's suicide (*Ann.* 15.60 and 64).

he got to Nomentum, but warns that ultimately a man carries his own troubles within him. No matter how far you travel, you cannot escape the evils of your own soul.[58] Seneca again admonishes the reader to think of his nearest and dearest as mortal, like a flourishing plant that will eventually wither (104.11), and emphasizes the importance of study over travel to heal one's mental state. If you must move, then move to be close to sensible people like Cato, Laelius, and Tubero – and if you must have Greeks, then spend time with Socrates, Zeno, Chrysippus, and Posidonius (104.21–22). The letter closes by praising the models of Socrates and Cato the Younger, who faced death bravely and on their own terms.

The portrait of husbandly affection at the start of this letter, where Paulina and Seneca seem to live with the same breath, is almost completely undermined by its content. As soon as Seneca gets away from Paulina, he recovers his health – as Henderson puts it:

> He bolts by carriage to an estate of his "at Nomentum." Away from fever, and for that reason from the City [of Rome]: from his wife, his wife, his brother, his health, his (Senecan) old age, his wife, his fear. From Pompeia Paulina. From Gallio. The moment he touched the vines, it was a case of "Once let into pasture, I went for my food" (104.6) and the recovery of his SELF (full concentration on study). (Henderson 2004, 40)

Seneca *explicitly* runs away from his family. For all his later protestations that travel does not help one escape from one's own demons, it seems to do him a power of good. The reader will also just have perused the admonition of *Letter* 103. This short letter warns that man delights to ruin man,[59] and tells the reader to guard against the everyday danger which comes from other people.

Seneca's decision to bolt, then, makes sense – he *has* to get away in order to be free of the dangers posed by others. The extreme caution of *Letter* 103 does not extend as far as abandoning social interaction altogether, so Seneca's criticism of his own journey to Nomentum acknowledges that one will not eradicate one's problems by fleeing from them. Yet he has still chosen to run, implying that the place in which he finds himself causes him sickness, just as Gallio told him his fever came from sojourning in Achaia. Seneca is not just escaping from Rome, of course, but also from his wife – it is surely not coincidental that Paulina is the only family mem-

---

58 The travel motif frequently appears in the collection, both as a description of a literal journey and as a metaphor for the soul's philosophical journey; Henderson 2006 explores this theme in *Letter* 57. Other letters that develop this idea include *Letters* 28.1–4, 53.1–5, and 70.1–6.
59 Sen. *Ep*. 103.2: "homini perdere hominem libet."

ber who truly intrudes on Seneca's voice in the *Epistulae Morales*, and from whom he has to escape to be his old self again.[60]

Seneca's choice to use Socrates as one of his examples towards the end of the letter further complicates any sentimental interpretation we might apply to the opening section. In sketching the hardships with which Socrates lived, Seneca emphasizes the difficulties of his home life:

> Si tamen exemplum desideratis, accipite Socraten, perpessicium senem, per omnia aspera iactatum, invictum tamen et paupertate, quam graviorem illi domestica onera faciebant, et laboribus, quos militares quoque pertulit. Quibus ille domi exercitus, sive uxorem eius moribus feram, lingua petulantem, sive liberos indociles et matri quam patri similiores [...][61]

> However, if you want an example, take Socrates, a hard-bitten old man, tossed through all harsh things, nonetheless unconquered by poverty, which his domestic burdens made heavier for him, and by the military service which he also endured. By these things he was harassed at home, either by his wife, fierce in her habits and insolent in her speech, or his unteachable children, who were more similar to their mother than their father [...] (Sen. *Ep.* 104.27)

Seneca highlights the toils and tribulations that Socrates suffered because of his wife and children, yet also remarks that nobody ever saw him excessively sad or happy – he maintained his equanimity.[62] Of course, plenty of other things caused Socrates discomfort, not only his family, but Seneca foregrounds that element, providing a stark contrast to his portrait of affectionate home life with Paulina. A detractor might suggest that the mention of Xanthippe should signal that all families cause some degree of stress for their members; Seneca provides two sides of the same coin to portray accurately the complexity of these relationships in our lives.

The fundamental messages of *Letter* 104 clash. On the one hand, Paulina's love reinvigorates Seneca's care for himself; on the other, he has to run away from her to Nomentum to regain his mental clarity and sense of self. Travel cannot help us escape from our mental turmoil, yet Seneca travels precisely to relieve his mental as well as physical fever. The letter in which Paulina plays the greatest part is also the one in which Seneca makes it clear he can do perfectly well without her. These conflicting ideas emphasize the ambivalent nature of the family. On the one hand, it supports and nurtures Seneca, but on the other, he occasionally needs to escape it to regain his equilibrium. This negotiation reflects the wider need

---

60 Sen. *Ep.* 104.6: "Repetivi ergo iam me."
61 The text is uncertain here; it seems likely that the sentence continued after *similiores*, but Reynolds *ad. loc.* obelizes the word that follows in his edition.
62 Sen. *Ep.* 104.28: "usque ad extremum nec hilariorem quisquam nec tristiorem Socraten vidit."

to find the fine balance between dedication to self and interaction with community, between isolation and participation.

Letter 108, another lengthy piece coming in at thirty-nine sections, is the final letter in which Seneca mentions his own family; it discusses knowledge and the best way to obtain it. Seneca reminisces about the advice his teacher Attalus gave him about learning, and takes as his central theme how one should learn philosophy from a philosopher. He outlines various sorts of pedagogical approaches, continuously returning to his own experiences as a pupil of Attalus, and of Sotion and Sextius.[63] After Sotion explained the Pythagorean rationale for vegetarianism and abstention from animal foods (108.17: "animalibus") to him, he ardently pursued it, but eventually gave up the diet because of political factors that brought such dietary practices under suspicion:

> Quaeris quomodo desierim? In primum Tiberii Caesaris principatum iuventae tempus inciderat: alienigena tum sacra movebantur et inter argumenta superstitionis ponebatur quorundam animalium abstinentia. Patre itaque meo rogante, qui non calumniam timebat sed philosophiam oderat, ad pristinam consuetudinem redii; nec difficulter mihi ut inciperem melius cenare persuasit.

> How did I stop, you ask? The time of my youth fell during the early reign of Tiberius Caesar. Foreign religious rites were being stirred up then, and among the evidence for superstition was included refraining from certain animal flesh. And so when my father asked me, who himself was not frightened of false accusation but hated philosophy, I returned to my previous habits. Nor was it difficult for him to persuade me to begin to eat better. (Sen. *Ep.* 108.22)

The concern with disrupting foreign religious cults, some marked by abstention from eating certain animals, would have caught up those who observed Pythagorean vegetarianism as well, although we have no record of Sotion himself being involved in this episode. Seneca the Elder's main motivation for asking his son to stop being a vegetarian is not fear that he might be caught up in the elimination of cults, as one might have supposed, but because he detested philosophy. In this case, his distaste is arguably misplaced. Vegetarianism was seen by the Pythagoreans as a mark of respect for one's parents; they argued against eating meat in case one

---

63 Sextius was the founder of a philosophical school at Rome that combined both Stoic and Pythagorean doctrines, as seen from Seneca's comment on his doctrinal affiliations in *Letter* 64.2; although the school did not last long as an institution, it seems to have been influential on Neronian philosophers. See Hadot 2007 and Manning 1987 for a discussion of the school, its members and its doctrines. Sotion was a Pythagorean, whom Seneca discusses separately from the Sextii, but as associated with them. Attalus was a Stoic philosopher, Seneca's first teacher to profess "pure" Stoicism; according to Seneca the Elder, he was banished by the machinations of Seianus (*Suasoriae* 2.12). For more on Seneca's philosophical education, see Inwood 2005, 13–16.

should accidentally attack the reincarnated souls of one's parents by using a knife or teeth on the bodies of the unfortunate animals into which they had been reincarnated (108.19). Yet Seneca's respect for his father manifests itself in precisely the opposite behavior. Seneca does not explain if his father took advantage of the political situation to persuade him to begin eating meat again or if he explicitly opposed the practice because of its philosophical origin; in some ways, that is as irrelevant to the function of this anecdote as whether it ever actually happened. The passage's important message is that it was under his father's influence that Seneca chose to disregard the philosophical teachings of Sotion.

Interestingly, Seneca is only wooed away from Sotion's teachings, not those of Attalus. The comparison between the two men returns to the idea of philosophical parentage Seneca explored earlier in the *Epistulae Morales*, especially in *Letter* 44. One "parent," Attalus, stays in the ascendant and has considerable influence over the young Seneca's moral development, while Sotion is eclipsed by Seneca the Elder. Seneca does not regret this. As he himself says, he did not require a great deal of persuasion to return to eating meat. Indeed, almost to reinforce the difference between Attalus and Sotion, Seneca immediately follows this incident with the fact that he still uses a hard pillow that resists the body, just as Attalus recommended, even though he is now an old man (108.23).[64] The juxtaposition of these anecdotes implies that our philosophical family's advice will survive our biological family's interference if that advice is founded in true wisdom. If it does not, then our biological family's requests to abandon it might help us separate out sound advice from more eccentric positions. *Letter* 94 acknowledges that the world at large can give misguided precepts. Now we see that people who call themselves philosophers can mislead too. Our two families can co-exist, and check the more excessive impulses of each other. Through weighing the two options presented to him and considering which one is more appropriate, Seneca is able to come to a rational decision.

This letter presents a complex vision of a student's loyalties to his biological and philosophical fathers and negotiations between the two. Seneca neither encourages us to separate ourselves from our biological family as he did in earlier letters nor to rely solely on the advice from our philosophical family. He juxtaposes the two, but can only do so because he draws on his own experience; he offers no general theory on the relative importance of philosophical authority and family commitments. A particular case must

---

64 This is not the only habit from his early philosophical training that Seneca maintains; in *De Ira* 3.36.1–3, he attributes his practice of self-scrutiny before falling asleep to Sextius, who had the same habit.

demonstrate it. Seneca the Elder, in advising his son to give up vegetarianism, provided him with valuable moral guidance despite the fact that his motivations came from his dislike of philosophy. Seneca cannot write a definitive guide to how interactions between the familial environment and the wider world of philosophy should operate. However, he can provide a concrete example from his own experience and let the reader draw his own conclusions about how the two spheres can interact. By juxtaposing the positive influence of his two fathers, Seneca the Elder and Attalus, he reminds the reader that there can be more than one place to learn about virtue.

VII. Conclusion

Our journey through the *Epistulae Morales* has shown how Seneca initially omits all references to the family from his work, before gradually introducing them as the reader gains philosophical expertise and establishes a solid moral foundation. Certain key elements need to be in place before any useful discussion can begin, such as a correct understanding of what is good and the true nature of virtue. Once Seneca is confident that his student has a firm grounding in these important concepts, he slowly reintroduces the family – always cautiously and always buttressed with reminders of other important ideas the reader needs to have in mind; all the same, an ethics of the family gradually emerges from a work seemingly obsessed with the individual.

The family still presents dangers. The fundamental complexity of Seneca's attitude towards the family cannot be reduced to easy precepts, although they have a part to play in guiding our behavior. The initial suspicion that we are encouraged to have of our parents and their misguided intentions for us gives way to a vignette of Seneca's father pointing him in the right direction – and ultimately to a discussion about the theory which makes parents love their children and want to protect them (*Ep.* 121). We advance from a skeptical attitude towards family members to one which cautiously accepts them as a positive influence in our lives, although we cannot allow ourselves to be misled by their mistaken concepts about what is good and what is virtuous. The process of adjustment is a slow one, but reflects the fundamental nature of this change.

What also emerges from the letters is that it does not much matter which family member is involved or what issue is at stake. Each family member, whether sibling, spouse, parent, aunt, or uncle, occupies the same relational position to the aspiring sage and thus has the same potential to offer good (or indeed bad) advice. Similarly, every issue is of equal importance in terms of moral guidance. While the choice of suicide may appear more important than one's choice of dietary habits, both are equally valid fields for the exercise of virtue. Relatives can thus offer useful moral guidance on both matters of life and death and the smaller issues of day-to-day life. Indeed, the role of the family members in the *Epistulae Morales* suggests that if they are trustworthy, they *should* offer advice across the spectrum of human activity, given their proximity to the moral agent.

The *Epistulae Morales*, then, are not unambiguously positive about the family but eventually allow the possibility that the family can provide positive moral formation as part of the wider project of individual moral education. They also recognize the fact that membership in a family entails a set of moral obligations as well as a potential support network and ultimately incorporate this aspect of the family into the broader discussion of how an individual may progress towards virtue. The didactic elements of the work and its emphasis both on the development of the individual soul and the need for cautious interaction with other people of necessity play a more prominent role in the text's themes. Yet when the collection touches on the theme of familial ethics, despite an emphasis on rational prudence and self-governance, the picture that Seneca eventually constructs preserves the possibility that as well as sometimes being a hindrance, one's biological family can contribute to successful moral development.

Bibliography

Bartsch, Shadi, and David Wray, eds. 2009. *Seneca and the Self*. Cambridge: Cambridge University Press.

Bellincioni, Maria, ed. and trans. 1979. *Lucio Anneo Seneca, Lettere a Lucilio: Libro XV: Le lettere 94 e 95*. Brescia: Paideia.

Borkowski, Andrew, and Paul du Plessis. 2005. *Textbook on Roman Law*. Oxford: Oxford University Press.

Bradley, Keith R. 1991a. *Discovering the Roman Family: Studies in Roman Social History*. Oxford; New York: Oxford University Press.

Bradley, Keith R. 1991b. "Remarriage and the Structure of the Upper-Class Roman Family." In *Marriage, Divorce, and Children in Ancient Rome*, edited by Beryl Rawson, 79–98. Canberra; Oxford: Humanities Research Centre; Clarendon Press.

Cancik, Hildegard. 1967. *Untersuchungen zu Senecas Epistulae Morales*. Hildesheim: Olms.

Cancik-Lindemaier, Hildegard. 1998. "Seneca's Collection of Epistles: A Medium of Philosophical Communication." In *Ancient and Modern Perspectives on the Bible and Culture: Essays in Honor of Hans Dieter Betz*, edited by Adela Yarbro Collins, 88–109. Atlanta: Scholars Press.

Carlon, Jacqueline M. 2009. *Pliny's Women: Constructing Virtue and Creating Identity in the Roman World*. Cambridge: Cambridge University Press.

Claassen, Jo-Marie. 1996. "Documents of a Crumbling Marriage: The Case of Cicero and Terentia." *Phoenix* 50: 208–232.

De Pretis, Anna. 2003. " 'Insincerity', 'Facts', and 'Epistolarity:' Approaches to Pliny's 'Epistles' to Calpurnia." *Arethusa* 36: 127–146.

Dixon, Suzanne. 1992. *The Roman Family*. Baltimore: Johns Hopkins University Press.

Donini, Pierluigi. 1999. "Stoic Ethics." In *The Cambridge History of Hellenistic Philosophy*, edited by Keimpe Algra, Jonathan Barnes, Jaap Mansfeld, and Malcolm Schofield, 675–738. Cambridge: Cambridge University Press.

Edwards, Catharine. 1997. "Self-Scrutiny and Self-Transformation in Seneca's Letters." *G&R* 44: 23–38.

Edwards, Catharine. 2009. "Free Yourself! Slavery, Freedom and the Self in Seneca's Letters." In *Seneca and the Self*, edited by Shadi Bartsch and David Wray, 139–159. Cambridge: Cambridge University Press.

Engberg-Pedersen, Troels. 1986. "Discovering the Good: Oikeiōsis and Kathēkonta in Stoic Ethics." In *The Norms of Nature: Studies in Hellenistic Ethics*, edited by Malcolm Schofield and Gisela Striker, 145–183. Cambridge; Paris: Cambridge University Press: Maison des Sciences de l'Homme.

Evans Grubbs, Judith. 2002. *Women and the Law in the Roman Empire: A Sourcebook on Marriage, Divorce and Widowhood*. London; New York: Routledge.

Flower, Harriet I. 1996. *Ancestor Masks and Aristocratic Power in Roman Culture*. Oxford: Oxford University Press.

Gardner, Jane F. 1986. *Women in Roman Law and Society*. Bloomington: Indiana University Press.

Gardner, Jane F. 1998. *Family and Familia in Roman Law and Life*. Oxford: Clarendon Press.

George, Michele, ed. 2005. *The Roman Family in the Empire: Rome, Italy, and Beyond*. Oxford: Oxford University Press.

Graver, Margaret R. 1996. *Therapeutic Reading and Seneca's "Moral Epistles."* PhD diss., Brown University.

Graver, Margaret R. 2007. *Stoicism and Emotion*. Chicago: University of Chicago Press.

Grebe, Sabine. 2003. "Marriage and Exile: Cicero's Letters to Terentia." *Helios* 30: 127–146.

Griffin, Miriam T. 1992. *Seneca: A Philosopher in Politics*. 2nd ed. Oxford: Clarendon Press.

Grimal, Pierre. 1978. *Seneca: Macht und Ohnmacht des Geistes*. Darmstadt: Wissenschaftliche Buchgesellschaft.

Hachmann, Erwin, ed. 2006. *L. Annaeus Seneca, Epistulae Morales, Brief 66: Einleitung, Text und Kommentar*. Frankfurt am Main et al.: Peter Lang.

Hadot, Ilsetraut. 1969. *Seneca und die griechisch-römische Tradition der Seelenleitung*. Berlin: De Gruyter.

Hadot, Ilsetraut. 2007. "Versuch einer doktrinalen Neueinordnung der Schule der Sextier." *RhM* 150: 179–210.

Henderson, John. 2004. *Morals and Villas in Seneca's Letters: Places to Dwell*. Cambridge: Cambridge University Press.

Henderson, John. 2006. "Journey of a Lifetime: Seneca, 'Epistle' 57 in Book VI in EM." In *Seeing Seneca Whole: Perspectives on Philosophy, Poetry and Politics*, edited by Katharina Volk and Gareth Williams, 123–146. Leiden: Brill.

Hierocles. 2009. *Elements of Ethics, Fragments, and Excerpts*. See Ramelli and Konstan 2009.

Inwood, Brad. 1983. "Comments on Professor Görgemanns' Paper: The Two Forms of Oikeiosis in Arius and the Stoa." In *On Stoic and Peripatetic Ethics: The Work of Arius Didymus*, edited by William W. Fortenbaugh, 190–201. New Brunswick: Transaction Books.

Inwood, Brad. 1999. "Stoic Ethics." In *The Cambridge History of Hellenistic Philosophy*, edited by Keimpe Algra, Jonathan Barnes, Jaap Mansfeld, and Malcolm Schofield, 675–705. Cambridge: Cambridge University Press.

Inwood, Brad. 2005. *Reading Seneca: Stoic Philosophy at Rome*. Oxford: Clarendon Press.

Inwood, Brad, trans. 2007a. *Seneca, Selected Philosophical Letters: Translation with an Introduction and Commentary*. Oxford; New York: Oxford University Press.

Inwood, Brad. 2007b. "The Importance of Form in Seneca's Philosophical Letters." In *Ancient Letters: Classical and Late Antique Epistolography*, edited by Ruth Morello and Andrew D. Morrison, 133–148. Oxford: Oxford University Press.

Kidd, Ian G. 1978. "Moral Actions and Rules in Stoic Ethics." In *The Stoics*, edited by John M. Rist, 247–258. Berkeley: University of California Press.

Kidd, Ian G. 1988. *Posidonius, II: The Commentary, 2: Fragments 150–293*. Cambridge: Cambridge University Press.

Langlands, Rebecca. 2006. *Sexual Morality in Ancient Rome*. Cambridge: Cambridge University Press.

Manning, Charles E. 1987. "The Sextii." *Prudentia* 19: 16–27.

Maurach, Gregor. 1970. *Der Bau von Senecas Epistulae Morales*. Heidelberg: Winter.

Mazzoli, Giancarlo. 1989. "Le 'Epistulae morales ad Lucilium' di Seneca: Valore letterario e filosofico." *ANRW* II 36.3: 1823–1877.

Milnor, Kristina L. 2005. *Gender, Domesticity, and the Age of Augustus: Inventing Private Life*. Oxford: Oxford University Press.

Pembroke, Simon G. 1971. "Oikeiōsis." In *Problems in Stoicism*, edited by Anthony A. Long, 114–149. London: University of London, Athlone Press.

Ramelli, Ilaria, and David Konstan, eds. and trans. 2009. *Hierocles the Stoic: Elements of Ethics, Fragments, and Excerpts*. Atlanta: Society of Biblical Literature.

Rawson, Beryl. 1986. "The Roman Family." In *The Family in Ancient Rome*, edited by Beryl Rawson, 1–57. Ithaca: Cornell University Press.

Rawson, Beryl, and Paul R. Weaver, eds. 1997. *The Roman Family in Italy: Status, Sentiment, Space*. Canberra; Oxford; New York: Humanities Research Centre; Clarendon Press; Oxford University Press.

Reydams-Schils, Gretchen. 2002. "Human Bonding and Oikeiōsis in Roman Stoicism." *OSAPh* 22: 221–251.

Reydams-Schils, Gretchen. 2005. *The Roman Stoics: Self, Responsibility, and Affection*. Chicago: University of Chicago Press.

Reynolds, Leighton D., ed. 1965. *L. Annaei Senecae Ad Lucilium epistulae morales*. 2 vols. Oxford: Oxford University Press.

Richardson-Hay, Christine. 2006. *First Lessons: Book 1 of Seneca's "Epistulae Morales" – A Commentary*. Frankfurt et al.: Peter Lang.

Saller, Richard P. 1984. " 'Familia,' 'Domus,' and the Roman Conception of the Family." *Phoenix* 38: 336–355.

Schafer, John. 2009. *Ars Didactica: Seneca's 94th and 95th Letters*. Göttingen: Vandenhoeck & Ruprecht.

Schofield, Malcolm. 2003. "Stoic Ethics." In *The Cambridge Companion to the Stoics*, edited by Brad Inwood, 233–256. Cambridge: Cambridge University Press.

Schofield, Malcolm. 1995. "Two Stoic Approaches to Justice." In *Justice and Generosity: Studies in Hellenistic Social and Political Philosophy: Proceedings of the*

Sixth Symposium Hellenisticum, edited by Andre Laks and Malcolm Schofield, 191–212. Cambridge: Cambridge University Press.

Seneca. 1965. *Ad Lucilium epistulae morales*. See Reynolds 1965.

Seneca. 1979. *Lettere a Lucilio: Libro XV: Le lettere 94 e 95*. See Bellincioni 1979.

Seneca. 2006. *Epistulae Morales, Brief 66*. See Hachmann 2006.

Seneca. 2007. *Selected Philosophical Letters*. See Inwood 2007a.

Treggiari, Susan. 2007. *Terentia, Tullia and Publilia: The Women of Cicero's Family*. London; New York: Routledge.

Wildberger, Jula. 2006. *Seneca und die Stoa: Der Platz des Menschen in der Welt*. 2 vols. Berlin; New York: De Gruyter.

Wilson, Marcus. 1997. "The Subjugation of Grief in Seneca's Epistles." In *The Passions in Roman Thought and Literature*, edited by Susanna Morton Braund and Christopher Gill, 48–67. Cambridge: Cambridge University Press.

Honeybee Reading and Self-Scripting: *Epistulae Morales* 84

Margaret R. Graver
Dartmouth College

Classicists have been intrigued to see the strong reaction of Michel Foucault to the philosophy of the early Roman Empire. In the opening essay to a 2009 volume *Seneca and the Self*, A.A. Long speaks movingly of how fresh and challenging Seneca appears, even to those who know him well, when situated by Foucault at the center of an emerging discourse about the cultivation of one's own selfhood as the essential requirement of ethics.[1] It is with similar excitement that I engage here with a particular letter of Seneca that was of interest to Foucault, seeking to bring out what is valuable and correct in his reading of it even if (as I shall argue) his understanding falls short in some respects. In his letter, Seneca speaks in a suggestive way about the activities of reading and writing and about the shaping of oneself as a person through these activities. Foucault picks up on this and speaks of a process of "scripting the self," by which he means constituting oneself as a better and more consistent moral agent through the very act of writing, writing which is in some way dependent on prior acts of reading. In this, I argue, Foucault was on the right track, though he may not fully have understood what Seneca had in mind. With deeper philological study we can bring out what is radical and of great significance in Seneca's thought even as we recognize the embeddedness of that thought in Roman literary culture.

Caution is required, certainly, as concerns the psychological model to be attributed to an author who considers himself an adherent of Stoic thought. Brad Inwood, writing for the same volume, reviews the expressions cited by Foucault for a particular concern with the self in Seneca and concludes that there is no evidence for innovation in terms of mental ontology.[2] Seneca is not in general very inclined to multiply psychological entities in the way that Plato does, and we should not expect him to be add-

---

1   Long 2009; the volume is Bartsch and Wray 2009. The essay was first published as Long 2006, 360–376.
2   Inwood 2009, first published as Inwood 2005, 322–352. For Seneca's understanding of Stoic moral psychology, see also now Graver 2014.

ing extra parts or organs to the unitary rational psyche posited by Chrysippus and other Stoics of the Hellenistic period. Inwood thus rejects the implication he finds in Foucault that Seneca conceives of the self in a way that departs from the analysis of mind and action he inherited from the Stoic tradition. Yet Inwood also acknowledges that Seneca does at least give the impression of emphasizing selfhood in a novel and distinctive way, because his frequent claims of intellectual independence seem like self-assertion *vis-à-vis* the Stoic tradition, and because of certain literary devices in his writing: his strong first-person voice and his habit of using his own experience to exemplify various points he is making. In his tendency toward self-exemplification, Seneca does create a kind of self, a self-portrayal that makes "Seneca" a fully realized character throughout the prose works and especially in the fictive correspondence that is the *Epistulae Morales*.

Like Inwood, I read Seneca's moral psychology as Chrysippan in all its essentials. Nonetheless, I believe that in the eighty-fourth letter, and implicitly elsewhere, Seneca does envision a novel ontology of the self. The novelty in his conception is not in the kind of psychological entities posited but in an exceptional philosophical adaptation of some familiar Roman ideas about what can be achieved through the medium of writing. I am not speaking now of Seneca's first-person perspective, nor of the many self-portraits we find in his writings: Such represented selves will not always capture the real identity of the maker. I mean rather that writing as Seneca describes it becomes a means of externalizing one's locus of identity, one's very thoughts, reasonings, and reactions, fixing them for the future and making them available to others. More than that, it becomes a means of transcending oneself: In his conception, artistic achievement surpasses and ultimately replaces one's unstable and fleeting sentience within the body with an externalized self that is more consistent and more admirable as well as more stable. This is what Foucault realized, at least in part, about Seneca, but his grasp was tentative and lacked the awareness of literary context that made it a natural thought for Seneca to have. I try here to fill in some of what is missing in his account.

I.

Seneca opens his letter by mentioning a journey, or rather a series of journeys (*itinera*), perhaps a succession of day-trips. It appears that Lucilius, the "you" of the correspondence, has suggested these, for *ista* in the first line gestures toward the second person point of view; we are perhaps expected to imagine an intervening letter urging Seneca to alter the sedentary habits described in *Ep.* 83.3. Moving about, Seneca now admits, has benefited both his health and his studies – more obviously the former, since it has aroused him from his scholarly lassitude, but also the latter. If this seems odd, he will explain: It is because "I have gotten away from readings."[3] Yet reading is a necessary activity, which both informs and refreshes the mind of the writer. The fact is that neither reading nor writing should be practiced to the exclusion of the other: Writing alone will "exhaust" our powers ("exhauriet"); reading alone will "dilute" them ("diluet"). The proper approach is to take what is collected by reading and "assimilate it to the body" by writing ("redigat in corpus").

This imagery of transfer of fluids, collection, and digestion sets up an easy transition to the extended metaphor of bees and the hive, the most highly developed image in the letter and one that has made a deep impression on many readers.[4] Seneca's description of the work of bees is beautifully detailed: They first move about and seize upon flowers suitable for honey-making, then arrange what they have collected and distribute it through the hive, and finally, in the words of Vergil, "pack away the liquid honey, and swell the comb with sweet nectar" (*Aeneid* 1.432–433). All this is worthy of imitation: We should first store away the things we have gathered from our diverse reading, keeping them distinct in our minds, then make an effort to combine those varied elements into a uniform product different in character from what existed before. Even if it is apparent where a thing is taken from, Seneca says, it should still appear to be different from that from which it was taken. A series of further metaphors then adds emphasis to the theme of assimilation and transformation. The process is like that of digestion in the body, which changes the mix of foods in the stomach into one's own flesh and blood; or like a numerical calculation which combines many numbers into one sum; or like human reproduction – for the later work should resemble earlier compositions in the way that a child resembles a parent, not in the way a statue resembles its model. "A statue is a dead thing" (84.8). When the process is carried out successfully, the features of the prior text will not be distinguishable at all, just as in a symphonic performance the sounds of bass and treble voices, trumpet, flute, and organ are all mingled into a unison. This, Seneca says, is what

---

3 I follow the received text. Some editors insert *non* before *recessi;* I argue against that insertion in section 3 below. Translations from the *Epistulae Morales* are those of Graver and Long forthcoming; other translations are my own throughout.

4 Summers 1910, 284 traces the influence of the passage through a series of authors from Macrobius (who plagiarizes shamelessly from it in the preface to his *Saturnalia*) through Petrarch (*Epistulae de rebus familiaribus* 1.7). See further De Rentiis 1998.

our mind should be like: It should harmonize many skills, many precepts, many examples from every age, into one.

To achieve such integration requires constant concentration and attentiveness to rational standards of conduct. One must act, or refrain from acting, only as reason directs (84.11: "ratione suadente"). No longer speaking solely about reading and writing, Seneca at the close of the letter reflects more generally on the values that should inform our behavior. One must abandon wealth, pleasure, and ambition, and seek wisdom instead. In so doing, one will find tranquillity as well as excellence, for while eminence in civic life is achieved only by struggle and difficulty, the *summum bonum* of the moral philosopher is reached via "level ground" (84.13); that is, by consistency in thought and action.

II.

Foucault's interest in this letter belonged to the last phase of his life, in 1981–1984; it was part of a topic he would no doubt have pursued further if he had lived to do so.[5] He had become intrigued by the work of the Parisian classical philosopher Pierre Hadot on certain "spiritual exercises" which, according to Hadot, were practiced throughout antiquity by the philosophically inclined of all schools.[6] He thus approached *Ep*. 84 as just one witness (though a key witness) to widely shared habits of reading and writing in the ancient world, and reading and writing themselves as belonging to a larger set of cultural practices aimed at the cultivation and care of one's individual identity.

Of course, Foucault was not primarily a classicist, and his fascination with Hadot's exercises, which he relabels "techniques of the self," has more to do with his own philosophical concerns than with a strictly historical understanding.[7] His response to this particular letter is nonetheless instructive. He is quite taken with what Seneca says about the need to alter-

---

5   Davidson 1997, 16.
6   Foucault knew Hadot's articles even before the first edition of *Exercices spirituels et philosophie antique* was published in Paris in 1981. The second edition (Hadot 1993) is available in English translation as Hadot 1995. Compare Foucault 1984, 53–85.
7   Hence the historically oriented critique in Strozier 2002, 139–174, is not entirely apposite. Vogt 2012 rightly draws attention to the more sympathetic assessment by Paul Veyne: "Greek ethics is quite dead, and Foucault judged it as undesirable as it would be impossible to resuscitate this ethics; but he considered one of its elements, namely, the idea of a work of the self on the self, to be capable of acquiring a contemporary meaning, in the manner of one of those pagan temple columns that one occasionally sees reutilized in more recent structures" (Veyne 1997, 231).

nate between reading and writing: that neither is beneficial without the other and that the two processes both limit one another and aid one another. The idea that a reading program needs to be restricted is one that he had found elsewhere in Seneca, notably in the second letter, where Seneca recommends concentrating on just a few works and excerpting small portions of these for further reflection. In a lecture given in Paris in 1982, and again in his 1983 essay "Self-Scripting" ("L'écriture de soi"), Foucault connects this notion of a restricted reading program with the writing of *hypomnēmata*, personal notebooks filled with extracts copied out from a variety of sources.[8] *Hypomnēmata* as Foucault imagines them are not written merely as an aid to memory or a tool for developing one's understanding of the source text; rather, they are an aid to ethical living. By copying, rereading, and reflecting upon selected aphorisms, one trains oneself to recognize "scattered truth" (*la verité disparate*) in writings from the past and then, further, to keep that truth always "at hand" (*ad manum*, Greek: *procheiron*) to influence one's actions on future occasions. This is one of two ways in which writing can be a spiritual exercise. The other is epistolography; that is, the writing of personal letters, in which one reveals oneself to another through personal narrative. Letters are written partly to educate the addressee, and reciprocally oneself, toward right action, but also partly to "objectify" oneself; that is, to give oneself over to the gaze of the addressee and to the much larger number of people who may eventually come to read the letter. By teaching and exhorting another, or many others, one is also training oneself to live in the eyes of others, "as though some other person could gaze into our inmost breast," as Seneca says in *Ep.* 83.1.

With his emphasis on the subsequent transformation of material learned through reading, Foucault goes a long way to resolve what might seem to be a striking discrepancy between the tightly controlled reading program recommended in *Ep.* 2.1–4 and the *diversa lectio* of *Ep.* 84.5. Seneca regularly urges Lucilius not to indulge in a wide range of readings, pleasurable as that might be, but to concentrate on just a few volumes.[9] Ill-advised browsing in many different authors and genres is compared in *Ep.* 2.2–4 to pointless travel (which Lucilius prudently avoids in 2.1), to frequent changes of medication for the sick, and above all to the consumption of a medley of foods. All these are indications of inward restlessness

---

8   For the lecture see Foucault 2001, 338–353. The essay was first published in Foucault 1983 and reprinted in Foucault 1994, vol. 4, pp. 415–430. In what follows I supply my own translations; a complete English translation by Ann Hobart may be found in Davidson 1997, 23–47.
9   The most important passages are *Ep.* 2.1–4, 6.5, 45.1–2, 88.35–38, 108.1–2 and 24–35; detailed analysis in Graver 1996; also Schöpsdau 2005.

(something "vagum et instabile," 2.1) and will only make one's condition worse: Where readings are "varied and diverse," they will not nourish the soul but "pollute" it (2.4: "inquinant non alunt"). By contrast, *Ep.* 84 speaks favorably of travel and appears also to recommend an eclectic program of reading, for the model of the honeybee surely suggests movement from place to place and nourishment drawn from a wide variety of sources. As Foucault realizes, however, the underlying implication is the same in both instances. What is important to Seneca in both letters is not so much the choice of readings as it is the process that goes on afterward within the reader, as multiple elements are combined into a single substance. This is the thought that is expressed by the motif of the many which become one, which appears constantly in *Ep.* 84, and in particular by the metaphor of digestion, which is prominent in both letters.[10] It is assimilation by digestion that makes reading successful or unsuccessful: If *Ep.* 2 dissuades Lucilius from the "varia et diversa," it is only because they are difficult to digest, and if *Ep.* 84 then endorses "diversa lectio," it is only insofar as digestion can transform diversity into uniformity.[11] It is a single idea, even though this metaphoric digestion takes different forms: in 2.4 an entirely inward activity of meditation, in 84.7 the more visible activity of writing. For Foucault, the two processes are essentially the same:

> Writing, as a personal exercise done by oneself and for oneself, is an art of scattered truth (*la verité disparate*). Or, more precisely, it is a reflective means of combining the traditional authority of the prior text with the singularity of the truth affirmed in it and with the particularity of the circumstances determining its use. (Foucault 1983, 11)

On this model the composition of *hypomnēmata* is in itself essentially reflective and integrative. One copies down a miscellany of excerpts, as Seneca describes in *Ep.* 2.4, then ponders each to find in it a personal truth which will be applicable to the circumstances of one's own life.

A further development of this idea brings Foucault to the insight which is at one and the same time the most valuable of his essay and the most problematic. Studying the implications of the digestion metaphor, he points out that digestion is not merely a process of assimilating what one has

---

10 Note *Ep.* 84.4: "in unum diversa;" 84.5: "in unum saporem varia libamenta;" 84.7: "unum quiddam fiat ex multis;" 84.8: "in unitatem illa competant;" 84.9: "unus tamen ex omnibus;" 84.10: "multa in unum conspirata." Compare *Ep.* 2.4: "cum multa percurreris, unum excerpe." Digestion is mentioned explicitly in 84.7: "concoquamus illa" and 2.4: "quod illo die concoquas," and is implied also in 2.3: "non prodest cibus nec corpori accedit qui statim sumptus emittitur" and 2.4: "fastidientis stomachi."

11 *Ep.* 2.4: " 'Sed modo,' inquis, 'hunc librum evolvere volo, modo illum.' Fastidientis stomachi est multa degustare; quae ubi varia sunt et diversa, inquinant non alunt."

ingested to one's own existing nature. It is also the process by which one's own nature is constituted and comes into being. The *corpus* to which one's reading is to be assimilated is thus in a real sense the very self that each of us is constantly creating. It is not a body of doctrine, but rather "the actual body of the one who, by transcribing his readings, has appropriated them and made their truth his own."[12] This is to say that the writing which he calls "assimilative writing" (*l'écriture assimilatrice*) creates from the material of prior texts a new self, a new identity, which is in some sense the real identity of the writer. He traces the same idea in the sentence about resembling one's ancestors "as a son does, not as a statue does." Again, there is an idea of artistic creation, but the artifact is not separable from its creator: Artwork and artist are one.

> It is one's own soul that must be composed in one's writings. But as a man bears on his visage a natural resemblance to his ancestors, so likewise it is well that we should be able to recognize in his writings the ancestry of those thoughts which have been engraved on his soul. Through the interplay of selected readings and assimilative writing, one should be able to form for oneself an identity, upon which can be read an entire spiritual genealogy. (Foucault 1983, 13)

Of course this notion of consciously creating an integrated self through deliberate spiritual practices of stylized reading and writing is one that combines easily with Foucault's own thoughts about self-actualization and an aesthetics of existence.[13]

As a generalization about Seneca's thought, this way of understanding *Ep.* 84 is problematic on several fronts. Even if it remains clear of the objections raised by Inwood to Foucault's other readings in the *Moral Epistles* (and I am not sure that it does), it certainly encounters the point made in direct response by Pierre Hadot, that Foucault is too quick to dismiss Seneca's commitment to Stoicism. Hadot objects strongly to Foucault's claim that therapeutic writing is eclectic by nature, that it is "not a body of doctrine" but is actually opposed to the doctrinal unity of any avowed philosophical school.[14] In addition, some readers have felt that Foucault's emphasis on reflexivity misrepresents Seneca's larger concern with normativity. As Hadot reminds us, Seneca urges Lucilius not to turn toward himself as he is but to discover "the best part of himself" (*Ep.* 23.6); that is, to learn what is required of him if he is to live as members of the human species were designed by the providential deity to live: rational-

---

12 Foucault 1983, 12.
13 Helpful discussions include Davidson 1994; Bernauer and Mahon 1994, 152–156; Veyne 1997.
14 Hadot 1989, 264–265, responding to Foucault 1983, 12.

ly, virtuously, happily.[15] These objections may not be entirely fair, for Foucault's own underlying concern is with transcendence. Still, the point is of such broad importance for Seneca's ethics that it is well to bring it out more clearly than he does, and with a more solidly doctrinal basis.

As an interpretation of *Ep.* 84 itself, however, Foucault's assertions have a good deal to recommend them. He is correct in believing that Seneca is promoting a kind of self-training toward moral action, for this model is clearly stated toward the end of the letter, where he mentions the criterion of action and avoidance and the values that should inform our actions (84.11–13). The urgency of this recommendation should be kept in view even if, as I argue below, Seneca's point in some earlier paragraphs is rather different from what Foucault supposed. Even more important, Foucault is right to insist on the deeply personal and intimate nature of Seneca's metaphors of nourishment, bodily processes, and sonship. "It is *one's own soul* that must be composed in one's writings."[16] In this letter of all his letters, Seneca's interest in personhood goes beyond his usual ethical concerns to express some definite ideas about how one creates a self out of the stuff of experience and how that self-in-progress may be shaped for maximum impact upon the world.

The trouble with Foucault's account in my view is just that it does not go far enough to bring out the full dimensions of Seneca's thought on these issues. For there are in fact several layers to that thought, all of which are suggestive for Foucault's own interests in ethics as well as for Seneca's. Although it is not wrong to speak of informal writing, such as journals and private letters, Foucault ought also to have considered the more ambitious and public literary forms favored by Seneca and Lucilius as members of Rome's educated elite. These are essential here, for at its core Seneca's notion of self-scripting is one of literary artistry, of harmonizing disparate stylistic inheritances within the written artifact. His criteria for success in this endeavor are aesthetic criteria which refer to the perceptions of those who read or hear what one has produced. Nonetheless the product of this artistry is a real self, an "I" whose thoughts are one's own, but improved, stabilized, and externalized for the long term. It is thus that self-scripting becomes for Seneca, as for others in his tradition, a means of self-transcendence.

---

15 Hadot 1989, 262; but cf. Davidson 1994. Seneca's concern with normativity has been emphasized in (for example) Long 2009 (who speaks of the "normative" vs. the "occurrent" self) and Gill 2009 (the "natural" vs. the "actual" self).

16 Foucault 1983, 13.

III.

The full understanding of Seneca's point necessarily begins with particulars of his language. I concentrate first on the word *studium*, a pivotal term in his discussion but one which lacks any precise functional equivalent in English (in what follows I render it, not very satisfactorily, as "study"). The difficulty both medieval and modern readers have had in understanding Seneca's usage of this word is indicated at the outset by a long-standing textual crux in the first paragraph of the letter. I must now quote in Latin. According to the received text, Seneca writes:

> Itinera ista quae segnitiam mihi excutiunt et valetudini meae prodesse iudico et studiis. Quare valetudinem adiuvent vides: cum pigrum me et neglegentem corporis litterarum amor faciat, aliena opera exerceor. Studio quare prosint indicabo: a lectionibus recessi. Sunt autem, ut existimo, necessariae, primum ne sim me uno contentus, deinde ut, cum ab aliis quaesita cognovero, tam et de inventis iudicem et cogitem de inveniendis.
>
> Those trips are shaking the laziness out of me; they have been beneficial, I believe, both to my health and to my studies. Why they should improve my health is plain to you: Since my love of letters makes me lazy and neglectful of my body, I get some exercise through the labor of others.[17] Why they should aid my study I will explain: I have withdrawn from readings. To be sure, reading is necessary, first that I may not be wrapped up in myself alone and second that after finding out about the inquiries of others, I may both judge concerning their discoveries and ponder what remains to be discovered. (Sen. *Ep.* 84.1)

L. D. Reynolds, editing for the Oxford Classical Text, inserts *non* in angled brackets before *recessi*, making Seneca say, "I have *not* gotten away from readings." François Préchac in the Budé edition and most other modern editors do approximately the same.[18] The preference for the negative is an old one: It goes back to the Renaissance edition by Justus Lipsius and appears also in the manuscript tradition, though only in a few late copies.[19] Despite its long pedigree among textual critics, however, the insertion of *non* is certainly a mistake. Seneca has offered to explain a benefit to his

---

17   I.e., his litter bearers. Seneca "exercises" via sedan chair.
18   The exception is Beltrami 1937. Axelson 1939, 144–145 defends the negative at length. Gummere follows Buecheler and Hense, who strengthen *non* to *nihil*. Summers omits the negative and interprets Seneca to mean: "I have of late given them up, and now am encouraged to resume them;" this saves the received text, but at the cost of making it say the opposite of what the words mean. Alexander 1941, 149 improves on Summers's interpretation by emphasizing the adversative force of *autem*, but still fails to draw an adequate distinction between *lectio* and *studium*.
19   Lipsius was influenced by *Ep.* 15.6, as is shown by his comment: "Quare itinera prosint studiis? quia gestatio legere non impedit, vel certe legentem audire." For the MS tradition I rely on the *apparatus criticus* in Reynolds 1965 and Préchac 1945.

studies, something he egregiously fails to do if we make him say no more than that he has "not withdrawn" from a previous activity. A person may say, if he wants, that he has improved his health while doing no harm to his scholarship, but he cannot claim to have gained something merely by continuing in his former habits. The improvement must be due to some change, and with *recessi*, the change must be a cessation of some kind, although that may be a temporary cessation.[20]

But can someone improve his studies – that is, his *studia* – by ceasing to read even temporarily? Not if *studia* and *lectiones* are synonymous, clearly, but when we look at the continuation of the paragraph it seems quite clear that Seneca does not simply equate the two; in fact, he sets up an opposition between them:

> Alit lectio ingenium et studio fatigatum, non sine studio tamen, reficit. Nec scribere tantum nec tantum legere debemus: altera res contristabit vires et exhauriet (de stilo dico), altera solvet ac diluet. Invicem hoc et illo commeandum est et alterum altero temperandum, ut quidquid lectione collectum est stilus redigat in corpus.
>
> Reading nourishes one's *ingenium* and refreshes it when it is worn out with study, even though reading itself requires study. We ought neither to write exclusively nor read exclusively: The first – writing, that is – will deaden and exhaust our powers; the second will weaken and dilute them. One must do both by turns, tempering one with the other, so that whatever is collected through reading may be assimilated into the body by writing. (Sen. *Ep.* 84.1–2)

"Study" now appears in a reciprocal relation to reading: Reading nourishes the *ingenium* when it is (somehow) worn out by study, but reading in the absence of study would not have this effect. Then in the following sentence it appears as if "study" is interchangeable not with reading but with writing (*scribere*, *stilus*).[21] At the very least we will have to say that *studium* is a nonspecific term for a wider range of intellectual activities.

A brief survey of other passages in the *Moral Epistles* will help to resolve the issue. As background, one needs to know that the usual signification of *studium* in Latin is something like "dedication" to any specific object: It may refer to zeal for a cause, enthusiasm for a hobby, support for a candidate, or any other form of devotion.[22] The more specific sense of energy and attention devoted to books and other intellectual pursuits may likewise be expressed by *studium* without additional limiting words, but this meaning does not predominate over other uses. Seneca's own usage of the word reflects his personal interests and priorities as a writer. He often

---

20 It is relevant that *recedere* in Latin frequently refers to a temporary withdrawal, like the waning of the moon or ebbing of the tides (*OLD* s.v. recedo 2ab, 4).
21 This is pointed out already in the note *ad loc.* in Motto 1985; similarly Schöpsdau 2005, 98.
22 *OLD* s.v. 1–6.

uses it to signify a zeal for virtue or for moral progress,[23] and it is in the same spirit that he speaks at *Ep.* 40.14 of the risks of putting one's *studium* into words rather than deeds. *Studium* in the sense of enthusiasm for objects other than virtue or philosophical progress is correspondingly rare: The entire *Moral Epistles* yields only one example.[24] On the other hand, in some contexts it seems clear that *studium* is being used in a sense similar to the English word "study." At *Ep.* 15.6 and 26.6, for instance, *studium* consists in a variety of intellectual pursuits, giving dictation, delivering and listening to speeches, and conversing, as well as reading; at 21.2 and 108.29 it is more specifically reading; and at 55.10 and 56.1 the point is about the quiet and seclusion needed to concentrate.[25]

Quite frequently the ideas of dedicated effort and of book learning both seem to be present: After all, Seneca as a Stoic does consider intellectual development to be essential to moral progress. For example, at *Ep.* 72.2 he speaks of the need to give over other occupations and to devote one's entire mind to philosophy, and of the excuses one might make for failing to do so. "Si hanc rem molestam composuero, studio me dabo," he imagines the prospective philosopher saying: "As soon as I get through this troublesome task, I will give myself over to study." *Studium* here is primarily a particular sort of activity which requires time and thought, and it seems inevitable (though Seneca does not say so) that this activity will consist largely in mastering terms, concepts, principles, and the like through reading or oral instruction. At the same time, though, *studium* distinctly conveys the frequent Senecan theme of a reorientation of one's attitude and commitment to the fullness of human potential. Thus he continues, just below: "There is no time that is not well suited to these healing studies; yet there are many who fail to study when caught up in the problems that give one reason to study."[26] *Studium* in this enriched sense is especially frequent at the beginnings of letters, where it has programmatic force: Examples may be found in *Ep.* 8, *Ep.* 16, *Ep.* 21, *Ep.* 56, *Ep.* 62, and, as we have just seen, in *Ep.* 72.

Still, even though a zeal for moral philosophy ($studium_1$, as it were) will often take the form of secluded, time-consuming study ($studium_2$), it is not to be expected that every kind of concentrated bookish activity will

---

23 E.g. at 16.1: "sapientiae studio [...] adsiduo studio;" 75.15: "adsidua intentione studii;" 89.5: "studium virtutis;" 124.12: "longo studio intentoque;" *De ira* 2.12.5: "tam pertinacis studii."
24 *Ep.* 76.4, on the enthusiasm of a theater crowd for certain musicians.
25 For *studium* as reading specifically, compare also *Prov.* 2.11, on the *studia* of Cato's last night (referring to his reading of Plato's *Phaedo*).
26 "Tempus quidem nullum est parum idoneum studio salutari; atqui multi inter illa non student propter quae studendum est."

qualify as *studium* in the sense that matters most to Seneca. Literary or academic work that is pursued for the wrong reasons or directed toward the wrong topics may be *studium₂* without being *studium₁*, in which case the two significations will be at odds with each other. A scholarly endeavor pursued merely for ostentation would be a *studium*, but not a *studium salutare* (17.5): it would "fail to heal what is amiss" (59.15). Seneca likes to explore the ironies of the term, especially when it is paired with the similarly bivalent adjective *liberalis*, "befitting a freeborn person," i.e. not a slave.[27] The phrase *liberalia studia* refers, as usual in Latin authors, to the various expensive forms of education favored by the elite, but Seneca also applies it to the one *studium* he continually recommends, commenting that it alone renders a person truly free:

> That sternness will turn out well with age, as long as he persists in working toward virtue and in imbibing the liberal studies. By which I do not mean those studies of which a smattering is enough; I mean *these* liberal studies. In these, the mind needs thorough steeping. (Sen. *Ep*. 36.3)

> It's obvious why they are called "liberal" studies: because they are worthy of a free person. But there is only one study that is truly liberal, and that is the one that liberates a person, which is to say, the study of philosophy. (Sen. *Ep*. 88.2)

Such doubling or twinning in the application of a term is a favorite device of Senecan rhetoric. A common word is invested with a special meaning in keeping with Seneca's ethical agenda, and this second meaning is then asserted as the dominant meaning on grounds of superior value. Thus "real friendship" exists only where there is complete trust (*Ep*. 3.2; 20.7); "real well-being" is when one is practicing philosophy (*Ep*. 15.1); "real joy" is only the special satisfaction of the Stoic sage in possession of "real goods," that is, goods of the mind (*Ep*. 23.4–6); and so on.

We can now discern the progression of ideas that Seneca is developing in the first portion of *Ep*. 84. The recent day trips which (on the face of things) occasion the letter benefit both Seneca's health, in the ordinary sense, and his *studia*, in a special sense which a reader accustomed to Seneca's devices will easily recognize as programmatic: They have helped his true intellectual endeavor, namely his progress in philosophy. With some irony, he proceeds to explain that this second benefit consists in a remission of his reading program, his study in the sense of *studium₂* (84.1: "litterarum amor"). But in this instance the objection to *studium₂* is not that Seneca or his readers have indulged in scholarly pursuits of the wrong sort. Reading is in fact an important part of philosophical activity, but it is not and cannot be the entirety of that activity. His true *studium* consists in

---

[27] In claiming the term "liberal studies" for philosophy alone, Seneca aligns himself with Posidonius as reported in *Ep*. 88.21–23. In addition to the passages quoted here, see *Ep*. 59.15, 62.1, 88 *passim*, and 95.23.

something else which is practiced in alternation with reading. The philosophical pursuit *par excellence*, for the moment anyway, is writing. Seneca did not have his books with him in the sedan-chair; he had his notebooks, or a nimble slave trotting alongside to take dictation.

IV.

Less unconventional, but still puzzling for English speakers, is Seneca's particular way of using the word *ingenium*. This word plays a starring role amid the many images of the letter. It is that which is fed by reading[28] and also that which enables one to combine the many elements collected by reading into one homogenous product.[29] Crucially, it is also that which is constituted from the elements one has digested;[30] and finally, it is the distinguishing feature of one who succeeds completely in the task of assimilation.[31] It is therefore very important to understand what this term means to Seneca and his readers.

The usual English renderings "mind," "intellect," or "character" are misleading in many contexts, and "talent," which I sometimes adopt as the closest English equivalent, also falls short of the mark. *Ingenium* does sometimes refer to one's intellectual aptitude in a broad sense, and with qualifiers added it may also indicate other aspects of temperament; a *saevum ingenium*, for instance, is a warlike temperament.[32] But in Seneca it often refers much more narrowly to a person's rhetorical and literary abilities as demonstrated in actual pieces of writing. In *Ep.* 2, he instructs

---

28 *Ep.* 84.1: "alit lectio ingenium;" 84.6: "in his quibus aluntur ingenia."
29 *Ep.* 84.5: "adhibita ingenii nostri cura et facultate."
30 *Ep.* 84.7: "concoquamus illa; alioqui in memoriam ibunt, non in ingenium."
31 *Ep.* 84.8: "si magni vir ingenii omnibus quae ex quo voluit exemplari traxit formam suam inpressit." I follow Reynolds 1965 for the emendation at 84.8.
32 Both senses were well established in Latin; see *OLD* s.v. Examples in Seneca referring to general intelligence or aptitude for philosophy include 29.4: "magna in illo ingeni vis est, sed iam tendentis in pravum" – "his intellect is very forceful, but tending just now toward ill;" 52.6: "quaedam ingenia facilia, expedita" – "some minds are easy and unencumbered;" 94.30: "alium esse ingenii mobilis et erecti, alium tardi et hebetis" – "one has a quick and lively intelligence, another is slow and dense;" similarly 7.6, 11.1, 24.3, 34.1, 51.11, 52.3, 66.1, 70.24, 71.31, 90.13, and 94.50. For aspects of temperament with more specific qualifiers, note "saeva ingenia" in *Ep.* 51.6, 27.5: "libertini ingenium" – "the character of a freedman;" 39.2: "neminem excelsi ingenii virum" – "no man of exalted character;" 56.12: "leve ingenium" – "a fickle mind;" 71.25: "ingenio vegetum" – "quick-witted;" 95.5: "obsequens ingenium" – "a compliant nature;" 105.4: "ingeni lenitas" – "a gentle character."

Lucilius to apply himself to specific *ingenia*, meaning that he is to concentrate on just a few books:

> Be careful, though, about your reading in many authors and every type of work. It may be that there is something wayward and unstable in it. You must stay with specific talents (*ingenia*) and be fed by them if you mean to derive anything that will dwell reliably with you. (Sen. *Ep.* 2.2)

In *Ep.* 33, where the topic is Lucilius' desire for brief maxims excerpted from Stoic rather than Epicurean books, Seneca advises him that the close texture of Stoic *ingenia* prevents this:

> For this reason you must give up hope that you will ever be able to take just a quick sampling from the *ingenia* of the greatest men. You must read them as wholes, come to grips with them as wholes. The subject matter is treated continuously and the work of the talent (*ingenium*) is structured along the lines that are proper to it. From this, nothing can be removed without a collapse. (Sen. *Ep.* 33.5)

In *Ep.* 75, Seneca remarks that although a philosopher's writing style should not be elaborate, still there is room within philosophy for the graces of style:

> It is not – by heaven – that I want what is said about such great themes to be jejune and arid (for there is a place for the talent [*ingenium*] even in philosophy); still, it is not proper to expend a great deal of effort over the words. (Sen. *Ep.* 75.3)

A bit paradoxically, he remarks in this context that philosophy is concerned with the *animus* and *not* with the *ingenium* – by which he means that elegant language per se is not the aim. One could hardly ask for a clearer illustration of this narrow sense of *ingenium*. Note, too, that the word can and often does convey the narrow meaning of "ability as a writer" even without added words to fix the reference.[33] When Seneca speaks merely of the *ingenium*, rather than of a certain kind of *ingenium*, this is what he most often has in mind.

Ep. 114 goes on to discuss Seneca's views on the relationship between the *ingenium* and the *animus* itself. His project in that letter is to explore the vagaries of literary and rhetorical style over time, how there comes to be a tendency of *ingenia* toward certain faults.[34] Why are certain stylistic devices, such as innuendo or metaphor, more prevalent in one time period

---

33 Additional examples are 7.9: "gloria publicandi ingenii;" 19.3: "in medium te protulit ingenii vigor;" 21.5: "pauca ingenia caput exerent;" 21.6: "ingeniorum crescit dignatio;" 24.9: "non in hoc exempla nunc congero ut ingenium exerceam;" 46.2: "materia [...] quae capiat ingenium;" 79.7: "ingenii tui vires;" 82.16: "multorum ingeniis certatum est;" 92.35: "habuit enim ingenium et grande et virile;" 108.23: "propositum adferunt ad praeceptores suos non animum excolendi sed ingenium;" 114.12: "nullum sine venia placuit ingenium;" examples from other works in Graver 1998, 613 n. 15.

34 I say "literary and rhetorical" because some (though not all) of what Seneca says appears equally applicable to the use of language in formal public speaking.

than another? His answer is that literary style is a direct manifestation of one's moral character: If an individual is morally degenerate, his speech and writing will reflect this, and if certain moral and intellectual traits are prevalent throughout the culture at a certain time, corresponding literary devices will then become the fashion.

> The condition of the talent (*ingenium*) cannot be different from that of the mind (*animus*). If the mind is healthy, well put together, serious, self-controlled, the *ingenium* is likewise completely sober; if the mind is flawed, the talent is likewise inflamed. Do you not see that if the mind has lost its vigor, the limbs trail along, and the feet shuffle? If the mind is effeminate, the softness is seen even in the walk; if it is energetic and fierce, the stride is quick; if it raves or is angry (a condition similar to raving), the movement of the body is disturbed and goes hurtling along rather than walking. Must not this be all the more true of the *ingenium*, which is completely mixed with the mind, and receives from it its shape, direction, and principle? (Sen. *Ep.* 114.3)

In this admittedly tendentious claim Seneca draws out the fullest implications of his key word *ingenium*. On the one hand, the *ingenium* is a distinctly psychological entity, a relatively stable capacity or characteristic of persons, and as such is "completely mixed" with the mind; on the other, it is something perceptible to the outside observer in the same way as one's gait and other bodily movements are perceptible. It thus provides a means of observing the character of the *animus*, a link between the external and the internal. Even a person's way of walking provides a means of judging character; a fortiori, the *ingenium*, being more closely allied to the *animus*, does the same. Indeed it is not clear that the *ingenium* is numerically distinct from the *animus*. The language of mixing may only be metaphoric: If pressed to explain his psychological model, Seneca would presumably retreat to the usual Stoic analysis and say that the *ingenium* just is the *animus* (the directive faculty or *hēgemonikon*) considered for its capacity to produce speech or writing. One should remember, though, that within the Stoic tradition the capacity to produce speech or writing is an extremely important capacity. Indeed it is the most important capacity the human mind exhibits, the one capacity that makes us distinctively human. For the human being is by definition a rational animal, a being endowed with a *hēgemonikon* that has the power of *logos*, both of speech and of reason.[35] It

---

35 Stoic thought on the vocal faculty is collected in Long and Sedley 1987, chapter 53. See especially Aët. 4.21.1–4 = LS 53H (utterance is one of eight main "parts" or faculties of the soul); Panaetius *apud* Nemesius 15, p. 202 Matthaei, 72 Morani = *Frg.* 86 van Straaten, 125 Alesse = LS 53I (the vocal faculty is governed by impulse); Sext. Emp. *Math.* 8.275 = LS 53T (internal speech differentiates humans from non-rational animals); Diog. Bab. *apud* Gal. *P.H.P* 2.5.11–12 = LS 53U (language has its source in thoughts within the chest and is imprinted with the conceptions present in thought).

therefore makes philosophical sense for Seneca to insist that the *ingenium* is more revelatory of a person's character than are other capacities, such as his manner of walking.

With this in mind we can now revisit Seneca's statements about the *ingenium* in *Ep.* 84. Here, just as in the three letters quoted above, his point is not about a person's general intelligence, character, or temperament, but about the specific faculty of his or her mind which generates spoken or written discourse. When he says that reading "nourishes the *ingenium*," he does not mean that reading makes a person more intelligent or better suited to put his philosophy into practice. He means that continued reflection on prior treatments of a theme will help a writer to develop his or her own talent. Similarly, his remarks about combining the various elements derived from books into a unity have a great deal to do with the creation of a richly allusive yet homogenous style in prose or verse, and his "man of great *ingenium*" is first and foremost a great writer. For much of the letter, this is how one's reading becomes part of oneself: It enriches and enlivens that aspect of oneself that will be open to the eyes of the public – the reading public.

V.

But this is not to say that the self that is so constituted is anything other than the real self of the writer. For the *ingenium* is not merely a represented self – an avatar, as when Seneca appears as a character in his own book. A clever writer could easily invent a character that would bear his name and resemble him in some respects but not in others. He could even make that character speak in the first person throughout his book. What cannot be hidden is the way the very book is written – the texture of the writing itself, the design and progression of the whole, all the characteristics we respond to when we say that we "know" an author. A book can lie, in that it can offer fictions or misrepresentations of fact, but one thing it cannot lie about is its author's capacity to write. That capacity is necessarily just what the actual writing shows it to be. If we add to this that a person's ability to write just is his or her mind *qua* producer of language, we arrive at a notion of selfhood revealed in written language: a scripted self.

The metaphor of digestion is indeed presented in such a way as to make it almost impossible to distinguish what we would consider inward or private thoughts from the thoughts that are manifested to the world through oral or written expression. Seneca says first that writers should imitate the honeybee in that they should apply the care and ability of their own *ingenium* to the various materials gathered, "so that even if it is apparent where a thing has been taken from, it may yet appear to be different from that from which it was taken." This entails digestion, and digestion requires change:

> It is what we see nature do in our bodies through no effort of our own. For the nutriments we have taken are burdensome for just so long as they retain their own character and swim as solids in the stomach, but when they have been changed from what they were, then at last they are added to our strength, passing into our bloodstream. Let us accomplish the same with these things that nourish the *ingenium*, not permitting the things we have consumed to remain whole but making them part of ourselves (*ne aliena sint*). Let us digest them; otherwise they will pass into the memory, not into the *ingenium*. Let us faithfully adjust our thinking to theirs and make them our own, so that from the many there may come to be some sort of unity. (Sen. *Ep.* 84.5–7)

This is to say that a writer should not merely string together quotations from older works but should develop a voice of his own which will be recognizable to readers. It is in this way that one produces "some sort of unity" ("unum quiddam"); that is, writing of a uniform character. But the relevant changes are not ones that can be brought about externally, on the page and not in the mind. They are accomplished entirely by inward reflection. We must not only ingest the things that nourish the *ingenium* but "faithfully adjust our thinking to theirs and make them our own,"[36] altering our thinking even as we alter the thoughts we have extracted from books. One melds into the other.

But what does it mean to "change" a piece of discourse so as to make it one's own? Nature may accomplish digestion in our bodies without any effort from us, but in the things by which the *ingenium* is nourished, we ourselves are to perform the assimilation, and we need therefore to know the standard by which assimilation is judged successful. How does one determine whether a unity has in fact been achieved? Seneca's answer to this all-important question takes the form of an appeal to the external observer. At 84.5, imitating the bees, we are to combine the bits derived from prior texts in such a way that even if their derivation is still discernible to readers, they may yet appear different.[37] Then in what follows Seneca reiterates that this is the standard:

> "What do you mean? Won't readers realize whose style, whose argumentation, whose well-turned remarks you are imitating?" It is possible they will not, I think, if a greatly talented man stamps his own form upon all the elements that he draws from his chosen model so that they all fit together into a unity. (Sen. *Ep.* 84.8)

---

36 *Ep.* 84.7: "Adsentiamur illis fideliter et nostra faciamus."
37 *Ep.* 84.5: "[...] ut etiam si apparuerit unde sumptum sit, aliud tamen esse quam unde sumptum est appareat."

The "greatly talented man" or "man of great *ingenium*" ("magni vir ingenii") is the one who succeeds in giving others the impression of a single mind at work even as he draws in elements from a multiplicity of sources. To be sure, there must also exist some principle or formula that explains what gives rise to that uniform impression. There might, for instance, be a consistent set of preferences in diction or word order, or a certain rhythmic pattern that is regularly employed at the ends of sentences; more substantively, there must also be a clear progression of thought from each word, sentence, or paragraph to the next. In theory, the talented writer might be aware of all these principles and refer to them as part of the writing process. But such awareness is not strictly necessary, for writers are also typically readers of their own work and can assess it from that perspective, revising as needed.

VI.

Looking still at that scripted self which is the Senecan *ingenium*, let us now consider the nature and format of this scripting, this writing, that both shapes and reveals one's inner nature. Foucault speaks of the composition of personal journals or commonplace-books (*hypomnēmata*) and of day-to-day correspondence with an intimate friend, like Marcus Aurelius' correspondence with Fronto. But writings of this sort would not easily be described by Seneca's language of organic unity. For a classicist reading *Ep.* 84, it is hard to escape the impression that Seneca has in mind a more consciously literary activity, productive not of jottings and journals but of long poems or ambitious works of prose. Of course this is the sort of writing Seneca himself produced, in his treatises and consolations, in the conspicuously literary *Natural Questions*, and in the *Moral Epistles* themselves, which are certainly not the casual personal letters they sometimes pretend to be.[38] But the source of the impression here is in features of *Ep.* 84 itself.

The image of the honeybee is itself suggestive of literary artistry. For bee-similes are a standard *topos* of the more exalted forms of poetry, where they regularly evoke the figure of the author ranging freely among topics and sources and producing from them a product of the highest quality. The image is as old as Pindar ("the finest of encomia darts from one theme to another like a bee") and figures prominently in Callimachus' famous *Hymn to Apollo*:[39]

---

38 This issue is treated also in Inwood 2007.
39 Call. *Ap.* 110–112. The lines from Pindar are *Pythian* 10.53–54.

> Not from every stream do the bee-maidens carry water to Demeter,
> but from that which flows thin, pure, and undefiled from the sacred spring,
> the finest and best.

At Rome, the application to acts of reading is made directly in Lucretius and in Horace's *Ode* 4.2.25–32, where the poet compares himself to Pindar.[40] Seneca's manner of introducing the bee simile actually announces these connections, for he includes the phrase *ut aiunt* ("as they say"), marking the comparison as a *topos* borrowed from multiple sources. The passage is thus a cleverly self-referential gesture, enacting its own recommendation. It is Seneca in his most consciously literary mode.

Even apart from the honeybee, the middle portion of *Ep.* 84 is redolent of writerly ambition, just because of the repeated appeal to the *ingenium*. Like "talent" or "genius" in English, *ingenium* referring to the ability of writers is a strongly valorizing term, applicable to the most admired works of the past. When Seneca uses it at *Ep.* 21.6 and 82.16, it is in reference to Vergil's *Aeneid;* at 33.5, it refers to the treatises of his favorite Stoic authors. He also uses it a number of times to refer to Lucilius' growing reputation as an author and to praise his talents: At 79.7, for instance, he urges Lucilius not to curb his *ingenium* from writing his poem on Mt. Etna merely because the theme was already treated by Vergil, Ovid, and Cornelius Severus.[41] When he applies it to a more dubious literary achievement the use is contrafactual: Of Gaius Maecenas, whose peculiar style he quotes with derision, he remarks more than once that he would have been a man of *ingenium* if he had not been corrupted by his luxurious manner of living.[42] The "man of great *ingenium*" of *Ep.* 84 will achieve what Maecenas failed to achieve. He will create a consistently impressive body of work – a *corpus*, as we and the Romans both say – in which there will be nothing that is not admirable.[43]

These belletristic implications of *Ep.* 84 are bound up in their own way with the notion of self-actualization through the act of writing. There was in antiquity a close connection between the concept of literary achievement and that of personal survival. The two ideas are linked already in Plato, in Diotima's speech in the *Symposium*, where Homer and Hesiod are called fortunate that their literary "offspring" perpetuate their names.[44] But the

---

40 Lucr. 3.11–12: "As bees in flowery meadows sample everything, so do I feed upon your [sc. Epicurus'] golden sayings."
41 See also *Ep.* 7.9, 19.3, and 46.2.
42 *Ep.* 19.9; 92.35; 114.4. Maecenas fails in that he does not control his diction nor establish clear syntactical relations among words: see Graver 1998.
43 *Corpus* in the sense of a single author's total literary production occurs in *Tranq. an.* 9.6 and *Ep.* 46.1; *OLD* (s.v. *corpus* 16a) cites instances also in Ovid and Pliny the Younger.
44 *Smp.* 209a, d.

Romans gave the notion of literary survival their own strongly first-personal cast, with the circulated work taking on the identity of its author. Over and over in Latin poetry, the book speaks in the voice of its author and claims a life that continues beyond the author's death. The passages are known to every Latinist: Ennius' "Alive I roll through mouths of men;" Horace's "I shall not die entire; a great part of me will evade Libitina;" Ovid's "in the mouths of the people [...] I will live."[45] More obliquely, Vergil addresses two minor characters in his poem: "If my songs have any power, no future day will ever erase you from the memory of ages" – by which he means that his poems do have power and will last for many ages, carrying with them the names and reputations of anyone the poet chooses to include.[46] The ideology expressed in such claims is that a talented writer can create in his work a kind of external self that will speak with his voice and exercise his influence after his life in the body is over. The literary product will not be just an image or representation of himself; it will be a genuine self, something that he can call "me" and that readers will legitimately refer to by his name. As one's texts are replicated over and over by successive hand copying, this scripted self carries on its existence independent of any particular copy, for it "lives" not in ink marks on papyrus but in the voices and memories of generations of readers, the "mouths of men." It is not immortal: when the last copy is burnt and the memory of Roman culture is extinguished, it too will cease to exist. But a work that wins admiration may last for a very long time.

That Seneca recognizes and participates in this ideology is made clear in an extended passage from *Ep.* 21. "Your studies will make you famous," he tells Lucilius. Like Idomeneus, whom Epicurus addresses in several of his letters, or Atticus, who is addressed in so many letters of Cicero, Lucilius will win lasting fame not by anything he himself has done but because of the literary reputation of Seneca who writes to him.

> Deep is the abyss of time that will close over us. A few talented minds (*pauca ingenia*) will raise their heads above it, and although they too must eventually depart into silence, yet for long will they resist oblivion and lay claim to themselves. What Epicurus was able to promise his friend, I promise to you, Lucilius: I shall find favor with posterity, and I can bring others' names along with me, so that they will endure as well. (Sen. *Ep.* 21.5)

---

45 Ennius' epitaph is quoted in Cicero's *Tusculanae disputationes* 1.34 and imitated by Vergil in *Georgica* 3.9 as well as Horace, *Carmen* 3.30 (Libitina is the funeral goddess) and Ovid, *Metamorphoses* 15.871–879. Compare also Persius 1.37–43 and later Martial 1.107.

46 *Aeneid* 9.446–449 (addressing Nisus and Euryalus); compare Propertius 3.9.32 (addressing Maecenas) "venies tu quoque in ora virum."

He then quotes from Vergil the apostrophe mentioned above, and continues:

> Those whom fortune has thrust into the midst of things, who have been the members and partakers of others' power, have great prestige and many visitors – while they are on their feet. The moment they are gone, they cease to be remembered. But minds of talent are held in growing esteem (*ingeniorum crescit dignatio*), and this extends not only to the authors themselves but to anything that is associated with their memory. (Sen. *Ep.* 21.6)

To one not familiar with Roman literary conventions it might seem that this is not very complimentary to Lucilius, to be told that his own achievements are as nothing compared with what he gains by being named in someone else's book. But a remark that could have been derogatory in a private conversation comes out very differently when made as part of the literary work itself. The real Lucilius will understand that just as the dedication of a literary work is highly honorific to him, so the author's claim to lasting fame within the work redounds also to the credit of the addressee. And although Seneca here minimizes Lucilius' independent achievements, he does also take every opportunity to honor the products of Lucilius' own literary *ingenium*.

VII.

All these ideas are so familiar a part of the Roman literary tradition, and so well established already in Seneca's work, that it requires only a few phrases to bring them to mind in the context of *Ep.* 84. But Seneca is not merely evoking the cherished aestheticism of Rome's elite class. When he speaks of crafting one's own *ingenium* as a kind of self, and of high standards in doing so, he has more in mind than the usual idea of personal survival through literary achievement. For his *ingenium* continues to be one manifestation of the rational mind itself, in Stoic thought the seat of consciousness and sole origin of ethically significant behavior. Right after the digestion metaphor of 84.5–7, we find a further comparison which is structured in much the same way:

> Do you not see how many voices combine to form a choir? Yet all of them sound as one. One is a high voice, another low, and another in the middle; women join the men, and flutes accompany them; yet one cannot make out the voices of individuals but only the one voice of them all. [...] When the line of singers fills the aisles and the seating-area is ringed with trumpeters and every kind of flute and water-organ sounds together from the stage, then from the different sounds is produced a unison. This is what I want our mind (*animus*) to be like: in it are many skills, many precepts, examples from many ages, but all harmonized into one. (Sen. *Ep.* 84.9–10)

As before, we have the notion of many components being combined into a homogenous artistic product; and as before, the success of the combination is to be judged by external observers. But here the point is about action-readiness, much more than about literary talent, for the elements combined, the "many skills, many precepts, examples from many ages," are surely all included primarily for what they might contribute to effective or principled agency. These are things that might indeed be gathered from books, but also things whose value can never be realized without some sort of action in the world.[47] The drawing into one is now the procedure of an orderly mind collecting and organizing various types of information, whether from books or from other sources, and integrating them into whatever it is in a person that produces moral acts – which is, once again, the *animus* itself.

The brief remainder of the letter confirms this observation. Seneca goes on to ask himself how this last remarkable result can be achieved, and to give himself an answer which is clearly oriented toward moral action, with "constant concentration" (*adsidua intentio*) playing the role that literary artistry played earlier:

> "How is this to be done?" you ask. By constant concentration: if we do nothing except at the prompting of reason and avoid nothing except at the prompting of reason. (Sen. *Ep.* 84.11)

He then provides a little speech in the voice of reason, urging the moral agent to turn aside from the commonly accepted values of wealth, bodily pleasure, and high social status, and to turn instead toward wisdom, which promises great serenity and also great abundance. In particular, one should turn one's back on political ambition, which leads to nothing of real value and also involves a person in much difficulty and danger. The letter ends with a comparison between "what seems most eminent in human affairs" and the true eminence attained by the philosopher: The former is reached by steep and difficult paths, "even though in reality it is puny and stands out only by comparison with what is the lowest;" the philosopher's summit is far above all conventional goals, but the path to it lies "upon level ground" (84.13: "per planum").

These last are familiar themes in Seneca's work: the appeal to rationally derived criteria, the inadequacy of conventional values, the inherent rewards of a life governed by moral philosophy. What is exceptional here is the way these themes are made continuous with the discussion of reading and writing that precedes. The transition from the honeybee and statue analogies of 84.3–8 (referring to literary style) to the orchestra analogy of 84.9 (referring to moral action) is virtually without seam; among modern

---

47 For Seneca's thought on the necessity of enacting that which is thought or spoken (*lekta*, "sayables"), see especially Wildberger 2006, 180–197.

editors, only Préchac indicates a paragraph division at this point. Seneca, who later insists that the *ingenium* "is completely mixed with the *animus* and receives from it its shape, direction, and principle" (*Ep.* 114.3), here mingles the two completely in his argument. It is as if there is no clear distinction to be made between self-formation in the sense of melding multiple literary influences to craft a unified and impressive voice in one's writings and self-formation in the sense of applying a single rational standard to the business of living.

VIII.

What happens in *Ep.* 84, then, is that Seneca superimposes one thing upon another. He works at first with an idea about writing which would be familiar to his readers – for members of the educated elite, like the Lucilius of the letters, nursed their own writerly ambitions and were deeply interested in anything connected with literary achievement. He sketches for them a rich notion of the *ingenium* or literary talent as a manifestation of one's intellectual capacity and force of character, and he urges them to devote themselves wholeheartedly to the work of rethinking and bringing coherence to various elements taken from earlier works. When he speaks repeatedly of the carefully constituted *ingenium* as a kind of self, he perhaps reminds them as well of the potential of the written artifact to perpetuate not only one's name and influence but even one's very identity, the very nature of one's mind, through the long-enduring medium of textual transmission. But then, having done all this, he invests that same model with a further dimension of meaning which extends beyond the activity of writers to every activity of the human mind. The productive intellect that is responsible for a person's literary achievements is in the end not distinct from the *animus* as productive of everything he or she does. What has been said about the one applies also to the other. As reading alternates with writing, so discovery in general alternates with response, and as one's quality and ultimate survival as a writer depends on one's success in integrating multiple literary influences, so one's self-actualization as a human being depends on one's success in setting in order all the many impressions gained from experience and rectifying them by the single mechanism of rational thought.

The conception of self that is operative in this distinctively Senecan project is strongly marked with transcendence. Our present writings do not achieve the perfect integration that the man of great *ingenium* would exhibit: As the interlocutor suggests, readers can generally discern whose style, whose argumentation, whose well-turned remarks we are imitating.

But the proper task of the writer is to work toward that integration, because it is only in so doing that one "stamps his own form" upon the elements drawn from one's chosen models (*Ep.* 84.8). In the same way, our occurrent selves – the moral agents we are at present – fail for the time being to act consistently in accordance with normative reason. Seneca insists nonetheless that the standards of reason are *our* standards, the ones that will enable us to be what we fundamentally are. In this, more than anything else, he betrays his Stoic allegiance.

Bibliography

Alexander, William H. 1941. "Seneca's Epistulae Morales: The Text Emended and Explained (XCIII–CXXIV)." *University of California Publications in Classical Philology* 12, no. 8: 135–164.
Axelson, Bertil. 1939. *Neue Senecastudien*. Lund: Gleerup.
Bartsch, Shadi, and David Wray, eds. 2009. *Seneca and the Self*. Cambridge: Cambridge University Press.
Beltrami, Achille, ed. 1937. *L. Annaei Senecae Ad Lucilium epistulae morales*. 2 vols. 2nd. ed. Rome: Regia Officina Polygraphica.
Bernauer, James, and Michael Mahon. 1994. "The Ethics of Michel Foucault." In *The Cambridge Companion to Foucault*, edited by Gary Gutting, 141–158. Cambridge: Cambridge University Press.
Davidson, Arnold. 1994. "Ethics as Ascetics." In *The Cambridge Companion to Foucault*, edited by Gary Gutting, 115–140. Cambridge: Cambridge University Press.
Davidson, Arnold. 1997. "Structures and Strategies of Discourse: Remarks towards a History of Foucault's Philosophy of Language." In *Foucault and His Interlocutors*, edited by Arnold Davidson, 1–17. Chicago: University of Chicago Press.
De Rentiis, Dina. 1998. "Der Beitrag der Bienen: Überlegungen zum Bienengleichnis bei Seneca und Macrobius." *RhM* 141: 30–44.
Foucault, Michel. 1983. "L'écriture de soi." *Corps écrit* 5: 3–23.
Foucault, Michel. 1984. *Histoire de la sexualité*. Vol. 3: *Le souci de soi*. Paris: Gallimard.
Foucault, Michel. 1994. *Dits et écrits, 1954-1988*. 4 vols. Paris: Gallimard.
Foucault, Michel. 2001. *L'herméneutique du sujet: Cours au Collège de France (1981–1982)*. Paris: Gallimard.
Gill, Christopher. 2009. "Seneca and Selfhood: Integration and Disintegration." In *Seneca and the Self*, edited by Shadi Bartsch and David Wray, 65–83. Cambridge: Cambridge University Press.
Graver, Margaret R. 1996. *Therapeutic Reading and Seneca's "Moral Epistles."* Ph.D. diss., Brown University.
Graver, Margaret R. 1998. "The Manhandling of Maecenas: Senecan Abstractions of Masculinity." *AJPh* 119: 607–632.
Graver, Margaret R. 2014. "Action and Emotion." In *Brill's Companion to Seneca: Philosopher and Dramatist*, edited by Gregor Damschen and Andreas Heil, 257–275. Boston; Leiden: Brill.
Graver, Margaret R., and Anthony A. Long, trans. Forthcoming. *Seneca, Letters on Ethics*. Chicago: University of Chicago Press.
Gummere, Richard Mott, ed. and trans. 1920. *Seneca, Ad Lucilium epistulae morales*. Vol. 2. London; Cambridge: Heinemann; Harvard University Press.

Hadot, Pierre. 1993. *Exercices spirituels et philosophie antique*. 2nd ed. Paris: Études Augustiniennes.
Hadot, Pierre. 1989. "Réflexions sur la notion de 'culture de soi'." In *Michel Foucault philosophe: Rencontre internationale, Paris 9, 10, 11 janvier 1988*. 261–270. Paris: Éditions du Seuil.
Hadot, Pierre. 1995. *Philosophy as a Way of Life: Spiritual Exercises from Socrates to Foucault* edited by Arnold I. Davidson, translated by Michael Chase. Oxford: Blackwell.
Inwood, Brad. 2005. *Reading Seneca: Stoic Philosophy at Rome*. Oxford; New York: Oxford University Press.
Inwood, Brad. 2007. "The Importance of Form in Seneca's Philosophical Letters." In *Ancient Letters: Classical and Late Antique Epistolography*, edited by Ruth Morello and Andrew D. Morrison, 133–148. Oxford; New York: Oxford University Press.
Inwood, Brad. 2009. "Seneca and Self-Assertion." In *Seneca and the Self*, edited by Shadi Bartsch and David Wray, 39–64. Cambridge: Cambridge University Press.
Long, Anthony A. 2006. *From Epicurus to Epictetus: Studies in Hellenistic and Roman Philosophy*. Oxford; New York: Oxford University Press.
Long, Anthony A. 2009. "Seneca on the Self: Why Now?" In *Seneca and the Self*, edited by Shadi Bartsch and David Wray, 20–37. Cambridge: Cambridge University Press.
Long, Antony A., and David N. Sedley, eds. 1987. *The Hellenistic Philosophers*. 2 vols. Cambridge: Cambridge University Press.
Motto, Anna Lydia. 1985. *Seneca, Moral Epistles*. Chico: Scholars Press.
Préchac, François, ed. and trans. 1945. *Sénèque: Lettres à Lucilius*. 3 vols. Paris: Les Belles Lettres.
Reynolds, Leighton D., ed. 1965. *L. Annaei Senecae Ad Lucilium epistulae morales*. 2 vols. Oxford: Clarendon Press.
Schöpsdau, Klaus. 2005. "Seneca über den rechten Umgang mit Büchern." *RhM* 148: 94–102.
Seneca. 1910. *Select Letters*. See Summers 1910.
Seneca. 1920. *Ad Lucilium epistulae morales*. See Gummere 1920.
Seneca. 1937. *Ad Lucilium epistulae morales*. See Beltrami 1937.
Seneca. 1945. *Lettres à Lucilius*. See Préchac 1945.
Seneca. 1965. *Ad Lucilium epistulae morales*. See Reynolds 1965.
Seneca. 1985. *Moral Epistles*. See Motto 1985.
Seneca. Forthcoming. *Letters on Ethics*. See Graver and Long forthcoming.
Strozier, Robert. 2002. *Foucault, Subjectivity, and Identity: Historical Constructions of Subject and Self*. Detroit: Wayne State University Press.
Summers, Walter C., ed. 1910. *Select Letters of Seneca: Edited with Introduction and Explanatory Notes*. London: Macmillan.
Veyne, Paul. 1997. "The Final Foucault and His Ethics." In *Foucault and His Interlocutors*, edited by Arnold Davidson, 225–233. Chicago: University of Chicago Press.
Vogt, Katja M. 2012. "Seneca." *The Stanford Encyclopedia of Philosophy*. Winter 2012 Edition. Accessed May 20, 2013. http://plato.stanford.edu/archives/win2012/entries/seneca/.
Wildberger, Jula. 2006. *Seneca und die Stoa: Der Platz des Menschen in der Welt*. 2 vols. Berlin; New York: De Gruyter.

The Philosopher as Craftsman: A Topos between Moral Teaching and Literary Production

Linda Cermatori
Università degli Studi di Firenze

The purpose of this paper is to investigate some uses Seneca makes in his works of the image of the philosopher as artist and craftsman and to emphasize some of its conceptual implications. My analysis is related to studies that underline the deep interdependence between literary form and philosophical thought in Seneca's prose.[1] In particular Armisen-Marchetti has shown that the study of images and metaphorical language can improve our understanding of both Seneca's literary and philosophical legacy.[2]

The field of material art, as much as the fields of jurisprudence and medicine (Lotito 2001), not only provides the philosopher with a repertoire of illustrative images aimed at facilitating comprehension and at a more effective reception of his ethical message; it also substantially inspires the

---

1   I refer mainly to Traina 1995, who describes the dualism between the care for oneself, which inspires the style of sentences that constitutes the language of "inner life," and the care for others, which produces the "centrifugal" force of moral exhortation. See also Mazzoli 1970, who highlights the importance of poetic style and the Platonic theory of divine frenzy. Seneca's thoughts on rhetoric are studied by Setaioli 2000. For an analysis of certain topics whose treatment by Seneca is influenced by Julio-Claudian literature, see Degl'Innocenti Pierini 1990 and 1999. Crucial for understanding Seneca's awareness of the importance of language and style as specific instruments of philosophical education is von Albrecht 2008. For a systematic examination of poetic vocabulary used by Seneca philosophus, see Hine 2005.
2   Armisen-Marchetti 1989. For an approach by *topoi* and motives, see Motto 2001 and Motto and Clark 1993. Concerning Seneca's epistolary work, Inwood 2007 has shown the influence of literary genre on philosophical content: Self-consciously Seneca writes letters that aim at more than just expressing admiration for Epicurus and a keen desire to rival Cicero (whose letters he quotes just often enough to signal awareness) and the influence of Horace's *Epistles* (again signaled by occasional quotations). Accordingly, the dismissive attitude in the letters towards logic and physics should not be taken to reflect Seneca's philosophical tastes, but is reflective of the fact that these two disciplines where thought less suitable for letters than personal experiences and moral advice.

content and ideology of his writings. Moreover, I would like to demonstrate how an observation of the terminology of art in Seneca's prose indicates the presence of his implicit self-conception as an author and, especially within the corpus of his letters, reveals a significant link between philosophy and epistolography.[3] Similarly, von Albrecht (2000) has shown that in *Epistles* 95 and 108 some expressions that allude to the image of philosophy as food for the disciple and are often derived from Horace's poetry are used by Seneca to communicate both a didactic and a literary theory.

Seneca uses the traditional image of youth as a malleable substance[4] and describes education with a multivalent language that evokes the craft of an artisan busy at work on the soul: "[...] for it's easy to set minds in good order (*componere*) while they're still tender, but difficult to prune away vices that have grown up with us."[5] On the other hand, Lucilius objects to the philosophical training of a middle-aged man:

> Respice aetatem eius iam duram et intractabilem. Non potest reformari; tenera finguntur.
>
> Consider his age, how hardened it now is, and past handling! Only young minds are moulded. (Sen. *Ep.* 25.1, trans. Gummere)[6]

A forty-year-old pupil cannot be re-shaped, and he is described with the adjectives *durus* and *intractabilis* that combine both moral and material meanings, referring to the stiffness of adulthood as opposed to the flexibility and tenderness of youth. Similarly, the verb *fingere* is invested with a figurative meaning and chosen to express moral education as a manual labor, in the sense of molding and modeling to produce virtue. Another noteworthy feature is the occurrence of the word *componere* in the first passage in the sense of composing by setting in a perfect order. This verb is used several times by the philosopher not only with reference to the improvement of a human soul and ethically significant behavior[7] but also

---

[3] This is an aspect not considered by Bartsch 2009, who investigates the importance of figural language in relation to Seneca's philosophical pedagogy. Bartsch also deals with the metaphorical concept of the self as a work of art, but ignores important literary implications of Senecan style and hardly explores meanings and forms of the corresponding images construed by Seneca in the tragedies.

[4] Plato, for example, refers to the constant sensitivity to flattery on the part of youths, even when they seem to be unimpressionable, in *Leg.* 633d: "τῶν σεμνῶν οἰομένων εἶναι τοὺς θυμοὺς ποιοῦσιν κηρίνους."

[5] *De ira* 2.18.2: "Facile est enim teneros adhuc animos componere, difficulter reciduntur vitia quae nobiscum creverunt." Translation by Robert A. Kaster 2010.

[6] All translations from the *Epistulae morales* are by Richard M. Gummere. See Laudizi 2003, 161; Armisen-Marchetti 1989, 79.

[7] See *Ep.* 29.9; 95.5; 119.10; *Polyb.* 18.9; *Helv.* 18.8.

to natural elements that are perfectly combined by the divine creator[8] and to a literary style that results from accurate and balanced writing aimed at the transmission of moral values.[9] The use of the same verb unifies the various types of creation, which all seem to be achieved by the same kind of molding action aimed at perfection and harmony, in accordance with the optimistic view of Stoic pantheism that considers virtue, rationality, and nature as aspects of the same divine principle.

Seneca represents the master as a craftsman who molds the disciple by education and uses terms that belong to the framework of material art, thus alluding to the image of philosophy as a creative force and developing our understanding of philosophical teaching. Education as a craftsmanship is also recognizable in the interaction between predisposition and learning (*institutio*), when Seneca defines Lucilius' natural potential to become a morally perfect man as a material for or "stuff of virtue" (*virtutis materia*):

> Deerat illis iustitia, deerat prudentia, deerat temperantia ac fortitudo. Omnibus his virtutibus habebat similia quaedam rudis vita; virtus non contingit animo nisi instituto et edocto et ad summum adsidua exercitatione perducto. Ad hoc quidem, sed sine hoc nascimur, et in optimis quoque, antequam erudias, virtutis materia, non virtus est.

> Justice was unkown to them, unknown prudence, unknown also self-control and bravery; but their rude life possessed certain qualities akin to all these virtues. Virtue is not vouchsafed to a soul unless that soul has been trained and taught, and by unremitting practice brought to perfection. For the attainment of this boon, but not in the possession of it, were we born; and even in the best of men, before you refine them by instruction, there is but the stuff of virtue, not virtue itself. (Sen. *Ep.* 90.46, trans. Gummere)

By the use of the pivotal term *materia*, Seneca can allude to a Stoic theory of human existence which derives from the Aristotelian distinction between actuality and potentiality: Although human beings do not feature a perfect innate rationality, they are endowed with a predisposition to virtue and can aspire to moral perfection thanks to the benefits of philosophy. The word *materia* also belongs to art terminology and represents the natural disposition of Lucilius as a good material, alluding to the image of education as a form of molding or sculpting. Furthermore it refers to a specific concept of Stoic cosmology according to which the universe is

---

[8] See *Ep.* 71.12: "Were it not so, the mind would endure with greater courage its own ending and that of its possessions, if only it could hope that life and death, like the whole universe about us, go by turns, that whatever has been put together (*componere*) is broken up again, that whatever has been broken up is put together again (*componere*), and that the eternal craftsmanship of God, who controls all things, is working at this task."

[9] See *Ep.* 110.8, for example, where *componere* is used both for the soul and the style of Fabianus.

constituted by two principles, matter (*materia*) and cause (*causa*). In that doctrine of causes, explained by Seneca in *Ep.* 65.2–3, the divine creator, as perpetual and active principle,[10] contributes to the formation of reality through his direct action on matter, the complementary passive principle, which suffers the actions but also limits[11] the power of the rational order. This constant penetration is the result of the monistic and pantheistic vision of Stoic orthodoxy recognized and explained by Seneca in clear opposition to the plurality of causes claimed by Aristotelianism and Platonism (*Ep.* 65).[12] The divine creator, the demiurge (*dēmiourgos*), is also compared to an artist (*technitēs*), and Seneca uses precisely this analogy to discuss the Aristotelian and Platonic theory of causes (*Ep.* 58.19–21; 65.4–10). In fact, from the beginning of the explication in *Ep.* 65, Seneca states to Lucilius that the creation of the universe is an artistic production: God is a sculptor and matter is like the bronze of a statue, which takes form (*forma*) under the divine impulse. On the other hand, all art is defined by Seneca as an imitation of nature and, we can infer, necessarily ruled by the same principles and by the same penetration.

> Dicunt, ut scis, Stoici nostri duo esse in rerum natura ex quibus omnia fiant, causam et materiam. Materia iacet iners, res ad omnia parata, cessatura, si nemo moveat. Causa autem, id est ratio, materiam format et quocumque vult versat, ex illa varia opera producit. Esse ergo debet, unde fiat aliquid, deinde a quo fiat. Hoc

---

10 Wildberger 2006, 14 has clarified the role of passive *materia* (τὸ πάσχον, *quod fit, quod patitur*), completely unable to change itself, and the role of God as the only active principle (τὸ ποιοῦν, *quod facit*), capable of altering itself and being subject to its own causal action, unlike the Aristotelian unmoved mover.

11 Seneca's adaptation of a passage of *Timaeus* (29d) in *Ep.* 65.10 ("What was God's reason for creating the world? God is good, and no good person is grudging of anything that is good. Therefore, God made it the best world possible") raises the question of the limits of creation, unlike the original Greek text, which presents a God who created a universe as similar to himself as possible. – In this section Seneca introduces the concept of a *materia* not completely suitable to the perfect goodness of creation, probably referring to an exegetical tradition following Plato, which would later circulate in Neoplatonic commentaries (Setaioli 1988, 136–140). Wildberger 2006, 51–56 has collected evidence for limits possibly set by matter in Stoic sources.

12 Some scholars interpret Seneca's physical setting as strictly dualistic and related to the Platonic tradition, for example Donini 1979, 158, who reads *Ep.* 65.2–3 and 12 as a denial of the corporeity of God under the influence of certain Middle-Platonic texts. All the same, the opinion of those who recognize the adherence to orthodox Stoicism by Seneca is prevailing: God is corporeal and immanent, while the two principles, cause and matter, are involved in the formation of a single cosmos, which is physical and divine at the same time, through constant permeation. Scarpat 1970 proposes a particular conception of "Stoic dualism," but a terminology of "monism" vs. "dualism" seems inadequate to define the view of Seneca (Wildberger 2006, 4f.; 456).

causa est, illud materia. Omnis ars naturae imitatio est. Itaque quod de universo dicebam ad haec transfer quae ab homine facienda sunt. Statua et materiam habuit quae pateretur artificem et artificem qui materiae daret faciem. Ergo in statua materia aes fuit, causa opifex. Eadem condicio rerum omnium est; ex eo constant quod fit et ex eo quod facit.

Our Stoic philosophers, as you know, declare that there are two things in the universe which are the source of everything – namely, cause and matter. Matter lies sluggish, a substance ready for any use, but sure to remain unemployed if no one sets it in motion. Cause, however, by which we mean reason, moulds matter and turns it in whatever direction it will, producing thereby various concrete results. Accordingly, there must be, in the case of each thing, that from which it is made, and next, an agent by which it is made. The former is its material, the latter its cause. All art is but imitation of nature; therefore, let me apply these statements of general principles to the things which have to be made by man. A statue, for example, has afforded matter which was to undergo treatment at the hands of the artist, and has had an artist who was to give form to the matter. Hence in the case of the statue, the material was bronze, the cause was the workman. And so it goes with all things – they consist of that which is made, and of the maker (Sen. *Ep.* 65.2–3, trans. Gummere).

Observing the language used by Seneca in the passages quoted, we can see that also moral education is often imagined as a work of art and that therefore we can regard the work of the philosopher as a conscious form of imitation of nature and of divine creation. If Lucilius is defined as the matter of virtue, a malleable soul, the action of the master who molds the soul of his disciple according to correct principles of God and what is good coincides with the power of a moral "cause."

In *Ep.* 50.5–6 the soul is not only matter but finer and more adaptable than any other substance, and the work of the teacher is like the heat that can straighten timber and girders; individual *ethos* is described as a material reality in a process of coming-into-being, sensitive to the corrective impact of philosophy:

Laborandum est et, ut verum dicam, ne labor quidem magnus est, si modo, ut dixi, ante animum nostrum formare incipimus et recorrigere quam indurescat pravitas eius. Sed nec indurata despero. Nihil est quod non expugnet pertinax opera et intenta ac diligens cura; robora in rectum quamvis flexa revocabis. Curvatas trabes calor explicat et aliter natae in id finguntur quod usus noster exigit: quanto facilius animus accipit formam, flexibilis et omni umore obsequentior. Quid enim est aliud animus quam quodam modo se habens spiritus? Vides autem tanto spiritum esse faciliorem omni alia materia, quanto tenuior est.

No, we must work. To tell the truth, even the work is not great, if only, as I said, we begin to mould and reconstruct our souls before they are hardened by sin. But I do not despair even of a hardened sinner. There is nothing that will not surrender to persistent treatment, to concentrated and careful attention; however much the timber may be bent, you can make it straight again. Heat unbends curved beams, and wood that grew naturally in another shape is fashioned artificially according to our needs. How much more easily does the soul permit itself to be shaped, pliable as it is and more yielding than any liquid! For what else is the soul than air in a certain state? And you see that air is more adaptable than any other matter, in proportion as it is rarer than any other. (Sen. *Ep.* 50.5–6, trans. Gummere)

In this passage Seneca uses multivalent terminology: the term *pravitas*, that means both "deformity" and "sin," for instance, and the verb *induro*, "to harden," effectively express at the same time a moral perversity and a material anomaly. On the other side, philosophical teaching is described as a moral and material correction, defined a hard work (*labor*) and a force (*robur*) that can mold (*fingere*), shape (*formare*), straighten (*in rectum revocare*), and bend (*explicare*) the defects of the matter. It is thanks to philosophy that the soul can finally take its form (*forma*), adds Seneca, using a term that like *materia* appears in *Ep.* 65 to express a specific concept of the doctrine of causes: the form, which Aristotle equates with the shape of a statue and which, according to the Platonist view, constitutes "the shape and the arrangement of the visible world" (*Ep.* 65.9: "habitus et ordo mundi quem videmus") that God contains in himself and by which the artist is inspired.[13] This concept loses its causal autonomy for Seneca and, in his view, coincides directly with the action and the essence of the divine craftsman:[14] God necessarily gives the *idos* (*Ep.* 65.4–5), the immanent and perceptible form of things, as a motive force compliant with the demands of universal nature.

The analysis of the vocabulary has shown that education is also conceived as an art (*technē*) and Seneca, the philosopher, as the craftsman who can penetrate the suitable but imperfect soul of his pupil-material, which is able to take the best possible form. Seneca also defines the formative

---

13 Sen. *Ep.* 65.7: "To these four Plato adds a fifth cause, – the pattern which he himself calls the 'idea:' for it is this that the artist gazed upon when he created the work which he had decided to carry out. Now it makes no difference whether he has his pattern outside himself, that he may direct his glance to it, or within himself, conceived and placed there by himself. God has within himself these patterns of all things, and his mind comprehends the harmonies and the measures of the whole totality of things which are to be carried out; he is filled with these shapes which Plato calls the 'ideas,' – imperishable, unchangeable, not subject to decay. And therefore, though men die, humanity itself, or the idea of man, according to which man is moulded, lasts on, and though men toil and perish, it suffers no change."

14 Stoics have probably taken that image from an Academic-Platonic tradition derived from the *Timaeus*. However, some sources for the ancient Stoa highlight the difference between these creative efforts: While a statue is made only from outside and the inside remains formless, God creates his works entirely, shaping them from within. See, e.g., Alex. Aphr. *Mixt.* p. 225 Bruns = *SVF* 2.1044 or Sen. *Ben.* 4.8.2: "Quocumque te flexeris, ibi illum [sc. deum] videbis occurrentem tibi; nihil ab illo vacat, opus suum ipse implet;" Wildberger 2006, 15–16.

relationship according to the terms of universal creation: It looks to an ethical purpose (*telos*), is consciously in harmony with the order and homology (*homologia*) of the macrocosm, and thus combines nature, art, and ethics.

Furthermore, Lucilius' virtue is considered Seneca's product and called an *opus*, by a keyword used in Latin to signify a work of art. The result of divine creation is called *opus* by the philosopher as well,[15] and so there exist strong connections between the activity of God, the artist *par excellence* and molder of the cosmos, and human activity.[16] This is so fundamental, that the intention of men to collaborate on the divine plan, the most beautiful work (*opus pulcherrimum*), is clearly expressed in *Ep.* 107.10, in accordance with the thought of Cleanthes.[17] In this regard also the enthusiastic words of *Ep.* 34.1–2[18] are suggestive: Seneca expresses his satisfaction with the progress made by Lucilius and calls him his own *opus*, comparing virtue to products of physical work:[19]

> Cresco et exulto et discussa senectute recalesco quotiens ex iis quae agis et scribis intellego quantum te ipse, nam turbam olim reliqueras, superieceris. Si agricolam arbor ad fructum perducta delectat, si pastor ex fetu gregis sui capit voluptatem, si alumnum suum nemo aliter intuetur quam ut adulescentiam illius suam iudicet; quid evenire credis iis, qui ingenia educaverunt et quae tenera formaverunt adulta subito vident? Adsero te mihi; meum opus es.

---

15 See *Ep.* 65.9: "The pattern is doubtless the model according to which God has made this great and most beautiful creation (*opus*)."

16 In *Ep.* 31.6, for instance, the wise man is the craftsman of his own life, and what is needed for his creation is dispensed with rationality and caution: "Your wise man, who is also a craftsman, will reject or choose in each case as it suits the occasion; but he does not fear that which he rejects, nor does he admire that which he chooses, if only he has a stout and unconquerable soul." Self-engagement leads the sage once again close to the divine *artifex* who, with equal skill, can include everything in a small space, as we read in *Ep.* 53.11: "But, by my faith, it is the sign of a great artist to have confined a full likeness to the limits of a miniature. The wise man's life spreads out to him over as large a surface as does all eternity to a god."

17 Mazzoli 1970, 47. Posidonius in particular explicitly defines the end (*telos*) of a person's life as "to live contemplating the truth and order of all things together and helping in promoting it as far as possible, in no way being led by the irrational part of the soul" (Clem. Al. *Strom.* 2.21.129.4 = *Frg.* 186 Edelstein and Kidd: "τὸ ζῆν θεωροῦντα τὴν τῶν ὅλων ἀλήθειαν καὶ τάξιν καὶ συγκατασκευάζοντα αὐτὴν κατὰ τὸ δυνατόν, κατὰ μηδὲν ἀγόμενον ὑπὸ τοῦ ἀλόγου μέρους τῆς ψυχῆς," translation by Kidd 1999).

18 See Mazzoli 1991, 74.

19 In *Ep.* 1.2.64–68, Horace uses a group of examples in order to exhort Lollius to a certain behavior and Seneca seems to elaborate a similar priamel in the letter 34. This form of exhortation (*parainesis*), which uses images from nature and becomes a mannerism in the elegiac poets (Race 1982, 125), is also introduced by Horace with a didactic purpose.

> I grow in spirit and leap for joy and shake off my years and my blood runs warm again, whenever I understand, from your actions and your letters, how far you have outdone yourself; for as to the ordinary man, you left him in the rear long ago. If the farmer is pleased when his tree develops so that it bears fruit, if the shepherd takes pleasure in the increase of his flocks, if every man regards his pupil as though he discerned in him his own early manhood, – what, then, do you think are the feelings of those who have trained a mind and moulded a young idea, when they see it suddenly grown to maturity? I claim you for myself; you are my handiwork. (Sen. *Ep.* 34.1–2, trans. Gummere)

In a similar fashion Horace, at the end of his *Epistle* to Lollius (1.2), highlights the malleability of his friend's young age and his ability to put moral advice to the best use. The comparison with a farmer who raises a colt or a puppy dog[20] indicates the author's educational motivations and emphasizes the recipient's potential:

> Fingit equum tenera docilem cervice magister
> ire viam quam monstret eques; venaticus, ex quo
> tempore cervinam pellem latravit in aula,
> militat in silvis catulus. Nunc adbibe puro
> pectore verba puer, nunc te melioribus offer.
>
> While the colt has a tender neck and is able to learn, the groom trains him to go the way his rider directs. The hound that is to hunt does service in the woods from the time that it first barked at a deer-skin in the yard. Now, while still a boy, drink in my words with clean heart, now trust yourself to your betters. (Hor. *Ep.* 1.2.64–68, trans. Fairclough)

Since the student's growth is both expressed in the letters and caused by the productive force of these philosophical writings, the metaphors for both moral edification and the process of literary art seem to converge and finally become one: The subject is forged by the transmission of philosophical instruction, and its moral portrait is handed over as a work of art to the wider audience. The ethical and literary purposes seem to merge and complete each other, as it is suggested by the statement "meum opus es" ("you are a product of my work"), which can be read as a claim by an author at all levels, similar to inscriptions of the poets that testify their self-conception as writers. In particular the triple set of verbs opening this letter, which describes the reaction of the philosopher to Lucilius' progress, may be compared with an idea expressed by Ovid in another corpus of literary letters (*Epistulae ex Ponto* 3.9.9–22). When describing his relationship to

---

20 In reference to the colt, Kiessling and Heinze 1957 cite a gnome by Aristippus and for the pup a passage by Hieronymus of Rhodes related by Plutarch, while Gigante 2002, 28 identifies Philodemus as the main source of these lines: The Epicurean philosopher compares the young person to a colt or a pup, develops the analogy with animal training and describes how susceptibility to improvement depends on the age.

his own poems (*opus*), he outlines the correspondence between the poet's soul and the poem's soul, which are growing in common fervor:

> Scribentem iuvat ipse labor minuitque laborem,
>   cumque suo crescens pectore fervet opus.
>
> While writing the very toil gives pleasure and itself is lessened, and the growing work glows with the writer's heart. (Ov. *Pont.* 3.9.21–22, trans. Wheeler)

In the poem that opens Ovid's collection, the concept of ownership of the art product is explicitly introduced to define the relationship between the debtor-poet and his patron.[21] At the same time, the multifaceted image of the work of art (*opus*) within the inscription also conjures up the idea of poetry's power aimed to immortalize its addressee as a monument.

> Unde rogas forsan fiducia tanta futuri
>   sit mihi? quod fecit, quisque tuetur opus.
> Ut Venus artificis labor est et gloria Coi,
>   aequoreo madidas quae premit imbre comas:
> arcis ut Actaeae vel eburna vel aerea custos
>   bellica Phidiaca stat dea facta manu:
> vindicat ut Calamis laudem, quos fecit, equorum:
>   ut similis verae vacca Myronis opus:
> sic ego pars rerum non ultima, Sexte, tuarum
>   tutelaeque feror munus opusque tuae.
>
> Whence, perchance you ask, have I so much confidence in the future? Every man watches over the work he has wrought. Just as Venus is at once the work and glory of the Coan artist, as she presses her locks damp with the spray of the sea; as the war goddess who guards the Actaean citadel stands in ivory or bronze wrought by the hand of Phidias, as Calamis claims renown for the steeds he has made, as the lifelike cow is Myron's work, so I am not the last of your possessions, Sextus; I am known as the gift, the work of your guardianship. (Ov. *Pont.* 4.1.27–36, trans. Wheeler)

In this text, similarities with works produced by the Greek masters clarify the polysemous value of *opus* that is the creative effort of the poet to fix a beautiful portrait of the recipient in the eternal universe of Latin literature.

Also in Seneca's epistolary a Greek master, Phidias, becomes the symbol of artistic excellence and ideal creation. In *Ep.* 85.40[22] for example, Seneca writes that this famous sculptor could make wonderful statues with any material; he is compared to the creative power of philosophy, that is, the ability of the wise man to accomplish memorable things in any situation, both at home and in exile, in wealth or in poverty:[23]

> Non ex ebore tantum Phidias sciebat facere simulacra; faciebat ex aere. Si marmor illi, si adhuc viliorem materiam obtulisses, fecisset quale ex illa fieri optimum pos-

---

21 See Helzle 1989, 53–59; Viarre 1991, 135; Wulfram 2008, 264–270.
22 Cf. Marino 2005, 133f.
23 On such paradoxes, see Motto and Clark 1993, 65–86.

> set. Sic sapiens virtutem, si licebit, in divitiis explicabit, si minus, in paupertate; si poterit, in patria, si minus, in exilio; si poterit, imperator, si minus, miles; si poterit, integer, si minus, debilis. Quamcumque fortunam acceperit, aliquid ex illa memorabile efficiet.
>
> It was not of ivory only that Phidias knew how to make statues; he also made statues of bronze. If you had given him marble, or a still meaner material, he would have made of it the best statue that the material would permit. So the wise man will develop virtue, if he may, in the midst of wealth, or, if not, in poverty; if possible, in his own country – if not, in exile; if possible, as a commander – if not as a common soldier; if possible, in sound health – if not enfeebled. Whatever fortune he finds, he will accomplish therefrom something noteworthy. (Sen. *Ep.* 85.40, trans. Gummere)

The wise man can serenely tolerate the loss of a friend, since he has gained the power to make another friendship whenever he desires, just as Phidias can fashion new sculptures to replace the old ones:

> Sine amico quidem numquam erit. In sua potestate habet, quam cito reparet. Quomodo si perdiderit Phidias statuam, protinus alteram faciet, sic hic faciendarum amicitiarum artifex substituet alium in locum amissi.
>
> But he need never lack friends, for it lies in his own control how soon he shall make good a loss. Just as Phidias, if he lose a statue, can straightway carve another, even so our master in the art of making friendships can fill the place of a friend he has lost. (Sen. *Ep.* 9.5, trans. Gummere)

An absolute self-sufficiency is thus also outlined in the domain of interpersonal relations, as a reflection of the universal and divine constructive power of wisdom. Seneca uses Phidias to represent the creative inexhaustibility of the wise craftsman with regard to friends. They are the result of his virtue and his philosophy: Just like the statues of Phidias, like the noteworthy works of a wise man (*Ep.* 85.40), and like the literary works traditionally compared to the statues of Greek masters by Latin authors,[24] they also seem to be destined for immortal appreciation. The relationship between Seneca and Lucilius, which is a process of artistic "construction" according to the beneficial laws of philosophy, can fit into the same equation: It is achieved through literary epistolography, and the disciple's virtue becomes an enduring monument of a teacher-author. In *Epistle* 21 Seneca expressly claims to be able to "extract and erect names for eternity"[25] due to the value of his own writing. Just like Epicurus, Cicero, and Vergil, he is

---

24 The comparison with Phidias is a reference to literary texts in which the sculptor's canon is established explicitly as an aesthetic symbol. I am thinking, for example, of Ovid's poem mentioned above (*Pont.* 4.1.27–36) or of Propertius' elegy 3.9, in which the poet claims to be the *alter ego* of famous sculptors who were bold enough to mold in the style that was best suited to their natures.

25 Sen. *Ep.* 21.5: "duratura nomina educere."

capable of delivering the soul of the recipient to posterity.[26] Seneca states that the glory of virtuous spirits grows with the passage of time and that very few of them will know how to "raise their heads"[27] and defeat oblivion. In those images, too, which communicate the philosopher's self-awareness by reprocessing the metaphor of commemorative monuments, language conveys the idea of a philosophical construction, combining the moral, affective, and literary spheres for the purpose of educating mankind and of creating virtue as a work of art.

The most important precedent for the comparison between a literary author and Phidias is the programmatic description that Cicero puts forward in the *Orator*:

> Atque ego in summo oratore fingendo talem informabo qualis fortasse nemo fuit. Non enim quaero quis fuerit sed quid sit illud quo nihil esse possit praestantius, quod in perpetuitate dicendi non saepe atque haud scio an numquam, in aliqua autem parte eluceat aliquando, idem apud alios densius, apud alios fortasse rarius. 8 Sed ego sic statuo, nihil esse in ullo genere tam pulchrum quo non pulchrius id sit unde illud, ut ex ore aliquo quasi imago exprimatur. Quod neque oculis neque auribus neque ullo sensu percipi potest, cogitatione tamen et mente complectimur. Itaque et Phidiae simulacris, quibus nihil in illo genere perfectius videmus, et eis picturis quas nominavi cogitare tamen possumus pulchriora. 9 Nec vero ille artifex cum faceret Iovis formam aut Minervae, contemplabatur aliquem e quo similitudinem duceret, sed ipsius in mente insidebat species pulchritudinis eximia quaedam, quam intuens in eaque defixus ad illius similitudinem artem et manum dirigebat.
>
> Consequently in delineating the perfect orator I shall be portraying such a one as perhaps has never existed. Indeed I am not inquiring who was the perfect orator, but what is that unsurpassable ideal which seldom if ever appears throughout a whole speech but does shine forth at some times and in some places, more frequently in some speakers, more rarely perhaps in others. But I am firmly of the opinion that nothing of any kind is so beautiful as not to be excelled in beauty by that of which it is a copy, as a mask is a copy of a face. This ideal cannot be perceived by the eye or ear, nor by any of the senses, but we can nevertheless grasp it by the mind and the imagination. For example, in the case of the statues of Phidias, the most perfect of their kind that we have ever seen, and in the case of the paintings I have mentioned, we can, in spite of their beauty, imagine something more beautiful. Surely that great sculptor, while making the image of Jupiter or Minerva, did not look at any person whom he was using as a model, but in his own mind there dwelt a surpassing vision of beauty; at this he gazed and all intent on this he guided his artist's hand to produce the likeness of the god. (Cic. *Orat.* 7–9, trans. Hubbell)

---

26   Cf. Cermatori 2010.
27   Sen. *Ep.* 21.5: "pauca ingenia caput exerent."

Cicero presents himself as an artist determined to imitate the form of the ideal orator, a model not perceptible to the senses but only to the mind.[28] He follows the Platonic hierarchy of Being and accepts the inferiority of a copy, but claims that the Ideas can appear in the artist's mind. Like Phidias, who creates the statues of Jupiter and Minerva following a mental model, Cicero can produce a copy of the perfect orator in his literary work because the author's mind is imagined to be like the divine Demiurge. We can find in this passage many expressions used by Cicero also to explain the process of universal creation in his translation of Plato's *Timaeus*.[29] In any case, he expressly defines his own activity as a codifier with terms that imply a constant overlapping between the metaphor of sculpture, the orator's creative potential, and the creation of the rhetorical theory devised for Brutus and the audience in the treatise. On the other hand, the Stoic Seneca does not conceive art as an inferior imitation of the form of Good, aimed at producing a flawed copy of Being, and his texts do not aspire to the pure Idea. According to Stoic pantheism, Seneca considers the artist an *alter ego* of the divine cause and contributes to the creation of virtue by interacting directly with matter in his teaching.

We can say that the two authors have different points of view that influence the conception and purpose of their literary work: Cicero dedicates to Brutus a treatise that delineates a theoretical model as a perfect and immutable portrait, which the reader can only try to imitate. Seneca, on the other hand, wants to convey his values by direct intervention, correcting the soul on its path of wisdom. He chooses a dialog with the recipient, an

---

28 Through the analysis of the language, Dross 2004–2005, 277 shows that the artistic creation conceived by Cicero is founded on an intellectual activity similar to φαντασία as it is defined in Quint. *Inst.* 6.2.9: The model to be imitated only exists in the mind and cannot be derived from reality or perceived by the senses; Dross also underlines the special importance of the Platonic theory of Ideas for this passage of the *Orator*.

29 Degl'Innocenti Pierini 1979 has shown the correspondence between *Orat.* 7 and the text of the *Timaeus*, as it is translated by Cicero (*Tim.* 11 and 34): "[…] videndum est, cuiusnam animantium deus in fingendo mundo similitudinem secutus sit. Nullius profecto id quidem, quae sunt nobis nota animantia. […] 34 Quot igitur et quales animalium formas mens in speciem rerum intuens poterat cernere, totidem et tales in hoc mundo secum cogitavit effingere." See also the brief considerations of Moretti 1995, 83 n. 29, who underlines not only an "explicit allusion to the Platonic doctrine of Ideas" in *Orator* 7 ("atque ego in summo oratore fingendo talem informabo qualis fortasse nemo fuit") but also the influence of Stoic expressions on Cicero's program. In this regard compare the language of Seneca's statement at *Const.* 7.1 (quoted below, on p. 307) and Chrysippus' affirmation at Plu. *Stoic. rep.* 1041f = *SVF* 3.545: "Διὸ καὶ διὰ τὴν ὑπερβολὴν τοῦ τε μεγέθους καὶ τοῦ κάλλους, πλάσμασι δοκοῦμεν ὅμοια λέγειν, καὶ οὐ κατὰ τὸν ἄνθρωπον καὶ τὴν ἀνθρωπίνην φύσιν."

epistolary exchange able to reinforce Lucilius' struggle in pursuit of moral perfection. Seneca's moral exhortations must develop and change depending on the disciple's successes, and the epistolary genre, a sort of literary "work in progress"[30] where author and addressee can evolve in parallel, conforms to the action of a *sapiens*-craftsman and to that of a philosophy which "is no trick to catch the public; it is not devised for show. It is a matter, not of words, but of facts. [...] It moulds and constructs (*format et fabricat*) the soul" (*Ep.* 16.2–3).[31] In the end it involves also the work of the writer for his readers, who are "built" and "molded" by the very epistles: The more fragile the foundations and the more marshy the ground, the harder it gets (in *Ep.* 52.5); some spirits are ready, while others need to be constructed from the ground up, and their foundations take a much greater effort.[32] On the other hand, in *Ep.* 76.31, a wise man's moral greatness is imagined as a statue with unchanging proportions, a colossus immune to all material conditions of the outer world. When Seneca refers to the form (*forma*) of the wise man fixed forever in the artist's work, he considers it as something achievable in real life, not just as an immaterial derivative of a purely mental model: In *Const.* 7.1, Seneca claims to shape (*fingere*) the portrait (*imago*) of a perfect wise man, materially derived from a real example (*exemplar*):[33]

> Non fingimus istud humani ingenii vanum decus nec ingentem imaginem falsae rei concipimus, sed qualem conformamus exhibuimus, exhibebimus, raro forsitan magnisque aetatium intervallis unum.

> This wise man is not a fiction of us Stoics, a sort of phantom glory of human nature, nor is he a mere conception, the mighty semblance of a thing unreal, but we have shown him in the flesh just as we delineate him, and shall show him – though perchance not often, and after a long lapse of years only one. (Sen. *Const.* 7.1, trans. Basore)

---

30 See Mazzoli 1989, 1860–1863.
31 We can compare Seneca's expressions with the words that describe the educational tasks of poets in Hor. *Ep.* 2.1.126–129: "Os *tenerum* pueri balbumque poeta *figurat* / torquet ab obscaenis iam nunc sermonibus aurem, / mox etiam pectus *praeceptis format* amicis, / asperitatis et invidiae corrector et irae." See also Brink 1982, 169.
32 Sen. *Ep.* 52.5: "Suppose that two buildings have been erected, unlike as to their foundations, but equal in height and in grandeur. One is built on faultless ground, and the process of erection goes right ahead. In the other case, the foundations have exhausted the building materials, for they have been sunk into soft and shifting ground and much labour has been wasted in reaching the solid rock. As one looks at both of them, one sees clearly what progress the former has made, but the larger and more difficult part of the latter is hidden."
33 See Sen. *Const.* 2.1 and 7.1, directly after the quoted passage, where Cato is called an *exemplar*.

In the treatise *On the Constancy of the Wise Man*, the artist-philosopher consciously intends to shape (*conformare*) the portrait of a perfect but feasible wisdom, far from the barren descriptions of those who want to mold (*fingere*) empty images that are irrelevant to real human betterment.

The correspondence between literary and moral project, between words and actions, is recognizable also in Seneca's description of ideal studies, where moral improvement and moral writing become the good result of the same readings, as a perfect artistry of the self. The teaching of moral values and rhetorical skills follows the same rules of harmony that inspires divine creation as well. It is consciously described by words and imagines that unify natural process, philosophical theory, and literary judgment. In *Epistle* 84, Lucilius receives the advice that he should consult the authors of the past regularly because knowledge acquired through reading must merge into an organic whole: Just as bees that fly around and select those flowers that are suitable to make honey, arranging in honeycombs everything that they bring back with them to their beehives, so other people's works, once understood and learnt, must be digested in order to make a personal product. As a man of genius, the recipient will give an original shape to his writing because, claims Seneca, from various models one must create a harmonious unity.[34] In this description, the criterion of "concentus ex dissonis" (84.10), the "harmony from discordant elements," as Mazzoli (1998) has already observed, combines literary composition and lifestyle in line with the providential law of the universe that gives shape to the macrocosm and microcosm alike. This ethical and aesthetic principle, whereby individuality is construed as the original and rational combination of preceding elements, however unharmonious they may have been before, explains the positive and consistent connection between Seneca the moralist, Seneca the literary critic, and Seneca the author of philosophical texts, capable of devising an ethical education by consciously following and developing ideas of others in the name of virtue: An author may be an "active product" of his studies and not merely a pale imitation:[35]

> Etiam si cuius in te comparebit similitudo quem admiratio tibi altius fixerit, similem esse te volo quomodo filium, non quomodo imaginem: imago res mortua est […] Puto aliquando ne intellegi quidem posse, si imago vera sit; haec enim omnibus quae ex quo velut exemplari traxit formam suam impressit, ut in unitatem illa conpetant.

---

34 For this metaphor see Cicu 2005, 133–142 and the contribution by Margaret Graver in this volume.

35 The value of artistic imitation in Seneca is recognized and discussed by Setaioli 2000, 197–217. See also Gianotti 1979. Significant observations are offered by Picone 1984, 53–58.

Even if there shall appear in you a likeness to him who, by reason of your admiration, has left a deep impress upon you, I would have you resemble him as a child resembles his father, and not as a picture resembles its original; for a picture is a lifeless thing. [...] I think that sometimes it is impossible for it to be seen who is being imitated, if the copy is a true one; for a true copy stamps its own form upon all the features which it has drawn from what we may call the original, in such a way that they are combined into a unity. (Sen. *Ep.* 84.8, trans. Gummere)

Such integration requires constant concentration and attentiveness to rational standards of conduct: One must both act and refrain from acting only as reason directs. Lucilius should harmonize many skills, many precepts, many examples from every age into one, and he must become not an inferior and immutable copy, a dead statue, but another "author" of virtue by consistency in thoughts, actions, and words.[36] The author and his text are as inseparable as the moral and artistic purposes, as soul and words.[37] Seneca is capable of elaborating a multivalent language that can convey moral education as an aspect of divine creation, and philosophical writing as the portrait of the soul, through the medium of the images and terms of art and craftsmanship.

I shall complete my analysis by turning to the complex universe of Senecan tragedy, where it is possible to find further evidence for the multivalent idea of "construction" of the individual and to identify elements related to the imagery of craftsmanship. They are used to reflect the degenerate and negative side of human souls caused by the loss of natural order and morality. In *Phaed.* 1265f., in particular, the failure of a harmonious and rational creation is symbolized by Hippolytus' body: Irreversibly dismembered, it is described with a judgment that is at once aesthetic and moral as "forma carens / et turpe," an ugly, formless thing.[38] Consequently, the useless attempt of Theseus, who approaches the body to count the corpse's limbs and "model" (*fingere*) his son's body in order to restore its proper shape,[39] becomes the signal of inhuman and insurmountable

---

36 For this interpretation of Seneca's *Epistle* 84, see also Graver, who writes in her contribution to this volume (290f.): "It is as if there is no clear distinction to be made between self-formation in the sense of melding multiple literary influences to craft a unified and impressive voice in one's writings and self-formation in the sense of applying a single rational standard to the business of living."
37 Graver in this volume has perfectly shown the strict relationship that holds, in Seneca's view, between *animus* ("soul") and *ingenium* ("mind").
38 Most 1992, 394f. shows the various forms of the substantive *forma* that appear in the *Phaedra*. The analysis of the numerous occurrences (especially those in the choral ode which follows Hippolytus' rejection of Phaedra and emphasizes the youth's *forma*) clarifies the imaginative unity of this tragedy.
39 Lanza 1988–1989, 150 discusses the dismemberment of the young body and the funeral lament as evocative dramatic devices, used by Seneca to produce a representation of cruelty by insisting on paternal devotion (*pietas*).

distortion of the natural order. The father's claim of ownership is the acknowledgment of destruction:[40]

> [Theseus] Durate trepidae lugubri officio manus,
> fletusque largos sistite arentes genae,
> dum membra nato genitor adnumerat suo
> corpusque fingit.[41] Hoc quid est forma carens
> et turpe, multo vulnere abruptum undique?
> Quae pars tui sit dubito; sed pars est tui:
> hic, hic repone, non suo, at vacuo loco.
>
> [Theseus speaking] Trembling hands, be firm for this sad service; eyes, be dry, check your copious tears, while the father is portioning out limbs to his son and fashioning his body. What is this ugly formless thing, that multiple wounds have severed on every side? What part it may be I am uncertain, but it is part of you. Here, set it down here, in an empty place if not in its proper place. (Sen. *Phaed.* 1262–1269, trans. Fitch)

The value of *fingo* which in Seneca's prose works indicates the realization of education, here conveys the concrete, yet illusory, nature of the father's effort to restore the human form (*forma*) destroyed forever by the perverse and guilty desire of revenge:

> [Theseus] Hyppolytus hic est? crimen agnosco meum:
> ego te peremi [...]
> [Chorus] Disiecta, genitor, membra laceri corporis
> in ordinem dispone et errantes loco
> restitue partes. Fortis hic dextrae locus,
> hic laeva frenis docta moderandis manus
> ponenda: laevi lateris agnosco notas.
>
> [Theseus] Is this Hippolytus? I recognise my crime: it was I that killed you [...]
> [Chorus leader] Arrange in order, father, his torn body's sundered limbs, put back in place the straying parts. This is the place for his strong right hand; here must be set his left hand, skilled in controlling the reins. I recognise the signs of his left side. (Sen. *Phaed.* 1249f. 1256–1260, trans. Fitch)

Theseus is the main culprit of his son's and his own annihilation. The torment of his effort to recompose and to shape that body is in contrast with the didactic action Seneca plans to apply to his addressee, Lucilius, so that he may assume his shape following the principles of philosophical and rational composition and grow harmoniously under the molding action of

---

40 For the meaning of this final and perpetual lament, see Degl'Innocenti Pierini 2008, 233f., and for the literary value of that violent dismemberment (*sparagmos*) in the light of indicative parallels, *ibid.* 241–250.

41 Coffey and Mayer 1990, 195 comment: "The technical term for arranging a body for burial is 'corpus componere.' S. wittily chooses a synonym for the verb which stresses how unusual this 'laying-out' is."

this master.[42] In contrast to this, Theseus defines himself as a cruel author of death and describes the horror of the events in language that overturns the metaphoric idea of creation of the self; he speaks of the extraordinary ravages done to his own humanity:

> [Theseus] Donator atrae lucis, Alcide, tuum
> Diti remitte munus; ereptos mihi
> restitue manes. Impius frustra invoco
> mortem relictam. Crudus et leti artifex,
> exitia machinatus insolita effera
> nunc tibimet ipse iusta supplicia irroga.

> Giver of light that is darkness, Alcides, return your gift to Dis; restore to me the world of shades you have stolen from me. But as a godless man I pray in vain for death, which I abandoned. You man of blood, you craftsman of death, who contrived bizarre, barbaric destructions, now inflict just punishments on yourself. (Sen. *Phaed.* 1217–1222, trans. Fitch)

Other protagonists of the drama are also masters of this perverse machination, instigators of those tragic turns of events that are the very basis of the plot, hence authors (*auctores*) of that infamous distortion that seems to inspire and motivate the literary development of the genre of which they are a part. Even the expressions related to this iconography contribute to emphasizing the creative power of evil.[43] For instance, in outlining his picture of progressive decline of human morality, Hippolytus accuses women of being "mistresses of corruption," thus foreshadowing his own fate:

> Sed dux malorum femina: haec scelerum artifex
> obsedit animos.

> But the leader in evil is woman. This artificer of crimes besets our minds. (Sen. *Phaed.* 559f., trans. Fitch)

Medea is defined in a similar manner by Creon: He calls her an "artificer" of crimes (266), by an expression linked to the idea of ingenious fabri-

---

42 Compare the images created by Seneca to warn Lucilius in *Ep.* 33.5 that *ingenium*, *ars*, and *corpus* follow the same criterion of harmony of parts: "For this reason, give over hoping that you can skim, by means of epitomes, the wisdom of distinguished men. Look into their wisdom as a whole; study it as a whole. They are working out a plan and weaving together, line upon line, a masterpiece, from which nothing can be taken away without injury to the whole. Examine the separate parts, if you like, provided you examine them as parts of the man himself. She is not a beautiful woman whose ankle or arm is praised, but she whose general appearance makes you forget to admire her single attributes." See Mazzoli 1970, 66.

43 In this regard, see the figure of tyrant as an *auctor* explored in Schiesaro 2000, 145–160 by analyzing some programmatic expressions delivered by Atreus. Compare also Picone 1984, 37–68.

cation.⁴⁴ Indeed, here the noun *machinator* combines the metaphorical meaning of "conspirator" or "schemer" with the primary meaning of "architect."⁴⁵ In verse 734, Medea is also called "mistress of corruption" by the Nurse as she sets about her fatal plan and begins mixing potent poisons while the images of the previous crime recur obsessively.⁴⁶ She killed her brother Absyrtus, dismembered his body and scattered his parts on an island to distract her father Aeëtes so that Jason could escape with her from Colchis. Now, the dead brother becomes the symbol of the devastating decomposition put in motion by the burning passion back in her home country. Finally, once the murder of her sons has been perpetrated, the protagonist is condemned by Jason as the "author of horrible crime,"⁴⁷ while the royal palace burns and collapses under the weight of its own misfortunes (879–890), offering the perfect symbolic atmosphere for a universal disaster. As Rita Degl'Innocenti Pierini (2012) highlights in a recent paper, Medea defines herself in the prologue as the master of her own fate and not only as an unfortunate victim: Her words reveal the awareness that she is the bearer both of female cruelty (*nequitia*) and manly force (*robur*); she intends to destroy Creusa together with Jason, her own children, the city of Corinth, the entire cosmos by fire,⁴⁸ and even the isthmus (35–36), contemplating the disaster of natural order like an anti-God.⁴⁹

---

44 Littlewood 2004, 298–301. – The hapax *machinatrix* appears quite well suited to Seneca's style, but the poet may have had in mind Cic. *Cat.* 3.6: "horum omnium scelerum improbissimum machinatorem" (Costa 1973, 96).

45 Sen. *Med.* 979: "sceleris auctorem horridi." In Tacitus' *Annales* 15.42.1, for instance, Severus and Celer are referred to as *machinatores* in their function as the designers of Nero's luxurious mansion, the *domus aurea*, which we know comprised a series of villas and pavilions covering one third of Rome as it was then: Open porticos to enjoy the artificial views were created where the heart of Rome had recently been; the grounds included forests, an altar in a sacred grove, pastures with flocks, vineyards, and a man-made lake in the center. It was a never-witnessed *rus in urbe*, a "countryside in the city." The endeavor was characterized by some intellectuals as an outrage against the city and nature itself. Probably Seneca alludes to it at *Ep.* 90.42–43, while describing the turning ceilings of some excessively luxurious residences, which are also equipped, among other things, with insidious and monstrous contraptions similar to stage devices (Degl'Innocenti Pierini 2008, 125f.).

46 Sen. *Med.* 452–453, 910–915; Edgeworth 1990.

47 Cf. Sen. *Ag.* 983–985, where Aegisthus is also defined the "artificer of an impious crime" and as a symbol of natural disorder: "one criminally begot, whom even his own parents cannot name, son of his sister, grandson of his sire" (trans. Fitch 2004). See Tarrant 1976, 357.

48 Picone 2002.

49 Concerning Medea's programmatic affirmation endowed with a metaliterary value, see Németi 2003, 151; Biondi 1984, 16–25. Mazzoli 2002, 621 f. explains the

Ulysses, too, is addressed by Andromache in the *Troades* with similar terms linked to the image of the fall of Troy as a "schemer of deception and artist of crime" (750: "machinator fraudis et scelerum artifex").[50] Indeed, Ulysses is the author of the fall of Priam's city: He designed the wooden horse, but also caused the final demise of Hector's house. The culmination of evil is represented by the tale of Astyanax's sacrifice, when the messenger describes the child's deformed and dismembered body after the terrible fall from the rock. The destruction of the son is compared by Hecuba to the destruction of Hector, who was dragged by Achilles' chariot and completely disfigured.

In another tragedy, delirious Phaedra laments about the inefficacy of all possible interventions. She sees no god nor a Daedalus who could truly quench the flame that is consuming her soul:

> Quis meas miserae deus
> aut quis iuvare Daedalus flammas queat?
> Non si ille remeet, arte Mopsopia potens,
> qui nostra caeca monstra conclusit domo,
> promittat ullam casibus nostris opem.

> What god or what Daedalus could assist my unhappy flames of passion? Not even if that master of Mopsopian arts should return, who enclosed our monster in his blind house, could he promise any aid in my misfortune. (Sen. *Phaed.* 119–123, trans. Fitch)

In these verses the architect who locked the monstrous product of her mother Pasiphaë's passion in the famous labyrinth in Crete, the native land of Phaedra, becomes, next to the divine power, a symbol of the dominance of self-restraint over impulse, which is irremediably lost in the passionate maelstrom and by now reduced to a distant past. No work (*opus*) can be built to contain the protagonist's inner horror, no work can divert her from her forbidden desire while she destroys herself, transforming into a frenzied Minotaur.[51] The queen identifies herself with the terrifying and violent monster when, just before her suicide, she faces the torn body of Hippolytus and his scattered limbs: The Minotaur is capable of equally "inhuman"

---

creative effort of Medea in the prologue (Sen. *Med.* 8f.: "quos [...] Medea magis / fas est precari"): "É l'autopresentazione incipitaria di cui parlavo prima: sintomaticamente non in prima ma in terza persona, la persona dell'oggettività. [...] Il personaggio si fa al tempo stesso non soltanto consigliere (tratto già presente in Euripides), ma anche cronista del proprio 'artistico' *nefas*, nel travaglio creativo che lo porta alla potenza dell'atto."

50 For some important literary parallels, see Fantham 1982, 314.
51 This may be read as a result of the urgency of Phaedra's self-representation. Cf. Fitch and McElduff 2008, 171–173.

atrocities (1169).[52] The violent passion indeed produces a distortion of the natural world, a subversive craftsmanship opposed to wisdom, both as a moral and as an aesthetic disharmony: It is the cause of a youth's dismemberment effected by the father and of the deformation of a woman who becomes a monster.

We can conclude that, in the world of tragedy, some characters like Hecuba and Theseus are assigned roles as victims of events, suffering the effects of the passions of others. They describe the experience of destruction, declaring the annihilation of their rational world, which is represented by the dismemberment of their sons. On the other hand, Phaedra, Medea, and Ulysses are clearly defined artificers and creators of horrible crimes because, as leaders in evil, they implement the "production" of tragedy in the moral and literary sense, fully self-conscious of their anti-heroism and in a certain manner aware of their own myths.[53] The creation of the tragic world unfolds under the deadly force of passion that usurps the creative power of wisdom and becomes a perverse cause directed at the realization and description of a world that is paradoxically construed by disharmony. The words of these characters contain the images of "art," the destructive art of creating evils directly opposed to the constructive role of wisdom (*sapientia*) of Seneca's prose and to the wise man as the "artificer" (*artifex*) whose main skill lies "in mastering evils."[54] Also in the dialogs between characters of the tragedies, the language of art mirrors the strict connection found elsewhere in Seneca's works between literary project and moral content: The protagonists of crime that shape the portraits of evils and passions as their work of art subvert the action of Stoic principles. They become autonomous constructors and absolute rulers of their world, conceiving themselves both as persons and as literary products. The crafting of evil by Seneca's tragic anti-heroes is thus the binary opposite of the crafting of virtue by the sage, both in his own soul and in those he advises.

---

52 The importance of the recurring image of the bull in Seneca's *Phaedra*, which seems to create a new symbolic interaction between mythological traditions and various aspects of the crime (*nefas*), is emphasized by Petrone 1984, 107–111. See also Davis 1983, 117–120, an essay that shows the allusions to the tragic sexual history of the house of Minos and the force of heredity that lies behind Phaedra's behavior and words.
53 Littlewood 2004, 148.
54 *Ep.* 85.41: "sic sapiens artifex est domandi mala."

Bibliography

Albrecht, Michael von. 2000. "Sulla lingua e lo stile di Seneca." In *Seneca e il suo tempo*, edited by Piergiorgio Parroni, 227–247. Roma: Salerno Editrice.
Albrecht, Michael von. 2008. "Seneca's Language and Style." *Hyperboreus* 14: 68–90.
Armisen-Marchetti, Mireille. 1989. *Sapientiae facies: Étude sur les images de Sénèque*. Paris: Les Belles Lettres.
Bartsch, Shadi. 2009. "Senecan Metaphor and Stoic Self-Instruction." In *Seneca and the Self*, edited by Shadi Bartsch and David Wray, 188–217. Cambridge: Cambridge University Press.
Basore, John W., ed. and trans. 1928–1935. *Seneca, Moral Essays*. 3 vols. London; New York: Heinemann; Putnam.
Biondi, Giuseppe G. 1984. *Il nefas argonautico: Mythos e logos nella Medea di Seneca*. Bologna: Pàtron.
Brink, Charles O. 1982, ed. *Horace on Poetry: Epistles Book II: The Letters to Augustus and Florus*. Cambridge: Cambridge University Press.
Cermatori, Linda. 2010. "L'epistula come monumentum: Seneca e l'autocoscienza letteraria della filosofia (epist. 21, 3-6)." *Athenaeum* 98: 445–465.
Cicero. 1949. *On Invention; The Best Kind of Orator; Topics*. See Hubbell 1949.
Cicu, Luciano. 2005. *Le api, il miele, la poesia: Dialettica intertestuale e sistema letterario greco-latino*. Roma: Università La Sapienza.
Coffey, Michael, and Roland Mayer, eds. 1990. *Lucius Annaeus Seneca, Phaedra*. Cambridge: Cambridge University Press.
Costa, Charles D. N., ed. 1973. *Seneca, Medea*. Oxford: Clarendon Press.
Davis, Peter J. 1983. " 'Vindicat Omnes Natura Sibi:' A Reading of Seneca's Phaedra." *Ramus* 12: 114–127.
Degl'Innocenti Pierini, Rita. 1979. "Cicerone 'demiurgo' dell'oratore ideale: Riflessioni in margine a Orator 7-10." *SIFC* 51: 84–102.
Degl'Innocenti Pierini, Rita. 1990. *Tra Ovidio e Seneca*. Bologna: Pàtron.
Degl'Innocenti Pierini, Rita. 1999. *Tra filosofia e poesia: Studi su Seneca e dintorni*. Bologna: Pàtron.
Degl'Innocenti Pierini, Rita. 2008. *Il parto dell'orsa: Studi su Virgilio, Ovidio e Seneca*. Bologna: Pàtron.
Degl'Innocenti Pierini, Rita. 2012. "Medea tra terra, 'acque' e cielo: Sul prologo della Medea di Seneca." In *"Ibo, ibo qua praerupta protendit iuga / meus Cithaeron:" Paesaggi, luci e ombre nei prologhi tragici senecani: Incontri sulla poesia latina di età imperiale*, 31–50. Bologna: Pàtron.
Donini, Pierluigi. 1979. "L'eclettismo impossibile: Seneca e il platonismo medio." In *Modelli filosofici e letterari. Lucrezio, Orazio, Seneca*, by Pierluigi Donini and Gian Franco Gianotti, 209–242. Bologna: Pitagora.
Dross, Juliette. 2004–2005. "De l'imagination a l'illusion: Quelques aspects de la phantasia chez Quintilien et dans la rhetorique impériale." *Incontri triestini di filologia classica* 4: 273–290.
Edgeworth, Robert J. 1990. "The Eloquent Ghost: Absyrtus in Seneca's Medea." *C&M* 41: 151–161.
Fairclough, Rushton, ed. and trans. 1929. *Horace, Satires; Epistles; Ars Poetica*. London; Cambridge: Heinemann; Harvard University Press. Rpt. 1999.
Fantham, Elaine, ed. and trans. 1982. *Seneca's Troades*. Princeton: Princeton University Press.
Fitch, John G., ed. and trans. 2002. *L. Annaeus Seneca, Tragedies*. Vol. 1: *Hercules; Trojan Women; Phoenician Women; Medea; Phaedra*. Cambridge: Harvard University Press.

Fitch, John G., ed. and trans. 2004. *L. Annaeus Seneca, Tragedies.* Vol. 2: *Oedipus; Agamemnon; Thyestes; Hercules on Oeta; Octavia.* Cambridge: Harvard University Press.
Fitch, John G., and Siobhan McElduff. 2008. "Construction of the Self in Senecan Drama." in *Seneca,* edited by John G. Fitch, 157–180. Oxford: Oxford University Press.
Gianotti, Gian Franco. 1979. "Dinamica dei motivi comuni." In *Modelli filosofici e letterari: Lucrezio, Orazio, Seneca,* by Pierluigi Donini and Gian Franco Gianotti, 126–132. Bologna: Pitagora.
Gigante, Marcello. 2002. *Philodemus in Italy.* Ann Arbor: University of Michigan Press.
Gummere, Richard M. ed. and trans. 1917–1925. *Seneca, Ad Lucilium epistulae morales.* 3 vols. London; Cambridge: Heinemann; Harvard University Press. Rpt. 1996.
Helzle, Martin. 1989. *Publii Ovidii Nasonis, Epistularum ex Ponto liber IV: A Commentary on Poems 1 to 7 and 16.* Hildesheim; Zürich; New York: Olms.
Hine, Harry M. 2005. "Poetic Influence on Prose: The Case of the Younger Seneca." In *Aspects of the Language of Latin Prose,* edited by James N. Adams, Tobias Reinhardt, and Michael Lapidge, 211–237. Oxford: Oxford University Press.
Horace. 1929. *Satires; Epistles; Ars Poetica.* See Fairclough 1929.
Horace. 1957. *Briefe.* See Kiessling and Heinze 1957.
Horace. 1982. *Epistles Book II: The Letters to Augustus and Florus.* See Brink 1982.
Hubbell, Harry M., trans. 1949. *Cicero, On Invention; The Best Kind of Orator; Topics.* London; Cambridge: Heinemann; Harvard University Press. Rpt. 1971.
Inwood, Brad. 2007. "The Importance of Form in Seneca's Philosophical Letters." In *Ancient Letters: Classical and Late Antique Epistolography,* edited by Ruth Morello and Andrew D. Morrison, 133–148. Oxford; New York: Oxford University Press.
Kaster, Robert A., and Martha C. Nussbaum, trans. 2010. *Lucius Annaeus Seneca, Anger, Mercy, Revenge.* Chicago: University of Chicago Press.
Kidd, Ian G., ed. and trans. 1999. *Posidonius.* Vol. 3: *The Translation of the Fragments.* Cambridge: Cambridge University Press.
Kiessling, Adolf G., and Richard Heinze, eds. 1957. *Quintus Horatius Flaccus, Briefe.* Berlin: Weidmann.
Lanza, Diego. 1988–1989. "Finis Tragoediae." *QCTC* 6–7: 147–166.
Laudizi, Giovanni. 2003. *Lucio Anneo Seneca, Lettere a Lucilio. Libro III: epp. XXII–XXIX.* Napoli: Loffredo.
Littlewood, Cedric A. J. 2004. *Self-Representation and Illusion in Senecan Tragedy.* Oxford; New York: Oxford University Press.
Lotito, Gianfranco. 2001. *Suum esse: Forme dell'interiorità senecana.* Bologna: Pàtron.
Marino, Rosanna, ed. and trans. 2005. *Lucio Anneo Seneca: Ad Lucilium epistula 85.* Palermo: Palumbo.
Mazzoli, Giancarlo. 1970. *Seneca e la poesia.* Milano: Ceschina.
Mazzoli, Giancarlo. 1989. "Le 'Epistulae morales ad Lucilium' di Seneca: Valore letterario e filosofico." *ANRW* II 36.3: 1823–1877.
Mazzoli, Giancarlo. 1991. "Effetti di cornice nell'epistolario di Seneca a Lucilio." In *Seneca e la cultura,* edited by Aldo Setaioli, 67–87. Napoli: Edizioni Scientifiche Italiane.
Mazzoli, Giancarlo. 1998. "Seneca e la letteratura." In *Seneca nel bimillenario della nascita,* edited by Sergio Audano, 109–123. Pisa: ETS.
Mazzoli, Giancarlo. 2002. "Medea in Seneca: Il logos del furor." In *Medeas: Versiones de un mito desde Grecia hasta hoy,* edited by Aurora López and Andrés Pociña, 615–625. Granada: Universidad de Granada.

Moretti, Gabriella. 1995. *Acutum dicendi genus: Brevità, oscurità, sottigliezze e paradossi nelle tradizioni retoriche degli Stoici*. Bologna: Pàtron.
Most, Glenn W. 1992. " 'Disiecti membra poetae:' The Rhetoric of Dismemberment in Neronian Poetry." In *Innovations of Antiquity*, edited by Ralph Hexter and Daniel Selden, 391–419. London; New York: Routledge.
Motto, Anna L., and John R. Clark, 1993. *Essays on Seneca*. Frankfurt am Main et al.: Peter Lang.
Motto, Anna L. 2001. *Further Essays on Seneca*, Frankfurt am Main et al.: Peter Lang.
Németi, Annalisa, ed. and trans. 2003. *Lucio Anneo Seneca, Medea*. Pisa: ETS.
Ovid. 1988. *Tristia; Ex Ponto*. See Wheeler 1988.
Petrone, Gianna. 1984. *La scrittura tragica dell'irrazionale: Note di lettura al teatro di Seneca*. Palermo: Palumbo.
Picone, Giusto. 1984. *La fabula e il regno: Studi sul Thyestes di Seneca*. Palermo: Palumbo.
Picone, Giusto. 2002. "La Medea di Seneca come fabula dell'inversione." in *Medeas: Versiones de un mito desde Grecia hasta hoy*, edited by Aurora López and Andrés Pociña, 639–650. Granada: Universidad de Granada.
Posidonius. 1999. See Kidd 1999.
Race, William H. 1982. *The Classical Priamel from Homer to Boethius*. Leiden: Brill.
Scarpat, Guiseppe, ed. 1970. *La lettera 65 di Seneca*. 2nd ed. Brescia: Paideia.
Schiesaro, Alessandro. 2000. "Estetica della tirannia." In *Seneca e il suo tempo: Atti del Convegno internazionale di Roma-Cassino 11–14 novembre 1998*, edited by Piergiorgio Parroni, 135–159. Roma: Salerno.
Seneca. 1917–1925. *Ad Lucilium epistulae morales*. See Gummere 1917–1925.
Seneca. 1928–1935. *Moral Essays*. See Basore 1928–1935.
Seneca. 1970. *La lettera 65 di Seneca*. See Scarpat 1970.
Seneca. 1973. *Medea*. See Costa 1973.
Seneca. 1976. *Agamemnon*. See Tarrant 1976.
Seneca. 1982. *Troades*. See Fantham 1982.
Seneca. 1990. *Phaedra*. See Coffey and Mayer 1990.
Seneca. 2002. *Hercules; Trojan Women; Phoenician Women; Medea; Phaedra*. See Fitch 2002.
Seneca. 2003. *Medea*. See Németi 2003.
Seneca. 2004. *Oedipus; Agamemnon; Thyestes; Hercules on Oeta; Octavia*. See Fitch 2004.
Seneca. 2005. *Ad Lucilium epistula 85*. See Marino 2005.
Seneca. 2010. *Anger, Mercy, Revenge*. See Kaster and Nussbaum 2010.
Setaioli, Aldo. 1988. *Seneca e i Greci: Citazioni e traduzioni nelle opere filosofiche*. Bologna: Pàtron.
Setaioli, Aldo. 2000. *Facundus Seneca: Aspetti della lingua e dell'ideologia senecana*. Bologna: Pàtron.
Tarrant, Richard. J., ed. 1976. *Seneca, Agamemnon: Edited with a Commentary*. Cambridge: Cambridge University Press.
Traina, Alfonso. 1995. *Lo stile "drammatico" del filosofo Seneca*. 5th ed. Bologna: Pàtron.
Viarre, Simone. 1991. "Les Muses de l'exil ou les métamorphoses de la mémoire." In *Ovidio: poeta della memoria*, edited by Giuseppe Papponetti, 117–141. Roma: Herder.
Wheeler, Arthur L. 1988, ed. and trans. *Ovid, Tristia; Ex Ponto*. Cambridge: Harvard University Press.
Wildberger, Jula. 2006. *Seneca und die Stoa: Der Platz des Menschen in der Welt*. 2 vols. Berlin; New York: De Gruyter.

Wulfram, Hartmut. 2008. *Das römische Versepistelbuch: Eine Gattungsanalyse*. Frankfurt am Main: Verlag Antike.

Sententiae in Seneca

Martin T. Dinter
King's College London

Studies of Seneca's tragedies have firmly established the label "rhetorical tragedies" (Boyle 1997, 15–31). My contribution intends to examine what the label "rhetorical" in point of fact means. I will move away from talking about rhetorical tragedy in a generalizing fashion and ask how rhetoric, when pinned down to detailed verbal points, functions to produce the cosmos of these tragedies, Seneca's literary corpus, and last but not least the persona of Seneca tragicus (who was thought to be distinct from Seneca philosophus in the Middle Ages).[1] I will do so by looking at one specific rhetorical device, Seneca's *sententiae*, which appear throughout the tragedies in all shapes and sizes as an essential part of Seneca's poetic technique. In what follows, I examine how Seneca's *sententiae* serve as carriers of his rhetoric and make themselves indispensable for creating discourse, for characterizing the personae in Senecan tragedies, and for showcasing Seneca tragicus as well as philosophus. I propose reading Seneca's *sententiae* as the readers' digest, the best of, essential Seneca – and, most particularly, as Seneca's legacy to his text.

The slogan "rhetorical" flags the notion of verbal virtuosity, while warning of the dangers of vain declamation and lack of substance.[2] However, attempts to rescue Seneca's tragedies from the prejudice that Seneca falls among certain authors (such as Lucan) who have "rhetoric to offer rather than poetry" have led the way in rehabilitating some of Seneca's artful rhetorical devices.[3] What has often been ignored is that Quintilian's judgment on Lucan, which I have taken as exemplary for later attitudes towards literature peppered with *sententiae*, must be considered more compliment than rebuke, as it is part of a rhetorical treatise (Russell 2001 at Quint. *Inst.* 10.1.90). Indeed Quintilian actually states that an author can

---

1 Mayer 1994; Ker 2006, 19–41.
2 See Leo's damming indictment (1878, 158): "istae vero non sunt tragoediae sed declamationes ad traegodiae amussim compositae et in actus deductae."
3 Cf. Boyle 1977 and Quintilian's often repeated *dictum* on Seneca's nephew Lucan (*Inst.* 10.1.90): "magis oratoribus quam poetis imitandus." Translations of Quintilian are taken from Russell 2001.

seem "distinguished for his *sententiae*."[4] By Seneca's day, however, the term *sententia* had developed from its first-century BCE meaning "precept," "maxim," or "generally accepted commonplace." Already in the writings of Seneca's father, Seneca the Elder, it designates the format of both gnomic generalizations and penetrating epigrams.[5] The function of the former category, *gnomai*, when defined as generalizing statements about particular human actions or the gods, is akin to that of modern-day proverbs (Boeke 2007, 13). They "persuade the listener and move him to correct action by utterance of familiar, unassailable wisdom" (Russo 1997, 57). It comes as no surprise then that the contents of *gnomai* cover human experience, as can be seen from a modern edition of Menander's *gnomai* that is not ordered alphabetically as in the manuscript tradition but instead grouped by themes, such as "virtue," "wedlock," "old age," "women," "death," "happiness," and "modesty" (Jäkel 1986, 116). The same applies to the ancient collection of alphabetically ordered *sententiae* from the mimes of Publilius Syrus, in which the reader can also make out recurrent *topoi* (Duff and Fantham 1996). Indeed, some of Publilius' *sententiae* provide variation on the same theme. Below I provide a small selection focusing on avarice:[6]

> Avarus ipse miseriae causa est suae.
> The mean man is cause of his own misery. (A 14)
>
> Avarum facile capias, ubi non sis item.
> You want to catch a mean man? Just be generous! (A 21)
>
> Avarus nisi cum moritur, nihil recte facit.
> The mean man only does well when he dies. (A 23)
>
> Avarus damno potius quam sapiens dolet.
> Loss hurts the mean man more than the wise. (A 25)
>
> Avaro quid mali optes nisi: vivat diu?
> You want to curse a mean man? Say: Long may you live! (A 26)
>
> Avidum oportet esse neminem, minime senem.
> No one ought to be mean, especially not the old. (A 35)
>
> Avaro acerba poena natura est sua. (A 46, cf. A 14)
>
> Avaro non est vita, sed mors longior.
> The mean man does not live, but rather dies slowly. (A 47)

The gnomic form of the *sententia* subsequently retreats more and more in favor of rhetorical pointed expressions which are thought up to fit a parti-

---

4 Quint. *Inst.* 10.1.90: "Lucanus ardens et concitatus et *sententiis clarissimus*" – "Lucan is ardent, passionate, and particularly distinguished for his *sententiae*."
5 Sinclair 1995, 120–122 outlines the history of the term *sententia*.
6 Translations are my own unless indicated otherwise.

cular context and thus do not feature universal gnomic force.[7] From the selection of Publilius above we may take A 14 and A 46, which both express the same thought in a different wording as precursors of the rhetorical practice to create incidental or casual redefinitions of current values rather than complete gnomic statements. This prevailing rhetorical type of *sententia* coined in accordance with the needs of each specific occasion employs a large variety of stylistic features. These are, in the order in which Quintilian discusses them, surprise, allusion, transfer from one context into another, repetition, and finally contrast of opposites as well as comparison.[8] In his discussion Quintilian demonstrates how *sententiae* are incorporated and firmly attached to the body of the text.[9] He construes *sententiae* as the most beautiful parts of the textual body and compares them to eyes: "Personally I think these highlights are in a sense the eyes of eloquence."[10] Quintilian also presents the notion that *sententiae* are extracts from an author's mind. They can even convey something of the author himself according to an etymology he provides.[11]

> Sententiam veteres quod animo sensissent vocaverant. Id cum est apud oratores frequentissimum, tum etiam in usu cotidiano quasdam reliquias habet.
>
> The ancients used the word *sententia* to mean what they felt in their minds. This meaning is very common in the orators, and there are some vestiges of it in everyday usage. (Quint. *Inst.* 8.5.1).

What is more, Aristotle in his discussion of the use of *gnomai* in *Rhetoric* 2.21.16 suggests that there might be a relation between the moral character of the author and the ethical quality of his *gnomai*: "If the *gnomai* are morally sound, they make the speaker appear to be a man of morally sound

---

7   Cf. Sussman 1978, 36 and Kirchner 2001, 38–39. The latter promotes a "purist" approach and objects to the contamination of general *gnomai* with rhetorical *sententiae*. His study therefore confines itself to examining gnomic *sententiae*; cf. Kirchner 2001, 44–48.
8   Cf. Quint. *Inst.* 8.5.15: "ex inopinato;" 8.5.16: "sunt et alio relata;" 8.5.17: "et aliunde petita, id est in alium locum ex alio tralata;" 8.5.17: "geminatio;" 8.5.18: "ex contrariis;" 8.5.19: "cum aliqua comparatione clarescit."
9   Cf. Quint. *Inst.* 8.5.34, quoted in the following note, and also Carey 1995, 96–99 on the highly personalized poetic voice of Pindar, which finds its expression in pronouncing *gnomai* as first person statements – not unlike personal thoughts. Pindar thus assumes a moral character and establishes the speaker's authority.
10 Quint. *Inst.* 8.5.34: "Ego vero haec lumina orationis velut oculos quosdam esse eloquentiae credo." On the beauty of the eyes, cf. Russell's 2001 commentary on the passage. In the following sentence Quintilian carries this textual body imagery even further when arguing against an excess of *sententiae*: "Sed neque oculos esse toto corpore velim, ne cetera membra officium suum perdant" – "But I don't want there to be eyes all over the body, lest the other organs lose their function".
11 Already Anaximenes (*Ars Rhetorica ad Alexandrum* 11.1) defines *gnomai* as expressions of an author's opinion.

character," for "anyone who uses a [*gnome*] makes a declaration in general terms about the objects of moral purpose (or preference)."[12]

Consequently, *sententiae* not only stand out and attract the attention of the reader through their rhetorical beauty but might also provide access to the voice of the author in the text. This is not to mean that I will be retreating to naïve biographism in search of the author as moralist when relating *sententiae* to thoughts of the author. Rather I would like to emphasize that whatever skeptical view we might take as modern literary critics on this matter, it is a perspective that derives from ancient literary criticism itself and thus represents a point of view, indeed an interpretative convention, with which the ancient audience might have been expected to be familiar.

As we will see, Seneca has fully absorbed both the gnomic and the rhetorical form of *sententiae* into his tragedies.[13] This results in a high frequency of paradox and hyperbole, figures which are characteristic of Seneca's rhetorical style in his tragedies and made them popular objects of rhetorical study. At the rhetoricians' schools of imperial Rome "the poets were studied not only for examples of rhetorical techniques but especially for examples of epigram (*sententiae*)."[14] Epigrams from epic functioned as "cultural capital," eagerly excerpted by the studious reader (Keith 2000, 17). Accordingly, Seneca's tragedies can thus also be used as a gold mine for *sententiae*. The *Controversiae* of Seneca the Elder show that passing on rhetorical pearls from one generation of orators to the next and to future generations is high on the agenda.[15] Seneca the Elder has turned to this subject at the request of his sons and offers them rhetorical specimens for examination and imitation (*Con.* 1 praef. 6). Like so much else in Roman

---

12   Quoted after Sinclair 1995, 49.
13   Kunz 1897 provides a wealth of examples, which I have mined for this contribution.
14   Keith 2000, 17. Furthermore, at the beginning of the standard rhetorical training stood exercises, "in which the students worked up an anecdote climaxing in a pithy saying, elaborated a proverb or apophthegm, and composed a fable and a simple narrative" (Fantham 2004, 87). On the poetic afterlife of single and often also fragmented lines of Vergil in patchwork texts, so-called *centos*, see McGill 2005.
15   Cf. Sen. *Con.* 1.22: "Nec his argumenta subtexam, ne et modum excedam et propositum, cum vos sententias audire velitis et quidquid ab illis abduxero molestum futurum sit" – "But I won't add the arguments that went with the [*sententiae*]. That would be excessive and irrelevant, for it is the *sententiae* you want to hear, and any space I deprive them of will annoy you" (trans. Winterbottom 1974). Cf. further Sen. *Con.* 2. praef. 5: "Scio futurum ut auditis eius sententiis cupiatis multas audire" – "I know that when you hear his epigrams you will want to hear many," and also *Con.* 7. praef. 9: "Video quid velitis: sententias potius audire quam iocos. Fiat: audite sententias in hac ipsa controversia dictas" – "I can see what you want: to hear epigrams, not jokes. Very well, you may hear the epigrams that were spoken on this very *controversia*."

elite culture, *sententiae* run in families. So "close parallels between turns of phrase in the younger Seneca's works and *sententiae* recorded in his father's anthology" abound.[16] It can come as no surprise then that Lucan, too, shared in this family tradition.[17]

Seneca employs *sententiae* frequently in the *peroratio* ("summing up") of a monologue in his tragedies, so as to go out with a bang. Indeed, Quintilian compares the use of final *sententiae* to the concluding request for applause in the comedies and tragedies of old (*plodite*): The end of a speech is the place to use grand and ornate thoughts to move the audience.[18] If self-authored, their polished style profiles the author's education, while if they are copied into a text, they display the author's wide reading.[19] Since the right question to ask about a *sententia* "is not whether it is true in any absolute sense, but whether it is convincing in its own particular context" (Sinclair 1995, 35), *sententiae* help to furnish a plausible ethical basis for the presentation of the author's views. They oblige the reader to register events from a very particular and often partisan perspective.[20] Hence *sententiae* partake in an author's specific social ethos and, as we have seen above, were even thought in antiquity to offer a window into the author's mind. By depicting values and commonly shared beliefs, *sententiae* help to construct the world of the text for the reader. Consequently, *sententiae* place their user in a position of authority, which often finesses further justification. Correspondingly, in one of his *Letters*, Seneca fervidly defends the use of *sententiae* as engines of practical ethics:

> Quis autem negabit feriri quibusdam praeceptis efficaciter etiam imperitissimos? Velut his brevissimis vocibus, sed multum habentibus ponderis: "Nil nimis."

---

16 Fairweather 1981, 28 points to Rolland 1906, Preisendanz 1908, and Rayment 1969. Cf. also Sussman 1978, 157–158 and Danesi Marioni 1999. Many of the contributions to Gualandri and Mazzoli 2003 examine the political and cultural role played by the *Annaei* family. For Lucan, cf. Sussman 1978, 159–160. Bonner 1966, 263–264 points to possible influences of Seneca the Elder on Lucan and also unearths the roots of some of Lucan's *sententiae* in Seneca the Younger's writings.
17 For *sententiae* in Lucan, see Dinter 2012, 89–118.
18 Cf. Quint. *Inst.* 6.1.52: "[...] et, cum sit maxima pars epilogi amplificatio, verbis atque *sententiis* uti licet magnificis et ornatis. Tunc est commovendum theatrum, cum ventum est ad ipsum illud quo veteres tragoediae comoediaeque cluduntur, 'plodite' " – "[...] and, as the main business of an Epilogue is Amplification, we can use grand and ornate words and thoughts. The moment to move the audience is when we come to the phrase with which the old tragedies and comedies end: 'Now give us your applause'."
19 Accordingly, Sinclair 1995, 122–132 reads Seneca's *Controversiae* as a tool for the social advancement of the author's family – displaying the father's erudition and equipping the sons to put theirs on display.
20 Cf. Sinclair 1995, 6 and ch. 3 for a discussion of legalistic rhythms in *sententiae* and Tacitus' role as nomothetic historian.

> "Avarus animus nullo satiatur lucro." "Ab alio exspectes, alteri quod feceris." Haec cum ictu quodam audimus, nec ulli licet dubitare aut interrogare "quare?" Adeo etiam *sine ratione* ipsa veritas ducit.
>
> Moreover, who can deny that even the most inexperienced are effectively struck by the force of certain precepts? For example, by such brief but weighty saws as: "Nothing in excess." "The greedy mind is satisfied by no gains." "You must expect to be treated by others as you yourself have treated them." We receive a sort of shock when we hear such sayings; no one ever thinks of doubting them or of asking "Why?" So strongly, indeed, does mere truth, *unaccompanied by reason*, attract us. (Sen. *Ep.* 94.43, trans. Gummere, my emphasis)[21]

In short, employing *sententiae* economizes on argumentation: Sententious force renders further explanation unnecessary. In addition, this very force makes sure that no reader is left unclear about the premises of the text.

Finally, there is also a competitive element in employing *sententiae*, for "from Aristophanes to Quintilian, we repeatedly come across images of combat and struggle in the description and use of [...] *sententiae*" (Sinclair 1995, 41). This notion is most prominent in the writings of Seneca the Elder, who vividly describes clashes between declaimers, whose acuity and pugnacity rival that of gladiatorial encounters.[22] What is more, even the authorial self of Seneca the Elder is represented as staging gladiatorial bouts.[23] When applying this imagery to Seneca the Younger's tragedies, we will see how powerfully *sententiae* assist the tragic personae in fighting their literary cause.

What is more, these *sententiae*, even if not taken from one single work, create for Seneca, their author, a particular persona; they flesh him out through their consistency across his oeuvre and draw an image of Seneca tragicus that seems surprisingly different from the voice of Seneca philosophus. For according to ancient views *sententiae*, when pieced together, serve to convey a sense of an author, a figure behind the aphorisms with his own distinctive personal agenda. Mayer, in his work on the literary persona in antiquity, shows how this concept (alien as it might seem to the modern reader, who is used to distinguishing author and literary mask) might work in practice, using examples from Horace:

> In literary contexts persona is used by the Romans to refer both to the "person" who is imagined as speaking (say, Alfius) and to the writer (say, Horace). However disparate the characters of writer and speaker, nonetheless the Romans tended to believe that they could see through the mask: to parody theological terms, they detected only a distinction of person, not a distinction of being. The commentator

---

21　The final *sententia* has been identified as Publilius *Frg* 2. We can see here how Seneca himself excerpts. For a discussion of Seneca *Letters* 94 and 95 focused on the connections between *sententia* and *praeceptum*, cf. Sinclair 1995, 91–96.

22　Sinclair 1995, 123–128 offers ample documentation.

23　Cf. Sen. *Con.* 4. praef. 1 and Fairweather 1981, 29–30.

Porfyrio, therefore, was sure that the moneylender Alfius in the second *Epode* was really voicing Horace's own opinion: *quod vult intellegi neminem* [n.b.] *nescire quid iucunditatis habeat vita rustica.* [...] Roman readers seem generally reluctant to distinguish sharply between the writer's own character and that of his *personae*. (Mayer 2003, 65–66)

When transferring this concept to Senecan tragedy, a scene from *Thyestes* springs to mind in which an assistant (*satelles*) and the tyrant Atreus lead a sententious discourse on kingship (*Thy*. 204–219). In the past this passage seems to have been read as representing the emperor Nero talking to his tutor Seneca.[24]

SATELLES: Fama te populi nihil
adversa terret? ATREVS: Maximum hoc regni bonum est,
quod facta domini cogitur populus sui
tam ferre quam laudare. SATELLES: Quos cogit metus
laudare, eosdem reddit inimicos metus.
At qui favoris gloriam veri petit,
animo magis quam voce laudari uolet.
ATREVS: Laus vera et humili saepe contingit viro,
non nisi potenti falsa. Quod nolunt velint.
SATELLES: Rex velit honesta: nemo non eadem volet.
ATREVS: Ubicumque tantum honesta dominanti licent,
precario regnatur. SATELLES: Ubi non est pudor
nec cura iuris sanctitas pietas fides,
instabile regnum est. ATREVS: Sanctitas pietas fides
privata bona sunt; qua iuvat reges eant.
SATELLES: Nefas nocere vel malo fratri puta.

ASSISTANT: You have no fear at all of hostile talk among the people?
ATREUS (king of Mycene): The greatest advantage of kingship is that the people are obliged to praise as well as to endure their lord's doings.
ASSISTANT: When fear makes them praise, fear also turns them hostile.
But one who seeks the benefit of true goodwill will want to be praised from the heart rather than the tongue.
ATREUS: Even a poor man can earn sincere praise, false praise comes only to the mighty. For the people are made to want what they do not want.
ASSISTANT: The king should want what is right: then everybody will want the same.
ATREUS: Where a lord is only allowed what is right, he reigns by entreaty.
ASSISTANT: Without shame, law, righteousness, goodness, and loyalty rule is unstable.
ATREUS: Righteousness, goodness, and loyalty are private values: king's should go where they please.
ASSISTANT: Consider it sacrilege even to harm a treacherous brother.
(Sen. *Thy*. 204–219, translation adapted from Miller 1917)

---

24 The pseudo-Senecan *Octavia* plays out this reading at length by staging an exchange between Seneca and Nero at *Oct*. 440–592. See Ferri 2003, 70.

As we can see from the passage above, Seneca uses *sententiae* as an opportunity to construct a marked rhetorical discourse. He provides us with a condensed *sententiae*-only exchange that reveals the protagonists' moral positions. Atreus and his assistant battle each other by expressing their moral maxims in the form of *sententiae* which lay down the moral laws of Senecan tragedy. Picone in his discussion of this passage recognizes the pivotal role *sententiae* play in Seneca's Thyestes and comments:

> Sul piano formale, la delineazione di una vera e propria teoria del regnum viene attuata mediante l'impiego della sententia che [...] e la cellula stilistica di cui Seneca si serve. Atreo e il satelles espongono le loro contrapposte concezioni del potere utilizzando brevi massime [...]. (Picone 1984, 45)

Recurrent vocabulary connects maxim with anti-maxim in this duel of words, and the entire passage reads very much like one of Seneca the Elder's declamatory excerpts featuring a selection of *sententiae* arguing for and against a case.

Following the notion that *sententiae* always contain something of the poet himself, crystallizing his line of thought, we can read Seneca's *sententiae* as his very essence. If this ancient reading practice is adopted, Seneca's moralizing is not confined to his philosophical writings but his *sententiae*, too, demonstrate and enhance the (perturbed) values of his tragic cosmos. As we shall see in my analysis below, Seneca succeeds in forming a system with his *sententiae* that undergirds the ideology of his tragedies and simultaneously lends him presence in his own text. If we subscribe to the ancient view that *sententiae* flesh out the voice of the authorial persona, we will arrive at reading Seneca's *sententiae* as reflecting the authorial self within the tragedies but also constituting, as we will see later, Seneca's claim to fame.

In what follows I propose a reading of Seneca through his sententiousness. For his *sententiae* have more than a purely formal or structural function and make an important contribution to the meaning and unity of the tragedies. They connect different segments of a tragedy (or even one tragedy to another) by patterning the text and by highlighting particular ethical arguments. In this way they help to map out Seneca's tragic cosmos. *Sententiae* also allow Seneca to transcend the immediacy of his poem. In a culture where a text's excerptability was a matter of course, where audiences would eagerly scan texts and anticipate finding *sententiae* that could be added to their own collections, Seneca could even expect a condensed version of his tragedies put together from excerpted *sententiae* only, along the lines of the anthology compiled by his father, Seneca the Elder, or the recycled mimes of Publilius Syrus.²⁵ For fame and afterlife, that contemporary of Caesar now depends solely on a collection of *sententiae* extracted from his plays.²⁶ Studied as a school text in antiquity and praised by the younger Seneca and Gellius, they were still popular in the nineteenth century as edifying reading.²⁷

Desbordes imagines Publilius' *sententiae* re-contextualized as lines of a play and points to the important function they will have fulfilled in the author's mimes:

> If the *sententiae* could figure in the mimes by way of solemn or mocking remarks in the action of the play, moreover, if they, when the opportunity presented itself, could play on the particular situation of the enunciation, this seems linked to the fact that the *sententia* marks a kind of rupture in the discourse in which it appears and that it makes a transition from the particular to the general.²⁸

I thus ask: Might "*sententiae* only, à la Publilius Syrus" be a reading strategy usefully applied to Seneca's oeuvre as well?²⁹ Are Seneca's

---

25 The criticism leveled against Cicero's early speeches in Tacitus' *Dialogus* 22.3 embodies this idea: "Nihil excerpere, nihil referre possis, et velut in rudi aedificio, firmus sane paries et duraturus, sed non satis expolitus et splendens" – "There is nothing which you can pick out or quote, and the style is like a rough building, the wall of which indeed is strong and lasting, but not particularly polished and bright." Cf. also what Tacitus lets M. Aper report about students of rhetoric: "Non solum audire sed etiam referre domum aliquid inlustre et dignum memoria volunt; traduntque in vicem ac saepe in colonias ac provincias suas scribunt, sive sensus aliquis arguta et brevi sententia effulsit, sive locus exquisito et poetico cultu enituit" – "They are anxious not merely to hear but also to carry back home some brilliant passage worthy of remembrance. They tell it one to another, and often mention it in letters to their colonies and provinces, whether it is a reflection lighted up by a neat and pithy phrase, or a passage bright with choice and poetic ornament" (*Dial.* 20.4; this and the previous translation by Church and Brodribb 1942).
26 Giancotti 1967, 318–338 suggests various origins for this collection in the first century CE: rhetorical schooltext, grammatical gradus, or introduction to ethics and philosophy. Publilius is mentioned by Cicero at *Fam.* 12.18.2 and *Att.* 14.2 and Seneca the Elder at *Con.* 7.3.8, who quotes several of his *sententiae*, as does Gellius 17.14. Trimalchio (at Petr. 55) offers 16 pseudo-Publilian *sententiae*. Macrobius *Sat.* 2.7 provides Publilius' biography garnished with a wealth of *sententiae*.
27 Cf. Benz 2001. Seneca himself quotes one of Publilius Syrus' *sententiae* in *Ep.* 94.43. Knecht 1986, 53–55 points out that the frequent use of paronomasia in *sententiae* (as well as proverbs) made them useful school texts for teaching "beginners' Latin" in antiquity.
28 Desbordes 1979, 75: "Si les sentences ont pu figurer dans des mimes à titre de commentaires sérieux ou malicieux de l'action théâtrale, si de plus, à l'occasion, elles ont pu jouer sur la situation particulière de l'énonciation, cela semble lié au fait que la sentence marque une sorte de rupture dans le discours où elle apparaît et qu'elle fait passer du particulier au général."
29 That Seneca the Younger was aware of Publilius is demonstrated by the eight instances which Pare-Rey 2009, 204–207 lists as *loci* where Seneca the Younger

sententiae meaningful outside their immediate context? What would we as readers gain by lining them up as a chain of reflections in an extended series?[30]

There certainly are recurrent vocabulary and themes in Seneca's *sententiae*, as will become apparent from the examples cited below. Kunz's nineteenth-century study groups Seneca's *sententiae* into two main categories: [1] deficits of human life and [2] the correct way to lead one's life (Kunz 1897, 2). These two categories are then divided into numerous subcategories, such as

[1a] the inclination to be evil (sin and redemption – *in tyrannos* – belligerence and its consequences)
[1b] moral shortcomings and weaknesses (grief and pain – fear and anxiety – passion and torment – the power of habit – the power of love – fickleness of youth)
[1c] the limits of human experience (dependence on gods and fate – ever changing fortune – death)

[2a] ethical maxims
[2b] the golden mean
[2c] ways of wisdom

We will see from the material below how versatile the forms are that a *sententia* can take. Seneca's oeuvre offers a large variety, ranging from the gnomic and proverbial, which have a more general content, to highly rhetorical ones coined solely to shine for a brief moment in their individual context. For the moment, we shall mainly concentrate on the gnomic ones. But I shall make a suggestion on how to incorporate the rhetorical *sententiae* into my argument below. A further caveat to consider is that dramatic genres themselves pass on a tradition of *sententiae* down the line from Greek into Latin (Dangel 2011). We should thus keep in mind that Senecan tragedy brimming with *sententiae* is not Seneca's own novel invention but rather constitutes the rhetorical culmination of a development, the foundations of which were already laid centuries earlier in Greek comedy and tragedy.[31] Let me now look at a selection of *sententiae* (taken from the list provided by Kunz 1897) grouped around

---

    employs Publilius' *sententiae*: Sen. *Tranq. an.* 11.8–9; *Marc.* 9.5; *Ep.* 8.8; 9.21–22; 94.28–29; 94.43; 108.8–9 and 11–12.

30 Rieks 1978, 367 identifies recurrent topics in Publilius' output, such as life and death, change of fortune, justice and injustice, wisdom and stupidity, freedom and slavery. The latter pair he connects to Publilius' biography, his rise from slavery to freedom. Duff and Fantham 1996, 1276, however, remark: "One would not expect a common ethical standard among maxims spoken by different characters in a mime. Some contradict others, as proverbs often do. […] many advocate selfish pragmatism […]."

31 Mauduit and Paré-Rey 2011 have assembled contributions that showcase this tradition from Greek tragedy onwards.

some topics central to both Seneca's tragedies and Seneca's philosophical writings in order to explore whether we can identify any overlapping concerns.[32]

Death

Seneca's philosophical writings aim to deliver mental tranquillity by eradicating the fear of death.[33] According to Seneca, death together with all other external evils *and* values, such as health, wealth, and family, ought not to exert any influence on our mental well-being. By knowing our place in the universe, we may begin to free ourselves from the fear of death and the resulting incapacitating behavior and vices in our lives so that we become indifferent to death. Self-knowledge will lead to self-mastery, and overcoming the fear of pain, violence, cruelty, and death itself allows one to achieve the sublime mental tranquillity of the sage. Death is inevitable, unpredictable, and fated and, thus, subject to chance. But by learning to acquiesce to fate willingly and to face death, the Stoic *proficiens* ("progressor" toward virtue) can overcome chance, his prime adversary, and gain mastery of himself.

Below I list a selection of *sententiae* from across the tragedies devoid of context and without even denoting the speaker. This presentation will demonstrate that these single sentences link into wider issues about death and dying that feature throughout Seneca's *œuvre*. As the personae of Seneca philosophus and Seneca tragicus have risen out medieval readings of the Senecan corpus, I include examples from tragedies nowadays believed to be spurious but which medieval readers must have taken for actual works of Seneca. I have indicated some overarching concerns with the help of subheadings; categories, however, tend to overlap.

No man is safe from death

Prima mors miseros fugit.
Death is the first to shun the unhappy. (*Tro.* 954)

Felices sequeris, mors, miseros fugis.
You follow the fortunate, Death, but shun the wretched. (*Her. O.* 122)

Quam tenuis anima vinculo pendet levi.
How frail a life hangs on such fragile bond. (*Tro.* 952)

---

32 All translations of Senecan plays adapted from Fitch 2002 and 2004 (with the exception of Sen. *Thy.* 204–219, quoted on p. 325).
33 See a concise overview over Seneca's philosophical writings in Mannering 2013, who also provides further bibliography.

Animam senilem mollis exsolvit sopor.
A gentle sleep released his aged spirit. (*Oed.* 788)

Quam varia leti genera mortalem trahunt
carpuntque turbam.
How varied are the kinds of death that ravage
and deplete the human stock! (*Phaed.* 475–476)

Death is not necessarily an evil

Interim poena est mori,
sed saepe donum
Sometimes death is punishment,
but often a gift. (*Her. O.* 930)

Mortem misericors saepe pro vita dabit.
Often a compassionate man will grant death rather than life. (*Tro.* 329)

Mors misera non est commori cum quo velis.
To die with someone you want to die with is no wretched death. (*Ag.* 202)

Mortem aliquid ultra est? Vita, si cupias mori.
Is anything worse than death? Life, if you long to die. (*Ag.* 996)

Felix iacet quicumque quos odit premit.
To crush those one hates is to lie happy in death. (*Her. O.* 350)

Mecum omnia abeant. Trahere, cum pereas, libet.
Let everything fall along with me. It is sweet to wreak havoc as you perish. (*Med.* 428)

Felix quisquis bello moriens
omnia secum consumpta tulit.
Blessed he who dying in war
takes with him his whole world destroyed. (*Tro.* 162)

Mors optima est perire lacrimandum suis.
To die mourned by loved ones is the best of deaths. (*Phaed.* 881)

Optanda mors est sine metu mortis mori.
A death to be prayed for is to die without fear of death. (*Tro.* 869)

Suicide

Ubique mors est. Optime hoc cavit deus.
Eripere vitam nemo non homini potest;
at nemo mortem: mille ad hanc aditus patent.
Everywhere there is death. God has made excellent provision.
Anyone can deprive a person of life, but no one of death.
A thousand doorways open to it. (*Phoen.* 151–153)

Quicumque misero forte dissuadet mori,
crudelis ille est.
Anyone who attempts to dissuade the wretched from dying
acts cruelly. (*Her. O.* 929–930)

Prohibere nulla ratio periturum potest
ubi qui mori constituit et debet mori.
No consideration can prevent someone from dying
who has both the resolve and the duty to die. (*Phaed.* 265)

Death as benefactor

Fortem facit vicina libertas senem.
The closeness of freedom makes the aged brave. (*Phaed.* 139)

Mors innocentes sola deceptos facit.
Only death establishes the innocence of those who were deceived. (*Her. O.* 890)

Morte sanandum est scelus.
Crime must be healed by death. (*Her. F.* 1262)

Though hardly more than a sketch these few examples demonstrate how certain topics recur throughout Seneca's oeuvre and how Seneca has woven a discourse on death, dying, and what it means to die into the texture of his tragedies. It stretches out across the entire tragic corpus and links together the plays by moral discourse. While Seneca does not showcase a coherent moral system, no reader will be able to escape the pull of his *sententiae* and the constant hail of rhetorical blows Seneca directs at his audience. The next section collects *sententiae* that put on display a further thematic complex central to Senecan tragedy.

Tyranny

Seneca's tragedies and some of his prose treatises have been read in relation to his role as tutor to the young emperor Nero. The sources concede a good *quinquennium* (a period of five years) before Nero, the monstrous tyrant, was unleashed with the death of his mother Agrippina. In those years, the promising young emperor still followed the guidance of his mother and tutors. Some of Seneca's prose output, such as the treatises *On Clemency* (*De clementia*) and *On Anger* (*De ira*), has thus been directly related to educating the young man in the manner of a "prince's mirror."[34] As a result, we can establish literature that centers on the emperor early in Nero's life both with celebratory anticipation of his reign, such as the *Apocolocyntosis* and Calpurnius' *Eclogues*,[35] and with educational support, such as Seneca's treatises. Seneca's tragedies, too, have something to contribute to this debate as they contain a marked discourse on tyranny within

---

34 Braund 2008, 78 for the literary genre and Mannering 2013.
35 See Whitton 2013 and Henderson 2013, who point to very explicit allusions to a golden age in both these texts.

their *sententiae*, as we have already seen from the *Thyestes* passage quoted above (p. 325f.). Below I shall provide a selection of *sententiae* that further furnish this debate.

> Non capit regnum duos.
> A throne has no room for two. (*Thy.* 444)

> Ubicumque tantum honesta dominanti licent,
> precario regnatur.
> Where a lord is allowed only what is right,
> he reigns by entreaty. (*Thy.* 214–215)

> Aequum atque iniquum regis imperium feras.
> You must endure a king's command, just or unjust. (*Med.* 195)

> Id esse regni maximum pignus putant,
> si quidquid aliis non licet solis licet.
> They think it is the greatest assurance of their kingship,
> that they alone are permitted what others are not permitted. (*Ag.* 271–272)

> Nec me fugit, quam durus et veri insolens
> ad recta flecti regius nolit tumor.
> I am well aware how obdurate and unused to the truth
> is royal pride, how unwilling to be corrected. (*Phaed.* 136–137)

> Qui morte cunctos luere supplicium iubet
> nescit tyrannos esse.
> A man who imposes the death penalty on all
> does not know how to be a tyrant. (*Her. F.* 511–512)

> Rudis est tyrannus morte qui poenam exigit.
> One who punishes by death is an inept tyrant. (*Ag.* 995)

> Qui vult amari, languida regnat manu.
> One who wants to be loved rules with a feeble hand. (*Phoen.* 659)

> Odia qui nimium timet
> regnare nescit: regna custodit metus.
> A king unduly afraid of being hated
> does not know how to rule: a throne is safeguarded by fear. (*Oed.* 703–704)

> Regnare non vult, esse qui invisus timet.
> He who fears to be hated has no appetite for ruling. (*Phoen.* 654)

> Ars prima regni est posse invidiam pati.
> The foremost art of ruling is being able to suffer envy. (*Her. F.* 353)

> Quod civibus tenere te invitis scias
> Strictus tuetur ensis
> With the sword you must guard
> what you willingly hold against the will of the people. (*Her. F.* 343–344)

> Ferrum tuetur principem.
> Steel is the emperor's protection. (*Oct.* 456)

> Sanctitas pietas fides
> privata bona sunt; qua iuvat reges eant.

Righteousness, goodness, and loyalty
are private values: kings should go where they please. (*Thy.* 217–218)

Malus est minister regii imperii pudor.
Shame is a poor servant of royal authority. (*Phaed.* 430)

Quod Iovi hoc regi licet.
What is Jove's right, is a king's right, too. (*Her. F.* 489)

Imperia pretio quolibet constant bene.
Power is well purchased at any price. (*Phoen.* 664)

Tyranny and the ramifications of absolute power are clearly a major concern across the tragedies and permeate the thoughts of the tragic personae. Some of these *sententiae* even express identical thoughts and are rhetorical variations of each other. When taken out of their context and lined up as above, they help us visualize the thematic net that binds together the *corpus* of Senecan tragedy.

As dark as the world of Senecan tragedy might seem after wading through this wealth of examples there is also more edifying fare to be had, as I shall briefly outline in the section below.

Virtues

Seneca's writings conceptualize the philosopher withdrawn from public life. He simultaneously proposes and showcases a singular self that stands in virtuous autonomy. The philosopher can become a role model by example as well as by precept. The wise person benefits his community by his example and his pedagogy (*Tranq. an.* 3.3), while attracting the best sort of friends (*Tranq. an.* 3.6).[36] We will see in the examples that follow that the *sententiae* found in Seneca's tragedies are not merely gloomy and cynical but also reflect a tradition of upbeat moral edification. Below I shall put together examples for just a small selection of topics:

Shame and Remorse

Nam sera numquam est ad bonos mores via.
For the path to goodness it is never too late. (*Ag.* 242)

Redire cum perit nescit pudor.
Shame once lost cannot return. (*Ag.* 113)

Quod non vetat lex, hoc vetat fieri pudor.
What law does not forbid, a sense of restraint forbids. (*Tro.* 334)

---

36 See Mannering 2013 with further bibliography.

Justice

Id facere laus est quod decet, non quod licet.
Praise lies in doing what one should not what one can. (*Oct.* 454)

Minimum decet libere cui multum licet.
He who has much right should please himself last. (*Tro.* 336)

Qui non vetat peccare, cum possit, iubet.
One who does not forbid wrongdoing when he has the power, commands it. (*Tro.* 291)

Qui statuit aliquid parte inaudita altera,
aequum licet statuerit, haud aequus fuit.
He who decides an issue without hearing the other side
has not been just, however just the decision. (*Med.* 199–200)

Patiare potius ipse, quam facias, scelus.
One should suffer crime oneself, rather than commit it. (*Phoen.* 494)

Golden Mean

Feriunt celsos fulmina colles.
The lofty hills are struck by lightning. (*Ag.* 96)

Quatiunt altas saepe procellae
aut evertit Fortuna domos.
Towering houses are often shaken by storms
or overturned by Fortune. (*Oct.* 897–898)

Corpora morbis maiora patent.
Larger physiques are prone to disease. (*Ag.* 97)

Quidquid excessit modum
pendet instabili loco.
All that strays from the mean
is poised in an unsteady place. (*Oed.* 909–910)

Quisquis medium defugit iter
stabili numquam tramite curret.
Those who avoid the middle path
will never run a stable course. (*Her. O.* 675–676)

From these final examples emerges an image of Seneca tragicus that seems to come close to the voice we hear in his letters and philosophical writings. While I would not want to recommend reading the tragedies alongside the philosophical writings as some kind of illustration, taking a closer look at Seneca's *sententiae* nevertheless allows us to reconcile the two literary personae of Seneca philosophus and Seneca tragicus to a certain extent. As different as the tragedies seem compared with Seneca's philosophical *œuvre*, they provide a discourse on related topics, and as we will see below, they were mined for their edifying content.[37]

Morales has examined *sententiae* in another large-scale text, Achilles Tatius' novel *Leucippe and Clitophon* (Morales 2004, 96–151). She follows Bennington's notion that "[s]ententious formulations imply a value-judgement grounded in social norms; they transmit a cultural heritage and are inherently conservative" (Bennington 1985, 9). Morales then poses the question: "What are the values and norms in the society of the novel and thus *what sort* of plausibility is relevant to Achilles Tatius?" (Morales 2004, 108). This approach proves fruitful when looking, as Morales does, only at the generalizing and universalizing statements and descriptions in a text. However – and this will be of particular relevance to my study – Bennington takes such strategies a step further when he states:

> Sententiousness becomes no longer so much a "type of sentence" as a force in texts [...]. This force is not some irrational or metaphysical entity assumed to be at work in texts, but a force of law. If the "overt" forms of sententiousness lay down the law, the more concealed types [...] draw their force from a law laid down, or exploit that law surreptitiously. (Bennington 1985, 62)

When applied to Seneca, this will mean that not only *sententiae* classified as *gnomai* contribute to our understanding of the "laws" in a text, but that even those which are rhetorical and situational offer us insights into the workings of the tragic world. Accordingly the anthologies of *sententiae* mentioned above, Publilius Syrus and Seneca the Elder's excerpts, "are only spectacular surface manifestations" of sententiousness as they are taken out of speeches or even out of an entire oeuvre of comedies and mimes (Bennington 1985, 62). For what unites the eighteenth-century French novel, *Leucippe and Clitophon*, and Seneca's tragedy, and indeed what makes their sententious aspects comparable is their narrative trajectory, the fact that they create and put on display their own individual world with its system of values.[38] By looking only at the *sententiae* in any of these works we strip out the narrative and keep only the ideology. Seneca is then reduced to ideology, becomes purely ethos – and as a result we are confronted with its essence.

---

37 I am aware that many scholars have identified a shared moral outlook in Seneca's plays and philosophy and have argued for an implicitly didactic role of the tragedies; cf. Buckley 2013 for an overview. She points out Pratt 1983, Wray 2009, and Nussbaum 1994 but also remarks that there are in equal measure readings showing that Stoic doctrine is challenged and subverted in the tragedies, such as Dingel 1974, Henry and Henry 1985, Boyle 1997, and Schiesaro 2003.
38 Cf. Bennington 1985, 62: "[...] the text 'in' which sententiousness is found becomes dispersed in an intertext of which sententiousness is a significant trace," while "sententiousness 'itself' is dispersed throughout narratives."

In a similar way my reading also takes temporality out of Seneca and breaks down the linearity of his tragedies. We suddenly gain a timeless and holistic vision of what is at stake in Seneca's tragedies. In his discussion of the imagery of *Aeneid* 12, Hunt suggests an approach not dissimilar for making "visible" the patterns of Vergil's epic, whose overarching structure he imagines in the manner of a triptych:

> The principal point, in any case, is that although the story must unfold in time, its meaning emerges in a kind of spatial memory – i.e. its organic sense emerges only when the three parts [of the triptych] are held together in a simultaneous vision. If the disparate themes and images were unified into a mental complex grasped spatially as a whole, the pattern of related meanings would fuse in an instantaneous impact, a genuinely comprehensive view whose apprehension would give the true form of the poem. (Hunt 1973, 84)

Seneca himself invites the reader to transcend the linearity of his story. He locates his tragedies about tyranny in the (safe) past of mythology. However, here the past informs the present. Seneca thus leads the way for his audience to ask what his tragedies conveyed to the Neronian reader. By reading Seneca's *sententiae*, we are negotiating this question; we construe Seneca's message while asking what his tragedies mean to us today. My moralizing reading supplants the narrative in favor of its *sententiae* and degrades Seneca's tragedies into a fable that illustrates a moral, a *sententia*, an *epimythion* – or indeed many of them, which in turn then lay down the laws for the tragic world.[39] Just as the fable is supplemented by *sententiae*, "the maxim tends to *supplant* the fable, to stand in for it once the fiction has gone" (Bennington 1985, 85).

To conclude, let me take a brief look at one of the passages from Seneca's letters, in which he comments on the use and educational value of *sententiae*.

> Nec recuso quominus singula membra, dummodo in ipso homine, consideres: non est formosa cuius crus laudatur aut brachium, sed illa cuius universa facies admirationem partibus singulis abstulit. 6 Si tamen exegeris, non tam mendice tecum agam, sed plena manu fiet; ingens eorum turba est passim iacentium; sumenda erunt, non colligenda. Non enim excidunt sed fluunt; perpetua et inter se contexta sunt. Nec dubito quin multum conferant rudibus adhuc et extrinsecus auscultantibus; facilius enim singula insidunt circumscripta et carminis modo inclusa. 7 Ideo pueris et sententias ediscendas damus et has quas Graeci chrias vocant, quia complecti illas puerilis animus potest, qui plus adhuc non capit. Certi profectus viro captare flosculos turpe est et fulcire se notissimis ac paucissimis vocibus et memoria stare: sibi iam innitatur. Dicat ista, non teneat; turpe est enim seni aut prospici-

---

39 Cf. Henderson 2001, 37 on Phaed. 3.10, where "[t]he story is sandwiched between an aggressive warm-up and multilayered complex of *epimythia*, which together – believe it or not – amount to all but *one* third of this, the longest extant *fabula* in Phaedrus."

enti senectutem ex commentario sapere. "Hoc Zenon dixit:" tu quid? "Hoc Cleanthes:" tu quid? Quousque sub alio moveris? Impera et dic quod memoriae tradatur, aliquid et de tuo profer.

Nor am I objecting to your contemplating individual limbs so long as you view them as parts of the man himself. A woman is not beautiful if she is praised for a leg or arm, but if her entire appearance diverts admiration from each separate part. 6 But if you demand full payment I shall not deal with you in such beggarly fashion, but distribute with a full hand: there is a great crowd of sayings scattered here and there which need to be picked up individually, not gathered together. They do not drop but flow, they are unending and interwoven. In fact, I don't doubt that they greatly benefit still untrained men listening from outside the school; for short and single items shaped like a verse sink in more easily. 7 That is why we give boys sayings to memorize and what the Greeks call Chriae [a saying attributed to a specific person and situation] because the child's mind can embrace them when it still cannot contain more. But it is shameful for a man who has made some progress to hunt blossoms and prop himself up with a few famous sayings, and rely on his memory: now let him rely on himself. Let him say such things, not hold on to them; for it is shameful for an old man, or one anticipating old age, to get his knowledge from other men's notes. "Zeno said this!" And what do you have to say? "Cleanthes said this." And what do you have to say? How long will you move under another's guidance? Take command and say something worth committing to memory, say something of your own creation. (Sen. *Ep.* 33.5–7, translation adapted from Fantham 2010)

Besides *Letter* 33, there are further letters, such as *Letters* 94 and 95, in Seneca's oeuvre (cf. n. 21) considering the force and use of precepts, maxims and *sententiae*. Two subjects, however, crystallize in *Letter* 33. First and foremost, Seneca, too, perceives *sententiae* as "unending and interwoven" (33.6: "perpetua et inter se contexta"), extracted from an intertext to which they link back. My reading of Seneca's sententiousness is thus no modern imposition but emphasizes traits of Seneca's own conceptualization. Secondly, and that is a stance Seneca may well have inherited from his *sententiae*-collecting father, Seneca the Elder, *sententiae* make the man, are part of an orator's or writer's claim to fame. He actively encourages his pupil Lucilius: "Say something of your own creation" (i.e. do not just quote, regurgitate, and recycle other peoples' thoughts), and most importantly: "Say something worth committing to memory" (i.e. leave your own mark). For Seneca one of the purposes of literary activity is to be quoted by others eventually, as a seal of quality as well as approval for his writing.

And indeed posterity assembled three collections of maxims by Seneca, which have come down to us as pseudo-Senecan writings, all of which were frequently edited and printed and well-thumbed by students in the Renaissance:[40]

---

40 The website of the Bibliotheca Medicea Laurenziana (Florence) contains an annotated list of Seneca epitomes, collections of maxims and other pseudo-Senecan

De remediis: a brief text on life's adversities, possibly dating back to Late Antiquity (Palmer 1953).

De moribus: a collection of 145 moral maxims, possibly by a Christian living in Gaul and already quoted among Seneca's works in a Canon of the Tours Council (657). It knew a wide circulation in the 8th century.

Proverbia or *Sententiae*: a collection of 149 statements in alphabetical order. The first section comprises maxims in verse by Publilius Syrus, the second section is in prose and derives from *De moribus*.[41]

Seneca works hard to secure his afterlife in his *sententiae*, and that extends to both his letters and his tragedies. Indeed, sententiousness might well be seen as one of the many links between Seneca's tragedies and his philosophical writings, a means by which Seneca could highlight the issues at stake throughout his *œuvre*. He makes the readers notice and consequently reflect under the constant barrage of sententiousness whether they have thought any more about the central questions posed by Seneca tragicus = philosophus.[42]

Bibliography

Bennington, Geoffrey. 1985. *Sententiousness & the Novel: Laying down the Law in Eighteenth-Century French Fiction*. Cambridge: Cambridge University Press.

Benz, Lore. 2001. "Publilius Syrus." In *Der Neue Pauly*, edited by Hubert Cancik and Helmuth Schneider, Vol. 10, p. 582. Stuttgart: Metzler.

Boeke, Hanna. 2007. *The Value of Victory in Pindar's Odes: Gnomai, Cosmology and the Role of the Poet*. Leiden: Brill.

Bonner, Stanley F. 1966. "Lucan and the Declamation Schools." *AJPh* 87: 257–289.

Boyle, Anthony James. 1977. "Senecan Tragedy: Twelve Propositions."*Ramus* 16: 78–101.

Boyle, Anthony James. 1997. *Tragic Seneca: An Essay in the Theatrical Tradition*. London: Routledge.

Braund, Susanna Morton, ed. 2008. *Seneca, De clementia*. Oxford: Oxford University Press.

Buckley, Emma. 2013. "Senecan Tragedy." In *The Blackwell Companion to the Age of Nero*, edited by Emma Buckley and Martin T. Dinter, 204–224. Malden: Wiley-Blackwell.

Carey, Chris. 1995. "Pindar and the Victory Ode." In *The Passionate Intellect: Essays on the Transformation of Classical Traditions, Presented to Professor I. G. Kidd*, edited by Lewis Ayres, 85–101. New Brunswick; London: Transaction Publishers.

---

works, from which the following information derives: http://www.bml.firenze.sbn.it/Seneca/eng/pseudo_seneca_contenuto.html.

41 The Technical University of Darmstadt provides a permalink to a digitized 1495 copy: http://tudigit.ulb.tu-darmstadt.de/show/inc-ii-127.

42 Paré-Rey 2012, 208–242 discusses how Seneca's *sententiae* fit into his Stoic project and concludes that he offers diverse fare for a heterogeneous audience.

Church, Alfred John, and William Jackson Brodribb, trans. 1942. *Publius Cornelius Tacitus, A Dialogue on Oratory*. New York: Random House
Danesi Marioni, Giulia. 1999. "Di padre in figlio: Il 'vir fortis' in lotta con la fortuna nei due Seneca." *InvLuc* 21: 123–132.
Dangel, Jacqueline. 2011. "Les énoncés gnomiques de la tragédie romaine en flux intertextuel: Pour quelle théâtricalité?" In *Les maximes théâtrales en Grèce et à Rome: Transferts, réécritures, remplois: Actes du colloque organisé les 11–13 juin 2009 par l'Université Lyon 3 et l'ENS de Lyon*, edited by Christine Mauduit and Pascale Paré-Rey, 177–188. Paris: De Boccard
Desbordes, Françoise. 1979. "Les vertus de l'énoncé: Notes sur les 'Sentences' de Publilius Syrus." *La Licorne* 3: 65–84.
Dingel, Joachim. 1974. *Seneca und die Dichtung*. Heidelberg: Winter.
Dinter, Martin T. 2012. *Anatomizing Civil War: Studies in Lucan's Epic Technique*. Ann Arbor: The University of Michigan Press.
Duff, John W., and Elaine Fantham. 1996. "Publilius Syrus." In *The Oxford Classical Dictionary*, 3rd ed., edited by Simon Hornblower and Antony Spawforth, 1276. Oxford: Oxford University Press.
Fairweather, Janet. 1981. *Seneca the Elder*. Cambridge: Cambridge University Press.
Fantham, Elaine. 2004. *The Roman World of Cicero's De Oratore*. Oxford: Oxford University Press.
Fantham, Elaine, trans. 2010. *Seneca, Selected Letters*. Oxford: Oxford University Press.
Ferri, Rolando, ed. 2003. *Octavia: A Play Attributed to Seneca*. Cambridge: Cambridge University Press.
Fitch, John G., ed. and trans. 2002. *Lucius Annaeus Seneca, Tragedies*. Vol. 1: *Hercules; Trojan Women; Phoenician Women; Medea; Phaedra*. Cambridge; London: Harvard University Press.
Fitch, John G., ed. and trans. 2004. *Lucius Annaeus Seneca, Tragedies*. Vol. 2: *Oedipus; Agamemnon; Thyestes; Hercules on Oeta; Octavia*. Cambridge; London: Harvard University Press.
Giancotti, Francesco. 1967. *Mimo e gnome: Studio su Decimo Laberio e Publilio Siro*. Messina; Firenze: Casa Editrice G. D'Anna.
Gualandri, Isabella, and Giancarlo Mazzoli, eds. 2003. *Gli Annei: Una famiglia nella storia e nella cultura di Roma imperiale: Atti del Convegno internazionale di Milano-Pavia, 2–6 maggio 2000*. Como: New Press.
Gummere, Richard M., ed. and trans. 1917–1925. *Seneca, Ad Lucilium epistulae morales*. 3 vols. London; Cambridge: Heinemann; Harvard University Press.
Henderson, John. 2001. *Telling Tales on Caesar: Roman Stories from Phaedrus*. Oxford: Oxford University Press.
Henderson, John. 2013. "The Carmina Einsidlensia and Calpurnius Siculus' Eclogues." In *A Companion to the Neronian Age*, edited by Martin Dinter and Emma Buckley, 170–187. Malden: Wiley-Blackwell.
Henry, Denis, and Elisabeth Henry. 1985. *The Mask of Power: Seneca's Tragedies and Imperial Rome*. Warminster: Aris and Phillips.
Hunt, J. William. 1973. *Forms of Glory, Structure and Sense in Virgil's Aeneid*. Carbondale; Edwardsville: Southern Illinois University Press.
Jäkel, Siegfried, trans. 1986. *Menander, Sentenzen*. Leipzig: Teubner.
Keith, Allison. 2000. *Engendering Rome: Women in Latin Epic*. Cambridge: Cambridge University Press.
Ker, James. 2006. "Seneca, Man of Many Genres." In *Seeing Seneca Whole: Perspectives on Philosophy, Poetry and Politics*, edited by Katharina Volk and Gareth D. Williams, 16–41. Leiden: Brill.
Kirchner, Roderich. 2001. *Sentenzen im Werk des Tacitus*. Stuttgart: Steiner.

Knecht, Theodor. 1986. "Das römische Sprichwort – Abgrenzungen, Formen, Anwendung." In *Reflexionen antiker Kulturen*, edited by Peter Neukam, 47–59. München: Bayrischer Schulbuch-Verlag.
Kunz, Franz. 1897. *Sentenzen in Senecas Tragödien*. Wiener-Neustadt: Selbstverlag des k.u.k. Staats-Ober-Gymnasiums.
Leo, Friedrich. 1878. *De Senecae tragoediis observationes criticae*. Berlin: Weidmann.
Mannering, Jonathan. 2013. "Seneca's Letters and Philosophical Writings." In *The Blackwell Companion to the Age of Nero*, edited by Emma Buckley and Martin T. Dinter, 188–203. Malden: Wiley-Blackwell.
Mauduit, Christine, and Pascale Paré-Rey, eds. 2011. *Les maximes théâtrales en Grèce et à Rome: Transferts, réécritures, remplois: Actes du colloque organisé les 11–13 juin 2009 par l'Université Lyon 3 et l'ENS de Lyon*. Paris: De Boccard.
Mayer, Roland G . 1994. "Personata Stoa: Neostoicism and Senecan Tragedy." *Journal of the Warburg and Courtauld Institutes* 57: 151–174.
Mayer, Roland G. 2003. "Persona Problems." *MD* 50: 1–26.
McGill, Scott. 2005. *Virgil Recomposed: The Mythological and Secular Centos in Antiquity*. Oxford: Oxford University Press.
Menander. 1986. *Sentenzen*. See Jäkel 1986
Miller, Frank Justus, ed. and trans. 1917. *Seneca, Tragedies*. Vol. 2: *Agamemnon; Thyestes; Hercules Oetaeus; Phoenissae; Octavia*. London; Cambridge: Heinemann: Harvard University Press. Rpt. 1961.
Morales, Helen. 2004. *Vision and Narrative in Achilles Tatius' Leucippe and Clitophon*. Cambridge: Cambridge University Press.
Nussbaum, Martha C. 1994. *The Therapy of Desire: Theory and Practice in Hellenistic Ethics*. Princeton: Princeton University Press.
Quintilian. 2001. *Institutio Oratoria – The Orator's Education*. See Russell 2001.
Palmer, Ralph Graham. 1995. *Seneca's De Remediis Fortuitorum and the Elizabethans: An Essay on the Influence of Seneca's Ethical Thought in the Sixteenth Century*. Chicago: Institute of Elizabethan Studies.
Paré-Rey, Pascale. 2012. *Flores et acumina: Les sententiae dans les tragédies de Sénèque*. Paris: De Boccard.
Picone, Giusto. 1984. *La fabula e il regno: Studi sul Thyestes di Seneca*. Palermo: Palumbo.
Pratt, Norman. 1983. *Seneca's Drama*. Chapel Hill: University of North Carolina Press.
Preisendanz, Karl. 1908. "De Senecae rhetoris apud philosophum filium auctoritate." *Philologus* 67: 68–112.
Rayment, Charles S. 1969. "Echoes of the Declamations in the Dialogues of the Younger Seneca." *CB* 45: 51–63.
Rieks, Rudolf. 1978. "Mimus und Atellane." In *Das römische Drama*, edited by Eckard Lefèvre, 348–377. Darmstadt: Wissenschaftliche Buchgesellschaft.
Rolland, Émile. 1906. *De l'influence de Sénèque le père et les rhéteurs sur Sénèque le philosophe*. Ghent: van Goethern.
Russell, Donald A., ed. and trans. 2001. *Quintilian, Institutio Oratoria – The Orator's Education*. 5 vols. Cambridge: Harvard University Press.
Russo, Joseph 1997. "Prose Genres for the Performance of Traditional Wisdom in Ancient Greece: Proverb, Maxim, Apophthegm." In *Poet, Public, and Performance in Ancient Greece*, edited by Lowell Edmunds and Robert W. Wallace, 49–64. Baltimore: Johns Hopkins University Press.
Schiesaro, Alessandro. 2003. *The Passions in Play: Thyestes and the Dynamics of Senecan Drama*. Cambridge: Cambridge University Press.
Seneca. 1917. *Agamemnon; Thyestes; Hercules Oetaeus; Phoenissae; Octavia*. See Miller 1917.
Seneca. 1917–1925. *Ad Lucilium epistulae morales*. See Gummere 1917–1925.

Seneca. 2002. *Hercules; Trojan Women; Phoenician Women; Medea; Phaedra.* See Fitch 2002.
Seneca. 2004. *Oedipus; Agamemnon; Thyestes; Hercules on Oeta; Octavia.* See Fitch 2004.
Seneca. 2008. *De Clementia.* See Braund 2008.
Seneca. 2010. *Selected Letters.* See Fantham 2010.
[Seneca.] 2003. *Octavia.* See Ferri 2003.
Seneca the Elder. 1974. *Declamations.* See Winterbottom 1974.
Sinclair, Patrick. 1995. *Tacitus the Sententious Historian: A Sociology of Rhetoric in Annales 1–6.* University Park: Pennsylvania State University Press.
Sussman, Lewis A. 1978. *The Elder Seneca.* Leiden: Brill.
Tacitus. 1942. *A Dialogue on Oratory.* See Church and Brodribb 1942.
Whitton, Christopher. 2013. "Seneca, Apocolocyntosis." In *A Companion to the Neronian Age*, edited by Martin Dinter and Emma Buckley, 151–169. Malden: Wiley-Blackwell.
Winterbottom, Michael, ed. and trans. 1974. *The Elder Seneca, Declamations.* 2 vols. London; Cambridge: Harvard University Press.
Wray, David L.. 2009. "Seneca and Tragedy's Reason." In *Seneca and the Self,* edited by Shadi Bartsch and David Wray. 237–254. Cambridge: Cambridge University Press.

Having the Right to Philosophize: A New Reading of Seneca, *De Vita Beata* 1.1–6.2

Matheus De Pietro
Universidade Estadual de Campinas

The repetitive character of Senecan style was criticized not only by modern scholars.[1] Most notably, Marcus Cornelius Fronto highlights this feature as a one of the many stylistic flaws he finds in Seneca's works.[2] Seneca himself, however, held a different opinion. In several passages throughout his prose writings he expresses the belief that presenting the same idea repeatedly and in different ways is desirable from a didactic point of view. Others have shown that such repetition may in fact be one of Seneca's tools of psychagogy.[3] The thesis I wish to develop in the present paper concerns an apparent paradox. Although Seneca's stylistic "flaws" were often seen as a sign of his shortcomings as a philosopher – or at least as an inappropriate mode of presentation for serious philosophy[4] – his ostenta-

---

1   See, for instance, Sandbach 1989, 162: "When this man [sc. Seneca] writes books about moralising, they hardly ring true. Nor are they helped by his style; as Seneca piles epigram upon epigram, we sense his satisfaction with his own cleverness and remember he had been trained by rhetoricians, as well as the Stoic teachers Sotio and Attalus. He seems insincere and a windbag, 'repeating the same sentiment a thousand times'." – I would like to express my gratitude to Jula Wildberger, Marcia L. Colish, and Benedict Beckeld for the kind suggestions and careful corrections made during the elaboration of this paper.
2   The phrase quoted by Sandbach *supra* refers to Fro. *Aur. Orat.* 5. Further criticism concerning Seneca's life and style can be found in Fro. *Aur. Orat.* 2–7.
3   That repetition is an essential part of Stoic psychagogical practice (*askēsis*; *meditatio*) can be inferred from several passages in Roman Stoics (Sen. *Ep.* 2.4; 4.5; 16.1; 82.8; 94.46–47; 107.3; *De ira* 2.10.7; Arr. *Epict.* 1.1.25; 3.8.1–5; 3.12.1–17; M. Ant. 2.1; 4.10 and 6.47). A considerable part of Stoic *askēsis* consists in the correction of an individual's false conceptions, for which purpose the repetition of correct conceptions was acknowledged as a very useful resource. A number of studies have also argued for the existence of either an epistemological or didactic reasoning justifying this practice, e.g. Rabbow 1914; Hijmans 1959; I. Hadot 1969; Traina 1974; Bellincioni 1978; Newman 1989; P. Hadot 1992; Mutschler 1998; Wildberger 2006; von Albrecht 2008; Graver 2009; van Ackeren 2012.
4   It is interesting to note that similar criticism was voiced against Lucretius' didactic poetry, which was considered by some as an unusual way of philosophizing (Dalzell 1996, 45–46 and 70–71).

tious use of such variation in *De vita beata* has a function which contradicts that assumption: It showcases his skill in treating important philosophical topics.

I will argue that the repeated unfolding and condensing of the concept of happiness in *De vita beata* 3.2–6.2 may be considered as Seneca's deliberate demonstration of his mastery of Stoic doctrine and thus of his standing as a philosopher. This hypothesis is supported by several different features exhibited by the text, the first of which is the structural disposition of the work as a whole. Second, one can point to the context in which it was written, which may have required some form of discourse justifying the author's self-characterization as a Stoic philosopher. Third, the initial part of the work draws attention to Seneca in contrast to everyone else. Fourth, there is his insistence on the inadequacy of all other definitions and the consequent need that the author himself provide one of his own as a solid basis for the subsequent debate on the topic of happiness. The fifth and most relevant evidence in support of my thesis is the multifaceted definition extending from sections 3.2 to 6.2 itself. It displays to striking properties: On the one hand, it contains several methodological remarks which draw attention to the act of composition. Seneca ensures that the reader cannot help but be aware of what he is doing and, at the same time, emphatically clarifies that the passage, however repetitive, was deliberately written in this manner.[5] On the other hand, the multiple definitions provided are not a mere accumulation of doxographic notices. Rather, they develop different aspects of the Stoic doctrine concerning happiness. By offering the same definition over and over, in different formulations, vocabulary, and images, and by making the reader conscious of that process, Seneca effectively demonstrates that he fully understands the concept being discussed and does not just parrot what was said by former Stoics.

I.

Before arguing that the passage serves as a demonstration of Seneca's expertise, we must clarify why he may have felt the need to supply such a proof of his skills in the first place. In other words, why must the author produce evidence that he is a competent philosopher? Seneca was often criticized for his lack of philosophical authority. He did not exhibit the

---

5 Von Albrecht 2008, 79–83 argues that Seneca employs variation and changes of style (length of periods, *ornatus*, colloquialism, archaism, syllogistic discourse, and synonymy) as a means of keeping the reader's attention.

frugal and detached lifestyle usually expected of a philosopher, as it was manifested by Socrates, unquestionably the most significant role model for someone whose profession was the quest for wisdom. Instead, Seneca was one of the wealthiest and most powerful men of his time – while professing a doctrine which regarded political power and material goods as morally indifferent. This fact led to the charge of hypocrisy, and his status as a proper philosopher (i.e. a philosopher who is consistent and has expert knowledge of the doctrines he professes) was called into question. It is probable that *De vita beata* was written as a response to accusations of this nature.[6] This may be inferred from information in the text itself. Beginning from section 17.1, the work becomes a defense of the entire class of philosophers against generic accusations of inconsistency. Even though *De vita beata*'s genre remains uncertain,[7] one may at least, acknowledge that it has a strong apologetic tone.

Attested ancient accusations directed specifically at his lack of philosophical authority are rare and, for the most part, posthumous.[8] What we do find in plenty, however, are criticisms that draw attention to Seneca's apparent inconsistency.[9] The best documented accusation we have today,

---

6   Arguments supporting this hypothesis can be seen, for example, in Griffin 1992, 19–20, 302–311 and Chaumartin 1989, 1686–1692.
7   *De vita beata* contains elements of dialogue, diatribe, apology, and doxography, while not properly exhibiting their generic conventions in sufficient number or in their expected form, thus preventing us to acknowledge the book as belonging to a specific mode of writing.
8   Information regarding accusations contemporary to Seneca is provided by Tacitus, who claims to report Suilius' charges (Tac. *Ann.* 13.42–43), and also by Cassius Dio (61.10.2). In the charges reported by Tacitus, Seneca's philosophical skill is questioned in light of his wealth, while Cassius Dio points out that Seneca's conduct was incoherent with the teaching of his philosophical school. Quintilian, writing decades before Tacitus and more than a century before Cassius Dio, also highlights what he considers to be Seneca's stylistic flaws, and questions his philosophical dedication, even though he acknowledges the usefulness of his moral exhortations (Quint. *Inst.* 10.129). It is worth noting that Quintilian also points out Seneca's eagerness in the pursuit of intellectual matters in general and his extensive knowledge of many subjects (Quint. *Inst.* 10.128). Thus, by praising Seneca's intellectual capacity shortly before mentioning his alleged shortcomings in philosophical matters, Quintilian only contributes to demeaning the Stoic's status as a philosopher.
9   The criticisms presented by Quintilian, Tacitus, and Cassius Dio are echoed by modern readers. The exact form of their accusations varies, but all focus on the apparent inconsistency between the author's philosophy and manner of living. Noteworthy are Milton 1818, 52, first published in 1670; Macaulay in Trevelyan 2006, 272; Hegel 1986, 272–273, first published in 1833 = *GP* 1.2.2; Farrar 2005, 160–165, first published in 1874; Cruttwell 1909, 353, 380 and 382, first published in 1887; Rose 1954, 359–360; L'Estrange 1882, xii; Wedeck 1955; and Sandbach 1989, 161–162. Montaigne (at *Essais* 2.32.2–3) actually takes Seneca's side, but

coming from the former *consul suffectus* Suillius Rufus, was leveled in public and certainly a blow to Seneca's reputation. Furthermore, as Griffin argues, Suillius' charge may have been a reflection of a general opinion about Seneca's life held by many of his peers.[10] Both kinds of criticism, however, are ultimately grounded on the same premise: Hypocrisy (e.g. not practicing what one preaches) or inconsistency (e.g. upholding different values at different times) are severe flaws that no serious philosopher can exhibit and therefore incompatible with that status.

Indeed, if coherence was regarded as sign of a correct understanding and practice of the tenets of one's school,[11] it was even more relevant for a Stoic, whose very goal as a philosopher was to live harmoniously and lead a thoroughly consistent life.[12] Thus we understand how deeply a charge of incoherence or hypocrisy affected Seneca: It carried the implicit message not only that he did not practice what he was preaching but also that he did not *understand* what he was preaching. Had he done so, he would certainly have known that Stoics regarded wealth as indifferent for a happy life and not taken the trouble to acquire so much of it. For someone in Seneca's position, a simple explanation of why he was not hypocritical would therefore not have been sufficient. In this case, it was necessary to provide not only a clarification of the misunderstandings concerning his lifestyle

---

speaks about a certain book published at his time, which compared King Charles IX to Nero and the Cardinal of Lorraine to Seneca, both being extremely wealthy, politically powerful, and behaving in similar ways. While Montaigne does not name the book or its author, he points out that it considers Seneca "a false pretender to philosophy" (*contrefaisant le philosophe à fauces enseignes*). For a detailed analysis of Seneca's opulent condition and its influence on his philosophical *persona*, see Griffin 1992, 286–314. A more recent investigation on Seneca's life and public image, although not limited to Seneca's financial condition, can be found in Griffin 2008. See also Chaumartin 1989 and Motto 1966.

10 Griffin 1992, 309 and 427 understands *De vita beata* as a work that reflects charges raised against Seneca and that he answers them in a general manner. She also points out that we cannot reasonably establish Suillius' public accusation as the *terminus post quem* for the elaboration of the work, nor can we determine whether *De vita beata* was written precisely with them in mind. On the other hand, Griffin regards it as not unlikely that Seneca was indeed concerned with the difficulty of justifying his style of life during the production of the text.

11 Compare Socrates' repeated emphasis on doxastic coherence as a necessary component of knowledge, two instances of which are Pl. *Phd.* 67e; *Grg.* 482a2–5 and b2–c3. Seneca himself also lists accusations of improper conduct against ancient philosophers in *Vit. beat.* 27.5: "Obicite Platoni quod petierit pecuniam, Aristoteli quod acceperit, Democrito quod neglexerit, Epicuro quod consumpserit" – "You criticize Plato for having asked for money, Aristotle for having accepted it, Democritus for having neglected it, Epicurus for having spent it." Where not otherwise indicated, translations are my own.

12 See, e.g., Stob. 2.7.6a, vol. 2, p. 75,11–14 Wachsmuth = LS 63B.

but also some evidence that he actually knew the doctrine he was teaching so eagerly.

II.

That Seneca presents himself in his writings as an expert in Stoic philosophy is nothing new, and at any rate nothing exceptional or unexpected. This paper aims to highlight the fact that references to his authority either as a Stoic or as a philosopher, which are more or less implicit in other texts, have a specific rhetorical function and take on an apologetic force in *De vita beata*. I will point out various features of the text that invite us to read *De vita beata* 1.1–6.2 as a statement of philosophical proficiency and indicate possible effects Seneca may have intended to achieve with them. The evidence can be divided into two broad categories: textual structure and philosophical content. Naturally, there are instances in which these categories overlap, but they must be analyzed separately for a clearer exposition of the effects achieved by these different means. I begin with a structural feature.

De vita beata's initial sections exhibit a referential structure that starts from a broader range of social groups or categories of individuals and reaches its final point in only one person, Seneca. The author opens the work with a reference to all human beings: Even though all want to live happily, they have muddled ideas about how such a condition can be achieved. The author then proceeds to outline the content of his work in form of a *partitio*, the division and preview of the content that is to follow (*Vit. beat.* 1.1), and immediately introduces the first of his explanatory aims, namely to dismiss false conceptions of happiness and produce a definition of correct one for the reader.

In a narrowing sequence, Seneca limits the range of persons whose judgment can trusted until the only one that remains is he himself:

omnes (1.1)

populus (1.4, 1.5)

maior pars (2.1)

pluris (2.1)

turba (2.1)

vulgus (2.2)

chlamydati et coronati (2.2)

alii [philosophi] (3.2)

Stoici proceris (3.2)

Seneca (3.2, 3.3)

It is certainly not insignificant that the passage dealing with the dismissal of false conceptions of happiness has a centripetal directionality with humankind forming the widest circle and Seneca at the midpoint. The rejection of sources for knowledge about the conception of happiness begins with "all" (*omnes*), then trust is denied first to the people (*populus*), then to the majority (*maior pars*), the many (*pluris*), and the masses (*turba* and *vulgus*). He further refuses to attribute correct conceptual knowledge to two specific subsets of the elite, to those who are powerful (*chlamydati*)[13] and acclaimed (*coronati*).[14] This suggests that even those commonly regarded as "happy" have in fact no idea of what happiness is. The circle tightens even more when Seneca mentions only the philosophers, who, unlike the previous groups, are professionally bound to attempt a reasonable and well-grounded definition of happiness. Even their conceptions are incorrect and can easily be refuted by the author, which leaves the reader with the impression that only the Stoics can provide the right interpretation of the debated concept. But even this is not exactly what Seneca intends to offer. Instead of giving a complete account of the Stoic position, the author declares that he will adduce or omit certain aspects in conformity with his personal judgment. At this point the reader can already infer that he will not receive the Stoic opinion, but rather the Stoic opinion through Seneca's lens.

It is important that this "narrowing" of the circle of competent judges occurs not only at a purely numerical level, but also concerns the value of the opinions of the mentioned groups, so that, at the end, Seneca draws attention not only *to himself* but also *to his opinion* about the matter. He appears as the one whose interpretation the reader should hear. It is a Stoic

---

13   In its literal sense, *chlamydati* means "those who wear the *chlamys*." Here, however, we may understand the term as a reference to individuals belonging to privileged social positions. The *chlamys* was a Geek garment typically worn by nobles, soldiers, hunters, and even emperors, a fact that may be interpreted as a symbol of power (see *ThLL* 3.1011.64–71 and Hurschmann 2012a). Moreover, one may point out that the use of this Greek word in a context related to military power may be an allusion to renowned Greek military leaders, such as Alexander of Macedon. A similar allusion to Alexander is repeated in *Vit. beat.* 25.4, where the image of a certain conqueror of many tribes who is worshiped as a god is presented as an example of the popular conception of what could be considered a "happy circumstance."

14   Just as is the case with *chlamydati*, the term *coronati* (meaning "those who wear garlands or crowns") may be a reference to a specific group of people, namely those who were awarded with wreaths due to exceptional actions, such as a display of military valor or a victory in athletic contests (see *ThLL* 4.977.26–986.19 and Hurschmann 2012b). It is possible, therefore, to understand the use of *coronati* in this phrase as a reference to individuals who enjoy a certain degree of fame, honor, and distinction, and are thus looked upon with admiration by average folk.

account, but through Seneca's voice and according to his design. The textual structure thus focuses attention on the author as a source of philosophical expertise.

Another effect produced by the features described above is the creation of a very particular situation at *De vita beata* 3.2. The reader's attention has been drawn to the presence of the author Seneca himself, and now he expects that this author will define the concept of happiness at last. The most striking feature of the following sections (3.2 to 6.2) is their repetitive character. Seneca does not merely condense, expand, and transfigure his definition of the concept, but he is also explicit in drawing attention to this feature: There are three methodological remarks, each near the other (3.2, 4.1, 4.3), which direct the reader's attention to the author's expositional method. Stylistic variation, a technique that Seneca is considered to have employed already beyond what is conventionally accepted, is here used to excess:[15] Over thirteen paragraphs the same concept is defined in multiple ways, each time in a different manner. Moreover, the methodological remarks rule out the possibility that this excess is a stylistic slip. The author takes care to clarify that he is perfectly conscious of what he is doing. We may therefore state with confidence that Seneca *wants* us to pay attention to what he is doing here.

III.

There was a simple and convenient way to provide definitions of Stoic concepts: Seneca could have copied the standard formulae from a doxographic handbook. One does not even need to be an actual philosopher to perform such a task, as the work of the biographer Diogenes Laertius confirms. Seneca, however, set himself a much more difficult task.

For example, he complicates his exposition by changing the *definiendum*, the *genus*, and the *species* of the definition – thus varying the Aristotelian pattern[16] – while maintaining the same idea as the conceptual core. Thus he affirms at *Vit. beat.* 4.2 that the supreme good (*definiendum*) is a mind (*genus*) with the attribute of being disdainful of Fortune (*species*), then states that the happy person (*definiendum*) is a man (*genus*) who regards a good and a bad mind as the sole good and evil (*species*). All three components of a definition have been replaced by something else, but the underlying idea that correct evaluation of moral worth is essential for achieving happiness remains the same.

---

15 Compare Sandbach's criticism quoted above in n. 1.
16 See, for example, Arist. *Top.* 139a24–151b24; *Met.* 1033b34 – 1034a1.

Another way in which Seneca complicates his task is his use of three different explanatory movements: contracting, unfolding, and transfiguring, each one of them introduced by a remark indicating that a diverse approach to the concept will now be taken. By "contracting" (*Vit. beat.* 4.2) I mean the lexical shortening of a previously given statement, which may happen, for example, by way of avoidance of syntactic subordination and by the use of polysemous vocabulary, thus creating a concise, semantically dense phrase. "Unfolding" (*Vit. beat.* 4.2) indicates the lexical or semantic expansion of a statement. This procedure makes use of figures of amplification and is more complex than more concise alternatives, thus loosening semantic density but exhibiting periphrases or longer sequences of attributes and allows the use of more refined expressions. "Transfiguring" (*Vit. beat.* 4.3) does not refer to a form of lexical arrangement, but rather to a change in the aspect of the concept currently being dealt with or to a change in the image currently employed in association with the explanation of the concept.

The process of presenting the subtleties of a concept or of providing different descriptions and analogies without deviating from its essential meaning can only be carried out by someone with sufficient understanding of that concept's theoretical foundation. If considered in this light, Seneca's repeated unfolding and contracting of definitions begins to look less like a stylistic flaw and more like a conscious attempt to demonstrate his theoretical knowledge of the Stoic doctrine.

Furthermore, right at the beginning of the definitory part, Seneca indicates that his definitions will be the result of a serious and independent intellectual effort:

> Sed ne te per circumitus traham, aliorum quidem opiniones praeteribo – nam et enumerare illas longum est et coarguere: nostram accipe. Nostram autem cum dico, non alligo me ad unum aliquem ex Stoicis proceribus: est et mihi censendi ius. Itaque aliquem sequar, aliquem iubebo sententiam dividere, fortasse et post omnes citatus nihil inprobabo ex iis quae priores decreverint et dicam: "Hoc amplius censeo."

> But not wishing to haul you through circuitous details, I will pass over without comment the opinions of other thinkers – for it would be a tedious business to number and refute them all. Accept ours. But when I say 'ours', I do not bind myself to one particular Stoic representative: I, too, have the right to vote. And so I shall follow one individual, I will bid some other one to divide the proposition, and, maybe, when I have been summoned to speak after everyone else, I shall not disapprove what has been decreed by the predecessors, and I will say: "I have this further observation to make." (Sen. *Vit. beat.* 3.2, trans. Davie, slightly altered)

The assertion that Seneca could refute the opinions of other philosophical schools if he so wished indicates that he considers them to be flawed and insufficient. The sequence of correct definitions is preceded by a methodological remark concerning the manner in which the author will present the Stoic position: He will follow someone, agree partially with another, and maybe, without disagreeing, provide his own opinion. This remark is meaningful because it gives the author some appearance of independence. It occurs at the very moment in which Seneca has put himself at the center of the reader's attention. The image of the Senate, a place where the ruling figures of Roman society meet to decide its fate, is not chosen at random. The author affirms that he will exert his right to vote ("censendi ius") and that he is therefore free to agree or disagree with the senior Stoics' propositions and has also the right to ask that a proposition be divided ("sententiam dividere")[17] for him to assent to it only partially. Moreover, the final expression effectively puts him in the same rank as the noble predecessors mentioned shortly before ("proceribus"). This last phrase is modest and cautious: It *might* ("fortasse") happen, when he is called *after everyone else* ("post omnes citatus")[18] and disagrees with *nothing* ("nihil"), that he *also* ("et") adds something of his own ("amplius censeo"). The message is clear: Seneca wants to be seen not as a generic follower (perhaps equivalent to a regular Roman subject) but as a Stoic philosopher on his own merit (a senator), albeit one holding a minor position.

IV.

Still in regards to the method, the author establishes a common ground: No matter which particular Stoic interpretation Seneca chooses to follow, he assures the reader that he is in agreement with the nature of things – like every other Stoic:

> Interim, quod inter omnis Stoicos convenit, rerum naturae adsentior; ab illa non deerrare et ad illius legem exemplumque formari sapientia est.
>
> In the meantime, as is a consensus among all Stoics, I agree with the nature of things; wisdom lies in not wandering away from it and in molding oneself according to its law and example. (Sen. *Vit. beat.* 3.3, trans. Davie, slightly altered)

---

17 Cf. *ThLL* 5.1.1609.35–43. The same image occurs in Sen. *Ep.* 21.9.

18 During a regular session, members of the Republican Senate were called according to their ranks and seniority (Byrd 1995, 34). Being called last means, therefore, that Seneca pictures himself as the lowest rank senator in the *curia*. In addition to that protocol, we may also interpret this expression as a chronological reference: At the moment in which he writes, Seneca considers himself the last Stoic in the line of succession of the school, while Zeno, portrayed as the presiding magistrate, had spoken first and conducts the session.

The adverb *interim* ("in the meantime") establishes the simultaneity of two events:[19] Even though Seneca handles the interpretations of fellow Stoics independently, he does not deviate from the central assumption shared by all members of the school, namely that wisdom consists in not straying from the nature of things and in being molded by its law and model. Seneca has thus clarified the school of thought to which he will adhere, but has also raised expectations that he will do so in an original and creative manner. In what follows, I will analyze the chain of definitions presented by the author in more detail and ascertain the extent to which they reflect or make creative use of actual nuances of Stoic theories.

IV.1 *Apatheia* and the Correct Valuation of What Is Good, Bad, and Indifferent

One distinctive feature of Seneca's account is the introduction of an internal structure by ordering the definitions into four sections with different dominant themes. The first of these focuses on impassibility (*apatheia*) and the ability to recognize what is truly good or bad. Order is also highlighted within the thematic sections themselves. Seneca takes care to create the impression that information is not accumulated at random but carefully selected and presented in a rational sequence.

> Beata est ergo vita conveniens naturae suae, quae non aliter contingere potest quam si primum sana mens est et in perpetua possessione sanitatis suae, deinde fortis ac vehemens, tunc pulcherrime patiens, apta temporibus, corporis sui pertinentiumque ad id curiosa non anxie, tum aliarum rerum quae vitam instruunt diligens sine admiratione cuiusquam, usura fortunae muneribus, non servitura.

> Therefore, happy is the life that is in harmony with its own nature, and the only way it can be achieved is if, first, the mind is sound and constantly in possession of its soundness, and secondly, if it is brave and vigorous, and, in addition, capable of the noblest endurance, adapting to every situation, attentive to the body and to all that is related to it, but not in an anxious way, and, moreover, if it concerns itself with all other things that outfit life, without showing undue respect for any one of them, taking advantage of Fortune's gifts, but not becoming their slave. (Sen. *Vit. beat.* 3.3, trans. Davie, slightly altered)

A logical consequence (marked by the conjunction *ergo*) of the stated fact that happiness requires agreement with the nature of things (3.3: "rerum naturae adsentior") is that a happy life must be in agreement with its own nature (3.3: "conveniens naturae suae"), since agreeing with the nature of things implies agreeing with one's particular nature. Seneca breaks down

---

19 Cf. *ThLL* 7.1.2202.33–42.

the development of such a life into four steps, which, as he emphasizes, must be taken *necessarily* ("non aliter"). In the first step, introduced by the adverb *primum* ("before everything else"), the reader is informed that the mind must be sound and in continuous possession of its soundness. The following adverb *deinde* ("afterward") introduces further conditions: Once the mind has been set on the right path (i.e. once it knows what is correct and has extirpated its vices), it must follow this path unwaveringly, that is, it cannot let itself be influenced either by opinions of others or by Fortune's provocations. The two attributes bravery and vigor are defensive postures against the two kinds of disturbances mentioned later in 3.4, that a brave and vigorous mind resists what excites ("inritant") and what frightens ("territant"). Once the first two conditions are met, "then" (*tunc*) the mind must display three external characteristics: It must exhibit noble endurance and the ability to adapt to different circumstances ("apta temporibus"), and it must be able to take care of its body without allowing it to become a source of worries. Lastly, beginning with *tum* ("moreover"), in a fourth and final step, the author presents two additional characteristics: The mind must accept other useful things without any esteem for them, and it must make good use of Fortune's gifts without becoming their slave.

Four connective adverbs thus structure a list of requirements for the "life [...] in harmony with its own nature:" *primum, deinde, tunc,* and *tum.* We cannot specify whether they are supposed to enumerate those characteristics temporally or causally. However, regardless of what Seneca's intention was, it is clear that those four particles divide the listed attributes in four groups, which is an indication that there is also a difference among the elements presented by each of them.

Indeed, among those four groups we perceive a distinction in the form of a gradual progression from internal to external characteristics, in which the internal elements are emphasized by their antecedent position. The first and second steps refer exclusively to internal attributes or configurations of the soul. The third contains a description of the mind's attitude toward the body (the external object most closely related to the individual), and the fourth is associated with other external objects.[20]

The next section is then presented as the logical consequence of having fulfilled these four steps.

> Intellegis, etiam si non adiciam, sequi perpetuam tranquillitatem, libertatem, depulsis iis quae aut irritant nos aut territant; nam voluptatibus et *** pro illis quae parua ac fragilia sunt et †ipsis flagitiis noxia† ingens gaudium subit, inconcussum

---

[20] The exhortation to behave correctly with regard to *indifferentia* is repeated in 8.2, in a similar context of defining a "life in accordance with nature" (*vita secundum naturam*). Kuen (1994, 79–80) understands the excerpt differently. She considers the fourfold division a logical sequence from general to particular propositions.

> et aequale, tum pax et concordia animi et magnitudo cum mansuetudine; omnis enim ex infirmitate feritas est.
>
> You understand, even if I were not to make this further point, that, once the things that either excite or scare us are banished, a lasting tranquillity and freedom follow; for once pleasures ***, then, in place of those things that are insignificant, fragile and, †harmful because of their own outrageousness,† a great joy will arise, one that is firm and stable, then peace and harmony of mind, as well as the greatness that goes with gentleness – for every impulse to cruelty is born from weakness.[21] (Sen. *Vit. beat.* 3.4, trans. Davie, with alterations)

Once the individual has followed the four steps described above, he will no longer be subject to external disturbances, such as sources of excitement or dread. Without such agitation, he will be in possession of attributes essential to a happy life. The fundamental reasoning developed in this first definitory section is that the achievement of happiness is contingent upon the development of a correct attitude toward externals. The ablative absolute *depulsis* and the verb *sequi* are equivalent to a classic "if–then" statement of implication and thus stress the causal relation between those conditions.

By speaking about the elimination of all forms of emotional stimulus stemming from one's false opinions about morally neutral objects Seneca alludes to the Stoic notion of impassibility (*apatheia*), the state of being free from irrational passions (*pathē*), which constitutes one of the aspects of the ultimate good of the Stoics.[22] By describing the mind as "sane" (*sana*), he evokes the the opposite condition of such mental health, which may be either a consolidated disease, a psychic condition which was called *arrōstēma* or *nosēma* by the Greek Stoics and rendered in Latin with the term *morbus*, or only a temporary perturbation or passion (*pathos* in Greek), which could eventually become a disease. *Morbus*, one of the Ciceronian translations of the Greek *pathos*,[23] is adopted by Seneca on several occasions in his prose.[24] However, Seneca uses it also as a

---

[21] The asterisks indicate a lacuna in the transmitted text. The words marked off by so-called cruces are corrupt. The transmitted text cannot have been the original version, but no plausible restitution has been found.

[22] Seneca gives us his own account of *apatheia* in Sen. *Ep.* 9.2–5.

[23] Cic. *Tusc.* 3.22–23. Throughout this work Cicero uses semantically related terms in order to describe similar notions, such as "disturbance" (*perturbatio* at Cic. *Tusc.* 4.11), "mental disturbances" (*perturbationes animi* at Cic. *Tusc.* 4.22), and "illness" (*aegritudo* at Cic. *Tusc.* 4.14). In another work Cicero translates the Greek *pathē* as "mental disturbances" (*perturbationes animorum*), and remarks that the term "illness" (*morbus*) is not appropriate for conveying the meaning of the Greek on all occasions (Cic. *Fin.* 3.35), thus demonstrating his awareness of the distinction between the Stoic notions of "disease" and "perturbation" mentioned above.

[24] See for example Sen. *Ep.* 75.10–12; 85.10; 94.17; *De ira* 1.20.1.

translation for *arrōstēma* or *nosēma* when he defines *morbus* as "a judgment persevering in its fault"[25] and as the result of an accumulation of reprehensible movements of the soul.[26] *Apatheia* is therefore understood as the mind's quality of being morally healthy in the sense that it does not suffer any fits of passion

IV.2 The Virtuous Mind: Three Different Formulations

From a didactic point of view, Seneca could have stopped his exposition here. The notion of happiness has been defined with sufficient clarity, and the author could proceed to the explanation of the practical means for achieving a happy life, since the theoretical background has now been roughly laid out.[27] Surprisingly, however, instead of moving on, he continues the definitional discourse and chooses to refine his exposition of the concept. The distinctive feature of the next passage is the method of definition, which Seneca illustrates with an analogy of the varying tactical formations a military unit may assume:

> Potest aliter quoque definiri bonum nostrum, id est eadem sententia non isdem comprendi verbis. Quemadmodum idem exercitus modo latius panditur modo in angustum coartatur et aut in cornua sinuata media parte curvatur aut recta fronte explicatur, vis illi, utcumque ordinatus est, eadem est et voluntas pro eisdem partibus standi, ita finitio summi boni alias diffundi potest et exporrigi, alias colligi et in se cogi.
>
> There is another way in which this good of ours can be defined, that is, the same notion can be expressed in different words. Just as an army remains the same, though at one time it deploys with an extended line, at another it contracts into a narrow area and either stands with wings curved and centre hollowed, or stretches out with straightened front, and, whatever formation it adopts, it maintains the same energy and same resolve to fight for the same cause, so the definition of the

---

25 Sen. *Ep.* 75.11. Cf. also *SVF* 1.202; 205–206; 3.412.
26 Sen. *Ep.* 75.12.
27 An example of how concise and direct a definition of the happy life can be occurs in Sen. *Ep.* 92.3: "Quid est beata vita? Securitas et perpetua tranquillitas. Hanc dabit animi magnitudo, dabit constantia bene iudicati tenax. Ad haec quomodo pervenitur? Si veritas tota perspecta est; si servatus est in rebus agendis ordo, modus, decor, innoxia, voluntas ac benigna, intenta rationi nec umquam ab illa recedens, amabilis simul mirabilisque." – "What is the happy life? Calmness and lasting tranquillity. This will be given by greatness of soul; it will be given by the steadfastness that resolutely clings to a good judgment just reached. How does one reach that condition? By gaining a complete view of truth, by maintaining, in all that he does, order, measure, fitness, and a will that is inoffensive and kindly, that is intent upon reason and never departs therefrom, that commands at the same time love and admiration" (trans. Gummere, slightly altered)

highest good can at one time be made in a lengthy and protracted form, at another concisely and succinctly. (Sen. *Vit. beat.* 4.1, trans. Davie)

Seneca draws the reader's attention to his presentation method a second time, pointing out that the same idea can be expressed in different forms. The definition of happiness may be expanded (*diffundi*) and extended (*exporrigi*), or contracted (*colligi*) and confined to itself (*in se cogi*) like an army which changes its form to meet different demands but whose general composition remains the same. Similar thoughts occur elsewhere in Senecan prose, e.g. at *Tranq. an.* 2.3 and *Ep.* 9.2, but here the abundance of synonymous expressions is strinking. He presents the reader with three different formulations that convey the same idea. These formulations correspond to the military analogy in the sense that they vary in length and density, ranging from concise and asyndetic (marked with A in the passage below) to elaborate (C):

> Idem itaque erit, si dixero [A] "summum bonum est animus fortuita despiciens, virtute laetus" aut [B] "invicta vis animi, perita rerum, placida in actu cum humanitate multa et conversantium cura." Licet et ita finire, ut [C] beatum dicamus hominem eum cui nullum bonum malumque sit nisi bonus malusque animus, honesti cultorem, virtute contentum, quem nec extollant fortuita nec frangant, qui nullum maius bonum eo quod sibi ipse dare potest noverit, cui vera voluptas erit voluptatum contemptio.

> It will, then, be the same thing, if I say, [A] "The highest good is a mind that despises the operations of chance, rejoicing in virtue," or [B] "an unconquerable power of the mind, skilled, gentle in action, and possessed of much courtesy and care for those with whom it comes into contact." It may also be defined thus, [C] so that we consider happy that man who recognizes no good and evil apart from a good and an evil mind, who holds honour dear and is content with virtue, who is not the sort of person to let the workings of chance go to his head or crush his spirit, who does not recognize any good greater than the one he alone can confer upon himself, and who will find true pleasure in despising pleasures." (Sen. *Vit. beat.* 4.2; trans. Davie, slightly altered)

These three formulations also highlight the need for a correct appraisal of an object's value, which is the same as holding correct conceptions of what is good and bad. Thus it may be said that a soul that regards fortune and virtue according to their true value (definition A) is on the right path to happiness. In another way definition B describes these requirements by alluding to the virtues of *fortitudo* ("courage")*, prudentia* ("practical wisdom"), *magnanimitas* ("greatness of soul"), and *humanitas* ("kindness"), and virtues are even more explicitly evoked in definition C. The author refers to a correct attitude toward fortuitous events, correct evaluation of what is truly good or bad, fearlessness, and the humane treatment of fellow individuals. The mention of these attributes in particular is undoubtedly another allusion to Stoic doctrine as it is attested in the doxographic tradition to which Seneca and his readers had access.

All the same, he reframes and rephrases the characterization according to his needs. The Greek doxographies quote the Stoic definition of practical wisdom (*phronesis*) as "knowledge of good things, bad things and what is neither;"[28] greatness of soul (*megalopsuchia*) as "knowledge or a condition which makes one superior to those things which happen alike to base and viruous men;"[29] courage (*andreia*) as "the knowledge of what is terrible and what is not terrible and what is neither,"[30] and good companionship (*eukoinōnēsia*) as "the knowledge of fairness in a community."[31]

The creative manner in which Seneca makes use of Stoic descriptions of the virtues is notable. The philosopher seems to allude to Greek Stoicism but also appears to rewrite the definitions of his predecessors (*proceres*) with his own words, just as he proposes at 3.2. By rewording the traditional description of the virtues, Seneca demonstrates his familiarity with Stoic tenets and, at the same time, his thorough understanding that allows him to reformulate without distorting their content.

---

28 Stob. 2.7.5b1, vol. 2, p. 59,4–5 Wachsmuth = *SVF* 3.262 = LS 61H: "φρόνησιν εἶναι ἐπιστήμην κακῶν καὶ ἀγαθῶν καὶ οὐδετέρων." An almost identical definition is found in Diogenes Laertius 7.92 = *SVF* 3.265 and Pseudo-Andronicus 2.1.1, p. 239 Glibert-Thirry = *SVF* 3.226. The translations of definitions of virtue are taken from Inwood and Gerson 1997.

29 D.L. 7.93 = *SVF* 3.265: "τὴν δὲ μεγαλοψυχίαν ἐπιστήμην <ἢ> ἕξιν ὑπεράνω ποιοῦσαν τῶν συμβαινόντων κοινῇ φαύλων τε καὶ σπουδαίων." The definitions of Arius Didymus (Stob. 2.7.5b2, vol. 2, p. 61,15–17 Wachsmuth) and Pseudo-Andronicus (2.5.2, p. 247 Glibert-Thirry = *SVF* 3.369) are exactly the same, and both differ only slightly from that in Diogenes Laertius: Magnanimity is "knowledge which makes one superior to those things which naturally occur among both virtuous and base men" ("ἐπιστήμην ὑπεράνω ποιοῦσαν τῶν πεφυκόντων ἐν σπουδαίοις τε γίνεσται καὶ φαύλοις").

30 Stob. 2.7.5b1, vol. 2, p. 59,10–11 Wachsmuth = *SVF* 3.262 = LS 61H "ἀνδρείαν δὲ ἐπιστήμην δεινῶν καὶ οὐ δεινῶν καὶ οὐδετέρων." Diogenes Laertius has a different formulation that may be related to courage: "Endurance is knowledge of or a condition [concerned with] of what one is to stand firmly by and what is not and neither" (D.L. 7.93 = *SVF* 3.265: "τὴν δὲ καρτερίαν ἐπιστήμην ἢ ἕξιν ὧν ἐμμενετέον καὶ μὴ καὶ οὐδετέρων").

31 Stob. 2.7.5b2, vol. 2, p. 62,2 Wachsmuth = *SVF* 3.264: "ἐπιστήμην ἰσότητος ἐν κοινωνίᾳ." A similar idea of appropriate social behavior is conveyed by the virtues of *chrēstotēs* ("kindness") and *eusunallaxia* ("fair dealing"), as described by Arius Didymus at Stob. 2.7.5b2, vol. 2, p. 62,3–5 Wachsmuth = *SVF* 3.264. These virtues were regarded as species of justice (*dikaiosunē*).

IV.3 Freedom (*libertas*)

Just like the longer definition in 3.3, this sequence of three shorter formulations describes happiness as a certain mode of thought; more specifically, they refer to the possession of correct opinions with regard to the moral value of things. This aspect of the happy life is absent from the following definitions, in which Seneca emphasizes something of a very different nature. The transition is marked with another procedural comment.

> Licet, si evagari velis, idem in aliam atque aliam faciem salva et integra potestate transferre.
>
> If you want to digress, it is possible to convey the same notion in this or that appearance, with its meaning preserved and uninjured. (Sen. *Vit. beat.* 4.3)

The reader is introduced to yet another method of definition: instead of describing the same idea in different words (4.1), Seneca may also express the same idea in different images or aspects, still with no loss of content.[32]

A new theme is introduced as well. Elements of the Stoic theory of passions are now conjoined with the topic of freedom (*libertas*).

> Quid enim prohibet nos beatam vitam dicere *liberum* animum et erectum et interritum ac stabilem, extra metum, extra cupiditatem positum, cui unum bonum sit honestas, unum malum turpitudo, cetera vilis turba rerum nec detrahens quicquam beatae vitae nec adiciens, sine auctu ac detrimento summi boni veniens ac recedens? Hunc ita fundatum necesse est, velit nolit, sequatur hilaritas continua et laetitia alta atque ex alto veniens, ut qui suis gaudeat nec maiora domesticis cupiat. Quidni ista bene penset cum minutis et frivolis et non perseverantibus corpusculi motibus? Quo die *infra* voluptatem fuerit, et *infra* dolorem erit; vides autem quam malam et noxiosam *servitutem serviturus* sit quem voluptates doloresque, incertissima *dominia* inpotentissimaque, alternis *possidebunt*: ergo exeundum ad *libertatem* est. Hanc non alia res tribuit quam fortunae neglegentia: tum illud orietur inaestimabile bonum, quies mentis in tuto conlocatae et sublimitas expulsisque erroribus ex cognitione veri gaudium grande et inmotum comitasque et diffusio animi, quibus delectabitur non ut bonis sed ut ex bono suo ortis.
>
> [F]or what prevents us from saying that the happy life is to have a mind that is free, elevated, fearless, and unshakeable, a mind that exists beyond fear and beyond desire, that regards excellence as the only good and infamy as the only evil, and everything else as a trivial collection of things which come and go without subtracting anything from the happy life nor adding anything to it, and do not increase or diminish the highest good? It is necessary that someone with such a grounding, whether he wills it or not, will be accompanied by lasting cheerfulness and a profound joy that comes from a profound place, since he rejoices in what is his own and does not long for what is foreign to him. Would he not be justified in matching these joys against the measly, petty, and transitory sensations of that thing, the body? That day he finds himself under the yoke of pleasure is the day he will also

---

32 *Facies* may mean "form" or "appearance," see *ThLL* 6.1.49.60–51.60.

be under the yoke of pain; but you observe how wicked and harmful is the servitude to which a man will submit when he is enslaved in turn by pleasures and pains, those masters of the most inconstant and frivolous sort: accordingly, we must escape to freedom. This is won by no other means except by showing indifference to Fortune: then will arise that priceless good, the peace and elevation of a mind that has found a secure anchorage, and, once all error in the recognition of the truth has been eliminated, the great and unalterable happiness, together with kindness and generosity of spirit – by which he will be pleased not because they are good, but because they derive from a good that is his own." (Sen. *Vit. beat.* 4.3–4.5, trans. Davie, slightly altered)

The whole passage brims with vocabulary associated with the concept of freedom and imagery of control and compliance, such as the Latin terms marked with italics in the quotation above. It is, as the author has just proposed, the same idea viewed in a different "appearance" (*facies*). Seneca remarks that the notion of a happy life can also be seen from the point of view of "freedom." This "freedom" encompasses both the common notion of absence of hindrances and the Stoic concept of self-sufficiency (*autarkeia*). As several sources attest, the idea that virtue is sufficient (*autarkēs*) for the attainment of a happy life was a tenet of great relevance to the Stoic doctrine,[33] and this also seems to be alluded to by the passage.

Moreover, the soul is considered free because it is no longer liable to be upset by the passions since it has learned to distinguish indifferent things (*indifferentia*) from true good and evil.[34] The individual recognizes that he must not look for happiness in what is external to himself but should rely only on what is by nature his own. Seneca argues that submitting one's life to the guidance of something external such as bodily pleasure will yield bitter results since it has the same roots as physical pain and, at any rate, is not a reliable criterion. Consequently, a first connotation of "freedom," as presented in the passage, is freedom from the dominance that indifferents exert on the fools.[35]

Seneca does not abandon the theme of the passions but shifts its focus. While the previous passage emphasizes correct value judgments as an aspect of happiness, the present passage underscores the importance of

---

33 *SVF* 3.49–69; D.L. 7.127 = *SVF* 1.187 = LS 61I; 7.188 = *SVF* 3.685; Cic. *Fin.* 5.79 = *SVF* 1.187; Stob. 2.7.11h, vol. 2, p. 101,1 Wachsmuth = *SVF* 3.208; [Andronic. Rhod.] 2.6.2.7, p. 254 Glibert-Thirry = *SVF* 3.272;
34 A similar reasoning occurs in Sen. *Ep.* 75.18; 80.4–5; 123.3.
35 Compare Arr. *Epict.* 4.1.1: "Free is he who lives in the manner he wishes, who is not compelled, nor constrained, nor forced;" 4.7.10: "If […] he regards his good and advantage as residing in externals and things outside the sphere of his moral purpose, he must needs be hindered and restrained, be a slave to those who have control over these things which he had admired and feared;" trans. Oldfather, slightly altered.

such judgments for the freedom of the valuer. The relation between freedom and the theory of passions is indicated by Seneca's allusion to the four pathological movements of the soul, namely: fear (*phobos* in Greek), desire (*epithymia*), pleasure (*hēdonē*), and distress (*lypē*). According to Stoic philosophy, fear and desire consist in movements of repulsion from or attraction to something believed to be bad or good.[36] In contrast, pleasure and distress consist in the belief that something good or bad is currently experienced.[37] A correct appraisal of the moral value of things save us from suffering these four states unnecessarily. The four cardinal passions are immediately identifiable by a reader with elementary knowledge of Stoicism[38] when Seneca points out that a happy soul is placed beyond fear and desire (4.3: "extra metum, extra cupiditatem") or describes the submission to pleasure and distress as a noxious condition (4.4: "infra voluptatem […] infra dolorem). The immediate mention of freedom as an antithesis of this state of mind ("ergo exeundum ad libertatem est") brings the discourse back to the main topic of this section. Such a freedom originates exclusively ("non alia res tribuit") in the disregard of Fortune (4.5: "Fortunae neglegentia"), and in a sense it may be equated to the tranquility of a mind that holds no false conceptions.[39]

IV.4 Reason and Knowledge in Their Relation to Happiness

Still in accordance with his method of employing different themes in his definition of happiness, Seneca abandons the references to freedom and turns to a new topic, namely reason and the cognitive aspects of the happy life. This passage is characterized by an abundance of technical terms, often used in a polysemic manner, and an allusion to the epistemological theory in which this vocabulary was developed. The definition begins with wordplay, as often in his prose: The author uses the adverb *liberaliter*

---

36 Stob. 2.7.10, vol. 2, p. 88,16–18 Wachsmuth; Cic. *Tusc.* 3.24–25. Cf. also [Andronic. Rhod.] 1.1, p. 223 Glibert-Thirry = *SVF* 3.391= LS 65B.
37 Stob. 2.7.10, vol. 2, p. 88,19–21 Wachsmuth; Cic. *Tusc.* 3.24–25.
38 Seneca often hints at the fact that he expects his reader to demonstrate a certain level of philosophical education, which is required to recognize allusions to theoretical nuances (be they Stoic or Epicurean) and to perform philosophical tasks, such as basic logic reasoning, without much effort. One example for this are expressions to the effect that an implied conclusion should be evident even if they were not spelled out explicitly: *Brev. vit.* 3.4: "intellegis, etiam si non adiciam;" 8.3: "intellegitur, etiam si non adiecero".
39 Note that the association of freedom with the absence of cognitive errors and passions can also be found in Epictetus (e.g. Arr. *Epict.* 2.1.23–24; 2.17.29; 4.1.42–47; 4.3.7–8; 4.6.16).

("freehandedly," "liberally"), indicating that information about the new theme has been lavished on the reader before it was due, that is, before the conclusion of the previous topic in 4.4.

> Quoniam liberaliter agere coepi, potest beatus dici qui nec cupit nec timet beneficio rationis, quoniam et saxa timore et tristitia carent nec minus pecudes; non ideo tamen quisquam felicia dixerit quibus non est felicitatis intellectus.

> Since I have begun to treat this topic liberally, one may describe the happy man as someone who neither desires nor fears thanks to the gift of reason, inasmuch as even rocks are without fear and grief, and no less are farm animals; however, no one would call these things "happy," when they have no understanding of happiness. (Sen. *Vit. beat.* 5.1, trans. Davie, slightly altered).

As in the previous definitions, the individual is here considered happy because he does not fear or desire. However, the emphasis of this passage is now on the rational grounds for that condition. The motive is clarified immediately :

> Eodem loco pone homines quos in numerum pecorum et animalium redegit hebes natura et ignoratio sui. Nihil interest inter hos et illa, quoniam illis nulla ratio est, his prava et malo suo atque in perversum sollers; beatus enim dici nemo potest extra veritatem proiectus.

> Assign to the same category those people whose dull nature and ignorance of themselves have brought them down to the level of beasts of the field and animals. There is no difference between these people and those creatures, since the latter have no reason, while the former have a reason that is warped, and, because it expends its energy in the wrong direction, harmful to themselves; for no one can be considered happy if he has been cast beyond the border of truth. (Sen. *Vit. beat.* 5.2, trans. Davie, partially altered).

Seneca informs the reader that another aspect of Stoic happiness is its cognitive content. The condition of not experiencing passions leads an individual to happiness only if it is generated by reason, and this is why it would be incorrect to deem stones and beasts "happy." The following paragraph further explains the role of reason in this process.

> Beata ergo vita est in recto certoque iudicio stabilita et inmutabilis. Tunc enim pura mens est et soluta omnibus malis, quae non tantum lacerationes sed etiam vellicationes effugerit, statura semper ubi constitit ac sedem suam etiam irata et infestante fortuna vindicatura. 4. Nam quod ad voluptatem pertinet, licet circumfundatur undique et per omnis vias influat animumque blandimentis suis leniat aliaque ex aliis admoveat quibus totos partesque nostri sollicitet, quis mortalium, cui ullum superest hominis vestigium, per diem noctemque titillari velit et deserto animo corpori operam dare?

> Accordingly, the happy life has been firmly established on a judgment that is correct and fixed, and not it is not subject to change. For that is the time when the mind is unclouded and released from all evil, as it has escaped not only serious wounds but even scratches, and, determined to hold to the end whatever position it has taken, it will defend its post, however angrily Fortune makes her assault. For as

far as pleasure is concerned, though it pours itself all around us and flows in through every channel, charming our minds with its blandishments, and applying one means after another to tempt us wholly or partly, who on earth, who has any trace of humanity left in him, would wish to have his senses stimulated day and night and, abandoning the mind, to devote himself to the body? (Sen. *Vit. beat.* 5.3–5.4, trans. Davie, slightly altered).

In the previous section Seneca defined the happy life as a result of the disregard of Fortune and consequent freedom from the passions; here the reader learns that such life must be firmly based on a "correct and reliable judgment." This as a reference to *epistēmē* (here translated as "knowledge"), which Arius Didymus[40] and Sextus Empiricus[41] define as "a cognition which is secure and unchangeable by reason."

Stoic doxography indicates that happiness, indeed, requires *epistēmē*, which is the genus of a definition of wisdom as "knowledge of divine and human matters"[42] and of virtues such as those quoted above (p. 344). According to the cognitive theory that underlies that assumption, it is through the purging of false conceptions and the absolute control over one's ability to give or withhold assent (in Greek, *synkatathesis*) that the individual can accumulate cognitive impressions (*phantasiai kataleptikai*) and, with time and the proper processes, form a solid body of knowledge (*epistēmē*).[43] This "knowledge" is stable, true, and unchangeable because it is composed solely of cognitive impressions, which are characterized by their true and reliable representation of facts.[44] It is to this epistemological theory that Seneca seems to be alluding in this passage. Several elements of the section are evocative of knowledge in the Stoic sense, for example the references to purity of mind and to its stability or firmness.[45] Equally relevant is the mention of the removal of cognitive flaws concerning the true meaning of happiness at the end of section 4.5,[46] of the correct use of rational faculties (5.1–5.2), and of an absolute truth (5.2).

---

40 Stob. 2.7.5k, vol. 2, p. 73,19–21 Wachsmuth = *SVF* 3.112 = LS 41H.
41 Sext. Emp. *Math.* 7.151 = LS 41C.
42 Sext. Emp. *Math.* 9.13 = *SVF* 2.36; Aëtius 1 Proem. 2 = *SVF* 2.35.
43 The several steps of the cognitive process that leads an individual to wisdom have been the subject of a wide range of studies, including Görler 1977; Striker 1983; Inwood 1985 and 2005; Newman 1989; Annas 1992; Long and Sedley 2000; Brennan 2003; Hankinson 2003; Bees 2004; Wildberger 2006; Inwood and Donini 2008; Frede 2008; Vogt 2008.
44 Cf. Sext. Emp. *Math.* 7.257 = *SVF* 2.65 = LS 40E.
45 Sen. *Vit. beat.* 4.3: "pura mens," "stabilita et inmutabilis," "statura semper ubi consistit," "admoveat," "sollicitet."
46 Sen. *Vit. beat.* 4.5: "Expulsis erroribus ex cognitione veri gaudium."

IV.5 Mental Pleasures and Their Priority for the Mind

In the next paragraph Seneca brings the definition closer to the Epicurean concept of happiness – which is subsequently refuted with Stoic arguments. In the exposition that follows Seneca contrasts not only Epicurean and Stoic assessments of pleasure, but also the role that the mind should play in attaining them according to these doctrines:

> "Sed animus quoque" inquit "voluptates habebit suas." Habeat sane sedeatque luxuriae et voluptatium arbiter; inpleat se eis omnibus quae oblectare sensus solent, deinde praeterita respiciat et exoletarum voluptatium memor exultet prioribus futurisque iam immineat ac spes suas ordinet et, dum corpus in praesenti sagina iacet, cogitationes ad futura praemittat: hoc mihi videbitur miserior, quoniam mala pro bonis legere dementia est. Nec sine sanitate quisquam beatus est nec sanus cui futura pro optimis adpetuntur.

> "However," he says, "the mind, too, will have its own pleasures." Let it have them by all means, and let it preside as a judge over luxury and pleasures; let it cram itself with all the things that are accustomed to delight the senses, then let it look back to the past and, recollecting vanished pleasures, let it revel in former experiences and eagerly anticipate now those to come, laying its plans, and, while the body lies supine from cramming itself in the present, let it turn its thoughts to future indulgences! Yet all this, it seems to me, will bring the mind greater misery, since it is madness to choose bad things instead of good. And no one is happy without being sound of mind, just as that one is not sane who sets his heart on future pleasures in preference to what is excellent. (Sen. *Vit. beat.* 6.1, trans. Davie, slightly altered).

This paragraph's emphasis on the present moment and the contrast evoked by references to bodily conditions constitutes an allusion to Epicurean categorizations of pleasure as well as Seneca's rebuttal of Epicurus' theory. Epicureans are known to have considered pleasures of the mind more desirable than those of the body since the latter are limited to a specific moment in time, while the former can also be triggered by anticipation of future pleasures or by recollection of the past, as Epicurus tells us in his *Principal Saying* 20:

> Ἡ μὲν σὰρξ ἀπέλαβε τὰ πέρατα τῆς ἡδονῆς ἄπειρα καὶ ἄπειρος αὐτὴν χρόνος παρεσκεύασεν· ἡ δὲ διάνοια τοῦ τῆς σαρκὸς τέλους καὶ πέρατος λαβοῦσα τὸν ἐπιλογισμὸν καὶ τοὺς ὑπὲρ τοῦ αἰῶνος φόβους ἐκλύσασα τὸν παντελῆ βίον παρεσκεύασε, καὶ οὐθὲν ἔτι τοῦ ἀπείρου χρόνου προσεδεήθη· ἀλλ' οὔτε ἔφυγε τὴν ἡδονὴν οὐδ' ἡνίκα τὴν ἐξαγωγὴν ἐκ τοῦ ζῆν τὰ πράγματα παρεσκεύαζεν, ὡς ἐλλείπουσά τι τοῦ ἀρίστου βίου κατέστρεψεν.

> The flesh receives as unlimited the limits of pleasure; and to provide it requires unlimited time. But the mind, grasping in thought what the end and limit of the flesh is, and banishing the terrors of futurity, procures a complete and perfect life, and has no longer any need of unlimited time. Nevertheless it does not shun pleasure, and even in the hour of death, when ushered out of existence by circum-

stances, the mind does not lack enjoyment of the best life. (Epicur. *Sent.* 20; trans. Hicks)

Seneca not only defends the standard Stoic view that pleasure is an indifferent and thus irrelevant for a happy life. He even rejects the preference for intellectual pleasures defended by Epicurus. According to him, it is much more harmful to strive for intellectual instead of bodily pleasures since the mind must neglect what he sees as the true good in order to do so. Under no circumstance would he admit that they contribute to a happy life. Rather than expending mental effort on remembering, anticipating, or seeking pleasure he would recommend that one focus on reason, a human being's particular good. The contrast between Epicurean and Stoic approaches toward pleasure works thus highlights a more fundamental disagreement between the two schools: While Stoics believe that the mind must be actively used only to pursue virtue and agreement (*homologia*), Epicureans argue that it must be employed to actively seek pleasures – something which, from Seneca's perspective, is a function far too petty for such a noble faculty.

Three statements conclude the sequence of definitions from 3.2 to 6.2 with a typical anaphoric *accumulatio*, summarizing the concepts introduced in this and the previous section.

> Beatus ergo est iudicii rectus; beatus est praesentibus qualiacumque sunt contentus amicusque rebus suis; beatus est is cui omnem habitum rerum suarum ratio commendat.
>
> The happy man, therefore, is correct in his judgments; the happy man is satisfied with his present situation, no matter what it is, and likes what he has; the happy man is the one to whom reason renders agreeable whatever state his affairs are in. (Sen. *Vit. beat.* 6.2)

These final descriptions take the form of *sententiae* – short, asyndetic statements easy to memorize (see Dinter in this volume). There is no explanation of the premises underlying these formulations nor any argumentation to prove their truth. As it happens often in Senecan didactic, a long line of reasoning is wrapped up by a *sententia*, which helps the reader to remember the central idea and its most important premises. The conjunction *ergo* introduces the *sententiae* as conclusions following from the preceding paragraphs: Since happiness is caring about what is truly ours and having a sane mind, it follows that a happy person will be "correct in his judgments." Likewise, he will be content with his present condition, that is, with what is his own and what is laid out before him. Finally, the individual is able to agree with nature and thus practice the fundamental tenet that Seneca shares with all Stoics (as he declares in 3.2), because his situation and whatever may happen to him is rendered agreeable to him by his reason

V.

We thus observe that Seneca has fulfilled his promise and has extended, condensed, and transfigured a Stoic definition of happiness. Following a brief introduction that culminates in his self-portrayal as a legitimate member of the Stoic school (*Vit. beat.* 1.1–3.2), the author initiates a series of definitions of that notion and describes that same idea to an extent that may seem excessive or repetitive. However, the meta-discursive remarks found in *Vit. beat.* 3.2, 4.1 and 4.3 indicate to the audience that these variations follow a method, and a close reading has shown that the sequence of definitions is divided into thematic blocks, each dealing with the concept of happiness from a different angle.

In each of these topic sections Seneca demonstrates expert knowledge of Stoic theory. In *Vit. beat.* 3.3–3.4 he describes the idea of happiness according to the notion of *apatheia*, also discussing the stance one should ideally take toward external objects in order to achieve a happy life. In *Vit. beat.* 4.1–4.2 the author continues the theme of the previous sections, while changing both the defined objects (i.e. the supreme good and the happy person) and the characteristics attributed to each one of them. The following sequence of definitions (*Vit. beat.* 4.3–4.5) is enriched by a change in the theoretical background of the discussion. By introducing the images of freedom and self-sufficiency and by alluding to Stoic virtues, Seneca demonstrates that he understands the many facets of the important concept of happiness. With the additional thematic variation in *Vit. beat.* 5.1–5.4, the author defines the happy life according to the Stoic theory of cognition, and, therefore, focuses on its rational elements. Finally, in *Vit. beat.* 6.1, Seneca defends the Stoic idea of happiness against what seems to be an objection of Epicurean origin and concludes in the following paragraph (6.2) with a summary of the topics discussed since *Vit. beat.* 3.3. The beginning of *De vita beata* thus serves as a deliberate declaration of mastery on Seneca's part, and the apparently repetitive series of definitions play an important role in this demonstration of philosophical skill.

Bibliography

Ackeren, Marcel van, ed. 2012. *A Companion to Marcus Aurelius*. Hoboken: Wiley-Blackwell.

Albrecht, Michael von. 2004. *Wort und Wandlung: Senecas Lebenskunst*. Leiden; Boston: Brill.

Albrecht, Michael von. 2008. "Seneca's Language and Style." *Hyperboreus* 14: 68–90.

Annas, Julia. 1992. *Hellenistic Philosophy of Mind*. Berkeley: University of California Press. Rpt. 1994.

Bees, Robert. 2004. *Die Oikeiosislehre der Stoa: Rekonstruktion ihres Inhalts*. Würzburg: Königshausen & Neumann.
Bellincioni, Maria. 1978. *Educazione alla sapientia in Seneca*. Brescia: Paideia.
Brennan, Tad. 2003. "Stoic Moral Psychology." In *The Cambridge Companion to the Stoics*, edited by Brad Inwood, 257–294. Cambridge: Cambridge University Press.
Byrd, Robert C. 1995. *The Senate of the Roman Republic: Adresses on the History of Roman Constitutionalism*. Washington: US Government Printing Office.
Chaumartin, François-Régis. 1989. "Les désillusions de Sénèque devant l'evolution de la politique néronienne et l'aspiration à la retraite: 'De uita beata' et le 'De beneficiis'." *ANRW* II 36.3: 1684–1723.
Cruttwell, Charles Thomas. 1906. *A History of Roman Literature*. New York: Charles Scribner's Sons.
Dalzell, Alexander. 1996. *The Criticism of Didactic Poetry: Essays on Lucretius, Virgil,and Ovid*. Toronto: University of Torono Press.
Davie, John, trans., and Tobias Reinhardt., ed. 2007. *Seneca: Dialogues and Essays*. Oxford: Oxford University Press.
Diogenes Laertius. 1925. *Lives of Eminent Philosophers*. See Hicks 1925.
Epictetus. 1952. *The Discourses as Reported by Arrian, the Manual and Fragments*. See Oldfather 1952.
Farrar, Frederic. W. 2005. *Seekers after God*. New York: Cosimo.
Frede, Michael. 2008. "Stoic Epistemology". In *The Cambridge History of Hellenistic Philosophy*, edited by Keimpe Algra, Jonathan Barnes, Jaap Mansfeld, and Malcolm Schofield, 295–322. Cambridge: Cambridge University Press.
Görler, Woldemar. 1977. "Ἀσθενὴς συγκατάθεσις: Zur stoischen Erkenntnislehre." *WJA* 3: 83–92.
Graver, Margaret R. 2007. *Stoicism and Emotion*. Chicago: University of Chicago Press.
Griffin, Miriam T. 1992. *Seneca: A Philosopher in Politics*. 2nd ed. Oxford: Clarendon Press.
Griffin, Miriam T. 2008. "Imago vitae suae." In *Seneca*, edited by John. G. Fitch, 23–58. Oxford: Oxford University Press.
Gummere, Richard M., ed. and trans. 1920. *Seneca, Ad Lucilium epistulae morales*. Vol. 2. London; Cambridge: Heinemann; Harvard University Press.
Hadot, Ilsetraut. 1969. *Seneca und die griechisch-römische Tradition der Seelenleitung*. Berlin: De Gruyter.
Hadot, Pierre. 1992. *La citadelle intérieure: Introduction aus pensées de Marc Aurèle*. Paris: Les Belles Lettres.
Hankinson, Robert J. 2003. "Stoic Epistemology." In *The Cambridge Companion to the Stoics*, edited by Brad Inwood. 59–84. Cambridge: Cambridge University Press.
Hegel, Georg W. F. 1986. *Vorlesungen über die Geschichte der Philosophie*. Vol. 2. Frankfurt am Main: Suhrkamp Verlag, 1986.
Hicks, Robert D., ed. and trans. 1925. *Diogenes Laertius, Lives of Eminent Philosophers*. Vol. 2. London; Cambridge: Heinemann; Harvard University Press.
Hijmans, Benjamin L. 1959. *Ἄσκησις: Notes on Epictetus' Educational System*. Assen: Van Gorcum & Comp.
Hurschmann, Rolf. 2012a. "Chlamys." In *Brill's New Pauly*, edited by Hubert Cancik and Helmuth Schneider. Accessed April 15, 2012. http://referenceworks.brillonline.com/entries/brill-s-new-pauly/chlamys-e232850
Hurschmann, Rolf. 2012b. "Wreath, Garland." In *Brill's New Pauly*, edited by Hubert Cancik and Helmut Schneider. Accessed April 15, 2012. http://referenceworks.brillonline.com/entries/brill-s-new-pauly/wreath-garland-e622060
Inwood, Brad. 1985. *Ethics and Human Action in Early Stoicism*. Oxford: Clarendon Press.

Inwood, Brad. 2005. *Reading Seneca: Stoic Philosophy at Rome.* Oxford: Clarendon Press.
Inwood, Brad, and Pierluigi Donini. 2008. "Stoic Ethics." In *The Cambridge History of Hellenistic Philosophy*, edited by Keimpe Algra, Jonathan Barnes, Jaap Mansfeld, and Malcolm Schofield, 675–738. Cambridge: Cambridge University Press.
Inwood, Brad, and Lloyd P. Gerson, trans. 1997. *Hellenistic Philosophy: Introductory Readings.* 2nd ed. Indianapolis; Cambridge: Hackett.
Kuen, Gabriele. 1994. *Die Philosophie als "dux vitae:" Die Verknüpfung von Gehalt, Intention und Darstellungsweise im philosophischen Werk Senecas am Beispiel des Dialogs "De vita beata:" Einleitung, Wortkommentar und systematische Darstellung.* Heidelberg: Winter.
L'Estrange, Roger. 1882. *Seneca's Morals of a Happy Life, Benefits, Anger, and Clemency.* Chicago: Belford, Clarke & Co.
Long, Anthony A., and David N. Sedley, eds. and trans. 1987. *The Hellenistic Philosophers.* 2 vols. Cambridge: Cambridge University Press.
Milton, John. 1818. *The History of Britain.* London: R. Wilks.
Motto, Anna Lydia. 1966. "The Case of the Opulent Stoic." *CJ* 61: 254–258.
Mutschler, Fritz-Heiner. 1998. "Variierende Wiederholung: Zur literarischen Eigenart von Senecas philosophischen Schriften." In *Mousopolos Stephanos: Festschrift Herwig Görgemanns*, edited by Manuel Baumbach, Helga Köhler and Adolf M. Ritter, 143–159. Heidelberg: Winter.
Newman, Robert J. 1989. " 'Cotidie Meditare:' Theory and Practice of the Meditatio in Imperial Stoicism." *ANRW* II 36.3: 1473–1517.
Oldfather, William A., ed. and trans. 1952. *Epictetus: The Discourses as Reported by Arrian, the Manual and Fragments.* Vol. 2. Cambridge: Harvard University Press.
Rabbow, Paul. 1914. *Antike Schriften über Seelenheilung und Seelenleitung.* Vol. 1. Leipzig: B. G. Teubner.
Reynolds, Leighton D., ed. 1977. *L. Annaei Senecae dialogorum libri duodecim.* Oxford: Clarendon Press. Rpt. with corrections 1991.
Rose, Herbert. J. 1954. *A Handbook of Latin Literature: From the Earliest Times to the Death of St. Augustine.* 3rd ed. Wauconda: Bolchazy-Carducci. Rpt. 1996.
Sandbach, Francis H. 1989. *The Stoics.* 2nd ed. London: Duckworth.
Seneca. 1977. *Dialogorum libri duodecim.* See Reynolds 1977.
Seneca. 1920. *Ad Lucilium epistulae morales.* See Gummere 1920.
Seneca. 2007. *Dialogues and Essays.* See Davie 2007.
Striker, Gisela. 1983. "The Role of Oikeiosis in Stoic Ethics." *OSAPh* 1: 145–167.
Traina, Alfonso. 1974. *Lo stile "drammatico" del filosofo Seneca.* Bologna: Pàtron.
Trevelyan, George O., ed. 2006. *Life and Letters of Lord Macaulay.* Teddington: The Echo Library.
Van den Hout, Michael P. J., ed. 1988. *M. Cornelii Frontonis Epistulae.* Leipzig: Teubner.
Vogt, Katja M. 2008. *Law, Reason, and the Cosmic City: Political Philosophy in the Early Stoa.* Oxford: Oxford University Press.
Wedeck, Harry E. 1955. "The Question of Seneca's Wealth." *Latomus* 14: 540–544.
Wildberger, Jula. 2006. "Seneca and the Stoic Theory of Cognition: Some Preliminary Remarks." In *Seeing Seneca Whole: Perspectives on Philosophy, Poetry, and Politics*, edited by Katharina Volk and Gareth D. Williams, 75–102. Leiden; Boston: Brill.

In Praise of Tubero's Pottery:
A Note on Seneca, *Ep.* 95.72–73 and 98.13

Francesca Romana Berno
Sapienza Università di Roma

The importance of historical examples in Latin literature, and in the Roman world in general, is commonly acknowledged by scholars.[1] In Seneca, they are intended as special means of philosophical exhortation,[2] and in this regard, he sometimes offers an original rereading of an example. My aim is to focus on a minor example, that of Q. Aelius Tubero, which Seneca interprets differently from his predecessors (Cicero in particular), and to analyze it both from an intertextual and an intratextual point of view. First, I will examine the relationship between Seneca and his source Cicero, in order to show a deliberate polemic of the former against the latter. Then, I will turn to the structure of the letters in which Tubero appears, to understand why Seneca accords him signal positions, such as the end of *Letter* 95. The analysis will stress the philosophical significance of this rhetorical feature: Tubero's eulogy becomes an apology of Stoic rigorism.

I. Tubero's Story: Cicero and Valerius Maximus

Q. Aelius Tubero was the grandson of L. Aemilius Paulus and nephew of P. Scipio Africanus. He was also a pupil of Panaetius and famous for his competence in astronomy and meteorology and for his frugality.[3] Aspiring

---

1 There is a huge bibliography on this topic. See, e.g., Wheatland Litchfield 1914; Bettini 2000; Braun et al. 2000; Hölkeskamp 2004; Romano 2006; Linke and Stemmler 2000 (in particular Stemmler 2000); Coudry and Späth 2001 (in particular Mencacci 2001); Morgan 2009, 122–159. On the philosophical meaning and rhetorical *status* of *exempla*, Kornhardt 1936; Gazich 1990.
2 See Mayer 1991; Chaumartin 1997, 153–154; Armisen-Marchetti 2006, 197–200; Wildberger 2006, 192–197 (with reference to *Ep.* 6.5; 75.1–5); Richardson-Hay 2006, 101–105; Costa 2013 (on Tubero: 177f.).
3 On Tubero in general, see Klebs 1893; Elvers 1996; Garbarino 1973, vol. 1, pp. 104–108 and vol. 2, pp. 435–440; Garbarino 2003, 64–65. On his relationship with Panaetius, see Cic. *Ac.* 135; *Fin.* 4.23; *Tusc.* 4.4; *Off.* 3.63; on his expertise in as-

to become praetor, Tubero organized a sacrificial banquet to celebrate the memory of his uncle, but following the rigorous frugality of his Stoic doctrine, he used pottery instead of silver dishes and wooden stools covered with goatskins instead of padded sofas. As a result, he was defeated in the elections. This episode is narrated as an example by Cicero, later by Valerius Maximus, and then by Seneca: I will briefly present the first two texts before focusing on the last.

Cicero is our first source for this example,[4] which appears in his speech *Pro Murena* (63 BCE). It is used to demonstrate the undesirability of extreme behavior in politics: The same frugality that one admires in the private man is frowned upon in a political context. Cicero's critique is consistent with his particular aim in this text, which is to stigmatize the excesses of Stoic rigor in order to diminish Cato's authority (Cato being the prosecutor of his client Murena). The example is in fact preceded by a detailed critique directly addressed to Cato (*Mur.* 60–68). He is ironically[5] presented as the bearer of an anachronistic, paradoxical, and unhelpful philosophy, with self-defeating consequences in politics.

> Qua re noli, Cato, maiorum instituta quae res ipsa, quae diuturnitas imperii comprobat nimium severa oratione reprehendere. Fuit eodem ex studio vir *eruditus* apud patres nostros et honestus homo et nobilis, Q. Tubero. Is, cum epulum Q. Maximus, P. Africani patrui sui nomine, populo Romano daret, rogatus est a Maximo ut triclinium sterneret, cum esset Tubero eiusdem Africani sororis filius. Atque ille homo *eruditissimus ac Stoicus* stravit pelliculis haedinis lectulos Punicanos et exposuit vasa Samia quasi vero esset Diogenes Cynicus mortuus et non divini hominis Africani mors honestaretur [...] Huius in morte celebranda graviter tulit populus Romanus hanc *perversam sapientiam* Tuberonis. 76 Itaque homo integerrimus, civis optimus, cum esset L. Pauli nepos, P. Africani, ut dixi, sororis filius, his haedinis pelliculis praetura deiectus est. Odit populus Romanus privatam luxuriam, publicam magnificentiam diligit; non amat profusas epulas, sordes et inhumanitatem multo minus; distinguit ratione officiorum ac temporum, vicissitudinem laboris ac voluptatis.

> Do not then, Cato, condemn in too harsh terms the customs of our ancestors, which are vindicated by experience and by the longevity of our government. There was in

---

tronomy, Cic. *Rep.* 1.14–17, 23–29, 31–32; on his frugality, see also (in addition to the passages from Cicero, Valerius, and Seneca discussed in this paper) Athenaeus, who writes that only Tubero, Rutilius Rufus, and Mucius Scaevola followed the *lex Fannia* (161 BCE) against luxury at banquets (4.108, 274a–275b).

4 On historical *exempla* in Cicero, see Schoenberger 1910; Plumpe 1932; Roloff 1967, 274–322; David 1980; Stemmler 2000; Van Der Blom 2010.

5 About irony in this context, see Van der Wal 2007; Nótári 2008, 52–61. In particular on *Mur.* 75–76, see the commentary of Adamietz 1989, 226–229, who recalls *Flac.* 73–75 regarding the different evaluations of luxury in private and in public, and La Penna 1989, 18–23, who finds the source of this topic in Demosthenes' *Third Olynthiac* (3.25–26).

our father's day a *scholar and a Stoic* like yourself, a fine man and an aristocrat, Quintus Tubero. When Quintus Maximus was giving a feast to the Roman people in honor of his uncle Publius Africanus, Tubero who was the son of the sister of this same Africanus was asked by Maximus to fit out a dining room. Whereupon, being *deeply versed in Stoicism*, he covered Punic couches with goatskins and set out Samian crockery more appropriate for the death of Diogenes the Cynic than a banquet to honor the death of the mighty Africanus. [...] The Roman people took hard Tubero's *ill-timed philosophy* in the ceremony commemorating Africanus' death. 76 These goatskins cost this most upright of men and the best of citizens the praetorship although he was the grandson of Lucius Paulus and, as I have said, the son of Publius Africanus' sister. The Roman people loathe private luxury, but they love public splendour. They do not like extravagant banquets, but much less do they like shabbiness and meanness; they take into account the variety of obligations and circumstances and recognize the alternation of work and pleasure. (Cic. *Mur.* 75–76, trans. Macdonald, modified)

In this passage, we can note many ironic features, such as the redundant repetition of *eruditus* ("a scholar"),[6] the abundance of superlatives,[7] and the insistence on Tubero's nobility,[8] all of which contrast with the humiliating electoral defeat. Also ironic is the comparison between the misanthropic philosopher Diogenes the Cynic and Scipio, who was one of the most famous Roman generals. Nevertheless, this light tone contrasts with the harsh definition Cicero gives of Tubero's behavior: *perversa sapientia*. This expression represents a singularity in Latin literature and is also a paradox, in that it implies that Tubero turns the moral and intellectual perfection of the sage (*sapientia*) into its opposite, i.e. a vice (*perversa*, from *perverto*, "to subvert"). Since Cicero in this context underlines the philosophical competence of his audience,[9] this expression may be an intentional reference to Stoic *diastrophē* – the distortion of the natural impulse towards the good into its contrary – whose Latin translation was, indeed, *perversitas*.[10] The expression *perversa sapientia* condenses Cicero's over-

---

6 Cic. *Mur.* 75: "eodem ex studio eruditus [...] eruditissimus et Stoicus."
7 Cic. *Mur.* 75: "eruditissimus;" 76: "homo integerrimus, civis optimus."
8 Cic. *Mur.* 75: "honestus homo et nobilis;" 76: "L. Pauli nepos, P. Africani, ut dixi, sororis filius."
9 Cic. *Mur.* 61: "Et quoniam non est nobis haec oratio habenda aut in imperita multitudine aut in aliquo conventu agrestium, audacius paulo de studiis humanitatis quae et mihi et vobis nota et iucunda sunt disputabo" – "Seeing, too, that I do not have to address an ignorant crowd or some gathering of rustics, I shall be a little more venturesome in discussing the liberal studies which are so familiar and agreeable to us both" (trans. Macdonald).
10 *Perversitas* is the Ciceronian word for *diastrophē*, whereas Seneca generally prefers *pravitas* (and *pravus*); the "ratio [...] in *perversum* sollers" is the mind of vicious men (Sen. *Vit. beat.* 5.2). See Grilli 1963; Bellincioni 1978, 33–37; Bellincioni 1979, 36–37 and 163–164 *ad Ep.* 95.30; cf. *Ep.* 95.41 (quoted below, p. 379–380); Wildberger 2006, 58.

all judgment about Stoicism and politics: Stoic philosophy is not wrong per se, but if pursued inflexibly, it is self-defeating and entails negative consequences. In other works as well, such as the *Brutus*, Cicero repeats this judgment: If Tubero was not the equal of his noble ancestors in terms of political success, it was because of his harshness in life and speech.[11]

The same example appears as the first item in Valerius Maximus' chapter about electoral defeats. This passage is remarkable because here we find explicit references to Cicero's version, occasionally even literal quotation,[12] and an analogous final comment: The same frugality which was admirable at home was inacceptable in a political context, and so the Romans were right to punish Tubero by not electing him as a praetor.

> Q. Aelius Tubero a Q. Fabio Maximo epulum populo nomine P. Africani patrui sui dante rogatus ut triclinium sterneret, lectulos Punicanos pellibus haedinis stravit et pro argenteis vasis Samia exposuit. *Cuius rei deformitas* sic homines offendit ut, cum alioqui vir egregius haberetur comitiisque praetoriis candidatus in campum L. Paulo avo et P. Africano avunculo nixus descendisset, repulsa inde abiret notatus: nam ut privatim semper continentiam probabant, ita publice maxima cura splendoris habita est. Quocirca urbs non unius convivii numerum, sed totam se in illis pelliculis iacuisse credens *ruborem* epuli suffragiis suis vindicavit.

> Q. Aelius Tubero was asked by Q. Fabius Maximus, who was giving a feast to the Roman people in honor of his uncle P. Africanus, to fit out a dining room. He covered Punic couches with goatskins and set out Samian crockery instead of silver. *This shabby proceeding* gave such offence that although he otherwise passed for an excellent person and went down to the Campus as a candidate at the praetorian elections relying on his grandfather L. Paulus and his maternal uncle P. Africanus, he left it with the stigma of rejection. For while they always approved of private frugality, publicly they set much store on a handsome show. So the city felt that its whole entity, not just the complement of one dinner party, had lain on those skins and by its votes took its revenge for the *shame* of the banquet. (V. Max. 7.5.1 [*De repulsis*], trans. Shackleton Bailey, modified)

Tubero's behavior is here separated from philosophical considerations: There are no references to wisdom and the like. In fact, Valerius does not have Cicero's aim of criticizing Stoicism. He is simply listing famous examples of electoral defeats. Tubero's poor banquet is considered a pro-

---

11 Cic. *Brut.* 117: "Ut vita sic oratione *durus* incultus horridus, itaque honoribus maiorum respondere non potuit" – "Like his life, so his language was harsh, untrained, and rough: and so in the career of office he did not attain to the rank of his ancestors" (trans. Hubbell).

12 Together with Livy, Cicero is recognized as one of the most important of Valerius' sources, whether by a collection of *exempla* (Bosch 1929, 57–109) or directly, as most scholars maintain: Maslakov 1984, 457–461; Bloomer 1992, 59–146; Wardle 1998, 15–18. On the relationship between the work of Valerius and the Roman tradition of *exempla*, see Skidmore 1996 (16–21 about Cicero, 25–27 about Seneca).

voking *deformitas*, something which made the Romans blush with shame (*rubor*). This position is somewhat contradictory to Valerius' own attitude towards frugality, which he always praises and considers characteristic of Romans in contrast to the luxury of foreign people.[13] For example, Cato the Elder is praised for using goatskins in public (4.3.11). Moreover, the homonymous father of our protagonist, Q. Aelius Tubero, son-in-law of L. Aemilius Paulus, is described as an example of frugality in an episode which deals precisely with pottery (4.3.7; see also 4.4.9): The Aetolians send Tubero silver vessels, and he refuses to accept this gift, continuing to use his modest earthenware.[14]

> Curi et Fabrici Q. Tuberonem cognomine Catum discipulum fuisse merito quis existimaverit. Cui consulatum gerenti cum Aetolorum gens omnis usus vasa argentea [...] per legatos misisset, qui superiore tempore gratulandi causa ad eum profecti rettulerant fictilia se in eius mensa vidisse, monitos ne continentiae quasi paupertati succurrendum putarent cum suis sarcinis abire iussit.
>
> One might well think that Q. Tubero surnamed Catus had been a pupil of Curius and Fabricius. When he was consul, the Aetolian nation sent him silver vessels [...] by the hand of envoys who had gone to thank him earlier on and reported having seen some vessels of clay on his table. He advised them that they should not suppose continence to need assistance like poverty and told them to go away with their baggage. (V. Max. 4.3.7 [*De abstinentia et continentia*], trans. Shackleton Bailey, slightly modified)

The Tuberos were evidently fond of expressing their frugality with the demonstrative use of pottery.[15] The two episodes have many features in common.[16] This is indeed an example of private parsimony.[17] Neverthe-

---

13   See, e.g., 2.5.6; 6.9.3. For the concept and representation of *frugalitas* at Rome (the opposite of the vice *luxuria*: Sen. *Ep.* 71.23; Quint. *Inst.* 5.10.73), see in general Corbier 1989 and La Penna 1989. For Seneca, see Citroni Marchetti 1991, 116–137; Borgo 1998, 73–74; Classen 2010, 237, 240f., and 258f.; Richardson-Hay 2009; Sen. *Polyb.* 3.5; *Marc.* 2.3; *Tranq. an.* 2.9; *Ep.* 5.5–6; *Ep.* 95.32. See also below, nn. 15 and 30.
14   The anecdote is repeated in Pliny the Elder (33.142). According to Shackleton Bailey, 374–375 n. 10, both Valerius and Pliny wrongly attribute it to Q. Aelius Tubero. In his opinion, the consul was, in fact, Sex. Aelius Paetus Catus. Klebs 1893, 535, on the other hand, confirms the correctness of Valerius' reference.
15   The praise of *frugalitas* is often expressed with reference to *fictilia* in opposition to objects made of silver or gold: see Ov. *Met.* 8.688; *Fast.* 1.202 and 3.14; V. Max. 4.4.11. Philemon and Baucis, the famous Ovidian couple, behave in a way similar to Tubero: They offer to the gods first a stool covered with a rough carpet (*Met.* 8.639f.), then a couch with a poor mattress (655f.), and the food is served in earthenware dishes, "omnia fictilibus" (668).
16   This similarity is so clear that a fourteenth-century commentator of Seneca's letters, Domenico da Peccioli, quotes Valerius' anecdote about Tubero the Elder as a parallel to the Senecan passage about our Tubero in *Ep.* 95.72 (see Marcucci 2007, 588).

less, it is shown in public, to the Aetolian envoys. A difference between the two episodes can be found in the addressee of the exemplary behavior: in this case (Tubero the Elder), the foreign Aetolians; in the other (Tubero the Younger), gods and also Romans. However, Valerius' judgment about Tubero the Younger was probably most of all influenced by Cicero. Even if there is no hint at Stoic rigor as the cause of the wrong behavior in Valerius, the interpretation of the episode is very similar, grounded as it is on the distinction between laudable private frugality and public frugality, which is to be condemned. Even though Valerius' aim is far from Cicero's intention to denigrate Stoic rigor, Tubero remains a negative example.

II. *Ep.* 95.72–73: Seneca vs. Cicero[18]

Seneca refers to Tubero four times, in the last books of his *Letters to Lucilius* (95.72–73; 98.13; 104.21; 120.19). Of these passages, only the first two deal with the episode of the banquet.[19] Their significance becomes apparent if they are read in their broader context.

Tubero appears at the end of *Letter* 95, one of the most famous in the Senecan corpus, in the scene with the earthenware. Without a word about

---

17 Cf., in the passage quoted: "in eius mensa" – "on his table."
18 The intertextual relationship between Cicero and Seneca still awaits a comprehensive study (even if, for example, Mayer 1991, 150f. mentions Cicero as a source of Seneca's examples with reference to the *Consolationes*). An exception are Seneca's rare quotations from Cicero and not so positive explicit judgments about him, which have been widely analyzed. See Gambet 1970; Grimal 1984; Setaioli 2003; Fedeli 2006.
19 I quote the other two for quick reference: *Ep.* 104.21: "Si velis vitiis exui, longe a vitiorum exemplis recedendum est. Avarus, corruptor, saevus, fraudulentus, multum nocituri si prope a te fuissent, intra te sunt. Ad meliores transi: *cum Catonibus vive, cum Laelio, cum Tuberone*" – "If you would be stripped of your faults, leave far behind you the patterns of the faults. The miser, the swindler, the bully, the cheat, who will do you much harm merely by being near you, are within you. Change therefore to better associations: *live with the Catos, with Laelius, with Tubero* (after these, Seneca cites some exemplary Greeks);" *Ep.* 120.19: "Quidam alternis Vatinii, alternis Catones sunt; et modo parum illis severus est Curius, parum pauper Fabricius, parum frugi et contentus vilibus Tubero, modo Licinium divitiis, Apicium cenis, Maecenatem deliciis provocant" – "Some men are like Vatinius, or like Cato by turns; at times they do not think even Curius stern enough, or Fabricius poor enough, or Tubero sufficiently frugal and contented with simple things; while at other times they vie with Licinius in wealth, with Apicius in banqueting, or with Maecenas in daintiness" (trans. Gummere). Seneca the Elder also refers to Tubero once: *Con.* 2.1.8, quoted below, p. 383.

the electoral defeat, Seneca offers an interpretation of this episode that is the opposite of that in Cicero and Valerius.[20]

> Proderit non tantum quales esse soleant boni viri dicere formamque eorum et liniamenta deducere sed quales fuerint narrare et exponere, Catonis illud ultimum ac fortissimum vulnus per quod libertas emisit animam, Laeli sapientiam et cum suo Scipione concordiam, alterius Catonis domi forisque egregia facta, Tuberonis ligneos lectos, cum in publicum sterneret, haedinasque pro stragulis pelles et ante ipsius Iovis cellam adposita conviviis vasa fictilia. Quid aliud paupertatem in Capitolio consecrare? Ut nullum aliud factum eius habeam quo illum Catonibus inseram, hoc parum credimus? 73 Censura fuit illa, non cena. O quam ignorant homines cupidi gloriae quid illa sit aut quemadmodum petenda! Illo die populus Romanus multorum supellectilem spectavit, unius miratus est. Omnium illorum aurum argentumque fractum est et milliens conflatum, at omnibus saeculis Tuberonis fictilia durabunt.

> It will be helpful not only to state what is the usual quality of good men, and to outline their figures and features, but also to relate and set forth what men there have been of this kind. We might picture that last and bravest wound of Cato's, through which Freedom breathed her last; or the wise Laelius and his harmonious life with his friend Scipio; or the noble deeds of the elder Cato at home and abroad; or the wooden couches of Tubero, spread at a public feast, goatskins instead of tapestry, and vessels of earthenware set out for the banquet before the very shrine of Jupiter! What else was this except consecrating poverty on the Capitol? Though I know no other deed of his for which to rank him with the Catos, is this one not enough? 73 It was a censorship, not a banquet. How lamentably do those who covet glory fail to understand what glory is, or in what way it should be sought! On that day the Roman populace viewed the furniture of many men; it marvelled only at that of one! The gold and silver of all the others has been broken up and melted down times without number; but Tubero's earthenware will endure throughout eternity. (Sen. *Ep.* 95.72–73, trans. Gummere)

Far from being an example of *perversa sapientia*, as we had read in Cicero (*Mur.* 76), Tubero is here a model of morality for all time ("omnibus saeculis"), an example of the sage totally devoted to virtue, as it is described in the preceding section of the letter. Seneca not only omits the end of the story (and the particular occasion of the event), but also hints at the opposite: Claiming that the Roman people were amazed ("populus Romanus [...] miratus est") at Tubero's earthenware, he uses the ambivalent verb *mirari*, both alluding to the shock of the audience over Tubero's transgression of Roman habits (that is, in Seneca's eyes, the reaction of fools), and to the admiration of the philosopher for such an example of virtue. We find

---

20 Regarding the intertextual relationship and Cicero as a source of Valerius, see n. 12 above. Concerning Valerius, I have found no specific readings, except for Klotz 1942, 52–57. Adamietz 1989, 226–229 hints at Seneca's polemic against Cicero; cf. Mayer 1991, 164–165. A stylistic analysis of the passage is to be found in von Albrecht 2004, 92–96.

the reason for this positive evaluation in the previous section of the letter, in particular among the other examples quoted. There is in fact an intentional polemic against Cicero. It is not a coincidence that the main examples of perfect morality quoted in *Letter* 95 are Cato the Younger and Tubero, who are precisely, as we have seen, the objects of Cicero's anti-Stoic critique in *Pro Murena*.

A closer analysis of these two examples will demonstrate the differences in Cicero's and Seneca's evaluation. In *Letter* 95, Seneca arrives at Tubero via a reversed chronology, from the suicide of Cato the Younger to some typically Ciceronian examples from the second century BCE: Laelius with his friend Scipio and Cato the Elder. But while Laelius and Cato the Elder are only mentioned by their names and virtues (72: "Laeli sapientiam, Catonis [...] egregia facta"), Seneca grants Cato the Younger and Tubero a more elaborate characterization.[21] Cato, represented as opposing both Caesar and Pompey, is compared with the famous heroic horse of Vergil's *Georgics* in a long and complex argument just before the text quoted above (*Ep.* 95.68–71).[22] Tubero is not adduced in unspecific terms, as a generic example of parsimony in the commonly accepted version; instead, Seneca deliberately recalls the criticized banquet, offering an interpretation that runs counter to that of his predecessors. Here, Seneca evidently intends to contradict Cicero, who in *Pro Murena* combined Cato and Tubero, both defined as followers of the Stoic doctrine, and raised the same objection against both, that they were too radical to be effective in politics. Seneca, on the contrary, presents both of them, from a historical and not only philosophical point of view, as the really *extreme* examples suitable to the extreme times of Neronian tyranny. As Seneca repeats again and again in *Letter* 95, the progress of vice in his time necessitates a parallel progress in fighting it (95.29–35). As a consequence, philosophers can no longer remain moderate. On the contrary, as we shall see in the next section (III), they must take any measure for the sake of virtue, just as Tubero did. There is no time for political opportunism, only for a radical fight on a moral, if not also political level. It is a fight in which philosophers are condemned to defeat but destined to become examples for future generations.[23] Cicero could not be farther removed from this sentiment.

---

21 On Seneca's characteristic love for lists of *exempla*, see Mayer 1991, 153–157. This time, Seneca goes beyond the usual scheme of three examples, which is respected in *Ep.* 98.13 as in 104.21 and 120.19, quoted above, n. 19 (two antithetic series of three examples).

22 On this passage, see Berno 2006, 55–64; Berno 2011, 234–242.

23 See *Ep.* 51.13; *Nat.* 4b.13.1; Griffin 1988, 133–150; Grimal 1992, 253–257; Citroni Marchetti 1994, 4562–4574; Cambiano 2001; Inwood 2005, 271–352.

The intertextual relationship with Cicero does not end here. Tubero is not only a Ciceronian example, but also a Ciceronian character. In fact, we find him among the protagonists of *De re publica* (54 BCE),[24] together with Laelius and Scipio, to whom, as we have seen, Seneca refers in *Letter* 95 (as he does to the Catos). In *De re publica*, Tubero has a peculiar role, not directly regarding politics or ethics. He debates the interpretation of an astronomical phenomenon, the double sun. Nevertheless, the theme of frugality is still present, for in the first book, Scipio presents Tubero, who was famous for his interest in astronomy, with a eulogy of this form of contemplation as contempt of earthly things.

> Quid porro aut praeclarum putet in rebus humanis, qui haec deorum regna perspexerit, aut diuturnum, qui cognoverit quid sit aeternum, aut gloriosum, qui viderit quam parva sit terra [...] 27 agros vero et aedificia et pecudes et immensum argenti pondus atque auri qui bona nec putare nec appellare soleat, [...] quam est hic fortunatus putandus! [...] 28 Quod autem imperium, qui magistratus, quod regnum potest esse praestantius quam despicientem omnia humana et inferiora sapientia ducentem nihil umquam nisi sempiternum et divinum animo volutare? [...] 29 Quam ob rem, Tubero, semper mihi et doctrina et eruditi homines et tua ista studia placuerunt.

> Furthermore how can any man regard anything in human affairs either as exalted, if he has examined into yonder realms of the gods, or as of long duration, if he has realized the meaning of eternity, or as glorious, if he has perceived how small is the earth [...] 27 But as far as our lands, houses, herds, and immense stores of silver and gold are concerned, the man who never thinks of these things or speaks of them as 'goods' [...] how fortunate is he to be esteemed! [...] 28 What power, moreover, what office, what kingdom can be preferable to the state of one who despises all human possessions, considers them inferior to wisdom, and never meditates on any subject that is not eternal and divine? [...] 29 For these reasons, Tubero, I have always delighted in learning, in men of erudition, and in such studies as those which you pursue. (Cic. *Rep.* 1.26–29, trans. Walker Keyes).

Here, nine years after *Pro Murena*, Cicero defends the idea of radical frugality in the words of Scipio, the ideal prince.[25] He does not mention Tubero's goatskins and crockery, but praises the contempt of both wealth

---

24 On Tubero as a character in this work, see the introduction of Büchner 1984, 34f.

25 On the other hand, we have to acknowledge that Scipio's eulogy is followed by Laelius' critique, in which Tubero is blamed for his lack of interest in the critical political situation, despite the example of his noble ancestors (*Rep.* 1.31): "Quid enim mihi L. Pauli nepos, hoc avunculo, nobilissima in familia [...] natus, quaerit quo modo duo soles visi sint, non quaerit cur in una re publica duo senatus et duo paene iam populi sint?" – "For why is it that the grandson of Lucius Paulus, the nephew of our friends here, a scion of a most worthy family and of this most glorious republic, is asking how two suns could have been seen, instead of asking why, in one State, we have almost reached the point where there are two senates and two separate peoples?" (trans. Walker Keyes).

and a political career,[26] as well as the contemplative nature of Tubero's philosophy. Cicero also counts him among the "men of erudition," which is reminiscent of the description of Tubero in *Pro Murena*.[27]

Seneca perhaps wishes to correct Cicero with Cicero, mixing the Tubero of *Pro Murena*, inserted in a peculiar political context and criticized for his radical philosophy, with the character "Tubero" of *De re publica*, where we find the praise of radical virtues in the context of a theoretical discussion of politics as a philosophical ideal. Seneca aims to lead the political opportunism of the oration *Pro Murena* towards the ideal of philosophical coherence of the treatise *De re publica*.

III. *Ep.* 95: Tubero in Context

The Tubero *exemplum* in Sen. *Ep.* 95.72–73 is important not only because of its intertextual relationship with occurrences of Tubero in Cicero but also on an intratextual level, within the structure of the letter itself. We have already said that Tubero is a perfect example of the extremism of virtue that is necessary in Seneca's time to fight abnormal vices. This is a well developed idea in *Letter* 95, where Seneca stresses the need of a philosophy "of greater effort" (32: "operosior philosophia"), which should act in a way "stronger than usual" (34: "solito vehementius"), and which we should follow with *superstitio* (35), a somewhat religious scrupulousness.

> Adversus tam potentem explicitumque late furorem operosior philosophia facta est et tantum sibi virium sumpsit quantum iis adversus quae parabatur accesserat. [...] 34 [...] In hac ergo morum perversitate desideratur solito vehementius aliquid quod mala inveterata discutiat. 35 [...] quos velis ad beatam vitam perducere [...] huius [sc. virtutis] quadam superstitione teneantur, hanc ament, cum hac vivere velint, sine hac nolint.

> Against this overmastering and widespread madness philosophy has become a matter of greater effort, and has taken on strength in proportion to the strength which is gained by the opposition forces. [...] 34 [...] Amid this upset condition of morals, something stronger than usual is needed, something which will shake off these chronic ills. 35 [...] Let [those whom you would bring to happy life] be held by a sort of superstitious worship of virtue; let them love her; let them desire to live with her, and refuse to live without her. (Sen. *Ep.* 95.32–35, trans. Gummere)

---

26   Cic. *Rep.* 1.27: "immensum argenti pondus atque auri;" 28: "imperium [...] magistratus [...] regnum.
27   Cic. *Rep.* 1.29: "doctrina [...] tua ista studia;" 29: "eruditi homines," with which compare Cic. *Mur.* 75: "eodem ex studio eruditus [...] eruditissimus et Stoicus."

The importance of the Tubero example in this context, which is generally neglected by scholars,[28] is shown by its position, at the very end of one of the longest[29] of Seneca's letters, in which Seneca has dealt with the different ways of teaching philosophy.

Expounding the *ars vitae* (7), the art of living a good life, the philosopher first describes the difficulty of philosophy in his own times, as we have seen, and the fight against new vices. Then he tells us what should be the sole aim of our lives, namely virtue, the only real good, while any other good is to be ignored as transient (43–46). We must shape our lives according to this principle, following the teachings that he gives in the second part of the letter. Seneca then discusses correct behavior towards the gods ("quomodo sint dii colendi," in 47–50), men ("quomodo hominibus sit utendum," in 51–53), things ("quomodo rebus sit utendum," in 54), and finally virtues (55–59). He affirms that examples are just as useful as other modes of instruction since they provide models and rules for living our lives (66–67). It is at this point that he quotes Cato and Tubero, with whom he ends the letter.

Seneca may have chosen the example of Tubero because this figure sums up and condenses both the *pars destruens* and the *pars construens* of the letter: on the one hand, the fight against current vices and, on the other, the aim of our life, expressed in the precepts given here. Addressing the widespread immorality of his time, Seneca returns to a topic already expounded in *Ep.* 94.60–67: Some disgusting vices condemned in private (such as ambition, cruelty, greed, or luxury) are admired in public, sometimes even imposed by laws.

> Non privatim solum sed publice furimus. [...] Ex senatus consultis plebisque scitis saeva exercentur et publice iubentur vetata privatim.
>
> We are mad, not only individually, but nationally. [...] Cruelties are practised in accordance with acts of senate and popular assembly, and the public is bidden to do that which is forbidden to the individual. (Sen. *Ep.* 95.30, trans. Gummere)

Later, regarding the relativity of what is right in personal actions, Seneca refers precisely to the public banquet, this time without personal examples:

> Quid est cena sumptuosa flagitiosius [...]? Quid tam dignum censoria nota, si quis [...] sibi hoc et genio suo praestet? Et deciens tamen sestertio aditiales cenae frugalissimis viris constiterunt. Eadem res, si gulae datur, turpis est, si honori, reprensionem effugit: non enim luxuria sed inpensa sollemnis est.
>
> What is more shameful than a costly meal which eats away the income even of a knight? Or what so worthy of the censor's condemnation as to be always indulging

---

28 Only a hint in Schafer 2009, 23; more detailed remarks in Bellincioni 1979, 328f., but without attention to its key position in the letter. See also Costa 2013, 177f.
29 Seneca himself describes it as "a huge letter" (95.3: "ingens epistula"). Actually, *Letter* 94 is one paragraph longer than 95.

oneself and one's "inner man" [...]? And yet often has an inaugural dinner cost the more careful man a cool million! The very sum that is called disgraceful if spent on the appetite, is beyond reproach if spent for official purposes! For it is not luxury but an expenditure sanctioned by custom. (Sen. *Ep.* 95.41, trans. Gummere)

"The Roman people loathe private luxury, but they love public splendor," is Cicero's commentary on Tubero's defeat (*Mur.* 76, quoted in section I above), and it is repeated by Valerius. There is no such remark in Seneca's version at *Ep.* 95.72–73, but the comparison with the quoted passage about vices imposed by politics and the relevance of the final example of Tubero imply the philosopher's reprobation of public luxury as well. Moreover, it is also due to the passage at *Ep.* 95.41 that Tubero becomes a perfect example of the quoted extremism of virtue. While the virtuous *frugalissimi* of this passage give sumptuous banquets, Tubero consecrates on the Capitolium not the virtue of *frugalitas*, but poverty itself (*Ep.* 95.72). Tubero's behavior is significant also because it shows in public a virtue we practice in private but are ashamed to display in public, as Seneca observes elsewhere.[30]

Let us now turn to the *pars construens* of the letter and see how Tubero is shown to comply with its precepts. Regarding the gods, Seneca explicitly opposes public donations and the like: These are superstitious practices which assign to gods a human vice, ambition (47).[31] The right way to honor the gods is to be good,[32] and this is precisely what Tubero was. For human beings, Seneca recommends above all *mansuetudo*, kindness (51). This is less relevant in the case of Tubero, but he is admired for his lack of ambition and scorn for glory, as we have seen above and will see below. Together with the desire for glory, ambition is the main cause of cruelty, the vice opposite to kindness. As regards things, it is important to consider them for their effective value, i.e. the weight they assume with respect to our authentic happiness, and not for their appearance (54). This is what Tubero did by not giving importance to wealth. Finally, speaking about virtues, Seneca insists on the concepts of consistency[33] and correct evaluation. *Divitiae, gratia, potentia* – wealth, influence, and power – are not important (59). This is what Tubero demonstrated with his behavior.

---

30 Sen. *Ep.* 20.3: "Numquid cenes frugaliter, aedifices luxuriose" – "Whether you eat frugal dinners and yet build luxurious houses;" *Ep.* 87.5: "Nondum audeo frugalitatem palam ferre" – "I have not yet the courage openly to acknowledge my thriftiness" (trans. Gummere).
31 Sen. *Ep.* 95.47: "Vetemus salutationibus matutinis fungi [...] vetemus lintea et strigiles Iovi ferre" – "Let us forbid men to offer morning salutation [...] let us forbid bringing towels and flesh-scrapers to Jupiter" (trans. Gummere).
32 Sen. *Ep.* 95.50: "Vis deos propitiare? Bonus esto."
33 Sen. *Ep.* 95.58: "Si vis eadem semper velle, vera oportet velis" – "If you would always desire the same things, you must desire the truth" (trans. Gummere).

Tubero with his pottery embodies each and every one of these precepts. In fact he shows radical consistency towards men (by being the same in private and in public), respect and not superstition toward the gods (by not believing that they would appreciate luxury as vicious men do), and finally indifference towards things (using poor instead of luxurious furniture). In the more famous and impressive example of Cato's suicide, which precedes that of Tubero, we find only the first of these elements, and so this example was not suitable for concluding the letter. Seneca mentions it, but not at the end. The comparison between Tubero and Cato is significantly hinted at by Seneca when he defines Tubero's banquet as a censorship (with an alliterating paronomasia "censura fuit illa, non cena" at *Ep.* 95.73). It is an office that Tubero never held; Cato the Elder, on the other hand, was nicknamed "The Censor" for his rigor in holding it. The same rigor characterized Cato the Younger, even if he was not a censor himself. In other words: Tubero was not a censor, but acted like a censor, i.e. as a model of morality, perhaps more so than the Catos.

Shifting to a biographical level, we can add that Seneca's way of life while writing the *Letters to Lucilius*[34] had more affinity with Tubero's than Cato's. In fact, even though he was facing a tyrant, as Cato had been facing Caesar, Seneca did not choose Cato's solution, namely suicide, and so he could obviously not follow this example to the very end. Tubero chose to act consistently with his philosophy, knowing that it would mean his political defeat; in this respect, his choice is similar to the voluntary retirement of Seneca's final years.

IV. *Ep.* 98.13: Tubero Again

The similarity between Tubero and Seneca in his retirement – a man far from the contradictions and luxury which years before he had tried to excuse in *De vita beata*[35] – is still more evident in *Letter* 98. In *De vita*

---

34 For the chronology, as for any other question about this text, see the clear synthesis of Setaioli 2014.
35 Presumably, *De vita beata* appeared between 54 and 59 CE (the *quinquennium Neronis*), most likely about 58 (Grimal 1969, 17–21). On this dialogue, see Grimal 1969 (15–17, a discussion of *Vit. beat.* 17–28) and Schiesaro, 1996, 5–26, who stresses its political background. On its apologetic purpose, compare also the contribution of Matheus de Pietro in this volume. For inconsistencies connected to Seneca's wealth, see Citroni Marchetti 1991, 124–133; von Albrecht 2003; Beck 2010; about the exercise of poverty: Avotins 1977; Allegri 2004, 14–19; Chioccioli 2007. On the relationship between philosophy and wealth, see Dross 2010, 332–347. Seneca's defense is based on a particular interpretation of the doctrine of *indifferentia* (*Vit. beat.* 22.2–4, 25.2 and 26.1): see the commentaries of Grimal

beata, Seneca had written: "No one condemned wisdom to poverty" (23.1: "nemo sapientiam *paupertate* damnavit"),[36] and announced: "When I am able, I will live as I should (18.1: "cum potuero, vivam quomodo oportet"). At the time of the *Letters*, after trying to return to Nero all the gifts he had received from him, Seneca lived in sober and voluntary retirement, and acknowledged his political defeat. From the works written after he retired from the court emerges a deep desire for detachment from earthly things depending on fortune, and in this context, we can understand how Tubero, who consecrated his poverty in the Capitol (*Ep.* 95.72), could become a model for his life.

Letter 98 offers significant evidence to confirm this relevance of the example. Here, the Tubero scene is summarized, and two other examples, Fabricius and Sextius, are listed together with him. The letter deals with fortune, that is, all the things fate gives and then suddenly takes away from us. Accordingly, it is far better not to count on them, and most of all not to worry about their loss. We have to overcome fortune (*Ep.* 98.12), as did the examples just mentioned.

> Rursus ista quae ut speciosa et felicia trahunt vulgum a multis et saepe contempta sunt. Fabricius divitias imperator reiecit, censor notavit; Tubero paupertatem et se dignam et Capitolio iudicavit, cum fictilibus in publica cena usus ostendit debere iis hominem esse contentum quibus di etiamnunc uterentur. Honores reppulit pater Sextius, qui ita natus ut rem publicam deberet capessere, latum clavum divo Iulio dante non recepit; intellegebat enim quod dari posset et eripi posse. Nos quoque aliquid et ipsi faciamus animose; simus inter exempla.

> Again, those objects which attract the crowd under the appearance of beauty and happiness, have been scorned by many men and on many occasions. Fabricius when he was general refused riches, and when he was censor branded them with disapproval. Tubero deemed poverty worthy both of himself and of the deity on the Capitol when, by the use of earthenware dishes at a public festival, he showed that man should be satisfied with that which the gods could still use. The elder Sextius rejected the honors of office; he was born with an obligation to take part in public affairs, and yet would not accept the broad stripe even when the deified Julius offered to him. For he understood that what can be given can also be taken away.

1969, 98–99 (on *Vit. beat.* 21.4) and 111 (on *Vit. beat.* 25.1); Kuen 1994, 257–261 (on *Vit. beat.* 22.2–4); for Seneca's overall theory, Wildberger 2006, 115f., 149–152. This interpretation returns in *Ep.* 5.6: "Magnus est ille qui fictilibus sic utitur quemadmodum argento, nec ille minor est qui sic argento utitur quemadmodum fictilibus" – "He is a great man who uses earthenware dishes as if they were silver; but he is equally great who uses silver as if it were earthenware" (trans. Gummere).

36 Cf. Sen. *Vit. beat.* 23.2: "Ille vero fortunae benignitatem a se non summovebit; magnas opes, munus fortunae fructumque virtutis, non repudiabit nec excludet" – "But he, surely, will not thrust aside the generosity of Fortune, and an inheritance that has been honorably acquired will give him no cause either to blush or to boast" (trans. Basore).

Let us also, therefore, carry out some courageous act of our own accord; let us be
included among the ideal types of history. (Sen. *Ep.* 98.13, trans. Gummere)

This sequence of examples has a precedent in a passage from Seneca the
Elder. Here, within a discourse against wealth, we find our Tubero, who
made poverty a virtue,[37] Fabricius, who refused gifts from the Samnites,
and other ancestors, whose description alludes to the story of Cincinnatus,
as if the man were so well known that the orator had not even felt the need
to mention his name.

> Hoc animo scio nostros fuisse maiores, hoc illum Aelium Tuberonem, cuius pau-
> pertas virtus fuit, hoc Fabricium Samnitium non accipientem munera, hoc ceteros
> patres nostros, quos apud aratra ipsa mirantes decora sua circumsteterunt lictores.
>
> I know that this was the spirit of our ancestors, of the Aelius Tubero whose poverty
> was a virtue, of Fabricius who rejected the presents of the Samnites, of the rest of
> our forebears, who stood at the very plough in awe of the symbols of authority of
> the lictors who surrounded them. (Sen. *Con.* 2.1.8, trans. Winterbottom)

From the comparison between the two passages we can infer some conclusions. First, while Fabricius is a stock example of frugality (together with
Curius,[38] whom Seneca himself quotes in *Ep.* 120.19 along with Fabricius
and Tubero),[39] Sextius the Elder is not so famous,[40] and his importance
comes more from his being the founder of the philosophical school of the
Sextii, which was closely aligned to Stoicism, than from any specific
virtue.[41] Of the three examples, two are interested in philosophy and
characterized by their affinity with Stoicism. In other words, the stock

---

37 This attribution is not certain, since it could refer both to Tubero the Elder and
Tubero the Younger (the editors refer to one of them without considering the
question). In my opinion, the comparison with *Letter* 98 leaves no doubt about the
identification with the Tubero described in Seneca the Elder and that of Cicero,
Pro Murena and Seneca, *Letter* 95.
38 In the chapter *De abstinentia et continentia*, Valerius quotes Curius, then Fabricius, then Tubero's father, identified as "a disciple of Curius and Fabricius" (4.3.5–
7); for Fabricius see also 4.4.3: He had only one silver plate, for the sacrifices to
the gods; thus we can say that even Fabricius is more luxurious than Tubero with
regard to religion; 4.4.11 (*De paupertate*). For the exemplary role of Curius and
Fabricius at Rome, see Berrendonner 2001; Vigourt 2001.
39 The text is given above, n. 19.
40 To my knowledge, only Seneca the Elder and Seneca the Younger quote him.
About this character, see Lana 1992, 110–115; Hadot 2007.
41 Cf. Sen. *Ep.* 64.2: "Lectus est deinde liber Quinti Sexti patris, magni, si quid mihi
credis, viri, et licet neget Stoici" – "We then had read to us a book by Quintus
Sextius the Elder. He is a great man, if you have any confidence in my opinion,
and a real Stoic, though he himself denies it;" *Ep.* 73.15: "Credamus [...] Sextio
[...] clamanti: 'Hac itur ad astra, *hac secundum frugalitatem*, hac secundum tem-
perantiam, hac secundum fortitudinem' " – "Let us therefore believe Sextius when
he [...] cries: 'This is the way to the stars, this is the way, *by observing thrift*, self-
restraint, and courage' " (trans. Gummere).

sequence of examples of frugality (Fabricius – Curius) and the trio in Seneca the Elder (Tubero – Fabricius – Cincinnatus) are here altered to emphasize the philosophical reason for a choice of life: living far from wealth – and thus far from honor and politics. It is a classic Epicurean choice to "live unnoticed," according to Epicurus' famous motto *lathe biōsas*,[42] which Seneca here intends to apply to personages linked with Stoicism.

Moreover, there is an important difference between Fabricius and Sextius on the one hand and Tubero on the other: Fabricius and Sextius refused gifts, the former from a foreign people, the latter from Caesar; Tubero, however, refused to *make* splendid gifts to the gods as was customary, and so sacrificed his political career. Wealth is considered from both sides, received and given, but always linked with one's political career: Either way it is to be rejected because it is aleatory and because it does not lead to happiness.

In *Letter* 98, as in 95, the public sphere is polemically referred to and associated with the private one. A political career is here interpreted as something desirable only from the point of view of the populace, whereas to the sage it depends on fortune and is thus transient and indifferent. The public and/or political sphere does not differ from the reign of fools and vice; in this regard, Tubero's experience is a perfect example. The narratives of all examples – Fabricius, Tubero, and Sextius – contain references to episodes concerning some public behavior. They evidently represent political authority (an important foreign people like the Samnites, the Romans as electors, and then Caesar, in a sort of climax) as hypostases of Fortune,[43] who gives goods, but then suddenly takes them away. It is not exactly a positive representation of power. The examples are followed by an exhortation in the first person to be examples and to return to a lost integrity.[44]

---

42 Epicur. *Frg.* 551 Usener. On this very famous motto, see Roskam 2007. On Seneca and Epicurus, Motto and Clark 1968; Inwood 2005, 163–165; Wildberger, in this volume. *Ep.* 68.10: " 'Otium' inquis 'Seneca, commendas mihi? Ad Epicureas voces delaberis?' " – "Then you say: 'It is retirement, Seneca, that you are recommending to me? You will soon be falling back upon the maxims of Epicurus!' " (trans. Gummere).

43 Here personified: Sen. *Ep.* 98.11: "Rem nobis eripit casus" – "Chance robs us of the thing;" 98.14: "restituamur, ut possimus [...] fortunae dicere: 'Cum viro tibi negotium est: quaere quem vincas' " – "we may be restored [...] let us therefore be so, in order that we may be able to [...] say to Fortune: 'You have to deal with a man: seek someone whom you can conquer!' " (trans. Gummere).

44 Sen. *Ep.* 98.13: "simus inter exempla;" 98.14: "licet reverti in viam, licet in integrum restitui."

We can conclude by saying that in *Letter* 98, perhaps more explicitly than in 95, Seneca alludes to his personal, painful choice of retirement.[45] By supporting it with somewhat Stoic examples, he tries to present it as the coherent application of the philosopher's independence from Fortune.

The defeat of the unlucky Tubero, who lost the office of praetor but kept his parsimonious life, when interpreted in a sense opposite to the opportunistic reading dictated by common sense, is no less exemplary to us than the more famous and spectacular example of the Stoic sage Cato committing suicide. Maybe the rather obscure Tubero is even *more* exemplary, in that he shows the superficiality of political power, which depends on the populace and thus on the vices of the populace. From this point of view, Tubero is more reminiscent of Seneca's final years than are other historical examples: Seneca did not yet share with Cato his struggle to death, but at least in his retirement, he admired and practiced Tubero's radical consistency between private and public life. Seneca would have liked to be similar to Tubero. It was his destiny which later forced him to become similar to Cato.

V. Tubero after Seneca

In the contest against Cicero's and Valerius' interpretation of Tubero, Seneca is the loser. While Athenaeus remembers Tubero as a model of frugality (see above, n. 3), we find another, implicit, reference to the episode in Tacitus, an author who has no great love for Seneca.[46] In the last book of the *Annals*, we find Tubero's choice interpreted in a way similar to Cicero. The *delator* Capito Cossutianus is prosecuting the Stoic Thrasea Paetus on a charge of conspiracy against Nero.

> "Ut quondam C. Caesarem" inquit "et M. Catonem, ita nunc te, Nero, et Thraseam avida discordiarum civitas loquitur. Et habet sectatores […] qui nondum contumaciam sententiarum, sed habitum voltumque eius sectantur, *rigidi et tristes*, quo tibi lasciviam exprobrent. […] 4 […] Ista secta Tuberones et Favonios, veteri quoque rei publicae ingrata nomina, genuit. Ut imperium *evertant*, libertatem praeferunt; si *perverterint*, libertatem ipsam adgredientur."

---

45 Cf. Tac. *Ann.* 14.53.1–56.3; 15.45.3. In Sen. *Ep.* 98.15, after the *exempla* I have discussed, there is a lacuna in the text, after which Seneca refers to a *senex egregius* who is going to die. This *senex* is evidently some noble friend of Seneca's. He may be someone who did not accept anything from fortune (that is, from the *princeps*), perhaps a figure like Burrus, who died just before Seneca's retirement without accepting compromises with the tyrant (Tac. *Ann.* 14.51.1–2). The lacuna could be explained with a sort of censorship. But this is only speculation.
46 Among the recent contributions to this vexed question, see Zimmermann 2005; Schmal 2008; Woodman 2011.

"As once," he said, "this discord-loving state prated of Caesar and Cato, so now, Nero, it prates of yourself and Thrasea. And he has his followers [...] who affect, not as yet the contumacity of his opinions, but his bearing and his looks, and whose *stiffness and austerity* are designed for an impeachment of your wantonness. [...] 4 [...] It is the sect that produced the Tuberones[47] and the Favonii – names unloved even in the old republic. In order to *subvert* the empire, they make a parade of liberty:[48] the empire *overthrown*, they will lay hands on liberty itself." (Tac. *Ann.* 16.22.2–4, trans. Jackson)

Capito compares Thrasea with Cato, remaking the Ciceronian linkage of *Pro Murena*; he defines him as "stiff" (*rigidus*) – a typical attribute of the Stoics – and "austere" (*tristis*),[49] and then concludes that Romans belonging to this sect have always been unloved by the people because they aim to subvert the state. The *perversa sapientia* which Cicero attributed to Tubero (see p. 371, above) becomes here, with a significant play on words, an instrument to subvert (*evertere, pervertere*) the legitimate power. And, as we know, after this accusation Paetus – the Stoic Paetus – will commit suicide, just like Seneca, whose death Tacitus describes in the previous book of the *Annals* (*Ann.* 15.62.1–64.4). Moral rigor and consistency are not appreciated in politics. In the end, political opportunism wins.

---

47 No scholar considers the identification of these *Tuberones* as a problem. Köstermann 1968, 383 refers this allusion to our Tubero (so Furneaux 1974, 457 n. 5; Wuilleumier 1978, 227 n. 3); Franzoi 2003, 1570–1573 does not say anything about this character, but maintains that Capito's judgment about Stoicism is to some extent shared by Tacitus. (I will only say that this passage shows the success of the Ciceronian interpretation.) Since Favonius fought in the civil war between Caesar and Pompey (and then died after Philippi), maybe here Tacitus is referring to his contemporary Q. Aelius Tubero. On the other hand, Capito's prosecution clearly criticizes philosophical inclinations, and our Tubero was the philosopher of the family. In any case, the emphatic plural can include the whole family, which, as we have seen above (p. 373), was famous for its radical (and thus Stoic) frugality. Regarding the negative prejudice against Stoicism in the Neronian age, we can also quote a passage about another victim of the emperor, Rubellius Plautus (*Ann.* 14.57.3): "adsumpta etiam Stoicorum adrogantia sectaque, quae turbidos negotiorum adpetentes faciat" – "[He] had taken upon himself the Stoic arrogance and the mantle of a sect which inculcated sedition and an appetite for politics" (trans. Jackson).
48 Cf. Sen. *Ep.* 95.72: "*Catonis* illud fortissimum vulnus per quod *libertas emisit animam.*" The complete passage is quoted above, p. 375.
49 Seneca himself defines Stoicism as a "strict and virile school of [...] philosophy" (*Helv.* 12.4: "rigida ac virilis sapientia," trans. Basore), or a "rigid sect" (*Nat.* 2.35.1: "rigida secta;" cf. *Ep.* 99.26). The Academic in Lucilius' satire is a "tristis philosophus" (*Frg.* 754 Marx), but Seneca ironically uses this attribute for his doctrine (*Ep.* 48.7): "Hoc est, quod tristes docemus et pallidi?" – "Is this the matter which we teach with sour and pale faces?" (trans. Gummere).

Bibliography

Adamietz, Joachim, ed. and trans. 1989. *Cicero, Pro Murena*. Darmstadt: Wissenschaftliche Buchgesellschaft.
Albrecht, Michael von. 2003. "Soldi e ricchezza in Seneca: Temi ed immagini." In *Moneta, mercanti, banchieri: I precedenti greci e romani dell'Euro*, edited by Gianpaolo Urso, 257–269. Pisa: ETS.
Albrecht, Michael von. 2004. *Wort und Wandlung: Senecas Lebenskunst*, Leiden; Boston: Brill.
Allegri, Giuseppina. 2004. *Progresso verso la virtus: Il programma della Lettera 87 di Seneca*. Cesena: Stilgraf.
Armisen-Marchetti, Mireille. 2006. "Speculum Neronis: Un mode spécifique de cri de conscience dans le De clementia." *REL* 84: 185–201.
Avotins, Ivars. 1977. "Training in Frugality in Epicurus and Seneca." *Phoenix* 31: 214–217.
Basore, John W., ed. and trans. 1928–1935. *Seneca, Moral Essays*. 3 vols. London; Cambridge: Heinemann; Harvard University Press. Rpt. 1958.
Beck, Jan-Wilhelm. 2010. *"Aliter loqueris, aliter uiuis:" Senecas philosophischer Anspruch und seine biographische Realität*. Göttingen: Edition Ruprecht.
Bellincioni, Maria. 1978. *Educazione alla sapientia in Seneca*. Brescia: Paideia.
Bellincioni, Maria, ed. and trans. 1979. *Lucio Anneo Seneca, Lettere a Lucilio: Libro XV: Le lettere 94 e 95*. Brescia: Paideia.
Berno, Francesca Romana. 2006. "Il cavallo saggio e lo stolto Enea: Due citazioni virgiliane nelle Epistulae ad Lucilium di Seneca (56, 12–14; 95, 68–71)." *AClass* 49: 55–78.
Berno, Francesca Romana. 2011. "Seneca, Catone e due citazioni virgiliane (Sen. Ep. 95, 67–71 e 104, 31–32)." *SIFC* 104: 233–253.
Berrendonner, Clara. 2001. "La formation de la tradition sur M'. Curius Dentatus et C. Fabricius Luscinus: Un homme nouveau peut-il être un grand homme?" In *L'invention des grands hommes de la Rome antique – Die Konstruktion der großen Männer Altroms*, edited by Marianne Coudry and Thomas Späth, 97–116. Paris: De Boccard.
Bettini, Maurizio. 2000. "Mos, mores e mos maiorum: L'invenzione dei 'buoni costumi' nella cultura romana." In *Le orecchie di Hermes: Studi di antropologia e letterature classiche*, 241–292. Torino: Einaudi.
Bloomer, Martin W. 1992. *Valerius Maximus and the Rhetoric of the New Nobility*. Chapel Hill: University of North Carolina Press.
Borgo, Antonella. 1998. *Lessico morale di Seneca*. Napoli: Loffredo.
Bosch, Clemens Emin. 1929. *Die Quellen des Valerius Maximus: Ein Beitrag zur Erforschung der Literatur der historischen Exempla*. Stuttgart: Kohlhammer.
Braun, Maximilian, Andreas Haltenhoff, and Fritz-Heiner Mutschler, eds. 2000. *"Moribus antiquis res stat Romana:" Römische Werte und römische Literatur im 3. und 2. Jh. v. Chr.* München; Leipzig: Saur.
Büchner, Karl, ed. 1984. *Cicero, De re publica*. Heidelberg: Winter.
Cambiano, Giuseppe. 2001. "Seneca e le contraddizioni del sapiens." In *Incontri con Seneca: Atti della giornata di studio, Torino, 26 ottobre 1999*, edited by Giovanna Garbarino and Italo Lana, 49–60. Bologna: Pàtron.
Chaumartin, François-Regis. 1997. "Les Lettres à Lucilius: La transparence inaccessible?" In *Dire l'evidence*, edited by Carlos Lévy, 145–156. Paris; Montréal: L'Harmattan.

Chioccioli, Marco. 2007. "La ricchezza come 'materia' per la virtù politica: Un percorso esegetico fra Seneca vita b. 22.1 e Marziale 11.5." *Prometheus* 33: 137–143.
Cicero. 1928. *De re publica; De legibus*. See Walker Keyes 1928.
Cicero. 1939. *Brutus; Orator*. See Hendrickson and Hubbel 1939.
Cicero. 1976. *In Catilinam 1–4; Pro Murena; Pro Sulla*. See Macdonald 1976.
Cicero. 1984. *De re publica*. See Büchner 1984.
Cicero. 1989. *Pro Murena*. See Adamietz 1989.
Citroni Marchetti, Sandra. 1991. *Plinio il vecchio e la tradizione del moralismo romano*. Pisa: Giardini
Citroni Marchetti, Sandra. 1994. "Il sapiens in pericolo: Psicologia del rapporto con gli altri, da Cicerone a Marco Aurelio." *ANRW* II 36.7: 4546–4598.
Classen, Carl Joachim. 2010. *Aretai und Virtutes: Untersuchungen zu den Wertvorstellungen der Griechen und Römer*. Berlin; New York: De Gruyter.
Corbier, Mireille. 1989. "Le statut ambigu de la viande à Rome." *DHA* 15: 107–158.
Costa, Stefano. 2013. *Quod olim fuerat: La rappresentazione del passato in Seneca prosatore*. Hildesheim; Zürich; New York: Olms
Coudry, Marianne, and Thomas Späth, eds. 2001. *L'invention des grands hommes de la Rome antique – Die Konstruktion der großen Männer Altroms*. Paris: De Boccard.
David, Jean-Michel. 1980. "Maiorum exempla sequi: L'exemplum historique dans les discours judiciaires de Cicéron." *MEFRA* 92: 67–86.
Domenico da Peccioli. 2007. *Lectura Epistularum Senecae*. See Marcucci 2007.
Dross, Juliette. 2010. *Voir la philosophie: Les représentations de la philosophie à Rome, de Cicéron à Marc Aurèle*. Paris: Les Belles Lettres.
Elvers, Karl Ludwig. 1996. *Der Neue Pauly*, edited by Hubert Cancik and Helmuth Schneider, Vol. 1, p. 171, s.v. *Aelius* I 16. Stuttgart: Metzler.
Fedeli, Paolo. 2006. "Cicerone e Seneca." *Ciceroniana* 12: 211–237.
Franzoi, Alessandro, ed. and trans. 2003. *Tacito, Opera omnia*. Vol. 2: *Annales*, edited by Renato Oniga. Torino: Einaudi.
Furneaux, Henry, ed. 1974. *The Annals of Tacitus*. Vol. 2: *Books 11–16*. 2nd ed. revised by Henry Francis Pelham and Charles Dennis Fisher. Oxford: The Clarendon Press.
Gambet, Daniel George. 1970. "Cicero in the Work of Seneca Philosophus." *TAPhA* 101: 171–183.
Garbarino, Giovanna. 1973. *Roma e la filosofia greca dalle origini alla fine del II secolo*. 2 vols. Torino: Paravia.
Garbarino, Giovanna. 2003. *Philosophorum Romanorum fragmenta usque ad L. Annaei Senecae aetatem collegit I. Garbarino*. Bologna: Pàtron.
Gazich, Roberto. 1990. "Teoria e pratica dell'exemplum in Quintiliano". In *Aspetti della paideia di Quintiliano*, edited by Pier Vincenzo Cova et al., 61–121. Brescia: Pubblicazioni dell'Università Cattolica del Sacro Cuore.
Griffin, Miriam T. 1988. "Philosophy for Statesmen: Cicero and Seneca." In *Antikes Denken – Moderne Schule*, edited by Hans Werner Schmidt and Peter Wülfing, 133–150. Heidelberg; Zürich: Winter.
Grilli, Alberto. 1963. "Diastrophē." *Acme* 16: 87–101.
Grimal, Pierre, ed. and trans. 1969. *Senecae De vita beata – Sénèque, Sur le Bonheur*. Paris: Les Belles Lettres.
Grimal, Pierre. 1984. "Sénèque juge de Cicéron." *MEFRA* 96: 655–670.
Grimal, Pierre. 1992. *Seneca*, translated by Tuckery Capra. Milano: Garzanti (= *Sénèque ou La conscience de l'Empire*. Paris: Les Belles Lettres, 1978).

Gummere, Richard Mott, ed. and trans. 1917–1925. *Seneca, Ad Lucilium epistulae morales*. 3 vols. London; Cambridge: Heinemann; Harvard University Press. Rpt. 1962
Hadot, Ilsetraut. 2007. "Versuch einer doktrinalen Neueinordnung der Schule der Sextier." *RhM* 150: 179–210.
Hendrickson, George Lincoln, and Harry Mortimer Hubbell, eds. 1952. *Cicero, Brutus; Orator*. London; Cambridge: Heinemann; Harvard University Press, repr. [1939].
Hölkeskamp, Karl Joachim. 2004. "Exempla und mos maiorum: Überlegungen zum kollektiven Gedächtnis der Nobilität." In *Senatus populusque Romanus: Die politische Kultur der Republik – Dimension und Deutungen*, 169–198. Stuttgart: Steiner.
Inwood, Brad. 2005. *Reading Seneca: Stoic Philosophy at Rome*. Oxford: Clarendon Press.
Jackson, John, ed. and trans. 1937. *Tacitus, The Annals: Books 13–16*. London; Cambridge: Heinemann; Harvard University Press. Rpt. 1956.
Klebs, Elimar. 1893. *RE* I.1, 535–537, s.v. *Aelius* 155.
Klotz, Alfred. 1942. *Studien zu Valerius Maximus und den Exempla*. München: Verlag der Bayerischen Akademie der Wissenschaften.
Köstermann, Erich. 1968. *Tacitus Annalen*. Vol. 4: *Buch 14–16*. Heidelberg: Winter.
Kornhardt, Hildegard. 1936. *Exemplum: Eine bedeutungsgeschichtliche Studie*. Borna; Leipzig: Noske.
Kuen, Gabriele. 1994. *Die Philosophie als "dux vitae:" Die Verknüpfung von Gehalt, Intention und Darstellungsweise im philosophischen Werk Senecas am Beispiel des Dialogs "De vita beata:" Einleitung, Wortkommentar und systematische Darstellung*. Heidelberg: Winter.
Lana, Italo. 1992. "La scuola dei Sestii." In *La langue latine langue da le philosophie*, edited by Pierre Grimal, 197–211. Roma: École française de Rome.
La Penna, Antonio. 1989. "La legittimazione del lusso privato da Ennio a Vitruvio: Momenti, problemi, personaggi." *Maia* 41: 3–34.
Linke, Bernhard, and Michael Stemmler, eds. 2000. *"Mos maiorum:" Untersuchungen zu den Formen der Identitätsstiftung und Stabilisierung in der römischen Republik*. Stuttgart: Steiner.
Macdonald, Charles, ed. and trans. 1976. *Cicero, Orations: In Catilinam 1–4; Pro Murena; Pro Sulla; Pro Flacco*. London; Cambridge: Heinemann; Harvard University Press.
Marcucci, Silvia, ed. 2007. *Domenico da Peccioli, Lectura epistularum Senecae*. Firenze: Edizioni del Galluzzo.
Maslakov, George. 1984. "Valerius Maximus and Roman Historiography: A Study of the Exempla Tradition." *ANRW* II 32.1: 437–496.
Mayer, Roland G. 1991. "Roman Historical Exempla in Seneca." In *Sénèque et la prose latine*, edited by Pierre Grimal, 141–176. Vandœuvres-Genève: Fondation Hardt.
Mencacci, Francesca. 2001. "Genealogia metaforica e maiores collettivi: Prospettive antropologiche sulla costruzione dei viri illustres." In *L'invention des grands hommes de la Rome antique – Die Konstruktion der großen Männer Altroms*, edited by Marianne Coudry and Thomas Späth, 421–437. Paris: De Boccard.
Morgan, Teresa. 2009. *Popular Morality in the Early Roman Empire*. Cambridge: Cambridge University Press.
Motto, Anna Lydia, and John R. Clark. 1968. "Paradoxum Senecae: The Epicurean Stoic." *CW* 62: 37–42.
Nosarti, Lorenzo. 2010. *Forme brevi della letteratura latina*. Bologna: Pàtron.
Nótári, Támás. 2008. *Law, Religion and Rhetoric in Cicero's Pro Murena*. Passau: Schenkbuchverlag.

Plumpe, Joseph C. 1932. *Wesen und Wirkung der auctoritas maiorum bei Cicero.* Bochum; Langendreer: Pöppinghaus.
Richardson-Hay, Christine. 2006. *First Lessons: Book 1 of Seneca's "Epistulae Morales" – A Commentary.* Bern et al.: Peter Lang.
Richardson-Hay, Christine. 2009. "Dinner at Seneca's Table: The Philosophy of Food." *G&R* 56: 71–96.
Roloff, Heinrich. 1967. "Maiores bei Cicero." In *Römische Wertbegriffe*, edited by Hans Oppermann, 274–322. Darmstadt: Wissenschaftliche Buchgesellschaft.
Romano, Elisa. 2006. " 'Allontanarsi dall'antico:' Novità e cambiamento nell'antica Roma." *Storica* 12: 7–42.
Roskam, Geert. 2007. *Live Unnoticed – Λάθε βιώσας: On the Vicissitudes of an Epicurean Doctrine.* Leiden; Boston: Brill.
Schafer, John. 2009. *Ars Didactica: Seneca's 94th and 95th Letters.* Göttingen: Vandenhoeck & Ruprecht.
Schiesaro, Alessandro, ed. 1996. *Seneca, Sulla felicità,* trans. Donatella Agonigi. Milano: Rizzoli.
Schmal, Stephan. 2008. "Held oder Harlekin? Der Sterbende Seneca bei Tacitus." *Klio* 90: 105–123.
Schoenberger, Hans. 1910. *Beispiele aus der Geschichte: Ein rhetorisches Kunstmittel in Ciceros Reden.* Augsburg: Pfeiffer.
Seneca. 1917–1925. *Ad Lucilium epistulae morales.* See Gummere 1917–1925.
Seneca. 1928–1935. *Moral Essays.* See Basore 1928–1935.
Seneca. 1969. *De vita beata – Sur le Bonheur.* See Grimal 1969.
Seneca. 1979. *Lettere a Lucilio: libro XV: Le lettere 94 e 95.* See Bellincioni 1979.
Seneca. 1996. *Sulla felicità.* See Schiesaro 1996.
Seneca the Elder. 1974. *Controversiae, Books 1–6.* See Winterbottom 1974.
Setaioli, Aldo. 2003. "Seneca e Cicerone." In *Aspetti della fortuna di Cicerone nella cultura latina: Atti del III Symposium Ciceronianum Arpinas (Arpino 10 maggio 2002)*, edited by Emanuele Narducci, 55–77. Firenze: Felice Le Monnier.
Setaioli, Aldo. 2014. "The Epistulae morales." In *Brill's Companion to Seneca: Philosopher and Dramatist*, edited by Gregor Damschen and Andreas Heil, 191–200. Leiden; Boston: Brill
Shackleton Bailey, David Roy, ed. and trans. 2000. *Valerius Maximus, Memorable Doings and Sayings.* 2 vols. Cambridge; London: Harvard University Press.
Sirago, Vitantonio. 1997. "Frugalità." In *Enciclopedia oraziana* II.11, 545–546. Roma: Istituto dell'Enciclopedia Treccani.
Skidmore, Clive. 1996. *Practical Ethics for Roman Gentlemen: The Work of Valerius Maximus.* Exeter: University of Exeter Press.
Stemmler, Michael. 2000. "Auctoritas exempli: Zur Wechselwirkung von kanonisierten Vergangenheitsbildern und gesellschaftlicher Gegenwart in der spätrepublikanischen Rhetorik." In *Mos maiorum: Untersuchungen zu den Formen der Identitätsstiftung und Stabilisierung in der römischen Republik*, edited by Bernhard Linke and Michael Stemmler, 141–205. Stuttgart: Steiner.
Tacitus. 1937. *The Annals: Books 13–16.* See Jackson 1937.
Tacitus. 1974. *The Annals of Tacitus.* Vol. 1: *Books 11–16.* See Furneaux 1974.
Tacitus. 1978. *Annales, Livres XIII–XVI.* See Wuilleumier 1978.
Tacitus. 2003. *Annales.* See Franzoi 2003.
Valerius Maximus. 1998. *Memorable Deeds and Sayings, Book I.* See Wardle 1998.
Valerius Maximus. 2000. *Memorable Doings and Sayings.* See Shackleton Bailey 2000.
Van Der Blom, Henriette. 2010. *Cicero's Role Models: The Political Strategies of a Newcomer.* Oxford; New York: Oxford University Press.

Van der Wal, Rogier L. 2007. " 'What a Funny Consul we Have!' Cicero's Dealing with Cato Uticensis and Prominent Friends in Opposition." In *Cicero on the Attack: Invective and Subversion in the Orations and Beyond*, edited by Joan Booth, 183–205. Swansea: The Classical Press of Wales.

Vigourt, Annie. 2001. "M'. Curius Dentatus et C. Fabricius Luscinus: les grands hommes ne sont pas exceptionnels." In *L'invention des grands hommes de la Rome antique – Die Konstruktion der großen Männer Altroms*, edited by Marianne Coudry and Thomas Späth, 117–129. Paris: De Boccard.

Walker Keyes, Clinton, ed. and trans. 1928. *Cicero, De Re Publica; De Legibus*. London; Cambridge: Heinemann; Harvard University Press. Rpt. 1961.

Wardle, David, ed. and trans. 1998. *Valerius Maximus, Memorable Deeds and Sayings. Book I: Translated with Introduction and Commentary*. Oxford: Clarendon Press.

Wheatland Litchfield, Henry. 1914. "National 'Exempla Virtutis' in Roman Literature." *HSPh* 25: 1–71.

Wildberger, Jula. 2006. *Seneca und die Stoa: Der Platz des Menschen in der Welt*. 2 vols. Berlin; New York: De Gruyter.

Winterbottom, Michael, ed. and trans. 1974. *The Elder Seneca, Declamations.* Vol. 1: *Controversiae, Books 1–6*. London; Cambridge: Heinemann; Harvard University Press.

Woodman, Antony John. 2011. "Seneca in Tacitus." In *Form and Function in Roman Oratory*, edited by Dominic H. Berry and Andrew Erskine, 294–308. Cambridge: Cambridge University Press.

Wuilleumier, Pierre, ed. and trans. 1978. *Tacite, Annales, Livres XIII–XVI*. Paris: Les Belles Lettres.

Zimmermann, Bernhard. 2005. "Tacitus und Seneca." In *Seneca philosophus et magister: Festschrift für Eckard Lefèvre zum 70. Geburtstag*, edited by Thomas Baier, Gesine Manuwald, and Bernhard Zimmermann, 261–272. Freiburg; Berlin: Rombach Verlag.

Seneca's Letters to Lucilius: Hypocrisy as a Way of Life

Madeleine Jones
Princeton University

> L'hypocrisie est un hommage que le vice rend à la vertu.
> (François de la Rochefoucauld, ~~Epictetus Junior. Seneca Unmasqued.~~ *Maximes*)[1]
>
> Le dire est autre chose que le faire, il faut considerer le presche à part, et le prescheur à part.
> (Michel de Montaigne, ~~De Ira.~~ *De la colère.*)

If we are to believe Tacitus, Seneca the Younger has been dogged by the charge of hypocrisy for as long as he has been in the public eye. The historian reports that a certain Publius Suillius accused Seneca of betraying his philosophical principles and profiting from his friendship with Nero, and asked: "By what wisdom, by which precepts of the philosophers had he procured three hundred million sesterces within a four-year period of royal friendship?"[2] Suillius' barbed question implies that Seneca's enrichment demonstrated that instead of dedicating himself to the improvement of his soul, as would befit his philosophical interests, he had pursued wealth by courting political influence.

---

1   The crossed-out titles are those given to early English editions of the Maxims. See the brief but fascinating discussion in Wray 2009. – This paper is an expanded and adjusted version of one given at the *Seneca Philosophus* conference in Paris, in May 2011. I would like to thank Matheus De Pietro and Jula Wildberger for organizing the conference. I am also grateful to Ada Bronowski, Antje Junghanss, and Jula Wildberger, for their comments on my paper at the conference, and to Yelena Baraz, Andrew Feldherr, Sam Galson, and Jula Wildberger, who commented on drafts of the present version. I first worked on Seneca during my MPhil at Cambridge under the supervision of John Henderson, and his influence was extremely important to the development of my ideas.

2   Tac. *Ann.* 13.42: "Qua sapientia, quibus philosophorum praeceptis intra quadriennium regiae amicitiae ter milies sestertium paravisset?" (trans. Woodman 2004). Beck 2010, 11–27 examines the ancient literary evidence for accusations of Senecan hypocrisy. Rudich 1997, 52–59 looks at Seneca's declared political views and contradictions between them.

The biographical facts of Seneca's great wealth and political power are not to be doubted. The sources agree that he was immensely wealthy (Tac. *Ann.* 15.64.4: "praedives").[3] As Griffin notes, "[t]wo of our principal sources for the reign of Nero credit Seneca and Burrus with the excellence of the early years. Tacitus and Cassius Dio [...] both agree that, for a period, they effectively controlled Nero and exercised their control in the interest of good government."[4] Nor were Seneca's power and his wealth unrelated: Though he hailed from a well-to-do Spanish equestrian family, his friendship with the emperor no doubt enriched him.[5]

Seneca's philosophical writings, on the other hand, do preach the indifference of wealth and power, in accordance with orthodox Stoicism, which held that virtue was the only good.[6] In *Ep.* 67, for example, Seneca urges that Lucilius retire from political life, the better to concentrate on his philosophical progress. Seneca describes how wealth merely begets the desire for more and more indifferent things:

> Suppose that the property of many millionaires is heaped up in your possession. Assume that fortune carries you far beyond the limits of a private income, decks you with gold, clothes you in purple, and brings you to such a degree of luxury and wealth that you can bury the earth under your marble floors; that you may not only possess, but tread upon, riches. Add statues, paintings and whatever art has devised for the satisfaction of luxury; you will only learn from such things to crave still greater. (Sen. *Ep.* 16.8, trans. Gummere)

The passage succinctly expresses Seneca's attitude towards wealth, which was in line with Stoic teaching. It is not that wealth is in itself bad, but it is indifferent. To desire it is to be misguided about the nature of the good, and thus led further away from it. Thus, the problem is not having wealth, or potentially even choosing it in certain situations, but treating it as a

---

3   Griffin 1992, 286–294 discusses Seneca's wealth. Mratschek-Halfmann 1993, 307–308 lists briefly the ancient evidence, literary and papyrological, for Seneca's wealth and provides relevant bibliography.
4   Griffin 1992, 67; see n. 2 for references to the ancient historians. See Griffin 1992, 67–128 for Seneca's career under Nero.
5   This was certainly the accusation which Tacitus reports Suillius making: He enriched himself while imperial *amicus* through inheritance and loans to the provinces. Dio 62.2 corroborates the allegation of loan-making. Griffin 1992, 289 notes "the acquisition of legacies would be a natural consequence of Seneca's position as a principal friend of the Emperor. In the resignation speech in 62 Tacitus makes Seneca refer to the *pecunia* Nero had given him and the lands, suburban villas, and investments he owed to Nero's liberality. A Neronian date for the acquisition of at least one such villa, that at Nomentum, is confirmed by the Elder Pliny." (In a footnote, Griffin refers to *Ann.* 14.53.5–6 and Plin. *Nat.* 14.49ff.)
6   For the indifferents, see Long and Sedley 1987, section 58. All translations of Seneca's *Epistulae morales* are from Gummere 1917–1925.

good.⁷ Since it is easier to be good when one is poor, Seneca exhorts Lucilius to "cast away everything of that sort."⁸ But it is possible to be worthy and rich: In fact, at *Ep.* 20.10 Seneca suggests that since maintaining a healthy indifference to wealth is harder for the rich, it is for them a greater demonstration of virtue. Thus the fact of Seneca's wealth in itself had no bearing on his ability to live up to his principles. Suillius would have had to demonstrate that Seneca's attitude to his wealth was faulty to prove him a hypocrite.

But if the question of Seneca's hypocrisy rested solely on this contingency and could be settled by working out how much he really *wanted* his wealth, it would not have had the hold on the imagination of Seneca's readers that it has. I contend in this paper that there is more at stake in the *topos* of Seneca the hypocrite than the contrast between Seneca's works and his life, though this is the guise in which those writing about the *topos* – Seneca and his critics – cast it. I start from the assumption that proving or disproving the accusation with reference to Stoic doctrine or Seneca's own life is to reach a dead end. Deciding that Seneca was or was not hypocritical might be of biographical interest, but has no challenging implications. By attention to the theme, however, and the way Seneca uses it, I hope in this paper to lay bare some of the ideas and obligations governing the construction of the authorial voice in the document through which we (feel we) get to know Seneca best: the tricksily autobiographical *Epistulae Morales*.

I. Seneca's Hypocrisy in Scholarship

It is easy to see how the nice distinction that wealth is indifferent but not actually bad could be lost on an audience skeptical of *Seneca praedives*. This has certainly been true in the modern critical tradition. E. Philips Barker's article on Seneca for the 1949 edition of the *Oxford Classical Dictionary* is one of the entries in that book whose age is more apparent to the contemporary reader. Over a couple of pages, Barker gives an overview of the life and works of the philosopher steeped in a sort of character

---

7   As Seneca puts it clearly at *Ep.* 71.4, that which is honorable is the only good; all other goods are false and counterfeit, worthless imitations of the original ("unum bonum est, quod honestum est, cetera falsa et adulterina bona sunt"). Indifferents may be preferred or dispreferred, according to the situation. Thus there might be circumstances in which wealth is preferable – but treating it as a good and choice-worthy in itself is erroneous and harmful. The common mistake of non-Stoics is to take these *falsa bona* as real goods.

8   *Ep.* 17.1–3: "Proice omnia ista."

assessment (or even assassination) which is out of fashion in contemporary criticism. For Barker, Seneca's poetic writings are the "primitive thought-forms, rough-hewn idola, and nightmares risen out of a tormented egoist's unconscious mind," and his philosophy is the "readymade escape system of a man whose deep-seated neurotic maladjustment is evidenced by his early ill-health." In short, the causes of the defects of his writings – which are characterized by "sparkle" and "artifice" and which "ring truer in emotional appeal than in speculation" – can be found in his life:

> Seneca's character, with its lamentable rift between principle and practise in crises, is sometimes pronounced detestable. He preached detachment and was conspicuously a money-maker; defiance of circumstance, yet whined in Corsica and crawled before Polybius; contempt for death and pain, yet, till finally trapped evaded them by flagrant complaisance. He could vent spite, or curry favour, or both by clever sniggering at a dead and by no means contemptible emperor, yet five years later connives supinely at more than common murder by a vicious live one. With all this he affects the moral guide. Such is briefly the indictment. (E. Philips Barker in Cary, Rose, Harvey, and Souter 1949, 828)

In his 1936 *Handbook of Latin Literature*, Herbert J. Rose had pulled even fewer punches in his assessment of "that eloquent moral weakling," though he does at least begin with a warning to the reader that he finds it difficult to judge Seneca's works fairly, "owing to the loathing which his personality excites."

> That a man in exile should flatter basely those who have power to recall him is understandable; Ovid did as much. That a prime minister in difficult times should show himself neither heroic nor self-consistent is no more than is to be expected of the vast majority of statesmen. That the influential adviser of an impressionable and unbalanced young prince should allow his master's favours to take the form of making him prodigiously wealthy is not remarkable; we may discount the tales of Seneca using extortion to add to his riches. That, having flattered, he should bespatter with abuse the object of his sometime adoration is certainly not commendable, but shows no deep depravity, merely a desire to swim with the current. That, being the most popular author of the day and master of an eloquence calculated to make the worst case appear passable, he should frame an elaborate justification of a matricide, may be passed over as one of the hard necessities of his position; but when the man who has done and is doing all this takes the tone of a rigid moralist and a seeker after uncompromising virtue, preaching, from his palace, simplicity and the plainest living with almost the unction of a St Francis praising Holy Poverty, refusing all knowledge that does not tend to edification, and proclaiming, in verse worthy of a better man than Nero's hack, that the true king is he who fears nothing and desires nothing, the gorge of the reader rises and he turns for relief to someone who either made his life fit his doctrine or, if he behaved unworthily of the best that was in him, at least laid no claim to be a spiritual guide. (Rose 1936, 359–361)

These are just two examples from a more austere age which I present as a reminder of an old tradition of charging Seneca with hypocrisy. The charge these two writers make is the same as Publius Suillius': the apparent conflict between Seneca's advocacy of withdrawal and relinquishing attachment to material objects, on the one hand, and his vast fortune and deep involvement with imperial power, on the other.

But in these assessments the authors do not limit their scorn to a contrast between Seneca's life and his works. Rather, they see the author's personal defects reflected in his literary output. For Rose the distance of Seneca's life from his doctrine means that reading the latter makes the gorge rise, and the implication is that he considers Seneca's "claim to be a spiritual guide" to be spurious. What the reader knows about Seneca's life affects his appreciation of these writings, precisely because they misrepresent that life. Barker goes further by suggesting that the "sparkle" and "artifice" of his writing directly reflects Seneca's deceitfulness in life. Thus Barker and Rose seem to denounce both the literary and philosophical quality of Seneca's work. More generally, at the time when Barker and Rose wrote, Seneca's prose and dramatic works were held in low regard by scholars and dismissed as examples of "Silver Latin." (The aesthetic judgments which made Seneca and his contemporaries unfashionable were often themselves couched in moralizing terms: "Silver" literature was considered as decadent and unrestrained as the decaying society from which it emanated.)

The comments of Barker and Rose could not be uttered by current critics. The literature of the early empire is now more often read as a sophisticated commentary upon the society which produced it rather than a disgusting excrescence of it. Furthermore, scholars have learned to read the "I" of a literary work as a textual persona rather than a direct representation of the author and avoid allowing biographical details to govern their interpretations of texts or textual devices their sense of an author's biography.[9] It is also no longer fashionable to make moral assessments of classical authors or their characters.

However, this is not to say that contemporary criticism does not itself make assumptions which are open to analysis. In fact, contemporary judgments on the charge of Senecan hypocrisy are especially interesting in the light of Seneca's writings. There is a tendency in more recent books and articles on Seneca to begin by acknowledging the tradition of regarding Seneca as a hypocrite and then to distance their own approach from it. Here are a few examples from the last few years:

---

9   But see Habinek 2000, 286 n. 55 on his preference for the language of "theatricality and performance" (referring to Woodman 1993, Edwards 1994, Bartsch 1994, 1–62, and Boyle 1997, 112–137) over that of dissimulation (as Rudich 1997): The critic must take care lest he misleadingly "assumes a stable, 'authentic' personality independent of its manifestations in action."

> The hypocritical millionaire mouthing Stoic pieties, the tutor and courtier to Nero who lost the dangerous game of court intrigue and died at the bidding of his own pupil, the author of possibly unplayable closet dramas prized by early modern playwrights but once interesting to scholars only as derivative copies of lost Greek originals: these shopworn handbook commonplaces shrink and fade under the light of recent work on this enigmatic, intriguing figure whose life and work seems equally riddled with self-contradiction. (Bartsch and Wray 2009, 3)
>
> Although Seneca's immortality derives mainly from the style he created and the philosophy he transmitted, his conduct as a man has also earned him fame, and notoriety. Ring-burdened Seneca, "in his books a philosopher," fawning while praising liberty, extorting while praising poverty, is one of literature's great hypocrites. (Griffin 2008, 23)[10]
>
> Sénèque souffre aussi, auprès des philosophes modernes, d'une autre réputation, plus imméritée encore. On le considère comme un moraliste mondain, un vulgarisateur plutôt qu'un véritable philosophe, le colporteur d'un stoïcisme éclectique, affaibli et non dépourvu de contradictions. (Trovato 2005, 32)[11]

The passages quoted come from the beginnings of books and articles on Seneca: The tradition of his hypocrisy is regarded as worth mentioning first off the bat. The writers no longer denounce Seneca's hypocrisy, but nor do they bring up the tendency to accuse Seneca of hypocrisy in order to defend him of the charge. Instead, they highlight it as a criticism which they consider irrelevant and weak because, as I have pointed out, moralizing and biographical criticism is no longer regarded as good scholarship. They are concerned not to show that Seneca was in fact consistent in life with the values he propounds in his writings, but that whether he was or not should not affect our judgment of the latter.

Although one can easily call to mind the sort of denunciations against which these reassessments of Seneca construct themselves, the tradition from which they distinguish themselves is long dead. No one comes out and calls Seneca a hypocrite these days. When Griffin looks for examples to support her generalization in 2008, she is unable to find any later than the early twentieth century; the 1949 *Oxford Classical Dictionary* entry was the last really egregious example I could find, and even that ended with the grudging admission that it may be more profitable for the critic to try to understand Seneca than condemn him unconditionally.

---

10 Griffin cites Landor 1905 (first published 1824) and Macaulay 1837. The description of Seneca as "in his books a philosopher" comes from Milton 1738, 25, whom Griffin does not cite. More contemporary accusations of Senecan hypocrisy are not cited.

11 The quotation strictly treats the idea that Seneca is a bad philosopher but, as I have suggested, criticism of Seneca as philosopher and writer were not unrelated to conceptions about his life, as Trovato suggests by his use of the phrase "moraliste mondain." Beck 2010, 16 n. 18 gives more examples of this "positive-apologetic tendency" among critics.

The return to this old accusation of Senecan hypocrisy, in order to deny its relevance, but not outright to deny it, suggests that the charge has not gotten out from under the critics' skin. The accusation is cited as precisely the kind of comment the literary critic, the philosopher, the historian cannot legitimately make, as a proposition outside the proper remit of the serious scholar. That is, it is not flagged as false, but as an idea which *cannot* be expressed within a modern scholarly discourse, and so it hangs, unexamined, unrefuted, simply canceled, over the legitimate literary, philosophical, or historical investigation.

This critical move of drawing attention to the charge of hypocrisy and simultaneously indicating that it is not a proper object of discussion is, I will argue, one which Seneca himself makes. I contend that the tradition of Seneca's hypocrisy comes not only from the contrast between his life and his writings, but also from his own thematization, in his writings, of such a contrast and of his failure to live up to his own standards.

Accusing philosophers who set themselves up as moral arbiters of moral depravation was something of a *topos* by Seneca's day.[12] In a discussion of a passage of *De vita beata* to which I shall return, Fuhrer points out that, however appropriate it might have been to Seneca's own situation, the charge of hypocrisy was a "familiar accusation which in the ancient world was continually leveled at philosophers: the accusation of a division between the life a philosopher lived and the teaching he propounded" (Fuhrer 2000, 204). Juvenal, in the opening of his second *Satire*, claims that the bushy beard of a philosopher is a dead giveaway of the sexual passivity which is precisely the *opposite* of the rugged asceticism it is meant to suggest.[13] Socrates was both held up as the supreme example of a true philosopher and sniggered at as a pederast.[14] The Stoic school was continually dogged by unflattering comparisons to Cynicism and emphasis on Zeno's thought experiments in the *Republic* of situations in which incest and cannibalism could be acceptable.[15]

The moment in his writings where Seneca most explicitly raises the issue of his own hypocrisy is a passage of *De vita beata* (18.1–3). Fuhrer, in her discussion of this passage, takes at face value Seneca's own explana-

---

12 See Zanker 1995.
13 Juv. 2.7–13: "And do you rebuke foul practices, when you are yourself the most notorious of the Socratic reprobates? A hairy body, and arms stiff with bristles, give promise of a manly soul: but the doctor grins when he cuts into the growths on your shaved buttocks" (trans. Ramsay).
14 Commenting on the passage of Juvenal just quoted, Braund 1996 suggests that *Socraticos cinaedos* "may suggest Socrates' supposed homosexual relations with his pupils." See Keulen 2003 for Socrates as a satirical figure.
15 Sellars 2009, 98–99

tion for its inclusion. He is responding to criticism of his enormous wealth by the likes of Publius Suillius: "In his work *De vita beata* he replies to the charges which had been made against him; and at no point does he accuse his detractors of misrepresenting his wealth" (202).

Fuhrer may well be correct that the passage of *De vita beata* was in dialogue with contemporary criticism of Seneca's lifestyle. But this cannot be its whole significance: Seneca has chosen to mention the criticism and has placed it within his own text. He has chosen to present himself as unable to live up to his own ideals, even if he immediately shows that this is not a problem. Seneca's self-characterization of someone dodging charges of hypocrisy is worthy of attention in itself.

For Fuhrer, Seneca successfully refutes charges of his having "double standards," not by denying his wealth, nor by suggesting that his lavish lifestyle is philosophically desirable, but by reminding the reader, "forcefully with his refrain-like repetition of the Stoic formula of happiness in the first half of the work that there is only *one* standard for the Stoic, which only the sage attains, namely, moral perfection; thus the normal person who has not attained this ideal does *not* live according to another standard" (207).

Seneca emphasizes that the distance between his practice and his philosophy is not only excusable but inevitable since no one but the sage acts morally. But interestingly, Seneca then goes on to defend himself with a second argument, which appeals to genre. "Plato, Epicurus, Zeno ...: none of them spoke about how they themselves lived, but about how they themselves ought to live. So I am speaking of moral perfection and not about myself and when I condemn moral weaknesses, then I mean above all my own" (*Vit. beat.* 18.1).[16] The generic requirements of philosophy do not include reference to oneself as example. One can write perfectly good philosophy while leading a perfectly bad life, since one is not obliged to mention the latter when one is expounding the former. While I concur with Fuhrer's judgment of this passage as logically coherent, it does not put to bed Seneca's *own* preoccupation in his writings with inconsistency. Rather, this becomes a major theme, years later, in the *Epistles*.

---

16 Translation quoted from Fuhrer 2000, 216. Fuhrer makes a similar judgment regarding the charge of double standards in the *De vita beata*; her interpretation differs from mine in that she offers the optimistic defense that Seneca's status as *proficiens* excuses him from the charge of double standards, or hypocrisy, whereas I pessimistically conclude that it commits him to it.

II. Hypocrite and Lecteur

At *Ep.* 20.3, Seneca exhorts Lucilius to consistency, insisting, as in *Vit. beat.* 18, on a single norm:

> Observe yourself, then, and see whether your dress and your house are inconsistent, whether you treat yourself lavishly and your family meanly, whether you eat frugal dinners and yet build luxurious houses. You should lay hold, once for all, upon a single norm to live by, and should regulate your whole life according to this norm.[17] (Sen. *Ep.* 20.3, trans. Gummere)

But also in the *Epistles*, Seneca demonstrates that there are complexities surrounding adherence to that one norm beyond just standing by it or failing. There is also the continual pressure of how one is seen to be behaving in relation to the norm.

Thus, Seneca declares that conspicuous asceticism can be a sign of philosophical failure rather than success. In *Ep.* 5, he tells Lucilius:

> I warn you, however, not to act after the fashion of those who desire to be conspicuous rather than to improve, by doing things which will rouse comment as regards your dress or general way of living. Repellent attire, unkempt hair, slovenly beard, open scorn of silver dishes, a couch on the bare earth, and any other perverted forms of self-display, are to be avoided. (Sen. *Ep.* 5.1, trans. Gummere)

The philosophical problem with these "perverted forms of self-display" is that one is showing off, and thus implicitly having regard for the gaze of others rather than recognizing this to be indifferent. It is a sign that one has not yet aligned one's priorities with the pursuit of the good. This is rather similar to the assumption which Fuhrer imputes to critics of Seneca, that setting oneself up as a philosopher, with all the pretentions towards moral expertise that this entails, is itself a reason to think that one might have moral failings. Being seen to be virtuous can itself be a warning sign that one is not.

In the same passage, Seneca goes on to give another reason why overt asceticism should be avoided:

> The mere name of philosophy, however quietly pursued, is an object of sufficient scorn; and what would happen if we should begin to separate ourselves from the customs of our fellow-men [...] Let us try to maintain a higher standard of life than that of the multitude, but not a contrary standard; otherwise, we shall frighten away and repel the very persons whom we are trying to improve. We also bring it about that they are unwilling to imitate us in anything, because they are afraid lest they might be compelled to imitate us in everything. (Sen. *Ep.* 5.2–3, trans. Gummere)

This passage makes a different claim from that in *Vit. beat.* 18.1–3. While there the single standard is the Stoic good, of which everyone, including

---

17 "Unam semel ad quam vivas regulam prende et ad hanc omnem vitam tuam exaequa."

the writer himself, falls short, here Seneca urges that the standard adopted ought to be the quotidian sense of virtue, which is attainable but flawed by Stoic standards. The clear sense is that all other things being equal, Stoics *would* adopt a wholly different standard, but their commitment to the public good means that they will make compromises in order to coax more people onto the path to virtue.

But why would adoption of a different (and in Stoic terms necessarily false) standard of virtue attract more people to Stoicism? Presumably one reason is that the true standard is depressingly difficult to attain. For the Stoics virtue and reason (which are intimately linked)[18] are available only to the sage (attainment of virtue and reason being the defining feature of sagehood) – and sages are as rare as the phoenix, and perhaps not one has ever existed (*Ep.* 42.1). There are no degrees of virtue: It will be an absolute state which subsumes one's entire person.

But Seneca also writes that the philosopher is an object of scorn. One reason too must be that if the true standard of virtue is adopted, the teacher of Stoicism will be seen to fall short of it and dismissed as a hypocrite. Already early in the collection, one is presented with a problem: Conspicuous adherence to Stoic doctrine marks one out as a show-off, and hence not *actually* indifferent to worldly things as one attempts by one's behavior to imply, and hence a hypocrite. Promotion of the true, high standard of virtue will lead to one being treated with scorn, as a hypocrite (even though, as Seneca argues in *Vit. beat.* 18.1–3, this is not necessarily the case: One might just be a sincere failure). Adoption of a more palatable, everyday standard of virtue will forestall this accusation of hypocrisy and give the philosopher more credibility: But this will be a totally hypocritical credibility since the philosopher will gain *kudos* for seeming to be virtuous according to a false standard of virtue.

In fact, assuming that the Stoic writer is not a sage, there will always be elements of the philosophy he expounds which he has not taken fully on board, and thus even if he acts rightly, he will not be doing so for the right reason.[19] It is not that progress is impossible: At *Ep.*75.8–15, Seneca describes the stages through which a *proficiens* (learner Stoic) can hope to pass, and throughout the corpus there is a real sense of improvement.[20] In practice, all Stoics are *proficientes*, traveling along the path to wisdom. But the fact is that most *proficientes* will not become sages, and their lives will

---

18 The exercise of reason is virtue: D.L. 7.88; Sen. *Ep.* 76.9.
19 Brennan 2005, 282: "[…] there are a number of Stoic texts that spell out in a fairly straightforward way the claim that the sage deliberates only about indifferents." It is the sage's exercise of reason in the choosing of indifferents which makes him virtuous, not what is chosen.
20 For example, *Ep.*16.1.

have been as devoid of virtue as the lifes of the most ignorant of fools (*stulti*). Any Stoic writer will be describing a philosophical position to which he aspires but which he has not yet attained.[21] As Seneca argues in *Vit. beat.* 18.1–3, the fact that the Stoic writer does not live up to his teachings need not be a problem. The philosopher can write an impersonal tract whose truth is not in the least affected by the character of its writer. But Seneca's longest work of moral philosophy is not an impersonal tract. The generic requirements of *letters* are somewhat different.

The *Epistles* have variously been regarded as philosophical tracts with epistolary formulae attached to beginning and end,[22] as the published record of a genuine correspondence,[23] and as a carefully crafted fictional document whose epistolary form is crucial to its meaning.[24] The influence of various other genres has been detected in the letters.[25] I leave aside the question of whether or not the letters are "genuine," but I do contend that the choice of the epistolary form is implicated in the content of the letters and that it ought to be taken into account in their interpretation.

Demetrius' *De elocutione*, which includes the only surviving ancient theoretical treatment of letters, suggests that the personal voice is a generic requirement of the epistolary form:

---

21 Long 1996, 150–151 makes the related point that Stoic adherents are following tenets which may be internally coherent, but which they have no way of independently verifying: since non-sages are not privy to a true understanding of Nature, they cannot know for certain whether they are living in accordance with it. However, Inwood 2005, in chapter 4 "Rules and Reasoning in Stoic Ethics," argues that Stoicism assumes that ordinary folk are able to make moral judgments and are not merely expected to have recourse to rules they do not understand (95) and, in chapter 10, "Getting to Goodness," that this is possible because by nature people have a sense of "cognitive dissonance," with which they can extrapolate the idea of virtue from non-virtuous acts (Inwood 2007, 286, on *Ep.* 120.4–5). Bénatouïl 2009, 97–125 draws a similar conclusion, on *parakolouthēsis* ("understanding") in Epictetus and Marcus Aurelius: "Pour l'homme, l'objectivité est donc accessible mais n'est pas immédiate," (109, with further references in n. 17).
22 See Wilson 2001, 165–169 on "essayistic" readings of the *Epistles*.
23 Berno 2011: "Several stylistic features, such as the obscurity of the style, repetitions, the apostrophes to Lucilius, and even the internal differences in structure between separate groups of epistles, characterize them as real letters, even if collected and re-elaborated by the author himself;" see Berno 2011 and Berno 2006, 14 n. 10 for further bibliography on the debate over whether the letters are part of a real-life or fictional correspondence, or something in between.
24 Wilson 2001.
25 Wilson 2001 gives a critical overview of the history of "reclassifying" (sic) the *Epistles*, examining "three prominent strategies that have been used to dethrone the 'epistolary' as the defining mode of Seneca's texts, with focus on studies of the letters as essays, as hortatory, and as pedagogical literature" (164).

> The letter, like the dialogue, should abound in glimpses of character. It may be said that everybody reveals his own soul in his letters. In every other form of composition it is possible to discern the writer's character, but in none so clearly as in the epistolary. (Demetr. *Eloc.* 227, trans. Roberts)

Furthermore, as Griffin points out, the example of Cicero's letters was unavoidable for any Roman epistolographer: I follow her in seeing the Ciceronian influence as compelling Seneca to adopt a personal manner and drop in reality effects to give the collection the impression of being a "genuine correspondence" (she deems it not one), stylistic features absent from Seneca's other important model, Epicurus' letters.[26]

By staging the letters as a personal correspondence, albeit one focused around philosophical questions, Seneca brings himself – or rather the self of the "I" of the letters – into it. Clearly this in no way implies that the "I" of a letter must be in any naïve or unproblematic sense the "I" of the author, though equally clearly, by offering the letters as from the desk of L. Annaeus, Seneca asks the reader to identify the authorial persona with him. It scarcely matters whether Seneca thought, felt, and experienced in his everyday life what the Seneca of the letters is described as thinking, feeling, or experiencing, but the letters' inclusion of some personal account of thoughts, feelings, and experiences is a requirement of their being plausible as a personal correspondence.

In short, though a philosophical tract does not require any personal confession, a letter, on Seneca's own model, does. Thus the defense Seneca mounts in *Vit. beat.* 18.1–3, that philosophers need not talk about their own lives, cannot hold in the case of his letters. Seneca chooses to write in a genre which demands reference to daily life, fictionalized or otherwise. Seneca's chosen genre of the philosophical letter stages a reconciliation between two generic exigencies: philosophical argument, of the sort that in *De vita beata* Seneca claims is not affected by the character of whoever propounds it, and a personal account (or what stages itself as such) of the writer's own efforts to live according to his philosophy. These elements do not appear alongside one another as easily separable entities in the letters. Rather, Seneca tells anecdotes about his life to reinforce or even make philosophical points.[27]

---

26 Griffin 1992, 418. Unlike Cicero's letters, the *Epistles* are pointedly silent on contemporary political matters. Berno 2011:"The *EM* have nevertheless an 'ambiguous character', because they are halfway between the intimate correspondence of Cicero (e.g. in the *Letters to Atticus*, which Seneca explicitly critics for their improvisation: *EM* 118.1) and the literary letters of Pliny the younger [...] Seneca's model is rather to be found in the *Letters* of Epicurus." For Seneca's models in the *Epistles*, see Maurach 1970, 182, and Berno 2011 for further bibliography.

27 Wildberger 2010 draws a distinction between formal argumentation, and what she calls 'Big Talk'– the "contemplation of great things," in "a style that appeals to the

These two exigencies inherent in Stoic letter-writing commit the author to a sort of continual self-accusation of hypocrisy. The unrealistically high expectations of Stoicism mean that Seneca will always fall short of virtue; the genre of the philosophical letter obliges Seneca, as he expounds doctrine, to point out the discrepancy between his theory and his practice.[28]

Admissions of hypocrisy also have a more instrumental role in the *Epistles*. The letters treat and exemplify an important therapeutic tool in imperial Stoicism: *meditatio*.[29] Seneca describes daily *meditatio* at *De Ira* 3.36, where he recommends asking oneself every night: "What bad habit have you cured today? What fault have you resisted? In what respect are you better?" on the grounds that "anger will cease and become more controllable if it finds that it must appear before a judge every day" (trans. Basore). For Seneca, honest self-reflection gives one the opportunity to take stock of one's philosophical progress and provides oneself with an incentive to adhere to one's philosophical principles. In the letters, Seneca explicitly connects his acknowledgement of his own shortcomings with this practice of honest self-appraisal.[30]

As has been elucidated by scholars, most notably Bartsch, a great deal of the corpus is preoccupied with the difficult and paradoxical implications of the Stoic praxis of self-scrutiny, whereby the subject takes himself as object of study. As Seneca describes it, the practice of meditative self-scrutiny is necessary to keep the self honest, and is actually necessary for a conception of the self as an integral whole: It is only when the self can be seen as a scrutinized object that one can see how all its parts fit together. However, clearly self-scrutiny also introduces a schism into the self, sepa-

---

senses and the emotions" (208), and proceeds to demonstrate how meaning is created by both contrast and blending of the two. Berno 2006 notes that the letters often have a tripartite structure: "aneddoto / considerazioni filosofiche da esso suggerite / parenesi finale" (19). This is the structure of *Ep.* 87 discussed below.

28 Scholars have looked at contradictions in Seneca's writings in different ways. Mazzoli 1991 describes how Seneca's avowed views on poetry "oscillate" between two poles. Montiglio 2006, discussing apparent contradictions in Seneca's writings, resolves these by appeal to polyphony in Seneca's prose. Wilson 2001, 167 offers a model for how differing or contradictory viewpoints can be explained without recourse to the idea of polyphony: "later epistles do not cancel out earlier ones but revisit the ideas in new circumstances and combinations. It is never exhaustive, never definitive […] throughout the collection philosophical ideas as motifs are explored through a series of inversions and reversals, in dissimilar moods, in concordance and discordance with other ideas."

29 See Armisen-Marchetti 1986 for *meditatio* in Seneca, Hijmans 1959 and Newman 1989 for its place in Imperial Stoicism.

30 Edwards 1997 and Bartsch 2006, 191–208 explore the consequences of reading the letters as a textual representation of *meditatio*.

rating the self *qua* scrutinizing subject from the self *qua* scrutinized object or *exemplum*.[31] The following passage illustrates this point:

> You bid me give you an account of each separate day, and of the whole day too; so you must have a good opinion of me if you think that in these days of mine there is nothing to hide. At any rate, it is thus that we should live (*vivendum*) – as if we lived in plain sight of all men; and it is thus that we should think (*cogitandum*) – as if there were someone who could look into our inmost soul; and there is one who can so look. For what avails it that something is hidden from man? Nothing is shut off from the sight of God. He is witness of our souls, and he comes into the very midst of our thoughts – comes into them, I say, as one who may at any time depart. 2 I shall therefore do as you bid, and shall gladly inform you by letter what I am doing, and in what sequence. I shall keep watching myself continually, and – a most useful habit – shall review each day. For this is what makes us wicked: that no one of us looks back over his own life. Our thoughts are devoted to what we are about to do. And yet our plans for the future always depend on the past. (Sen. *Ep.* 83.1–2, trans. Gummere)

This passage illustrates Seneca's preoccupation with the notion of a cleaving of the self in self-scrutiny.[32] God is in between our minds ("interest animis nostris"). He comes into the midst of our thoughts ("cogitationibus mediis intervenit"). The point is not only that God is in the thick of things and so knows all, but that the mind is cleaved apart in order to make room for his insertion: By letting the Stoic god in, one splits open oneself. Furthermore, God comes in as one who might at any time leave: The important thing is not the subjective experience of god, but that there is a position for god to occupy. This fact is something we might have deduced from the resounding silence of Seneca's correspondent Lucilius, who is supposed to occupy the same structural position of privileged observer: This space where god may enter may also be vacated by god, leaving a blank space, which can be occupied by the subject himself, Seneca, or any reader.[33] In the above passage, *vivendum* and *cogitandum* are structurally equivocated as things to be scrutinized, but *cogitandum* is also the act of scrutiny: Self-scrutiny is itself part of the life to be scrutinized, and so the

---

[31] On the paradoxical splitting of the self in Seneca, see Bartsch 2001 and Gill 2005.

[32] The psychological dualism of Seneca (or his rejection thereof) is a vexed topic. Inwood 1993 rejects Seneca's seeming dualism in the letters by arguing that some of Seneca's imagery and metaphorical language can be regarded as theoretically irrelevant and by showing that the instances of dualism which do stand make a division between body and soul rather than within the soul. I am happy to accept Inwood's arguments for a body-soul division in Seneca's thought, but the literary critic is forbidden the option of dismissing parts of a text as "just" figures of speech, and I thus consider Seneca's dualistic imagery a legitimate subject of inquiry.

[33] See Bartsch's analysis (2006, ch. 2) of Seneca's account of the sexual exploits of Hostius Quadra in *Nat.* 1.16.

split in the self is never a clean cut, but rather part of an unending feedback loop.

Furthermore, Seneca suggests that his confessional letter writing to Lucilius is equivalent to self-scrutiny. In writing the letter Seneca is scrutinizing himself; Lucilius (and we, the reader) are offered a peek into Seneca's view of himself. To Lucilius he remarks: "You judge me kindly if you think that there isn't anything in them [sc. his days] that I would hide." This aside hints at the possibility that Seneca might be lying to Lucilius in his letters to him. If the letters are documents of Seneca's own self-scrutinizing therapy, this means that he is also lying to himself.

This split in the self, a necessary and important part of Stoic self-awareness, opens up the possibility of self-deceit. This is the ideal mechanism for facilitating hypocrisy: One can behave badly during the day, hide it in the letter one writes at the end of it, and thus regard oneself as having behaved well. Furthermore, in one sense, following Seneca's logic, self-scrutiny is necessarily deceitful since, although it introduces a split into the self, it facilitates the viewing of the self as an integral whole.

But *meditatio* is also a philosophical tool. Self-scrutiny, for Seneca, opens the way for, as Edwards (1997) puts it, self-transformation. And one important manner in which this happened was self-accusation. Self-scrutiny will also force us to be honest about our true position, a vital step towards transforming it. Early in the letters, Seneca finds that he is in need of total transformation – and is not discouraged, but heartened by this:

> I feel, my dear Lucilius, that I am being not only reformed, but transformed. I do not yet, however, assure myself, or indulge the hope, that there are no elements left in me which need to be changed. Of course there are many that should be made more compact, or made thinner, or be brought into greater prominence. And indeed this very fact is proof that my spirit is altered into something better, – that it can see its own faults, of which it was previously ignorant. In certain cases sick men are congratulated because they themselves have perceived that they are sick. (Sen. *Ep.* 6.1, trans. Gummere)

The transformation of himself which Seneca claims to have observed is not the final change that brings him into line with virtue, but the first change, which allows him to see how much needs to be changed. It is to be celebrated, since it is the first step towards making the necessary changes. So, in his philosophical letters, Seneca is obliged continually to acknowledge shortcomings, a discrepancy between theory and practice – to accuse himself of hypocrisy. But at the same time, this self-accusation is a necessary first step towards virtue. Hypocrisy, by being acknowledged, is transformed from a failure to live up to one's own standards into a first step on the road to being able to do so.

From this overview, it should be clear that Seneca's so-called hypocrisy, a contradiction between his Stoic convictions and his lifestyle, is a phenomenon integral to his *Epistles* and inseparable from several important aspects of its literary identity. I have argued that the letters stage a reconciliation between the communication of philosophical precepts and a personal account (or what stages itself as such) of Seneca's own efforts to keep up with them. The two elements meet in the practice of self-scrutiny, which demands both a very personal self-appraisal *and* constant attention to philosophical teaching, and puts both in the service of moving towards personal alignment with the Stoic ideal.

Seneca's Stoicism presented a standard of virtue which he could not plausibly (given the rareness of sages) portray himself as embodying. His decision to write about Stoic philosophy committed him to promoting this standard of virtue. The epistolary genre demanded that he at least purport to speak in a personal voice about his own life, thus calling attention to his own failure to achieve virtue. Seneca's decision to stage the letters as a medium for his own self-improving self-scrutiny transforms his frank admission of his own shortcomings into a step towards virtue. But by drawing attention to the necessary focalization of this self-scrutiny through Seneca's own perspective, Seneca underlines the possibility that he is flatteringly misrepresenting his own progress, thus encouraging the reader to speculate that what purports to be a warts-and-all veristic portrayal of a philosophical journey may in fact be a hypocritically self-serving vanity piece, with self-blaming details dropped in to give the *appearance* of ingenuousness, that the *Epistles* themselves might be "a perverted form of self-display," to borrow Seneca's own phrase (at *Ep.* 5.1, quoted p. 401).

The *topos* of hypocrisy lays bare a fundamental ambivalence in the authorial voice of the *Epistles*. Hypocrisy is simultaneously the inevitable condition of the Stoic *and* a vice whose acknowledgement is necessary for progress *and* a potential danger, which may prevent the author from being honest with himself and which forces the reader always to question the honesty of the authorial voice.

III. Self-Scrutiny and Self-Accusation

One reason why it seems so very naive to those modern scholars who denounce the earlier tradition of decrying Seneca's hypocrisy to go ahead and point out any discrepancy between Seneca's practice and his preaching is that he is the first to admit (and he admits it first of all) that he has not yet assimilated the principles of his philosophy. No one knows better than he how far he falls short of his own ideal, but he is doing what he can.

> You may desire to know how I, who preach to you so freely, am practicing. I confess frankly: my expense account balances, as you would expect from one who is

free-handed but careful. I cannot boast that I waste nothing, but I can at least tell you what I am wasting, and the cause and manner of the loss; I can give you the reasons why I am a poor man. My situation, however, is the same as that of many who are reduced to slender means through no fault of their own: everyone forgives them, but no one comes to their rescue. (Sen. *Ep.* 1.4, trans. Gummere)

Such a frank confession of culpability, already in the very first letter, sets the tone for the collection.

A personal letter from a Stoic is the true revelation of Stoicism coming from the pen of one who is generically bound also to give a picture of his life and thereby to reveal how far short of the Stoic ideal it falls. The genre thus effectively conveys what must be the experience of Stoicism for its adherents. Seneca can talk about virtue, but it is always out of reach for him, and his day-to-day existence is bathetically un-Stoic. Furthermore, though his philosophy compels him to give an account of his personal experience, this experience is ultimately irreconcilable with the truth of his philosophy. Only the sage has perfect access to reason, the only criterion by which the truth of a philosophical thesis might be measured: *Proficientes do* make progress towards it, but nonetheless they have not attained it. The only knowledge a Stoic has is how far short of the Stoic ideal he comes: He knows only that he does not really *know* virtue.

A man who knows only that he knows nothing sounds familiar. It recalls Socrates' famous ironic stance:[34] His laid-back, seen-it-all incredulity on being informed that he was the wisest man in the city, his self-assured naivety in his enquiries. A philosopher after Socrates *cannot* parade his own wisdom, his own virtue: Socrates subtly, smugly showed that those who do that are sophists. But Socrates had oracles coming in to tell him he was the wisest man in the city, a coterie of admiring devotees, and crucially, a Plato to write him: His self-ironizing only worked in the narrative frame of a man whose words and deeds were recorded for their wisdom. Seneca, on the other hand, has to be Socrates and Plato, both teacher and example.[35] If Seneca self-effacingly parades his own shortcomings, he also has to be the one who subtly, or not so subtly, hints that despite, or more radically but also more Socratically, *because of* these shortcomings he is a figure to be respected, to be imitated.

The difference in mode makes a big difference to the character of the philosophy as well as to our impression of the philosopher. Plato's dialogues were carefully designed so that the ideas were elevated above the

---

[34] For Socrates in the letters see Isnardi Parente 2000, Albrecht 2001, and Staley 2002. Compare Keulen 2003 on Socrates in Apuleius' *Metamorphoses*.

[35] Henderson's laconic description of Seneca's persona in the letters makes this point: "this chummy 'Teacher-and/as-Pupil' " (2004, 1). Henderson refers to his 1991 article on Persius' *Satires*.

text itself. Wise though Socrates was, no one thinks that he is in any straightforward sense a mouthpiece for Plato, an authorial persona. Plato's points come out from the dialogue between Socrates and his interlocutor. His dialogues consist in a continual sparking back and forth of thesis and antithesis: The philosophy is in the synthesis and the synthesis is in you, even less material than the spoken words that make up the dialogues.[36] But in letters, that most determinedly embodied of literary genres (a written-down speech act designed to have consequences in real world, which makes sense only as an actual material document, delivered by one person to another), meaning is produced by juxtaposition and contradiction immanent in the text and is anchored to the grubby materiality of the page.[37] Conflict – the clash of voices – in Plato gives rise to the beautiful purity of the idea, conflict in Seneca *is* the idea: His writing deals with the practical impasses of a Stoic's life.

The co-option of Socrates as model makes vices, including hypocrisy, the most inescapable vice, which governs all others, into philosophical credentials, prefigurations of virtue. This is incredibly irritating of course, and Seneca's self-portrait becomes a good deal less attractive when we realize that his self-effacing openness about his faults, this frank admittance of discrepancy between his preaching and his practice, this advertisement of his own hypocrisy, is itself a forestalling of any accusations of hypocrisy. How can we call him a hypocrite when he's already done it? Wouldn't that be the height of naivety?

But if we feel as if we have dug deeper, have gotten beyond Seneca's double bind, if we come out and say that Seneca's parading of own hypocrisy before anyone has the chance to come out and accuse him of it is itself slightly hypocritical, that is, if we feel as if we have *gotten somewhere* with Seneca, made some progress, then we are brought back to the start: *Well yes*, hypocrisy was his thing, right there on page one, letter one. The strategy is, interestingly, precisely the same one as that adopted by the contemporary scholars quoted above, which make a claim to authority and simultaneously draw attention to the areas which escape that authority (for those scholars, Seneca's hypocrisy is not the proper object of a scholarly discussion), and thereby apologize for the limitations of the discourse with-

---

36 Demetr. *Eloc.* 224 suggests that a letter can be thought of as half a dialogue, though Seneca himself says that a live dialogue is a better medium for philosophy than letters (*Ep.* 6.5).
37 This is what Henderson 2007 calls "epistoliterarity." Derrida 1980 meditates on a reproduction of a medieval engraving which depicts Socrates taking dictation from Plato: The implication of writer and subject is made analogous to the relationship between writer and recipient of a letter, in a way that is particularly fascinating for readers of Seneca's letters.

out precisely admitting them. This process itself teaches a lesson: One cannot make any progress in Stoicism if one fights it. The unfortunate thing is that one also does not make any real progress if one does not. The problem continually directs the reader back to square one, page one: This is the Senecan experience *par excellence*. And even if the letters do not set one back, they do not get one anywhere either.

Stasis is a particular problem in the Stoic journey towards wisdom: In point of fact, it is somewhat unfair to suggest that progress is impossible. Seneca often proclaims that he feels that he or Lucilius have had a breakthrough, and the increasing length and philosophical density of the letters suggests progress on either his or his correspondent's part, or both. But though the central metaphor in Stoic education is the *journey* (hence *proficiens*, the word for Stoic adepts), procedure itself is somewhat ambivalent.[38] For one thing, it can be difficult to tell whether one's journey is actually taking one in the right direction: Seneca tells Lucilius in *Ep.* 16 that he understands that he has come far (16.2: "intellego multum te profecisse"), presumably in his philosophical advancement, but just a few lines later darkly warns that Lucilius must scrutinize himself to see whether he has proceeded in philosophy or in life itself,[39] that is, whether he has merely gotten older and no wiser, after all. Or perhaps the idea here is that Lucilius must make sure that he is making progress in applying his philosophy in life, rather than merely becoming more philosophically learned. Either way, the point is that not all progress gets one closer to wisdom.

Furthermore, movement is itself somewhat negative.[40] In the second letter of the collection, Seneca tells Lucilius:

> Judging by what you write me, and by what I hear, I am forming a good opinion regarding your future. You do not run hither and thither and distract yourself by

---

38 For the theme of travel in Seneca's work see Bouquet 1979, Motto 1984, Jourdan-Gueyer 1991, Motto 1997, and Montiglio 2006. For a discussion of travel as a motif in ancient philosophy more broadly, see Sassi 1991. According to Chambert 2005, 29–36, an antipathy to the very idea of travel is a typically Epicurean position characterized by a thinking of journeys on the analogy of infectious diseases, an anxiety about agitation of matter, and a sense that movement is incompatible with *ataraxia*. She characterizes the Stoics, on the other hand, as being inclined by their cosmopolitanism to think of travel as an indifferent and notes that Seneca himself emphasizes this, for example in the consolation to Helvia (see Chambert 2005, 36–41). For a comprehensive list of metaphors of travel see the entry "Chemin et voyage" in Armisen-Marchetti 1989, 86–90.
39 *Ep.* 16.3: "Utrum in philosophia an in ipsa vita profeceris."
40 On travel in Seneca, see Garbarino 1997 and Montiglio 2006. Montiglio sees travel as comprising a "contradiction in Seneca's thought." I argue that the shipwreck that is beginning and end is an instantiation of that contradiction.

changing your abode; for such restlessness is the sign of a disordered spirit. The primary indication, to my thinking, of a well-ordered mind is a man's ability to remain in one place and linger in his own company. (Sen. *Ep.* 2.1, trans. Gummere)

In fact, progress towards sagehood may be best achieved by standing strong: In *Ep.* 32 Seneca expresses a fear that the influence of non-philosophers may hinder Lucilius' progress (32.2), and offers this advice:

I pray that you may get such control over yourself that your mind, now shaken by wandering thoughts, may at last come to rest and be steadfast, that it may be content with itself, and, having attained an understanding of what things are truly good – and they are in our possession as soon as we have this knowledge – that it may have no need of added years. (Sen. *Ep.* 32.5, trans. Gummere)

The suspicion against travel is motivated ultimately by the Stoic ideal of homology: The idea that the Supreme Good alone is always identical to itself, and thus provides a fixed point in a world of otherwise shifting ends.[41] Thus false desires are a journey without end:

Natural desires are limited; but those which spring from false opinion have no stopping point. The false has no limits. When you are traveling on a road, there must be an end; but when astray, your wanderings are limitless. Recall your steps, therefore, from idle things (*vanis*), and when you would know whether that which you seek is based upon a natural or upon a misleading desire, consider whether it can stop at any definite point. If you find, after having traveled far, that there is a more distant goal always in view, you may be sure that this condition is contrary to nature. (Sen. *Ep.* 16.9, trans. Gummere)

Hence the alternative movement offered instead of *progression* is a sort of dynamic staying still, a burrowing into the self and firming of one's own foundations whose characteristic action is introspection. This is why self-scrutiny can be such a powerful tool in philosophical progress: It allows us to discover the Stoicism that is within us.[42] The man who does achieve the Supreme Good will find himself equal always to himself:

This, I say, is the highest duty and the highest proof of wisdom, – that deed and word should be in accord, that a man should be equal to himself under all conditions, and always the same. (Sen. *Ep.* 20.2, trans. Gummere)

---

41 On *homologia* in the pursuit of the good, see Frede 1999, 82.
42 The question of the innate goodness or otherwise of mankind was a vexed one within the Stoic school. Inwood 2007, 185, on Sen. *Ep.* 71.4–5, points out that Seneca is not committed to the existence of innate concepts by maintaining that "we have within us the idea of the honourable as the (highest and only) good, but we often do not know it." Inwood points out the implications of this: "If we have within us the outline notion (or a natural conception: See D.L. 7.53) of the good but fail to realize its significance in our lives, then part of the way forward is to develop a kind of self-knowledge and part of it is to find a way to exploit the latent moral intuitions we have." For a different account, see the contribution of Ilsetraut Hadot in this volume, and also the lexical study of Antonello Orlando.

And wisdom may be defined as "always desiring the same things, and always refusing the same things. You may be excused from adding the little proviso – that what you wish, should be right; since no man can always be satisfied with the same thing, unless it is right" (*Ep.* 20.5).

Thus the Senecan mistrust of travel stems from the same source as a desire for a single standard: an end to hypocrisy. It is no surprise then, that a metaphor of travel is used to illustrate the attempt to find a single standard to live by. In a footnote, Atherton expresses the central problem: "Strictly, there is no 'progress' towards, virtue, in that the transition from vice to virtue is instantaneous."[43] I argue that in Seneca's conception it is more accurate to say that one can move *towards* virtue, one can get closer to it, but this approach is not the movement which will finally get one there: This will always be, as Atherton notes, an instantaneous and total transformation. Because, for the Stoics, virtue is the only good, and there are no degrees of virtue, if one has not arrived at virtue, it makes no difference how far towards it one has traveled: One is still un-virtuous, and just as un-virtuous as the most depraved or ignorant of all the *stulti*.

IV. Shipwreck on the Voyage to Virtue

To illustrate these general remarks and their relevance to the theme of hypocrisy, I finish with a reading of a single letter. *Ep.* 87 deals explicitly with the difficulty of truly abandoning the worldly values which one knows to be flawed.[44] It is a treatment of a famous Stoic paradox: that only the wise man is rich.[45] In it, Seneca confronts his pride in his material wealth, which lingers even as he attempts to practice frugality. This instance of acting one way and feeling another is a prime example of the hypocrisy we have been discussing, and in the letter Seneca anatomizes

---

43 Atherton 1993, 53 n. 19. The note continues, "Plutarch *quomodo ... profectus* 75C ([sc. LS] 61S). But some notion of "advance" to this goal was clearly accepted, as is shown by *e.g.* Plutarch *st. rep.* 1043D, despite such texts as Plutarch *comm. not.* 1063AD (61T)."
44 The letter has been treated by commentators as falling into two parts: the anecdotal introduction and the dialectical proofs. Summers 1910 prints only the former. Cancik 1967 puts a divide between the two parts. See especially Allegri 2004 (a monograph on the letter) and Inwood 2007 *ad loc.*
45 This is the final Stoic paradox which Cicero treats in his *Paradoxa Stoicorum*. At *Ep.* 17.10, Seneca makes the same point: "Repraesentat opes sapientia, quas cuicumque fecit supervacuas, dedit" – "Wisdom offers wealth in ready money, and pays it over to those in whose eyes she has made it superfluous," and at *Ep.* 81.11 refers to certain Stoic dogmata as paradoxes. On logical paradoxes in Stoicism see Mignucci 1999, 157–176.

that phenomenon. The letter begins with a dramatic and perplexing declaration:

> I was shipwrecked before I embarked. I shall not add how that happened, lest you may reckon this also another of the Stoic paradoxes; and yet I shall, whenever you are willing to listen, or even if you are unwilling, prove to you that these words are by no means untrue, nor so surprising as one at first sight would think. Meanwhile, the journey showed me this: how much we possess is superfluous; and how easily we can make up our minds to do away with things whose loss, whenever it is necessary to part with them, we do not feel. (Sen. *Ep.* 87.1, trans. Gummere)

The meaning of the opening phrase "I was shipwrecked before I embarked" is debated in the scholarship on this letter.[46] After that, the letter barely mentions sea travel again. And Seneca himself explicitly writes that he will not explain what he means by it, nor expand upon how his "shipwreck" came about, in case Lucilius places it among the Stoic paradoxes. As Wright (1991, 16–17) notes of Cicero's *Paradoxa Stoicorum*, our fullest record of the memorable saws which the Stoics promoted, these sayings, "are not paradoxes in the strictly logical sense in which apparently sound argument leads to an outright contradiction. [...] The Stoics also knew about the so-called paradoxes of material implication, and used them extensively in their propositional logic, but Cicero's essays are in the original sense of paradox: That which runs counter to generally accepted opinion (*doxa*)."

This assertion is again open to interpretation. One explanation is that the shipwreck is indeed a Stoic paradox, but that the paradoxes only *seem* contrary to what one might expect when one does not fully understand Stoic tenets about the world. Once one does, what had seemed paradoxical will seem perfectly obvious. After all, Seneca promises: "I will prove that nothing of these is false nor so surprising as it seems at first sight." So on that reading, Seneca declines to expand on the point because Lucilius will dismiss it as paradoxical before understanding why it is true. Another possibility is that the shipwreck is not one of the Stoic paradoxes at all, and that Seneca does not want Lucilius to mis-classify it as such. But if the shipwreck that happens before one embarks were not to be placed among the Stoic paradoxes, what might it be instead? This question, and the com-

---

[46] On the opening sentence, "Naufragium, antequam navem adscenderem, feci," see most recently, Garbarino 1997 and, in response, Allegri 1999. The former argues that the *naufragium* ought to be understood as a metaphor for deprivation at the start of a trip (following Summers and Gummere's note in his Loeb edition) and not as a symbol of moral failing. Allegri reasserts the sense of *naufragium* as a disaster on the journey towards sagacity. See Allegri 1999, 85 n. 2 for a comprehensive bibliography of the scholarly debate over this phrase. As will be seen, I argue that there are many valences at play in the phrase simultaneously.

plex implications of the strange opening gambit are, I argue, key to understanding this letter.

After this cryptic introduction, Seneca launches into an anecdote. When he first mentioned the *iter* ("journey") which taught him the superfluity of possessions at the start of this letter (*Ep.* 87.1), it was by no means obvious that he was talking about a particular trip as opposed to a metaphorical journey: As we have seen, in the letters, progress appears as a metaphor for both philosophical learning and the passage through life. Armisen-Marchetti notes that in Seneca's works, "symbole de la vie des hommes ordinaires, la navigation est figurée avant toute chose comme un épisode périlleux. Les tempêtes qui la troublent represéntent soit les malheurs inhérents à la condition humaine, soit les dangers de la vie sociale, soit enfin les passions dans lesquelles sombre le *stultus*,"[47] for example, at *Ep.* 73.5, where a ship's reaching land is a simple metaphor for security and shipwreck stands in for all the disasters which might afflict one in life. Given this common metaphorical valence, the reader is primed to see this particular *voyage* as a whole philosophical *iter* in miniature.[48] However, here we see that in fact, Seneca does mean to describe a specific journey, one undertaken not by sea but by land, a trip in a cart with a friend, Maximus.[49]

The sea-faring metaphor is particularly relevant to the theme which the carting holiday introduces: the superfluity of possessions. Merchant shipping was synonymous with the sort of trade with which the senatorial class

---

47 Armisen-Marchetti 1989, 270. For ships, sea storms, and shipwreck in classical literature see Poeschl 1964 s.v. Schiff, Kahlmeyer 1934, and Nisbet and Hubbard 1989, on Horace's *Carm.* 1.14. Harrison 2010 examines the sea voyage as a metapoetic symbol in Latin poetry.
48 The idea of a sea voyage ending in disaster also evokes the idea of the *iter* of life in a broader than the Stoic context: Ships were a fairly common motif in tomb decor, and the metaphor of death as a safe harbor at the end of an arduous voyage was a commonplace. In the *Satyricon,* for example, Trimalchio imagines a naval motif for his tomb (Petr. *Sat.* 71.9–10); Petrovic 2005 discusses the passage in the context of contemporary funerary art. Tombs 43 and 90 in the Isola Sacra necropolis, Portus, are examples of tombs depicting ships coming into port. See also the entry on "Port et terre ferme" in Armisen-Marchetti 1989 for examples in Seneca.
49 If Lucilius is a little Lucius – Berno 2006, 14: "Una sorta di Seneca in piccolo: a cominciare del nome, quasi un diminutive del prenome del maestro, Lucio, e dal *cognomen* che lo qualifica come più giovane, *Iunior*, comme infatti pare che fosse (di circa dieci anni)" – then this man seems greater than the teacher himself; Inwood 2007 *ad loc.* identifies him as Caesennius Maximus, an "influential friend of Seneca [...] who seems to have accompanied him in his Corsican exile many years before."

ought not concern itself.[50] Maritime trade and money-making are made synonymous at *Ep.* 4.10–11 and *Ep.* 119.5.

> My friend Maximus and I have been spending a very happy period of two days, taking with us very few slaves – one carriage-load – and no paraphernalia except what we wore on our persons. (Sen. *Ep.* 87.2, trans. Gummere)

Seneca's story, we learn, is about a theme weekend of pretend penury. The *exercitatio* (or, in Greek, *askēsis*) was the procedure by which Stoics put into practice what they had learned in their meditations.[51] Here, Seneca is at pains to emphasize the frugality of his trip: As he has said, it taught him how much we possess is superfluous and how much of what we have we can do away with.[52]

Seneca describes the ascetic simplicity of the trip in terms which are surely meant to be amusing: He and Maximus took with them very few slaves – those which one carriage could hold.[53] Not quite reaching the extreme of making the ground his bed, he points out that he at least put his mattress on the ground, and himself on top of that.[54] The lunch, from which "nothing could have been subtracted," took "not more than an hour" to prepare.[55] Seneca remarks high-mindedly that, "the soul is never greater than when it has laid aside all extraneous things, and has secured peace for itself by fearing nothing, and riches by craving no riches" (*Ep.* 87.3), but of course the sentiment is amusingly undercut by the deeply compromised nature of his reported attempts at asceticism. The description is a satirical depiction of a man unwilling to give up his comfortable life but attracted by the idea of self-deprivation, and settling on a comically cosmetic version of it.

Here, Seneca connects the anecdote to the letter's opening gambit. He claims that he went out on his trip as stripped down as a shipwrecked man who has lost everything at sea.[56] The shipwreck of the opening line seems then to be a metaphor for the abandonment of attachment to material things that is necessary for an approach to wisdom. In the case of Stoicism, shipwreck is a particularly potent metaphor. As Garbarino notes, shipwreck is a

---

50 See the evidence collected in Verboeven 2009, 132.
51 Allegri recognizes the importance of this practice for the letter and opens her discussion with consideration of it (2004, 13). See her note 1 for bibliography on the topic.
52 As Allegri 2004, 16 points out, at *Ep.* 18.5–6 Seneca recommends an exercise in poverty.
53 *Ep.* 87.2: "quos unum capere vehiculum potuit."
54 *Ep.* 87.2: "culcita in terra iacet, ego in culcita."
55 *Ep.* 87.3: "De prandio nihil detrahi potuit; paratum fuit non magis hora."
56 Huxley 1965, 124: The shipwrecked sailor appears in literature as coming to land and telling of disasters at sea at Cic. *N.D.* 3.89, Prop. 2.1.43, Juv. 12.81–82, and Martial 12.57.12.

topos in the biographical tradition of several philosophers:[57] Aristippus the Cyrenaic, Zeno's teacher Stilpo of Megara, and the founder of Stoicism, Zeno himself, are all supposed to have had their philosophical visions on being shipwrecked.[58] In the tradition, losing one's possessions in such a dramatic fashion was a catalyst for the discovery of true wealth.

But here, of course, the comparison underscores the irony of the passage: Seneca, with his entourage and camping equipment, is in stark contrast to the proverbial shipwrecked (*naufragus*). The description recalls passages like *Ep.* 5.1, quoted above p. 401, where Seneca denounces those who hypocritically indulge their vanity with the shallow appearance of austere living. This self-satire sets up the real point of the letter: that something is missing from the trip. Describing the farmer's cart, led by knackered mules and a barefoot driver, Seneca breaks down and admits: "I can scarcely force myself to wish that others shall think this cart mine" (*Ep.* 87.4). He explains:

> My false embarrassment about the truth still holds out, you see; and whenever we meet a more sumptuous party I blush in spite of myself – proof that this conduct which I approve and applaud has not yet gained a firm and steadfast dwelling-place within me. He who blushes at riding in a rattle-trap will boast when he rides in style. (Sen. *Ep.* 87.4, trans. Gummere)

Seneca reveals that he has not been able fully to commit to the view that what we own is regarded as superfluous. His language makes it clear that he is torn between two value sets which contradict one another, but which he nonetheless holds simultaneously: He cannot help but notice that the carriage at whose passage he blushes is "more sumptuous" ("lautiorem"), but at the same time, he is frustrated that at his lack of commitment to those things which he praises ("quae laudo"), that is, the indifference to wealth he is attempting to cultivate. The phonic similarity between "lautiorem" and "laudo" reinforces their parallel demands for Seneca's approval. That his lingering attachment to material things and reputation is part of a fully developed value system, albeit one that is perverse, is signaled by Seneca's use of the word *verecundia* to describe his embarrassment: The word designates a traditional Roman virtue.[59]

57　Garbarino 1997 156. See also Blumenberg 1997.
58　Diogenes Laërtius 7.2–5 gives three versions of the story of Zeno's shipwreck. Similarly, in the consolation addressed to his mother Helvia on his own exile, Seneca uses the conduct of his aunt, his mother's sister, on her husband's death in a shipwreck as an exemplum of unselfishness and disregard for material things (*Helv.* 19.4–19.7).
59　Graver 2007, 56–59: The Stoics distinguished two types of shame: *aischyne* (a passion) and *aidos* (a virtue). See further 206–210.

Seneca holds double standards. The problem with which he is dealing is a kind of hypocrisy, but one that Seneca is sincerely trying to resolve. This doubleness is emphasized in the language in which the trip is described, full of doubles: two men, two happy days, two blankets.[60] And the disastrous end of Seneca's trip is doubly embarrassing: He is embarrassed at being seen by the chic in such a humble vehicle *and* embarrassingly finds that his ostentatious attempts at austerity amount to nothing rather than to the virtue which he takes pride in seeming to display (of course, they come to nothing *because* of this pride).[61] Seneca's attempts at practicing virtue were scuppered because he did not jettison enough in the putative shipwreck that occurred before he set out on his *voyage*: He had not abandoned his perverse embarrassment at the truth.[62]

Armisen-Marchetti and Allegri both note that "in portu naufragium facere" – "to be shipwrecked in port" – was a proverbial phrase for the failure of an enterprise at the moment of its inception. This is a second sense in which Seneca was "shipwrecked before he set out." His chances of progress in this particular leg of the journey to wisdom were sabotaged from the beginning because he had not yet fully excised the attachment to material values which would hold him back. He set out, doomed to failure, and in that sense already shipwrecked.[63]

This second sense of the opening phrase allows us, too, to have a secondary understanding of Seneca's claim that the shipwreck should not be placed among the Stoic paradoxes. The Stoic paradoxes are truths which seem strange to the uninitiated. But the disastrous end of Seneca's journey, the shipwreck which prevented him from getting to his destination, was caused by a continued commitment to values outside Stoicism. The shipwreck is thus not a truth to be expressed within the terms of Stoicism, but the problem which arises when Stoicism confronts a false set of values in the mind of a fool.

As the trip comes to an end, he notes, "parum adhuc profeci:" He has not come far enough.[64] The echo of the opening line, "I was shipwrecked"

---

60 *Ep.* 87.2: "ego et Maximus meus;" "biduum [...] beatissimum;" "duabus penulis."
61 Inwood 2007, commenting on *Ep.* 71.7: "Seneca seems to be claiming here that being held in contempt is a necessary condition for being a genuinely good man."
62 "Perversa recti verecundia."
63 Commenting on *Ep.* 87.1, Inwood 2007 points out that Seneca the Elder "includes, in his *Controversiae* 7.1.4, a sentence crafted by Quintus Haterius describing someone doomed to failure from before the beginning of his voyage: *naufragus a litore emittitur*, 'he left shore shipwrecked already.' In that case the claim was literal, not figurative." Summers 1910, in his commentary on the passage, makes the same observation.
64 Allegri 2004, 90 argues, *contra* Garbarino 1997, 150, that the phrase is "una ripresa stilisticamenta marcata dell'incipit [...] in una sorta di 'Ringkomposition'."

("naufragium feci"), reminds us that this is the point to which he is brought back. The problem is not merely a conflict between his theory and his practice, or his writings and his real life. Rather, the opposition is within Seneca's own declarations. Seneca laments that he *ought* to voice Stoic paradoxes (*Ep.* 87.5: "I should really have uttered an opinion counter to that in which mankind believe"). He ought to say: "You are mad, you are misled, your admiration devotes itself to superfluous things! You estimate no man at his real worth!" (*Ep.* 87.5), that is, he ought to be able to voice the Stoic paradox that only the wise man is rich. But his shipwreck amounts to the fact that he *cannot* express Stoic truths in his own voice. He has not yet taken them on as his own. This is the problem which makes the *Epistles* more deeply hypocritical than the sort of abstract philosophical texts about which Seneca hypothesizes in *Vit. beat.* 18.1–3. Seneca has committed himself in the letters to expounding Stoic truth in his own personal voice. But he cannot use his own voice to tell that truth because it is a truth he has not yet taken on.

Seneca moves on to illustrate the superfluity of wealth. He no longer emphasizes that he is presenting a view that is not fully his own, but having read *Ep.* 87.5, the reader knows that that is the case. He offers another anecdote, this time about Cato, drawing a contrast between Cato's manner of traveling light with contemporary travelers who carry superfluous items with them and thus reveal their depraved luxury. Seneca delightedly imagines an encounter between Cato on a loaded-up nag, and someone of "these dandies" of his own day, traveling amidst Numidian slaves and a cloud of dust. The latter would doubtless appear "more refined and better attended" with his "luxurious paraphernalia."[65]

However, details in Seneca's description of Cato and the dandies seem to undercut the overt point of the comparison. Emphasis is placed upon the amount of baggage with which Cato loaded his nag: "Cato used to ride a gelding, and a gelding, at that, which carried saddle-bags containing the master's necessaries;"[66] "O what a glory to the times in which he lived [...] to be content with a single nag, and with less than a whole nag at that! For part of the animal was pre-empted by the baggage that hung down on either flank."[67] In each instance the great weight of Cato's luggage beneath which his single nag strains is stressed as evidence of virtuous parsimony in itself. Meanwhile, the so-called dandy has his retinue rather than what they carry emphasized, and though he is amidst *apparatus delicati*, his

---

65 *Ep.* 87.9: "ex his trossulis;" "cultior comitatiorque;" "apparatus delicatos."
66 *Ep.* 87.9: "cantherio vehebatur et hippoperis quidem inpositis, ut secum utilia portaret" (trans. Gummere, modified).
67 *Ep.* 87.10: "O quantum erat saeculi decus [...] uno caballo esse contentum et ne toto quidem! partem enim sarcinae ab utroque latere dependentes occupabant."

mind is on the sword and the hunting-knife. Noble engagement in gladiatorial games is here an emblem of society's perversion, but nonetheless the machismo of gladiatorial combat is dangerously close to the ideal of the Roman man who takes pride in physical activity and spurns effeminate luxuries.[68]

The passage as a whole is characterized by a worrying affinity between the two items Seneca purports to contrast: Cato has less than modern-day dandies, but greater emphasis is laid on what he carries about. After jettisoning his excess baggage, what he is left with looks alarmingly like what he started out with. On the one hand, this could be taken as an illustration of the Stoic paradox: The wise man, who has abandoned his attachment to material wealth, discovers that he has thereby become truly wealthy. But on the other hand it poses a problem: How to tell the difference between the wealth attachment to which must be abandoned and the wealth of Stoic wisdom that is the ultimate goal? One might find that the wealth one is left with is not the true wealth of Stoic wisdom after all, and then one will find oneself where one started.

The dangerous similarity of vice and virtue was a preoccupation of Seneca's.[69] Perhaps the distinction between Cato and the dandies is illusory. At *Ep.*87.6, Seneca had encouraged Lucilius to think about how examining a man's wealth may show that a portion of it is borrowed. But in the next section it is revealed that this examination is an example of how one can go some distance in *seeming* to strip away illusory measures: In fact, *all* wealth is borrowed – from fortune (*Ep.* 87.7). Two rich men appear identical, but investigation may prove that one is in the black, one in the red. This investigation seems to have gotten further to the truth, but in fact, it obscures the truth of the matter: There is no distinction between the men after all, no distinction between what is borrowed and what is owned. Similarly, the difference between Cato and the dandies might turn out to be cosmetic.

Seneca refrains from drawing a conclusion either way on that point, but changes the subject with an ambiguous statement: "video non futurum finem in ista materia ullum, nisi quem ipse mihi fecero" (*Ep.* 87.11), which

---

68 See Edwards 2007, 46–77 and Barton 1993, 47 on this double-edged status. At *Ep.* 30.8, Seneca advises the philosopher to die willingly like a gladiator.

69 Inwood 2007 326, *ad* 120.8–9: "The similarity of vice to virtue helps us to learn what true virtue is like, if only because the close but ultimately disappointing resemblance of the virtue forces the reflective observer to concentrate and analyse." Berno 2003 45–49 and *passim*, writing about the relationship between descriptions of the natural world and moralizing digressions denouncing vice in the *Naturales Quaestiones*, finds that for Seneca virtue and vice act in parallel ways to achieve opposite goals: They are in a relationship of what she calls "specularità."

Gummere translates as "I see that there will be no end in dealing with such a theme unless I make an end myself." As we saw in the discussion of Seneca's attitude to travel above, the philosophical journey only ends with wisdom, when one is totally self-consistent. And that journey's end only comes with the total act of will by which one commits oneself to virtue, and renounces attachment to indifferents, including material possessions. Here "ista materia" could just as well mean "material possessions," implying a continuum of materialism between Cato and the dandies, upon which Seneca himself is also situated and to which an end can only be made if he takes action himself and renounces his own *materia*. Seneca notes that whoever named luggage *inpedimenta* was prescient in doing so, for it is only a "hindrance" – baggage, to which he is irrationally, emotionally attached, which stands in his way to sagehood (*Ep.* 87.10). This baggage must be abandoned. That abandonment is not a process, a journey, but a single act which will bring an end to journeying.[70] When the baggage is renounced, sagehood is realized. If it is not, any journey towards it will be prematurely cut off: The ship will be wrecked before it leaves port.

At that Seneca abruptly ends the anecdotal opening section of the letter and turns his attention to "the syllogisms, as yet very few, belonging to our school and bearing upon the question of virtue, which, in our opinion, is sufficient for the happy life" (*Ep.* 87.11). In fact, the rest of the letter is taken up with syllogistic discussion. Seneca's moving on to the arguments of the schools at this point is a literary staging of his own refusal to take the step he knows he must in order to proceed and renounce his attachment to wealth. We see that the opening, "I was shipwrecked before I embarked," functions as a comment on the shape of the letter as a whole as well. If he was wrecked before he set out, then the jettisoning of baggage when the inevitable wreck is reached can only bring him back to where he was and what he had at the start of his journey, the primal scene of shipwreck, from where he can do nothing but start all over again, this time with logic. But Seneca proceeds to cycle through syllogism after syllogism proving the indifference of wealth, only to reject the validity of each in turn. Arguments that bring Seneca to the point of accepting the single, simple Stoic truth that virtue is the only good and that wealth and the opinion of others are thus indifferent are continually staged but none manages to get him to acceptance. As each one is scuppered, the end of the doomed voyage is enacted again. Seneca finally asks Lucilius to imagine

---

70 See also *Ep.* 71.29–31 for the importance of wanting to learn. Chapter 5 of Inwood 2005, "The Will in Seneca," is the fullest treatment of this issue. For further scholarly treatment of the theme, see Inwood 2005, 134–139. Inwood argues that for Seneca the will is affected by cognitive causation.

an act dealing with the abolition of riches being brought before the Roman people. Would these syllogisms convince us he asks? The answer, he caustically spells out, is clearly "no." The reader is left in the same state of abandonment from which he began.

Shipwreck is the beginning and end of a voyage of philosophical enquiry that is repeated interminably: Seneca writing letter after letter with the same Stoic message, with themes and imagery recurring periodically, and Lucilius' unremitting silence, throughout a corpus which eventually cuts off rather than ending, whose formlessness is unparalleled in ancient literature, and which is written in a much imitated style known to categorists as "the Senecan amble." In a way, then, the abortive end, the acknowledgement of stupidity and vice, is the destination, or at least it is all we ever get to. For Zeno, the trauma of a sea-journey that ended in shipwreck turned out to be the start of his voyage to enlightenment; for Seneca, shipwreck represents the traumatic event to which he keeps returning. For him it is also the start of a philosophical journey, but he is consistently brought back to the start because any progress he makes in Stoicism that does not bring him all the way to his destination of sagehood succeeds only in revealing to him how far he has to go and how hard the journey is; this is the shipwreck that brings him back to port, but this port, which consists of acknowledgement of his own shortcoming, is the only port from which he can, as a Stoic, sail.

He is wrecked too soon, and lost at sea, because he has not come far enough along the journey which *is* abandonment and shipwreck and prevents him from fully, and openly, committing to his philosophy (*Ep.* 87.5: "nondum audeo frugalitatem palam ferre"). This is not to say that he has not made any progress. He has made, as he says, a little. And he has learned a lesson from the failure of the enterprise: "Meanwhile, the journey showed me this: how much we possess that is superfluous; and how easily we can make up our minds to do away with things whose loss, whenever it is necessary to part with them, we do not feel" (*Ep.* 87.1). He has learned that what was easy to condemn in *meditatio* is more difficult to renounce in *exercitatio*.[71] And at least learning what one does not know is learning something. The first step for the *proficiens* is the acknowledgement that he is one of the *stulti*: (*Ep.* 28.9: "initium est salutis notitia peccati"). The precondition for the Stoic's journey towards wisdom is acknowledging that he is bereft of wisdom. Paradoxically, this self-knowledge is, as Allegri (2004, 91–92) points out in this context, a step towards virtue. This is why failure is the start of the philosophical journey, why Zeno started off with a

---

71 As Allegri 2004, 90 notes: "Due giorni di vita austera non danno la certezza di essere saggi."

shipwreck. The disastrous revelation that one has been committed to a totally illusory value set, even as one tried to pursue virtue, is itself a necessary step in the pursuit of virtue. It sets one back to the very start of one's journey but it is at the same time the first step because the journey one was on before was in the wrong direction. Misguided and vain self-perception is the *inpedimentum* that must be abandoned (p. 421). Only after one has emerged stripped of this, like someone shipwrecked, is one ready to embark on the voyage.

Shipwreck is hardly a positive motif. It is synonymous with disaster in general: At *Nat.* 3.28.2, Seneca describes the end of world (admittedly for him a watery end) as a shipwreck ("tam grande naufragium"). Elsewhere in his writings, Seneca evokes shipwreck to stand for both disasters in general[72] and the particular disaster of being without Stoicism. The man who is left to face the disasters of life without philosophy is as a man left to face the high seas without a raft.[73] And though there is, as I have argued, a way in which, short of getting to sagehood, this disaster is the best that can be hoped for, this points to the gloomy prognosis for the Stoic *proficiens*. His Stoic journey is almost certainly doomed to end in shipwreck: Practically no one reaches the shores of virtue. Even as he begins his journey, the *proficiens* knows that the likelihood of his reaching his destination is slim to zero. And just as the Stoics grimly note that it makes no difference how far under water you are when you drown, so they might remark that it is no matter how far along your voyage you are when your ship is wrecked.[74] More pessimistically, then, we are *all* shipwrecked before we set out: We know in advance that we cling onto the vices which will prevent us from ever arriving at our destination though, at the same time, we all have with-

---

72 See Armisen-Marchetti 1989, 141 for a comprehensive catalogue: "Les tempêtes et le naufrage sont le lot normal d'une existence que ne guide pas la sagesse. L'image est donc très fréquente."
73 Again, see Armisen-Marchetti 1989, 141–142 for many more examples and, e.g., *Brev. vit.* 2.2: "nihil quo cursum derigant placet."
74 Fools are like the drowning: They die inches beneath the surface just as well as if 500 feet under: Plutarch, *Comm. not.* 1063a = *SVF* 3.539. Compare Cic. *Parad.* 20: "auri navem evertat gubernator an paleae, in re aliquantulum, in gubernatoris inscitia nihil interest" and *Ep.* 49.11 with Armisen-Marchetti's gloss: "[...] dans la vie, comme lorsqu'on navigue, on n'est séparé de la mort que par une mince paroi" (1989, 140). Schofield 2003, 252 cites another Stoic *exemplum* which uses the analogy of shipwreck to show that life can be a lose-lose situation: "The instance of the shipwrecked traveler in the water who gets the opportunity to dislodge someone else from a plank that floats past: if he pushes him off, he behaves unjustly (committing an act of violence against another); if he does not, he is a fool (sparing another's life at the expense of his own)." The reference is to Cicero (as reported in Lactantius *Inst.* 5.16) and the anonymous commentary on the *Theaetetus* (col. 5.18–6.31).

in ourselves the capacity for virtue. All we have to do is embrace it. In fact, arriving at sagehood must be instantaneous: a transformation from being not-at-all virtuous, to being wholly so. Since there are no degrees of virtue, it cannot be arrived at gradually. In setting off towards virtue, one has already refused to leap instantaneously into it. Although one might hope to come to a point where one can make that leap, one has already made the decision that puts one among the shipwrecked souls of the world.

This is the non-paradox which Seneca will teach Lucilius, whether he wants it or not: When one is traveling towards wisdom, realization of the residual vices in one's character will bring the journey to an abrupt halt. The staging of advancement and dismissal of dialectical argument, voyage and shipwreck, is an illustration of the attempt and failure to subscribe to Stoic doctrine. It is not merely an example of Seneca's supposed inability to engage with dialectic,[75] but a strategy which hints at the ineffable gulf in Stoic experience, the gulf between being aware of Stoic precepts and fully believing them. Seneca finishes the letter by telling Lucilius: "If we can, let us speak more boldly; if not, let us speak more frankly."[76] The substitute for bravely committing to virtue is openly telling of one's failure to do so. The hypocrisy is not only the contrast between teaching and practice but the way in which acknowledging failure and vice is the most promising step towards virtue the Stoic can make.

Seneca lets slip, at *Ep.* 87.7, that he is speaking in a borrowed voice: He cannot *really*, for himself, denounce wealth as indifferent. But he is generically bound to preach that doctrine, and generically bound to speak in his own personal voice. He is thus committed to a position where any time he offers Stoic doctrine, it will be in another's voice, since he has not embraced the truth of Stoicism. He cannot, in what is avowedly a Stoic tract, offer counter-arguments against Stoicism in a philosophical letter,

---

[75] Seneca is frequently dismissive of dialectical philosophy in the letters. See, Barnes 1997 and, for example, *Ep.* 49.5–6: "Cicero declared that if the number of his days were doubled, he should not have time to read the lyric poets. And you may rate the dialecticians in the same class; but they are foolish in a more melancholy way. The lyric poets are avowedly frivolous; but the dialecticians believe that they are engaged on more serious business. I do not deny that one must cast a glance at dialectic; but it ought to be a mere glance, a sort of greeting from the threshold, merely that one may not be deceived, or judge these pursuits to contain any hidden matters of great worth." Cooper 2004, 317–320 sees Seneca's disinterest in dialectic as a philosophical shortcoming. Inwood 2007, 218, arguing against Cooper, remarks that "the dismissal of technical philosophy [...] must be weighed alongside the fact that he chooses to introduce the technical material and to engage with it in a manner which more or less forces his readers to do the same." For dialectic in the Stoic tradition see Long 1978.

[76] "Si possumus, fortius loquamur; si minus, apertius." Compare Ahl 1984 on the distinction between the loaded terms *palam* and *apertus*.

even though we must assume some to occur to him (otherwise he would embrace Stoicism). The only thing he can sincerely do is point out his own shortcomings, his own hypocrisy.

Bibliography

Ahl, Frederick M. 1984. "The Art of Safe Criticism in Greece and Rome." *AJPh* 105: 174–208.
Albrecht, Michael von. 2001. "Sokrates bei Seneca." *Sokrates: Nachfolge und Eigenwege*, edited by Herbert Kessler. 261–279. Zug: Die Graue Edition.
Allegri, Giuseppina. 1999. " 'Naufragium feci:' Autoanalisi di un fallimento." *Paideia*, 54: 85–93.
Allegri, Giuseppina. 2004. *Progresso verso la virtus: Il programma della Lettera 87 di Seneca*. Cesena: Stilgraf.
Armisen-Marchetti, Mireille. 1986. "Imagination et méditation chez Sénèque: L'exemple de la praemeditatio." *REL* 64: 185–195.
Armisen-Marchetti, Mireille. 1989. *Sapientiae facies: Étude sur les images de Sénèque*. Paris: Les Belles Lettres.
Armisen-Marchetti, Mireille. 1996. "La langue philosophique de Sénèque : Entre technicité et simplicité." *A&A* 42: 76–84
Atherton, Catherine. 1993. *The Stoics on Ambiguity*. Cambridge: Cambridge University Press.
Barnes, Jonathan. 1997. *Logic and the Imperial Stoa*. Leiden: Brill.
Barton, Carlin A. 1993. *The Sorrows of the Ancient Romans: The Gladiator and the Monster*. Princeton: Princeton University Press.
Bartsch, Shadi. 1994. *Actors in the Audience: Theatricality and Doublespeak from Nero to Hadrian*. Cambridge; London: Harvard University Press.
Bartsch, Shadi. 2001. "The Self as Audience: Paradoxes of Identity in Imperial Rome." *Pegasus* 44: 4–12.
Bartsch, Shadi. 2006. *The Mirror of the Self: Sexuality, Self-Knowledge, and the Gaze in the Early Roman Empire*. Chicago: University of Chicago Press.
Bartsch, Shadi, and David Wray, eds. 2009. *Seneca and the Self.* Cambridge: Cambridge University Press.
Basore, John W., ed. and trans. 1928–1935. *Seneca. Moral Essays*. 3 vols. London; New York: Heinemann; Putnam. Rpt. 1989.
Beck, Jan-Wilhelm. 2010. *"Aliter loqueris, aliter uiuis:" Senecas philosophischer Anspruch und seine biographische Realität*. Göttingen: Ruprecht.
Bénatouïl, Thomas. 2006. "L'usage de soi dans le stoicism impérial." In *Vivre pour soi, vivre dans la cité*, edited by Carlos Lévy and Perrine Galand-Hallyn. Paris: Presses de l'Université Paris-Sorbonne.
Bénatouïl, Thomas. 2009. *Les stoïciens III: Musonius – Épictète – Marc Aurèle*. Paris: Les Belles Lettres.
Berno, Francesca Romana. 2003. *Lo specchio, il vizio e la virtù: Studio sulle Naturales Quaestiones di Seneca*. Bologna: Pàtron.
Berno, Francesca Romana. 2006. *L. Anneo Seneca, Lettere a Lucilio libro VI: Le lettere 53–57*. Bologna: Pàtron.
Berno, Francesca Romana. 2011. "Epistulae morales ad Lucilium." *The Literary Encyclopedia*. Accessed September 28, 2012. http://www.litencyc.com/php/sworks. php?rec=true&UID=32192.

Blumenberg, Hans. 1997. *Shipwreck with Spectator: Paradigm of a Metaphor for Existence*, translated by Steven Rendall. Cambridge: MIT Press.
Bouquet, Jean. 1979. "La notion de progrès chez Lucrèce et Sénèque." *ALMarv* 6: 13–22.
Boyle, Anthony James. 1997. *Tragic Seneca: An Essay in the Theatrical Tradition*. London: Routledge.
Braund, Susanna Morton, ed. 1996. *Juvenal, Satires, Book 1*. Cambridge: Cambridge University Press.
Brennan, Tad. 2005. *The Stoic Life: Emotions, Duties, and Fate*. Oxford; New York: Oxford University Press.
Cancik, Hildegard. 1967. *Untersuchungen zu Senecas Epistulae morales*. Hildesheim: Olms.
Cary, Max, H. J. Rose, Paul Harvey, and Alexander Souter, eds. 1949. *Oxford Classical Dictionary*. Oxford: Oxford University Press.
Chambert, René. 2005. *Rome: Le mouvement et l'ancrage: Morale et philosophie du voyage au début du Principat*. Bruxelles: Latomus.
Cicero. 1991. *On Stoic Good and Evil*. See Wright 1991.
Cooper, John M. 2004. "Moral Theory and Moral Improvement: Seneca." in *Knowledge, Nature and the Good: Essays on Ancient Philosophy*, 309–334. Princeton: Princeton University Press.
Demetrius. 1927. *On Style*. See Roberts 1927.
Derrida, Jacques. 1980. *La carte postale de Socrate à Freud et au-delà*. Paris: Flammarion.
Edwards, Catharine. 1994. "Beware of Imitations: Theatre and the Subversion of Imperial Identity." In *Reflections of Nero: Culture, History, and Representation*, edited by Jas Elsner and Jamie Masters, 83–97. Chapel Hill: University of North Carolina Press.
Edwards, Catharine. 1997. "Self-Scrutiny and Self-Transformation in Seneca's Letters." *G&R* 44: 23–38.
Edwards, Catharine. 2007. *Death in Ancient Rome*. New Haven: Yale University Press.
Frede, Michael. 1999. "On the Stoic Conception of the Good." In *Topics in Stoic Philosophy*, edited by Katerina Ierodiakonou, 71–94. Oxford: Oxford University Press.
Fuhrer, Therese. 2000. "The Philosopher as Multi-Millionaire: Seneca on Double Standards." In *Double Standards in the Ancient and Medieval World*, edited by Karla Pollmann, 201–219. Göttingen: Duehrkohp und Radicke.
Garbarino, Giovanna. 1997. "Naufragi e filosofi: A proposito dell'epistola 87 a Lucilio." *Paideia* 52: 147–156.
Gill, Christopher. 2005. "Tragic Fragments, Ancient Philosophers and the Fragmented Self." In *Lost Dramas of Classical Athens*, edited by Fiona McHardy, James Robson, and David Harvey, 151–172. Exeter: University of Exeter Press.
Graver, Margaret R. 2007. *Stoicism and Emotion*. Chicago: University of Chicago Press.
Griffin, Miriam. T. 1992. *Seneca: A Philosopher in Politics*. Oxford: Clarendon Press.
Griffin, Miriam. T. 2008. "Imago Vitae Suae." In *Seneca*, edited by John Fitch, 23–58. Oxford: Oxford University Press.
Gummere, Richard M., ed. and trans. 1917–1925. *Seneca, Ad Lucilium epistulae morales*. 3 vols. London; Cambridge: Heinemann; Harvard University Press.
Habinek, Thomas. 2000: "Seneca's Renown: 'Gloria,' 'Claritudo,' and the Replication of the Roman Elite." *ClAnt* 19: 264–303.
Harrison, Stephen. 2010. "The Primal Voyage and the Ocean of Epos: Two Aspects of Metapoetic Imagery in Catullus, Virgil and Horace." *Dictynna* 4: 1–17.

Henderson, John. 1991. "Persius' Didactic Satire: The Pupil as Teacher." *Ramus* 20: 123–148.
Henderson, John. 2004. *Morals and Villas in Seneca's Letters: Places to Dwell.* Cambridge: Cambridge University Press.
Henderson, John. 2007. " 'When Who Should Walk into the Room but...:' Epistoliterarity in Cicero, Ad. Qfr. 3, 1." In *Ancient Letters: Classical and Late Antique Epistolography*, edited by Ruth Morello and Andrew D. Morrison, 37–85. Oxford: Oxford University Press.
Hijmans, Benjamin L. 1959. Ἄσκησις: *Notes on Epictetus' Educational System.* Assen: Van Gorcum.
Huxley, Herbert H. 1965. "Storm and Shipwreck in Roman Literature." *G&R* 21: 117–124.
Inwood, Brad. 1993. "Seneca and Pychological Dualism." In *Passions and Perceptions: Studies in Hellenistic Philosophy of Mind*, edited by Jacques Brunschwig and Martha C. Nussbaum, 150–183. Cambridge: Cambridge University Press.
Inwood, Brad. 2005. *Reading Seneca: Stoic Philosophy at Rome.* Oxford: Clarendon Press.
Inwood, Brad, trans. 2007. *Seneca, Selected Philosophical Letters: Translation with an Introduction and Commentary.* Oxford; New York: Oxford University Press.
Isnardi Parente, Margherita. 2000. "Socrate e Catone in Seneca: Il filosofo e il politico." In *Seneca e il suo tempo: Atti del Convegno internazionale di Roma-Cassino 11–14 Novembre 1998*, edited by Piergiorgio Parroni, 215–225. Roma: Salerno Editrice.
Jourdan-Gueyer, Marie-Ange. 1991. "Iter vitae: De l'image du chemin à l'expérience du voyage dans l'œuvre philosophique de Sénèque." In *La route: Mythes et réalités antiques : Actes du colloque organisé par l'ARELAD dans le cadre de la MAFPEN*, 33–44. Dijon: Université de Bourgogne.
Juvenal. 1940. *Satires.* See Ramsay 1940.
Juvenal. 1996. *Satires, Book 1.* See Braund 1996.
Kahlmeyer, Johannes. 1934. *Seesturm und Schiffbruch als Bild im antiken Schrifttum.* Hildesheim: Fikuart.
Keulen, Wytse. 2003. "Comic Invention and Superstitious Frenzy in Apuleius' 'Metamorphoses:' The Figure of Socrates as an Icon of Satirical Self-Exposure." *AJPh* 124: 107–135.
Landor, Walter S. 1905. *Imaginary Conversations.* London: Routledge.
Long, Anthony A. 1978. "Dialectic and the Stoic Sage." In *The Stoics*, edited by John M. Rist, 101–124. Berkeley: University of California Press.
Long, Anthony A. 1996. *Stoic Studies.* Cambridge: Cambridge University Press.
Long, Anthony A., and David N. Sedley. eds. and trans. 1987. *The Hellenistic Philosophers.* 2 vols. Cambridge: Cambridge University Press.
Macaulay, Thomas. 1873. *Lord Bacon.* London: Longmans, Green and co.
Maurach, Gregor. 1970. *Der Bau von Senecas Epistulae morales.* Heidelberg: Winter.
Mazzoli Giancarlo. 1991. "Seneca e la poesia." In *Sénèque et la prose latine: Neuf exposés suivis de discussions*, edited by Pierre Grimal, 177–217. Vandœuvres-Genève: Fondation Hardt.
Mignucci, Mario. 1999. "8: Paradoxes." In *The Cambridge History of Hellenistic Philosophy*, edited by Keimpe Algra, Jonathan Barnes, Jaap Mansfeld, and Malcolm Schofield, 157–176. Cambridge: Cambridge University Press.
Milton, John. 1738. *A Complete Collection of the Historical, Political, and Miscellaneous Works of John Milton: Correctly Printed from the Original Editions.* Vol. 2. London: A. Millar.
Montiglio, Silvia. 2006. "Should the Aspiring Wise Man Travel? A Conflict in Seneca's Thought." *AJPh* 127: 553–586.

Motto, Anna Lydia. 1984. "The Idea of Progress in Senecan Thought." *CJ* 79: 225–240.
Motto, Anna Lydia. 1997. "Seneca on Restlessness and Inconstancy." *Eirene* 33: 96–105.
Mratschek-Halfman, Sigrid. 1993. *Divites et praepotentes: Reichtum und soziale Stellung in der Literatur der Prinzipatszeit*. Stuttgart: Steiner.
Newman, Robert J. 1989. " 'Cotidie Meditare:' Theory and Practice of the 'Meditatio' in Imperial Stoicism." *ANRW* II 36.3: 1473–1517.
Nisbet, Robin G. M., and Margaret Hubbard. 1989. *A Commentary on Horace: Odes, Book I*. Oxford: Oxford University Press.
Petrovic, Andrej. 2005. "Under Full Sail: Trimalchio's Way into Eternity: A Note on Petr. Sat. 71.9–10." *AAntHung* 45: 85–90.
Poeschl, Viktor. 1964. *Bibliographie zur antiken Bildersprache*. Heidelberg: Winter.
Ramsay, George G., ed. and trans. 1940. *Juvenal and Persius*. London, Cambridge: Heinemann; Harvard University Press.
Roberts, William Rhys, ed. and trans. 1927. "Demetrius, On Style." In *Aristotle, Poetics; Longinus, On the Sublime; Demetrius, On Style*, ed. and trans. William H. Fyfe and William Rhys Roberts. London; Cambridge: Heinemann; Harvard University Press. Rpt. 1995.
Rose, Herbert J. 1936. *A Handbook of Latin Literature from the Earliest Times to the Death of St. Augustine*. London: Methuen.
Rudich, Vasily. 1997. *Dissidence and Literature under Nero: The Price of Rhetoricization*. London: Routledge.
Sassi, Maria Michela. 1991. "Il viaggio e la festa: Note sulla rappresentazione dell' ideale filosofico della vita." In *Idea e realtà del viaggio*, edited by Giorgio Camassa and Silvana Fasce, 17–36. Genova: ECIG.
Schofield, Malcolm. 2003. "Stoic Ethics." In *The Cambridge Companion to the Stoics*, edited by Brad Inwood, 233–256. Cambridge: Cambridge University Press.
Sellars, John. 2009. *The Art of Living: The Stoics on the Nature and Function of Philosophy*. Bristol: Bristol Classical Press.
Seneca. 1910. *Select Letters*. See Summers 1910.
Seneca. 1917–1925. *Ad Lucilium epistulae morales*. See Gummere 1917–1925.
Seneca. 1928–1935. *Moral Essays*. See Basore 1928–1935.
Seneca. 2007. *Selected Philosophical Letters*. See Inwood 2007a.
Staley, Gregory. A. 2002. "Seneca and Socrates." *Noctes Atticae: 34 Articles on Graeco-Roman Antiquity and its Nachleben*, edited by Bettina Amden, Pernille Flensted-Jensen, Thomas Heine Nielsen, Adam Schwarz, and Chr. Gorm Tortzen, 281–285. Copenhagen: Museum Tusculanum Press, University of Copenhagen.
Summers, Walter C., ed. 1910. *Select Letters of Seneca: Edited with Introduction and Explanatory Notes*. London: Duckworth. Rpt. 1983.
Tacitus. 2004. *The Annals*. See Woodman 2004.
Trovato, Vincent. 2005. *L'oeuvre du philosophe Sénèque dans la culture européenne*. Paris: Harmattan.
Verboven, Koenraad. 2009. "A Funny Thing Happened on My Way to the Market: Reading Petronius to Write Economic History." In *Petronius: A Handbook*, edited by Jonathan R. W. Prag and Ian D. Repath, 125–139. Malden; Oxford; Chichester: Wiley-Blackwell
Wildberger, Jula. 2010. " 'Praebebam enim me facilem opinionibus magnorum uirorum:' Platonic Readings in Seneca Ep. 102." In *Aristotle and the Stoics Reading Plato*, edited by Verity Harte, Mary M. McCabe, Robert A. Sharples, and Ann Sheppard, 205–232. London: Institute of Classical Studies.
Wilson, Marcus. 2001. "Seneca's Epistles Reclassified." In *Texts, Ideas and the Classics: Scholarship, Theory, and Classical Literature*, edited by Stephen J. Harrison, 164–187. Oxford: Oxford University Press.

Woodman, Anthony J. 1993. "Amateur Dramatics at the Court of Nero: Annals 15.48–74." In *Tacitus and the Tacitean tradition*, edited by Torrey J. Luce and Anthony J. Woodman, 104–128. Princeton: Princeton University Press.
Woodman, Anthony J., trans. 2004. *Tacitus, The Annals: Translated, with Introduction and Notes.* Indianapolis: Hackett.
Wray, David L. 2009. "Seneca and Tragedy's Reason." In *Seneca and the Self*, edited by Shadi Bartsch and David L. Wray, 237–254. Cambridge: Cambridge University Press.
Wright, Margaret, ed. and trans. 1991. *Cicero, On Stoic Good and Evil.* Warminster: Aris & Phillips.
Zanker, Paul. 1995. *The Mask of Socrates: The Image of the Intellectual in Antiquity*, translated by Alan Shapiro. Berkeley: University of California Press.

The Epicurus Trope and the Construction of a "Letter Writer" in Seneca's *Epistulae Morales*

Jula Wildberger
The American University of Paris

Whereas older scholarship took Seneca's interest in Epicurus as a showcase example of a Roman philosopher's eclecticism, or at least softened Stoicism, more recent contributions highlight the careful selectivity with which Seneca plunders valuables from the "enemy camp" for his own unambiguously Stoic discourse. He clearly sides with the Stoics against incompatible Epicurean positions wherever the two schools disagree on tenets fundamental to their respective systems, e.g. in the fields of physics, theology, social anthropology, axiology, or about the definition of the good life. However, this does not prevent him from appreciating Epicurus as one of his stylistic and generic models, from adapting Epicurean methods of therapy, or from integrating ideas and concepts to supplement the ethical teachings offered in his own school.[1]

In this paper I wish to add a further dimension to such observations and to explore the literary function of Epicurus' presence in the *Epistulae morales*. I will argue that in this work engagement with Epicurus has become a multifaceted stylistic device essential to the fabric of this epistolary

---

1   For the Epicureans as "the enemy," see Sen. *Ep.* 2.5: "aliena castra." Unless indicated otherwise, translations are my own. Original quotations of the *Epistulae morales* are adapted from Reynold's edition, with changes of orthography and punctuation. For quotations of Epicurus, I have used the editions of Arrighetti and Usener. An excellent recent introduction to "Seneca's reception of Epicurus" is Margaret Graver's chapter in the forthcoming *Oxford Handbook of Epicureanism*. See also, e.g., Weissenfels 1886; Mutschmann 1915; Schildhauer 1932; Pohlenz 1941; Hermes 1951; Schottlaender 1955; Schmid 1955; Motto and Clark 1968; André 1969; Grimal 1969 and 1970; Hadot 1969, 41–56; Avotins 1977; Maso 1979–1980; Setaioli 1988, 171–256 (with detailed doxography) and 1997; Freise 1989; Lana 1991; Mazzoli 1989; Obstoy 1989; Degl'Innocenti Pierini 1992; Hachmann 1995, 220–237 and 1997; Casadesús Bordoy 1997; Grilli 1998; Gigante 1998 and 1999 (= 2000); Schwaiger 2000; Cooper 2004, 337–346; Henderson 2004; Inwood 2007b; Graver 2009. A list of "main references" is supplied by Ferguson 1999, 2280–2282. I was unable to access Sacheli 1925. – I wish to thank Hynd Lalam for her help with editing this paper. All remaining errors are my own.

Bildungsroman. As I have argued elsewhere,[2] it is not only the addressee "Lucilius" who appears as an exemplary reader and student of philosophy. Also the sender "Seneca" is a learner whose grasp of the issues he studies is evolving constantly, so that he can serve as a role model in his efforts to make progress toward the life of a seriously practicing Stoic. In this context, the Epicurus trope – as I will call the phenomenon from now on[3] – contributes to the creation of a Letter Writer, the persona "Seneca," who must be distinguished from L. Annaeus Seneca (henceforth "L. Annaeus"), the man who crafted "Seneca" together with the *Epistulae morales.* As an important element of the corpus' overall structure,[4] the Epicurus trope marks turning points in the Letter Writer's methodology and mode of thinking.

In what follows, I will first point out evidence, both well known and new, that references to Epicurus in the *Epistulae morales* should not be read as mere scholarly source citations. I will show that it is at least sometimes possible to distinguish two layers of reception: naive endorsement by the Letter Writer Seneca and cunning manipulation by the author L. Annaeus (section I). In a next step, I will outline the relation between Seneca and Epicurus as it is depicted in the earlier letters and indicate how this image is painted, at least partly, through conscious misrepresentation and reinterpretation of Epicurean ideas by L. Annaeus (section II). In a third section (III), I will use conceptions of pleasure as an example to demonstrate how an increasingly sophisticated account of Stoic thought is paralleled by a gradually sharper demarcation from Epicurean tenets.[5] This

---

2   Wildberger 2006, 141–152; Wildberger 2010. I agree with the thesis proposed by Margaret Graver in her contribution to this volume that for L. Annaeus there is no clear division between the man and book, and only wish to clarify that the "Letter Writer" is just one aspect of this much more complex and multilayered "externalized self" created through writing and publication.
3   "Trope" seems to be the appropriate term in this context, insofar as I wish to refer to something which is both a recurrent motif and an intricate figure of style and thought.
4   On the structure of the corpus, see in particular Cancik 1967; Maurach 1970 (a summary in Maurach 2005, 158–173); Hachmann 1995; Henderson 2004. Compare also the paper by Elizabeth Gloyn in this volume as well as the contribution by Gareth Williams about an even larger superstructure comprising the *Epistulae morales,* the *Naturales quaestiones,* and possibly the *Libri moralis philosophiae.* The structural importance of Seneca's engagement with Epicurus in the *Epistulae morales* is discussed by André 1969 and Hachmann 1995, 220–237.
5   Hachmann 1995, 220–237 observes more criticism of Epicurean positions toward the end of the collection, especially in the last third (229). Already André 1969, 473 had noted this and explained it with a "raidissement doctrinal:" "[…] les lettres du dernier tiers, LXXX à CXXIV, apparaissent dominées par le souci du 'système'." I wish to develop these approaches by showing that there are no clear-

will lead to a few final conclusions about the philosophical significance of the Epicurus trope in the *Epistulae morales* (section IV). I thus hope to both advance our understanding of the *Epistulae morales* as a work of literature and contribute to a better informed assessment of the thought of its author. Unless we begin to take serious account of the developmental story of the Letter Writer Seneca that L. Annaeus has plotted for us, we are in constant danger of equating the utterances of a character on stage with the opinions of the dramatist.[6]

I.

Discussions of the Epicurus trope usually begin with a survey of sources that the author of the *Epistulae morales* might have used. Did he read original works or only the available collections of sayings and maybe excerpts compiled by his research assistants? Did his Stoic professor Attalus, who has surprisingly much to say about pleasure, introduce him to the other school? What was the impact of contemporary Epicureans, whose lectures the author may have attended?[7] As concerns L. Annaeus, it is difficult to reach any certainty. Given that philosophical letters, such as those of Epicurus, were the closest model for the genre he chose for the *Epistulae morales*, it is very likely that L. Annaeus read at least some of these in the original. A collection of letters by various Epicureans may have been a source for the compilation of sayings known as the *Sententiae Vaticanae*, and among extant testimonies for Epicurean thought, this gnomology yields the largest number of parallels.[8] One borrowing can be traced back

---

  cut breaks. Rather, the demarcation takes the form of a continuous and gradual process of distancing, interwoven with a complex and equally gradual process of building a refined conceptual toolbox of Stoic ethical theory.

6 The dramatic nature of the letters, which has long been seen as such, was recently highlighted by Schafer 2011. He and others observe a didactic drama in which Seneca plays the teacher, while Lucilius undergoes a development, e.g. Schafer 2010, 33: "The Letters teach teaching by example; they are a literary case-study, an articulated, carefully drawn *exemplum* of Stoic and Senecan pedagogy." On the role of Epicurus in this drama, including a possible conversion of Lucilius, see, e.g., Mutschmann 1915, Schottlaender 1955, or Hachmann 1996. The more interesting drama, to my mind, is the development of the Letter Writer Seneca himself.

7 See Schottlaender 1955, 133–134 and Sen. *Ep.* 9.7; 63.5–7, and compare also *Ep.* 99.25 = Metrod. *Frg.* 34 Körte; 67.15; 72.8; 81.22–23; 110.18 with Epicur. *Sent. Vat.* 33.

8 See, e.g., Usener 1887, liv–lvii (who, however, believes that Seneca used only a collection of sayings – some ancestor of the collection transmitted to us – and not original letters); Mutschmann 1915; Hermes 1951, 7–16; Setaioli 1988, 171–181; Gigante 1998 and 1999.

to the extant *Letter to Menoeceus*, a famous elementary introduction to Epicurean ethics (D.L. 10.28). Surprisingly, Seneca expresses his inability to locate the source in this case: "It's by Epicurus or Metrodorus or someone else from that workshop."[9] This does not mean, however, that L. Annaeus himself did not know which source he was quoting. One might even speculate that he wished to avoid the impression that his Letter Writer was studying Epicurus from elementary textbooks.

Whatever the truth about L. Annaeus – as concerns the Letter Writer, it is striking to which extent our author, in an artfully crafted pretense of randomness, has Seneca make casual remarks that bear witness to his close and intensive engagement with original works by Epicureans. At *Ep.* 2.5, for example, Seneca has perused long stretches of text from which *he himself* excerpted the saying to be digested.[10] Since Seneca is "accustomed" to explore the "enemy's camp" and thus reads Epicurus *regularly*, the reader may conclude that Epicurus does not belong to the secondary writers greedy Lucilius may gorge on in addition to the ordinary fare and is rather one of the few authors approved for constant perusal (2.4).[11] So the reader is not surprised to learn a few letters later (*Ep.* 8.7) that Seneca is still "pillaging" (*compilamus*) this same author.

There are further hints that the Letter Writer tackles Epicurean philosophers themselves and not just digests of their thought. At *Ep.* 13.17, Seneca adds the information that the quoted sentence is not one of the better known sayings of Epicurus. At *Ep.* 46.1, he remarks in passing that a book sent to him by Lucilius had the voluminous appearance of a scroll by Livy or Epicurus, thus implying that the look and feel of the Greek philosopher's original books is just as familiar to him as his old copy of the Latin classic. Frequently, Seneca provides fuller citations and indicates not only the authors of quotes but also the works in question, all but one letters by Epicurus.[12] The addressee is indicated in the case of a letter to Idomeneus, and once Seneca even copies out the date in addition to the name. Exceptional is the quotation of a few Greek words from Metrodorus' consolatory letter to his sister.[13]

---

9   Sen. *Ep.* 14.17; the quote is: "Is maxime divitiis fruitur qui minime divitiis indiget," which corresponds to Epicur. *Ep. ad Men.* 130: "ὅτι ἥδιστα πολυτελείας ἀπολαύουσιν οἱ ἥκιστα ταύτης δεόμενοι,"
10 On this reading habit of browsing continuous texts for *sententiae*, which is characteristic of L. Annaeus' times, see the contribution by Martin Dinter in this volume.
11 See already Mutschmann 1915, 335.
12 "In quadam epistula:" *Ep.* 9.1 and 79.15–16; "cum scriberet:" *Ep.* 7.11 and 21.3.
13 Letter (or letters?) to Idomeneus: *Frg.* 128–138 Usener, 52–61 Arrighetti, quoted by name of the addressee at *Ep.* 21.3, 21.7, and 22.5; without naming the addressee at *Ep.* 66.47 and 92.25. – Addressee and date: *Ep.* 18.9: "in iis epistulis […] quas scripsit Charino magistratu ad Polyaenum." – Metrodorus' letter: *Ep.* 98.9; 99.25.

Referencing of this kind might have seemed too pedantic for the kind of informal exchange that the *Epistulae morales* purport to be, and accordingly, L. Annaeus makes sure to counter this impression. At *Ep.* 7.11, for example, the citation provides the context necessary to identify the referents of the pronouns in the quote. At the same time, we learn that Epicurus' assertion arose in a situation similar to that discussed in Seneca's letter: Epicurus "was writing to one of the partners with whom he shared his studies." Thus, the citation appears motivated by Seneca's wish to clarify how Epicurus' remark applies to himself and Lucilius and their shared studies too. The elaborate citation with addressee and date at *Ep.* 18.9 supports a claim that Seneca himself seems to regard as almost incredible, just as if he had felt the need to provide more substantial evidence in order to forestall the addressee's incredulity over Epicurus, of all men, recommending ascetic exercises.

In comparison, references to works of other authors are rare in the *Epistulae morales*, and not even one Stoic title is given. We may therefore surmise that this aspect of the Epicurus trope serves specific purposes. One of these may be the aim of placing L. Annaeus' literary innovation – Latin philosophical prose epistle – in its generic context.[14] This assumption is supported by the fact that the work referred to most often after Epicurean letters is the collection of Cicero's letters to Atticus.[15] Another effect achieved by these references is the impression that Seneca is seen literally with Epicurus' books in hand, just as the first-person perspective in *Ep.* 46.1 (see p. 434) encourages us to imagine him weighing a particularly hefty Epicurus scroll. Dealing with Epicurean philosophy has become a material part of Seneca's studious practices.[16]

This only underscores the Letter Writer's engagement with a school not his own; the *thematic* presence of Epicurus is even more pervasive than the debt expressly acknowledged by Seneca. A detailed account of this phenomenon would far exceed the scope of this paper. I will therefore limit

---

14 Compare Henderson 2004, 15, 30, and 44, and see also Lana 1991; Wilson 2001; Ker 2006; Inwood 2007b; Wilcox 2012, 17–22; Setaioli 2014a, section 6; Griffin (forthcoming), with n. 30.
15 Mentioned at *Ep.* 21.4; 97.3–4; 118.1–2. – In *Ep.* 108.30 and the Gellius fragment (Gel. 12.2), Seneca discusses readings of Cicero's *De re publica*. A book *Prometheus* by Maecenas appears at *Ep.* 19.9 ("Maecenas de cultu suo" at *Ep.* 114.4 seems to be a gloss); see also Setaioli 1997. – The only other citations of work titles that I have found are: Ep. 94.25: "in Vatinium Calvi […] sententia;" *Ep.* 114.18: "L. Arruntius, vir rarae frugalitatis, qui historias belli Punici scripsit." Not quite a title is *Ep.* 115.15: "in tragoedia Euripidis."
16 On the importance of *studia* for the *Epistulae morales* and their Letter Writer, see the contribution by Margaret Graver in this volume.

the discussion to a few selected examples that illustrate the extent and sophistication of L. Annaeus' borrowings.[17]

One example of a tenet adapted together with its stylistic form is Seneca's repeated use of the idea that pain is either bearable or short, which found striking expression in the fourth *Vatican Saying* and in the *Letter to Menoeceus*.

> Πᾶσα ἀλγηδὼν εὐκαταφρόνητος· ἡ γὰρ σύντονον ἔχουσα τὸ πονοῦν σύντομον ἔχει τὸν χρόνον, ἡ δὲ χρονίζουσα περὶ τὴν σάρκα ἀβληχρὸν ἔχει τὸν πόνον.

> All bodily pain is easy to despise. That which is sharp (*suntonon*) in its toiling is short (*suntomon*) in its time, and that which lasts longer in the flesh causes only mild toiling. (Epicur. *Sent. Vat.* 4)

> [...] τὸ δὲ τῶν κακῶν ὡς ἢ χρόνους ἢ πόνους ἔχει βραχεῖς.

> [...] the [limit] of bad things, that either their times (*chronous*) or toils (*ponous*) are short. (Epicur. *Ep. ad Men.* 133)

The same idea occurs in the deathbed lectures of Seneca's Epicurean friend Bassus,[18] but also before that letter, and there still without any explicit

---

17 Further examples are to be found, e.g., in Mutschmann 1915, 33; Hermes 1951, 17–53; Schottlaender 1955, 142–143; Setaioli 1988, 240–248; Grilli 1998; Graver (forthcoming). Compare also *Ep.* 3.5–6 with *Sent. Vat.* 11: "Τῶν πλείστων ἀνθρώπων τὸ μὲν ἡσυχάζον ναρκᾷ, τὸ δὲ κινούμενον λυττᾷ" or the "viscata beneficia" of *Ep.* 8.3 with *Sent. Vat.* 16: "Οὐδεὶς βλέπων τὸ κακὸν αἱρεῖται αὐτό, ἀλλὰ δελεασθεὶς ὡς ἀγαθῷ πρὸς τὸ μεῖζον αὐτοῦ κακὸν ἐθηρεύθη." Pacuvius' daily funeral party at *Ep.* 12.8 and the following reflections might echo *Sent. Vat.* 47 = Metrod. *Frg.* 49 Körte: "Προκατείλημμαί σε, ὦ Τύχη, καὶ πᾶσαν <τὴν> [Usener] σὴν παρείσδυσιν ἐνέφραξα. Καὶ οὔτε σοὶ οὔτε ἄλλῃ οὐδεμίᾳ περιστάσει δώσομεν ἑαυτοὺς ἐκδότους· ἀλλ᾽ ὅταν ἡμᾶς τὸ χρέων ἐξάγῃ, μέγα προσπτύσαντες τῷ ζῆν καὶ τοῖς αὐτῷ κενῶς περιπλαττομένοις ἄπιμεν ἐκ τοῦ ζῆν μετὰ καλοῦ παιῶνος [πλείονος V., corr. Usener], *ἐπιφωνοῦντες ὡς εὖ ἡμῖν βεβίωται*." It is also noteworthy that strong expressions of contempt, such as προσπτύω in this fragment, appear to be a characteristic of Epicurean style (compare also Epicur. *apud* Athen. 12, 547a = 512 Usener, 136 Arrighetti; *Frg.* 181 Usener, 124,2 Arrighetti, quoted in n. 23; and *Sent. Vat.* 4, quoted on p. 436). So Seneca's almost terminological use of the verb *contemnere* for the correct evaluation of indifferents (see, e.g., Lotito 2001, 78f.) might have had an Epicurean and not a Cynic pedigree, as one would assume at first sight. – In a forthcoming paper, Hans Bernsdorff argues that the shipwreck narrative at the beginning of Sen. *Ep.* 53 might allude to a similar account of Epicurus' own shipwreck experience on his way to Lampsacus which, as Plutarch tells us, Epicurus himself shared with his friends in one of his letters (Plu. *Non posse suaviter vivi secundum Epicurum* 1010e = *Frg.* 189 Usener; a new fragment of that letter was published in 2011: POxy 76.5077). The narrative itself was discovered in 1970 on the monumental inscription set up by Diogenes in his home town Oenoanda (*Frg.* 72 [NF 7], ed. Smith 1993). On the importance of shipwreck imagery, see the contribution by Madeleine Jones in this volume.

18 Sen. *Ep.* 30.14: "nullum enim dolorem longum esse qui magnus est" (indicated by Reynolds 1965 *ad* 94.7).

acknowledgment of its Epicurean origin. At *Ep.* 24.14, Seneca addresses pain in a form reminiscent of Epicurus' wordplays, which combine phonetic similarity with antithesis of meaning.[19]

Levis es si ferre possum; brevis es si ferre non possum.

You're slight if I can bear you; you're short if I can't bear you. (Sen. *Ep.* 24.14)

Ep. 18 is an example of how borrowings may extend beyond the explicitly cited gobbet and exemplifies how a letter by Epicurus may have also served as a structural model for one of the *Epistulae morales*. The letter has four parts: It begins with the question whether a philosopher should participate in public festivals, such as the currently celebrated Saturnalia (18.1–4). Then Seneca recommends an ascetic exercise, for which Epicurus is mentioned as a model and authority at *Ep.* 18.9. This is followed by an assessment of this practice. Seneca highlights the greatness of mind one can derive from it, a greatness that makes the agent "worthy of god" (18.10–13, quoting Verg. *Aen.* 8.364f. at § 12). The letter closes with another quote from Epicurus,[20] now about anger as the first step to madness (18.14–15). This looks as if Seneca had integrated Epicurean ideas in a web of his own reflections. In fact, however, the letter "to Polyaenus under the archonship of Charinus" cited at *Ep.* 18.9, if supplemented correctly by Usener and Philippson, may have also dealt with the appropriate involvement of the Epicurean philosopher in religious festivals, even using expressions not very different from what we read in *Ep.* 18.2.[21]

The evaluation of the recommended ascetic practice in the third part (*Ep.* 18.10–13), which the uninitiated reader would tend to regard as Seneca's own Stoic commentary on what he has read,[22] seems to draw either on the same letter to Polyaenus or some other Epicurean text. A reference to Zeus would not be surprising in a letter that dealt with religious practices, and parallels to main ideas in *Ep.* 18.10–13 can be

---

19 The idea reoccurs with some wordplay at Sen. *Ep.* 78.7: "Nemo potest valde dolere et diu" and 94.7: "[…] quod non potest nec qui extenditur magnus esse nec qui est magnus extendi," both collected as *Frg.* 446 Usener. Sen. *Ep.* 4.3 might be another example, but this is uncertain because of the lacuna. On *Ep.* 24.14 and the imitation of Epicurus' pointed expression by Seneca, see Hermes 1951, 20 and 75–77.
20 Epicur. *Frg.* 484 Usener, 246 Arrighetti.
21 Philodemus, *On Piety*, PHerc 1077, col. 30, line 865–870 Obbink, p. 105 Gomperz = *Frg.* 157 Usener, 86 Arrighetti = Philippson 1921, 373 (cited according to Obbink's text): ἀλλὰ κα[ὶ πρὸς Πο]λύαινον [συνεορτασ]τέα κἀν[θεστήρι]α καὶ γὰρ τῷ[ν θεῶν] | ἐπιμνηστέ[ον. There is further evidence that the letter dealt with religious matters (see Obbink 1996, 430–435 in the commentary to this passage, also concerning the attribution of the passage to the same letter as the one cited by Seneca). Note the syntactical parallel between the verbal adjectives συνεορταστέα and ἐπιμνηστέον and the gerundives in Sen. *Ep.* 18.2.
22 This is, e.g., how Hachmann 1995, 151–153 discusses the section.

found in Epicurus' extant fragments. In the *Letter to Menoeceus*, Epicurus states that "water and barley porridge provide the greatest pleasures,"[23] while Seneca refers to the same provisions (*aqua et polenta*)[24] together with "a piece of barley bread" and explains that such sustenance is not pleasurable by itself but something that gives occasion to the "greatest pleasure" of "having reduced oneself to a minimum that no injustice of Fortune could ever take away" (*Ep.* 18.10). Of course, Epicurus highlights the physiological as well as the mental pleasures generated by this frugal fare, while Stoic Seneca is interested only in the mental pleasure deriving from such greatness of mind. All the same, Epicurus also mentions fearlessness in the face of Fortune as one of the advantages of asceticism.[25] What is more, Seneca's Vergilian exhortation to be daring and become worthy of God through contempt of earthbound riches is, most likely, inspired by an Epicurean conceit, echoes of which can be found in other passages of the *Epistulae morales* too.[26]

> Σαρκὸς φωνὴ τὸ μὴ πεινῆν, τὸ μὴ διψῆν, τὸ μὴ ῥιγοῦν· ταῦτα γὰρ ἔχων τις καὶ ἐλπίζων ἕξειν κἂν <Διὶ> ὑπὲρ εὐδαιμονίας μαχέσαιτο.
>
> The cry of the flesh: not to be hungry, not to be thirsty, not to be cold. For if someone has these things and is confident of having them in the future, he might contend even with <Zeus> for happiness. (Epicur. *Sent. Vat.* 33, trans. Inwood and Gerson 1997)

One of these passages is the digestive exercise performed at *Ep.* 4.10–11, where Seneca first quotes and then comments on a part of another *Vatican*

---

23 Epicur. *Ep. ad Men.* 131: "Καὶ μᾶζα καὶ ὕδωρ τὴν ἀκροτάτην ἀποδίδωσιν ἡδονήν […]." Compare also Epicur. *apud* Stob. 3.17.33, vol. 3, p. 501 Hense = *Frg.* 181 Usener, 124 Arrighetti: "Βρυάζω τῷ κατὰ τὸ σωμάτιον ἡδεῖ, ὕδατι καὶ ἄρτῳ χρώμενος, καὶ προσπτύω ταῖς ἐκ πολυτελείας ἡδοναῖς οὐ δι' αὐτάς, ἀλλὰ διὰ τὰ ἐξακολουθοῦντα αὐταῖς δυσχερῆ."
24 The Latin word *polenta* refers to barley groats or the porridge cooked from these. Unlike a *polenta* as it is now served in Italy, the Roman *polenta* did, of course, not yet contain any Indian corn.
25 Epicur. *Ep. ad Men.* 131: "[…] καὶ πρὸς τὴν τύχην ἀφόβους παρασκευάζει;" Sen. *Ep.* 18.10: "[…] sed summa voluptas est posse capere etiam ex his voluptatem et ad id se deduxisse quod eripere nulla Fortunae iniquitas possit."
26 Compare, e.g., Sen. *Ep.* 21.11: "Venter praecepta non audit: poscit, appellat." That Seneca knew the whole saying transpires from *Ep.* 25.4 = *Frg.* 602 Usener: "Ad legem naturae revertamur: divitiae paratae sunt. Aut gratuitum est quo egemus aut vile: panem et aquam natura desiderat. Nemo ad haec pauper est, intra quae quisquis desiderium suum clusit cum ipso Iove de felicitate contendat, ut ait Epicurus, […]" and *Ep.* 119.7:" 'At parum habet qui tantum non alget, non esurit, non sitit.' Plus Iuppiter non habet." A Stoic correction of the same tenet is *Ep.* 110.20, where Attalus lectures that someone who would want to compete with Iuppiter ("Iovem provocare") should desire nothing, not even water and porridge ("aqua et polenta").

Saying. This last example illustrates how Seneca's own elaborations of quoted sayings are not necessarily the original creative productions that one might expect.[27] He first presents the following sentence from Epicurus as the saying to be pondered that day.

> Magnae divitiae sunt lege naturae composita paupertas.
> Great wealth is poverty settled according to the law of nature. (Sen. *Ep.* 4.10 = Epicurus *Frg.* 477 Usener, 219 Arrighetti)
> Ἡ πενία μετρουμένη τῷ τῆς φύσεως τέλει μέγας ἐστὶ πλοῦτος· πλοῦτος δὲ μὴ ὁριζόμενος μεγάλη ἐστὶ πενία.
> Poverty measured by the end of nature is great wealth, while unlimited wealth is great poverty. (Epicur. *Sent. Vat.* 25).

In addition to this acknowledged literal borrowing, Seneca's elaboration at *Ep.* 4.10–11 refers to the "limits" (*terminos*) implied in the word "unlimited" in the second half of *Sent. Vat.* 25, which is omitted in his quotation. When explaining the content of the law prescribing natural wealth, he quotes the threesome "not to be hungry, not to be thirsty, not to be cold" from *Vatican Saying* 33 and then uses various expressions (*parabile, appositum, ad manum est*) to translate the Epicurean key term *euporistos* ("easy to procure"), which we find in several still extant pointed statements by Epicurus, of which one is, again, a *Vatican Saying*, to the effect that the natural desires of a human being are easy to fulfill since "the wealth of nature is limited and easy to procure, [...]."[28]

Such borrowings, which could not have been very difficult to spot for someone even superficially acquainted with Epicurus' writings, may be taken as an example for the kind of thorough reading that Seneca himself recommends in *Ep.* 2 and whose effects are described later, at *Ep.* 84.8: Whenever someone else's writings have made a deeper impression on the mind of the admiring recipient, the similarity will be apparent like that between a father and a son.[29] However, a more attentive reader will note

---

27 See also Setaioli 1988 for further examples of such cases "in cui un centone di sentenze epicuree [...] serve da cornice per presentarne poi una formalmente tradotta" (194).
28 Epicur. *Sent.* 15 = *Sent. Vat.* 8, quoted on p. 445. Compare also *Ep. ad Men.* 130: "[...] καὶ ὅτι τὸ μὲν φυσικὸν πᾶν εὐπόριστόν ἐστι, τὸ δὲ κενὸν δυσπόριστον;" *Sent.* 21: "Ὁ τὰ πέρατα τοῦ βίου κατειδὼς οἶδεν ὡς εὐπόριστόν ἐστι τὸ <τὸ> ἀλγοῦν κατ' ἔνδειαν ἐξαιροῦν καὶ τὸ τὸν ὅλον βίον παντελῆ καθιστάν." For the Latin term *parabilis* see already Cic. *Tusc.* 5.93 = Epicur. *Frg.* 456 Usener ("divitias enim naturae esse parabiles") and *Fin.* 2.90 = Epicur. *Frg.* 468 Usener, 221 Arrighetti.
29 On *Ep.* 84 see Margaret Graver's paper in this volume. For the differences between the reading recommended in *Ep.* 2 and *Ep.* 84 see the remarks by Ilsetraut Hadot quoted at the end of this paper (p. 459) and also Setaioli 2000, 206–215 as well as

that professed endorsement often goes hand in hand with rather shameless manipulation.

In several cases, Seneca praises the words of Epicurus as universal truths while endowing them with a sense quite far from the meaning intended by the author of the Greek original. The statement that "necessity is bad but [that] there is no need to live in necessity," for example, was probably part of Epicurus' polemic against determinists, among whom he would have counted the Stoics who talk themselves into believing – erroneously, according to Epicurus – that everything happens by necessity. Yet Seneca blithely takes it as an exhortation to consider the fact that human mortality opens many "pathways to freedom" for us.[30]

In addition to such blunt misreading, we also encounter more subtle manipulation to fit Epicurean ideas into a Stoic mindset. For example, the translation of the Greek words that we know as *Vatican Saying* 25 in *Ep.* 4.10 (quoted on p. 439), substitutes "the law of nature" for "the end of nature." Epicurean "nature" is the physiology of each individual human being, which determines the desires that must be fulfilled for that individual to live without bodily pain. Epicurus is talking about *finite* needs – needs with an end point – that set a quantitative *measure*. Someone who speaks of a "law of nature," on the other hand, whether that of an individual human being's nature or the law of the cosmos' universal nature, implies a rationally ordered universe. So we read later in the *Epistulae morales* about someone "who takes Nature as his teacher and settles himself according to her laws, living in the manner that she prescribes" or about the "founder of the cosmos, who set out for us the laws of life."[31] In such a providential universe, quantitative wealth becomes a quality, a "settled poverty" characterized by the very adjective *compositus* which is used almost as a technical term in the *Epistulae morales* and denotes a mind that is both calm and well ordered because it has achieved internal and external agreement; it thus epitomizes the combination of Epicurean tranquility of mind with a

---

Setaioli 2014b, § 7. For the present purpose, it suffices that in both cases reading is seen as an assimilation process by which what is read becomes a part of the reader.

30 Epicur. *Sent. Vat.* 9: "Κακὸν ἀνάγκη, ἀλλ' οὐδεμία ἀνάγκη ζῆν μετὰ ἀνάγκης;" Sen. *Ep.* 12.10 = Epicur. *Frg.* 487 Usener: "Malum est in necessitate vivere, sed in necessitate vivere necessitas nulla est." Note how Seneca's reading is facilitated by replacing "necessity" with "living in necessity" already in the first half of the saying. On its interpretation, see Setaioli 1988, 215–216. On the significance of suicide in Seneca's philosophy, see the contributions by Rita Degl'Innocenti Pierini and Tommaso Gazzarri in this volume.

31 Sen. *Ep.* 45.9: "qui natura magistra utitur, ad illius leges componitur, sic vivit quomodo illa praescripsit;" *Ep.* 119.15: "ab illo mundi conditore qui nobis vivendi iura discripsit."

Stoic "structured self" which is so characteristic of the earlier part of the *Epistulae morales*.[32]

The Letter Writer Seneca, however, shows no awareness of such ambiguities in his elaborations of the sentences he quotes. With regard to one of Heraclitus' sayings, he admits the possibility of different readings (*Ep.* 12.7), but not as concerns Epicurus. On the contrary, Seneca repeats again and again that Epicurus is just a mouthpiece for universally shared, general convictions.[33] At *Ep.* 9.20, he insists that the ideas (*res*) of Epicurus are important, not the actual words (*verba*) with which they are expressed, and a quotation from the letter to Idomeneus is even characterized as "too clear to need interpretation" (*Ep.* 21.8).

On the other hand, there is evidence that L. Annaeus, the author of the *Epistulae morales* himself, was well aware of the mismatch between Seneca's interpretations and Epicurean doctrine. In *Vit. beat.* 19.1, for example, the author reports a controversy over the suicide of an Epicurean by the name of Diodorus, which shows that this practice was at least not as unequivocally endorsed in Epicurus' school as one might believe when reading Sen. *Ep.* 12.10 (p. 440, n. 30). At the same time, a quotation of Epicurus' *Principal Saying* 16 at *Const.* 15.4[34] indicates that L. Annaeus knew more about Epicurus' rejection of determinism than we would surmise from Seneca's interpretation in *Ep.* 12. The problem of determinism and human agency, which L. Annaeus discusses in the *Naturales quaestiones* (2.32–38), was not only a fervently debated topic of Epicurean and Stoic physics; it was also such a central point of Epicurus' ethical theory and receives so much attention in his *Letter to Menoeceus* (133–135) that it would have been very surprising, indeed, if an educated man like L.

---

32 For the connotation of order, see, e.g., Sen. *Ep.* 11.9: "ut [...] se componat atque ordinet;" *Vit. beat.* 8.3: "compositum ordinatumque fore talem virum;" for the idea of tranquility: *Ep.* 56.6: "nulla placida est quies, nisi quam ratio composuit;" *Ep.* 100.8: "ad animi tenorem quietum compositumque formata;" *Nat.* 7.30.1: "si intramus templa compositi." Further relevant occurrences in the *Epistulae morales* are: 2.1; 4.1; 7.1; 11.6 and 9; 29.9; 40.2; 56.6 and 14; 61.3; 89.9; 94.1, 33, 49, and 60; 95.5; 98.5; 99.20; 114.3; 123.6. For the artistic connotation of *componere*, see the paper of Linda Cermatori in this volume (p. 296f.). The term "structured self" is Christopher Gill's (2006).

33 See, e.g., *Ep.* 8.8; 12.11; 14.18; 21.9; 33.2; Freise 1989, 537; Casadesús Bordoy 1997, 545–547. These are the natural or common conceptions discussed in the contributions of Ilsetraut Hadot and Antonello Orlando. The learning experience of the Letter Writer, as I will outline it below, gradually takes him beyond this basic consensus and thus illustrates the third level of concept formation posited by both scholars, at which a universal, naturally formed concept is further refined in an intellectual process that requires reflection and formal instruction.

34 Epicur. *Sent.* 18: "Βραχέα σοφῷ τύχη παρεμπίπτει, [...];" Sen. *Const.* 15.4: [...], " 'Raro' inquit 'sapienti fortuna intervenit.' "

Annaeus had had no inkling of these views. Similarly, there is evidence in the *Epistulae morales* themselves that their author had all the philosophical knowledge required to see that his Latin translation at *Ep.* 4.10 of the words in *Sent. Vat.* 25 (p. 439) was a distortion of Epicurean thought. In a section of *Ep.* 97 we learn that Epicurus rejected the idea of natural justice,[35] and thus also natural law, and I have already collected evidence (n. 26) that L. Annaeus must have known the full text of what has been transmitted to us as *Sent. Vat.* 33. So L. Annaeus must also have known that, according to Epicurus, it was not the "law of Nature" that set the limit at not being hungry, thirsty, and cold but rather the "cry of the flesh."[36]

From such observations we can conclude that the *Epistulae morales* do not present two static conceptual grids, here the Stoic system and there Epicurean thought, which are compared, contrasted, or integrated according to a philosopher's unchanging rational criteria. This is what one would expect in an ethical treatise. Instead we encounter an intellectual drama, designed by L. Annaeus, whose protagonist, the Letter Writer Seneca, changes his mind and develops his own Stoic thought with increasing precision. This drama is also reflected in Seneca's readings of Epicurus.

II.

In his actual practice, the Letter Writer of the early *Epistulae morales* is the living likeness of an Epicurean.[37] He retreats from public life, limits his intellectual endeavors to what is wholesome for the troubled mind, cultivates friendship with a small circle of like-minded students of philosophy, and communicates with the outside world through letters. It is thus important that this same Seneca takes care to stress emphatically that he is *not* at all an Epicurean in his ethics of social relations. His own philosophy endorses the principle that human beings are sociable by nature (*Ep.* 5.4; 6.4; 9.17); his retreat is a form of active service for the general good (*Ep.* 8.1–6); and his idea of friendship is based on Stoic altruism (*Ep.* 6.2–4; *Ep.* 9) and contrasted with the material interests allegedly pursued by the self-serving

---

35 Sen. *Ep.* 97.15 = Epicur. *Frg.* 531 Usener: "[...] dicit nihil iustum esse natura." Interestingly, a similar connection between the Epicurean discourse on ascetic autarky and a "law of human nature" is made in Porphyry's *Letter to Marcella* 25. Since it also involves a universal cosmic law, this distinction cannot be Epicurean.

36 See also Schottlaender 1955, 143–145, who characterizes the phenomenon as "superficial citation."

37 Similarly Hachmann 1995, 220.

Epicurean.[38] A Stoic sage, asserts Seneca, seeks friendship to practice his virtue,

> non ad hoc quod dicebat Epicurus in hac ipsa epistula, "ut habeat qui sibi aegro assideat, succurrat in vincula coniecto vel inopi" [Epicur. *Frg.* 175 Usener, 132 Arrighetti], sed ut habeat aliquem cui ipse aegro assideat, quem ipse circumventum hostili custodia liberet. Qui se spectat et propter hoc ad amicitiam venit male cogitat.
>
> not for the purpose that Epicurus was indicating in that very same letter, "to have someone who would sit at his bedside when he is sick and help him should he be taken captive or destitute of means," but to have someone at whose bedside he himself could sit, whom he himself could free from the enemy's guard that imprisons him. Someone who thinks only of himself and comes to friendship for this purpose has the wrong intentions. (Sen. *Ep.* 9.8)

At this point, L. Annaeus has Seneca exaggerate the difference between Epicurus and his own school. He does so by omission and concentration on the very point over which Epicurus and Stoics disagree. *Ep.* 9 replies to Epicurus' objection against a thesis defended by the philosopher Stilbo of Megara: While Stilbo insisted that a sage is self-sufficient and therefore not in need of friends, Epicurus believes that friendship presupposes some form of need and thus cannot occur between completely self-sufficient agents (*Ep.* 9.1). In stark contrast to this, Seneca insists that self-serving motivations cannot form the basis of a true friendship (9.8–11) and argues that "friendship is to be sought for its own sake" and so "can be approached by someone who is self-sufficient" (*Ep.* 9.12). However, what appears as a complete refutation of an Epicurean social theory is much closer to Epicurus' own position than one would suspect just from Seneca's reply in this letter. Epicurus, too, regards friendship as something to be sought for its own sake; he only gives a different account of its origin, an origin that he may even have located in the remote past, at the primitive phylogenetic beginnings of human society, as the resultative perfect tense of the verb *eilēphen* suggests. Like the first communities and state, friendship did not arise from a natural drive toward social interaction *per se* (as the Stoics believed) but from the need for mutual support and the practical benefits that accrue from the cooperation with others. This is why it can occur only among agents that are in need of such benefits.

> Πᾶσα φιλία δι' ἑαυτὴν αἱρετή [Usener; ἀρετή codd.].[39] ἀρχὴν δ' εἴληφεν ἀπὸ τῆς ὠφελείας.

---

38 Similar remarks occur also later, e.g. at *Ep.* 48.2 and 68.10.
39 Usener's emendation (which was rejected, e.g., by Long and Sedley 1987, vol. 2, p. 132, on LS 22F) is confirmed by the context. Whereas a "virtue because or through itself" would be a theoretical monstrosity, the conception of something to be sought because of its intrinsic value is commonplace in ancient ethics. A de-

> All friendship is to be sought for its own sake, but it has (*eilēphen*) its beginning in benefit. (Epicur. *Sent. Vat.* 23)

Given the fact that we know this, again, from the *Vatican Sayings* that have yielded so many other parallels to the *Epistulae morales*, it is safe to assume that L. Annaeus was aware of this point as well.[40] As it seems, he wanted to introduce us to a Stoic Letter Writer emphatically at odds with Epicurean social ethics. It was not L. Annaeus' intention to present us with a fair and balanced assessment of the merits to be found in each side's viewpoint.

Apart from this early demarcation between sociable Stoic and self-centered Epicurean, which serves to forestall misunderstanding and clarifies the respectable, Stoic nature of Seneca's enterprise right from the start, the earlier books of the *Epistulae morales* are characterized by ingenious blending and reinterpretation of Epicureanism. The Letter Writer crafted by L. Annaeus is a man who treats his desires and fears with a Stoico-Epicurean therapy[41] that intermingles and adapts Epicurean ideas into a not yet very clearly defined Stoicism.

According to a Stoic, passions such as fear, distress, or desire, are erroneous judgments (or the direct consequence of these).[42] A desire arises when an indifferent of limited value is regarded as a good with absolute value and thus not taken with the necessary reservation but rather as something the agent must have in any case and cannot ever do without. The Epicurean distinguishes natural from unnatural and necessary from unnecessary desires. An Epicurean passion and the ensuing displeasure arise through "opining in addition" (*prosepidoxazein*), when agents entertain the mistaken belief that it is natural, or even necessary for them, to fulfill a certain desire, even if it is not. Seneca blends these two conceptions by emphasizing the error of mistaken opining and the frustration of the misdirected desire. Someone who is guided by opinions will *never* be rich.

> Istuc quoque ab Epicuro dictum est: "Si ad naturam vives, numquam eris pauper; si ad opiniones, numquam eris dives."
>
> This here too was said by Epicurus: "If you align your life with nature, you'll never be poor. If with opinions, you'll never be rich." (Sen. *Ep.* 16.7 = Epicur. *Frg.* 201 Usener, 217 Arrighetti)

---

fense of Usener's correction and discussion of Epicurean altruism is Mitsis 1987. See also O'Keefe 2001, 278–289.

40 Schottlaender 1955, 137–138.
41 Compare also the paper by David Kaufman in this volume, about a treatment of passions that Seneca may have adapted from Epicurean therapeutics.
42 For the Stoic theory of passions, see the excellent and comprehensive account by Graver 2007.

The precise source of this saying is difficult to spot. There are close similarities to one of the sayings we find in both of the two collections of Epicurean sayings transmitted to us (see also p. 439).

> Ὁ τῆς φύσεως πλοῦτος καὶ ὥρισται καὶ εὐπόριστός ἐστιν, ὁ δὲ τῶν κενῶν δοξῶν εἰς ἄπειρον ἐκπίπτει.
>
> The wealth of the nature is limited and easy to procure, but that of hollow opinions escalates into infinity. (Epicur. *Sent.* 15 = *Sent. Vat.* 8)

However, an even closer parallel occurs in a section from Porphyrius' *Letter to Marcella*, which presents a digest of some Epicurean discussion of these ideas.

> Ὁ τῆς φύσεως πλοῦτος <ὁ> [supp. des Places] ἀληθῶς φιλόσοφος ὥρισται καὶ ἔστιν εὐπόριστος, ὁ δὲ τῶν κενῶν δοξῶν ἀόριστός τε καὶ δυσπόριστος. Ὁ οὖν τῇ φύσει κατακολουθῶν καὶ μὴ ταῖς κεναῖς δόξαις ἐν πᾶσιν αὐτάρκης· πρὸς γὰρ τὸ τῇ φύσει ἀρκοῦν πᾶσα κτῆσίς ἐστι πλοῦτος, πρὸς δὲ τὰς ἀορίστους ὀρέξεις καὶ ὁ μέγιστος πλοῦτός ἐστιν οὐ<δέν> [suppl. Nauck]. [= 202 Usener; 216 Arr.] *Σπάνιόν γε εὑρεῖν ἄνθρωπον πρὸς τὸ τῆς φύσεως τέλος <πένητα>* [suppl. Usener] *καὶ πλούσιον πρὸς τὰς κενὰς δόξας.* [...] [= 471 Usener, 214 Arr.]
>
> The truly philosophical wealth of nature is limited and easy to procure, but that of hollow opinions unbounded and difficult to procure. And so the one following [his][43] nature and not hollow opinions is in all things self-sufficient. For with regard to what suffices for [one's] nature, every possession is wealth, but with regard to unlimited desires, even the largest wealth is nothing. *A rare find, indeed, is the man who is <poor> with regard to the end of [his] nature and rich with regard to [his] hollow opinions.* [...] (Porph. *Marc.* 27)

The idea of incompatibility is enhanced when Seneca speaks not just of a rare occurrence, as Porphyrius does at the end of the quoted passage, but about something that "never" happens. Seneca relates the idea to a second-person addressee, and also gives a more condensed expression of the two opposite benchmarks "with which" (Porphyrius: *pros*, Seneca: *ad*) the agent must align his behavior: "nature" instead of "the end of the nature" and "opinions" instead of "hollow opinions."[44]

For an Epicurean the frustration of unnecessary desires results from the fact that there is no natural limit to them. "Nature," explains Seneca, "desires only very little, but opinion an immeasurable amount" (*Ep.* 16.8). "Natural desires are finite; those arising from a wrong opinion have no point where they could desist" (*Ep.* 16.9). For the Stoic, however, frustration follows from the fact that the agent commits a *category* error: The agent wants a good but only gets an indifferent, if he gets it at all. The

---

43 Pronouns were added to indicate that the individuating article does not point to one cosmic Nature but to the nature of the individual agent.
44 See already Setaioli 1988, 193, who regards this sentence in the *Letter to Marcella* as the original for Seneca's version.

desire, Seneca continues to explain, is unlimited because "there is no boundary to what is false" (*Ep.* 16.9). What in Epicurus is the problem – the undefined, unlimited quantity of what is desired – becomes for Seneca an epistemic criterion by which to recognize the error.

> Retrahe ergo te a vanis, et cum *voles scire* quod petes utrum naturalem habeat an caecam cupiditatem, considera num possit alicubi consistere: si longe progresso semper aliquid longius restat, *scito* id naturale non esse.
>
> Therefore pull back from such hollow things, and if *you wish to know* what you should go for, whether it arouses a natural or a blind desire, consider whether it can come to a halt somewhere. If you have progressed far and there is still something left even further ahead, *you should know* that this is not natural. (Sen. *Ep.* 16.9)

Seneca's Stoicism is also betrayed by the manner in which the natural becomes for him a *qualitative* and not just a quantitative category.[45] What is at stake for the Epicurean is the quantity of pleasure to be achieved. Unnatural, unnecessary desires are to be avoided not because there is anything intrinsically wrong with them[46] but because of their unpleasant consequences. Since they are difficult to fulfill, they are often frustrated, and this frustration is painful.[47] It is for this practical reason that Epicureans seek to understand the limits of human nature,[48] i.e. complete freedom from pain, the maximum amount of pleasure that can ever be obtained (Epicur. *Sent.* 3). For the Stoic, on the other hand, there is only one end, a life of virtue and what partakes of it,[49] and all other objects of desires, including the objects of desires which an Epicurean would deem natural or even necessary, cannot satisfy the agent. This difference in the category of values, which corresponds to the category error of the erroneous passion opinion, is expressed by Seneca when he transfers the imagery of hollowness from the opinions to the objects themselves, which are either *vana* ("hollow")[50] or *solida* ("solid").

> Finem constitue quem transire ne possis quidem si velis; discedant aliquando ista insidiosa bona et sperantibus meliora quam assecutis. Si quid in illis esset solidi, aliquando et implerent: nunc haurientium sitim concitant.
>
> Define an end that you cannot transgress even if you wanted to. May these treacherous goods finally leave us alone, which are so much better when you aspire to

---

45 Compare the interpretation of *Sent. Vat.* 35 in Sen. *Ep.* 4.10 discussed on p. 440.
46 See, e.g., Epicur. *Frg.* 181 Usener, 124 Arrighetti, quoted in n. 23; *Sent.* 10; *Ep. ad Men.* 129.
47 A second reason, which is however not the one given in the passages quoted above, may be collateral pain, so to speak, for example when over-eating leads to health problems.
48 Referred to by words like πέρας, ὅρος, τέλος, *terminus*, or *finis*.
49 Compare D.L. 7.101.
50 See Sen. *Ep.* 16.9 (quoted above) and p. 452.

them than when you've achieved them. If they had any solidity, they would finally lead to satisfaction: Now they just inflame the drinkers' thirst. (Sen. *Ep.* 15.11)

Another famous example of Epicurus on the procrustean bed of Seneca's Stoicism is the assimilation of the concept of gratitude. Epicurus praises gratitude because it implies the recollection of past pleasures. A recollected past pleasure is, at the same time, an occurrent present mental pleasure. Gratitude is thus the art of deriving pleasure from one's past experiences. Seneca refers to this concept in a context in which he has just quoted Metrodorus (*Ep.* 98.9 = *Frg.* 35 Körte).

> Quid ergo adversus has amissiones auxili invenimus? Hoc, ut memoria teneamus amissa nec cum ipsis fructum excidere patiamur quem ex illis percepimus. Habere eripitur, habuisse numquam. Peringratus est qui, cum amisit, pro accepto nihil debet.
>
> What help can we muster against such losses? The following: that we retain the lost things in our memory and do not let the joy we've drawn from them slip away together with the things themselves. Possession can be taken away, but never that one has had the possession. It would be terribly ungrateful if someone felt he owed nothing for what he had received once he lost it. (Sen. *Ep.* 98.11)

The Epicurean Lucretius compares the minds of fools to leaky containers through which all "advantages percolate and perish unappreciated."[51] Since fools always forget already perceived pleasures, they are in constant need of new gratifications to keep up their pleasure balance, and this is why their "ungrateful life" – as Seneca calls it, quoting Epicurus and possibly alluding to Lucretius – is carried away into the future.[52] It is most likely this same thought that Epicurus had in mind when he said:

> Πᾶς ὥσπερ ἄρτι γεγονὼς ἐκ τοῦ ζῆν ἀπέρχεται.
>
> Everyone leaves life as if he had just been born. (Epicur. *Sent. Vat.* 60)

Fools are like new-born infants who have not yet experienced anything to which they could gratefully look back with pleasure.[53] Close to this saying

---

51 Lucr. 3.935–938: "Nam si grata fuit tibi vita ante acta priorque / et non omnia pertusum congesta quasi in vas / commoda perfluxere atque ingrata interiere, / cur non ut plenus vitae conviva recedis?" The meaning of the passage is elucidated by Görler 1997. On Seneca and Lucretius, see Schottlaender 1955, 141–142; Mazzoli 1970, 206–209; Lana 1991, 263–268; Setaioli 1991; La Penna 1994; Gigante 1999, 11.
52 Sen. *Ep.* 15.9 = Epicur. *Frg.* 491 Usener, 242 Arrighetti: "Ecce insigne praeceptum: 'Stulta vita ingrata est, trepida; tota in futurum fertur.' " A clear allusion to the idea expressed by Lucretius occurs at Sen. *Ep.* 99.5: "Acquiescamus iis quae iam hausimus, si modo non perforato animo hauriebamus et transmittente quicquid acceperat." Compare also *Ep.* 22.17, quoted in n. 58.
53 I read πᾶς ("everyone") as a rhetorical hyperbole. A different interpretation of both the Epicurean saying and Seneca's interpretation is suggested by Schmid 1955, followed by Setaioli 1988, 206–211.

we find two similar ideas in the same gnomology: that ingratitude of the mind creates unbounded desire for variegated pleasures and that one shows an ungrateful attitude to the goods received in the past if one says that a long life can only be judged at its end.[54] A wise old man, we learn in another *Vatican Saying*, has "safely closed away in the storehouse of gratitude the goods about whose possession he had despaired before,"[55] while yet a fourth *Vatican Saying*, no. 55, advises us to remedy losses with gratitude and the knowledge that the past cannot be undone, just as Seneca had advised in *Ep.* 98, in the passage quoted above.[56] Even the conceit that the length of life is malleable according to one's grateful or ungrateful attitude has parallels in attested Epicurean fragments, although there we encounter the opposite effect of that described in *Vatican Saying* 60. Gratitude appears as a rejuvenating force and lack of memory as an aging factor, probably because one still enjoys, and in a sense, lives the rich and pleasurable life of a youth, while the forgetful person's life is limited to the fleeting perceptions of the present moment and thus as short as that of an old man.

> Τοῦ γεγονότος ἀμνήμων ἀγαθοῦ γέρων τήμερον γεγένηται.
>
> Who forgets the good that happened has become an old man today. (Epicur. *Sent. Vat.* 19)

Accordingly, we learn in the *Letter to Menoeceus* that a young man should devote himself to philosophy "so that, while growing old, he stays young in goods because of his gratitude for what happened."[57]

We can still recognize a reflection of this Epicurean idea when Seneca explains that we die in such an immature and bad condition because we are "empty of all goods" and that "no part of life has stayed and settled in us: it passed through and was discharged."[58] However, while Epicurus wished to refer to the ingratitude of people who do not collect past pleasures, Stoic Seneca connects the saying with the problem of a lack in moral progress. He gives us two versions:

---

54 Epicur. *Sent. Vat.* 69: "Τὸ τῆς ψυχῆς ἀχάριστον λίχνον ἐποίησε τὸ ζῷον εἰς ἄπειρον τῶν ἐν διαίτῃ ποικιλμάτων;" *Sent. Vat.* 75: "Εἰς τὰ παρῳχηκότα ἀγαθὰ ἀχάριστος φωνὴ ἡ λέγουσα τέλος ὅρα μακροῦ βίου."

55 Epicur. *Sent. Vat.* 17: "τὰ πρότερον δυσελπιστούμενα τῶν ἀγαθῶν ἀσφαλεῖ κατακλείσας χάριτι."

56 Epicur. *Sent. Vat.* 55: "Θεραπευτέον τὰς συμφορὰς τῇ τῶν ἀπολλυμένων χάριτι καὶ τῷ γινώσκειν ὅτι οὐκ ἔστιν ἄπρακτον ποιῆσαι τὸ γεγονός."

57 Epicur. *Ep. ad Men.* 122: "τῷ μὲν ὅπως γηράσκων νεάζῃ τοῖς ἀγαθοῖς διὰ τὴν χάριν τῶν γεγονότων."

58 Sen. *Ep.* 22.17: "Causa autem haec est, quod inanes omnium bonorum sumus, vitae *** laboramus. Non enim apud nos pars eius ulla subsedit: transmissa est et effluxit."

"Nemo non ita exit e vita tamquam modo intraverit."

"Everyone leaves life as if he had just entered." (Sen. *Ep.* 22.14 = Epicur. *Frg.* 495 Usener, 241 Arrighetti)

"Nemo" inquit "aliter quam quomodo natus est exit e vita."

He says: "No one leaves life (in a way) different from how he was born." (Sen. *Ep.* 22.15 = Epicur. *Frg.* 495 Usener, 241 Arrighetti)

Especially in the second version, which is immediately interpreted further as "worse than when we were born" (*Ep.* 22.15), quantity – the amount of pleasure collected in the mind – is turned again[59] into quality, whether one is a good person or bad and encumbered with all kinds of vices.

For Seneca, lack of progress is the consequence of a lack in determination. Because of their inconsistency (*inconstantia*), fools do not persevere in pursuing the aim they have set themselves. Instead they change their plans and always begin something new (Sen. *Ep.* 52.1–2). It is precisely in this sense that Seneca interprets Epicurean assertions about the foolishness of always starting life anew.

"Molestum est semper vitam inchoare," aut si hoc modo magis sensus potest exprimi: "Male vivunt qui semper vivere incipiunt."

"Always embarking upon a new life is unpleasant," or if the idea can be expressed better in this way: "Those who always begin their life live a bad life." (Sen. *Ep.* 23.9 = Epicur. *Frg.* 493 Usener, 243 Arrighetti)

Again we observe how the second translation redirects the issue toward a Stoic concern. What is at stake is no longer the inability to collect past pleasures but the difficulty of acquiring moral value. The fool's life is bad, not just unpleasant. And the reason why it is bad has already been indicated at the first occurrence of the Epicurean motif of the ingrate's unhappiness.

"Inter cetera mala hoc quoque habet stultitia: semper incipit vivere." Considera quid vox ista significet, Lucili virorum optime, et intelleges quam foeda sit hominum levitas cotidie nova vitae fundamenta ponentium, novas spes etiam in exitu inchoantium.

"Among all other evils, foolishness also suffers from this one: It always begins its life." Consider what this saying means, dear Lucilius, best of men, and you'll realize how shameful the temerity of such people is who lay out a new basis for their life every day and embark on new hopes even while they are leaving. (Sen. *Ep.* 13.16 = Epicur. *Frg.* 494 Usener, 244 Arrighetti)

In a way, this interpretation transforms Epicurus' thought into its opposite. Epicurus wants us to realize that what we need *has already been achieved*. The pleasure has been enjoyed, and now we simply need to remember it in order to enjoy it again. For Seneca it is important that the agent remembers

---

59   See already pp. 440 and 446.

and keeps up his resolve, as he explains in three letters that are framed by the quotations we have discussed (*Ep.* 16.1; 20.4–6; 23.7–8). In this sense, he demands a continuous but consistent orientation toward a *future* aim.[60] At the same time, the quotations from Epicurus also provide Seneca with an occasion to draft that very aim itself and thus imagine a state in which the Stoic too, having achieved goodness and a perfect life, can *look back*, content with himself, and say that he has lived enough (*Ep.* 23.10).[61]

III.

Such adaptations and assimilations by which Epicurean thought is fitted into a Stoic world view are characteristic of the earlier books of the *Epistulae morales*. I now wish to show how gradual demarcation of Epicurean tenets from Stoic conceptions serves as an element of the intellectual drama played out in the corpus of letters. This will become evident if we look at Seneca's treatment of pleasure, the highest – and only – Epicurean good.[62]

It has long since been seen that Stoic tenets are introduced gradually in the *Epistulae morales*, and the manner in which this happens has partly been outlined by authors such as Hildegard Cancik, Gregor Maurach, or Erwin Hachmann. In contrast to Maurach and Hachmann, I would not wish to define clearly delimited sections (*Briefkreise*), even though Seneca marks off an early Epicurean part by explicitly announcing the end of the regular quotation installments in *Ep.* 29 and commenting on this change in *Ep.* 33.[63] One might even read *Ep.* 30 as a symbol for Seneca's departure from his previous alignment with Epicurus, which is laid to rest, so to speak, with the dying Epicurean Bassus. In general, however, it seems methodologically safer to point out areas in which certain concepts occur for the first time or predominate.[64] In these terms it can be shown how an increasingly clear-cut and at the same time more technical understanding of the Stoic good is evolving throughout the corpus.

While the first few letters deal with the therapy of fear and greed and present a rather hazy idea of moral improvement as "becoming a better

---

60 The psychology of this orientation by the impulses of *prothesis* and *epibolē* is outlined in my forthcoming paper on Seneca's new concept of progressor friendship.
61 Compare also, e.g., *Ep.* 12.8–9 (on which see n. 17) and *Ep.* 32.5.
62 On this topic, see also Hachmann 1995, 227–237.
63 Sen. *Ep.* 29.10: "ultimam […] pensionem," "in finem aeris alieni;" *Ep.* 33.1.
64 In practice, this is the method applied by Hachmann 1995. Compare also Elizabeth Gloyn's contribution to this volume.

person every day" (*Ep.* 5.1),⁶⁵ definitions of goodness and the good begin to occur from *Ep.* 20. The good is described as internal agreement (20.5; 23.7; 31.8), and the following letters introduce further features of the perfect mind of a Stoic sage: In *Ep.* 31, virtue appears as that which constitutes all goods; at *Ep.* 31.6 and 32.5, we encounter Stoic intellectualism; reason in the emphatic Stoic sense is introduced at *Ep.* 36.12 and 37.4.

This image of the good as a perfect internal mental disposition is then set in a wider cosmic context, beginning from *Ep.* 41, in which human beings are set at the top of a scale of beings. It is their reason that distinguishes them from other animals and places them in the vicinity of the divine. *Ep.* 58 and 65 encourage a comparison between the divine world order and the order in man (in particular *Ep.* 58.28–29) and serve as an exhortation to share God's cosmic concerns through contemplation (*Ep.* 65.18–22). Parallel to such ventures into the sphere of physics, the idea of external agreement is introduced with the advice that we must assent to whatever happens to us (*Ep.* 55.7; *Ep.* 61).

A next level of conceptualization is reached when the distinction between goods and indifferents, which was only adumbrated in *Ep.* 31, is systematically introduced together with a sustained discussion of the tenet that only what is honorable is a good (*Ep.* 66; 67; 71; 74; 76; 82; 85; 87; 92).

After the Stoic theory of value has thus been developed in its entirety, Seneca and Lucilius turn to even more specialized questions, such as the physics of the good: its place in the body (*Ep.* 92); whether there can be goods composed of separate parts (*Ep.* 102); the corporeality of goods (*Ep.* 106 and 117); whether the virtues, which constitute goodness, are living beings (*Ep.* 113); or whether there are future goods (*Ep.* 117.26–29).

The last part of the collection, as we have it now, deals with a topic that one might call *notitia boni*:⁶⁶ The concept of good is spelled out in a series of definitions (*Ep.* 118) and described in form of a portrait of the exemplary good man (*Ep.* 120.10–14). Seneca and Lucilius also investigate the epistemology of the good: how knowledge of the good is acquired through concept formation (*Ep.* 120) and through self-perception and appropriation (*oikeiōsis*) to the constitution thus perceived (*Ep.* 121). Finally, Seneca clarifies that the good of a human being is perceived by intellection and not by sense experience (*Ep.* 124).

Parallel to this increasingly subtle understanding of the Stoic theory of value and the human good, Seneca introduces clearer distinctions between

---

65 The concern persists throughout the corpus. See, e.g., *Ep.* 7.8; 31.1; 50.1; 58.26; 79.11; 87.8; 93.8; 104.15; 121.2.
66 On this topic, see also the papers by Ilsetrout Hadot and Antonello Orlando in this volume.

Epicurus' pleasure ethics and his Stoic attitude to various forms of pleasurable experiences. In the earliest letters, virtue ethics and hedonism form an inseparable unity. At *Ep.* 2.5, Epicurus is praised for characterizing "joyful poverty" ("laeta paupertas") as something honorable. Stoic *honestum*, what is morally good and beautiful, and Epicurean delight are intermingled also when Seneca describes Lucilius' aim as "enjoying a corrected and settled mind" and depicts the "pleasure" ("voluptas") that awaits the one who can contemplate such a perfectly purified mind.[67] Without any hint of reservation, Seneca discusses the pleasures of friendship (*Ep.* 9.6–7), old age (*Ep.* 12.4–5), asceticism (*Ep.* 18.9–10), and reduced desires (*Ep.* 21.8–11).

It is only with the introduction of the more specifically Stoic idea of internal agreement, that he also makes a distinction between the right things in which one should rejoice and pleasures to be avoided (*Ep.* 23). The recommended object of joy is now the perception of one's own consistent and virtuous mind (*Ep.* 23.3, 23.7) and emphatically *not* the external goods that satiate bodily desires, as natural as these might be (*Ep.* 23.3, 23.6). However, the advice not to rejoice in "empty things" (*Ep.* 23.1: "ne gaudeas vanis;" see p. 446) is still reminiscent of Epicurus' warnings not to seek pleasures suggested by "hollow opinions" (see p. 444f.), and the distinction made in *Ep.* 23 does not yet constitute a fundamental rejection of hedonism, insofar as the virtuous mind does not appear as an end in itself but still as a means to enjoy a happy feeling.

> Sola virtus praestat gaudium perpetuum, securum.
>
> Only virtue guarantees lasting, certain joy. (Sen. *Ep.* 27.3).

The next level is reached when Seneca admits that, according to the distinction made by his Stoics, there is a difference between the passion *voluptas* ("delight") and the good feeling *gaudium* ("joy"). Only the sage has joy, while the delight of ordinary people is a "disreputable thing," an instable, uncontrollable, and immoderate motion of the mind, which uninformed people suffer because of their wrong opinions about what is

---

67 Sen. *Ep.* 4.1: "Persevera ut coepisti et quantum potes propera, quo diutius frui emendato animo et composito possis. Frueris quidem etiam dum emendas, etiam dum componis: alia tamen illa voluptas est quae percipitur ex contemplatione mentis ab omni labe purae et splendidae." The idea that already the study of philosophy is pleasurable is expressed in *Sent. Vat.* 27: "Ἐπὶ μὲν τῶν ἄλλων ἐπιτηδευμάτων μόλις τελειωθεῖσιν ὁ καρπὸς ἔρχεται, ἐπὶ δὲ φιλοσοφίας συντρέχει τῇ γνώσει τὸ τερπνόν· οὐ γὰρ μετὰ μάθησιν ἀπόλαυσις, ἀλλὰ ἅμα μάθησις καὶ ἀπόλαυσις." Compare also Sen. *Ep.* 50.8: "Deinde non est acerba medicina; protinus enim delectat dum sanat. Aliorum remediorum post sanitatem voluptas est, philosophia pariter et salutaris et dulcis est."

good.[68] It follows that any mental pleasure that an imperfect person like Seneca or Lucilius might perceive is, at least in this sense, bad. There are no harmless natural pleasures, and it happens not just exceptionally that foolish "opining in addition" (*prosepidoxazein*) causes excessive and unnatural desires: Wrong opinions are all-pervasive. However, the Stoic distinction is still introduced as a somewhat exaggerated zeal for legalistic precision,[69] and even more importantly, mental pleasure in the form of joy continues to appear as something valuable in itself. Virtue is still presented as a means to the end of perpetual joy: All human beings strive for joy (*Ep.* 59.15), but do not know how to achieve it. "Evenness of joy" is the product of wisdom, and this is a good reason why Lucilius should want to become a wise man. The perfect joy of a sage "can only arise from the awareness of one's virtues."[70]

It is in *Ep.* 66, with the systematic introduction of the concept of indifferents, that bodily pain and the pleasures caused by external goods clearly appear as irrelevant for happiness, insofar as the different kinds of goods that are equal, according to Seneca's argument, occur when a sage is either in a state of great pain or experiences something that is an obvious cause for elation. It follows that Epicurean pleasures and pains are irrelevant for the attribution of the predicate "good" and that the Epicurean distinction of goods by degree, as more or less pleasurable or painful, is impossible.[71] Furthermore, it turns out that even the joy (*gaudium*) of a Stoic sage is not

---

68 Sen. *Ep.* 59.2: "Scio, inquam, et voluptatem, si ad nostrum album verba derigimus, rem infamem esse et gaudium nisi sapienti non contingere; est enim animi elatio suis bonis verisque fidentis. [...] 4 Quamvis enim ex honesta causa imperitus homo gaudeat, tamen affectum eius impotentem et in diversum statim inclinaturum voluptatem voco, opinione falsi boni motam, immoderatam et immodicam."

69 With *album* at *Ep.* 59.2, Seneca alludes to the praetor's edict, a code of civil procedure, and thus to the extreme formality of Roman legal language. The same metaphor was applied to the study of sophisms by dialecticians at *Ep.* 48.10, which Seneca rejects vigorously in that context.

70 Sen. *Ep.* 59.16: "Hoc ergo cogita, hunc esse sapientiae effectum, gaudii aequalitatem. Talis est sapientis animus qualis mundus super lunam: semper illic serenum est. Habes ergo et quare velis sapiens esse, si numquam sine gaudio est. Gaudium hoc non nascitur nisi ex virtutum conscientia: non potest gaudere nisi fortis, nisi iustus, nisi temperans."

71 See, e.g., Sen. *Ep.* 66.5: "Quaedam, ut nostris videtur, prima bona sunt, tamquam gaudium, pax, salus patriae; quaedam secunda, in materia infelici expressa, tamquam tormentorum patientia et in morbo gravi temperantia;" 66.12: "Paria itaque sunt et gaudium et fortis atque obstinata tormentorum perpessio;" 66.14: "Quid ergo? nihil interest inter gaudium et dolorum inflexibilem patientiam?;" 66.15: "Ergo aequalia sunt bona, ultra quae nec hic potest se melius in hoc gaudio gerere nec ille melius in illis cruciatibus;" 66.29: "Ita dico: in aequo est moderate gaudere et moderate dolere. Laetitia illa non vincit hanc animi firmitatem sub tortore gemitus devorantem."

the only good nor the ultimate aim for a human being. All the same, there is still some conceptual fuzziness since the sage's elation is occasioned by indifferents, such as peace or the safety of one's country, that are highly valued but not goods in the full Stoic sense, and thus by themselves no reason for the good feeling *gaudium* a wise person has when perceiving the presence of a real good. In fact, Seneca still acknowledges common ground between Stoics and Epicureans, not only by distinguishing categories of goods by the criteria of concomitant pain or pleasurable feelings, to which he also refers with the non-technical word *laetitia* (*Ep.* 66.29) that also denotes the passion of delight. He also stresses that both Stoic and Epicurean sages are in the possession of goods even under duress since the Epicurean will remain in a state of pleasure even when he is subjected to torture or the pains of a severe illness (*Ep.* 66.45–48 = *Frg.* 434 Usener, 186 Arrighetti). It is only in the next letter, at *Ep.* 67.15, that Seneca, together with his Stoic teacher Attalus, rejects the "soft" name *dulce* ("sweet") for the good of a sage under such conditions. Another fundamental objection to hedonism, which is inherent already in the argument of *Ep.* 66, is spelled out even later, at *Ep.* 82.18: The Epicurean pleasure calculus requires that one sometimes chooses something bad (i.e. pain) in expectation of a good (i.e. pleasure). According to Seneca's Stoic position, such reasoning can never lead to consistent and whole-hearted motivation since it is natural for a human being to abhor what it perceives to be bad, with the consequence that the agent is torn in different directions.

In the next topic area, the one concerned with the physics of the good, Seneca's and Epicurus' views, at last, appear as completely irreconcilable. At *Ep.* 85.18 Seneca reports Epicurus' assertion that virtue is only a necessary but not a sufficient condition for the happy life since it is pleasure – arising from virtue – that makes a man happy and not virtue itself. At this point, Seneca calls Epicurus' distinction "silly," explaining that, after all, virtue is always accompanied by pleasure. (For a Stoic, this is so because a virtuous person perceives the presence of this good and, accordingly, enjoys the good feeling *gaudium*.) Here, just as in *Ep.* 66.45–48 and at *Ep.* 67.15, Seneca seems to relate to Epicurus as someone who shares the central tenets of Stoicism but is somehow confused about the right way to conceptualize them properly. A very different picture emerges from *Ep.* 92, where Seneca finally seems to have understood the full significance of Epicurus' distinction.[72]

---

[72] A short critique directed at the subordination of virtue to pleasure occurs already at *Ep.* 90.35, where Epicureanism is the philosophy "that handed virtue over to the pleasures." The passage is also significant as a summary rejection of Epicureanism as an unsuitable form of philosophy.

This letter combines first considerations about the physics of the good with the various ideas introduced at earlier stages in the letter corpus. Its argument draws on ideas about the position of man within the cosmos as they were introduced starting from *Ep.* 41. At the same time it concludes the discussion of the tenet that only the honorable is good, which began with *Ep.* 66, here in form of the assertion that virtue on its own is sufficient for a perfectly good life (*vita beata*). Seneca assumes Lucilius' approval of the thesis that there is a hierarchical relation of means and ends according to which external goods are acquired for the sake of the body, the body is maintained for the soul, and in the soul itself there are "serving parts" for nutrition and locomotion, "given to us because of the leading part (*principale*) itself. In this leading part there is something irrational and also something rational; the former is the slave (*servit*) of the latter. This is the only [thing] that is not oriented at something else but orients everything toward itself." What is rational within the leading part is then compared to the divine reason in charge of everything in the cosmos and even described as originating from it. From this hierarchy Seneca concludes that the good life must consist in having perfected reason. [73] A little later, he adds that the irrational in the soul, which he now calls a "part," is again subdivided into two "parts" reminiscent of the two inferior powers *thumoeides* and *epithumētikon* in the tripartite model of the soul presented in Plato's *Republic*. One of them is "spirited, ambitious, unrestrained, concerned with affections, the other lowly, flaccid, given to pleasures" (*Ep.* 92.8). On the basis of this psychology,[74] the debate whether it is virtue or pleasure that brings

---

73 Sen. *Ep.* 92.1–2: "Puto, inter me teque conveniet externa corpori acquiri, corpus in honorem animi coli, in animo esse partes ministras per quas movemur alimurque, propter ipsum principale nobis datas. In hoc principali est aliquid irrationale, est et rationale; illud huic servit, hoc unum est quod alio non refertur sed omnia ad se refert. Nam illa quoque divina ratio omnibus praeposita est, ipsa sub nullo est; et haec autem nostra eadem est, quae ex illa est. 2 Si de hoc inter nos convenit, sequitur ut de illo quoque conveniat, in hoc uno positam esse beatam vitam, ut in nobis ratio perfecta sit."

74 A discussion of its sources and the degree of orthodoxy is impossible here. Most likely it was inspired by Posidonius. See *Ep.* 92.10 = Posidon. *Frg.* 184 Edelstein and Kidd and on Posidonius' psychology Tieleman 2003, 202–230. Posidonius did not speak of "parts" or "powers." Instead, he used substantive neuter adjectives (τὸ ἄλογον etc.) to refer to the rational and irrational aspect of the leading part of the soul (Tieleman 2003, 228). This would explain why Seneca uses the rather unusual Latin expressions "aliquid rationale" and "aliquid irrationale" at the beginning of the letter. On the question of sources see also the – skeptical – chapter of Inwood 2005, 23–64. Inwood highlights the importance of literary form (see also Inwood 2007b). However, as far as I can see, no discussion of the sources for the psychology in *Ep.* 92 has yet taken into account that the division is presented by Seneca and not by L. Annaeus.

about the good life is no longer an attempt to make "a silly distinction" (*Ep.* 85.18). Pleasure, the good of what is irrational in the soul and of that part of it which is less manly (*Ep.* 92.8), is now "the good of cattle" (*Ep.* 92.6), whereas virtue is the good of divine reason and of man as a being "shaped by nature for this purpose: to equal the gods in his volition" and to "return" to the heavens where he belongs.[75] Accordingly, the hedonist is subhuman (*Ep.* 92.7) as well as "degenerate and of the most lowly mind" (*Ep.* 92.6), even though he agrees that the sage will be happy in spite of physical pain (*Ep.* 92.5 = *Frg.* 138 Usener, 52 Arrighetti).

Hedonism is now unequivocally criticized as a perverted account of human nature. Man, a member of "the most beautiful class of animals and second to the gods" (*Ep.* 92.7) is debased from his divine status and treated like a beast. The Epicurean understanding of the relation between virtue and pleasure as one of means and end, which Seneca so far had either endorsed or downplayed as irrelevant, is now seen as an unacceptable monstrosity. Reason, the natural ruler (*Ep.* 92.1), is enslaved to the most humble part of the mind (*Ep.* 92.9), and even the mere conjunction of the two values as equal elements of one functional unit is as inacceptable as if one would generate a Scylla-like hybrid of two incompatible species. It is an abnormal compound of "venerable and heavenly parts" coupled with "an inert and nerveless" brute (*Ep.* 92.10).

In *Ep.* 92, the critique of a hedonist position is based on objective considerations about the hierarchy of faculties in a human being and its position in the world. Just as a third-person observer can identify the values of a plant or a beast by analyzing its biological make-up, so Seneca concludes from the internal structure of human beings and the factual relation of the human organism to the cosmic whole that the human good must be virtue in the form of perfected reason. A last sequence of letters in the corpus works on defining the good more precisely from the internal first-person viewpoint of the agent himself who is seeking it. Seneca discusses the perception of the good and the implications that its epistemological status has for the nature of the good and *vice versa*. In this context,

---

75 Sen. *Ep.* 92.30: "Sed 'si cui virtus animusque in corpore praesens' [≈ Verg. *Aen.* 5.363], hic deos aequat, illo tendit originis suae memor. Nemo improbe eo conatur ascendere unde descenderat. Quid est autem cur non existimes in eo divini aliquid existere qui dei pars est? Totum hoc quo continemur et unum est et deus; et socii sumus eius et membra. Capax est noster animus, perfertur illo si vitia non deprimant. Quemadmodum corporum nostrorum habitus erigitur et spectat in caelum, ita animus, cui in quantum vult licet porrigi, in hoc a natura rerum formatus est, ut paria dis vellet; et si utatur suis viribus ac se in spatium suum extendat, non aliena via ad summa nititur. Magnus erat labor ire in caelum: redit."

he rejects a version of the Epicurean cradle argument,[76] according to which animals and infants would learn the correct use of their body parts through the deterrent of pain (*Ep.* 121.7–8).[77] Instead, he posits the Stoic tenet that human and animal agents have some perception of their biological make-up (*constitutio*), understood as "the soul in a certain disposition relative to the body,"[78] and explains that they are "appropriated" to that make-up, i.e. constituted in such a way that they like it and wish to preserve it. This is the subjective account that complements the objective discussion in *Ep.* 92. Rational animals perceive and like themselves as rational beings (*Ep.* 121.14–15),[79] and so they see and cherish their rational mind as related to their body in the very hierarchy that was described from a third-person perspective in *Ep.* 92.

The difference is laid out even more sharply in the last letter of the collection. For the Epicurean, "all good and bad consists in sense experience," to quote from a famous argument in the *Letter to Menoeceus*.[80] The Stoic Seneca, on the other hand, has shown that the good is perceived by the *mind's* eye (*Ep.* 115.6) through a complex process of concept formation (*Ep.* 120) and self-cognition (*Ep.* 121), which he calls *intellectus*.[81] Also in this respect, hedonism and Seneca's Stoicism now appear as incompatible.

> Quaeritur utrum sensu comprendatur an intellectu bonum. Huic adiunctum est in mutis animalibus et infantibus non esse. 2 Quicumque voluptatem in summo ponunt sensibile iudicant bonum, nos contra intellegibile, qui illud animo damus.
>
> The question is whether the good is grasped by sense experience or by intellection. Connected with this is the fact that the good is not present in dumb animals and in infants. 2 All those who treat pleasure as the most important thing take the view that the good is perceptible to sense experience (*sensibile*); but we, who locate what is most important in the mind, think it is intelligible. (Sen. *Ep.* 124.1–2, trans. Inwood 2007a, with alterations)

---

76 On this type of argument, see Brunschwig 1986.
77 A precursor to this rejection is the remark at Sen. *Ep.* 116.3 that "Nature has infused an ingredient of pleasure into necessary things, not for us to seek pleasure [itself] but so that its addition would make that without which we cannot live more welcome to us." Neither this nor the passage in *Ep.* 121 precludes a positive evaluation of pleasure as one of the preferred indifferents.
78 Sen. *Ep.* 121.10: "principale animi quodam modo se habens erga corpus." Translation by Inwood 2007a.
79 See also *Ep.* 118.14, where Seneca shows how perfection and the achievement of the good is a matter of quality and not just of reaching the level of a certain optimum quantity, as it would be for an Epicurean. Other instances of Stoic quality in contrast to Epicurean quantity were discussed on pp. 440, 446, 449, and 453.
80 Epicur. *Ep. ad Men.* 124: "ἐπεὶ πᾶν ἀγαθὸν καὶ κακὸν ἐν αἰσθήσει." Translation by Inwood and Gerson 1997.
81 For a more detailed discussion of this term, see Wildberger 2006, section 3.1.2.9.

If the good were measured by the senses, then the intricate distinctions made by an Epicurean would be impossible.

> Si de bono sensus iudicarent, nullam voluptatem reiceremus; nulla enim non invitat, nulla non delectat; et e contrario nullum dolorem volentes subiremus; nullus enim non offendit sensum.
>
> If the senses passed judgment on the good, then we would never reject a pleasure, for every pleasure entices us and all of them please us. And conversely we would never willingly undergo any pain, for every pain hurts our senses. (Sen. *Ep.* 124.2, trans. Inwood 2007a, with minor changes to orthography and punctuation)

There would also be no reason to blame agents for greedy and self-indulgent behavior when they do what their senses, the arbiters of good and bad, tell them.

> Quid autem peccant si sensibus, id est iudicibus boni ac mali, parent? His enim tradidistis appetitionis et fugae arbitrium.
>
> Yet what is their offence if they are just listening to their senses, that is, to the judges of what is good and bad? For you have surrendered to the senses the power to decide about what to pursue and what to avoid. (Sen. *Ep.* 124.3, trans. Inwood 2007a)

The theoretical problems raised in *Ep.* 66 (p. 454f.) and the perversion criticized in *Ep.* 92 (pp. 455f.) now reappear from an epistemological point of view (*Ep.* 124.4–5). The hedonist chooses the wrong modality for his decision making: The senses simply cannot perceive what is really important for him.

> Sed videlicet ratio isti rei praeposita est: illa quemadmodum de beata vita, quemadmodum de virtute, de honesto, sic et de bono maloque constituit.
>
> But of course it is reason which is in charge of that business. Just as reason decides about the happy life and about virtue and about what is honorable, so too reason decides about what is good and what is bad. (Sen. *Ep.* 124.4, trans. Inwood 2007a)

IV.

In the last two letters we have discussed, Epicurus is no longer mentioned by name.[82] Seneca has outgrown the teacher of his earlier studies. The Greek philosopher served as an intellectual inspiration, as a model for paraenesis and therapeutic practices, and even once Seneca has moved beyond his early Stoico-Epicurean philosophy of carefree and joyful happiness, Epicurus is still adduced as the opponent who, despite himself, has to agree

---

82 The disappearance of Epicurus' name is noted by André 1969, 474 and Hachmann 1995, 235; see also Henderson 2004, 16 n. 2.

with the Stoic truth.[83] Now, Seneca and Lucilius have moved on to a different type of philosophy, a philosophy of questions and fine conceptual distinctions that takes the form of a debate between experts, even experts of the same school.

Ilsetraut Hadot observes a progression in technicality both within and "*outside* the epistolary exchange" (my emphasis). She parallels the methodological progress in the *Epistulae morales*[84] with the readings that Lucilius is given for the accompanying "course in philosophy." First he reads noteworthy sayings, then handbooks or abridged versions of longer works, and finally complete treatises:

> Daneben lassen sich folgende Stadien des philosophischen, außerhalb des Briefwechsels stattfindenden Lehrgangs, aus den Briefen ablesen: *I. Phase (Sentenz)* [...] *II. Phase (Epitome)* [...] *III. Phase (commentaria)*. (I. Hadot 1969, 54–55)

Hadot argues that this development is inspired by Epicurean didactics. What is more important with regard to the argument of this paper is, however, her observation that the different phases pertain not only to Lucilius' readings but at the same time also to Seneca's own intellectual activity and literary production. Seneca *himself* advances as a recipient of philosophical instruction and as a writer. First he reads extensively and collects interesting highlights, marking them out for Lucilius' benefit (*Ep.* 2.4–5; *Ep.* 6.5); then he engages with complete works which he summarizes (e.g. *Ep.* 39); finally he writes his own comprehensive books (e.g. *Ep.* 106.1–2).[85]

As Seneca reasserts once again near the end of our collection (*Ep.* 123.14, 123.16), the fundamental aim of both friends is still to become better men and make moral progress, to resist the vanities sought by the people around them and the downward pull of pleasures.[86] But it has by

---

83   Compare Freise 1989, 535–542.
84   Hadot 1969, 54: "[...] ein allmähliches Fortschreiten von lapidaren philosophischen Grundsätzen, die so allgemein sind, daß Seneca sie unbeschadet seines Stoikertums aus dem Munde Epikurs nehmen kann, bis hin zu philosophischen Quisquilien." A new French version of this book, entitled *Sénèque: Direction spirituelle et pratique de la philosophie*, is forthcoming with the publisher Vrin in Paris. On Epicurus' role in the context of generic change within the *Epistulae morales*, compare already Mutschmann 1915, 324.
85   It remains to be discussed how this literary activity of the Letter Writer relates to the actual oeuvre of L. Annaeus, in particular if one agrees with Gareth Williams's thesis in this volume that we are to read the *Epistulae morales* and the *Naturales quaestiones* as contemporaneous witnesses to L. Annaeus' literary persona.
86   This is one of the many allusions in the *Epistulae morales* to the twofold explanation for what the Stoics call "perversion" or *diastrophē*, the distortion of a human being's natural development toward perfect goodness as a result of "the persuasiveness of the things [themselves]" and "the voices of the many echoing around us" (D.L. 7.89 = *SVF* 3.228; further evidence is collected in *SVF* 3.229–236).

now become clear to them that it does not suffice to repeat universally acclaimed "public voices."[87] Real philosophical progress can only be made by someone who does not shun the technical discussions in which he trains his *intellectus*, accustoms himself to using his mind's eye, and learns the proper criteria for discerning good and bad with this faculty of reason.

> Mores alia aliter attingunt: quaedam illos corrigunt et ordinant, quaedam naturam eorum et originem scrutantur. 3 Cum <quaero> quare hominem natura produxerit, quare praetulerit animalibus ceteris, longe me iudicas mores reliquisse? Falsum est. Quomodo enim scies qui habendi sint nisi quid homini sit optimum inveneris, nisi naturam eius inspexeris? Tunc demum intelleges quid faciendum tibi, quid vitandum, cum didiceris quid naturae tuae debeas.

> Different things have different impacts on our character. Some improve it and make it orderly, while others investigate its nature and origin. 3 When <I ask> why nature made human beings, why she made us superior to the rest of the animals, do you think I have left character far behind? Not so. For how will you know what character you should have unless you find out what is best for a human being, unless you look into its nature. You won't really understand (*intelleges*) what you should do and what you should avoid until you have learned what you owe to your own nature. (Sen. *Ep.* 121.2–3, trans. Inwood 2007a, slight alterations)

Accordingly, Lucilius follows Seneca's lead in no longer refusing to engage in subtle discussions of finer points and in his new willingness to look carefully even at minute matters as long as there is some purpose to the activity (*Ep.* 121.1–2). And, as Seneca underscores, driving home once again the divide between beastly hedonism and the god-like aspirations of the Stoic, there *is* a benefit to the discussion.

> Quo nunc pertineat ista disputatio quaeris, et quid animo tuo profutura sit? Dico: et exercet illum et acuit et utique aliquid acturum occupatione honesta tenet. Prodest autem etiam quo moratur ad prava properantes. Sed <et> illud dico: nullo modo prodesse possum magis quam si tibi bonum tuum ostendo, si te a mutis animalibus separo, si cum deo pono.

> What, you ask, is the relevance now of this debate, and how will it benefit your own mind? I'll tell you. It exercises and sharpens the mind and, at the least, since the mind is bound to be doing something in any case, keeps it busy with an honorable employment. And it is also beneficial in that it slows down people who are rushing into moral error. But I will <also> say this: I can in no way be of greater benefit to you than if I show you what your good is, if I distinguish you from the dumb animals, if I place you alongside God. (Sen. *Ep.* 124.21, trans. Inwood 2007a, orthography altered)

For Erwin Hachmann (1995, 237), this letter marks the logical end point of the engagement with Epicurean thought that he observes in the *Epistulae morales*, and he takes this as an indication that not much of the work has been lost. Indeed, the only evidence that the corpus continued beyond that

---

87 *Ep.* 8.8; see also n. 33.

letter, the quotations by Aulus Gellius from a letter in which Seneca discusses Cicero's assessment of Ennius' style in *De re publica*, would fit very well into that part of the extant corpus in which Seneca talks about matters of style himself (e.g. in *Ep.* 100 and 114). The topic is particularly close to the second half of *Ep.* 108, which belongs to book 17 or 18. In that letter, Seneca distinguishes different ways of reading and also quotes from Cicero's *De re publica*. It is well known that we have only a fragment of the second half of the *Epistulae morales*, and there are signs that something has been lost also in this part of the collection. The extant letters do not feature an *incipit* marking off book 17 from book 18, and what remains is too short to fill two whole books properly. So there would have been a place for the Gellius fragment in that section. Unfortunately, however, Gellius himself cites the source of his quotations as the twenty-second book,[88] while our extant collection ends with book 20. So, unless we wish to assume a misreading of the book number (if, e.g., an original XIIX was read as XXII), we must accept the fact that the work continued beyond *Ep.* 124.

Whatever may be the case – an analysis of the Epicurus trope in the *Epistulae morales* allows us to see more clearly the manner in which L. Annaeus uses his Letter Writer "Seneca" to endow this work with a dramatic structure that serves both aesthetic and philosophical functions. Not only does the progression from simple to more refined debates contribute to shaping the corpus into an accessible and lively introduction to Stoic ethics. The *Epistulae morales* become an introduction to philosophy itself, to the practices and methodologies it entails. As such, they present men of the Roman upper classes with an authoritative and appealing model of how they might embark into an exemplary philosophical life themselves.[89]

Bibliography

André, Jean-Marie. 1969. "Sénèque et l'Épicurisme: ultime position." In *Actes du VIIIe Congrès de l'Association Guillaume Budé*, 469–480. Paris: Les Belles Lettres.

Arrighetti, Graziano, ed. 1973. *Epicuro, Opere*. 2nd ed. Torino: Einaudi.

Avotins, Ivars. 1977. "Training in Frugality in Epicurus and Seneca." *Phoenix* 31: 214–217.

Brunschwig, Jacques. 1986. "The Cradle Argument in Epicureanism and Stoicism." In *The Norms of Nature: Studies in Hellenistic Ethics*, edited by Malcolm Schofield

---

88 Gel. 12.2.3: "In libro enim vicesimo secundo Epistularum moralium quas ad Lucilium composuit [...]."

89 On this socio-political function of the *Epistulae morales* of presenting new role models for the Roman elite, see my two forthcoming publications on friendship and exemplary retreat from the public sphere in Seneca.

and Gisela Striker, 113–144. Paris; Cambridge: Maison des Sciences de l'Homme; Cambridge University Press.
Cancik, Hildegard. 1967. *Untersuchungen zu Senecas Epistulae morales.* Hildesheim: Olms.
Casadesús Bordoy, Francesco. 1997. "Citas epicúreas en las 'Epistulae morales' de Séneca." In *Séneca dos mil años después: Actas del congreso internacional conmemorativo del bimilenario de su nacimiento (Córdoba, 24 a 27 de septiembre de 1996)*, edited by Miguel Rodríguez-Pantoja, 541–549. Córdoba: Servicio de Publicaciones de la Universidad de Córdoba.
Cooper, John M. 2004. *Knowledge, Nature, and the Good: Essays on Ancient Philosophy.* Princeton: Princeton University Press.
Degl'Innocenti Pierini, Rita. 1992. " 'Vivi nascosto:' riflessi di un tema epicureo in Orazio, Ovidio, Seneca." *Prometheus* 18: 150–172.
Diogenes of Oenoanda. 1993. *The Epicurean Inscription.* See Smith 1993.
Epicurus. 1887. See Usener 1887.
Epicurus. 1973. See Arrighetti 1973.
Ferguson, John. 1990. "Epicureanism under the Roman Empire." *ANRW* II 36.4: 2257–2327.
Freise, Hermann. 1989. "Die Bedeutung der Epikur-Zitate in den Schriften Senecas." *Gymnasium* 96: 532–556.
Gigante, Marcello. 1998. "Seneca in partibus Epicuri." In *Seneca nel bimillenario della nascita: Atti del convegno internazionale di Chiavari del 19–20 aprile 1997*, edited by Sergio Audano, 13–18. Pisa: ETS.
Gigante, Marcello. 1999. "Connobbe Seneca l'opera di Filodemo?" *CronErc* 21: 5–15.
Gigante, Marcello. 2000. "Seneca, ein Nachfolger Philodems?" In *Epikureismus in der späten Republik und der Kaiserzeit: Akten der 2. Tagung der Karl-und-Gertrud-Abel-Stiftung vom 30. September – 3. Oktober 1998 in Würzburg*, edited by Michael Erler and Robert Bees, 32–41. Stuttgart: Steiner.
Gill, Christopher. 2006. *The Structured Self in Hellenistic and Roman Thought.* Oxford; New York: Oxford University Press.
Görler, Woldemar. 1997. "Storing up Past Pleasures." In *Lucretius and His Intellectual Background*, edited by Keimpe Algra, Mieke H. Koenen, and Piet H. Schrijvers, 193–207. Amsterdam et al.: North-Holland.
Graver, Margaret R. 2007. *Stoicism and Emotion.* Chicago: University of Chicago Press.
Graver, Margaret R. 2009. "The Weeping Wise: Stoic and Epicurean Consolations in Seneca's 99th Epistle." In *Tears in the Graeco-Roman World*, edited by Thorsten Fögen, 235–252. Berlin; New York: De Gruyter.
Graver, Margaret R. Forthcoming. "Not as a Deserter, but as a Spy: Seneca's Reception of Epicureanism." In *The Oxford Handbook of Epicureanism*, edited by Jeffrey Fish and Kirk Sanders. Oxford; New York: Oxford University Press.
Grilli, Alberto. 1998. "Epicuro tra Seneca e Orazio." *RIL* 132: 39–51.
Grimal, Pierre. 1969. "L'epicureisme romain." In *Actes du VIIIe Congrès de l'Association Guillaume Budé*, 139–168. Paris: Les Belles Lettres.
Grimal, Pierre. 1970. "Nature et limites de l'éclectisme philosophique chez Sénèque." *LEC* 38: 3–17.
Hachmann, Erwin. 1995. *Die Führung des Lesers in Senecas "Epistulae morales."* Münster: Aschendorff.
Hachmann, Erwin. 1996. "Die Spruchepiloge in Senecas Epistulae morales." *Gymnasium* 103: 385–410.
Hadot, Ilsetraut. 1969. *Seneca und die griechisch-römische Tradition der Seelenleitung.* Berlin: De Gruyter.

Henderson, John. 2004. *Morals and Villas in Seneca's Letters: Places to Dwell.* Cambridge: Cambridge University Press.
Hermes, Theodor. 1951. *Epikur in den Epistulae morales Senecas.* Dr. phil. diss., Marburg.
Inwood, Brad. 2005. *Reading Seneca: Stoic Philosophy at Rome.* Oxford; New York: Oxford University Press.
Inwood, Brad, trans. 2007a. *Seneca, Selected Philosophical Letters: Translation with an Introduction and Commentary.* Oxford; New York: Oxford University Press.
Inwood, Brad. 2007b. "The Importance of Form in Seneca's Philosophical Letters." In *Ancient Letters: Classical and Late Antique Epistolography*, edited by Ruth Morello and Andrew D. Morrison, 133–148. Oxford; New York: Oxford University Press.
Inwood, Brad, and Lloyd P. Gerson, trans. 1997. *Hellenistic Philosophy: Introductory Readings.* 2nd ed. Indianapolis; Cambridge: Hackett.
Ker, James. 2006. "Seneca: Man of Many Genres." In *Seeing Seneca Whole: Perspectives on Philosophy, Poetry and Politics*, edited by Katharina Volk and Gareth D. Williams, 19–42. Leiden; Boston: Brill.
Lana, Italo. 1991. "Le 'Lettere a Lucilio' nella letteratura epistolare." In *Sénèque et la prose latine*, edited by Pierre Grimal, 253–311. Vandœuvres-Genève: Fondation Hardt.
La Penna, Antonio. 1994. "Un'altra eco di Lucrezio in Seneca? (con qualche riflessione sulla tradizione indiretta)." *Maia* 46: 319–322.
Long, Anthony, and David N. Sedley, eds. and trans. 1987. *The Hellenistic Philosophers.* 2 vols. Cambridge: Cambridge University Press.
Lotito, Gianfranco. 2001. *Suum esse: Forme dell'interiorità senecana.* Bologna: Pàtron.
Maso, Stefano. 1979–1980. "Il problema dell'epicureismo nell'epistola 33 di Seneca." *AIV* 138: 573–589.
Maurach, Gregor. 1970. *Der Bau von Senecas Epistulae morales.* Heidelberg: Winter.
Maurach, Gregor. 2005. *Seneca: Leben und Werk.* 4th ed. Darmstadt: Wissenschaftliche Buchgesellschaft.
Mazzoli, Giancarlo. 1970. *Seneca e la poesia.* Milano: Casa Editrice Ceschina.
Mazzoli, Giancarlo. 1989. "Le 'Epistulae morales ad Lucilium' di Seneca: Valore letterario e filosofico." *ANRW* II 36.3: 1823–1877.
Mitsis, Philip T. 1987. "Epicurus on Friendship and Altruism." *OSAPh* 5: 127–153.
Motto, Anna Lydia, and John R. Clark. 1968. "Paradoxum Senecae: The Epicurean Stoic." *CW* 62: 37–42.
Mutschmann, Hermann. 1915. "Seneca und Epikur." *Hermes* 50: 321–356.
Obbink, Dirk, ed. 1996. *Philodemus, On Piety. Part 1: Critical Text with Commentary.* Oxford: Clarendon Press.
Obstoj, Angelika. 1989. *Seneca und Epikur: Untersuchungen zu Senecas Verhältnis zur epikureischen Philosophie.* Dr. phil. diss., Hannover.
O'Keefe, Tim. 2001. "Is Epicurean Friendship Altruistic?" *Apeiron* 34: 269-305.
Philippson, Robert. 1921. "Zur Philodems Schrift über die Frömmigkeit." *Hermes* 56: 355–410.
Philodemus. 1996. *On Piety.* See Obbink 1996.
Pohlenz, Max. 1941. "Philosophie und Erlebnis in Senecas Dialogen." *Nachrichten von der Akademie der Wissenschaften in Göttingen: Philosophisch-historische Klasse* I, 4.3: 55–118.
Reynolds, Leighton D., ed. 1965. *L. Annaei Senecae ad Lucilium epistulae morales.* 2 vols. Oxford: Clarendon Press.
Sacheli, Agostino. 1925. *Lineamenti epicurei nello stoicismo di Seneca.* Genova: Libreria Editrice Moderna.

Schafer, John. 2011. "Seneca's 'Epistulae Morales' as Dramatized Education." *CPh* 106: 32–52.
Schildhauer, Hans. 1932. *Seneca und Epikur: Eine Studie zu ihrer Ethik und Weltanschauung.* Dr. phil. diss., Greifswald.
Schmid, Wolfgang. 1955. "Eine falsche Epikurdeutung Senecas und seine Praxis der erbauenden Lesung (Epic. Gnom. Vat. 60)." *Acme* 8: 119–129.
Schottlaender, Rudolf. 1955. "Epikureisches bei Seneca: Ein Ringen um den Sinn von Freude und Freundschaft." *Philologus* 99: 133–148.
Schwaiger, Clemens. 2000. "Die Idee des Selbstdenkens in der römischen Philosophie aufgezeigt am Beispiel Senecas." *Gymnasium* 107: 129–142.
Seneca. 1965. *Ad Lucilium epistulae morales.* See Reynolds 1965.
Seneca. 2007. *Selected Philosophical Letters.* See Inwood 2007a.
Setaioli, Aldo. 1988. *Seneca e i Greci: Citazioni e traduzioni nelle opere filosofiche.* Bologna: Pàtron.
Setaioli, Aldo. 1991. "Seneca e gli arcaici." In *Seneca e la cultura: Atti del Convegno di Perugia, 9–10 novembre 1989*, edited by Aldo Setaioli, 33–45. Napoli: Edizioni Scientifiche Italiane. Revised version in Setaioli 2000, 219–231.
Setaioli, Aldo. 1997. "Séneca, Epicuro y Mecenas." In *Séneca, dos mil años después: Actas del Congreso Internacional conmemorativo del bimilenario de su nacimiento (Córdoba, 24 a 27 de septiembre de 1996)*, edited by Miguel Rodríguez-Pantoja, 563–576. Córdoba: Servicio de Publicaciones de la Universidad de Córdoba. Revised version in Setaioli 2000, 255–274.
Setaioli, Aldo. 2000. *Facundus Seneca: Aspetti della lingua e dell'ideologia senecana*, Bologna: Pàtron.
Setaioli, Aldo. 2014a. "The Epistulae Morales." In *Brill's Companion to Seneca: Philosopher and Dramatist*, edited by Gregor Damschen and Andreas Heil, 191–200. Leiden; Boston: Brill.
Setaioli, Aldo. 2014b. "Philosophy as Therapy, Self-Transformation, and 'Lebensform'." In *Brill's Companion to Seneca: Philosopher and Dramatist*, edited by Gregor Damschen and Andreas Heil, 239–256. Leiden; Boston: Brill.
Smith, Martin Ferguson, ed. 1993. *Diogenes of Oinoanda: The Epicurean Inscription.* Napoli: Bibliopolis.
Tieleman, Teun. 2003. *Chrysippus' On Affections: Reconstruction and Interpretation.* Leiden; Boston: Brill.
Usener, Hermann, ed. 1887. *Epicurea.* Leipzig: Teubner.
Weissenfels, Oskar. 1886. *De Seneca Epicureo (Programme d'invitation à l'examen public du Collège Royal Français, 1837–1890).* Berlin: Starcke.
Wilcox, Amanda. 2012. *The Gift of Correspondence in Classical Rome: Friendship in Cicero's Ad Familiares and Seneca's Moral Epistles.* Madison: University of Wisconsin Press.
Wildberger, Jula. 2006. *Seneca und die Stoa: Der Platz des Menschen in der Welt.* 2 vols. Berlin; New York: De Gruyter.
Wildberger, Jula. 2010. " 'Praebebam enim me facilem opinionibus magnorum uirorum:' Platonic Readings in Seneca Ep. 102." In *Aristotle and the Stoics Reading Plato*, edited by Verity Harte, Mary M. McCabe, Robert A. Sharples, and Ann Sheppard, 205–232. London: Institute of Classical Studies.
Wildberger, Jula. Forthcoming. "Amicitia and Eros: Seneca's Adaptation of a Stoic Concept of Friendship for Roman Men in Progress." In *Philosophie in Rom*, edited by Gernot Michael Müller. Schwabe: Basel.
Wildberger, Jula. Forthcoming. " 'Simus inter exempla!' Formen und Funktionen beispielhafter Weltflucht in der frühen Kaiserzeit." In *Menschenbilder zwischen Weltflucht und Verantwortung*, edited by Heinz-Günther Nesselrath and Meike Rühl. Tübingen: Mohr Siebeck.

Wilson, Marcus. 2001. "Seneca's Epistles Reclassified." In *Texts, Ideas, and the Classics: Scholarship, Theory, and Classical Literature*, edited by Stephen J. Harrison, 164–187. Oxford; New York: Oxford University Press.

Abbreviations

Abbreviations of ancient authors and works are those of the *Greek-English Lexicon* by Henry George Liddell, Robert Scott and Henry S. Jones (with a revised supplement, Oxford: Clarendon Press, 1996, accessible online at http://www.stoa.org/abbreviations.html) and the *Oxford Latin Dictionary*, edited by P. G. W. Glare (Oxford: Clarendon Press, 1982; also used by the Packard Humanities Institute for its online collection of *Classical Latin Texts* at http://latin.packhum.org/browse). Wherever necessary, these are supplemented by the *Thesaurus linguae Latinae: Index librorum scriptorum inscriptionum ex quibus exempla afferuntur* (2nd ed. Teubner: Leipzig 1990) and the list of works and authors published online by The Diccionario Griego-Español Project at http://dge.cchs.csic.es /lst/2lst1.htm. Square brackets around an author's name indicate spurious attribution.

Journal titles are abbreviated according to the *Année Philologique*. Seneca's *Dialogi* are not quoted by number but by title, abbreviated thus:

Brev. vit.	*De brevitate vitae* (Dial. 10)
Const.	*De constantia sapientis* (Dial. 2)
Helv.	*Ad Helviam matrem de consolatione* (Dial. 12)
Marc.	*Ad Marciam de consolatione* (Dial. 6)
Polyb.	*Ad Polybium de consolatione* (Dial. 11)
Prov	*De providentia* (Dial. 1)
Tranq. an.	*De tranquillitate animi* (Dial. 9)
Vit. beat.	*De vita beata* (Dial. 7)

Further abbreviations in alphabetical order:

Aëtius or Aët.	"Ἀετίου περὶ τῶν ἀρεσκόντων συναγωγή," in: Hermann Diels. *Doxographi Graeci*, 267-444. Berlin: De Gruyter, 1879
Galen *P.H.P.*	Galen, *De Placitis Hippocratis et Platonis*, usually quoted after Galen. *On the doctrines of Hippocrates and Plato: Edition, Translation and Commentary* by Phillip H. De Lacy. Berlin: Akademie-Verlag, 1978 (Corpus Medicorum Graecorum V 4.1.2)

LS	Passage quoted from Anthony A. Long and David Sedley, eds. *The Hellenistic Philosophers.* 2 vols. Cambridge: Cambridge University Press, 1987.
Sext. *Emp. Math.*	Sextus Empiricus, *Adversus mathematicos*
Plu. *Comm. not.*	Plutarch, *De communibus notitiis adversus Stoicos* (*Moralia* 1058e-1086b)
Plu. *Stoic. rep.*	Plutarch, *De Stoicorum repugnantiis* (*Moralia* 1033a-1057b)
Plu. *Virt. mor.*	Plutarch, *De virtute morali* (*Moralia* 44d-462d)
PIR²	*Prosopographia Imperii Romani saec. I. II. III.* 2nd ed. Berlin: De Gruyter, 1933–
SVF	Hans von Arnim, ed. *Stoicorum veterum fragmenta.* 3 vols. Leipzig, 1903–1905 (quoted by volume and fragment number)
ThLL	*Thesaurus linguae Latinae.* Leipzig: Teubner, 1900–

Index of Passages Cited

Accius
Acc. Trag. 549–551 Ribbeck: 171 n. 16.

Aelianus
Ael. V.H. 2.20: 181 n. 67

'Aëtius'
Aët. 1 Pr. 2: 362 n. 42
Aët. 1.7.33: 12 n. 12
Aët. 2.11.1: 44 n. 8
Aët. 4.11: 11, 17, 26–29, 34 n. 83
Aët. 4.11.1–4: 44
Aët. 4.11.1: 45 n. 10
Aët. 4.11.4–5: 27f.
Aët. 4.21.1–4: 283 n. 35
Aët. 5.13.3: 214 n. 5

Alcinous
Alc. Intr. 24, p. 177 Hermann: 68 n. 12

Alexander Aphrodisiensis
Alex.Aphr. De An. 2, p. 188, 6–8 Bruns: 68 n. 13
Alex.Aphr. Mixt. p. 224, 23–25 Bruns: 12 n. 15
Alex.Aphr. Mixt. p. 225 Bruns: 300 n. 14

Anaximenes Lampsacenus
Rh.Al. 11.1: 321 n. 11

Ps.-Andronicus Rhodius
[Andronic. Rhod.] 1: 111 n. 3
[Andronic. Rhod.] 1.1, p. 223 Glibert–Thirry: 360 n. 36
[Andronic. Rhod.] 2.1.1, p. 239 Glibert–Thirry: 357 n. 28
[Andronic. Rhod.] 2.5.2, p. 247 Glibert–Thirry: 357 n. 29
[Andronic. Rhod.] 2.6.2.7, p. 254 Glibert–Thirry: 359 n. 33

Anonymi
Anon. Aetna: 145 n. 38
Anon. in Tht. col. 5.18–6.31: 423 n. 74
Anon. Cramer 1839, vol. 1, p. 171 (Quomodo homines boni et mali fiant?): 14 n. 23

Apollodorus
Apollod. 2.116–117: 195 n. 54

Apuleius
Apul. Met. 8.28: 58, 58 n. 67
Apul. Met. 9.14: 58 n. 68
Apul. Met. 10.10: 58 n. 67

Aristophanes
Ar. Lys. 107–110: 215 n. 12

Aretaeus
Aret. S.D. 1.1: 200 n. 75

Aristoteles
Arist. E.N. 2, 1103a–b: 13 n. 21
Arist. E.N. 7.3: 78 n. 44
Arist. E.N. 7.3, 1145b25–27: 65 n. 2
Arist. E.N. 7.3, 1146a35–1147b3: 114 n. 7
Arist. G.A. 727a16–19: 220 n. 25
Arist. G.A. 728a17–25: 219 n. 23
Arist. G.A. 783b33–784a12: 220 n. 25
Arist. G.A. 784a: 213 n. 3
Arist. Met. 7, 1033b34 – 1034a1: 349 n. 16
Arist. P.A. 2.7, 653a28–29: 218
Arist. Pol. 1.3, 1253b: 252 n. 47
Arist. Rh. 2.21.16: 321
Arist. Top. 139a24–151b24: 349 n. 16
[Arist.] M.M. 2.4, 1200b 25–28: 65 n. 2

Arrianus: see Epictetus

Athenaeus
Athen. 4, 274a–275b: 370 n. 3, 385
Athen. 12, 547a: 436 n. 17

Caesar
Caes. Civ. 1.31.2: 49 n. 22
Caes. Gal. 6.24.5: 49 n. 22
[Caes.] B. Hisp. 20.5: 191 n. 22

Callimachus
Call. Ap. 110–112: 286f.

Celsus
Cels. pr. 26: 199 n. 73
Cels. 4.31.1: 213 n. 3

Chryippus
Chrysipp. On Goals, book 1: 30
Chrysipp. apud D.L. 7.180 = SVF 2.1: 66
Chrysipp. apud Gal. PHP 4.6.7–9 = SVF 3.473: 127 n. 38
Chrysipp. apud Gal. P.H.P. 4.6.19 = SVF 3.473: 76 n. 39
Chrysipp. apud Gal. P.H.P. 4.6.27 = SVF 3.475: 120 n. 21
Chrysipp. apud Orig. Cels. 8.51 = SVF 3.474: 111 n. 2, 115 n. 9, 117 n. 14
Chrysipp. apud Plu. Stoic. rep. 1041e = SVF 3.69: 17f., 44f. n. 9
Chrysipp. apud Plu. Stoic. rep. 1041f = SVF 3.545: 306 n. 29
Chrysipp. apud Plu. virt. mor 450c = SVF 3.390: 123 n. 24
Chrysipp. apud Stob. 4.39.22, vol. 5, p. 906 Wachsmuth and Hense = SVF 3.510: 37 n. 89

Cicero
Cic. Ac. 1. 41: 51
Cic. Ac. 1.38: 20 n. 42
Cic. Ac. 135: 369 n. 3
Cic. Ac. 2.44: 57
Cic. Att.: 404
Cic. Att.: 245 n. 36
Cic. Att. 1.5: 245
Cic. Att. 13.31.3: 170
Cic. Att. 14.2: 327 n. 26
Cic. Att. Frg.: 169 f.
Cic. Brut. 117: 372 n. 11
Cic. Catil. 3.11: 50 n. 29
Cic. Clu. 66: 191 n. 21
Cic. Clu. 187: 191 n. 22
Cic. De orat. 1.38: 238 n. 17
Cic. De orat. 3.10: 172 n. 20
Cic. Div. 1.1: 49 n. 16
Cic. Div. 2.108: 57
Cic. Dom. 108: 177 n. 49
Cic. Fam. 12.18.2: 327 n. 26
Cic. Fat. 42–43: 105 n. 42
Cic. Fin. 1.31: 53–55, 59 n. 73, 60
Cic. Fin. 1.57: 127 n. 39
Cic. Fin. 2.90: 439 n. 28
Cic. Fin. 2.104–106: 127 n. 39
Cic. Fin. 2.106: 130 n. 48
Cic. Fin. 3.33: 52
Cic. Fin. 3.16–25: 231 n. 5
Cic. Fin. 3.16–17: 30
Cic. Fin. 3.21: 31, 49, 52
Cic. Fin. 3.33–34: 32
Cic. Fin. 3.33: 23 n. 53, 24
Cic. Fin. 3.35: 354 n. 23
Cic. Fin. 3.60f.: 236 n. 15
Cic. Fin. 3.62–68: 55 n. 52
Cic. Fin. 4.18: 54 n. 42
Cic. Fin. 4.23: 369 n. 3
Cic. Fin. 5.43: 56, 56 n. 54
Cic. Fin. 5.79: 359 n. 33
Cic. Flac. 73–75: 370 n. 5
Cic. Font. 39: 51 n. 33
Cic. Leg. 1.22: 13 n. 19
Cic. Leg. 1.26: 49
Cic. Leg. 1.33: 15 n. 26
Cic. Leg. 2.10: 52 n. 38
Cic. Mil. 21.57: 192 n. 29
Cic. Mur. 60–68: 370
Cic. Mur. 61: 371 n. 9
Cic. Mur. 75–76: 370f., 376
Cic. Mur. 75: 278 n. 27
Cic. Mur. 76: 280, 375
Cic. N.D. 1.100: 54 n. 42
Cic. N.D. 1.43–45: 54
Cic. N.D. 1.43: 16, 16 n. 29, 48f., 54 n. 43
Cic. N.D. 1.44: 15, 16 n. 29, 43, 54
Cic. N.D. 1.45: 54 n. 43
Cic. N.D. 2.12: 17 n. 31, 29, 48
Cic. N.D. 2.45: 48
Cic. N.D. 3.89: 416 n. 56
Cic. Off. 1.40: 52 n. 37
Cic. Off. 1.90: 169 n. 9
Cic. Off. 1.142: 37 n. 87
Cic. Off. 1.149: 202 n. 94
Cic. Off. 2.29: 56 n. 59
Cic. Off. 3.17: 38 n. 92

Cic. Off. 3.63: 369 n. 3
Cic. Off. 3.89: 201 n. 84
Cic. Orat. 116: 49
Cic. Orat. 133: 54
Cic. Orat. 7–9: 305f.
Cic. Orat. 7: 306 n. 29
Cic. Parad.: 413f.
Cic. Parad. 12: 52 n. 38
Cic. Parad. 20: 423 n. 74
Cic. Parad. 34: 174
Cic. Parad. 48: 52 n. 37
Cic. Part. 113: 194 n. 41
Cic. Part.123: 57
Cic. Phil. 1.2: 191 n. 21
Cic. Phil. 11.2–3: 194 n. 41
Cic. Phil. 2.55: 56
Cic. Phil. 5.26: 50 n. 30
Cic. Pis. 1: 242 n. 29
Cic. Pis. 89: 192 n. 30
Cic. Planc. 48: 51 n. 33
Cic. Red. sen. 36: 172 n. 20
Cic. Rep.: 435 n. 15, 461
Cic. Rep. 1.14–17: 370 n. 3
Cic. Rep. 1.23–29: 370 n. 3
Cic. Rep. 1.26–29: 377
Cic. Rep. 1.27: 278 n. 26
Cic. Rep. 1.28: 278 n. 26
Cic. Rep. 1.29: 278 n. 27
Cic. Rep. 1.31–32: 370 n. 3
Cic. Rep. 1.31: 377 n. 25
Cic. Rep. 3.15: 195 n. 54
Cic. Sull. 87: 171 n. 19
Cic. Tim. 11: 306 n. 29
Cic. Tim. 13: 52 n. 36
Cic. Tim. 34: 306 n. 29
Cic. Top. 31: 50
Cic. Tusc. 1.30: 46f.
Cic. Tusc. 1.34: 288
Cic. Tusc. 1.57: 53, 54 n. 42
Cic. Tusc. 2.33: 171
Cic. Tusc. 2.94–95: 171
Cic. Tusc. 3.2: 15
Cic. Tusc. 3.22–23: 354 n. 23
Cic. Tusc. 3.24–25: 360 n. 36, 360 n. 37
Cic. Tusc. 3.32: 127
Cic. Tusc. 3.33: 128
Cic. Tusc. 3.35: 128
Cic. Tusc. 3.63: 54 n. 42
Cic. Tusc. 3.76–79: 111
Cic. Tusc. 3.76: 115 n. 9
Cic. Tusc. 3.77: 124 n. 28
Cic. Tusc. 3.79: 115 n. 9

Cic. Tusc. 4.4: 369 n. 3
Cic. Tusc. 4.11: 354 n. 23
Cic. Tusc. 4.14: 111 n. 3
Cic. Tusc. 4.22: 354 n. 23
Cic. Tusc. 4.61: 124 n. 28
Cic. Tusc. 4.84: 52 n. 39
Cic. Tusc. 5.85: 52 n. 39
Cic. Tusc. 5.93: 439 n. 28
Cic. Tusc. 5.96: 127 n. 39
Cic. Ver. 2.3.23: 194 n. 41
Cic. Ver. 2.4.23: 51 n. 33
Cic. Ver. 2.5.139: 54 n. 42
Cic. Ver. 2.5.62: 194 n. 41
Cic. Ver. 2.5.63: 191 n. 16

CIL VI.10229: 244 n. 34

Clemens Alexandrinus
Clem.Al. Strom. 1.6.34.1–35.2: 13 n. 20
Clem.Al. Strom. 2.21.129.4: 301 n. 17
Clem.Al. Strom. 7.3.19.3–4: 13 n. 20

Demetrius
Demetr. Eloc. 224: 409 n. 36
Demetr. Eloc. 227: 403f.

Demosthenes
Dem. 3.25–26: 370 n. 5

Dexippus
Dexipp. in Cat. p. 50, 31 Busse: 13 n. 17

Digesta
Dig. 9.41.1a.196: 194 n. 42
Dig. 34.2.16: 244 n. 34
Dig. 48.9.9: 192 n. 34
Dig. Frg. 1.9, Ad Leg. Pomp. de Parricid. 48.9: 192 n. 33

Dio Cassius
D.C. 49.12: 191 n. 22
D.C. 54.23.2–4: 192 n. 35
D.C. 60.24: 195 n. 48
D.C. 61.10.2: 345 n. 8

Dio Chrysostomus
D.Chr. 6.40: 182 n. 73
D.Chr. 6.60: 182

Diocles: see Diogenes Laërtius

Diodorus Siculus
D.S. 13.90.4: 195 n. 53
D.S. 19.108.71: 195 n. 53

Diogenes Babylonius
Diog.Bab. apud D.L. 7.61: 21 n. 50
Diog.Bab. apud Galen, P.H.P 2.5.11–12: 283 n. 35

Diogenes Laërtius
D.L. 7.2–5: 416 n. 58
D.L. 7.46: 24f. n. 62
D.L. 7.49–54: 11
D.L. 7.49: 21
D.L. 7.50–54: 20–25
D.L. 7.50–51: 27
D.L. 7.50: 21, 23
D.L. 7.51: 21f., 23, 26 n. 66, 27f.
D.L. 7.52–53: 20
D.L. 7.52: 22–24, 24 n. 57, 52
D.L. 7.53: 23f., 28f., 32 n. 76, 412 n. 42
D.L. 7.54: 24f., 29, 44 n. 5, 44 n. 8
D.L. 7.61: 21, 23, 27, 28 n. 68
D.L. 7.85–86: 30, 231 n. 5
D.L. 7.88: 402
D.L. 7.89: 13 n. 21, 14 n. 23, 35 n. 84, 459 n. 86
D.L. 7.92: 357 n. 28
D.L. 7.93: 357 n. 29, 357 n. 30
D.L. 7.101: 446 n. 49
D.L. 7.110: 68 n. 13, 83 n. 60
D.L. 7.111: 72 n. 29
D.L. 7.113: 125 n. 32
D.L. 7.127: 359 n. 33
D.L. 7.130: 236 n. 15
D.L. 7.135–136: 12 n. 11
D.L. 7.147: 11 n. 9
D.L. 7.156: 12 n. 12
D.L. 7.180: 66
D.L. 7.188: 359 n. 33
D.L. 10.22: 127 n. 39
D.L. 10.28: 434
D.L. 10.33: 44 n. 2

Diogenes Oinoandensis
Diog.Oen. Frg. 72 [NF 7], ed. Smith 1993: 436 n. 17

Ennius
Enn. apud Cic. Tusc.1.34: 288

Epictetus
Arr. Epict. 1.1.25: 343 n. 3
Arr. Epict. 1.16.10: 219 n. 24
Arr. Epict. 1.2.29: 219 n. 24
Arr. Epict. 1.22.9: 25 n. 64
Arr. Epict. 1.22.39: 25 n. 64
Arr. Epict. 1.28: 67 n. 9
Arr. Epict. 1.28.7–10: 67 n. 9
Arr. Epict. 1.28.8–9: 73 n. 31
Arr. Epict. 1.28.28: 67 n. 9
Arr. Epict. 2.1.23–24: 360 n. 39
Arr. Epict. 2.11: 18–20
Arr. Epict. 2.11.2: 19 n. 39, 25 n. 64
Arr. Epict. 2.11.3–6: 19f., 24
Arr. Epict. 2.11.6–14: 44 n. 6
Arr. Epict. 2.11.6: 19 n. 41, 24 n. 58
Arr. Epict. 2.17.7: 25 n. 64
Arr. Epict. 2.17.19–22: 67 n. 9
Arr. Epict. 2.17.29: 360 n. 39
Arr. Epict. 3.8.1–5: 343 n. 3
Arr. Epict. 3.12.1–17: 343 n. 3
Arr. Epict. 4.1.1: 359 n. 35
Arr. Epict. 4.1.42–47: 360 n. 39
Arr. Epict. 4.3.7–8: 360 n. 39
Arr. Epict. 4.4.18: 100 n. 21
Arr. Epict. 4.6.16: 360 n. 39
Arr. Epict. 4.6.34–35: 100 n. 20
Arr. Epict. 4.7.10: 359 n. 35
Epict. Ench. 1.5: 100 n. 20
Epict. Ench. 17: 106 n. 44

Epicurus
Epicur. Ep. ad Men. 122: 448
Epicur. Ep. ad Men. 124: 457 n. 80
Epicur. Frg. 128–138 Usener, 52–61 Arrighetti: 434 n. 13
Epicur. Ep. ad Men. 129: 446 n. 46
Epicur. Ep. ad Men. 130: 434 n. 9, 439 n. 28
Epicur. Ep. ad Men. 131: 438, 438 n. 25
Epicur. Ep. ad Men. 133–135: 441
Epicur. Ep. ad Men. 133: 436
Epicur. Frg. 138 Usener, 52 Arrighetti: 127 n. 39, 456
Epicur. Frg. 157 Usener, 86 Arrighetti: 437 n. 21
Epicur. Frg. 175 Usener, 132 Arrighetti: 443
Epicur. Frg. 181 Usener, 124 Arrighetti: 438 n. 23, 446 n. 46, 436 n. 17
Epicur. Frg. 189 Usener: 436 n. 17

Epicur. Frg. 201 Usener, 217 Arrighetti: 444
Epicur. Frg. 202 Usener; 216 Arrighetti: 445
Epicur. Frg. 423 Usener: 127 n. 39
Epicur. Frg. 434 Usener, 186 Arrighetti: 454
Epicur. Frg. 436 Usener: 130 n. 48
Epicur. Frg. 446 Usener: 437 n. 19
Epicur. Frg. 456 Usener: 439 n. 28
Epicur. Frg. 468 Usener, 221 Arrighetti: 439 n. 28
Epicur. Frg. 471 Usener, 214 Arrighetti: 445
Epicur. Frg. 477 Usener, 219 Arrighetti: 439
Epicur. Frg. 484 Usener, 246 Arrighetti: 437 n. 20
Epicur. Frg. 487 Usener: 440
Epicur. Frg. 491 Usener, 242 Arrighetti: 447 n. 52
Epicur. Frg. 493 Usener, 243 Arrighetti: 449
Epicur. Frg. 494 Usener, 244 Arrighetti: 449
Epicur. Frg. 495 Usener, 241 Arrighetti: 449
Epicur. Frg. 512 Usener, 136 Arrighetti: 436 n. 17
Epicur. Frg. 531 Usener: 442 n. 35
Epicur. Frg. 551 Usener: 384 n. 42
Epicur. Frg. 602 Usener: 438 n. 26
Epicur. in POxy 76.5077: 436 n. 17
Epicur. Sent. 15: 439 n. 28, 445
Epicur. Sent. 16: 441
Epicur. Sent. 18: 441 n. 34
Epicur. Sent. 20: 363f.
Epicur. Sent. 21: 439 n. 28
Epicur. Sent.Vat. 4: 436, 436 n. 17
Epicur. Sent.Vat. 8: 439 n. 28, 445
Epicur. Sent.Vat. 9: 440
Epicur. Sent.Vat. 11: 436 n. 17
Epicur. Sent.Vat. 16: 436 n. 17
Epicur. Sent.Vat. 17: 448
Epicur. Sent.Vat. 19: 448
Epicur. Sent.Vat. 23: 443f.
Epicur. Sent.Vat. 25: 439, 440, 442
Epicur. Sent.Vat. 27: 452 n. 67
Epicur. Sent.Vat. 33: 433 n. 7, 438, 439, 442
Epicur. Sent.Vat. 35: 446 n. 45
Epicur. Sent.Vat. 47: 436 n. 17
Epicur. Sent.Vat. 55: 448
Epicur. Sent.Vat. 60: 447f.
Epicur. Sent.Vat. 69: 448 n. 54
Epicur. Sent.Vat. 75: 448 n. 54

Euripides
Eur. Andr. 629–630: 127 n. 38
Eur. Med.: 82 n. 56
Eur. Med. 374f.: 79 n. 49
Eur. Med. 446f.: 69 n. 16
Eur. Med. 791–796: 79 n. 49
Eur. Med. 1021–1080: 66
Eur. Med. 1078f.: 79 n. 47
Eur. Med. 1080: 69 n. 16

Eusebius
Eus. P.E. 15.14.1–2: 11f., 12 n. 10

Florus
Flor. Epit. 1.47.8: 172 n. 19

Fronto
Fro. Aur.Orat. 2–7: 343 n. 2
Fro. Aur.Orat. 5: 343 n. 2

Galenus
Gal. In Hippocratis librum VI epidemiarum, commentarius V, vol. 17b, p. 251, 1–9 Kühn: 12 n. 16
Gal. P.H.P. 2.5.11–12: 283 n. 35
Gal. P.H.P. 4–5: 67f.
Gal. P.H.P. 4.1.16–17: 72 n. 29
Gal. P.H.P. 4.2.6: 72 n. 29
Gal. P.H.P. 4.2.8–18: 75 n. 38
Gal. P.H.P. 4.2.15–18: 117 n. 13
Gal. P.H.P. 4.2.19–27: 86 n. 73
Gal. P.H.P. 4.2.27: 76 n. 39
Gal. P.H.P. 4.4.24–25: 117 n. 13
Gal. P.H.P. 4.4.24: 75
Gal. P.H.P. 4.5.13: 75
Gal. P.H.P. 4.5.28: 124 n. 28
Gal. P.H.P. 4.6.6–17: 86 n. 71
Gal. P.H.P. 4.6.7–9: 127 n. 38
Gal. P.H.P. 4.6.19: 76 n. 39
Gal. P.H.P. 4.6.20–22: 76 n. 39
Gal. P.H.P. 4.6.27: 120 n. 21
Gal. P.H.P. 4.7.12–17: 85 n. 66
Gal. P.H.P. 4.6.7–9: 127 n. 38
[Gal.] Definitiones medicae 29, vol. 19, p. 355, 11–13 Kühn: 12 n. 13
[Gal.] Definitiones medicae 95, vol. 19, p. 371, 4–9 and 12–14 Kühn: 12 n. 10, 12 n. 12

[Gal.] Introductio seu medicus, p. 20, 21–22 Petit: 12 n. 16

Gellius
Gel. 7.2.11–12: 105 n. 42
Gel. 12.2: 232 n. 6, 460f.
Gel. 12.2.3: 138 n. 13, 461
Gel. 12.7: 34 n. 79
Gel. 17.14: 327 n. 26
Gel. 17.21–24: 194 n. 44
Gel. 19.1: 126 n. 35

Hierocles
Hierocles apud Stob. 4.84.23, vol. 4, pp. 671–673 Hense: 231 n. 5

Hippocrates/Corpus Hippocraticum
Hp. Aph. 6.28–29: 212 f. n. 3
Hp. Epid. 6.8.32: 219–221

Homerus
Hom. Il. 1.459–469: 204 n. 105
Hom. Il. 2.422–432: 204 n. 105
Hom. Il. 9.206–217: 204 n. 105
Hom. Od. 3.448–473: 204 n. 105

Horatius
Hor. Carm. 1.14: 415 n. 47
Hor. Carm. 3.30: 288
Hor. Carm. 4.2.25–32: 287
Hor. Ep. 1.15.36: 191 n. 16
Hor. Ep. 1.2.64–68: 301 n. 19, 302
Hor. Ep. 2.1.126–129: 307 n. 31
Hor. S. 1.3.80–81: 191 n. 22
Hor. S. 1.6.12–17: 242 n. 29
Hor. S. 1.6.110–115: 182

Hyginus
Hyg. Fab. 31: 195 n. 54
Hyg. Fab. 56: 195 n. 54
Hyg. Fab. 257: 195 n. 53

Isidorus
Isid. Orig. 9.4.47: 238 n. 17

Iuvenalis
Juv. 2.7–13: 399 n. 13
Juv. 6.219–223: 191 n. 22
Juv. 6.614: 195 n. 53
Juv. 8.80: 195 n. 53
Juv. 8.212–214: 192 n. 34
Juv. 8.235: 191 n. 19
Juv. 12.81–82: 416 n. 56

Lactantius
Lact. Inst. 5.16: 423 n. 74
Lact. Ira 17.13: 72 n. 27, 125 n. 32

Livius
Liv. 3.8.10: 191 n. 22
Liv. 22.12.11: 171 n. 19
Liv. 22.23: 191 n. 22
Liv. 22.33.2: 191 n. 22
Liv. 24.14.7: 191 n. 22
Liv. 30.44.13: 191 n. 22
Liv. 33.73: 195 n. 53

Lucanus
Luc. 2.380–395: 236 n. 15
Luc. 3.674–675: 172 n. 19
Luc. 9.211–212: 173

Lucilius
Lucil. Frg. 601 Marx: 179 n. 56
Lucil. Frg. 754 Marx: 386 n. 49

Lucilius Iunior
Lucil. Iun. Frg. 4 Courtney: 144 n. 36

Lucretius
Lucr. 3.11–12: 287 n. 40
Lucr. 3.935–938: 447 n. 51
Lucr. 4.478: 54f.
Lucr. 5.182: 54 n. 48
Lucr. 5.1046–1049: 54 n. 48
Lucr. 6.588–591: 172 n. 19

Macrobius
Macrob. Sat. 2.7: 327 n. 26

Marcus Aurelius
M.Ant. 1.1–4: 99 n. 16
M.Ant. 1.7: 99 n. 15
M.Ant. 1.8: 99 n. 15
M.Ant. 1.11: 99 n. 15
M.Ant. 1.14: 99 n. 16
M.Ant. 1.16–17: 99 n. 15, 99 n. 16, 99 n. 17
M.Ant. 2.1: 99 n. 15, 343 n. 3
M.Ant. 2.3: 99 n. 13
M.Ant. 2.16: 99 n. 15
M.Ant. 3.2: 99 n. 13
M.Ant. 3.5: 99 n. 19
M.Ant. 3.6: 99 n. 17
M.Ant. 3.10: 99 n. 13
M.Ant. 4.3: 99 n. 13, 99 n. 18
M.Ant. 4.6: 99 n. 13
M.Ant. 4.10: 343 n. 3

Index of Passages Cited 475

M.Ant. 4.19: 99 n. 13
M.Ant. 4.25: 99 n. 18
M.Ant. 4.32–33: 99 n. 13
M.Ant. 4.32: 99 n. 16
M.Ant. 4.48: 99 n. 13
M.Ant. 4.50: 99 n. 13
M.Ant. 5.1: 99 n. 15
M.Ant. 5.11: 99 n. 18
M.Ant. 5.23: 99 n. 13
M.Ant. 5.31: 99 n. 18
M.Ant. 5.33: 99 n. 17
M.Ant. 6.4: 99 n. 13
M.Ant. 6.13: 99 n. 17
M.Ant. 6.15: 99 n. 13
M.Ant. 6.16: 99 n. 17
M.Ant. 6.24: 99 n. 13
M.Ant. 6.30: 99 n. 14, 99 n. 15, 99 n. 16
M.Ant. 6.36: 99 n. 13
M.Ant. 6.47: 99 n. 13, 343 n. 3
M.Ant. 7.6: 99 n. 13
M.Ant. 7.19: 99 n. 13
M.Ant. 7.21: 99 n. 13
M.Ant. 7.26: 99 n. 15
M.Ant. 7.34: 99 n. 13
M.Ant. 8.3: 99 n. 13
M.Ant. 8.8–9: 99 n. 15, 99 n. 17
M.Ant. 8.15: 99 n. 15
M.Ant. 8.25: 99 n. 13
M.Ant. 8.31: 99 n. 13
M.Ant. 8.37: 99 n. 13
M.Ant. 8.44: 99 n. 13
M.Ant. 8.45: 99 n. 13
M.Ant. 9.12: 99 n. 17
M.Ant. 9.27: 99 n. 15
M.Ant. 9.29: 99 n. 13
M.Ant. 9.30: 99 n. 17
M.Ant. 9.42: 99 n. 15
M.Ant. 10.8: 99 n. 13
M.Ant. 10.9: 99 n. 15
M.Ant. 10.13: 99 n. 15
M.Ant. 10.27: 99 n. 13
M.Ant. 10.31: 99 n. 13
M.Ant. 10.33: 105 n. 43
M.Ant. 10.37: 99 n. 18
M.Ant. 11.1: 99 n. 18
M.Ant. 11.18: 99 n. 15
M.Ant. 11.19: 99 n. 13, 99 n. 18
M.Ant. 11.28: 99 n. 13
M.Ant. 12.27: 99 n. 13
M.Ant. 12.35: 99 n. 18
M.Ant. 12.36: 106 n. 45
Martial

Mart. 1.90.6–8: 216 n. 15
Mart. 1.107: 288 n. 45
Mart. 4.86.8: 191 n. 19
Mart. 7.67.13–17: 216 n. 16
Mart. 10.25.5–6: 191 n. 19
Mart. 12.57.12: 416 n. 56

Metrodorus
Metrod. Frg. 34 Körte: 433 n. 7
Metrod. Frg. 35 Körte: 447
Metrod. Frg. 49 Körte: 436 n. 17

Musonius Rufus
Muson. Diatr. 2, p. 37, 21–22 Lutz: 18 n. 37
Muson. Diatr. 2, p. 38, 1–14 Lutz: 18f., 20, 24
Muson. in Stob. 2.9.8, vol. 2, p. 183f. Wachsmuth: 13 n. 21
Muson. in Stob. 2.31.126, vol. 2, p. 244f. Wachsmuth: 13 n. 21

Nemesius
Nemesius 15, p. 202 Matthaei, 72 Morani: 283 n. 35

Olympiodorus
Olymp. in Alc. p. 37 Westerink = vol. 2, p. 54 Creuzer: 127 n. 37

Origines
Orig. Cels. 4.48, 15–24: 12 n. 10
Orig. Cels. 8.51: 111 n. 2, 115 n. 9, 117 n. 14
Orig. Princ. 2.1.3 (2): 14 n. 23

Ovidius
Ov. Am. 1.14: 213 n. 3
Ov. Am. 1.14.25: 200 n. 75
Ov. Ars 1.645–650: 195 n. 54
Ov. Ars 1.653: 195 n. 53
Ov. Fast. 1.202: 373 n. 15
Ov. Fast. 3.14: 373 n. 15
Ov. Her. 12: 82 n. 56
Ov. Ib. 437: 195 n. 53
Ov. Met. 7.20f.: 66 n. 6
Ov. Met. 8.639f.: 373 n. 15
Ov. Met. 8.655f.: 373 n. 15
Ov. Met. 8.668: 373 n. 15
Ov. Met. 9.183–84: 195 n. 54
Ov. Met. 15.871–879: 288
Ov. Pont. 3.6.41: 195 n. 54
Ov. Pont. 3.9.9–22: 302

Ov. Pont. 3.9.21–22: 303
Ov. Pont. 4.1.27–36: 303, 304 n. 24
Ov. Tr. 3.11.39: 195 n. 54
Ov. Tr. 3.11.51: 195 n. 53
Ov. Tr. 5.1.53: 195 n. 53

Panaetius
Panaet. Frg. 86 van Straaten, 125 Alesse: 283 n. 35

Persius
Pers. 1.37–43: 288 n. 45

Petronius
Petr. 55: 327 n. 26
Petr. 71.9–10: 415 n. 48
Petr. 94.8–11: 179 n. 56

Phaedrus
Phaed. 3.10: 336 n. 39

Philo
Ph. De aeternitate mundi 8: 12 n. 10
Ph. De aeternitate mundi 75: 13 n. 17
Ph. Legum allegoriae 2.22: 13 n. 17
Ph. Quod deus sit immutabilis 35: 13 n. 17
Ph. Quod deus sit immutabilis 41: 13 n. 17

Philodemus,
Phld. De pietate, PHerc 1077, col. 30, line 865–870 Obbink, p. 105 Gomperz: 437 n. 21

Pindarus
Pi. P. 1.95–98: 195 n. 53
Pi. P. 10.53–54: 286

Plato
Pl. Grg. 456b: 200 n. 75
Pl. Grg. 479a: 200 n. 75
Pl. Grg. 480c: 200 n. 75
Pl. Grg. 482a–c: 346 n. 11
Pl. Grg. 522a: 200 n. 75
Pl. Grg. 525b: 199 n. 73
Pl. Lg. 633d: 296 n. 4
Pl. Lg. 854e: 199 n. 73
Pl. Lg. 862e: 199 n. 73
Pl. Lg. 934b: 199 n. 73
Pl. Phd.: 279 n. 25
Pl. Phd. 67e: 346 n. 11
Pl. Phdr. 237d: 45
Pl. Phdr. 250d: 15 n. 25
Pl. Plt. 271e: 203 n. 101
Pl. Prt. 351b–358e: 65 n. 2, 85 n. 67
Pl. R. 4: 67f.
Pl. R. 5, 449a–457c: 217
Pl. R. 5, 455d: 217
Pl. R. 8, 565e: 196 n. 60
Pl. Smp. 207a5–212c3: 246 n. 38
Pl. Smp. 209a: 287 n. 44
Pl. Smp. 209d: 287 n. 44
Pl. Ti: 300 n. 14, 306
Pl. Ti. 29d: 298 n. 11
Pl. Ti. 90e: 218

Plautus
Pl. As. 481: 190 n. 11
Pl. Bac. 362: 191 n. 22
Pl. Mil. 372: 191 n. 22
Pl. Mil. 502: 190 n. 11
Pl. Mil. 511: 190 n. 11
Pl. Mos. 991: 194 n. 41
Pl. Poen. 832: 238 n. 17
Pl. Truc. 623: 49 n. 19

Plinius maior
Plin. Nat. 2.157: 200 n. 75
Plin. Nat. 7.200: 195 n. 53
Plin. Nat. 9.77: 118 n. 16, 192 n. 35
Plin. Nat. 9.167: 192 n. 35
Plin. Nat. 11.133: 218 n. 20
Plin. Nat. 14.49ff.: 394 n. 5
Plin. Nat. 14.89f.: 213 n. 4
Plin. Nat. 16.71: 200 n. 75
Plin. Nat. 28.82: 220 n. 25
Plin. Nat. 29.13: 200 n. 75
Plin. Nat. 33.142: 373 n. 14
Plin. Nat. 34.89: 195 n. 53

Plinius minor
Plin. Ep. 3.16.13: 248 n. 42
Plin. Ep. 4.1: 245 n. 36
Plin. Ep. 4.19: 245 n. 36
Plin. Ep. 5.14: 245 n. 36
Plin. Ep. 8.10: 245 n. 36
Plin. Ep. 8.11: 245 n. 36
Plin. Ep. 8.19: 245 n. 36
Plin. Ep. 9.36: 245 n. 36
Plin. Ep. 10.120: 245 n. 36

Plutarchus
Plu. Comm.not. 1059c: 44 n. 4
Plu. Comm.not. 1063a–d: 412 n. 43
Plu. Comm.not. 1063a: 423 n. 74

Plu. Comm.not. 1077b: 12 n. 10
Plu. Comm.not. 1084f–1085c: 44 n. 4
Plu. De puerorum educatione 12: 201 n. 83
Plu. De sollertia animalium 959d: 204 n. 111
Plu. Non posse suaviter vivi secundum Epicurum 1010e: 436 n. 17
Plu. Non posse suaviter vivi secundum Epicurum 1091b: 127 n. 39
Plu. Non posse suaviter vivi secundum Epicurum 1099d: 130 n. 48
Plu. Quomodo quis suos in virtute sentiat profectus 75c: 412 n. 43
Plu. Stoic.rep. 1041e: 17f., 44f. n. 9
Plu. Stoic.rep. 1041f: 306 n. 29
Plu. Stoic.rep. 1043d: 412 n. 43
Plu. Virt.mor.: 82
Plu. Virt.mor. 6–9: 82 n. 58
Plu. Virt.mor. 7, 446f–447a: 82f.
Plu. Virt.mor. 450c: 123 n. 24
Plu. Virt.mor. 441c–d: 83 n. 59
Plu. Virt.mor. 441c: 20 n. 42
Plu. Virt.mor. 446c: 86 n. 71
Plu. Virt.mor. 450c: 117 n. 13
Plu. Virt.mor. 451b: 13 n. 17

Polybius
Plb. Frg. 12.5: 195 n. 53

Porphyrius
Porph. Marc. 25: 442 n. 35
Porph. Marc. 27: 445

Posidonius
Posidon. Frg. 184 Edelstein and Kidd: 455 n. 74
Posidon. Frg. 186 Edelstein and Kidd: 301 n. 17
Posidon. apud Gal. P.H.P. 4.5.28: 124 n. 28

POxy 76.5077: 436 n. 17

Propertius
Prop. 2.1.43: 416 n. 56
Prop. 2.25.11: 195 n. 53
Prop. 3.9: 304 n. 24
Prop. 3.9.32: 288 n. 46

Publilius Syrus
Pub. Sent. A 14: 320, 321
Pub. Sent. A 21: 320

Pub. Sent. A 23: 320
Pub. Sent. A 25: 320
Pub. Sent. A 26: 320
Pub. Sent. A 35: 320
Pub. Sent. A 46: 320, 321
Pub. Sent. A 47: 320

Quintilianus
Quint. Decl. 17.9: 192 n. 34
Quint. Decl. 18.11.15: 191 n. 16
Quint. Decl. 19.15: 191 n. 16
Quint. Inst. 1.4–5: 34 n. 81
Quint. Inst. 2.17: 195 n. 54
Quint. Inst. 5.10.60: 238 n. 17
Quint. Inst. 5.10.73: 373 n. 13
Quint. Inst. 6.1.18: 200 n. 75
Quint. Inst. 6.1.52: 323 n. 18
Quint. Inst. 6.2.9: 306 n. 28
Quint. Inst. 8.5.1: 321
Quint. Inst. 8.5.15–19: 321 n. 8
Quint. Inst. 8.5.34: 321 n. 9, 321 n. 10
Quint. Inst. 8.6: 195 n. 53
Quint. Inst. 10.1.90: 319f.
Quint. Inst. 10.128: 345 n. 8
Quint. Inst. 10.129: 345 n. 8
[Quint.] Decl. maior 7: 194 n. 41

Scribonius Largus
Larg. ep. 2: 200 n. 75

Seneca maior
Sen. Con. 1 pr. 6: 322
Sen. Con. 1.6–7: 195 n. 51
Sen. Con. 1.22: 322 n. 15
Sen. Con. 2 pr. 5: 322 n. 15
Sen. Con. 2.1.8: 374 n. 19, 383f.
Sen. Con. 2.4.4: 169 n. 5
Sen. Con. 2.5: 195 n. 51
Sen. Con. 3.6: 195 n. 51
Sen. Con. 4 pr. 1: 324 n. 23
Sen. Con. 4.7: 195 n. 51
Sen. Con. 5.4: 192 n. 34
Sen. Con. 5.8: 195 n. 51
Sen. Con. 7 pr. 9: 322 n. 15
Sen. Con. 7.1.4: 418 n. 63
Sen. Con. 7.3.8: 327 n. 26
Sen. Con. 7.6: 195 n. 51
Sen. Con. 9.4: 195 n. 51
Sen. Suas. 2.12: 262 n. 63
Sen. Suas. 6.1: 173
Sen. Suas. 6.22: 169 n. 6
Sen. Suas. 6.23: 172 n. 21
Sen. Suas. 6.24: 169 n. 7

Sen. Suas. 7.1: 173
Sen. Suas. 7.3: 173 n. 25

Seneca minor
Sen. Ag. 44–48: 197 n. 63
Sen. Ag. 96: 334
Sen. Ag. 97: 334
Sen. Ag. 108–124: 88 n. 78
Sen. Ag. 113: 333
Sen. Ag. 202: 330
Sen. Ag. 242: 333
Sen. Ag. 271–272: 332
Sen. Ag. 589: 176
Sen. Ag. 590: 176
Sen. Ag. 609: 177 n. 46
Sen. Ag. 983–985: 312 n. 47
Sen. Ag. 988–997: 197 n. 63
Sen. Ag. 995: 332
Sen. Ag. 996: 330
Sen. Apocol.: 331
Sen. Ben. 2.9.2: 50 n. 25
Sen. Ben. 2.12.2: 196 n. 59
Sen. Ben. 2.23.1: 50 n. 25
Sen. Ben. 2.31.1: 51 n. 33
Sen. Ben. 3.4.1–2: 130 n. 48
Sen. Ben. 3.20.1: 176
Sen. Ben. 3.29.4: 56, 56 n. 58 and 59
Sen. Ben. 4.6.6: 55
Sen. Ben. 4.7: 11 n. 9
Sen. Ben. 4.7.1: 55 n. 50
Sen. Ben. 4.8.2: 300 n. 14
Sen. Ben. 4.12.4: 102 n. 35
Sen. Ben. 4.21.5: 102 n. 35
Sen. Ben. 4.21.6: 191 n. 17, 192 n. 27
Sen. Ben. 4.31.2: 196 n. 60
Sen. Ben. 4.34.4: 58 n. 65
Sen. Ben. 5.16.3: 196 n. 60
Sen. Ben. 7.1.7: 202 n. 92
Sen. Ben. 7.19.5: 195 n. 52
Sen. Ben. 7.19.7: 195 n. 52
Sen. Ben. 7.19.8: 191 n. 17, 193 n. 38, 196
Sen. Brev. vit. 2.2: 423 n. 73
Sen. Brev. vit. 3.4: 360 n. 38
Sen. Brev. vit. 4.4: 361
Sen. Brev. vit. 4.5: 196 n. 60
Sen. Brev. vit. 5.1–3: 167f., 180
Sen. Brev. vit. 5.1: 169 n. 8, 5.1: 172
Sen. Brev. vit. 5.2: 169f.
Sen. Brev. vit. 5.3: 174, 175
Sen. Brev. vit. 8.3: 360 n. 38
Sen. Brev. vit. 10.2: 101 n. 30
Sen. Brev. vit. 10.2–4: 130 n. 48

Sen. Brev. vit. 12.4: 203 n. 100
Sen. Brev. vit. 13.6: 192 n. 30, 192 n. 31, 203 n. 103
Sen. Brev. vit. 13.7: 196 n. 60
Sen. Brev. vit. 15.3: 241 n. 27
Sen. Brev. vit. 18.6: 197 n. 62
Sen. Brev. vit. 19.3: 191 n. 23
Sen. Cl.: 331
Sen. Cl. 1.1.1–2: 103
Sen. Cl. 1.1.1: 181 n. 64
Sen. Cl. 1.1.2: 180
Sen. Cl. 1.1.3: 196 n. 60
Sen. Cl. 1.1.4: 103
Sen. Cl. 1.1.8: 180
Sen. Cl. 1.2.2: 200 n. 76
Sen. Cl. 1.3.1: 202 n. 92
Sen. Cl. 1.3.2: 202
Sen. Cl. 1.3.5: 183 n. 75
Sen. Cl. 1.5.1: 197 n. 67, 200 n. 75
Sen. Cl. 1.7.3: 196 n. 60
Sen. Cl. 1.7.4: 181 n. 69
Sen. Cl. 1.8.1: 181
Sen. Cl. 1.8.2: 181f., 183
Sen. Cl. 1.10.3: 197 n. 66
Sen. Cl. 1.11.1: 196 n. 60
Sen. Cl. 1.12.2: 196 n. 60
Sen. Cl. 1.13.2: 192 n. 27, 200 n. 75, 204 n. 108
Sen. Cl. 1.15.1: 198 n. 68
Sen. Cl. 1.15.7: 192 n. 32, 192 n. 34
Sen. Cl. 1.16.3: 197 n. 66, 198 n. 68
Sen. Cl. 1.17.2: 200 n. 75
Sen. Cl. 1.18.1: 202 n. 94
Sen. Cl. 1.18.2: 192 n. 30, 192 n. 35, 201 n. 85, 203 n. 103
Sen. Cl. 1.23.1: 191 n. 23, 192 n. 32, 195 n. 49, 196 n. 56, 197 n. 61, 198 n. 71
Sen. Cl. 1.24.1: 198 n. 70
Sen. Cl. 1.25.1: 196 n. 55, 202 n. 96
Sen. Cl. 1.25.2: 203 n. 97
Sen. Cl. 1.26.1: 191 n. 23
Sen. Cl. 2.14.1: 193 n. 37
Sen. Cl. 2.2.2: 198 n. 68
Sen. Cl. 2.3.1: 197 n. 65
Sen. Cl. 2.4.1: 191 n. 17, 195 n. 54, 201 n. 81
Sen. Cl. 2.4.3: 195 n. 52
Sen. Cl. 2.5.3: 202 n. 91
Sen. Cl. 2.6.2: 192 n. 30
Sen. Cl. 2.7.4: 51 n. 33
Sen. Const. 1.1: 214 n. 8
Sen. Const. 2.1: 307 n. 33

Sen. Const. 2.2: 171, 177
Sen. Const. 5.3: 123
Sen. Const. 7.1: 306 n. 29, 307, 307 n. 33
Sen. Const. 7.3–8: 124 n. 30
Sen. Const. 10.3–4: 126 n. 35
Sen. Const. 15.4: 441, 441 n. 34
Sen. Const. 19.2: 174
Sen. De ira: 67, 71f., 331
Sen. De ira 1.1.1: 72, 125 n. 33, 203 n. 99
Sen. De ira 1.1.2: 72, 74 n. 33, 76
Sen. De ira 1.1.3–7: 71 n. 22
Sen. De ira 1.2.2–3: 203 n. 99
Sen. De ira 1.2.2: 191 n. 23
Sen. De ira 1.2.3b: 72 n. 27, 125 n. 32
Sen. De ira 1.3.4: 72
Sen. De ira 1.5.2: 72 n. 25, 72 n. 26
Sen. De ira 1.6.1: 198f., 202 n. 90
Sen. De ira 1.6.2–4: 124 n. 29
Sen. De ira 1.6.3: 193 n. 39
Sen. De ira 1.6.4: 199 n. 73
Sen. De ira 1.7: 76
Sen. De ira 1.7.3–4: 76
Sen. De ira 1.7.4: 116 n. 11
Sen. De ira 1.8.4–7: 82
Sen. De ira 1.9.2–3: 116
Sen. De ira 1.9.2: 119 n. 19
Sen. De ira 1.10.1: 112 n. 5, 113
Sen. De ira 1.10.2: 77
Sen. De ira 1.15.2: 200 n. 78
Sen. De ira 1.16.2–4: 124 n. 29
Sen. De ira 1.16.4: 200 n. 77
Sen. De ira 1.16.5: 190 n. 13, 192 n. 32, 200 n. 78, 201 n. 81
Sen. De ira 1.17.4–6: 90
Sen. De ira 1.17.7: 121
Sen. De ira 1.18.1–2: 74 n. 33
Sen. De ira 1.18.1: 119 n. 18
Sen. De ira 1.18.2: 121
Sen. De ira 1.18.6: 78 n. 46
Sen. De ira 1.19.1: 121 n. 23
Sen. De ira 1.19.7: 124 n. 29
Sen. De ira 1.20.1–5: 90 n. 80
Sen. De ira 1.20.1: 354 n. 24
Sen. De ira 2.1–4: 72, 74 n. 32
Sen. De ira 2.1.3: 119 n. 20, 123 n. 26
Sen. De ira 2.1.4: 72 n. 28, 125 n. 32
Sen. De ira 2.2: 75 n. 36, 119 n. 20
Sen. De ira 2.2.2: 119 n. 20, 120 n. 20, 123 n. 26, 126 n. 34
Sen. De ira 2.3: 75 n. 36
Sen. De ira 2.3.1: 126 n. 34
Sen. De ira 2.3.2: 126 n. 36
Sen. De ira 2.3.4: 76 n. 4, 1119 n. 19, 120 n. 22
Sen. De ira 2.3.5: 72 n. 28, 75 n. 37, 119 n. 20, 123 n. 26, 126 n. 34
Sen. De ira 2.4: 112, 122
Sen. De ira 2.4.1: 74f., 116 n. 12, 119f.
Sen. De ira 2.4.2: 120 n. 20, 126 n. 34
Sen. De ira 2.5: 91, 119 n. 19
Sen. De ira 2.5.1: 195 n. 52
Sen. De ira 2.5.4: 196 n. 60
Sen. De ira 2.10.7: 343 n. 3
Sen. De ira 2.11.4: 198 n. 68
Sen. De ira 2.12.5: 279 n. 23
Sen. De ira 2.18.2: 296
Sen. De ira 2.23.1: 196 n. 55
Sen. De ira 2.27.3: 199 n. 72
Sen. De ira 2.31: 88 n. 76
Sen. De ira 2.31.6: 202 n. 96, 203 n. 97, 204 n. 106
Sen. De ira 2.31.7: 197 n. 67, 202 n. 92, 202 n. 94
Sen. De ira 2.35: 76
Sen. De ira 2.35.4: 126
Sen. De ira 2.36.5–6: 72 n. 25
Sen. De ira 2.36.5: 71 n. 24
Sen. De ira 2.37.3: 58 n. 65
Sen. De ira 3.1.3: 72
Sen. De ira 3.2.6: 119 n. 18, 125
Sen. De ira 3.3.2: 205 n. 112
Sen. De ira 3.3.3: 72 n. 25, 72 n. 26
Sen. De ira 3.3.6: 191 n. 15, 191 n. 17, 191 n. 18, 191 n. 23, 192 n. 27, 192 n. 28, 192 n. 30, 203 n. 103
Sen. De ira 3.5.5: 72 n. 26
Sen. De ira 3.13.1: 74 n. 33
Sen. De ira 3.15.3: 179, 179 n. 55
Sen. De ira 3.15.4: 178
Sen. De ira 3.17.2: 196 n. 55, 197 n. 61
Sen. De ira 3.17.3: 192 n. 36, 196 n. 55, 197 n. 61, 203 n. 103
Sen. De ira 3.17.4: 192 n. 36, 204 n. 107
Sen. De ira 3.18.1: 196 n. 56, 197 n. 61, 197 n. 62
Sen. De ira 3.18.3: 194, 199 n. 74
Sen. De ira 3.19.1–4: 196 n. 56
Sen. De ira 3.19.1: 190 n. 13, 191 n. 17, 192 n. 27, 192 n. 28, 195 n. 46, 197 n. 62, 197 n. 64
Sen. De ira 3.19.2: 191 n. 17, 194f.

Sen. De ira 3.20.1: 196 n. 55, 197 n. 61, 203 n. 103
Sen. De ira 3.28.3: 198 n. 69, 203 n. 103
Sen. De ira 3.29.2: 121 n. 23
Sen. De ira 3.32.2: 192 n. 36
Sen. De Ira 3.36: 405
Sen. De ira 3.36.1–3: 100–102, 263 n. 64
Sen. De ira 3.36.4–3.38.1: 101 n. 28
Sen. De ira 3.39.2: 257 n. 53
Sen. De ira 3.39.4: 112 n. 5, 113, 118, 128
Sen. De ira 3.40.2–4: 118 n. 16
Sen. De ira 3.40.2: 192 n. 35
Sen. De ira 3.40.4: 192 n. 35
Sen. De ira 3.40.5: 112 n. 5, 118 n. 16
Sen. De ira 3.42.2–4: 146 n. 42
Sen. De ira 3.43.5: 91 n. 86
Sen. De otio 5.5–6: 152 n. 73
Sen. De otio: 102 n. 32
Sen. Ep.: 135
Sen. Ep. 1–18: 138, 141, 160 n. 101
Sen. Ep. 1–12: 232f.
Sen. Ep. 1: 154
Sen. Ep. 1.1: 153
Sen. Ep. 1.2: 153
Sen. Ep. 1.4: 408
Sen. Ep. 2: 439, 439 n. 29
Sen. Ep. 2.1–4: 273, 273 n. 9
Sen. Ep. 2.1: 274, 411, 441 n. 32
Sen. Ep. 2.2–4: 273
Sen. Ep. 2.2: 281f.
Sen. Ep. 2.3: 274 n. 10
Sen. Ep. 2.4–5: 459
Sen. Ep. 2.4: 274, 274 n. 10, 274 n. 11, 343 n. 3, 434
Sen. Ep. 2.5: 431 n. 1, 434, 452
Sen. Ep. 3.2: 280
Sen. Ep. 3.4: 102 n. 31
Sen. Ep. 3.5–6: 436 n. 17
Sen. Ep. 4: 230 n. 3
Sen. Ep. 4.1: 441 n. 32, 452 n. 67
Sen. Ep. 4.2: 240 n. 23
Sen. Ep. 4.3: 146 n. 41, 437 n. 19
Sen. Ep. 4.4: 191 n. 15
Sen. Ep. 4.5: 343 n. 3
Sen. Ep. 4.10–11: 415, 438f.
Sen. Ep. 4.10: 439, 440, 442, 446 n. 45
Sen. Ep. 5: 230 n. 3
Sen. Ep. 5.1: 401, 408, 417, 451
Sen. Ep. 5.2–3: 401
Sen. Ep. 5.4: 203 n. 100, 442

Sen. Ep. 5.5–6: 373 n. 13
Sen. Ep. 5.6: 382 n. 35
Sen. Ep. 6.1. 407
Sen. Ep. 6.2–4: 442
Sen. Ep. 6.4: 442
Sen. Ep. 6.5: 273 n. 9, 409 n. 36, 459
Sen. Ep. 7: 154, 233 n. 10
Sen. Ep. 7.1: 441 n. 32
Sen. Ep. 7.2: 149 n. 62, 149 n. 63
Sen. Ep. 7.3–5: 192 n. 30
Sen. Ep. 7.3: 204 n. 110
Sen. Ep. 7.4: 192 n. 31, 200 n. 75, 203 n. 103, 204 n. 111, 191 n. 16, 204 n. 109
Sen. Ep. 7.6: 281 n. 32
Sen. Ep. 7.8: 140: 451 n. 65
Sen. Ep. 7.9: 282 n. 33, 287 n. 41
Sen. Ep. 7.11: 434 n. 12, 435
Sen. Ep. 8: 230 n. 3, 279
Sen. Ep. 8.1–6: 442
Sen. Ep. 8.1: 102 n. 32, 140
Sen. Ep. 8.2–3: 153 n. 76
Sen. Ep. 8.3: 436 n. 17
Sen. Ep. 8.5: 154 n. 83
Sen. Ep. 8.7: 434
Sen. Ep. 8.8: 328 n. 29, 441 n. 33, 460 n. 87
Sen. Ep. 9: 230 n. 3, 233, 442
Sen. Ep. 9.1: 434 n. 12, 443
Sen. Ep. 9.2–5: 354 n. 22
Sen. Ep. 9.2: 356
Sen. Ep. 9.5–12: 158 n. 90
Sen. Ep. 9.5: 304
Sen. Ep. 9.6–7: 452
Sen. Ep. 9.7: 433 n. 7
Sen. Ep. 9.8–11: 443
Sen. Ep. 9.8: 236, 443
Sen. Ep. 9.12: 443
Sen. Ep. 9.15: 233
Sen. Ep. 9.17: 235, 442
Sen. Ep. 9.18–19: 234
Sen. Ep. 9.20: 441
Sen. Ep. 9.21–22: 328 n. 29
Sen. Ep. 9.21: 234
Sen. Ep. 11.1: 281 n. 32
Sen. Ep. 11.6: 441 n. 32
Sen. Ep. 11.9: 441 n. 32
Sen. Ep. 12: 154, 230 n. 3, 233 n. 10
Sen. Ep. 12.4–6: 157 n. 89
Sen. Ep. 12.4–5: 452
Sen. Ep. 12.7: 441
Sen. Ep. 12.8–9: 450 n. 61
Sen. Ep. 12.8: 436 n. 17

Sen. Ep. 12.10: 440, 441
Sen. Ep. 12.11: 441 n. 33
Sen. Ep. 13: 230 n. 3
Sen. Ep. 13.12: 112f., 117
Sen. Ep. 13.14: 177
Sen. Ep. 13.16: 449
Sen. Ep. 13.17: 434
Sen. Ep. 14: 140
Sen. Ep. 14.1: 55 n. 51
Sen. Ep. 14.4: 191 n. 17, 192 n. 30, 203 n. 103
Sen. Ep. 14.5: 191 n. 19, 191 n. 23, 191 n. 25, 192 n. 27
Sen. Ep. 14.8: 140, 140 n. 26, 172 n. 20
Sen. Ep. 14.17: 434 n. 9
Sen. Ep. 14.18: 441 n. 33
Sen. Ep. 15.1: 280
Sen. Ep. 15.6: 277 n. 19, 279
Sen. Ep. 15.9: 447 n. 52
Sen. Ep. 15.11: 446f.
Sen. Ep. 16–17: 158 n. 91
Sen. Ep. 16: 230 n. 3, 279
Sen. Ep. 16.1: 279 n. 23, 343 n. 3, 402, 450
Sen. Ep. 16.2–3: 307
Sen. Ep. 16.2: 101 n. 30, 411
Sen. Ep. 16.3: 411
Sen. Ep. 16.7: 444
Sen. Ep. 16.8: 394, 445
Sen. Ep. 16.9: 412, 445f.
Sen. Ep. 17: 230 n. 3
Sen. Ep. 17.1–3: 395 n. 8
Sen. Ep. 17.5: 143, 280
Sen. Ep. 17.9: 157 n. 88
Sen. Ep. 17.10: 413 n. 45
Sen. Ep. 18: 437f.
Sen. Ep. 18.1–4: 437
Sen. Ep. 18.1: 138
Sen. Ep. 18.2: 437, 437 n. 21
Sen. Ep. 18.5–6: 416 n. 52
Sen. Ep. 18.5: 257
Sen. Ep. 18.9–10: 452
Sen. Ep. 18.9: 434 n. 13, 435, 437
Sen. Ep. 18.10–13: 437
Sen. Ep. 18.10: 438, 438 n. 25
Sen. Ep. 18.12: 437
Sen. Ep. 18.14–15: 437
Sen. Ep. 19–23: 138
Sen. Ep. 19–22: 142
Sen. Ep. 19.3: 50 n. 25, 282 n. 33, 287 n. 41
Sen. Ep. 19.9: 287 n. 42

Sen. Ep. 20: 451
Sen. Ep. 20.2: 412
Sen. Ep. 20.3: 380 n. 30, 401
Sen. Ep. 20.4–6: 450
Sen. Ep. 20.5: 412, 451
Sen. Ep. 20.7: 280
Sen. Ep. 20.10: 395
Sen. Ep. 21: 279
Sen. Ep. 21.2: 279
Sen. Ep. 21.3: 434 n. 12, 434 n. 13
Sen. Ep. 21.4: 435 n. 15
Sen. Ep. 21.5: 282 n. 33, 288, 304f.
Sen. Ep. 21.6: 282 n. 33, 287, 289
Sen. Ep. 21.7: 434 n. 13
Sen. Ep. 21.8–11: 452
Sen. Ep. 21.8: 441
Sen. Ep. 21.9: 351 n. 17, 441 n. 33
Sen. Ep. 21.11: 438 n. 26
Sen. Ep. 22.5: 434 n. 13
Sen. Ep. 22.14: 449
Sen. Ep. 22.15: 449
Sen. Ep. 22.17: 447 n. 52, 448 n. 58
Sen. Ep. 23: 452
Sen. Ep. 23.1: 138, 138 n. 13, 452
Sen. Ep. 23.3: 452
Sen. Ep. 23.4–6: 280
Sen. Ep. 23.6: 154 n. 83, 275, 452
Sen. Ep. 23.7–8: 450
Sen. Ep. 23.7: 102 n. 33, 451, 452
Sen. Ep. 23.9: 449
Sen. Ep. 23.10: 450
Sen. Ep. 24–67: 138
Sen. Ep. 24–35: 273 n. 9
Sen. Ep. 24: 258
Sen. Ep. 24.1: 58 n. 65
Sen. Ep. 24.3: 281 n. 32
Sen. Ep. 24.6–8: 222
Sen. Ep. 24.9: 282 n. 33
Sen. Ep. 24.11–14: 146 n. 41
Sen. Ep. 24.12: 102 n. 34
Sen. Ep. 24.13: 191 n. 17
Sen. Ep. 24.14: 190 n. 13, 192 n. 27, 437, 437 n. 19
Sen. Ep. 25.1: 296
Sen. Ep. 25.4: 438 n. 26
Sen. Ep. 26.1–7: 154 n. 79
Sen. Ep. 26.5–6: 106 n. 46
Sen. Ep. 26.6: 279
Sen. Ep. 26.8–10: 146 n. 41
Sen. Ep. 27.1: 153 n. 76, 154
Sen. Ep. 27.3: 452
Sen. Ep. 27.5: 281 n. 32
Sen. Ep. 28.1–4: 260 n. 58

Sen. Ep. 28.9: 422
Sen. Ep. 28.10: 100 n. 25, 101 n. 30
Sen. Ep. 29: 450
Sen. Ep. 29.4: 281 n. 32
Sen. Ep. 29.9: 296 n. 7, 441 n. 32
Sen. Ep. 29.10: 450 n. 63
Sen. Ep. 29.12: 106 n. 46
Sen. Ep. 30: 257f., 450
Sen. Ep. 30.2: 157 n. 89
Sen. Ep. 30.3: 257
Sen. Ep. 30.5–11: 146 n. 41
Sen. Ep. 30.5: 257
Sen. Ep. 30.8: 419 n. 68
Sen. Ep. 30.14: 246 n. 18
Sen. Ep. 31: 236, 239, 241, 248, 451
Sen. Ep. 31.1: 451 n. 65
Sen. Ep. 31.2: 237, 238
Sen. Ep. 31.5: 237
Sen. Ep. 31.6: 237, 301 n. 16, 451
Sen. Ep. 31.8: 451
Sen. Ep. 31.9: 13 n. 21, 140, 140 n. 22, 237
Sen. Ep. 31.10: 50 n. 25, 238
Sen. Ep. 31.11: 238
Sen. Ep. 32: 236, 239, 242
Sen. Ep. 32.2: 149 n. 63, 154 n. 78, 239 n. 18, 411
Sen. Ep. 32.4: 239
Sen. Ep. 32.5: 411, 450 n. 61, 451
Sen. Ep. 33: 236, 239f., 450
Sen. Ep. 33.1: 450 n. 63
Sen. Ep. 33.2: 441 n. 33
Sen. Ep. 33.5–7: 336f.
Sen. Ep. 33.5: 282, 287, 311 n. 42
Sen. Ep. 33.6: 337
Sen. Ep. 33.10: 239 n. 20
Sen. Ep. 34: 301 n. 19
Sen. Ep. 34.1–2: 301f.
Sen. Ep. 34.1: 281 n. 32
Sen. Ep. 35.1: 154 n. 82, 158 n. 90
Sen. Ep. 36.3: 280
Sen. Ep. 36.8: 146 n. 41
Sen. Ep. 36.12: 451
Sen. Ep. 37.4: 451
Sen. Ep. 38.2: 56, 56 n. 60
Sen. Ep. 39: 459
Sen. Ep. 39.2: 281 n. 32
Sen. Ep. 40.2: 441 n. 32
Sen. Ep. 40.7: 105 n. 43
Sen. Ep. 40.14: 279
Sen. Ep. 41: 451, 455
Sen. Ep. 42.1: 402
Sen. Ep. 43.4–5: 104

Sen. Ep. 44: 241, 263
Sen. Ep. 44.1: 154 n. 82, 241, 242
Sen. Ep. 44.2: 241 n. 26
Sen. Ep. 44.3: 241
Sen. Ep. 44.4: 241
Sen. Ep. 44.5: 242
Sen. Ep. 44.6: 243 n. 30
Sen. Ep. 45.1–2: 273 n. 9
Sen. Ep. 45.3–5: 153 n. 76
Sen. Ep. 45.5: 148, 174
Sen. Ep. 45.9: 440 n. 31
Sen. Ep. 46.1: 287 n. 43, 434, 435
Sen. Ep. 46.2: 282 n. 33, 287 n. 41
Sen. Ep. 47.4: 201 n. 86
Sen. Ep. 47.5: 201, 202
Sen. Ep. 47.19: 201 n. 88
Sen. Ep. 48.2: 433 n. 39
Sen. Ep. 48.7: 386 n. 49
Sen. Ep. 48.10: 453 n. 69
Sen. Ep. 49.1: 155
Sen. Ep. 49.4: 146 n. 44
Sen. Ep. 49.5–6: 424 n. 75
Sen. Ep. 49.11: 14 n. 23, 423 n. 74
Sen. Ep. 50: 243
Sen. Ep. 50.1: 451 n. 65
Sen. Ep. 50.2: 243, 244 n. 33, 256
Sen. Ep. 50.5–6: 299f.
Sen. Ep. 50.8: 452 n. 67
Sen. Ep. 50.9: 243
Sen. Ep. 51: 155
Sen. Ep. 51.6: 281 n. 32
Sen. Ep. 51.9: 174 n. 34
Sen. Ep. 51.11: 281 n. 32
Sen. Ep. 51.13: 376 n. 23
Sen. Ep. 52.1–2: 449
Sen. Ep. 52.3: 153 n. 76, 281 n. 32
Sen. Ep. 52.5: 307, 307 n. 32
Sen. Ep. 52.6: 281 n. 32
Sen. Ep. 53.1–5: 154 n. 81, 260 n. 58
Sen. Ep. 53.1–4: 436 n. 17
Sen. Ep. 53.11: 301 n. 16
Sen. Ep. 54: 230 n. 3
Sen. Ep. 54.1–3: 154 n. 80
Sen. Ep. 54.7: 172 n. 22
Sen. Ep. 55.1–2: 154 n. 81
Sen. Ep. 55.3–4: 170
Sen. Ep. 55.3: 170 n. 15
Sen. Ep. 55.4: 170 n. 14, 170 n. 15
Sen. Ep. 55.7: 451
Sen. Ep. 55.10: 279
Sen. Ep. 56: 279
Sen. Ep. 56.1: 150, 203 n. 100, 279
Sen. Ep. 56.2: 203 n. 100

Sen. Ep. 56.3: 150
Sen. Ep. 56.5–6: 150
Sen. Ep. 56.6: 441 n. 32, 441 n. 32
Sen. Ep. 56.12: 281 n. 32
Sen. Ep. 56.14: 441 n. 32
Sen. Ep. 57.1–3: 154 n. 81
Sen. Ep. 57.3: 153 n. 76
Sen. Ep. 58: 451
Sen. Ep. 58.6: 57
Sen. Ep. 58.19–21: 298
Sen. Ep. 58.21: 58f.
Sen. Ep. 58.26: 451 n. 65
Sen. Ep. 58.28–29: 451
Sen. Ep. 58.33–36: 157 n. 88
Sen. Ep. 59.2: 453 n. 68, 453 n. 69
Sen. Ep. 59.15: 280, 280 n. 27, 453
Sen. Ep. 59.16: 452 n. 70
Sen. Ep. 61: 451
Sen. Ep. 61.1: 154 n. 80
Sen. Ep. 61.3: 441 n. 32
Sen. Ep. 62: 279
Sen. Ep. 62.1: 280 n. 27
Sen. Ep. 63: 258
Sen. Ep. 63.1: 258 n. 55
Sen. Ep. 63.5–7: 433 n. 7
Sen. Ep. 64.2: 100 n. 26, 262 n. 63, 383 n. 41
Sen. Ep. 65: 152, 298, 300, 451
Sen. Ep. 65.1: 154 n. 80
Sen. Ep. 65.2–3: 298f., 298 n. 12
Sen. Ep. 65.4–10: 298
Sen. Ep. 65.4–5: 300
Sen. Ep. 65.7: 300 n. 13
Sen. Ep. 65.9: 300, 301 n. 15
Sen. Ep. 65.10: 298 n. 11
Sen. Ep. 65.12: 298 n. 12
Sen. Ep. 65.15: 148
Sen. Ep. 65.16–22: 152, 154 n. 83, 158 n. 92
Sen. Ep. 65.16: 148, 152
Sen. Ep. 65.18–22: 451
Sen. Ep. 65.23: 152 n. 73
Sen. Ep. 66: 158 n. 91, 246, 451, 453, 455, 458
Sen. Ep. 66.1: 281 n. 32
Sen. Ep. 66.5: 453 n. 71
Sen. Ep. 66.12: 13 n. 19, 453 n. 71
Sen. Ep. 66.14: 453 n. 71
Sen. Ep. 66.15: 453 n. 71
Sen. Ep. 66.18: 191 n. 17, 192 n. 27, 193 n. 38, 195 n. 52, 197 n. 61
Sen. Ep. 66.19–20: 123f. n. 27
Sen. Ep. 66.26: 246

Sen. Ep. 66.27: 246
Sen. Ep. 66.29: 453 n. 71, 454
Sen. Ep. 66.45–48: 454
Sen. Ep. 66.47: 434 n. 13
Sen. Ep. 67: 394, 451
Sen. Ep. 67.1: 138, 138 n. 13
Sen. Ep. 67.2: 154 n. 80, 155 n. 85, 156 n. 86
Sen. Ep. 67.3: 191 n. 17, 192 n. 27, 222
Sen. Ep. 67.6: 222 n. 31
Sen. Ep. 67.7: 222
Sen. Ep. 67.15: 433 n. 7, 454
Sen. Ep. 68–86: 138
Sen. Ep. 68: 141 n. 27
Sen. Ep. 68.8–9: 153 n. 76
Sen. Ep. 68.10: 384 n. 42, 433 n. 39
Sen. Ep. 68.13: 157 n. 89
Sen. Ep. 69.6: 146 n. 41
Sen. Ep. 70.1–6: 260 n. 58
Sen. Ep. 70.1–2: 154 n. 79
Sen. Ep. 70.6: 192 n. 36, 196 n. 55, 203 n. 103
Sen. Ep. 70: 173, 247, 249, 258
Sen. Ep. 70.3: 247
Sen. Ep. 70.4: 247 n. 41
Sen. Ep. 70.10: 248
Sen. Ep. 70.12: 179 n. 56
Sen. Ep. 70.15: 223
Sen. Ep. 70.16: 179 n. 57, 223
Sen. Ep. 70.17: 146 n. 41
Sen. Ep. 70.24: 281 n. 32
Sen. Ep. 71: 451
Sen. Ep. 71.1: 154 n. 82
Sen. Ep. 71.4–5: 412 n. 42
Sen. Ep. 71.4: 395 n. 7
Sen. Ep. 71.7: 417 n. 61
Sen. Ep. 71.12: 297 n. 8
Sen. Ep. 71.19: 37 n. 88
Sen. Ep. 71.21: 192 n. 27
Sen. Ep. 71.23: 373 n. 13
Sen. Ep. 71.25: 281 n. 32
Sen. Ep. 71.29–31: 421 n. 70
Sen. Ep. 71.31: 281 n. 32
Sen. Ep. 72: 279
Sen. Ep. 72.2: 279
Sen. Ep. 72.8: 433 n. 7
Sen. Ep. 73.5: 415
Sen. Ep. 73.15: 383 n. 41
Sen. Ep. 74: 451
Sen. Ep. 74.33: 58 n. 65
Sen. Ep. 75.1–2: 155 n. 85, 156 n. 86
Sen. Ep. 75.3: 282

Sen. Ep. 75.8–15: 402
Sen. Ep. 75.10–12: 354 n. 24
Sen. Ep. 75.11: 355 n. 25
Sen. Ep. 75.12: 355 n. 26
Sen. Ep. 75.15: 279 n. 23
Sen. Ep. 75.18: 175, 359 n. 34
Sen. Ep. 76: 451
Sen. Ep. 76.1–5: 154 n. 79
Sen. Ep. 76.4: 279 n. 24
Sen. Ep. 76.9: 402
Sen. Ep. 76.10: 158 n. 91
Sen. Ep. 76.15–16: 20 n. 42
Sen. Ep. 76.31: 307
Sen. Ep. 77: 258
Sen. Ep. 78: 249
Sen. Ep. 78.1–2: 249, 256
Sen. Ep. 78.1: 249
Sen. Ep. 78.4: 158 n. 90
Sen. Ep. 78.7: 437 n. 19
Sen. Ep. 78.14: 192 n. 27
Sen. Ep. 78.18: 129 n. 45
Sen. Ep. 78.19: 191 n. 16, 191 n. 17, 192 n. 27
Sen. Ep. 79.1: 145, 145 n. 37
Sen. Ep. 79.2: 145
Sen. Ep. 79.4: 145
Sen. Ep. 79.7: 282 n. 33, 287
Sen. Ep. 79.10–12: 145
Sen. Ep. 79.11: 451 n. 65
Sen. Ep. 79.13–18: 158 n. 91
Sen. Ep. 79.14: 50 n. 25
Sen. Ep. 79.15–16: 434 n. 12
Sen. Ep. 80.2: 150
Sen. Ep. 80.4–5: 359 n. 34
Sen. Ep. 81.11: 413 n. 45
Sen. Ep. 81.12: 158 n. 90
Sen. Ep. 81.21: 100 n. 22
Sen. Ep. 81.22–23: 433 n. 7
Sen. Ep. 82: 451
Sen. Ep. 82.8: 343 n. 3
Sen. Ep. 82.15: 55 n. 51
Sen. Ep. 82.16: 282 n. 33, 287
Sen. Ep. 82.18: 454
Sen. Ep. 83.1–2: 406
Sen. Ep. 83.1: 273
Sen. Ep. 83.2: 100 n. 25, 101 n. 29
Sen. Ep. 83.3: 271
Sen. Ep. 83.7: 150
Sen. Ep. 83.25: 196 n. 60
Sen. Ep. 84: 269–292, 308, 439 n. 29
Sen. Ep. 84.1–2: 278
Sen. Ep. 84.1: 154 n. 81, 277f., 280, 281 n. 28

Sen. Ep. 84.3–8: 290
Sen. Ep. 84.4: 274 n. 10
Sen. Ep. 84.5–7: 285, 289
Sen. Ep. 84.5: 273, 274 n. 10, 281 n. 29, 385 n. 37
Sen. Ep. 84.6: 210, 281 n. 28
Sen. Ep. 84.7: 274, 274 n. 10, 281 n. 30, 285 n. 36
Sen. Ep. 84.8: 271, 274 n. 10, 281 n. 31, 285, 292, 308f., 439
Sen. Ep. 84.9–10: 289
Sen. Ep. 84.9: 274 n. 10, 290
Sen. Ep. 84.10: 274 n. 10, 308
Sen. Ep. 84.11–13: 276
Sen. Ep. 84.11: 272, 290
Sen. Ep. 84.13: 272, 290
Sen. Ep. 85: 451
Sen. Ep. 85.8: 116
Sen. Ep. 85.10: 354 n. 24
Sen. Ep. 85.18: 454 456
Sen. Ep. 85.26: 191 n. 17
Sen. Ep. 85.27: 190 n. 13
Sen. Ep. 85.31: 172 n. 20
Sen. Ep. 85.40: 303f.
Sen. Ep. 85.41: 314 n. 54
Sen. Ep. 86.10: 203 n. 100
Sen. Ep. 86.11: 203 n. 100
Sen. Ep. 86.16: 138
Sen. Ep. 87–91: 138
Sen. Ep. 87: 405 n. 27, 413–425, 451
Sen. Ep. 87.1: 413, 418 n. 63, 422
Sen. Ep. 87.2: 415, 416, 417 n. 60
Sen. Ep. 87.3: 416
Sen. Ep. 87.4: 138, 417
Sen. Ep. 87.5: 380 n. 30, 418 n. 63, 419, 422
Sen. Ep. 87.6: 420
Sen. Ep. 87.7: 420, 424
Sen. Ep. 87.8: 451 n. 65
Sen. Ep. 87.9: 419 n. 65, 419 n. 66
Sen. Ep. 87.10: 419 n. 67, 421
Sen. Ep. 87.11: 420, 421
Sen. Ep. 88–124: 159 n. 99
Sen. Ep. 88: 280 n. 27
Sen. Ep. 88.1: 154 n. 82
Sen. Ep. 88.2: 280
Sen. Ep. 88.21–23: 280 n. 27
Sen. Ep. 88.29: 191 n. 17
Sen. Ep. 88.35–38: 273 n. 9
Sen. Ep. 89.5: 279 n. 23
Sen. Ep. 89.9: 441 n. 32
Sen. Ep. 89.18: 148
Sen. Ep. 90.1: 13 n. 21

Sen. Ep. 90.13: 281 n. 32
Sen. Ep. 90.19: 150
Sen. Ep. 90.20: 51 n. 33
Sen. Ep. 90.35: 454 n. 72
Sen. Ep. 90.42–43: 312 n. 45
Sen. Ep. 90.44–6: 35 n. 84
Sen. Ep. 90.44: 13 n. 20
Sen. Ep. 90.46: 31 n. 72, 34, 37 n. 88, 37f. n. 90, 297
Sen. Ep. 91: 138, 146f.
Sen. Ep. 91.1: 146
Sen. Ep. 91.2: 146
Sen. Ep. 91.8: 58 n. 65
Sen. Ep. 91.12: 146
Sen. Ep. 91.13: 146 n. 48
Sen. Ep. 92–122: 138
Sen. Ep. 92: 451, 454–456, 458
Sen. Ep. 92.1–2: 455
Sen. Ep. 92.1: 456
Sen. Ep. 92.3: 355 n. 27
Sen. Ep. 92.5: 456
Sen. Ep. 92.6: 456
Sen. Ep. 92.7: 456
Sen. Ep. 92.8: 455, 456
Sen. Ep. 92.9: 456
Sen. Ep. 92.10: 455 n. 74, 456
Sen. Ep. 92.25: 434 n. 13
Sen. Ep. 92.27: 13 n. 19
Sen. Ep. 92.30: 456 n. 75
Sen. Ep. 92.35: 282 n. 33, 287 n. 42
Sen. Ep. 93.3: 170, 170 n. 14
Sen. Ep. 93.8: 451 n. 65
Sen. Ep. 94: 32f., 40, 251, 254, 255, 263, 337, 379 n. 29
Sen. Ep. 94.1: 252, 441 n. 32
Sen. Ep. 94.3: 252
Sen. Ep. 94.7: 246 n. 18, 437 n. 19
Sen. Ep. 94.15: 252
Sen. Ep. 94.17: 354 n. 24
Sen. Ep. 94.25–26: 103 n. 37
Sen. Ep. 94.25: 252, 435 n. 15
Sen. Ep. 94.26: 253
Sen. Ep. 94.28–29: 328 n. 29
Sen. Ep. 94.29: 15 n. 24, 33, 56
Sen. Ep. 94.30: 15 n. 27, 281 n. 32
Sen. Ep. 94.31: 33
Sen. Ep. 94.33: 441 n. 32
Sen. Ep. 94.42: 33
Sen. Ep. 94.43: 33, 324, 327 n. 27, 328 n. 29
Sen. Ep. 94.45: 34 n. 82
Sen. Ep. 94.46–47: 343 n. 3
Sen. Ep. 94.49: 441 n. 32

Sen. Ep. 94.50: 281 n. 32
Sen. Ep. 94.52: 253 n. 50
Sen. Ep. 94.53–54: 149 n. 63, 154 n. 78
Sen. Ep. 94.54: 254
Sen. Ep. 94.56: 254
Sen. Ep. 94.58: 183 n. 79
Sen. Ep. 94.60: 441 n. 32
Sen. Ep. 95: 40, 251, 254, 296, 337, 369, 379 n. 29
Sen. Ep. 95.3: 202, 254 n. 51, 379 n. 29
Sen. Ep. 95.5: 296 n. 7, 441 n. 32
Sen. Ep. 95.7: 379
Sen. Ep. 95.8–9: 103 n. 37
Sen. Ep. 95.14–15: 210
Sen. Ep. 95.15–23: 209–221, 223f.
Sen. Ep. 95.15–18: 211
Sen. Ep. 95.17: 210f.
Sen. Ep. 95.18: 200 n. 75, 211
Sen. Ep. 95.19: 211
Sen. Ep. 95.20–21: 212, 215
Sen. Ep. 95.20: 212, 214
Sen. Ep. 95.23: 211, 280 n. 27
Sen. Ep. 95.29–35: 376
Sen. Ep. 95.30: 379
Sen. Ep. 95.32–35: 378
Sen. Ep. 95.32: 373 n. 13, 378
Sen. Ep. 95.33: 199 n. 74
Sen. Ep. 95.34: 378
Sen. Ep. 95.35: 378
Sen. Ep. 95.37–41: 96 n. 2, 103 n. 37
Sen. Ep. 95.37: 255
Sen. Ep. 95.38: 255
Sen. Ep. 95.41: 379f.
Sen. Ep. 95.43–46: 379
Sen. Ep. 95.43–45: 103 n. 37
Sen. Ep. 95.45: 256
Sen. Ep. 95.47–50: 379
Sen. Ep. 95.47: 380, 380 n. 31
Sen. Ep. 95.50: 380 n. 32
Sen. Ep. 95.51: 380
Sen. Ep. 95.51–53: 379
Sen. Ep. 95.52: 197 n. 67
Sen. Ep. 95.54: 379, 380
Sen. Ep. 95.55–59: 379
Sen. Ep. 95.57–64: 96 n. 2, 103 n. 37
Sen. Ep. 95.57: 37 n. 88
Sen. Ep. 95.58: 380 n. 33
Sen. Ep. 95.59: 380
Sen. Ep. 95.60–67: 379
Sen. Ep. 95.66–67: 379
Sen. Ep. 95.68–71: 376

Sen. Ep. 95.72–73: 280, 374–381, 375, 378
Sen. Ep. 95.72: 177, 373 n. 16, 376, 380, 382, 386 n. 48
Sen. Ep. 95.73: 381
Sen. Ep. 97.3–4: 435 n. 15
Sen. Ep. 97.12: 104f.
Sen. Ep. 97.14: 104f.
Sen. Ep. 97.15–16: 105 n. 40
Sen. Ep. 97.15: 104f., 442 n. 35
Sen. Ep. 98: 259
Sen. Ep. 98.5: 257, 441 n. 32
Sen. Ep. 98.9: 258 n. 56, 434 n. 13, 447
Sen. Ep. 98.11: 384 n. 43, 384 n. 44, 447, 448
Sen. Ep. 98.12: 191 n. 23, 191 n. 24, 382
Sen. Ep. 98.13: 374, 376 n. 21, 381–385, 384 n. 44
Sen. Ep. 98.14: 384 n. 43
Sen. Ep. 98.15: 385 n. 45
Sen. Ep. 98.16: 157 n. 88
Sen. Ep. 99: 256, 258
Sen. Ep. 99.1: 257
Sen. Ep. 99.2: 256
Sen. Ep. 99.3–5: 129 n. 46
Sen. Ep. 99.3: 258 n. 56
Sen. Ep. 99.5: 447 n. 52
Sen. Ep. 99.11: 259
Sen. Ep. 99.16: 257
Sen. Ep. 99.18: 126 n. 35
Sen. Ep. 99.20–21: 257 n. 52
Sen. Ep. 99.20: 441 n. 32
Sen. Ep. 99.25: 433 n. 7
Sen. Ep. 99.26: 386 n. 49
Sen. Ep. 100: 461
Sen. Ep. 100.8: 441 n. 32
Sen. Ep. 101.10: 192 n. 26
Sen. Ep. 101.11: 192 n. 26, 203 n. 103
Sen. Ep. 101.12: 191 n. 23
Sen. Ep. 101.14: 191 n. 23
Sen. Ep. 102: 451
Sen. Ep. 102.20–22: 149 n. 61
Sen. Ep. 102.28–29: 96 n. 2
Sen. Ep. 103: 260
Sen. Ep. 103.1–2: 149 n. 63, 154 n. 78
Sen. Ep. 103.2: 260 n. 59
Sen. Ep. 104: 259, 261
Sen. Ep. 104.1: 144 n. 34, 259
Sen. Ep. 104.2: 259, 376 n. 21
Sen. Ep. 104.6: 259, 261 n. 60
Sen. Ep. 104.11: 260

Sen. Ep. 104.15: 451 n. 65, 50 n. 27
Sen. Ep. 104.21–22: 149, 260
Sen. Ep. 104.21: 374
Sen. Ep. 104.27: 261
Sen. Ep. 104.28: 180, 261 n. 62
Sen. Ep. 104.30: 172 n. 23
Sen. Ep. 105.4: 281 n. 32
Sen. Ep. 105.7–8: 105 n. 39
Sen. Ep. 106: 135 n. 5, 451
Sen. Ep. 106.1–3: 158f.
Sen. Ep. 106.1–2: 459
Sen. Ep. 106.11: 148
Sen. Ep. 107.3: 343 n. 3
Sen. Ep. 107.4: 58 n. 65
Sen. Ep. 107.10: 301
Sen. Ep. 108: 262, 296, 461
Sen. Ep. 108.1–2: 159, 273 n. 9
Sen. Ep. 108.8–9: 328 n. 29
Sen. Ep. 108.8: 13 n. 21, 15, 15 n. 24, 33 n. 78, 35 n. 84
Sen. Ep. 108.11–12: 328 n. 29
Sen. Ep. 108.17: 262
Sen. Ep. 108.19: 263
Sen. Ep. 108.22: 262
Sen. Ep. 108.23: 263, 282 n. 33
Sen. Ep. 108.28: 157 n. 89
Sen. Ep. 108.29: 279
Sen. Ep. 108.30: 435 n. 15
Sen. Ep. 110.1: 144 n. 34
Sen. Ep. 110.8: 297 n. 9
Sen. Ep. 110.18: 433 n. 7
Sen. Ep. 110.20: 438 n. 26
Sen. Ep. 112.4: 105 n. 41
Sen. Ep. 113: 451
Sen. Ep. 113.26: 148
Sen. Ep. 114: 461
Sen. Ep. 114.3: 282f., 291, 441 n. 32
Sen. Ep. 114.4: 287 n. 42, 435 n. 15
Sen. Ep. 114.12: 282 n. 33
Sen. Ep. 114.18: 435 n. 15
Sen. Ep. 115.3–4: 15 n. 25
Sen. Ep. 115.6–7: 158 n. 91
Sen. Ep. 115.6: 38 n. 91, 457
Sen. Ep. 115.15: 435 n. 15
Sen. Ep. 116.3: 457 n. 77
Sen. Ep. 117: 451, 46
Sen. Ep. 117.6: 15 n. 27, 17 n. 31, 25, 29, 46, 48, 50, 51, 59
Sen. Ep. 117.7: 47 n. 15
Sen. Ep. 117.18: 148
Sen. Ep. 117.26–29: 451
Sen. Ep. 118: 451
Sen. Ep. 118.1–2: 435 n. 15

Sen. Ep. 118.1: 404 n. 26
Sen. Ep. 118.2–3: 101 n. 30
Sen. Ep. 118.14: 457 n. 79
Sen. Ep. 119.5: 415
Sen. Ep. 119.7: 438 n. 26
Sen. Ep. 119.10: 296 n. 7
Sen. Ep. 119.15: 440 n. 31
Sen. Ep. 120: 1–2, 35–39, 46, 55, 451, 457
Sen. Ep. 120.3–4: 51f.
Sen. Ep. 120.3: 34
Sen. Ep. 120.4: 31 n. 73, 32 n. 75, 35, 51, 52 n. 40, 53, 55–58
Sen. Ep. 120.5: 35
Sen. Ep. 120.6–7: 36, 52
Sen. Ep. 120.8–9: 420 n. 69
Sen. Ep. 120.8: 36
Sen. Ep. 120.9–11: 36f.
Sen. Ep. 120.10–14: 451
Sen. Ep. 120.11–14: 38
Sen. Ep. 120.13–16: 154 n. 83
Sen. Ep. 120.14: 38
Sen. Ep. 120.19: 374, 376 n. 21, 383
Sen. Ep. 121: 231, 231 n. 5, 264, 451, 457
Sen. Ep. 121.1–2: 460
Sen. Ep. 121.2–3: 460
Sen. Ep. 121.2: 451 n. 65
Sen. Ep. 121.7–8: 457
Sen. Ep. 121.10: 457 n. 78
Sen. Ep. 121.14–15: 457
Sen. Ep. 122.1: 138
Sen. Ep. 122.14: 104 n. 38
Sen. Ep. 123–124: 138
Sen. Ep. 123.3: 359 n. 34
Sen. Ep. 123.6: 441 n. 32
Sen. Ep. 123.8–12: 149 n. 63
Sen. Ep. 123.11: 50 n. 30
Sen. Ep. 123.14: 459
Sen. Ep. 123.16: 459
Sen. Ep. 124: 38, 451, 461
Sen. Ep. 124.1–2: 457
Sen. Ep. 124.1: 38
Sen. Ep. 124.2: 38 n. 92, 458
Sen. Ep. 124.3: 458
Sen. Ep. 124.4–5: 458
Sen. Ep. 124.4: 458
Sen. Ep. 124.9–12: 30 n. 71
Sen. Ep. 124.12: 40, 279 n. 23
Sen. Ep. 124.21: 460
Sen. Frg. De amicitia: 135
Sen. Frg. De matrimonio 50 Vottero, 78–79 Haase: 224 n. 36

Sen. Frg. Exhortationes: 135
Sen. Frg. Libri moralis philosophiae: 135, 158, 161
Sen. Frg. Libri moralis philosophiae, 96 Vottero, 124 Haase: 191 n. 16
Sen. Helv.: 411 n. 38
Sen. Helv. 1–2: 147 n. 52
Sen. Helv. 5.2: 153 n. 76
Sen. Helv. 8.5–6: 152 n. 73
Sen. Helv. 12.4: 386 n. 49
Sen. Helv. 13.2: 146 n. 42
Sen. Helv. 16.3: 215 n. 9
Sen. Helv. 17.1–2: 115, 129 n. 44
Sen. Helv. 17.1: 116 n. 11
Sen. Helv. 17.2: 115
Sen. Helv. 18.8: 296 n. 7
Sen. Helv. 19.4 –19.7: 416 n. 58
Sen. Helv. 19.6: 215 n. 9
Sen. Helv. 20.2: 152
Sen. Her.F. 75–122: 88 n. 78
Sen. Her.F. 343–344: 332
Sen. Her.F. 353: 332
Sen. Her.F. 489: 333
Sen. Her.F. 511–512: 332
Sen. Her.F. 1262: 331
Sen. Marc. 1.2: 179
Sen. Marc. 1.3: 179 n. 58
Sen. Marc. 2.3: 373 n. 13
Sen. Marc. 3.4: 129 n. 46
Sen. Marc. 6.3: 172 n. 20
Sen. Marc. 7.4: 58 n. 65
Sen. Marc. 9.2: 100 n. 24
Sen. Marc. 9.5: 100 n. 23, 328 n. 29
Sen. Marc. 12.1–3: 129 n. 46
Sen. Marc. 16.1: 214 n. 7
Sen. Marc. 17.5: 191 n. 17, 196 n. 55
Sen. Marc. 18.2–8: 152 n. 73
Sen. Marc. 19.1: 51
Sen. Marc. 20: 179
Sen. Marc. 20.3: 179 n. 59, 190 n. 13, 191 n. 23, 191 n. 24, 191 n. 25, 192 n. 28
Sen. Marc. 20.6: 177
Sen. Marc. 22.5: 196 n. 60
Sen. Med. 1–55: 70
Sen. Med. 1–8: 70
Sen. Med. 8–18: 70
Sen. Med. 8f.: 313 n. 49
Sen. Med. 35–36: 312
Sen. Med. 40–55: 88 n. 77
Sen. Med. 40–43: 89
Sen. Med. 40–42: 70
Sen. Med. 49–52: 70

Sen. Med. 116f.: 73
Sen. Med. 116: 80 n. 51
Sen. Med. 120: 73
Sen. Med. 123f.: 82
Sen. Med. 124: 73
Sen. Med. 134–136: 71
Sen. Med. 139–149: 80
Sen. Med. 140–149: 88 n. 77
Sen. Med. 150–154: 74 n. 33
Sen. Med. 155: 73
Sen. Med. 171: 89
Sen. Med. 174f.: 74 n. 33
Sen. Med. 195: 332
Sen. Med. 198: 80
Sen. Med. 199–200: 334
Sen. Med. 203f.: 76
Sen. Med. 235–246: 80
Sen. Med. 266: 311
Sen. Med. 272–275: 80
Sen. Med. 382–396: 71 n. 22
Sen. Med. 382–392: 89
Sen. Med. 385: 76, 82
Sen. Med. 401–414: 88 n. 77
Sen. Med. 423f.: 74
Sen. Med. 425f.: 74 n. 33
Sen. Med. 428: 330
Sen. Med. 431–443: 73
Sen. Med. 434–443: 89
Sen. Med. 444–446: 70 n. 19
Sen. Med. 447: 80 n. 51
Sen. Med. 452–453: 312 n. 46
Sen. Med. 465–487: 80
Sen. Med. 489: 80
Sen. Med. 500–503: 80
Sen. Med. 515–527: 80
Sen. Med. 518: 89
Sen. Med. 527f.: 74
Sen. Med. 531–537: 80 n. 51
Sen. Med. 538: 81
Sen. Med. 544–550: 81
Sen. Med. 558f.: 74 n. 33
Sen. Med. 591f.: 76
Sen. Med. 734: 312
Sen. Med. 752f.: 71 n. 21
Sen. Med. 771–774: 71 n. 21
Sen. Med. 805–811: 71 n. 21
Sen. Med. 849: 71 n. 21
Sen. Med. 866–869: 82
Sen. Med. 866f.: 76
Sen. Med. 879–890: 312
Sen. Med. 893–977: 70 n. 19
Sen. Med. 910–915: 312 n. 46
Sen. Med. 910: 89, 91

Sen. Med. 911–917: 89
Sen. Med. 914: 70 n. 19
Sen. Med. 916: 70 n. 19
Sen. Med. 917f.: 73
Sen. Med. 926–932: 89 n. 79
Sen. Med. 930: 70 n. 19
Sen. Med. 933–936: 89 n. 79
Sen. Med. 935: 77
Sen. Med. 937–944: 83, 89 n. 79
Sen. Med. 943f.: 77, 84
Sen. Med. 944–947: 89 n. 79
Sen. Med. 948–953: 89 n. 79
Sen. Med. 951–953: 78
Sen. Med. 969–971: 78
Sen. Med. 979: 312 n. 45
Sen. Med. 988–990: 88
Sen. Med. 992–994: 88
Sen. Med. 1020f.: 88
Sen. Med. 1027: 91
Sen. Nat.: 135, 286
Sen. Nat. 1: 140f., 160
Sen. Nat. 1 pr.: 137, 160
Sen. Nat. 1 pr. 1–2: 160f.
Sen. Nat. 1 pr. 1: 156 n. 86
Sen. Nat. 1 pr. 3: 149
Sen. Nat. 1 pr. 5: 156 n. 86
Sen. Nat. 1 pr. 6–13: 158
Sen. Nat. 1 pr. 6: 141, 142 n. 28, 156 n. 86
Sen. Nat. 1 pr. 7: 144
Sen. Nat. 1 pr. 11: 153
Sen. Nat. 1 pr. 12: 161
Sen. Nat. 1 pr. 13: 161
Sen. Nat. 1 pr. 14: 156 n. 86
Sen. Nat. 1 pr. 17: 148 n. 55
Sen. Nat. 1.16: 149 n. 58, 158 n. 92, 406 n. 33
Sen. Nat. 1.17.4: 50 n. 26
Sen. Nat. 1.17.6: 55 n. 51
Sen. Nat. 2: 135 n. 5, 145
Sen. Nat. 2.1.1–2: 160
Sen. Nat. 2.2.1: 58 n. 69
Sen. Nat. 2.3.1: 52 n. 35
Sen. Nat. 2.17–20: 150
Sen. Nat. 2.26.4–6: 145
Sen. Nat. 2.27–28: 150
Sen. Nat. 2.30.1: 145
Sen. Nat. 2.32–38: 441
Sen. Nat. 2.35.1: 386 n. 49
Sen. Nat. 2.46: 135 n. 5
Sen. Nat. 2.51.1: 50 n. 26
Sen. Nat. 2.59.1: 148, 148 n. 57
Sen. Nat. 2.59.2: 148

Index of Passages Cited

Sen. Nat. 3 pr.: 140, 153, 155–157, 160
Sen. Nat. 3 pr. 1–4: 153f.
Sen. Nat. 3 pr. 1: 144f., 146 n. 43
Sen. Nat. 3 pr. 2: 139, 144, 146 n. 44, 155
Sen. Nat. 3 pr. 3: 153
Sen. Nat. 3 pr. 4: 153
Sen. Nat. 3 pr. 10–16: 156f.
Sen. Nat. 3.1.1: 144 n. 36
Sen. Nat. 3.1.2: 143 n. 32
Sen. Nat. 3.17–18: 149 n. 58, 158 n. 92
Sen. Nat. 3.25.5: 144 n. 36, 172 n. 19
Sen. Nat. 3.25.7: 172 n. 19
Sen. Nat. 3.26.1: 143 n. 32
Sen. Nat. 3.26.5: 144 n. 36
Sen. Nat. 3.27–30: 150, 153
Sen. Nat. 3.28.2: 422
Sen. Nat. 3.29.7: 144 n. 36
Sen. Nat. 3–4b: 144
Sen. Nat. 4a: 140, 143
Sen. Nat. 4a pr.: 145, 153, 156 n. 86
Sen. Nat. 4a pr. 1: 142–144, 155
Sen. Nat. 4a pr. 3–6: 143
Sen. Nat. 4a pr. 14: 142
Sen. Nat. 4a pr. 17: 191 n. 17, 196 n. 56, 197 n. 62
Sen. Nat. 4a pr. 20: 140, 140f. n. 26, 155f. n. 86
Sen. Nat. 4a pr. 21–22: 144
Sen. Nat. 4a.1.1: 143
Sen. Nat. 4a.2: 153
Sen. Nat. 4b: 145, 145 n. 39
Sen. Nat. 4b.13: 149 n. 58
Sen. Nat. 4b.13.1: 147, 148 n. 57, 376 n. 23
Sen. Nat. 5.12–13: 150
Sen. Nat. 5.18: 149 n. 58, 153, 158 n. 92
Sen. Nat. 6: 145, 147, 153
Sen. Nat. 6.1.2: 139
Sen. Nat. 6.8.2: 144
Sen. Nat. 6.14–15: 150
Sen. Nat. 6.17–18: 150
Sen. Nat. 6.30.1: 144 n. 36
Sen. Nat. 6.30.2: 150
Sen. Nat. 6.30.3: 144
Sen. Nat. 6.32.1: 147
Sen. Nat. 6.32.4: 150
Sen. Nat. 7: 139, 153
Sen. Nat. 7.6.1: 139 n. 17
Sen. Nat. 7.11.1: 58, 58 n. 69
Sen. Nat. 7.17.2: 139 n. 17
Sen. Nat. 7.21.3–4: 139 n. 17
Sen. Nat. 7.22–27: 160
Sen. Nat. 7.22.1: 153 n. 75
Sen. Nat. 7.23.1: 139 n. 17
Sen. Nat. 7.27.6: 153 n. 75
Sen. Nat. 7.28.3: 139 n. 17
Sen. Nat. 7.29.2–3: 139 n. 17
Sen. Nat. 7.30.1: 441 n. 32
Sen. Nat. 7.31–32: 149 n. 58
Sen. Nat. 7.32.2: 241 n. 27
Sen. Oed. 13: 176
Sen. Oed. 687: 176
Sen. Oed. 703–704: 332
Sen. Oed. 788: 330
Sen. Oed. 909–910: 334
Sen. Phaed. 99–103: 70 n. 19
Sen. Phaed. 119–123: 313
Sen. Phaed. 136–137: 332
Sen. Phaed. 139: 331
Sen. Phaed. 177–184: 77
Sen. Phaed. 250–254: 84 n. 62
Sen. Phaed. 265: 331
Sen. Phaed. 372–373: 90
Sen. Phaed. 430: 333
Sen. Phaed. 475f.: 330
Sen. Phaed. 559f.: 311
Sen. Phaed. 592–599: 88 n. 78
Sen. Phaed. 604f.: 77 n. 42
Sen. Phaed. 698f.: 77 n. 42
Sen. Phaed. 881: 330
Sen. Phaed. 1156–1167: 70 n. 19
Sen. Phaed. 1159–1200: 84 n. 62
Sen. Phaed. 1169: 313f.
Sen. Phaed. 1217–1222: 311
Sen. Phaed. 1249f.: 310
Sen. Phaed. 1256–1260: 310
Sen. Phaed. 1262–1269: 310
Sen. Phaed. 1265f.: 309
Sen. Phoen. 151–153: 330
Sen. Phoen. 494: 334
Sen. Phoen. 654: 332
Sen. Phoen. 659: 332
Sen. Phoen. 664: 333
Sen. Polyb. 3.5: 373 n. 13
Sen. Polyb. 7.2: 181 n. 68
Sen. Polyb. 8.3–4: 129 n. 44
Sen. Polyb. 9.3: 176
Sen. Polyb. 10.3: 129f.
Sen. Polyb. 10.6: 129 n. 46
Sen. Polyb. 17.4–6: 115 n. 10
Sen. Polyb. 18.9: 296 n. 7
Sen. Prov.: 135, 136 n. 8

Sen. Prov. 2.9–10: 177
Sen. Prov. 2.10: 146 n. 40
Sen. Prov. 2.11: 279 n. 25
Sen. Prov. 3.2: 200 n. 75
Sen. Prov. 3.7: 196 n. 60
Sen. Prov. 3.9: 192 n. 36, 203 n. 103
Sen. Prov. 3.10: 191 n. 23
Sen. Prov. 5.8: 176 n. 44
Sen. Prov. 5.9: 172 n. 19, 172 n. 20
Sen. Prov. 6.7: 178 n. 51
Sen. Thy. 176–204: 88 n. 78
Sen. Thy. 204–219: 325
Sen. Thy. 214–215: 332
Sen. Thy. 217–218: 332f.
Sen. Thy. 437–439: 168f.
Sen. Thy. 444: 332
Sen. Thy. 720–775: 197 n. 63
Sen. Thy. 755–770: 204 n. 105
Sen. Tranq.an. 1.4–17: 96 n. 2
Sen. Tranq.an. 2.1–15: 96 n. 2
Sen. Tranq.an. 2.3: 356
Sen. Tranq.an. 2.9: 373 n. 13
Sen. Tranq.an. 3.3: 333
Sen. Tranq.an. 3.6: 333
Sen. Tranq.an. 6.1: 101 n. 30
Sen. Tranq.an. 9.6: 287 n. 43
Sen. Tranq.an. 11.6: 146 n. 42
Sen. Tranq.an. 11.8–9: 328 n. 29
Sen. Tranq.an. 14.3: 196 n. 60
Sen. Tranq.an. 14.4: 195 n. 52, 196 n. 58
Sen. Tranq.an. 16.1: 177, 178 n. 51
Sen. Tro. 162: 330
Sen. Tro. 291: 334
Sen. Tro. 329: 330
Sen. Tro. 334: 333
Sen. Tro. 336: 334
Sen. Tro. 750: 313
Sen. Tro. 869: 330
Sen. Tro. 952: 329
Sen. Tro. 954: 329
Sen. Vit.beat.: 381 n. 35
Sen. Vit.beat. 1.1–6.2: 343–365
Sen. Vit.beat. 1.1–3.3: 347f.
Sen. Vit.beat. 1.1–3.2: 365
Sen. Vit.beat. 1.1: 347
Sen. Vit.beat. 1.4: 347f.
Sen. Vit.beat. 1.5: 347f.
Sen. Vit.beat. 2.1: 347f.
Sen. Vit.beat. 2.2: 347f.
Sen. Vit.beat. 3.2–6.2: 344, 349, 364
Sen. Vit.beat. 3.2: 347f., 349, 350f., 357, 364, 365
Sen. Vit.beat. 3.3–3.4: 365
Sen. Vit.beat. 3.3: 203 n. 98, 347f., 351f., 352f., 358, 365
Sen. Vit.beat. 3.4: 353f.
Sen. Vit.beat. 4.1–4.2: 365
Sen. Vit.beat. 4.1: 349, 355f., 358, 365
Sen. Vit.beat. 4.2: 349, 350, 356f.
Sen. Vit.beat. 4.3–4.5: 358f., 365
Sen. Vit.beat. 4.3: 349, 350, 358, 360, 362 n. 45, 365
Sen. Vit.beat. 4.4: 360
Sen. Vit.beat. 4.5: 360, 362, 362 n. 46
Sen. Vit.beat. 5.1–5.4: 365
Sen. Vit.beat. 5.1–5.2: 362
Sen. Vit.beat. 5.1: 361
Sen. Vit.beat. 5.2: 361, 362, 371 n. 10
Sen. Vit.beat. 5.3–5.4: 361f.
Sen. Vit.beat. 6.1: 363, 365
Sen. Vit.beat. 6.2: 364, 365
Sen. Vit.beat. 8.2: 353 n. 20
Sen. Vit.beat. 8.3: 441 n. 32
Sen. Vit.beat. 10.3: 103 n. 36
Sen. Vit.beat. 10.5: 103 n. 36
Sen. Vit.beat. 15.7: 176 n. 44
Sen. Vit.beat. 17–28: 381 n. 35
Sen. Vit.beat. 17.1: 345
Sen. Vit.beat. 17.3–4: 101 n. 29
Sen. Vit.beat. 18: 401
Sen. Vit.beat. 18.1–3: 399f., 401, 402, 403, 404, 419
Sen. Vit.beat. 18.1: 382, 400
Sen. Vit.beat. 19.1: 102 n. 34, 441
Sen. Vit.beat. 20.4: 102 n. 34
Sen. Vit.beat. 20.5: 102 n. 34
Sen. Vit.beat. 21.4: 382 n. 35
Sen. Vit.beat. 22.2–4: 381 n. 35, 382 n. 35
Sen. Vit.beat. 23.1: 382
Sen. Vit.beat. 23.2: 382 n. 36
Sen. Vit.beat. 25.1: 382 n. 35
Sen. Vit.beat. 25.2: 381 n. 35
Sen. Vit.beat. 25.4: 348 n. 13
Sen. Vit.beat. 26.1: 381 n. 35
Sen. Vit.beat. 27.5: 346 n. 11
[Sen.] Her.O. 122: 329
[Sen.] Her.O. 350: 330
[Sen.] Her.O. 675–676: 334
[Sen.] Her.O. 890
[Sen.] Her.O. 929–930: 330
[Sen.] Her.O. 930: 330
[Sen.] Oct. 381–384: 175
[Sen.] Oct. 440–592: 325 n. 24
[Sen.] Oct. 454: 334

[Sen.] Oct. 456: 332
[Sen.] Oct. 897–898: 334

Sextus Empiricus
Sext.Emp. Math. 7.151: 362 n. 41
Sext.Emp. Math. 7.228–229: 21 n. 48
Sext.Emp. Math. 7.257: 362 n. 44
Sext.Emp. Math. 8.56–57: 22 n. 53
Sext.Emp. Math. 8.56: 29, 34 n. 83
Sext.Emp. Math. 8.275: 203 n. 102, 283 n. 35
Sext.Emp. Math. 8.409: 21 n. 51; 22 n. 53, 34 n. 83
Sext.Emp. Math. 9.13: 362 n. 42
Sext.Emp. Math. 9.88: 203 n. 102

Simplicius
Simp. in Cat. p. 237f. Kalbfleisch: 37 n. 88

Stobaeus
Stob. 1.17.3, vol. 1, p. 153, 7 Wachsmuth: 12 n. 10
Stob. 2.7.5b1, vol. 2, p. 59, 4–5 Wachsmuth: 357 n. 28
Stob. 2.7.5b1, vol. 2, p. 59, 10–11 Wachsmuth: 357 n. 30
Stob. 2.7.5b2, vol. 2, p. 61, 15–17 Wachsmuth: 357 n. 29
Stob. 2.7.5b2, vol. 2, p. 62, 2 Wachsmuth: 357 n. 31
Stob. 2.7.5b2, vol. 2, p. 62, 3–5 Wachsmuth: 357 n. 31
Stob. 2.7.5b3, vol. 2, p. 62 Wachsmuth: 14 n. 23
Stob. 2.7.5b8, vol. 2, p. 65, 7–10 Wachsmuth: 13 n. 21, 14 n. 23
Stob. 2.7.5k, vol. 2, p. 73, 19–21 Wachsmuth: 362 n. 40
Stob. 2.7.6a, vol. 2, p. 75, 11–14 Wachsmuth: 346 n. 12
Stob. 2.7.10, vol. 2, p. 88, 11f. Wachsmuth: 84 n. 64
Stob. 2.7.10, vol. 2, p. 88, 16–18 Wachsmuth: 360 n. 36
Stob. 2.7.10, vol. 2, p. 88, 19–21 Wachsmuth: 360 n. 37
Stob. 2.7.10a, vol. 2, p. 89 Wachsmuth: 117 n. 13
Stob. 2.7.10b, vol. 2, p. 90 Wachsmuth: 111 n. 3
Stob. 2.7.11d, vol. 2, p. 95 Wachsmuth: 201 n. 80
Stob. 2.7.11h, vol. 2, p. 101, 1 Wachsmuth: 359 n. 33
Stob. 2.7.11m, vol. 2, p. 111f. Wachsmuth: 86 n. 72
Stob. 2.9.7b, vol. 2, p. 88 Wachsmuth: 85 n. 69
Stob. 2.9.8, vol. 2, p. 183f. Wachsmuth: 13 n. 21
Stob. 2.10c, vol. 2, p. 91 Wachsmuth: 125 n. 32
Stob. 2.31.126, vol. 2, p. 244f. Wachsmuth: 13 n. 21
Stob. 3.17.33, vol. 3, p. 501 Hense: 436 n. 17, 438 n. 23, 446 n. 46
Stob. 4.27.23, vol. 4, pp. 671–673 Hense: 231 n. 5
Stob. 4.39.22, vol. 5, p. 906 Wachsmuth and Hense: 37 n. 89

Suetonius
Suet. Aug. 74: 238 n. 17
Suet. Cal. 27: 192 n. 30
Suet. Cl. 24: 238 n. 17
Suet. Cl. 34: 194 n. 44
Suet. Cl. 34.1: 195 n. 49
Suet. Iul. 75.3: 200 n. 75
Suet. Nero 15.44: 195 n. 50
Suet. Nero 49: 194 n. 44

Stoicorum veterum fragmenta
SVF 1.60: 51, 85 n. 69
SVF 1.98: 11f., 12 n. 10
SVF 1.102: 12 n. 11
SVF 1.187: 359 n. 33
SVF 1.199: 20 n. 42
SVF 1.205–206: 355 n. 25
SVF 1.202: 20 n. 42, 355 n. 25
SVF 1.206: 84 n. 64
SVF 1.497: 12 n. 10
SVF 1.529: 203 n. 102
SVF 1.566: 13 n. 21, 14 n. 23
SVF 2.1: 66
SVF 2.35: 362 n. 42
SVF 2.36: 362 n. 42
SVF 2.55: 20 n. 45
SVF 2.56: 26 n. 66
SVF 2.60: 20 n. 45
SVF 2.61: 20 n. 45
SVF 2.65: 362 n. 44
SVF 2.71: 20 n. 45
SVF 2.82–89: 39
SVF 2.83: 26–29
SVF 2.84: 20 n. 45

SVF 2.87: 20 n. 45
SVF 2.88: 29
SVF 2.94: 25
SVF 2.105: 20 n. 45
SVF 2.223: 203 n. 102
SVF 2.442: 12 n. 15
SVF 2.458: 13 n. 17
SVF 2.459: 13 n. 17
SVF 2.460: 13 n. 17
SVF 2.461: 13 n. 17
SVF 2.618: 12 n. 10
SVF 2.619: 12 n. 10
SVF 2.715: 12 n. 16
SVF 2.716: 12 n. 16
SVF 2.752: 214 n. 5
SVF 2.774: 12 n. 12
SVF 2.780: 12 n. 13
SVF 2.823: 68 n. 13
SVF 2.980f.: 85 n. 69
SVF 2.988: 14 n. 23
SVF 2.1021: 11 n. 9, 11 n. 9
SVF 2.1027: 12 n. 12
SVF 2.1044: 300 n. 14
SVF 2.1074: 12 n. 10
SVF 2.1133: 12 n. 10, 12 n. 12
SVF 3.49–69: 359 n. 33
SVF 3.69: 17f., 44f. n. 9
SVF 3.72: 32
SVF 3.112: 362 n. 40
SVF 3.117–168: 124 n. 27
SVF 3.171: 85 n. 69
SVF 3.178: 30
SVF 3.188: 31
SVF 3.208: 359 n. 33
SVF 3.214: 14 n. 23
SVF 3.219: 14 n. 23
SVF 3.224: 13 n. 20
SVF 3.225: 13 n. 20
SVF 3.226: 357 n. 28
SVF 3.228–236: 34 n. 80
SVF 3.228: 13 n. 21, 14 n. 23, 459 n. 86
SVF 3.229–236: 459 n. 86
SVF 3.262: 357 n. 28, 357 n. 30
SVF 3.264: 14 n. 23, 66 n. 4, 357 n. 31
SVF 3.265–270: 37 n. 88
SVF 3.265: 357 n. 28, 357 n. 29, 357 n. 30, 66 n. 4
SVF 3.272: 359 n. 33
SVF 3.339: 13 n. 19
SVF 3.369: 357 n. 29
SVF 3.378: 84 n. 64
SVF 3.389: 117 n. 13

SVF 3.390: 117 n. 13, 123 n. 24
SVF 3.391: 111 n. 3, 360 n. 36
SVF 3.393: 111 n. 3
SVF 3.394.: 111 n. 3
SVF 3.395: 125 n. 32
SVF 3.396: 125 n. 32
SVF 3.412: 355 n. 25
SVF 3.456: 72 n. 29
SVF 3.462: 117 n. 13
SVF 3.473: 76 n. 39, 127 n. 38
SVF 3.474: 111 n. 2, 115 n. 9, 117 n. 14
SVF 3.475: 120 n. 21
SVF 3.476: 117 n. 13
SVF 3.489: 127 n. 37
SVF 3.510: 37 n. 89
SVF 3.517: 37 n. 88
SVF 3.525: 37 n. 88
SVF 3.539: 423 n. 74
SVF 3.545: 306 n. 29
SVF 3.548: 86 n. 72
SVF 3.640: 201 n. 80
SVF 3.685: 359 n. 33

Tacitus
Tac. Agr. 3.1: 181
Tac. Agr. 41: 178 n. 54
Tac. Ann. 11.22: 195 n. 47
Tac. Ann. 13.42–43: 345 n. 8
Tac. Ann. 13.42: 393
Tac. Ann. 14.51.1–2: 385 n. 45
Tac. Ann. 14.52–56: 139
Tac. Ann. 14.53.1–56.3: 385 n. 45
Tac. Ann. 14.53f.: 183
Tac. Ann. 14.53.5–6: 394 n. 5
Tac. Ann. 14.54: 183 n. 79
Tac. Ann. 14.57.3: 386 n. 47
Tac. Ann. 15.22.2: 139
Tac. Ann. 15.42.1: 312 n. 45
Tac. Ann. 15.44: 203 n. 104
Tac. Ann. 15.45.3: 385 n. 45
Tac. Ann. 15.56: 195 n. 50
Tac. Ann. 15.60: 259 n. 57
Tac. Ann. 15.62.1–64.4: 386
Tac. Ann. 15.64: 222 n. 30, 259 n. 57
Tac. Ann. 15.64.4: 394
Tac. Ann. 16.13.3: 138 n. 11
Tac. Ann. 16.22.2–4: 385f.
Tac. Dial. 20.4: 327 n. 25
Tac. Dial. 22.3: 327 n. 25
Tac. Hist. 4.3: 191 n. 22
Tac. Hist. 4.11: 191 n. 22

Terentius
Ter. Ad. 313: 190 n. 11
Ter. An. 622: 190 n. 11
Ter. An. 786: 190 n. 11
Ter. Haut. 53: 49 n. 20

Valerius Maximus
V. Max. 2.5.6: 373 n. 13
V. Max. 3.3: 195 n. 53
V. Max. 4.3.5–7: 383 n. 38
V. Max. 4.3.7: 373
V. Max. 4.3.11: 373
V. Max. 4.4.3: 383 n. 38
V. Max. 4.4.9: 373
V. Max. 4.4.11: 373 n. 15, 383 n. 38
V. Max. 6.9.3: 373 n. 13
V. Max. 7.5.1: 372
V. Max. 9.2: 195 n. 53

Varro
Varro L.: 170 n. 10
Varro L. 8.78: 52 n. 39

Velleius Paterculus
Vell. 2.48.6: 171 n. 19
Vell. 2.110.5: 49 n. 22

Vergilius
Verg. A.: 287
Verg. A. 1.432–433: 271
Verg. A. 3.414–419: 144 n. 36
Verg. A. 5.363: 456 n. 75
Verg. A. 8.364f.: 437
Verg. A. 9.446–449: 288
Verg. A. 9.698–701: 190 n. 10
Verg. A. 12: 336
Verg. G. 3.5: 195 n. 54
Verg. G. 3.9: 288

Xenophon
X. Mem. 3.9.4: 65 n. 2

Index of Modern Authors

Abel, Karlhans: 126 n. 34, 129 n. 46, 138 n. 12
Ackeren, Marcel van: 99 n. 18, 106 n. 45, 343 n. 3
Adam, Traute: 181 n. 67
Adamietz, Joachim: 370 n. 5, 375 n. 20
Adams, Charles D.: 213 n. 3
Adams, James N.: 215 n. 10
Ahl, Frederick M.: 424 n. 76
Albrecht, Michael von: 295 n. 1, 296, 343 n. 3, 344 n. 5, 376 n. 20, 381 n. 35, 409 n. 34
Alexander, William H.: 277 n. 18
Algra, Keimpe: 97 n. 8
Allegri, Giuseppina: 381 n. 35, 413 n. 44, 413f. n. 46, 415 n. 51, 416 n. 52, 418, 418 n. 64, 422, 422 n. 71
Allen, Walter: 177 n. 49
André, Jean-Marie: 189 n. 6, 200 n. 79, 201 n. 82, 431 n. 1, 432 n. 4. 432 n. 5, 458 n. 82
Annas, Julia: 53, 69 n. 15, 98 n. 11, 362 n. 43
Armisen-Marchetti, Mireille: 146 n. 40, 146 n. 45, 146 n. 49, 167 n. 1, 178 n. 52, 295 n. 2, 296 n. 6, 369 n. 2, 405 n. 29, 415 n. 47, 415 n. 48, 418, 423 n. 72, 423 n. 73, 423 n. 74
Arpaly, Nomy: 114 n. 7
Arrighetti, Graziano: 431 n. 1
Asmis, Elizabeth: 44 n. 2, 54 n. 47, 127 n. 40
Atherton, Catherine: 412f. , 412 n. 43
Avotins, Ivars: 381 n. 35, 431 n. 1
Axelson, Bertil: 277 n. 18
Aygon, Jean-Pierre: 190 n. 9
Babut, Daniel: 17 n. 34
Bailey, Cyril: 54 n. 44
Barker, E. Philips: 395–397
Barnes, Jonathan: 59, 424 n. 75
Barton, Carlin. A.: 419 n. 68
Bartsch, Shadi: 96 n. 1, 167 n. 1, 230 n. 3, 269 n. 1, 296 n. 3, 397 n. 9, 398, 405, 405 n. 30, 406 n. 31, 406 n. 33

Basore, John. W.: 51 n. 34, 167f. , 168 n. 2, 171, 191 n. 15, 194f. , 196, 198f. , 222 n. 29, 307, 382 n. 36, 386 n. 47, 405
Bauman, Richard: 190 n. 12
Bäumer, Änne: 75 n. 36
Bayet, Albert: 223 n. 32
Bayet, Jean: 190 n. 9
Beck, Aaron. T.: 150f.
Beck, Jan-Wilhelm: 381 n. 35, 393 n. 2, 398 n. 11
Bedon, Robert: 146 n. 51
Bees, Robert: 362 n. 43
Bellincioni, Maria: 213 n. 3, 251 n. 45, 343 n. 3, 371 n. 10, 379 n. 28
Beltrami, Achille: 277 n. 18
Bénatouïl, Thomas: 105 n. 41, 105 n. 43, 403 n. 21
Bennington, Geoffrey: 335, 336
Benz, Lore: 327 n. 27
Berger, Adolf: 50 n. 31
Bernauer, James: 275 n. 13
Berno, Francesca Romana: 148 n. 55, 170 n. 14, 376 n. 22, 403 n. 23, 404 n. 26, 405 n. 27, 415 n. 49, 420 n. 69
Bernsdorff, Hans: 436 n. 17
Berrendonner, Clara: 383 n. 38
Berti, Emanuele: 189 n. 7
Bettini, Maurizio: 214 n. 4, 369 n. 1
Biondi, Giuseppe G.: 312 n. 49
Blair, Elena: 218 n. 19
Bloomer, Martin. W.: 372 n. 12
Blumenberg, Hans.: 416 n. 57
Bobonich, Christopher: 96 n. 1
Bobzien, Susanne: 103 n. 37, 105 n. 42
Bodéüs, Richard: 14 n. 21
Boehringer, Sandra: 216 n. 17
Boeke, Hanna: 320
Boeri, Marcelo D.: 66 n. 3, 86 n. 70
Bonhöffer, Adolf F.: 10f. , 10 n. 7, 17, 25 n. 64, 44 n. 6

Bonner, Stanley F.: 323 n. 16
Borgo, Antonella: 100 n. 22, 373 n. 13
Borkowski, Andrew: 240 n. 21
Bosch, Clemens E.: 372 n. 12
Bouquet, Jean: 411 n. 38
Bourgery, Abel: 138 n. 13. 159 n. 99
Boyancé, Pierre: 190 n. 12
Boyle, Anthony J.: 175 n. 39, 319, 319 n. 3, 335 n. 37, 397 n. 9
Bradley, Keith R.: 190 n. 12, 201 n. 82, 201 n. 86, 231 n. 4
Braun, Maximilian: 369 n. 1
Braund, Susanna M.: 331 n. 34, 399 n. 14
Brennan, Tad: 362 n. 43, 402 n. 19
Brink, Charles O.: 307 n. 31
Briquel, Dominique: 191 n. 20, 192 n. 33
Brodribb William J.: 327 n. 25
Brunschwig, Jacques: 457 n. 76
Büchner, Karl: 377 n. 24
Buckley, Emma: 335 n. 37
Buecheler, Franz: 277 n. 18
Burck, Erich: 189 n. 5
Bury, Robert G.: 22 n. 53
Byrd, Robert C.: 351 n. 18
Cambiano, Giuseppe: 97 n. 7, 376 n. 23
Cancik, Hildegard: 230 n. 2, 232, 413 n. 44, 432 n. 4
Cancik, Hubert: 104 n. 37
Cantarella, Eva: 191 n. 17, 217 n. 18
Carey, Chris: 321 n. 9
Carlon, Jacqueline M.: 245 n. 36
Casadesús Bordoy, Francesco: 431 n. 1
Castner, Catherine J.: 16 n. 28
Cermatori, Linda: 59 n. 72, 230 n. 2, 305 n. 26, 441 n. 32
Chambert, René: 411 n. 38
Chase, Michael: 9 n. *, 12 n. 10
Chaumartin: 345 n. 6, 346 n. 9, 369 n. 2
Chioccioli, Marco: 381 n. 35
Church, Alfred J.: 327 n. 25
Cicu, Luciano: 308 n. 34
Citroni Marchetti: 373 n. 13, 376 n. 23, 381 n. 35
Claassen, Jo-Marie: 244 n. 33
Clark, John. R.: 295 n. 2, 303 n. 23, 383 n. 42, 431 n. 1
Classen, Carl Joachim: 373 n. 13
Codoñer Merino, Carmen: 138 n. 14, 143 n. 31, 143 n. 32, 168 n. 3
Coffey, Michael: 310 n. 41

Cohoon, James W.: 182 n. 72
Colish, Marcia L.: 173 n. 28
Cooper, John. M.: 55 n. 49, 97 n. 9, 98 n. 11, 117 n. 13, 130 n. 49, 148 n. 56, 424 n. 75, 431 n. 1
Copeman, William S.: 213 n. 3
Corbier, Mireille: 373 n. 13
Costa, Charles D. N.: 312 n. 44
Costa, Stefano: 369 n. 2, 379 n. 28
Coudry, Marianne: 369 n. 1
Courtney, Edward: 144 n. 36
Cruttwell, Charles T.: 345 n. 9
Cupaiuolo, Fabio: 190 n. 8
D'Ippolito, Federico: 181 n. 65
Dalzell, Alexander: 343 n. 4
Danesi Marioni, Giulia: 323 n. 16
Dangel, Jacqueline: 328
Daremberg, Charles: 190 n. 13, 191 n. 16, 191 n. 17, 191 n. 20, 192 n. 27, 192 n. 28, 194 n. 41
David, Jean-Michel: 370 n. 4
Davidson, Arnold I.: 97 n. 11, 272 n. 5, 272 n. 8, 275 n. 13, 276 n. 15
Davie, John: 350, 351, 352, 354, 356, 358f., 361f., 363
Davies, Roy W: 50 n. 32
Davis, Peter J.: 314 n. 52
De Filippis Cappai, Chiara: 217 n. 18
De Lacy, Phillip: 75
De Pietro, Matheus: 381 n. 35
De Rentiis, Dina: 271 n. 4
De Vaan, Michiel: 54 n. 41 , 56 n. 56 , 57 n. 61
Decourt, Jean-Claude: 138 n. 11
Degl'Innocenti Pierini, Rita: 169 n. 5, 170 n. 13, 171 n. 16, 171 n. 17, 176 n. 42, 179 n. 56, 182 n. 71, 240 n. 23, 295 n. 1, 306 n. 29, 310 n. 40, 312, 312 n. 45, 431 n. 1, 440 n. 30
Delatte, Louis: 135 n. 1, 140 n. 21, 140 n. 25, 141 n. 26, 141 n. 27
Derrida, Jacques: 410 n. 37
Desbordes, Françoise: 327
Desideri, Paolo: 182 n. 74
Destrée, Pierre: 96 n. 1
Detel, Wolfgang: 97 n. 11
Detienne, Marcel: 204 n. 105
DeWitt, Norman: 53, 54 n. 44
Diller, Hans: 79 n. 47
Dillon, John: 66 n. 7, 73 n. 31
Dingel, Joachim: 335 n. 37

Dinter, Martin. T.: 323 n. 17, 364, 434 n. 10
Dixon, Suzanne: 231 n. 4
Dobbin, Robert F.: 97 n. 8, 103 n. 37
Domenico da Peccioli: 373 n. 16
Donini, Pierluigi: 58 n. 71, 239 n. 19, 298 n. 12, 362 n. 43
Dragona-Monachou, Myrto: 100 n. 21
Dross, Juliette: 306 n. 28, 381 n. 35
Dryden, Windy: 151 n. 65, 151 n. 67
Du Plessis, Paul: 240 n. 21
Duff, John. W.: 320, 328 n. 30
Durry, Marcel: 213 n. 4
Dyson, Henry: 9 n. *, 44 n. 7, 45 n. 9 and 10, 56 n. 54
Edelstein, Ludwig: 97 n. 8, 97 n. 9
Edgeworth, Robert J.: 312 n. 46
Edwards, Catharine: 100 n. 25, 168 n. 3, 177 n. 47, 178 n. 54, 230, 240 n. 23, 250 n. 43, 397 n. 9, 405 n. 30, 407, 419 n. 68
Elvers, Karl Ludwig: 369 n. 3
Ermann, Joachim: 191 n. 14
Ernout, Alfred: 49 n. 21, 50 n. 28, 54 n. 41, 56 n. 56, 57 n. 61
Evans Grubbs, Judith: 240 n. 22
Fairclough, Rushton: 302
Fairweather, Janet: 323 n. 16, 324 n. 23
Fantham, Elaine: 210, 211, 212, 222 n. 28, 313 n. 50, 320, 322 n. 14, 328 n. 30, 337
Farrar, Frederic. W.: 345 n. 9
Favez, Charles: 190 n. 8, 223 n. 35
Fedeli, Paolo: 373 n. 18
Ferguson, John: 431 n. 1
Ferraiolo, William: 152 n. 69
Ferri, Rolando: 325
Fillion-Lahille, Janine: 101 n. 27, 119 n. 19
Fitch, John. G.: 70 n. 18, 77, 80 n. 51, 83, 88, 310, 311, 312 n. 47, 313, 313 n. 51, 329 n. 32
Flemming, Rebecca: 215 n. 12, 217 n. 18, 218 n. 22
Flower, Harriet I.: 242, 242 n. 28
Föllinger, Sabine: 214 n. 5, 218 n. 19
Forschner, Maximilian: 84 n. 63, 97 n. 7
Fortenbaugh, William W.: 184 n. 82
Foucault, Michel: 97 n. 11, 151 n. 65, 269f. , 272–276, 286
Fox, Matthew: 52
Francia Somalo, Rosa: 223f. n. 35

Franzoi, Alessandro: 386 n. 47
Frede, Michael: 412 n. 41
Freise, Hermann: 431 n. 1, 441 n. 33, 459 n. 83
Fuhrer, Therese: 399–401
Furneaux, Henry: 386 n. 47
Gambet, Daniel G.: 373 n. 18
Garani, Myrto: 145 n. 38
Garbarino, Giovanna: 168 n. 3, 176 n. 45, 369 n. 3, 411 n. 40, 413 n. 46, 416, 416 n. 57, 418 n. 64
Gardner, Jane F.: 231 n. 4, 240 n. 21
Gauly, Bardo M.: 138 n. 14, 139 n. 15, 139 n. 16, 139 n. 19, 143 n. 31, 148 n. 57
Gazich, Roberto: 369 n. 1
Gazzarri, Tommaso: 176 n. 43, 440 n. 30
George, Michele: 231 n. 4
Gercke, Alfred: 142 n. 28
Gerson, Lloyd P.: 357 n. 28, 438, 457 n. 80
Giancotti, Francesco: 327 n. 26
Gianotti, Gian. Franco: 308 n. 35
Giavatto, Angelo: 106 n. 45
Gigante, Marcello: 302 n. 20, 431 n. 1, 433 n. 8, 447 n. 51
Gigon, Olof: 54 n. 44
Gill, Christopher: 65f. , 65 n. 3, 67 n. 8, 68 n. 14, 73 n. 31, 77 n. 43, 79 n. 47, 80 n. 50, 82 n. 58, 86 n. 71, 86 n. 73, 87 n. 74, 87 n. 75, 90 n. 83, 91 n. 84, 97 n. 7, 98 n. 11, 117 n. 13, 151 n. 66, 276 n. 15, 406 n. 32, 441 n. 32
Glidden, David K.: 44 n. 2
Gloyn: 432 n. 4, 450 n. 64
Goodyear, Francis R. D. 145 n. 38
Görler, Woldemar: 362 n. 43, 447 n. 51
Gosling, Justin: 66 n. 3, 95 n. 1
Gould , Josiah B.: 96
Goulet, Richard: 14 n. 22, 14 n. 23, 21 n. 46, 21 n. 49, 22 n. 53, 23 n. 54, 23 n. 56, 24 n. 61, 24 n. 62, 30 n. 70
Gourévitch, Danielle: 215 n. 11
Gourinat, Jean-Baptiste: 16 n. 29, 66 n. 3, 66 n. 4, 95 n. 1
Gowers, Emily: 215 n. 11
Graver, Margaret R.: 75 n. 35, 75 n. 36, 91 n. 85, 105 n. 42, 105 n. 43, 111 n. 1, 117 n. 13, 119 n. 19, 124 n. 28, 126 n. 34, 127 n. 39, 230 n. 2,

257 n. 52, 269 n. 2, 271 n. 3, 273 n. 9, 282 n. 33, 287 n. 43, 309 n. 36, 309 n. 37, 343 n. 3, 417 n. 59, 431 n. 1, 436 n. 17, 439 n. 29, 444 n. 42
Grebe, Sabine: 245 n. 36
Griffin, Miriam T.: 55, 135 n. 1, 138, 138 n. 12, 138 n. 13, 139 n. 19, 140 n. 22, 140 n. 23, 141 n. 27, 142 n. 28, 143 n. 29, 143 n. 30, 145 n. 39, 146 n. 47, 200 n. 82, 244 n. 33, 250 n. 43, 345 n. 6, 346 n. 9, 346 n. 10, 376 n. 23, 394, 394 n. 3, 394 n. 4, 394 n. 5, 398, 404, 435 n. 14, 435 n. 16
Grilli, Alberto: 135 n. 3, 371 n. 10, 431 n. 1, 436 n. 17
Grimal, Pierre: 98 n. 11, 100 n. 22, 135 n. 1, 140 n. 23, 167, 230 n. 2, 373 n. 18, 376 n. 23, 381 n. 35, 431 n. 1
Grisé, Yolande: 223 n. 32
Grollios, Constantine C.: 129 n. 46
Gross, Nikolaus: 143 n. 31
Gualandri, Isabella: 323 n. 16
Guckes, Barbara: 66 n. 3, 77, 95 n. 1
Gummere, Richard M.: 170 n. 14, 277 n. 18, 296, 296 n. 6, 297, 299, 300, 302, 304, 309, 324, 355 n. 27, 374 n. 19, 375, 376, 379, 380, 382 n. 25, 383, 383 n. 41, 384 n. 42, 384 n. 43, 386 n. 47, 394, 394 n. 6, 401, 406, 407, 408, 411, 412, 413, 414 n. 46, 415, 417, 419 n. 66, 420
Habinek, Thomas: 397 n. 9
Hachmann, Erwin: 136 n. 7, 246 n. 37, 246 n. 38, 431 n. 1, 432 n. 4, 432 n. 5, 433 n. 6, 437 n. 22, 442 n. 37, 450 n. 62, 450 n. 64, 458 n. 82, 460
Hadot, Ilsetraut: 33 n. 77, 38 n. 91, 45 n. 12, 54 n. 46, 96 n. 6, 97 n. 11, 130 n. 49, , 146 n. 45251 n. 45, 262 n. 63, 343 n. 3, 383 n. 40, 412 n. 42, 431 n. 1, 439 n. 29, 441 n. 33, 451 n. 66, 459
Hadot, Pierre: 97 n. 11, 100 n. 25, 103 n. 37, 151 n. 65, 152 n. 70, 272, 275, 276 n. 15, 343 n. 3
Hahm, David E.: 24f.
Halbig, Christoph: 66, 84 n. 63
Hallak, Laurence: 189 n. 1, 190 n. 8
Halm-Tisserant, Monique: 195 n. 52

Haltenhoff, Andreas: 369 n. 1
Hammerstaedt, Jürgen: 44 n. 2
Hammond, Mason: 168 n. 3, 181 n. 66
Hankinson, R. J.: 45 n. 10
Hankinson, Robert J.: 362 n. 43
Hanson, Ann. E.: 217 n. 18, 218 n. 22
Hard, Robin: 99 n. 14, 99 n. 19
Hardie, Philip: 141f.
Harris, William V.: 101 n. 27
Harrison, Stephen: 415 n. 47
Hegel, Georg W. F.: 345 n. 9
Heinze, Richard: 302 n. 20
Heldmann, Konrad: 73 n. 30, 81 n. 55, 82 n. 56
Helzle, Martin: 303 n. 21
Hembold, William: 82f.
Henderson, John: 140 n. 24, 144 n. 33. 155 n. 84, 157 n. 87, 229 n. 1, 232f. , 259, 260, 331 n. 35, 336 n. 39, 409 n. 35, 410 n. 37, 431 n. 1, 432 n. 4, 435 n. 14, 458 n. 82
Hengel, Martin: 191 n. 20
Henry, Denis: 90 n. 81, 335 n. 37
Henry, Elisabeth: 335 n. 37
Hense, Otto: 277 n. 18
Herbert, James M.: 151
Hermes, Theodor: 431 n. 1, 433 n. 8, 436 n. 17, 437 n. 19
Heuzé, Philippe: 190 n. 10
Hicks, Robert D.: 66, 364
Hijmans, Benjamin. L.: 343 n. 3, 405 n. 29
Hill, Timothy: 176 n. 43
Hine, Harry M.: 58 n. 70, 67 n. 10, 70 n. 17, 80 n. 51, 87 n. 75, 136 n. 9, 138 n. 14, 139 n. 15, 139 n. 16, 140 n. 20, 148 n. 57, 149 n. 60, 295 n. 1
Hoffman, Tobias: 96 n. 1
Hölkeskamp, Karl Joachim: 369 n. 1
Hubbard, Margaret: 415 n. 47
Hubbell, Harry M.: 305, 372 n. 11
Hunt, J. William: 336
Hurschmann, Rolf: 348 n. 14
Huxley, Herbert H.: 416 n. 56
Hyde, Walter W.: 145 n. 38
Impara, Paolo: 104 n. 37
Inwood, Brad: 9–11, 16, 20, 22–24, 26, 29, 32, 34–37, 39, 46, 51f. , 52 n. 38, 55, 58f. , 66 n. 3, 69 n. 15, 73 n. 32, 75 n. 35, 84 n. 63, 85 n. 68, 86 n. 72, 97, 97 n. 7, 136 n. 6, 159 n. 96, 161 n. 102, 117 n. 15, 168 n.

3, 184 n. 82, 229 n. 2, 231 n. 5, 232 n. 6, 246 n. 37, 247 n. 39, 250 n. 43, 253, 253 n. 49, 255, 262 n. 63, 269 n. 2, 286 n. 38, 295 n. 2, 357 n. 28, 362 n. 43, 362 n. 43, 376 n. 23, 383 n. 42, 403 n. 21, 406 n. 32, 412 n. 42, 413 n. 44, 415 n. 49, 417 n. 61, 418 n. 63, 420 n. 69, 421 n. 70, 424 n. 75, 431 n. 1, 435 n. 14, 438, 455 n. 74, 457, 457 n. 78, 457 n. 80, 458, 460
Isnardi Parente, Margherita: 171 n. 18, 221 n. 27, 223 n. 32, 409 n. 34
Jackson, John: 183 n. 79, 386, 386 n. 47
Jackson-McCabe, Matt: 10f. , 10 n. 7, 17 n. 35, 20, 22f. n. 53, 24f. , 26 n. 65, 29, 44, 45, 55, 96 n. 6, 97 n. 7
Jäkel, Siegfried: 320
Jaume, Jacques: 191 n. 20
Jones, Madeleine: 436 n. 17
Jones, William H. S.: 220 n. 25
Jourdan-Gueyer, Marie-Ange: 411 n. 38
Joyce, Richard: 66 n. 3, 86 n. 70, 95 n. 1
Kahlmeyer, Johannes: 415 n. 47
Kamtekar, Rachana: 97 n. 8
Kassel, Rudolf: 127 n. 40
Kaster, Robert A.: 72 n. 27, 75, 75 n. 37, 90, 123 n. 24, 125 n. 31, 296 n. 5
Kaufman, David H.: 82 n. 57, 118 n. 17, 257 n. 53, 444 n. 41
Keith, Allison: 322
Ker, James: 100 n. 25, 146 n. 43, 147, 168 n. 3, 222 n. 30, 319 n. 1, 435 n. 14
Keulen, Wytse: 399 n. 14, 409 n. 34
Kidd, Ian. G.: 251 n. 46, 301 n. 17
Kiessling, Adolf G.: 302 n. 20
King, John. E.: 47
Kirchner, Roderich: 321 n. 7
Klebs, Elimar: 369 n. 3, 373 n. 14
Klotz, Alfred: 375 n. 20
Knecht, Theodor: 327 n. 27
Kolbet, Paul R.: 97 n. 11
Konstan, David: 231 n. 5
Kornhardt, Hildegard: 369 n. 1
Köstermann, Erich: 183 n. 77, 386 n. 47
Kuen, Gabriele: 353 n. 20
Kullmann, Wolfgang: 71 n. 22, 78 n. 45
Kunz, Franz: 322 n. 13, 328
Kutzko, David: 215 n. 12
L'Estrange, Roger: 345 n. 9
La Penna, Antonio: 370 n. 5, 373 n. 13, 447 n. 51
Lamb, William R. M.: 218
Lana, Italo: 168 n. 3, 180 n. 61, 383 n. 40, 431 n. 1, 435 n. 14, 447 n. 51
Landor, Walter S.: 398 n. 10
Langlands, Rebecca: 253 n. 48
Lanza, Diego: 309 n. 39
Lanzarone, Nicola: 135 n. 1, 135 n. 3, 135 n. 5, 146 n. 40, 173 n. 24
Laudizi, Giovanni: 296 n. 6
Lazarus, Arnold A.: 151f.
Lefèvre, Eckard: 70 n. 19, 79 n. 48
Leo, Friedrich: 319 n. 2
Lévi-Strauss, Claude: 215 n. 11
Lévy, Carlos: 44 n. 7, 45 n. 10, 49, 50 n. 24
Liebich, Werner: 54 n. 44
Limburg, Florence J. G.: 138 n. 14, 146 n. 49
Lindsay, Jack: 215 n. 12
Linke, Bernhard: 369 n. 1
Lipsius, Justus: 277 n. 19
Littlewood, Cedric A. J.: 312 n. 44, 314 n. 53
Locke, John: 45 n. 10
Long, Anthony A.: 17 n. 34, 44, 45 n. 10, 68 n. 13, 68 n. 14, 83 n. 59, 84 n. 63, 84 n. 64, 85 n. 66, 97 n. 8, 124 n. 27, 231 n. 5, 269, 271 n. 3, 276 n. 15, 283 n. 35, 346 n. 12, 357 n. 28, 357 n. 30, 360 n. 36, 362 n. 40, 362, n. 43, 362 n. 44, 394 n. 6, 403 n. 21, 424 n. 75, 443 n. 39
Loretto, Franz: 223 n. 35
Lotito, Gianfranco: 175 n. 35, 295, 436 n. 17
Lucas, Gérard: 138 n. 11
Lutz, Cora: 18f.
Macaulay, Thomas B.: 345 n. 9, 398 n. 10
Macdonald, Charles: 371, 371 n. 9
MacGregor, Arthur: 214 n. 4
Madvig, Johan. N.: 53, 54 n. 44
Mahon, Michael: 275 n. 13
Malaspina, Ermanno: 56 n. 53, 181 n. 67, 182 n. 72, 196 n. 60, 198 n. 68

Mannering, Jonathan: 329 n. 32, 331 n. 34, 333 n. 36
Manning, Charles E.: 129 n. 46, 223 n. 35, 262 n. 63
Manuli, Paola: 217 n. 17
Manuwald, Anke: 54, 54 n. 44
Marcucci, Silvia: 373 n. 16
Marino, Patricia: 114 n. 7
Marino, Rosanna: 303 n. 22
Maslakov, George: 372 n. 12
Maso, Stefano: 431 n. 1
Mauduit, Christine: 328 n. 31
Maurach, Gregor: 71 n. 24, 74 n. 34, 75 n. 36, 81 n. 53, 91 n. 88, 136 n. 7, 230 n. 2, 232 n. 9, 403 n. 25, 432 n. 4
Mayer, Roland G.: 310 n. 41, 319 n. 1, 324f. , 369 n. 2, 373 n. 18, 375 n. 20, 376 n. 21
Mazzoli, Giancarlo: 176 n. 44, 177 n. 50, 183 n. 76, 230 n. 2, 295 n. 1, 301 n. 17, 301 n. 18, 307 n. 31, 308, 311 n. 43, 312 n. 49, 323 n. 16, 405 n. 28, 431 n. 1, 447 n. 51
McElduff, Siobhan: 313 n. 51
McGill, Scott: 322 n. 14
McGlinchey, Joseph B.: 151 n. 65, 151 n. 67
Meillet, Antoine: 49 n. 21, 50 n. 28, 54 n. 41, 56 n. 56, 57 n. 61
Mencacci, Francesca: 369 n. 1
Mignucci, Mario: 413 n. 45
Miller, Frank J.: 169 n. 4, 325
Miller, Walter: 169 n. 9
Milnor, Kristina L.: 231 n. 4
Milton, John: 345 n. 9, 398 n. 10
Minieri, Luciano: 213 n. 4
Mitsis, Philip T.: 444 n. 39
Molenaar, Gaspar: 50 n. 30
Mommsen, Theodor: 191 n. 14, 191 n. 22, 192 n. 33, 194 n. 41, 194 n. 43, 194 n. 45
Montaigne, Michel de: 345f. n. 9
Montgomery, Robert W.: 151 n. 65, 151 n. 67
Montiglio, Silvia: 405 n. 28 , 411 n. 38, 411 n. 40
Moore Brookshire, Sarah A.: 151 n. 65, 151 n. 67
Moore, Helen: 141f.
Morales, Helen: 335
Morel, Pierre-Marie: 44 n. 2
Moreschini, Claudio: 49 n. 18, 50 n. 24

Moretti, Gabriella: 306 n. 29
Morgan, Teresa: 369 n. 1
Most, Glen. W: 189 n. 1, 189 n. 4, 190 n. 8, 203 n. 101, 205 n. 105, 309 n. 38
Motto, Anna L.: 278 n. 21, 295 n. 2, 303 n. 23, 346 n. 9, 383 n. 42, 411 n. 38, 431 n. 1
Mratschek, Sigrid: 394 n. 3
Müller, Jörn: 65 n. 1, 66 n. 3, 67 n. 11, 85 n. 65, 86 n. 71, 95f. n. 1
Mutschler, Fritz-Heiner: 343 n. 3, 369 n. 1
Mutschmann, Hermann: 431 n. 1, 433 n. 6, 433 n. 8, 434 n. 11, 436 n. 17, 459 n. 84
Narducci, Emanuele: 177 n. 46, 177 n. 47
Németi, Annalisa: 312 n. 49
Newman, Robert J.: 97 n. 11, 343 n. 3, 362 n. 43, 405 n. 29
Nicholson, John: 170 n. 10
Nisbet, Robin. G. M.: 415 n. 47
Noailles, Pierre: 213 n. 4
Nótári, Tamás: 370 n. 5
Noyes, Russell: 146 n. 40
Nriagu, Jerome O.: 213 n. 3
Nussbaum, Martha C.: 66 n. 5, 72, 73 n. 31, 76 n. 40, 81 n. 52, 81 n. 54, 87 n. 74, 87 n. 75, 88 n. 76, 91 n. 87, 91 n. 88, 151 n. 65, 335 n. 37
O'Keefe, Tim: 444 n. 39
Obbink, Dirk: 437 n. 21
Obstoj, Angelika: 431 n. 1
Oldfather, William A.: 359 n. 35, William A.
Olligschläger, Uwe J.: 151 n. 65
Orlando, Antonello:: 96 n. 6
Orlando: 412 n. 42, 441 n. 33, 451 n. 66
Palmer, Ralph Graham: 338
Parente, Fausto: 191 n. 20
Paré-Rey, Pascale: 327 n. 29, 328 n. 31, 338 n. 42
Parroni, Piergiorgio: 138 n. 14
Pasche, Micheline: 189 n. 1
Pease, Arthur: 57 n. 53
Pecchiura, Paolo: 171 n. 18
Peck, Arthur L: 213 n. 3, 219 n. 23, 220 n. 26
Perkams, Matthias: 96 n. 1
Petrarca, Francesco: 271 n. 4
Petrone, Gianna: 314 n. 52

Petrovic, Andrej: 415 n. 48
Philippson, Robert: 437
Piccaluga, Giulia: 213 n. 4
Picone, Giusto: 308 n. 35, 311 n. 43, 312 n. 48, 326
Plumpe, Joseph C.: 370 n. 4
Poeschl, Viktor: 415 n. 47
Pohlenz, Max: 12, 23 n. 53, 45, 431 n. 1
Pomeroy, Sarah B.: 218 n. 19
Porter, Roy: 213 n. 3
Pratt, Norman: 335 n. 37
Préchac, François: 277 n. 19
Preisendanz, Karl: 323 n. 16
Price, Anthony: 66 n. 3
Procopé, J. F.: 55 n. 49
Rabbow, Paul: 97 n. 11, 343 n. 3
Race, William H.: 301 n. 19
Rackham, Harris: 43 n. 1, 48f. , 174 n. 32, 218 n. 20
Ramelli, Ilaria: 231 n. 5
Ramsay, George G.: 399 n. 13
Ramsey, John. T.: 56 n. 57, 139 n. 18
Rawson, Beryl: 231 n. 4
Rawson, Elizabeth: 209 n. 1
Rayment, Charles S.: 323 n. 16
Regenbogen, Otto: 70 n. 20, 78 n. 45, 189 n. 1
Reid, James: 54, 54 n. 44, 57 n. 64
Reiss, Steven: 151 n. 65
Reydams-Schils, Gretchen: 100 n. 25, 149 n. 63, 214 n. 5, 223 n. 35, 247 n. 40
Reynolds, Leighton. D.: 112 n. 5, 261 n. 61, 277, 277 n. 19, 281 n. 31, 431 n. 1, 436 n. 18
Richardson-Hay, Christine: 149 n. 62, 230 n. 2, 232 n. 9, 369 n. 2, 373 n. 13
Richlin, Amy: 216 n. 13
Ridley, Edward: 174 n. 29
Rieks, Rudolf: 328 n. 30
Rist, John: 69 n. 15
Roberts, William R.: 404
Robertson, Donald: 151f. , 156f.
Rolland, Émile: 323 n. 16
Roller, Matthew: 168 n. 3, 175 n. 36
Roloff, Heinrich: 370 n. 4
Romano, Elisa: 369 n. 1
Rosati, Gianpiero: 158f.
Rose, Herbert J.: 345 n. 9, 396f.
Roskam, Geert: 383 n. 42
Rousseau, George S.: 213 n. 3

Rudich, Vasily: 393 n. 2, 397 n. 9
Russell, Donald A.: 319, 319 n. 3, 321 n. 10
Russo, Joseph: 320
Rutherford, Richard B.: 97 n. 8, 98 n. 11, 152 n. 70
Sacheli, Agostino: 431 n. 1
Saglio, Edmond: 190 n. 13, 191 n. 16, 191 n. 17, 191 n. 20, 192 n. 27, 192 n. 28, 194 n. 41
Saller, Richard P.: 231 n. 4
Sandbach, Francis H.: 10, 10 n. 7, 17, 44 n. 3, 44 n. 7, 45, 96 n. 5, 343 n. 1, 343 n. 2, 345 n. 9, 349 n. 16
Sassi, Maria M.: 411 n. 38
Scarpat, Giuseppe: 173 n. 24, 298 n. 12
Schafer, John: 136 n. 8, 138 n. 13, 141 n. 27, 148 n. 56, 153 n. 77, 251 n. 45, 379 n. 28, 433 n. 6
Schiesaro, Alessandro: 90 n. 81, 169 n. 4, 189 n. 1, 311 n. 43, 335 n. 37, 381 n. 35
Schildhauer, Hans: 431 n. 1
Schmal, Stephan: 385 n. 46
Schmid, Wolfgang: 431 n. 1, 447 n. 53
Schoenberger, Hans: 370 n. 4
Schofield, Malcolm: 44, 44 n. 2, 423 n. 74
Schöpsdau, Klaus: 273 n. 9, 278 n. 21
Schottlaender, Rudolf: 431 n. 1, 433 n. 6, 433 n. 7, 436 n. 17, 442 n. 36, 444 n. 40, 447 n. 51
Schwaiger, Clemens: 431 n. 1
Sedley, David: 17 n. 34, 44, 68 n. 13, 68 n. 14, 83 n. 59, 84 n. 64, 85 n. 66, 124 n. 27, 231 n. 5, 283 n. 35, 346 n. 12, 357 n. 28, 357 n. 30, 360 n. 36, 362 n. 40, 362, n. 43, 362 n. 44, 394 n. 6, 443 n. 39
Segal, Charles: 189 n. 6, 190 n. 8
Sellars, John: 96 n. 6, 97 n. 7, 399 n. 15
Setaioli, Aldo: 170 n. 12, 180 n. 61, 189 n. 4, 295 n. 1, 298 n. 11, 308 n. 35, 373 n. 18, 381 n. 34, 431 n. 1, 433 n. 8, 435 n. 14, 435 n. 15, 436 n. 17, 439 n. 27, 439f. n. 29, 440 n. 30, 444 n. 44, 447 n. 51, 447 n. 53
Shackleton. Bailey, David R.: 56 n. 57, 170 n. 11, 216 n. 15, 216 n. 16, 372, 373
Sharples, Robert W.: 45 n. 10
Sherman, Nancy: 102 n. 35

Shorey, Paul: 217
Sinclair, Patrick: 320 n. 5, 322 n. 12, 323, 323 n. 19, 323 n. 20, 324, 324 n. 21, 324 n. 22
Sissa, Giulia: 214 n. 6, 216 n. 12, 217 n. 17
Skidmore, Clive: 372 n. 12
Smith, Wesley D: 219
Sorabji, Richard: 75 n. 35, 98 n. 11, 103f. n. 37, 111 n. 1, 120 n. 21, 121, 151 n. 65
Sørensen, Villy: 190 n. 12
Späth, Thomas: 369 n. 1
Staley, Gregory. A.: 409 n. 34
Steidle, Wolf: 78 n. 45, 79 n. 48, 81 n. 55
Stemmler, Michael: 369 n. 1, 370 n. 4
Stephens, William O.: 97 n. 8
Still, Arthur: 151 n. 65, 151 n. 67
Striker, Gisela: 362 n. 43
Strozier, Robert: 272 n. 7
Summers, Walter C.: 145 n. 37, 271 n. 4, 277 n. 18, 413 n. 44, 414 n. 46, 418 n. 63
Sussman, Lewis A.: 321 n. 7, 323 n. 16
Syme, Ronald: 174
Tarrant, Richard J.: 189 n. 1, 312 n. 47
Taub, Liba C.: 145 n. 38
Thorarinsson, Geir: 128 n. 43
Thraede, Klaus: 155 n. 85
Tieleman, Teun: 67 n. 8, 123 n. 25, 455 n. 74
Timpanaro, Sebastiano: 214 n. 4
Torre, Chiara: 223 n. 35
Traina, Alfonso: 168 n. 3, 170 n. 12, 174 n. 33, 175 n. 35, 175 n. 37, 189 n. 4, 295 n. 1, 343 n. 3
Treggiari, Susan: 245 n. 36
Trevelyan, George O.: 345 n. 9
Trovato, Vincent: 398
Tsouna, Voula: 54 n. 44
Usener, Hermann: 431 n. 1, 431 n. 1, 433 n. 8, 437
Van. Der Blom, Henriette: 370 n. 4
Van. der Wal, Rogier L.: 370 n. 5
Van. Mal Maeder, Danielle: 189 n. 4, 195 n. 51
Verboeven, Koenraad: 415 n. 50
Vernant, Jean-Pierre: 204 n. 105
Veyne, Paul: 100 n. 25, 103 n. 37, 223 n. 32, 272 n. 7, 275 n. 13
Viarre, Simone: 303 n. 21
Vigourt, Annie: 383 n. 38

Viti, Anastasia: 138 n. 11, 146 n. 47, 146 n. 50, 146 n. 51
Voelke, André-Jean: 96 n. 5, 97 n. 7, 98 n. 11, 103 n. 37, 105 n. 41
Vogt, Katja M.: 120, 123 n. 25, 125 n. 31, 272 n. 7, 362 n. 43
Volkmann, Hans: 181 n. 67
Vottero, Dionigi: 135 n. 1, 135 n. 2, 135 n. 4, 139 n. 15, 139 n. 16, 148 n. 57, 150 n. 64
Walker Keyes, Clinton: 377, 377 n. 25
Walker, Bessie: 90 n. 81
Wallace-Hadrill, Andrew: 139 n. 16
Wanke, Christiane: 189 n. 5
Wardle, David: 372 n. 12
Warmington, Eric H.: 171 n. 16
Watts, Nevile H.: 192 n. 29
Weaver, Paul R.: 231 n. 4
Wedeck, Harry E.: 345 n. 9
Wedeen, Richard P.: 213 n. 3
Weissenfels, Oskar: 431 n. 1
Wheatland Litchfield, Henry: 369 n. 1
Wheeler, Arthur L.: 303
White, Stephen. A.: 124 n. 28
Whitton, Christopher: 331 n. 35
Wiener, Claudia: 74 n. 33
Wilamowitz-Möllendorff, Ulrich von: 181 n. 67
Wilcox, Amanda: 435 n. 14
Wildberger, Jula: 46 n. 14, 72 n. 28, 91 n. 85, 96 n. 2, 98 n. 12, 148 n. 56, 149 n. 61, 117 n. 15, 127 n. 38, 130 n. 49, 174 n. 31, 178 n. 43, 230 n. 2, 232 n. 6, 240 n. 23, 290 n. 47, 298 n. 10, 298 n. 11, 298 n. 12, 300 n. 14, 343 n. 3, 362 n. 43, 369 n. 2, 371 n. 10, 383 n. 42, 403 n. 27, 432 n. 2, 450 n. 60, 457 n. 81
Williams, Craig A.: 215 n. 10, 217
Williams, Gareth D.: 138 n. 14, 144 n. 35, 146 n. 49, 147 n. 52, 149 n. 59, 153 n. 74, 230 n. 2, 432 n. 4, 459 n. 85
Wilson, Marcus: 258f., 403, 403 n. 22, 403 n. 25, 405 n. 28, 435 n. 14
Winterbottom, Michael: 169 n. 5, 322 n. 15, 383, 385 n. 46
Wirszubski, Chaim: 168 n. 3, 174 n. 31, 175 n. 36, 180 n. 60
Woodman, Anthony J.: 393 n. 2, 397 n. 9
Woolf, Raphael: 53

Wray, David L.: 230 n. 3, 269 n. 1, 335 n. 37, 393 n. 1, 398
Wright, Margaret: 414
Wuilleumier, Pierre: 386 n. 47
Wulfram, Hartmut: 303 n. 21

Zanker, Paul: 399 n. 12
Zimmermann, Bernhard: 385 n. 46
Zöller, Rainer: 103 n. 37, 105 n. 41
Zugibe, Frederick T.: 191 n. 20

General Index

adiaphora: see indifferents
advice: 74, 95, 100–102, 140, 156 n. 86, 159, 173, 200, 230, 237, 239, 242f., 248–250, 252–254, 257–260, 262–265, 273, 282, 295 n. 1, 295 n. 2, 302, 307f., 314, 345 n. 8, 353 n. 20, 412, 420 n. 68, 448, 451f.; precepts: 33, 251–256, 263, 264, 272, 290, 309, 320, 324, 333, 337, 379, 380f., 393, 408, 424; see also: exhortation
aesthetics: 98 n. 11, 189f., 275f., 289, 304 n. 24, 308f., 314, 322, 397, 461; see also: art
Aetna: 145, 287; the poem *Aetna*: 145 n. 38
akrasia: 65–91, 95f. 105
Alexander the Great: 196, 197 n. 61, 348 n. 13
ambition (or lack of it): 98f., 142f., 237f., 248, 272, 290, 377–379, 384
amplification: 146, 179, 323 n. 18, 350; before reduction: 146–147, 150
analogy: 10, 22–24, 31f., 35, 39, 51f., 55, 57, 60, 96
anger: 65–91, 99–101, 111–113, 116, 118–126, 127 n. 38, 129 n. 44, 193, 196 n. 57, 198, 200 n. 78, 203, 205, 257 n. 53; Stoic definition of anger: 125 n. 32
animal: 192, 196f. 201f., 203f., 215, 218, 262, 456–458, 460; animalization: 203f.
animus: see mind
Annaei: see family
Antipater: 25
Antonius (Mark Antony): 56, 169, 173
apatheia: see passion
aphormē ("starting point"): 11–20, 26 n. 65, 32–34
Apollodorus: 25
Aristippus: 302 n. 20, 417
Aristo: 20 n. 42, 32f., 40, 252

Aristoteles: 47, 65, 68, 72 n. 26, 78, 96 n. 1, 148, 220f., 297, 298, 300, 349
Arria: 248
Arrianus: 106
art, artist: 295–314; artisan: 205–207, 300, 304, 307, 309, 311, 314; *fingere*: 296, 299f., 307–310; *opus*: 301–303, 313; god as artist: 297–301, called *dēmiourgos*: 298, 306; *forma, formare*: 298–300, 306–308; lack of *forma*: 309f.; see also: *componere*; education
asceticism, *askēsis*: 343 n. 3, 401f., 415f., 422, 435, 437f.
Asclepiades of Bithynia: 209
Asinius Pollio: 169
assent (*sunkatathesis*): 69, 72, 75, 77, 83, 87, 119f., 124–126, 362; weak assent: 85–87, 96, 98 n. 12, 105, 127 n. 38
Attalus: 262–264, 262 n. 63, 433, 438 n. 26, 454
Atticus: 245, 288; *Letters to Atticus*: 168–170, 404, 435
Augustus: 118 n. 16, 192, 196 n. 60, 240
authorial persona: 137f., 149 n. 61, 152–154, 245 n. 36; 324, 395, 397, 410; self-scripting: 269–292; conveyed through *sententiae*: 324–326, 335; as artist-educator: 295–309; self-presentation as a Stoic philosopher: 343–365; Tubero as a model for Seneca: 369–386; author L. Anneaus vs. "Letter Writer:" 431–461; see also: hypocrisy
Balbus (character in Cicero's *De natura deorum*): 17, 29, 47f.
Bassa: 216f.
Bassus (Aufidius Bassus, orator): 172
Bassus (Betilienus Bassus): 194
Bassus (Epicurean friend of Seneca): 257, 436, 450

bee: 271, 285–287, 290, 308
belief: 112–126, 127 n. 38, 131, 444f., 453
body: 30, 35, 38f., 105, 176, 178, 189f., 249, 259, 263, 270, 277, 283, 288, 309–313, 352f., 363, 451, 455, 457; an author's work as a body: 275, 287 n. 43, 321; beard: 219f.; blood: 196, 199f.; in the tragedies: 309f, 312f.; see also: digestion; medicine; mind and body; sexuality; torture; women
Brutus (M. Brutus): 256, 306; Cicero's work *Brutus* dedicated to him: 371f.
Burrus: 385 n. 45, 394
Busiris: 195f.
Caesar (Julius Caesar): 177f., 222, 327, 376, 381, 384, 386
Caligula: 115 n. 10, 194–197, 199 n. 74
Calpurnius Siculus: 331
Campania: 139, 155
cannibalism: 399
Capito Cossutianus: 385f.
career criticism: 141f.
Cato the Elder: 419
Cato the Younger (Uticensis): 169, 171 n. 19, 171–174, 177f., 221f., 236 n. 15, 258, 260, 270f., 279 n. 25, 307 n. 33, 376f., 379, 381, 385
chronology of Seneca's works: 134–42, 381 n. 34, 381 n. 35
Chrysippus: 9, 17f., 19, 20f., 24–26, 28–30, 34, 37 n. 89, 44f., 60, 65f., 68, 72, 75, 76, 79, 85, 86, 87 n. 74, 95 n. 1, 96, 105, 111f., 111 n. 2, 113, 115 n. 9, 116f., 120 n. 21, 123 n. 24, 124 n. 28, 127, 260, 270, 306 n. 29
Cicero: 43–60, 111, 127f., 167–174, 244 n. 33, 245 n. 36, 304, 369–378
Cincinnatus: 383f.
Claudius: 195f., 197 n. 61, 248 n. 42
Cleanthes: 14, 21 n. 47, 26 n. 66, 28, 30, 33, 40, 111f., 113, 117, 241
clemency: 169, 193, 197, 201f., 205
componere: 296, 297 n. 8, 310 n. 41; 440f.
concept (*notitia, notio, opinio; ennoia*): 19, 25, 27, 43, 49–51, 58, 52; concept formation: 32f., 52; 441 n. 33, 451, 459; see also: *prolēpsis*

conscience: 95–106; *conscientia*: 100; see also: self; self-examination; self-knowledge
consistency (*homologia*): 39 n. 93, 95, 102, 173, 269f., 272, 292, 301, 346, 350–352, 364, 412, 440f., 451f., 454; inconsistency: 90, 168–169, 172, 449f.; intrinsical vs. incidental inconsistency: 113f.
consolation: 111f., 115–118, 127–130, 146f., 152, 249, 257–259
Corsica: 135 n. 3, 152, 175, 396, 415 n. 49
cosmic viewpoint: 144–5, 152–161, 451
craft: see art
Cremutius Cordus: 179
crimen maiestatis: 194
cruelty: 71, 118 n. 16, 180, 190, 192, 195–198, 200–205, 215, 309 n. 39, 311, 312, 329, 379f.; *feritas*: 119 n. 19; see also: pleasure; torture
Curius (M. Dentatus): 383f.
Cynics, Cynicism: 182, 203 n. 101, 370f., 399, 436 n. 17
death: 38f., 98, 102, 106, 257f., 329–331; fear of death: 230; see also: consolation; grief; suicide
declamation: 173, 189, 195, 319, 322, 324, 326, 336
definition: 349
Demetrius Poliorcetes: 233f.
diastrophē: 20, 32–34; 149–150, 204, 238f., 253f., 371f., 419, 459f.; *perversitas*, wordplay with *pervertere*: 371, 371 n. 10; 378f., 386
digestion: 40, 211, 214f., 271, 273–275, 281, 284f., 289, 308, 434, 438; see also: food
Diogenes the Dog: 182, 371
Dionysius of Syracuse: 196, 204
Drusus Libo: 247–249
earthquake: 139, 144, 147, 150, 153, 172 n. 19; Pompeii devastated by it: 139f.
eclecticism: 431
education: 2, 96f., 114 n. 8, 189, 229, 247, 251–256, 262, 265, 273, 280, 295–7, 299f., 302, 307 n. 31, 308 n. 10, 323, 331, 336f., 360 n. 38, 411; education as art: 295–318; punishment as education: 201
Ennius: 288, 461

Epictetus: 10, 16, 18–20, 25, 95, 97 n. 11, 99f., 102, 106, 360 n. 39, 403 n. 21
Epicurus, Epicureanism: 15–17, 38, 43, 44 n. 2, 45, 48–50, 53f., 59, 112, 127–131, 130 n. 49, 233, 288, 304, 363f., 384, 404, 411 n. 38
epistemology: 9–40, 96, 403 n. 21, 446, 451, 456–458; see also: assent; concept; knowledge; *phantasia*; *prolēpsis*; sense perception; self-knowledge
Epistulae morales: relation to *Nat.*: 135–161; question of fictionality: 137–140, 143, 229, 229f. n. 2, 276, 403f., 431–461; epistolography: 273, 304, 442; genre of *Ep.*: 400, 403–413, 424, 431, 433, 435; 433, 459 n. 84; letter vs. treatise: 158f., 442; epistolary form: 143–5; 150–161; developmental reading of *Ep.*: 229–265, 431–461; spatial coordinates of *Ep.*: 154f., 233
ethics vs. physics: 147–149, 160f.
eudaimonia: 95–97, 455; see also: good
Euripides: 65f., 71, 73, 79, 80 n. 50, 82 n. 56, 90, 313 n. 49
excerpts: see reading
exemplum, exemplification: 36, 38 n. 93, 52, 96f., 193, 221f., 270, 307, 369–386, 369 n. 1, 400, 405f., 417 n. 58, 432, 433 n. 6, 451, 461; see also: Cato; Fabricius; Socrates; Tubero
exhortation: 70, 76, 179, 237, 239, 273, 295 n. 1, 307, 345, 353 n. 20, 369, 384, 395, 401, 438, 440, 451; *parainesis*: 301 n. 19; Seneca's *Exhortationes*: 135
exile: 70, 129, 182, 219, 222 n. 29, 303f.; Cicero's exile: 172 n. 20, 177 n. 49, 245 n. 36; exile of Diogenes the Dog: 182; Seneca's exile: 117 n. 14, 135 n. 3, 152, 175, 396, 415 n. 49, 417 n. 58
Fabricius (C. Luscinus): 36, 52, 373, 374 n. 19, 382–384
fame and glory: 50, 176–178, 224 n. 36, 237, 288f., 305, 326f., 337, 348 n. 14, 380
family: 71, 77, 79, 80, 91, 214, 224 n. 35, 229–265, 329; the Annaei family: 322f., 323 n. 16, 323 n. 19,

394; definition of *familia*: 230f.; philosopher's family: 240–243, 262–264; *imagines*: 242f.; friendship more important: 257; see also: father; marriage; wife
father: 179, 197, 239f., 249f., 252, 256, 260f., 262–265; see also: Seneca the Elder
food: 209–215, 221, 223, 262, 296, 373 n. 15, 434, 437f.; see also: digestion
fool: 359, 375, 384, 403, 413, 415, 418, 422–424, 447–450, 453; Seneca's household fool (*fatua*): 243–245
Fortuna: 100, 102, 168, 174, 230, 233, 240 n. 23, 242, 328, 334, 349, 352f., 356, 360, 383f., 438
Foucault, Michel: 269–292; see also the Index of Modern Authors
freedom: 77, 79, 100, 144, 155, 167–184, 168 n. 3; 221f., 358–360, 440; freedom of speech: 182f.; *semiliber*: 167f., 170; see also: slave; suicide
friend, friendship: 101f., 114, 135, 142, 146, 148, 157, 233, 235, 236, 246, 250, 254, 257, 258, 280, 286, 304, 333, 393f., 415f. 442–444
Fronto: 286, 343
frugalitas: see wealth
Galen: 66f., 105 n. 43
Gallio (Seneca's brother): 259f.
Gellius (A. Gellius): 327
gender: 209–224; see also: family; women
genre: see *Epistulae morales*; genre of *Vit. beat*: 345 n. 7
glory: see fame
god: 297–301, 312f., 406, 451, 455–458, 460; belief in and common notion of gods: 17f., 25, 44, 46–49; active principle: 11f.; inner *daimōn*: 97; God as artist: 297–301
good: 280, 290, 444, 446, 453; notion of good: 9–40, 44, 50, 51–53, 451; supreme good (*summum bonum*): 130, 233, 351–365, 446, 450–458; see also: agreement; *eudaimonia*; sage; virtue; wisdom
gratitude: 99, 103 n. 35, 183, 447f.
greatness of mind: 37, 91, 174, 238, 307, 356f., 382 n. 36, 416, 437f.,

440f., 447, 449, 451, 452, 455–457; greatness of *ingenium*: 284–287, 291; see also: cosmic viewpoint
grief: 74, 114f., 118, 128, 146, 245, 250, 256–259, 328; sage weeps at funeral: 256f. n. 52; see also: consolation
habitus; *hexis*: 31, 37f., 37 n. 90
Haterius (Q. Haterius): 173, 418 n. 63
hatred: 80, 90, 201, 300f.
hēgemonikon: see mind
Helen: 127 n. 38
Helvia: 117 n. 14, 152, 417 n. 58
Heraclitus: 441
Hesiod: 287
Hieronymus of Rhodes: 302 n. 20
Hippolytus: 77, 84, 309–311, 313
Homer: 190, 287
homologia: see consistency
Horace: 288, 296, 324
Horatius Cocles: 36, 52
hormē: see impulse
humanitas: 72, 91, 190, 201f., 205, 311, 356
hypocrisy: 103, 105, 345f., 381 n. 35, 393–425
hypomnēma: 273f., 286;
Idomeneus: 288, 434, 434 n. 13, 441
imagery: 15, 55, 76, 98, 105, 167–169, 171f., 177–179, 183, 189f., 197f., 199, 203, 209–224, 246, 271, 281, 286, 295–314, 321 n. 10, 324, 336, 344, 350, 351, 358f., 365, 406 n. 32, 422, 446; see also: bee; digestion; food; body; journey; ship
impression: see *phantasia*
impulse: 13, 14 n. 22, 14 n. 23, 30, 60, 68f., 72, 75f., 78f., 83, 85–87, 113, 119 n. 18, 124 n. 28, 246, 257, 263, 283 n. 35, 298, 371, 450 n. 60; *hormē pleonazousa*: 75; see also: *phantasia hormētikē*
incest: 399
indifferents (*adiaphora*): 38f., 96, 123f., 150, 174, 184, 205, 236, 257–259, 272, 290, 329, 345, 346, 352–355, 381f. n. 35, 384, 394f., 401f., 411 n. 38, 417, 421, 424, 436 n. 17, 444–446, 452–454, 457 n. 77; see also: wealth
ingenium: 278, 281–291, 309 n. 37, 311 n. 42

innatism (*innatus, insitus; emphutos*): 9–40, 44f., 48f., 53–60, 96, 297, 412 n. 42; see also: *aphormē*; concept; *prolēpsis*; seed
Inwood, Brad: 9–40; see also the Index of Modern Authors
Iulius Bassus: 169
see Bassus
Jason: 66, 69 n. 16, 70–74, 77, 79–82, 84, 87–91, 312
journey: 148, 178, 184, 260 n. 58, 270f., 281, 410–425; mind-travel: 145, 153; see also: ship; wisdom
Jupiter, Zeus: 11, 305f., 375, 437f., 380 n. 31, 438
justice, injustice: 15 n. 25, 71–73, 75, 78, 81, 201, 297, 328 n. 30, 334, 357 n. 31, 442
knowledge: 9, 15, 35, 37, 39, 44, 49–52, 69, 78f., 113, 128, 148, 210, 262, 308, 345, 346 n. 11, 348, 350, 360, 365, 409, 442, 448; *scientia, epistēmē*: 35, 48 n. 16, 52, 56, 96, 237f., 357, 361f., 451; self-knowledge: 97, 104f., 329, 412 n. 42, 422; see also: epistemology; seeds
Laelius: 149, 260, 374 n. 19, 375–377
law: 47, 50, 95, 175, 194, 198, 205, 230f., 239f., 304, 308, 323 n. 20, 326, 335f., 352, 379, 439f., 442, 453; legal language: 50, 453 n. 69
libertas: see freedom
Livy: 169, 372 n. 12, 434
logic: 46 n. 14, 59, 148, 149 n. 61, 295 n. 2, 344 n. 5, 352f., 360 n. 38, 413 n. 45, 414, 421f.; terms for premises: 57
Lollius: 301 n. 19, 302
love: 71, 76f., 79–84, 88–91; self-love: 55, 102, 105, 146, 205, 237f., 246, 248, 254, 259, 261, 264, 328
Lucan: 319, 323
Lucilius: 140–145, 158; as dedicatee: 135, 289; relation to the reader of *Ep.*: 232 n. 7, 244 n. 31; Lucilius *Iunior* vs. Seneca *senex*: 146 n. 43; his *ingenium*: 287f.; representative of elite: 276
Lucretius: 53–55, 343 n. 4, 447
Lugdunum destroyed by fire: 138, 146f.
luxury: see wealth
Lysimachus: 196, 197 n. 61

Macrobius: 271 n. 4, 327 n. 26
Maecenas: 287f., 374 n. 19, 435 n. 15
Marcellinus (Tullius Marcellinus): 258
Marcia: 179
Marcus Aurelius: 95, 97–99, 101f., 105f., 286, 403 n. 21
marriage: 70, 73, 80, 214 n. 5, 224 n. 35, 235, 245 n. 36, 252f.
Marullus: 256–259
materia: 295–300, 305f., 307; *materia virtutis*: 34, 38 n. 90, 59, 297; passive principle: 298; possessions: 420f.
Maximus (Caesennius Maximus): 415f.
Medea: 65–91, 311–314
medicine: 18, 199f., 209–224, 243, 295; gout: 212f., 215f., 220f.; baldness: 212f., 215, 220f.
meditatio: 152, 245, 274, 343 n. 3, 405, 407, 416, 422; *meditatio mortis*: 145f.: see also: *praemeditatio*
Menelaus: 127 n. 38
Metrodorus: 258 n. 56, 434, 447
mind, soul: 16, 35f., 38, 45, 52f., 56f., 60, 72f., 75, 77–79, 81–84, 96, 97f., 144, 147f., 149 n. 61, 155f., 156 n. 86, 174–176, 182, 233, 237f., 243, 249, 260, 265, 270, 271, 272, 280, 296f., 299f., 303, 306f., 309, 314 321, 323, 349, 352–357, 360–364, 398, 406, 416, 418, 424; mind and body: 13 n. 19, 39 n. 93, 152f., 175f., 257, 270, 288, 406 n. 32, 457; mindless: 72, 83; mind's eye: 153, 306, 457, 460; *animus*: 282f., 289–291; *hēgemonikon*: 21, 26, 28, 68f., 77, 83, 96, 455, 457; *hēgemonikon = animus*: 283; vocal faculty: 283 n. 35; definition of soul: 12; immortality of soul: 47, 305; metempsychosis: 218, 262f.; see also: greatness of mind; *ingenium*; journey; psychological monism vs. dualism
Minerva: 305f.
Minotaur: 313
mother, motherhood: 213 n. 3, 223, 232 n. 8, 252, 261, 313, 331; see also: Helvia; Medea; parent(s)
Murena: 370
Musonius Rufus: 18–20, 214

natural, unnatural: 13f., 17, 24, 26, 28f., 34, 47, 54, 55, 202–204, 235, 444f., 454
Naturales quaestiones: relation to *Ep.*: 135–161; book ordering: 135 n. 5, 138f., 140f., 152f.; see also: chronology
Nero: 103, 135, 137, 139f., 142, 180–184, 192 n. 34, 195, 197, 244 n. 32, 312 n. 45, 325, 331, 346 n. 9, 376, 381 n. 35, 382, 385f., 393f., 396, 398
Nile: 143, 153
noise in *Ep.* and *Nat.*: 149f.
notio, notitia: see concept; *prolēpsis*
oikeiōsis: 11, 29–32, 45, 55, 60, 96, 224 n. 35, 231, 362 n. 43, 451, 457
Ovid: 66, 82 n. 56, 288
Panaetius: 98 n. 11, 283 n. 35, 369
parent(s): 20, 56, 84, 214 n. 5, 224 n. 35, 231, 237–239, 241f., 246f., 250, 254, 256, 258, 262–264, 271, 312 n. 47
parricide: 192, 195
passion (*pathos*): 65–91, 95f., 111–131, 256f. n. 52, 354f., 359f., 444f., 451, 453; pre-passion (*propatheia*): 75 n. 36, 119, 125f.; impassibility (*apatheia*): 352–355
Paulina (Pompeia Paulina, Seneca's wife): 244, 259–261; see also: wife
Paulus (L. Aemilius Paulus): 369, 371–373, 377 n. 25
Peripatetics: 49, 68, 72, 75
persona: see authorial persona
pessum: 171f. n. 19
Phaedra: 77, 84, 88 n. 78, 90, 309; 313f.
Phaëtusa: 219
Phalaris: 193, 195f., 197 n. 61
phantasia ("representation" or "impression"): 12, 21–25, 27f., 34, 38 n. 91, 39, 44f., 69, 72, 75 n. 37, 85f., 96, 115, 119f., 123–126, 291, 362; *phantasia hormētikē*: 85; 127 n. 38
Phidias: 303–306
Philainis: 216
Philoctetes: 171
Philodemus: 302 n. 20
phusikōs: see natural
pity (*misericordia*): 90, 201, 247 n. 39

Plato, Platonism: 10 n. 3, 12, 13 n. 18, 15 n. 25 and 26, 26 n. 65, 34 n. 79, 38f., 43, 45, 47, 50, 53, 57–60, 65, 67f., 73f., 77, 82, 84, 148, 176, 217f., 220f., 241, 269, 295 n. 1, 296 n. 4, 298, 300, 306, 409f., 455; Ideas: 45, 53, 58f., 305f.

pleasure and joy: 38 n. 92, 53f., 65, 83, 115, 125, 127–130, 174, 175, 240 n. 23, 259, 272, 290, 356, 359f. 363f., 432, 433, 438, 444, 446–450, 452–459; *gaudium*: 280, 454f.; sadism: 190, 193, 202f., 204

Plutarch: 67, 82f., 85, 204 n. 11

pneuma: 11f., 22, 38, 126, 214 n. 5

politics, political: 36, 47 n. 15, 98–102, 106, 167–184, 190, 193, 194–202, 205, 224 n. 36, 237, 238, 242f., 244 n. 32, 246, 262f., 345, 345f. n. 9, 370–372, 376–378, 380f., 383–386, 393f.; see also: ambition; Cato the Younger; fame and glory; sociability; Tubero; tyranny

Polyaenus: 434 n. 13, 437

Polybius (freedman of Claudius): 129f., 175, 396

Pompeii: 139, 147

Pompey: 167f., 173, 196 n. 60, 376, 386 n. 47

Posidonius: 68, 87 n. 74, 124 n. 28, 149, 260, 280 n. 27, 455 n. 74.

poverty: see wealth

praemeditatio futurorum malorum: 38, 98, 100, 151

praesumptio: see *prolēpsis*

precepts: see advice

progress, progressor (*proficiens*): 37 n. 89, 141, 147–149, 154, 156 n. 86, 159, 236f., 239, 251, 265, 276, 278–280, 301f., 306f., 329, 394, 400 n. 16, 402, 405, 408–413, 415, 416–418, 421–424, 448–450; see also: *aphormē*

prolēpsis: 9–40, 43–60

propatheia: see passion

psychological monism vs. dualism: 65–91, 95f., 269f., 406 n. 32, 455f.

Publilius Syrus: 320f., 327, 335, 338

pudicitia: 215, 224 n. 36, 253 n. 48

punishment: 70, 72, 78–80, 104f., 119f., 123–125, 189–205, 213 n. 4, 311, 330, 332, 372

Pythagoras, Pythagoreans: 100, 262f.

reading: 269, 271–274, 277–282, 284, 286f., 290f.; excerpting as reading: 273f., 282, 319, 322, 324 n. 21, 326–338, 434; variety: 273f.; digestion metaphor: 274f.; as *studium*: 277f.; "Seneca," the Letter Writer as reader of Epicurus: 434f., 439, 441

reason (*ratio*; *logos*): 13, 28, 95–97, 105, 197, 200–203, 205, 235, 272, 283, 290, 292, 360–362, 402, 455–458; right reason: 99; reason-responsiveness, or lack of it, of empassioned people: 112f. 116f., 119, 122, 127, 131

regret: 88, 114 n. 8, 118 n. 17, 121, 333

repetition: 321, 343–365, 371, 400, 403 n. 23; as *meditatio*: 343 n. 3

representation: see *phantasia*

retirement (*conversio ad se*, withdrawal, etc.): 102, 135, 137, 139–142, 381f., 384f., 394, 397, 442

rhetoric: 189, 209, 223, 258, 280, 281, 282, 295 n. 1, 306, 308, 319, 321–323, 326, 331, 333, 335, 343 n. 1, 347, 369; meaning of "rhetorical:" 319; rhetorical vocabulary: 51, 60; see also: declamation

sage: 37–39, 91, 95f., 100, 102, 151, 167f., 172–176, 222, 233, 235f., 250, 256f. n. 52, 280, 290, 301 n. 16, 303f., 306–308, 314, 400, 402, 450, 453f.

scale of being: 12, 30, 451; Platonic: 306

Scipio Aemilianus: 375–377

Scipio Africanus: 369, 371

Scribonia: 248f.

seed, semen (*semen*; *sperma*, *logos spermatikos*): 11–20, 26 n. 65, 32–34, 35, 53–57, 96, 213 n. 4, 214 n. 5, 218–220

Seianus: 179, 196 n. 60, 262 n. 63

self: 84, 89, 90 n. 81, 90 n. 83, 91, 97, 101, 103 n. 37, 138, 150, 157, 229f., 231 n. 5, 260–262, 269–292, 296 n. 3, 308, 311, 333; care of: 230, 233, 442; see also: authorial persona; *conscientia*; Foucault; knowledge; love

self-examination: 97–103, 106, 154, 230, 263 n. 64, 405–413; *meditatio* as self-examination: 405–408

self-sufficiency: 103, 174, 233–236, 304, 365, 442 n. 35, 443, 445
Seneca the Elder: 169, 173, 249f., 256, 262–264, 320, 322, 324, 326f., 335, 337
Seneca tragicus, relation to Seneca philosophus: 56–91, 309–314; 319, 324, 329, 334, 338
sense perception: 10, 14 n. 21, 15 n. 25, 17–29, 38f., 53, 55, 68f., 96, 101, 305f., 456–458
sententiae: 319–338, 363f., 433–442; uses and functions: 320–325; *gnomai*: 320–322, 328, 335; in the tragedies: 325–334; as timeless law: 335–337; reception: 337f.
severity (*severitas*): 201, 205
Sextius pater: 100f., 262, 262 n. 63, 263 n. 64, 382, 383f.
sexuality: 209, 212–221, 314 n. 52; *tribas*: 216f., 219f., 223, 399, 406 n. 33; see also: body; *pudicitia*; women
shame: 84, 88, 104, 114, 114 n. 8, 118 n. 17, 333, 372f., 308, 417, 417f.
ship: 98, 168, 172: shipwreck: 346 n. 17, 413–425; see also: journey
Sicily: 140, 141 n. 26, 143–145, 153, 155; see also: Aetna
slaves, slavery: 99, 118 n. 16, 173, 175, 179, 180, 191–195, 201f., 205, 223 n. 33, 231, 238, 244, 252, 254, 280, 281, 328 n. 30, 416, 419; *endoxos douleia*: 181; slave of vices or passions: 33, 76–79, 174 n. 34, 240 n. 23, 352f., 359, 455f.
sociability, social relations: 91, 182 n. 74, 197, 202, 255, 260, 323, 357, 442–444; see also: family; friendship
social status: 99, 144, 194, 238, 241f., 254, 290
Socrates: 65, 149, 173, 180, 221–223, 241, 260f., 345, 399, 409f; Socrates and his wife: 261
Sotion: 262f.
soul: see mind
spiritual exercise: 14 n. 21, 34, 38, 40, 97 n. 11, 272f., 275; spiritual guide: 136 n. 6, 396f.
Stilbo: 233–236, 416, 443
Stoics, Stoicism: 9–40, 43–47, 49–51, 53–55, 58–60, 65–69, 72–75, 77,
79, 82–87, 91, 95–100, 105f., 111f., 117, 122f., 125, 126f., 129–131, 190, 201–204, 229f., 231 n. 5, 235f., 238, 239 n. 19, 241, 242, 242 n. 9, 247, 248, 250f., 255, 253 n. 49, 256, 257 n. 54, 262 n. 63, 269, 269 n. 2, 274, 279, 280, 282, 283, 287, 289, 292, 297f., 300 n. 14, 306, 306 n. 29, 314, 329, 335 n. 37, 338 n. 42, 343–365, 351f., 369–372, 373, 383f., 385f., 394f., 398, 399, 401–403, 407–425, 437f., 440–458; Stoic paradoxes: 413f., 418
studia: 271, 277–281, 288; *studia liberalia*: 280; see also: *ingenium*; reading; writing
style: 98, 177, 189f., 232 n. 6, 276, 282–285, 287, 290f., 295 n. 1, 296 n. 3, 297, 304 n. 24, 312 n. 44, 321–323, 327 n. 25f., 343f., 345 n. 8; 349, 350, 375 n. 20, 398, 403 n. 23, 404, 431f., 436, 461; see also: amplification; imagery; *ingenium*; repetition; rhetoric
suicide: 84, 157, 171–173, 176–180, 209, 221–224, 235f., 248–250, 330f., 440, 441: suicide as path to freedom: 178; in Seneca's tragedies: 179
Suillius (P. Suillius Rufus): 345f., 393–395, 397, 400
Sulla: 169, 196f.
Tacitus: 183f., 244 n. 32, 323 n. 20
Telesphorus: 197 n. 61, 204
theater: 33 n. 78, 118, 190, 279 n. 24; world as a stage: 106; *mise-en-scène* and theatricality: 177, 183, 397 n. 9; see also: Seneca tragicus
therapy: 74 n. 33, 76, 98, 98 n. 11, 111–131, 199, 233, 275, 405, 431, 444–446, 451; cognitive-behavioral therapy: 100, 137, 150–158; *revocatio* and *avocatio*: 127–131; see also: consolation (for medical therapy, see: medicine)
Thrasea Paetus: 385f.
Thyestes: 168f.
Torquatus (Lucius Manlius): 53
torture: 99, 125 n. 33, 179, 189–205, 223, 454; *crematio*: 191; crucifixion: 191f.; *culleus* 192; *damnatio ad bestias*: 192, 203f., dismem-

berment: 203 f.; flagellation: 190f., 194; imprisonment: 192f.; interrogation of slaves: 192f., 195; mutilation: 189f., 193, 196f., 203; rack (*eculeus* or *fidicula*): 192, 195, 197 n. 64, 204 n. 108

translation: 15–18, 22 n. 53, 23 n. 55, 48, 50f., 52, 54, 55, 57–59, 440, 440 n. 30, 442, 449

Troy, fall of: 127 n. 38, 146, 313

Tubero, Q. Aelius: the Younger: 149, 260, 369–386; the Elder: 373f., 383 n. 37

tutela: 239f.

tyrant, tyranny: 99, 100, 177 n. 47, 179f., 182, 193, 194–197, 204f., 222, 235, 311 n. 43, 325f., 331–333, 336, 376, 381, 385 n. 45; tyranny of passions: 77

Ulysses: 237, 313f.

utility: 9 n. 2, 201, 205

Valerius Maximus: 369–375, 372 n. 12, 375 n. 20, 380, 383, 385

Vedius Pollio: 118 n. 16, 192

Velleius (C. Velleius, character in Cicero's *De natura deorum*): 16, 48,

Vergil: 190, 287–289, 304, 336, 438

vice: 32f., 35f., 37 n. 88, 82, 100, 103–105, 113, 117, 123f., 149, 158 n. 92, 171, 199, 202, 204, 211, 214, 221, 224, 254, 296, 329, 353, 371, 376, 378–380, 384f., 395, 408, 410, 413, 420, 422–424, 449

virtue: 10, 11, 13–16, 18–20, 26 n. 65, 26f. n. 66, 31, 33–40, 51f., 60, 75, 97, 99, 100, 102f., 123f., 130 n. 47, 145, 148, 157, 172, 177, 181, 197, 202, 212, 214f., 218, 221, 223f., 236, 246f., 296f., 299, 301, 304–306, 308f., 314, 297, 301, 333f., 355–357, 380, 394, 402, 403 n. 21, 420, 446, 451–454

wealth and the attitude to it: 183, 192, 210, 230, 254, 329, 382, 422, 452; wealth and poverty are indifferents: 123, 141, 184, 272, 290, 303f., 345f., 377f., 380, 384f., 394f., 417, 419–421, 424, 438;

avarice and greed: 320, 379, 450, 458; luxury, self-indulgence: 147, 287, 312 n. 45, 373, 379–381, 383 n. 38, 394, 419f., 458; public luxury: 370, 379f.; frugality (*frugalitas*, see also: asceticism): 211, 344f., 369–386, 373 n. 13, 413, 416, 422, 438; poverty as virtue: 380, 382, 383; true wealth: 413, 417, 419f., 439, 444f.; Seneca's wealth: 345, 381, 393–395, 396, 400, 413; see also: hypocrisy

wife: 219, 223, 234–236, 243–245, 252f., 254f., 257, 261; Seneca's wife Paulina and his other wives: 101, 243f., 245 n. 35, 256, 259f.; Medea as a wife: 82, 88f.

will: 95f., 103 n. 37, 105, 174 n. 31, 421 n. 70; see also: *akrasia*; impulse; weak assent

wisdom: 15 n. 25, 46, 145, 252, 263, 304, 308, 314, 328, 351f., 356f., 362, 372, 382, 393, 409, 413, 416, 453; to be sought instead of indifferents: 272, 290; progress toward wisdom: 159, 345, 411, 416; journey to wisdom: 148f., 178, 184, 306, 402, 411, 418, 420–422, 424

women: 209–221, 223f., 248; as advisors: 244–246; in letters: 245 n. 36; stomach vs. uterus: 214f.; wine: 213 n. 4; Plato on women: 217f.; inferior to men: 217f.; illness: 212–216, 219f.; importance of reproduction and sex: 220, 223; menstruation: 213 n. 3, 218–220; see also: Arria; body; gender; Medea; Paulina; Phaedra; Scribonia; sexuality; wife; Xanthippe

writing: 269–276, 278, 281–287, 290f.

Xanthippe: 261

Zeno: 11f., 32, 44, 97, 149, 337, 351 n. 18, 260, 400, 416f., 422; Zeno's *Republic*: 399

Zeus: see Jupiter